Practical Guide to Assessing Infants and Preschoolers with Special Needs

Judith A. Bondurant-Utz

Buffalo State College
State University of New York

Merrill
Prentice Hall

Upper Saddle River, New Jersey
Columbus, Ohio

Library of Congress Cataloging-in-Publication Data
Bondurant-Utz, Judith A.
    Practical guide to infant and preschool assessment in special education/Judith Bondurant-Utz.
        p. cm.
    Includes bibliographical references (p.) and index.
    ISBN 0-13-025521-1
        1. Handicapped children—Education (Preschool)—United States. 2. Handicapped
    children—Services for—United States. 3. Handicapped—United States—Functional
    assessment. I. Title.

LC4019.2 .B66 2002
371.9'0472—dc21

                                                                                    2001044013

Vice President and Publisher: Jeffery W. Johnson
Executive Editor: Ann Castel Davis
Editorial Assistant: Keli Gemrich
Production Editor: Sheryl Glicker Langner
Production Coordination: Clarinda Publication Services
Design Coordinator: Diane C. Lorenzo
Photo Coordinator: Valerie Schultz
Cover Designer: Melissa J. Cullen
Cover Photo: FPG
Production Manager: Laura Messerly
Director of Marketing: Kevin Flanagan
Marketing Manager: Amy June
Marketing Coordinator: Barbara Koontz

This book was set in Zapf Book, Novarese, and Helvetica by The Clarinda Company. It was printed and bound by
Maple Vail Book Manufacturing Group. The cover was printed by The Lehigh Press, Inc.

Photo Credits: 3, 23, 51, 105, 213, 285, 315, 361, 393: Anne Vega/Merrill; 81, 343: Scott Cunningham/Merrill; 119, 135,
173, 189, 245, 263, 417: Barbara Schwartz/Merrill.

Pearson Education Ltd., London
Pearson Education Australia Pty. Limited, Sydney
Pearson Education Singapore, Pte. Ltd.
Pearson Education North Asia Ltd., Hong Kong
Pearson Education Canada, Ltd., Toronto

Pearson Educación de Mexico, S.A. de C.V
Pearson Education—Japan, Tokyo
Pearson Education Malaysia, Pte. Ltd.
Pearson Education, Upper Saddle River, New Jersey

10 9 8 7 6 5 4 3 2 1
ISBN: 0-13-025521-1

Merrill
Prentice Hall

⟨ Preface ⟩

This book is intended for early intervention/ early childhood special educators, evaluators, related service staff, supervisors, and professionals involved in preparing personnel who work with young children with disabilities. In this text, early intervention is defined as occurring from birth to 3 years and early childhood special education as 3 to 5 years. At times, the entire age span is referred to as young children with special needs.

Practical Guide to Assessing Infants and Preschoolers with Special Needs is designed to be an introductory text which provides the basic guidelines for early childhood assessment. The material is developed to provide a functional overview of the variety of assessment instruments available, important points to consider for choosing assessment instruments, and a compilation of resources, examples, and practical suggestions for individuals, families, and training personnel. In preparing this second edition, the author has attempted to update the information in the original edition, incorporate current practices in the field that are preferred in the identification and assessment of young children with special needs, and provide more depth of content than in the original publication.

The current practices outlined in Part I and emphasized throughout the text include the integration of a family-centered philosophy, collaborative decision making among the professionals and parents, and an understanding that any assessment must be made realizing that many of the children and families with whom we work are culturally and linguistically diverse. Therefore, the first section includes chapters on family involvement, cultural diversity, and the team process.

The development of this book was stimulated by the recognition that assessing young children is a process that requires different skills and knowledge than those used for assessing school-aged children. Part II provides some basic considerations when assessing young children and making qualitative observations. Chapter 7 takes a practical approach and discusses assessment of infants, toddlers, and preschoolers with sensory or physical disabilities, behavioral disabilities, autism, and diseases such as HIV/AIDS or cancer.

Part III discusses the stages in the assessment from the very beginning to the end of the process. Emphasis is placed on the understanding that assessment is a process of information gathering about a child's typical behaviors; therefore, assessment must occur in a child's typical environment. Assessment of children in their typical environment will result in a decision about further evaluation, eligibility, and programming planning, which will more accurately reflect the child's behavior. The chapters have been updated with the most current assessment instruments and approaches. The chapter on behavioral assessment provides depth of content and includes a section on functional behavioral assessment as required by the reauthorization of the IDEA in 1997.

Part IV presents assessment within specific areas that are key domains in the assessment process. The domains presented are cognition, communication, social-emotional, sensorimotor, and adaptive. Chapter 15 on communication assessment is written by two speech/language pathologists, and Chapter 17 on sensorimotor development is written by an occupational therapist. These viewpoints provide a more comprehensive understanding of the domains and further emphasize the need for a collaborative approach to assessment of infants, toddlers, and preschoolers with special needs. The final chapter provides an assessment of adaptive skills.

This book is intended only as a beginning. Each child is different and programs have different philosophies; therefore, each professional must choose what is appropriate for each individual child. Competence in the evaluation process comes with experience and supervised practice. This book is intended to be a good beginning in this difficult task but is *not* meant as a substitute for comprehensive personnel preparation. This preparation must include quality field-based experiences with children and families in a collaborative setting.

For those readers who have experience with very young children with disabilities and their families, it is hoped that this will be a useful resource book. For those who are new to the field of early intervention and early childhood special education, we hope that *Practical Guide to Assessing Infants and Preschoolers with Special Needs* will be an excellent beginning point.

Acknowledgments

Special recognition and thanks go to the chapter authors who contributed their expertise and time to this book. I am grateful for their hard work. I would also like to acknowledge the contributions of the reviewers of the manuscript: Brent A. Askvig, Minot State University; Peggy A. Gallagher, Georgia State University; Melanie B. Jephson, Stephen F. Austin State University; and Pam Robinson, Oklahoma Baptist University.

Special thanks to Ms. Elizabeth Largeman-Kalnitz for her assistance in obtaining all of the copyright permissions for this book. I couldn't have done it without her.

The skilled, committed, patient personnel at Merrill/Prentice Hall deserve my special thanks also. I would especially like to recognize Ann Davis, executive editor, who provided continuous support, encouragement, and guidance throughout the process; and to Sheryl Langner, production editor. Also, I would like to recognize Emily Autumn at Clarinda Publication Services for her patience and expertise in the publication process.

Finally, I would like to express my appreciation to my husband, Russ, who constantly supported and encouraged me in this long and time-consuming endeavor. Without his kindness, patience, and understanding, I would not have completed this book.

⌒ Discover the Companion Website Accompanying This Book ⌒

The Prentice Hall Companion Website: A Virtual Learning Environment

Technology is a constantly growing and changing aspect of our field that is creating a need for content and resources. To address this emerging need, Prentice Hall has developed an online learning environment for students and professors alike—Companion Websites—to support our textbooks.

In creating a Companion Website, our goal is to build on and enhance what the textbook already offers. For this reason, the content for each user-friendly website is organized by topic and provides the professor and student with a variety of meaningful resources. Common features of a Companion Website include:

For the Professor—

Every Companion Website integrates **Syllabus Manager**™, an online syllabus creation and management utility.

- **Syllabus Manager**™ provides you, the instructor, with an easy, step-by-step process to create and revise syllabi, with direct links into Companion Website and other online content without having to learn HTML.
- Students may log on to your syllabus during any study session. All they need to know is the web address for the Companion Website and the password you've assigned to your syllabus.
- After you have created a syllabus using **Syllabus Manager**™, students may enter the syllabus for their course section from any point in the Companion Website.
- Clicking on a date, the student is shown the list of activities for the assignment. The activities for each assignment are linked directly to actual content, saving time for students.
- Adding assignments consists of clicking on the desired due date, then filling in the details of the assignment—name of the assignment, instructions, and whether or not it is a one-time or repeating assignment.
- In addition, links to other activities can be created easily. If the activity is online, a URL can be entered in the space provided, and it will be linked automatically in the final syllabus.
- Your completed syllabus is hosted on our servers, allowing convenient updates from any computer on the Internet. Changes you make to your syllabus are immediately available to your students at their next logon.

For the Student—

Topic Overviews—outline key concepts in topic areas

Characteristics—general information about each topic/disability covered on this website

Read About It—a list of links to pertinent articles found on the Internet that cover each topic

Teaching Ideas—links to articles that offer suggestions, ideas, and strategies for teaching students with disabilities

Web Links—a wide range of websites that provide useful and current information related to each topic area

Resources—a wide array of different resources for many of the pertinent topics and issues surrounding special education

Electronic Bluebook—send homework or essays directly to your instructor's email with this paperless form

Message Board—serves as a virtual bulletin board to post—or respond to—questions or comments to/from a national audience

Chat—real-time chat with anyone who is using the text anywhere in the country—ideal for discussion and study groups, class projects, etc.

To take advantage of these and other resources, please visit the *Practical Guide to Assessing Infants and Preschoolers with Special Needs* Companion Website at

www.prenhall.com/bondurant-utz

≈ Contents ≈

Part III
Stages in the Assessment
Process

10 _____

Curriculum-Based Assessment for Instructional Planning   **213**

11 _____

Ecological Assessment   **245**

15

Communication Assessment   343

Contributed by Ellenmorris Tiegerman and Christine Radziewicz

16

Assessing Social and Emotional Development   361

17

Assessing Sensory-Motor Development   393

Contributed by Shelly J. Lane

18

Assessing Adaptive Behavior   417

Contents

Introduction to Assessment
with Young Children

1

Introduction

The role of high-quality assessment practices has been a central focus throughout the history of services to young children with disabilities and their families (McConnell, 2000). Assessment determines which children have a need for special services, defines the services to be provided, and measures the success of early intervention/early childhood special education efforts. Assessment is an important and ongoing responsibility for professionals who serve young children and their families.

The purpose of this text is to provide basic guidelines for early intervention (birth to 3 years) and early childhood special education (3 to 5 years) assessment, an overview of the assessment process, examples of the variety of assessment instruments available, and a rationale for decision making when choosing an instrument. The development of this text was stimulated by the recognition that assessing young children is a process that requires different skills and knowledge than does the process of assessing school-aged children. Faced with the large amount of important information that needs to be presented in a usable format, it is not intended to be a comprehensive text, but a basic informational guide which can refer an individual to more comprehensive sources.

This chapter provides an overview of the purpose of assessment, the legal basis for assessment, and the various functions of assessment. The chapter ends with the unique characteristics, qualities, and basic considerations that should be made when assessing infants, toddlers, and preschoolers with disabilities and their families.

Purpose of Assessment

The purpose of assessment in early childhood is to derive information to facilitate decision making for an individual child. Assessment decisions revolve around the possible existence of a problem within the child or family as well as the treatment or intervention needs for the child and family. Bricker (1996) stated ". . . an assessment process should yield information and insights on children and their families which accurately reflect their usual modes of behaving, accurately pinpoint their strengths, and accurately target areas in need of intervention . . ." (p. 170).

The purpose of the assessment must be established before assessment materials are selected. Assessment serves four distinct purposes or functions: identification, diagnosis and determination of eligibility, assessment for program planning and service delivery, and monitoring of progress during intervention. The purpose of the assessment is the basis for selecting, using, and reporting the results of assessment instruments (Bagnato, Neisworth, & Munson, 1989).

An introduction to the legislative mandates for each of these functions is essential for understanding the assessment process for young children with disabilities. The next section of this chapter addresses the legal mandates that directly affect the assessment of young children.

Legislative Mandates for Young Children

The field of early intervention (birth to age 3) and early childhood special education (ages 3 to 5) is relatively new. The laws governing assessment of young children with special needs have been passed fairly recently. Under PL 94–142, the Education for All Handicapped Children Act, states were allowed to choose whether or not to serve preschool children. Passage of PL 99–457 in 1986 amended PL 94–192 and required states to provide a free and appropriate public education to preschool children. States provided guidelines for the assessment of preschool children. Part H of PL 99–457 added incentives for serving infants and toddlers with special needs.

PL 99–457 (the 1986 Amendments to the Education for All Handicapped Children Act) was retitled in 1990 as the Individuals with Disabilities Education Act [IDEA] (PL 101–476). Part H of IDEA called for establishing statewide services for infants and toddlers with disabilities and their families and required states to provide a free and appropriate public education to preschool children with disabilities. Regulations which governed school-aged children were then mandated for preschoolers. In 1991, PL 102–119 reauthorized and amended both Part H (infants/toddlers) and Part B (preschool) legislation. On June 4, 1997, the IDEA was reauthorized and signed into law as PL 105–17. This law focuses on improving results for children with disabilities by promoting early identification and early provision of services, ensuring their access to the general curriculum and general education reforms. The reauthorization of IDEA focuses on six major themes:

- Improving outcomes for children with disabilities by ensuring they are included in ongoing reform efforts
- Early identification and provision of services
- Focus on services in inclusive settings with children without disabilities
- Strengthening parent involvement and partnerships with families
- Strengthening collaboration with general education and with other service agencies
- Focus on paperwork and procedures that detract from teaching and learning

The IDEA Amendments of 1997 restructured IDEA into four parts, which reflect the major provisions in the Amendments. A major structural change within the law moved Part H (infants/toddlers) to Part C and included preschoolers

in Part B with school-aged children. The four parts are:

- Part A (Definitions)
- Part B (Assistance for Education of All Children with Disabilities)
- Part C (Infants and Toddlers with Disabilities)
- Part D (National Activities to Improve the Education of Children with Disabilities)

Six principles constitute a framework for IDEA. According to Turnbull and Cilley (1999), this framework makes IDEA a sensible, seamless approach to the education of students with disabilities. These principles are:

- *Zero reject* requires the inclusion in school of every student ages 3 through 21, regardless of the type or extent of the child's disability;
- *Nondiscriminatory evaluation* assures a fair, unbiased evaluation of the child's educational needs and strengths across all relevant domains;
- *Appropriate education* requires professionals to comply with important processes in providing an appropriate education;
- *Least restrictive environment* reflects the presumption that the child's education will take place in a typical setting and with nondisabled students;
- Procedural *due process* is a way for parents to hold the program or school accountable for that education and for the schools to hold the parents accountable to their child;
- *Parent participation* ensures that the parents and the child collaborate with educators in having a say about the child's education.

The IDEA Amendments ensure that every child with a disability has access to a free appropriate public education that emphasizes special education and services to meet their unique needs (Section 1400(d)). Each child must receive a nondiscriminatory evaluation that becomes the basis for the child's appropriate education and for placement in the least restrictive environment. IDEA favors educating children with disabilities with their peers who do not have disabilities. Schools are required to offer a continuum of placements from less to more restrictive, and within that continuum, students must be placed in the setting that is the least restrictive possible and also provides an appropriate education. If IDEA is not followed, then due process procedures give parents and schools the opportunity to hold each other accountable for the appropriate education of the child. The parent participation principle requires shared decision-making (Turnbull & Cilley, 1999).

IDEA and Evaluation

The aspects of parent involvement, flexibility, improved outcomes, and access to general education programs for students with disabilities are reflected in the law's requirements concerning evaluation procedures. The importance of parent involvement was underscored in the reauthorization of IDEA. The Amendments require that the Individual Family Service Plan (IFSP) be designed to include necessary participation of the family members. The IDEA Amendments of 1997 further stressed the importance of parent participation by including parents on the Individualized Education Program (IEP) team and by encouraging parents to submit additional information to be used during the eligibility and planning process. The regulations implementing IDEA require that the parents be given a copy of the evaluation report and the documentation of eligibility on completion of administration of tests and other evaluation materials.

IDEA contains mandates to promote fair, objective assessment practices and due process procedures. Due process is the foundation for legal recourse when parents or schools disagree with evaluation or placement recommendations. Early interventionists/early childhood special educators not only should be aware of

the law but also strive to maintain compliance in testing young children, recommending placement, and developing Individualized Family Service Plans (IFSPs) and IEPs.

Specific aspects relevant to assessment of infants, toddlers, and preschoolers include:

- A definition of the term "developmentally delayed" to be used for determining eligibility.
- The extension of the use of the term "developmental delay" from 3 to 9 years if the state so chooses.
- Mulitidisciplinary evaluations of the service needs of infants, toddlers, and preschoolers with disabilities and their families.
- An IFSP for each eligible infant and toddler which outlines services designed to meet the child's and family's needs. Part C requires justification of the extent, if any, to which early intervention services will not be provided in the natural environment.
- Identification of each family's needs must be "family-directed."
- Placement in law of the regulatory requirement that the determination of whether a child has a disability is made by "a team of qualified professionals and the parent of the child."
- Parents can review *all* records, not just all relevant records.

The relationship of all aspects of the IDEA relevant to the assessment process with infants, toddlers, and preschoolers will be highlighted throughout this text. The assessment process begins with finding children who may need special services and the determination of whether a child is eligible for special services. Therefore, the eligibility criteria used are a key factor in this process and will be discussed in the next section.

Eligibility Criteria

The infant and toddler regulations require states to find eligible infants and toddlers

(Child Find) and to develop procedures for evaluation and services. A general definition of children who are eligible for Early Intervention/Early Childhood Special Education (EI/ECSE) services is provided in federal law. However, each state or territory is responsible for the exact definition of eligibility as well as designation of the diagnostic instruments or procedures to be used.

Infant and Toddler Eligibility. Three groups of infants and toddlers may be eligible for early intervention services:

1. Children who are experiencing a developmental delay, as measured by appropriate diagnostic instruments and procedures in one or more of the following areas: cognitive development (learning and thinking), physical development (growth, gross and fine motor abilities), communication (understanding and using words) development, social or emotional development (relating to others), or adaptive development (self-help skills such as feeding).
2. Children who have a diagnosed physical or mental condition which has a high probability of resulting in developmental delay.
3. Children who are at risk for developmental delay if early intervention is not provided. This provision allows, but does not require, a state to serve children who are at-risk.

Each state or territory has established criteria for determining where a measurable developmental delay exists for infants and toddlers. The specific criteria vary according to the type of measure used and in terms of the level of delay required. The delay may be expressed in the number of standard deviations below the mean, the percent of delay, or the number of months of delay in a developmental area. For example, in Iowa a child who has a 25% delay in one or more areas is eligible for special services. Delay is defined in Texas as performance at a certain number of months below age level, and the number of months varies based on the age of the child. Colorado defines delay as 1.5 standard deviations (SD) below the mean in one or more areas. Some states have chosen to rely on professional judgment rather than on test scores in determining eligibility.

Preschooler Eligibility. For preschoolers, the current legal description for "children with disabilities" means children with mental retardation, hearing impairments, speech or language impairments, visual impairments, serious emotional disturbance, orthopedic impairments, autism, traumatic brain injury, other health impairments, or specific learning disabilities. PL 105–17 (1997 Amendments to IDEA) allowed states to utilize "developmental delay" eligibility criteria as an alternative to specific disability through age 9. The term "developmental delay" may include a child who is experiencing developmental delays as defined by the state and as measured by appropriate diagnostic instruments and procedures in one or more of the following areas: physical development, cognitive development, communication development, social or emotional development, or adaptive development. Therefore, preschoolers with disabilities may be described according to progress in developmental domains.

Preschool eligibility definitions vary widely. The most common designation of delay is in SD or delay expressed as a percentage of the chronological age. Some states allow the use of qualitative criteria or "professional judgment" (McLean, Bailey, & Wolery, 1996).

Infants, toddlers, and preschoolers are evaluated based on the individual state's criteria to determine whether the child has a disability or is at-risk for developmental delay if early intervention is not provided. The evaluation should also provide information related to the content of the IFSP or IEP and information regarding the preschool child's participation in appropriate activities [Section 1414(b)(2)(A)]. The requirement that evaluation information be related to the IFSP or IEP emphasizes the link between assessment and intervention. The assessment model provided by Bagnato, Neisworth, and Munson (1989) makes the link between assessment and intervention required by IDEA and will be used as the basis for this text. An overview of this model is presented in the next section.

The Stages in the Assessment Process

Bagnato, Neisworth, and Munson (1989) offered a model which provides a process for making these decisions and more clearly linking evaluation and assessment to intervention. Their approach proposes that the assessment process should be structured by a sequence of activities that proceed from the general to the specific and are linked to the purpose of the assessment in early intervention (Bagnato, Neisworth, & Munson, 1997). The steps or stages in this model are (1) screen/identify, (2) assess/link, (3) program/intervene, and (4) monitor/evaluate. Appropriate assessment measures must be used to accomplish each function, but the steps are interrelated.

Each stage in this model is a part of the assessment process. Children are screened to determine if there may be a developmental delay. If the screening results indicate there may be a delay or disability, then a full evaluation is conducted. Based on this evaluation or diagnostic assessment, the child may or may not be referred for special services. If special services are required, a curriculum-based assessment is used for developing intervention plans and evaluating the effectiveness of the intervention. Each of the stages in this process is discussed in the sections that follow.

Screening

Screening is the first step in the process. The purpose of screening is to determine whether to refer the child for additional assessment for identifying a possible developmental delay or disability. Screening is usually completed in a short time period and examines a child's skills for a broad look at overall functioning. It does not provide comprehensive quantitative or qualitative information about the child's developmental status but indicates whether or not further evaluation is necessary. It assists in the identification of infants, toddlers, and preschoolers who may need further assessment so that services may begin as early as possible.

Screening is usually conducted by nurses, pediatricians, or other health professionals. It may be part of the Child Find process which is mandated by federal legislation and requires states to develop programs for finding and identifying young children with special needs.

Norm-referenced, developmental screening measures that address multiple domains are used. The professional administering these tests should look for signs of developmental concern in patterns of peaks and lows on the child's profile of domains. In other words, the profile from the screening instrument should identify areas of development which are in need of closer examination.

Assessment and Linkage

In this stage of the assessment process it is necessary to determine whether the child has a developmental delay or disability. The assessment measures and procedures used depend on the suspected delay or disability but frequently involve standardized measures conducted by professionals who are specifically trained to use them. They often are conducted in clinical settings.

The diagnostic assessment increases the magnification and provides more attention to detail. This assessment should provide a comprehensive and detailed analysis of the child's developmental capabilities which will assist in establishing the goals for intervention. Diagnostic assessment yields a score or product but, more important, should gather qualitative information about how the child earned that score. It should produce a profile of strengths and limitations with suggestions about the best way in which the child learns. Diagnostic assessment should also analyze development by focusing on the problem areas identified during the screening.

Programming and Intervention

The next stage in the process involves the planning of individualized curricular activities and adaptive strategies for teaching. The child's current level of developmental functioning must be determined. In this stage, curriculum-based assessments that address multiple developmental domains are conducted by teachers and relevant therapists. These are supplemented with direct observation of the child in multiple natural settings, informal testing, and interviews with others, including parents and caregivers.

Curriculum-based assessment assists in establishing the objectives as well as the particular instructional strategies for intervention. These assessments help to analyze the child's skills into subskills that can be more easily taught. They provide information about the adaptations and assistance needed for the child's performance. Direct observation, informal assessments, and interviews with parents/caregivers and others help to establish the child's usual patterns of responding and what environmental variables appear to influence the child's performance.

In addition to curriculum-based assessments, assessments in specific domains, such as speech and language, assist in determining

if related services are needed. Does the child need specialized services in speech/language therapy, physical therapy, or any other related area? These assessments determine the type(s) of service(s) needed and where the child could receive the necessary services (e.g., at home or in a center).

Evaluation of Progress

In this stage the intervention program is monitored for the child and the family. The purpose of this monitoring is to track ongoing progress, determine program effectiveness, and make modifications as needed. In this phase it must be determined if the child is making adequate progress in learning important skills. A wide view must be taken as well as paying attention to detail. Data are collected from unstructured and structured observations of the child in natural contexts as well as from periodic probes of the child's performance. It is important to include reports by family members of the child's use of skills outside of the classroom. The special educator or therapist uses repeated assessment to provide information on developmental gains across time and examines the child's progress in specific curricular areas in order to determine program effectiveness and to allow for subsequent modifications as indicated. This assessment evaluates the child's program from the perspective of family needs and expectations.

In summary, this model of the assessment stages can help to identify possible developmental problems and assist in making an accurate diagnosis. The process can provide an objective description of the child's abilities and deficits (functional assessment) as well as determining eligibility for various EI or ECSE programs. Developmental assessment can aid in planning for appropriate interventions and provide a baseline for measuring progress and the effects of interventions. Developmental assessment should not be viewed as a single event, but as an ongoing collaborative process between professionals and caregivers that follows the child over time in a variety of settings. Collecting information in this way will give useful outcomes for formulating and evaluating the process. This makes the process valid, efficient, and effective (Bricker, 1996). An example of an assessment which fits the assessment model of Bagnato, Neisworth, and Munson (1997) and directly links developmental assessment and evaluation is provided by Bricker (1987).

Linking Assessment and Evaluation

Bricker (1987) operationalized a type of linked assessment-evaluation model and published the first commercially available system, the Assessment, Evaluation, and Programming System (AEPS). This system has four components: (1) measurement or assessment for children from birth to age 3; (2) curriculum for children from birth to age 3; (3) measurement for children from ages 3 to 6; and (4) curriculum for children from ages 3 to 6. The AEPS provides specific activities for performing initial assessment and helps parents and professionals ensure that children meet IEP/IFSP objectives through formative and summative progress evaluations (Bricker, 1993; Bricker & Pretti-Frontczak, 1996; Bricker & Waddell, 1996; Cripe, Slentz, & Bricker, 1993).

The linked assessment approach (Bricker, 1993) is composed of three critical processes: assessment, intervention, and evaluation. The assessment process establishes a baseline or entry-level measurement of the child's skills and desired family outcomes. This process should produce the information necessary to select appropriate intervention goals and objectives. The intervention process arranges the physical and social environment to produce the desired growth and development outlined in the intervention plan for the child and family. The evaluation process compares the child's performance on selected intervention goals and objectives,

as well as the family's progress toward their family outcomes (Bricker, 1993).

Figure 1–1 illustrates the linked assessment, intervention, and evaluation approach. The major processes are shown in the boxes, which are linked by arrows to indicate the sequence in which the processes should occur. The vertical arrows show the desired participation of professionals and families in each of these three processes. An appropriate assessment should obtain information through collaboration between professionals and families and through careful and systematic observation of the child in a variety of settings and activities. Collecting information in this way will yield outcomes that can be used directly to formulate and evaluate intervention efforts which are valid, efficient, and effective (Bricker, 1996).

The assessment of an infant or young child with developmental disabilities must take into account the full complexity of the child's development (Greenspan & Meisels, 1996). All of the child's functional areas (cognitive, social emotional, language, motor, and sensory functioning) must be evaluated as well as the constitutional and maturational variations that influence the child's development as well as the caregiver, family, community and cultural patterns (Greenspan & Meisels, 1996). A linked developmental assess-

FIGURE 1–1
A Schematic of a Linked Assessment-Intervention-Evaluation Approach to Early Intervention with Joint Professional and Family Participation

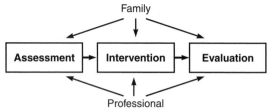

From "Assessment, Evaluation, and Programming System for Infants and Children," by D. Bricker (Ed.), 1993. *AEPS measurement for birth to three years* (Vol. 1), Baltimore, MD: Paul H. Brookes.

ment must try to understand infants and young children in the context of their families and their developmental abilities. The principles that will provide an appropriate, comprehensive developmental assessment will be introduced in this chapter.

Family Participation in the Assessment Process

Active family participation is an essential component in early childhood assessment. The family members are an integral part of the assessment team and have a voice in all decision-making. A key feature of the IDEA reauthorization (PL 105–17) is the clarification that parents have an opportunity to participate in the decision-making aspects of the identification, evaluation, and educational placement of their child.

The concept of family-centered services has evolved from the notion that parents should participate in the activities that professionals deemed important to the concept of building partnerships with parents to empower them for decision making (McWilliam, Tocci, & Harbin, 1998). The various approaches became known as *family focused*, *family friendly*, *family directed*, *family driven*, or *family centered*. The nuances of these different terms and the debate about which term is most appropriate emphasize the complexity of the concept of providing services to families (McWilliam, Tocci, & Harbin, 1998).

Two parents of children with disabilities have given us their perspectives on the assessment process. Rocco (1996), the parent of a child with a disability, characterized the assessment and planning process as a brainstorming session. The discussion should focus on giving families normal life opportunities, rather than creating "nearly normal" children. Rocco advocated that the team's job is identifying supports that will enhance the quality of life and the relationship between the child and family, rather than listing

the child's deficits and how to fix them. Popper (1996) pointed out that well-trained, sensitive professionals are aware of parents' feelings and try to make every phase of an assessment an opportunity to share knowledge, observe the child together, and plan collaboratively. In this situation, professionals and parents see themselves as allies on behalf of the child.

Family participation must be self-defined along a number of dimensions and levels of intensity. Including the family as an integral part of the team will encourage a higher level of participation. "Collaboration will take place only when the family is the final decision maker and when the team's the implementer of decisions (Vincent & McLean, 1996, p. 63).

These concepts pertain to the entire assessment process for all children from birth to age 5 and their families. Further consideration is given to family participation in the assessment process in Chapter 2 on family involvement.

Considering Linguistic, Cultural, and Family Contexts

A child's life is embedded within both a cultural and family context. When assessing children with possible developmental delays, it is essential to consider:

- The family's culture
- Parents' priorities
- Parenting styles
- Family support systems

It is important to recognize that there may be cultural and familial differences in expectations when evaluating a child.

If English is not the primary language of the family, it is important for professionals to look for ways to communicate effectively with the child and the family, including finding professionals and translators who speak the child's and family's language. The IDEA provides that the assessments used for evaluation must be

selected and administered so as not to be discriminatory on a racial or cultural basis [Section
1414(b)(3)(A)(i)]. The test must be provided
and administered in the child's native language
or other mode of communication [Section
1414(b)(3)(A)(ii)].

Cultural and linguistic differences must be
considered throughout the evaluation process.
These variables will be discussed further in
Chapter 3.

Characteristics and Qualities of Multidimensional Assessment

Developmental assessment must be based on
an integrated developmental model (Greenspan
& Meisels, 1996). Assessment, programming,
and evaluation information should include
multiple types of data obtained from multiple
sources (McCune, Fleck, Kalmanson, Glazewski,
& Sillari, 1990). The 1997 IDEA reauthorization
places much more emphasis on functional
assessments than did the original law. The
types of tests or other evaluation materials
must be tailored to assess specific areas of
concern and not merely result in a single score.
These types of tests must be validated for the
specific purposes for which the tests are administered (Turnbull & Turnbull, 1997). It also
mandates that a variety of assessment tools be
used. Therefore, although special educators may
still use assessment tools that measure a child's
overall achievement, they may also be expected
to administer tests that provide a more fine-
tuned analysis of the specific skills a child has
mastered. Performance assessment tools may
not be restricted to formal, standardized tests.
Informal, curriculum-based assessments may
be used to help determine a child's functional
abilities.

Neisworth and Bagnato (1988) defined multidimensional assessment as "a comprehensive
and integrated approach that employs multiple

measures, derives data from multiple sources,
surveys multiple domains, and fulfills multiple
purposes" (p. 24). Bagnato and Neisworth
(1991) formalized these assessment practices
with their convergent assessment model.

> Convergent assessment refers to the synthesis of
> information gathered from several sources, instru-
> ments, settings, and occasions to produce the
> most valid appraisal of developmental status and
> to accomplish the related assessment purposes of
> identification, prescription, progress evaluation,
> and prediction. (Bagnato & Neisworth, 1991, p. 57)

Early childhood assessment should be a
flexible, collaborative decision-making process
between parents and professionals who may
repeatedly revise their judgments and reach
consensus about the changing developmental,
educational, medical, and mental health status
of the young child and family (Bagnato &
Neisworth, 1991). The criteria comprising a
convergent assessment process must be considered when planning a young child's developmental assessment. The criteria include multiple
measures, multiple sources, multiple domains,
and multiple purposes. Each of these will be discussed in the next sections.

Multiple Measures

A variety of assessment measures should be
used in early childhood assessment. A battery
of developmental scales provides more
information and, therefore, a more comprehensive assessment of the child. The measures
most commonly used by preschool teachers
are curriculum-based assessments. School psychologists and related service professionals
(i.e., speech and language pathologists, occupational therapists, physical therapists) often
employ norm-based scales. Many practitioners
may be aware of only norm-based or curriculum-
based assessments and may not realize the
variety of assessments available which will provide a more comprehensive assessment when

used with norm-based and curriculum-based assessment. A thorough diagnostic battery for a child might include norm-based, curriculum-based, and clinical judgment scales, which require impressions of developmental or behavioral traits (Neisworth & Bagnato, 1988).

Neisworth and Bagnato (1988) categorized these diverse assessment instruments to help the practitioner decide which type of assessment is needed. Their multidimensional model provides a practical guide for categorizing these assessment measures to match the needs of the early interventionist. Neisworth and Bagnato (1988) used an eight-category scheme for differentiating the variety of assessment instruments. Table 1–1 summarizes these categories and gives examples of the different types of instruments. In the next sections, a more thorough explanation of each category and the purpose for each type of test are provided.

Norm-based Assessment. Norm-based assessment compares a child's developmental skills with those of a referent or normative group that is comparable in child and demographic dimensions (Neisworth & Bagnato, 1988). Because norm-based assessments compare a child's performance with that of a norm group, they are often used for screening or diagnostic assessment. Screening tests provide information to determine if a child's development may be delayed and thus in need of further assessment. Diagnostic tests often are used to determine eligibility for special services. Norm-based assessment is discussed further in Chapter 9.

Curriculum-based Assessment. Curriculum-based assessment allows the early interventionist to track a child's performance on specific program objectives and compare current performance with past performance, thus monitoring the child's progress. Curriculum-based assessment is a form of criterion-referenced evaluation but gives the EI/ECSE a direct link between testing

and teaching because the assessment provides the specific developmental objectives which make up the instructional curriculum for the child. These objectives may be major developmental goals within each developmental domain or sequences of prerequisite skills leading to these general goals within domains. The early interventionist or early childhood special educator determines if the child has acquired the skills addressed in the curriculum or if they are emerging. These skills then become the point at which to begin intervention. This assessment yields a basis for evaluation of the child's mastery of skills and program effectiveness and provides a common instrument to coordinate interdisciplinary team members' assessments. Curriculum-based assessment will be discussed at length in Chapter 10.

Adaptive to Disability. A child's disability may interfere with an examiner's ability to obtain a valid measure of the child's ability. A sensory, motor, or behavioral deficit may prevent many young children from showing what they have learned. For example, a motor impairment will hinder the child's ability to respond to test items which require a motor performance, even in other domains, such as language or cognition. Some assessments are designed to circumvent a disability and, thus, are used to obtain a more valid or fair estimate of the capability of the child who has a sensory or motor impairment. Procedures are provided for excluding biased items, rescoring performance, or using new technologies, such as computers, assistive devices, and CD/ROMs. These modifications are necessary to avoid penalizing a child who cannot see, hear, or make voluntary movements.

Neisworth and Bagnato (1988) offered three types of adaptive approaches. A test may permit modification of items where necessary; it is up to the test administrator to decide how and when to make these adaptations. A second type of test modification outlines systematic

TABLE 1–1
Types of Assessments in Early Childhood Special Education

Type of Measure	Description	Example
Norm-Based	Describes the child's functional skills by comparing child's skills with appropriate referent group. Classifies the degree of the child's deficit using a preexisting diagnostic category.	Bayley Scales of Infant Development, 2nd ed. (Bayley, 1993) (0–30 mos.) Battelle Developmental Inventory (Newborg, Stock, Wnek, Guidubaldi, & Svinicki, 1988) (0–95 mos.) Kaufmann Assessment Battery for Children (Kaufman & Kaufman, 1984) (30–244 mos.)
Curriculum-Based	Tracks a child's performance on a continuum of objectives. Skills emerging or not acquired then become the point to begin intervention.	Early Learning Accomplishment Profile (Glover, Preminger, & Sanford, 1995) (0–36 mos.) Hawaii Early Learning Profile (VORT, 1995) (0–72 mos.)
Adaptive to Disability	Designed to circumvent the child's disabilities to produce a more accurate picture of abilities. Modifies content of assessment to allow adaptation of test items or alternative responses to obtain a more valid estimate of capability when a sensorimotor disability is present.	Carolina Curriculum for Infants and Toddlers with Special Needs, 2nd ed. (Johnson-Martin, Jens, Attermeier, & Hacker, 1991) (0–24 mos.) Developmental Programming for Infants and Young Children (Brown et al., 1981) (36–62 mos.)
Process	Provides a way to estimate the cognitive, adaptive, or social communication capabilities when direct assessment is not feasible (e.g., child reactions such as smiling and vocalizing to a change in stimulus). Includes both formal and informal methods for estimating the child's capabilities and probing information-processing abilities.	Clinical and Educational Manual for Use with the Uzgiris and Hunt Scales of Infant Psychological Development (Dunst, 1980) (0–30 mos.) Dynamic Assessment (Feuerstein, 1979;1980)
Judgment-Based	Samples ambiguous characteristics and response classes that are not discrete (e.g., temperament, activity level). Quantifies perceptions of professionals and caregivers about child/environmental characteristics using Likert scale or checklist.	Early Coping Inventory (Zeitlin, Williamson, & Szczepanski, 1988) (4–36 mos.) Child Behavior Checklist (Achenbach, 1986) (24–72 mos.) Social Skills Rating System (Gresham & Elliott, 1990) (36+ mos.)

Type of Measure	Description	Example
Ecological	Looks at physical, social, and psychological features of child's environment (e.g., preschool or home environment, peer interaction, consequences of behavior). Describes the nature and qualities of child/environment interactions and identifies specific child and milieu dimensions that can be added or rearranged to improve interactions.	Infant/Toddler Environmental Rating Scale (Harms, Cryer, & Clifford, 1990) (0–36 mos.) Home Observation for Measurement of the Environment (Caldwell & Bradley, 1978) (0–72 mos.) Family Needs Survey (Bailey & Simeonsson, 1990)
Interactive	Assesses the content and effect of caregiver-child interactions and the capabilities of both partners in this process by dissecting typical elements of these interactions.	Parent Behavior Progression (Bromwich, 1979) (0–36 mos.) Parenting Stress Index (Abidin, 1990) (1–60+ mos.)
Systematic Observation	Structures collection of data on observable, measurable behavior (e.g., frequency or rate of behavior). Analyzes specific target behaviors to detect emerging or present behavior patterns.	Social Interaction Scan (Guralnick, 1988) Planned Activities Check (Doke & Risley, 1972)

From "Assessment in early childhood special education: A typology of dependent measures," by J. T. Neisworth & S. J. Bagnato. In Odum, S. L., and Karnes, M. B. (Eds.) (1988). *Early intervention for infants and children with handicaps: An empirical base* (pp. 26–27). Baltimore: Paul H. Brookes. Adapted with permission.

guidelines for altering the task or response mode. The examiner follows these guidelines to accommodate for the disability. Third, some instruments have been designed and standardized for a specific disability. For example, these instruments exclude tasks and procedures that would limit the performance of the child with a visual or hearing impairment.

Using these assessments with adaptions for disabilities will give a more representative assessment of the child's functioning and true capabilities, rather than relying solely on comparisons to the norm (Neisworth & Bagnato, 1988). Adaptive assessments or adapting items also assist in determining the types of specific teaching strategies and therapeutic modifications that will help the child learn despite the disability as well as identify appropriate goals for instruction.

Process. Atypical behavior patterns and other severe limitations in functioning limit the child's ability to attend, interact, and follow task requirements. Process assessment provides a means with which to estimate the capabilities of children with severe impairments who seem to be untestable. For example, process assessment looks at changes in child reactions, such as smiling or vocalizing, as a result of changes in stimulus events. These responses are used to infer the child's capacity to understand concepts or events. Process assessment allows the examiner to probe a child's abilities when more conventional assessment is not feasible and estimate the status of children with absent or impaired response methods. This type of assessment may be used to evaluate the cognitive, adaptive, and social communication capabilities of a child with severe impairments.

Judgment-based. Judgment-based assessment quantifies the perceptions and clinical judgments of professionals and caregivers about child/environmental characteristics. These assessment measures may require actual observation of a child and immediate judgment, or they may be the result of accumulated impressions across time, people, and situations. Judgment-based measures may be very useful in assessing children with more severe disabilities because such measures can be more sensitive to small changes in behavior. These types of scales also provide a way for caregivers and professionals to have personal input into the assessment results. By using a Likert type scale, judgment-based measures can examine such traits as temperament, activity level, and attention, which are difficult to observe and measure. Although these measures are retrospective and highly subjective, they may provide social validity if a variety of people in various settings have similar judgments (Neisworth & Bagnato, 1988).

Ecological. Ecological assessment looks at the child's development on the basis of the physical, social, and psychological features. These features may include preschool and home environments, peer interactions, caregiver responsiveness, and family program participation. Physical elements which are often evaluated include such features as room arrangement, materials available, and properties of toys. Social features often included are the extent of peer interaction, and caregiver sensitivity and responsiveness. The psychological or learning variables examine the antecedents (setting events), the child's behavior, and the consequences of the behavior. Ecological assessment is based on an interactive model which stresses that behavior is a function of personal variables

(Neisworth & Bagnato, 1988). The ecological emphasis is important to the development of the IFSP, which requires the team not only to evaluate the child but also the child's physical and social environment. The family's self-appraisal is integral to this process (Bagnato & Neisworth, 1991). (See also Chapter 11.)

Interactive. Interactive assessment is a result of the discovery that caregiver-child interactions are reciprocal. Instruments have been developed to assess the content and effect of interactions and the capabilities of both partners in this process. Interactive assessment provides information regarding the content and quality of these interactions. For example, does the caregiver read the infant's cues and provide reinforcing consequences to the infant? Interactive assessment yields information about the match between the child's competencies and the content and pacing of the caregiver's responses (Neisworth & Bagnato, 1988).

Systematic Observation. Systematic observation is the direct observation and recording of behavior. It is a structured way to collect data on observable, measurable behaviors. The child may be observed in his natural setting, a situation that has been staged, or in a role play or setting which has been prompted. Dimensions of behavior which may be assessed are frequency or rate, duration, latency, intensity, topography, and locus. Direct systematic observation provides an objective measure of actual overt behavior. Specific target behaviors can be analyzed to detect emerging or present behavior patterns. Systematic observation can provide a close look at behavior and detect small changes (Neisworth & Bagnato, 1988); this type of observation is discussed in Chapter 12.

Multiple Techniques

Assessment instruments include formats for observation, protocols for interviews, standardized test sequences, and so forth. The multiple measures discussed previously are examples of some of the materials available to professionals and families. Assessment should include the use of several types of instruments and methods, such as formal and informal testing, observation, and interviews. Formal testing has standardized content and procedures. Its strengths and limitations will be discussed further in Chapter 9. Informal testing includes procedures related to ecological surveys, checklists, and other less-structured means of assessing a child's functioning. Real life observations perhaps offer the best information. Interviews of family members and others who are familiar with the child can be very helpful and guide us to more focused assessment (Bagnato, Neisworth, & Munson, 1997).

Multiple Occasions

Assessments should occur on multiple occasions. Conducting assessments at different times of the day and on different days of the week enables the EI/ECSE to determine the consistency of a child's behavior and the impact of fatigue, endurance, and sleep requirements on a child's ability to learn. This is especially important for children with medical conditions and special developmental needs (Bagnato, Neisworth, & Munson, 1997). Careful observation of the child's behavior in multiple but familiar contexts on multiple occasions will provide a rich picture of the child's current strengths and challenges (Greenspan & Meisels, 1996).

Multiple Sources or Perspectives

The assessment of an infant or preschooler should include information and findings from several professionals and from the child's caregivers. Young children tend to be person- and situation-specific. Information from the family and a variety of professionals allows the early interventionist to see the child's behavior in a variety of situations. This input should

validate findings from norm-referenced and curriculum based assessments and thus provide a more accurate appraisal of the child's skills. Team members who can provide relevant information in a variety of settings include the caregivers, psychologist, teacher, speech/language pathologist, occupational or physical therapist, nurse, pediatrician, social worker, and any paraprofessionals who are familiar with the child.

Parents are valuable partners in providing information and perspectives which may not always be available to professionals. However, all team members may not see the child in the same way. The issue should not be a question of which perspective is right or more accurate but that multiple observers should contribute multiple perspectives from multiple contexts. These multiple perspectives provide a more complete picture of the child's status (Bagnato, Neisworth, & Munson, 1997).

Multiple Domains

Assessment of multiple domains refers to examining the child's strengths and weaknesses in several developmental and behavioral areas. Curriculum-based assessments usually examine such areas as cognitive, language, socioemotional, gross and fine motor, and self-care domains. Behavioral processes which may be assessed include mastery motivation, social competence, play, temperament, attention, emotional expression, and early coping behavior. Assessment information should include information on the processes the child is employing in his learning or how the child learns as well as the product of his learning (the demonstration of a skill). These domains and behavioral processes will be discussed in later chapters.

Multiple Purposes

Several different types of decisions must be made in working with young children. The purpose of the assessment must be clear to all involved. Multiple purpose measurement allows the early interventionist to screen, diagnose, place, prescribe, predict, or evaluate the intervention services. Screening instruments are used to provide a brief look at a child to see if further evaluation is warranted; a curriculum-based assessment assists in planning a child's intervention program. The assessment measurement chosen must be consistent with the purpose of the assessment. A screening instrument would not be appropriate to use when planning a child's intervention program. In addition, the assessment measures that are chosen must also be compatible with the goals and content of the curriculum. If increasing the quality of parent-child interaction is a goal of the curriculum, then an assessment must be chosen which will measure this interaction. The framework or typology as shown in Table 1–1 should assist in the choice of an appropriate assessment instrument.

Additional Assessment Models

Authentic/Performance Assessment Model

Authentic assessment recommends the use of developmentally appropriate assessment techniques for all young children and advocates eliminating standardized norm-referenced testing in early childhood settings. Authentic procedures have been endorsed by the National Association for the Education of Young Children (NAEYC) and the Division for Early Childhood (DEC) of the Council for Exceptional Children.

Coutinho and Malouf (1992) emphasized three major features of performance-based or authentic assessment: performance dimension, authentic dimension, and instructional linkage. The performance dimension is a student's active response and highlights the fact that the response is directly or indirectly observable,

e.g., a permanent product (Coutinho & Malouf, 1992). The authentic dimension emphasizes the real-life nature or natural context in which the assessment occurs or the data are gathered. Instructional linkage emphasizes the extent to which the assessment tasks are consistent with curriculum outcomes (Coutinho & Malouf, 1992). An example of an authentic assessment would be to assess a nonverbal child's social and communication skills by observing the child's ability to initiate a social interaction with a peer through sounds, gestures, or other alternative forms of communication (Bagnato, Neisworth, & Munson, 1997).

Dynamic Assessment Model

The dynamic assessment model is based on the work of Feuerstein (1979) and was modified for use with preschoolers by Lidz (1991). Dynamic assessment uses the test-teach-test procedure to engage the child as an active learner in performing activities to assess the child's approach to problem solving. There are three central components of the dynamic assessment model: (1) active engagement of the child in the task; (2) emphasis on "learning to learn" strategies to foster independent problem solving; and (3) recommendations for arranging instructional techniques that are designed for a given child (Bagnato, Neisworth, & Munson, 1997). Dynamic assessment will be discussed further in Chapter 3.

Functional/Adaptive Assessment Model

A child's special needs are assessed in terms of the level of functional ability. Functional assessment enables professionals and parents to discuss the scope and intensity of services needed. Professionals attempt to identify those clusters of behaviors that have the greatest likelihood of increasing a child's competence in interacting with people and objects in his environment. This model stresses the use of alternative sensory and response capabilities with appropriate learning opportunities (Bagnato, Neisworth, & Munson, 1997).

Play-Based Assessment Model

Play-based assessment is considered the most natural and developmentally appropriate model for young children. Parents and professionals are involved in the child's play session using the child's own toys and in the natural setting for observing the child's play skills. Play-based assessment allows flexible accommodations to be made to situations and materials to better suit each child's unique functional limitations and temperament (Bagnato, Neisworth, & Munson, 1997). Linder's Transdisciplinary Play-Based Assessment (1993) is the most widely used play-based system and will be discussed in Chapter 10 (curriculum-based assessment).

Summary

Assessment is a process which must be family-directed. The overall purpose of this process is to facilitate decision making with respect to the infant, toddler, or preschooler and his family. These decisions focus on determining the provision of any special services which might be necessary to help the child develop to his full potential. Assessment must be a continuous process with each stage in the process linked to the next stage. An interdisciplinary or transdisciplinary approach must be used, involving the family and professionals from across several disciplines based on the individual child and family needs. The assessment process should be multidimensional, employing multiple measures from multiple sources, fulfilling multiple purposes, and allowing for the diversity of cultures in our society.

Neisworth and Bagnato (1996) emphasized that assessment for early intervention should yield outcomes that offer prescriptions for progress rather than diagnoses that may limit progress. These researchers advocate that assessment measures and procedures

- Be flexible for teams of caregivers and professionals;
- Produce functional and integrated intervention goals;

- Accommodate the child's sensory, neuromotor, communication, and behavioral deficits;
- Match the behavior styles characteristic of infants, toddlers, and preschoolers;
- Be sensitive enough to monitor small increments of change in the child's capabilities; and
- Have high reliabilities and show evidence of utility for instruction.

The process, the products, and the procedures of assessment have changed dramatically over the years, but the goals remain essentially the same: (1) to gain valid, reliable, useful information about children without penalizing them through the limits of our measurement system; and (2) to gather information that can be translated quite easily into improved instruction and services for children with special needs (Fewell, 2000).

References

Abidin, R. R. (1990). *Parenting Stress Index* (3rd ed.). Charlottesville, VA: Pediatric Psychology Press.

Achenbach, T. M. (1986). *Child Behavior Checklist.* Burlington, VT: University of Vermont.

Bagnato, S. J., & Neisworth, J. T. (1991). *Assessment for early intervention: Best practices for professionals.* New York: Guilford Press.

Bagnato, S. J., Neisworth, J. T., & Munson, S. M. (1989). *Linking developmental assessment and early intervention: Curriculum-based prescriptions.* Rockville, MD: Aspen.

Bagnato, S. J., Neisworth, J. T., & Munson, S. M. (1997). LINK*ing assessment and early intervention: An authentic curriculum-based approach.* Baltimore, MD: Paul H. Brookes.

Bailey, D. B., & Simeonsson, R. J. (1990). *Family needs survey.* Chapel Hill, NC: Frank Porter Graham Child Development Center, University of North Carolina.

Bayley, N. (1993). *Bayley Scales of Infant Development* (2nd ed.). San Antonio, TX: The Psychological Corporation.

Bricker, D. (1987). *Early intervention with at-risk and handicapped infants.* Glenview, IL: Scott-Foresman.

Bricker, D. (Ed.). (1993). *Assessment, Evaluation, & Programming System for infants and children. Vol. 1: AEPS measurement for birth to three years.* Baltimore: Paul H. Brookes.

Bricker, D. (1996). Assessment for IFSP development in intervention planning. In S. J. Meisels & E. Fenichel (Eds.), *New visions for the developmental assessment of infants and young children* (pp. 169–192). Washington, DC: Zero to Three/National Center for Infants, Toddlers, and Families.

Bricker, D., & Pretti-Frontczak, K. (Eds.). (1996). *AEPS Measurement for Three to Six Years.* Baltimore: Paul H. Brookes.

Bricker, D., & Waddell, M. (Eds.). (1996). *Assessment, Evaluation, and Programming System for infants and children: Vol. 4. AEPS curriculum for three to six years.* Baltimore: Paul H. Brookes.

Bromwich, R. (1979). *Parent Behavior Progression.* Austin, TX: PRO-ED.

Brown, S., D'Eugenio, D., Drews, J., Haskin, S., Whiteside-Lynch, E., Moersch, M., & Rogers, S. (1981). *Developmental Programming for Infants and Young Children.* Ann Arbor, MI: University of Michigan Press.

Caldwell, B., & Bradley, R. (1978). *Home Observation for Measurement of the Environment* (HOME). Little Rock, AR: University of Arkansas, Human Development.

Coutinho, L. P., & Malouf, L. (1992). Performance assessment and children with disabilities: Issues and possibilities. *Teaching Exceptional Children,* 25(4), 62–67.

Cripe, J., Slentz, K., & Bricker, D. (1993). *Assessment, Evaluation, and Programming System (AEPS) for infants and children. Vol. 2: AEPS curriculum for birth to three years.* Baltimore: Paul H. Brookes.

Doke, L. A., & Risley, T. R. (1972). The organization of day-care environments: Required vs. optional activities. *Journal of Applied Behavior Analysis,* 5, 405–420.

Dunst, C. J. (1980). *A clinical and educational manual for use with the Uzgiris and Hunt scales of infant psychological development.* Austin, TX: PRO-ED.

Feuerstein, R. (1979). *The dynamic assessment of retarded performers: The Learning Potential Assessment Device, theory, instruments, and techniques.* Baltimore: University Park Press.

Feuerstein, R. (1980). *Instructional enrichment.* Baltimore: University Park Press.

Fewell, R. R. (2000). Assessment of young children with special needs: Foundations for tomorrow. *Topics in Early Childhood Special Education,* 20(1), 38–42.

Glover, M. E., Preminger, J. L., & Sanford, A. R. (1995). *Early Learning Accomplishment Profile* (E-LAP). Chapel Hill, NC: Chapel Hill Training-Outreach Project.

Greenspan, S. I., & Meisels, S. J. (1996) Toward a new vision for the developmental assessment of infants and young children. In S. J. Meisels & E. Fenichel (Eds.), *New visions for the developmental assessment of infants and young children* (pp. 169–192). Washington, DC: Zero to Three/National Center for Infants, Toddlers, and Families.

Gresham, F. M., & Elliott, S. M. (1990). *Social Skills Rating System* (SSRS). Circle Pines, MN: American Guidance Service.

Guralnick, M. (1988). *Social Interaction Scan.* Seattle: University of Washington.

Harms, T., Cryer, D., & Clifford, R. M. (1990). *Infant/Toddler Environmental Rating Scale.* New York: Teachers College Press.

Johnson-Martin, N. M., Jens, K. G., Attermeier, S. M., & Hacker, B. J. (1991). *The Carolina Curriculum for Infants and Toddlers with Special Needs* (2nd ed.). Baltimore: Paul H. Brookes.

Kaufman, A. S., & Kaufman, N. L. (1984). *Kaufman Assessment Battery for Children.* Circle Pines, MN: American Guidance Service.

Lidz, C. S. (1991). *Practitioner's guide to dynamic assessment.* New York: Guilford Press.

Linder, T. W. (1993). *Transdisciplinary play-based assessment: A functional approach to working with young children* (rev. ed.). Baltimore: Paul H. Brookes.

McConnell, S. R. (2000). Assessment in early intervention and early childhood special education: Building on the past to project into our future. *Topics in Early Childhood Special Education,* 20(1), 43–48.

McCune, L., Fleck, M., Kalmanson, B., Glazewski, B., & Sillari, J. (1990). An interdisciplinary model of infant assessment. In S. J. Meisels & J. P. Shonkoff (Eds.), *Handbook of early childhood intervention* (pp. 221–245). New York: Cambridge University Press.

McLean, M., Bailey, D. B., & Wolery, M. (1996). *Assessing infants and preschoolers with special needs* (2nd ed.). Upper Saddle River, NJ: Merrill/Prentice Hall.

McWilliam, R. A., Tocci, L., & Harbin, G. L. (1998). Family-centered services: Service providers' discourse and behavior. *Topics in Early Childhood Special Education,* 18(4), 206–221.

Neisworth, J. T., & Bagnato, S. J. (1988). Assessment in early childhood special education: A typology of dependent measures. In S. L. Odom & M. B. Karnes (Eds.), *Early intervention for infants and children with handicaps: An empirical base* (pp. 23–51). Baltimore: Paul H. Brookes.

Neisworth, J. T., & Bagnato, S. J. (1996). Assessment for early intervention: Emerging themes and practices. In S. L. Odom & M. E. McLean (Eds.), *Early intervention/early childhood special education: Recommended practices* (pp. 23–58). Austin, TX: PRO-ED.

Newborg, J., Stock, J. R., Wnek, J., Guidubaldi, J., & Svinicki, J. S. (1988). *Battelle Developmental Inventory.* Chicago: Riverside.

Popper, B. K. (1996). Achieving change in assessment practices: A parent's perspective. In S. I. Greenspan & S. J. Meisels (Eds.), *Toward a new vision for the developmental assessment of infants and young children* (pp. 59–66). Washington, DC: Zero to Three/National Center for Infants, Toddlers, and Families.

Rocco, S. (1996). Toward a shared commitment and shared responsibility: A parent's vision of developmental assessment. In S. I. Greenspan & S. J. Meisels (Eds.), *Toward a new vision for the developmental assessment of infants and young children* (pp. 59–66). Washington, DC: Zero to Three/National Center for Infants, Toddlers, and Families.

Turnbull, A. P., & Turnbull, H. R. (1997). *Families, professionals and exceptionality: A special partnership*. Upper Saddle River, NJ: Merrill/Prentice Hall, Inc.

Turnbull, R., & Cilley, M. (1999). *Explanations and implications of the 1997 amendments to* IDEA. Upper Saddle River, NJ: Merrill/Prentice Hall, Inc.

Vincent, L. J., & McLean, M. E. (1996). Family participation. In S. L. Odom & M. E. McLean (Eds.), *Early intervention/ early childhood special education: Recommended practices* (pp. 59–66). Austin, TX: PRO-ED.

VORT Corporation. (1995). HELP *for Preschoolers*. Palo Alto, CA: Author.

Zeitlin, S., Williamson, G. G., & Szczepanski, M. (1988). *Early Coping Inventory* (ECI). Bensenville, IL: Scholastic Testings Service.

2

Family Involvement

Family-Centered Practices

"Family-centered" policies and practices in early intervention have been encouraged consistently in the literature (Dunst, Johanson, Trivette, & Hamby, 1991; Dunst, Trivette, & Deal, 1994). Orienting assessment, planning, and treatment of families as units is recommended for the programming of all young children and mandated in Part C for those children from birth to 2 years of age. Part B of the IDEA, which focuses on services to preschool children with disabilities, also stresses the important roles to be played by families. Parents of preschool children are given a significant role in the design and evaluation of services provided to their children; they are partners with the schools in developing IEPs. Dunst, Trivette, and Deal (1988, 1994) pointed out that the family—not the individual child—must be the focus of any plan and system of intervention in order to maximize its effectiveness. This recognition has stemmed, in part, from the awareness that the success of any early intervention program is dependent on the efforts coming from within as well as from outside the family unit.

In family-centered programs, families control the early intervention process. This family-centered approach requires a dramatic shift in the way that many professionals think about families. The interventionist must hold a set of attitudes or values that places the needs and desires of the family at the center of the intervention process. This value system is counter to the child-centered approach historically endorsed by early intervention professionals. Professional training programs have concentrated on teaching students how to be experts in a particular content area. A family-centered approach requires that the professionals relinquish this "expert" role and create a partnership with families in which both the professional and the family member have equal status.

Dunst, Trivette, and Deal (1988, 1994) advocated respect for families and meaningfulness of intervention in their commitment to enabling and empowering families. "Enabling" is defined as creating opportunities for all families to display and acquire competencies that strengthen family functioning; "empowerment" is the family's ability to meet needs and aspirations in a way that promotes a clear sense of intrafamily mastery and control over important aspects of family functioning. The key point is that family members must maintain ownership of their powerful, positive impact on one another, including the child with disabilities. Failure to display competence is not owing to deficits within the person, but rather the failure of social systems to create opportunities for competence to be displayed or learned (Dunst, Trivette, & Deal, 1994). The efficacy of early intervention programs will be enhanced to the extent that professionals can assist in meeting the needs and reaching the special goals of the family.

Families hold the power to make key decisions about their children in family-centered programs. Professionals believe that families are capable of making wise and responsible decisions. Parents are encouraged to take a leadership role on the intervention team, rather than acting as passive participants. Family decisions are respected, even when they conflict with the recommendations of the professionals (Stoneman & Manders, 1998).

Strengthening and supporting the family unit and not just the child considerably enhances the chances of making a significant positive impact on all family members (Dunst, Trivette, & Deal, 1994). Collaborative partnerships are now recognized as recommended practice for all early childhood programs (Vincent & McLean, 1996).

Winton and Bailey (1988) summarized the literature on best practice in working with families. Best practice is based on at least four assumptions:

1. Each family is unique. The same event will have different meanings and result in different

reactions from different families (McCubbin & Patterson, 1983a). It is essential to determine a family's definition and understanding of an event (Berger, 1986).

2. Because family needs are developmental and changing over time (Wikler, 1981; McCubbin & Patterson, 1983b), a mechanism for frequent monitoring and communicating with families regarding those needs is essential.

3. A truly family-centered approach means that the early interventionists focus on the needs of the child as a part of the family as well as the needs of other family members (Parke, 1986; Simeonsson & Bailey, 1986).

4. Consideration must be given to the degree to which the family is embedded within its social environment and the ways in which this context affects families (Aponte, 1986; Bronfenbrenner, 1979; Kazak & Wilcox, 1984).

Based on these assumptions, this chapter begins with the concept of family-centered services; presents the federal mandates regarding family involvement in the assessment process and the benefits of family involvement; considers the uniqueness of each family within their social context; and discusses how the level of participation families choose may vary between families and at different times in the assessment and intervention process. The latter part of the chapter addresses the identification of family resources, priorities, and concerns; methods for information gathering; family participation in collecting assessment information; and an ecocultural approach to intervention, including the development of IFSPs and IEPs.

Federal Mandates

In 1986, PL 99–457 furthered the practice of family involvement in early intervention by mandating the inclusion of families in the assessment process and program development for infants and toddlers with disabilities. As a result of this legislation, families were to be an integral part of the process of evaluating a young child's potential needs by their participation in assessment activities relating to child development and family functioning, as well as in the planning of the intervention program.

PL 105–17 (IDEA), the 1997 Amendments of PL 99–457, retained the requirements of prior law regarding the right of parents to examine their child's records, obtain an independent education evaluation, be given prior written notice of actions proposed or refused by the public agency in their native language, and initiate a due process hearing regarding such actions (Turnbull & Cilley, 1999). The 1997 amended IDEA clarifies that parents have an opportunity to participate in decision making with respect to identification, evaluation, and educational placement of their child, and the provision of a free appropriate public education to the child. PL 105–17 also specifies that a surrogate parent must be appointed whenever the parents of the child are not known or when the agency cannot locate the parents after reasonable efforts (Turnbull & Cilley, 1999).

Each family with an infant or toddler who is at risk or has a disability served under Part C of the IDEA must have an IFSP based on the assessment of priorities, resources, and concerns of the family. A variety of support services are available and the family and the other members of the interdisciplinary team determine the type and extent of services needed. Under Part B, an IEP is required for each preschool child served, although the multidisciplinary team also may include a family needs component in the IEP for this age group (Demers & Fiorello, 1999).

Family participation has moved to policy-making. Family members are viewed as stakeholders and decision makers. Their perspective, vision, and expertise are as necessary as those of various professionals and agencies in the development, implementation, and evaluation of the EI/ECSE system (Vincent & McLean, 1996). Family participation is now guided by the vision of an equal partnership between the family and the service system (Vincent & McLean, 1996; Turnbull & Turnbull, 1997).

Benefits of Family Involvement

The importance of family involvement in the young child's assessment far exceeds compliance with federal mandates. The family's input and participation are highly valued for many reasons. The family constitutes the young child's predominant environment. Even those children attending nursery and preschool programs do so for small portions of the day or week. Few preschool-age children are either afforded or are ready for the social independence needed to establish a community of peers/friends outside the family circle. Most of the young child's functioning occurs within, or closely related to, family life. Therefore, it is difficult to assess meaningfully a child's functioning without considering her in the context of that primary environment. An excellent model for including the family in the assessment process is demonstrated by Linder's Trans-disciplinary Play-Based Assessment Model (Linder, 1993). This model will be discussed further in Chapter 10 on curriculum-based assessment. The benefits of family involvement include:

- Source of information about the child
- Least restrictive environment
- Family investment in program
- Child comfort and security

Source of Information

The family's input is also highly valued because of the wealth of information it offers. Families, parents, and caregivers are the greatest source of information about the child. They are the experts with respect to this individual. Research has documented that parents are accurate appraisers of their young child's development, especially when they are asked to make judgments about behaviors their child currently exhibits (Bricker & Squires, 1989; Diamond & Squires, 1993; Henderson & Meisels, 1994). Birth, medical, and early developmental histories are vital to an understanding of the young child and her needs. Parent or caregiver responses to checklists, questionnaires, and inventories can provide a host of information regarding the child's overall development, skills, and behaviors. Adaptive and daily functioning measures are an important part of the child's developmental assessment and are best provided by those with whom the child lives.

Least Restrictive Environment

The 1997 Amendments clarified that infants and toddlers should receive services in the home or in other natural settings where possible. Our assessment of the child becomes fuller and richer when we examine the way the child functions within that most important and natural setting. Direct observation of child-caregiver-family interactions leads to a better understanding of the child's interpersonal relating skills, personality, temperament, and communication effectiveness. Developmental, behavioral, and social skills assessments are served well by family participation and report. PL 105-17 also improves the coordination and transition for children from infant and toddler programs to preschool programs.

Family Investment in Program

The parents, caregivers, and family also benefit from their involvement in the assessment process. By becoming active members and decision makers on the assessment and intervention team, the parents or caregivers also learn more about the child's functioning, strengths, and needs. The perspectives of the professional members of the multidisciplinary team add to the family's knowledge base by confirming what they had observed, ruling out suspected concerns, or offering new observations and impressions. Furthermore, by participating in the development of the intervention plan (IFSP), the family's personal investment in the plan is increased. Through increased understanding of and agreement with the assessed needs and how to address them, the family members become increasingly committed to the plan they help devise, and this plan reflects their concerns more accurately. Their competencies are enhanced in the process, enabling them to more effectively meet the needs of their own child and family system.

Child Comfort and Security

Among the greatest benefits of family involvement in the assessment process is that which it affords the child. The young child's feelings of comfort, safety, and security are very important if an adequate sample of the child's capabilities is to be assumed. The young child's perceptions of safety and security are often dependent on parent feedback and support and, in the case of infants, on the parent's own demeanor and feelings of comfort in the unfamiliar setting. The parent or caregiver's presence and participation in the assessment process can hasten the child's establishment of trust and rapport with the other members of the team.

Respect for Family Diversity

Recognition of the importance and value of the family's involvement in the assessment process must be matched by a respect for the family system and its unique set of circumstances. In our society, we currently recognize many variations of the family unit. Many families in today's world consist of a single parent and a child or children. Very often a grandparent or another relative or friend is an integral part of the family unit. The family has expanded from the traditional family unit to one that includes persons

who are legally responsible for a child's well-being and also those who care for the child as a parent would.

The changes in the structure of the family can be attributed to the variability in social arrangements for raising children. The changing family structure has direct relevance for interventionists or teachers who work with families of young children. There is a significant need for EI/ECSE interventionists to develop further their skills in working with families who are nontraditional, ethnic, or culturally diverse. Early childhood interventionists must accept as a family unit whomever the child's parents or guardians consider to be the child's family. Because all members of the family are affected by the child's special needs, they all need to be involved in the intervention plan to some degree.

Gathering family information necessitates entry into a family's world and way of functioning, which may not always be consistent with that of the interventionist. Family behaviors that are culture-specific could be misinterpreted by the interventionist who lacks an awareness of cultural or ethnic differences. Cross-cultural competence is not developed overnight. Practitioners cannot expect to know everything there is to know about every culture, ethnicity, and race. When forming working partnerships with families who are culturally diverse, the key is to remain sensitive, aware, and responsive. General issues that should be taken under consideration include cultural characteristics, cultural patterns, languages, values, beliefs, attitudes, behaviors, and the level of acculturation (Nuttall, Romero, & Kalesnik, 1999). This topic is given further consideration in Chapter 3 on cultural diversity.

It is recommended that the examiners/practitioners strive for the following when assessing an infant or young child:

- Recognize and be sensitive to the family's values, attitudes, and feelings, especially as they relate to the child.

- Respect and communicate awareness of the family's "expertness" with respect to the child.
- Come to understand the family's expectations, wishes, and goals regarding the child.
- Respect the "culture of the family," including its beliefs, customs, and parenting styles.
- Note how the family's style and expectations impact the child and how adaptive the child is within the context of the family and its routine practices.
- Assist and empower the family without diminishing or disregarding its responsibility for the child.
- Recognize the particular stress the assessment must present to the parents or caregivers. The assessment may confirm or refute some concerns that have been raised about the child.

Sensitivity and respect for the family's tension at this time are crucial to accurate data collection as well as to effective decision making regarding the child's potential programming. McWilliam, Tocci, and Harbin (1998) found that service providers' positiveness, sensitivity, friendliness, responsiveness, and child and community skills provide the path to the family orientation door. Family centeredness encompasses both philosophy (i.e., attitudes and beliefs) and behavior (i.e., practices) (Nuttall, Romero, & Kalesnik, 1999).

Levels of Family Involvement

Bailey (1996) suggested three questions that are essential to the process of determining the concerns, priorities, and resources of the family: (1) What role does the family want to play in the process of making decisions about their child and in providing educational or therapeutic interventions? (2) What does this family want from the service system? (3) How do family members perceive the service system and what constitutes an acceptable relationship between parents and service providers?

Families vary considerably in the extent to which they want to be involved in assessment, team meetings, decision making, and service delivery. Some families want to play a major role in determining the assessment information to be gathered, participating in the team meeting, and making decisions about goals and services for the child and the family. On the other hand, some families would prefer that professionals take the leadership role. The range of possible roles family members could fill is very wide (Bailey, 1996).

Hains, Rosenkoetter, and Fowler (1991) presented four roles that parents may assume during the child's transition from preschool to kindergarten, including teacher, information source, decision maker, and advocate. For example, the parents may wish to learn about the activities they can do with their child to promote her development. The family is an important source of information for understanding the child and, therefore, can assume this role of providing information about the child to the rest of the team. Bruns and Fowler (1999) suggested broadening these family roles to encompass the entire family, not only the parents. Bruns and Fowler (1999) recommended the family be viewed as guide, information specialist, decision maker, and ally (Figure 2–1). These same roles could be applied to the assessment process. Early interventionists/early childhood special educators must realize that all of these roles may not be appropriate or sensitive to all families. There may be within-group differences as well. For example, members of different Asian groups may assume a range of roles in their young child's education, based on the level of acculturation, family traditions, country of origin, or socioeconomic level (Chan, 1998). Some roles may conflict with cultural beliefs and practices. For instance, the parents of a young child may consult with many family members before they make a decision.

A family-centered approach does not force families to assume any particular role. Because wide variability exists, the level of involvement

FIGURE 2–1
Parent Roles

- Information source
- Information specialist
- Teacher
- Guide
- Decision Maker
- Advocate
- Ally

must be determined by each particular family. The level of involvement may vary depending upon the nature of the activity. One family may want to be more involved in the child's assessment or the child's intervention activities, but another's parents may prefer to leave the decision making about the child's assessment to the professionals and be involved only in the team meeting. The team needs to determine the family's choice of roles in each of the contexts (Bailey, 1996). It also should be noted that the family preference for involvement might change over time. Initially, a family may feel very insecure and uncomfortable in trying to play a leadership role surrounded by professionals, but eventually, the family may become more comfortable and confident in their opinions and skills and so choose to begin to exert more influence and play a greater role in the process (Bailey, 1996).

Identification of Family Resources, Priorities, and Concerns

The assessment, which strives to identify family resources, priorities, and concerns, is one component of the early intervention process. Information about the family's resources, concerns, priorities, and preferences comes from the child's family or primary caregivers and addresses their priorities for the child's development, skill acquisition, and behavior. This information reflects the family's traditions, culture, desire for involvement, family roles, and interactional styles. This information includes the family's own needs, which might include knowledge about child development, information about a specific disability, or advice on behavior management or teaching certain skills at home (Davis, Kilgo, & Gamel-McCormick, 1998).

The resources, priorities, and concerns which are identified by the family are used then in the development of the IFSP. The IFSP defines the intervention program for the child and family. (See "Individualized Family Service Plans" and "Individualized Education Programs" later in this chapter.)

Bailey (1996) pointed out that families differ in many respects. These differences include the meaning they attach to their child's disability, the way the family is organized, the goals they have for their child, their views of service providers and public assistance systems, and the ways in which they want to be involved in making decisions and providing services for their child. Gathering information regarding the family's priorities, resources, and concerns will ensure that family services are individualized and thus meet their particular needs. This process of information gathering or assessment should be ongoing and interactive and result in information which determines family priorities for goals.

The process for family information-gathering is often misunderstood. Families report that one of the most threatening and uncomfortable aspects of early intervention services is the process of assessing the family's concerns, priorities, and resources (Slentz, Walker, & Bricker, 1989). Early intervention professionals are not being asked to intrude on the privacy of families but are charged with providing opportunities for families to choose to share the challenges for which they want help and support (Berman & Shaw, 1996). Slentz and Bricker (1992) advocated a family-guided approach to family information-gathering and early intervention. With a family-guided approach, the child remains the primary focus of intervention and assessment. Resolution of family issues is facilitated by the interventionist as concerns or priorities related to the child's development are raised. Family outcomes are included in the IFSP as they arise, rather than being identified at the time of entry into the program. The family guides the content of assessment and intervention so that services are individualized according to family member priorities, values, culture, and activities.

The best way to find out what approach is preferred by families is to ask them. Parents have expressed a strong and consistent preference for informal approaches and open-ended conversations, rather than structured interviews (Summers et al., 1990). They prefer informality and nonintrusive questions. Parents wanted professionals to invest whatever time is necessary to develop rapport and friendships. Broad consensus was expressed about the need for keen listening skills and sensitivity to needs that may be expressed by indirect statements, such as "I didn't get much sleep last night" (Noonan & McCormick, 1993). Slentz and Bricker (1992) recommended an initial interview and a brief needs assessment. Discussing the family strengths sets a positive tone and allows the family the opportunity to participate in the intervention planning. A series of topics or questions focusing on family composition, history, and issues might be asked as well as questions about the child's early life and developmental milestones. The questions would be discussed with the families in the context of assessing their needs and planning to meet those needs (Kaiser & Hemmeter, 1989). The family also could be given the opportunity to complete a formal or informal needs assessment at this time or at a later meeting.

Another area of broad consensus found among parents was that only family strengths or needs clearly related to the child's specific IFSP objectives should be discussed and that the parents should be the ones to say precisely what would appear in writing on the IFSP (Summers et al., 1990). In essence, families are responsible for their children. Family priorities and concerns, as identified by the family, determine the professional's role. Families do not have to participate in the assessment of their resources, priorities, and concerns in order for their children to receive services. However, the most effective method of obtaining useful information for early intervention depends on collaboration between caregivers and professionals (Benner, 1992). The process of identifying family strengths and needs must be done on an individual basis. The purpose is to identify family strengths, resources, needs, and concerns relevant to an individual family's ability to enhance the development of the child (Johnson, McGonigel, & Kaufmann, 1989). A model for conducting a family-focused interview has been provided by Winton and Bailey (1988).

The Family-Focused Interview

Winton and Bailey (1988) provided a model for conducting a family-focused interview. The family-focused interview has a moderate degree of structure in that the interviewer identifies specific topics to cover during the interview. An interview guide is developed with a list of objectives and questions. However, the interviewer has great flexibility in the order and manner in which topics are discussed. The emphasis is on open-ended questions which allow unanticipated areas of concern to appear. Using this model, families are allowed to "tell their own story" in their own way and emphasize the aspects that are important to them (Glaser & Strauss, 1967; Gorden, 1969; Wilson, 1977). The interview process is described as building trust and rapport and increasing families' feelings of worth as persons whose opinions are valued and respected (Gorden, 1969). The ultimate goal of the interview is to generate family goals as a result of a truly collaborative effort between the interventionist and the family (Winton & Bailey, 1988). The steps in this interview process are outlined in the next sections.

Organizing the Interview. The interventionist should gather information from a variety of sources before the interview. This information may include medical records, prior contacts with the family and other professionals involved with the family, and any assessment information that has been gathered to date. Five types of information may be gathered: (1) family roles and needs for support, information, or training; (2) critical events which may necessitate family adaptation; (3) parent-child interaction; (4) information about the home environment; and (5) child variables relevant to family functioning, such as temperament or demand characteristics (Bailey et al., 1988; Winton & Bailey, 1988). This information may be organized into two areas: initial hypotheses about family goals, and areas that need to be explored further within the interview. The four phases of the interview are presented in Table 2–1.

Introductory Phase. This phase is used to reduce the family's anxiety and create an appropriate listening environment. This phase includes explaining the purpose of the interview, confirming the time allotted and the format to be followed, discussing issues of confidentiality (e.g., who will have access to the information and under what conditions), and structuring the physical environment (e.g., limiting interruptions and accommodating young children). The introductory phase is critical to the success of the interview (Winton & Bailey, 1988).

Inventory Phase. This is the significant portion of the interview. The purpose of this phase is to validate and elaborate on prior information and to identify additional areas of family concern, strengths, and resources. The interventionist's opening statement sets the tone for the interview and should be related to the purpose of the interview. The statement should be open-ended, nonthreatening, and allow the family to start the interview where they are most comfortable. The interventionist should convey the feeling that he is there to listen, and the family should do most of the talking.

Summary, Priorities, and Goal-Setting. The purpose of this phase is to reach agreement on the family's concerns, goals, and priorities. This is a key part of the interview. In this phase, assessment information is compiled and translated into meaningful and practical goals. It is important that target goals are defined in such a way that success is possible. This process will build a family's confidence and sense of competence and demonstrate the interventionist's ability to be a family helper (Aponte, 1976; Berger, 1986; Bryant, 1984).

Closure. In the final phase, the interventionist expresses recognition and appreciation of the family's contribution, makes plans for the next meeting, reiterates objectives to be addressed, and gives family members an opportunity to reflect on feelings about the interview or raise other questions or concerns. In this phase, family members may express concerns or critical information that had not been brought out in the earlier phases. Therefore, it is important to allow the family this opportunity for final thoughts. Turnbull and Turnbull's (1997) conversation guide (Table 2–2) provides some ideas for questions that might be used in any of the interview phases.

Domains of Family Information-Gathering

Many types of instruments have been developed or adapted to be used to assess the family's priorities, resources, and concerns in early intervention settings. A review of the literature reveals that many potential areas or domains have been used or considered for this assessment. Some examples of these domains

TABLE 2–1
Model for Conducting Family-Focused Interview

Interviewing Phase	Purpose

1. Introduction
   A. Explain purpose of the interview
   B. Confirm time allotted and format
   C. Discuss confidentiality
   D. Structure physical environment (if possible)
	Reduce parents' anxiety and create appropriate listening

2. Inventory
   A. Opening statement
   B. Major portion of the interview parents do most of the talking
	Validate and elaborate information from assessment
	
	Identify additional areas of family needs, strengths, and resources

3. Summary and Priority
   A. Summarizing statement
   B. Exploration of family's priorities
	Clarify consensus and disagreement between parents
	
	Agree on definition of family needs

4. Closure
   A. Recognition of and appreciation for parents' contribution to interventionist's understanding of family
   B. Statement of family and interventionist's objectives to be accomplished or worked on by next meeting
	Agree on order in which to consider needs
	
	Recognize parents' efforts
	
	Focus on objectives or actions to be accomplished by next meeting

From Winton, P. J., & Bailey, D. B. (1988). The family-focused interview: A collaborative mechanism for family assessment and goal-setting. *Journal of the Division for Early Childhood, 12*, p. 199.

include: stress, coping styles, teaching skills, parent-child interaction, the home environment, locus of control, support systems, and stages of grief. However, the purpose of family information-gathering for developing the IFSP suggests that these domains are not likely to be appropriate.

According to federal legislation, the appropriate domains for assessment are family resources, priorities, and concerns related to the care of the young child with a disability. Consideration first must be given to understanding what is meant by resources, priorities, and concerns.

TABLE 2–2
Possible Topics for Interview Questions

Focus	Areas
Family	Perceptions of assessment process
	Parent concerns
	Pertinent family information/Health history
Child	Health
	Feeding and oral behavior
	Independent toileting
	Sleep
	Social adaptation
	Coping skills
	Language and communication behaviors
	Preferred toys and play
	Experiences outside home
	Feelings, fears, and moods

From Meisels, S. J., & Provence, S. (1989). *Screening and assessment: Guidelines for identifying young disabled and developmentally vulnerable children and their families.* Arlington, VA: ZERO TO THREE: National Center for Clinical Infant Programs. Reprinted by permission.

Family Resources

Bailey and Simeonsson (1988) suggested three categories of family strengths and resources: (1) personal resources, (2) intra-family resources, and (3) extra-family resources. Personal resources are the personal characteristics that give meaning to life and allow individuals to address problems constructively. Examples of these resources might include an outgoing and assertive personality, a strong sense of competence and control over life, and religious or philosophical beliefs.

Intra-family resources are obtained within the nuclear or extended family, e.g., from a spouse, sibling, parents, or in-laws. Such resources include help with specific tasks, such as child care or housekeeping, and socioemotional support from family members who are good listeners and provide emotional support.

Extra-family resources come from outside the family. Individuals or groups who might be a resource include neighbors, friends, professionals, agencies, church, and so on. Generally, the more access the family has to resources, then the more coping mechanisms the family members have to assist them in their difficulties.

Families should identify and use their existing strengths and resources. They should be encouraged by professionals to use their own abilities to solve problems and obtain needed resources.

Family Priorities

This type of information tells professionals what the family wants the child to achieve. Teachers, therapists, administrators, and other ECSE professionals tend to focus their goals and objectives on skills that will allow the child to flourish in all settings. Families are usually more concerned about both developmental issues and the acquiring skills which she seems to need more often. For example, a parent may be concerned that her child has a way to tell her when she wants to play with another toy or child.

Family Concerns

An important dimension to family information-gathering is the identification and documentation of specific concerns with which each family would like assistance. These concerns may range from wanting information about their child's disability, including current and future services available, to developing strategies for teaching their child. They may want to obtain baby-sitting services, access specialized adaptive equipment, or find and access financial assistance for their child's medical expenses. The early interventionist should be able to help families meet certain concerns, refer them to other professionals, agencies, or resources, and help family members to build and reinforce their own resources.

The critical events facing a family influence the type of needs a family may have at a particular time. Three specific periods bring about increased stress for families with young children with disabilities: (1) the initial diagnosis of a disability, (2) the first efforts at seeking help or intervention, and (3) the transition from infant to preschool programs (Bernheimer, Young, & Winton, 1983). As the child approaches major developmental milestones, such as walking and self-feeding, and the family recognizes that the child cannot perform these tasks, families may need additional coping skills. Professionals need to be aware of these critical times and events so that support may be adjusted accordingly.

Early strains on parent-child relationships from health concerns, for example, can have long-term consequences. Information gained from parent-child interaction assessments can be used to foster positive interactions by helping parents become more sensitive to their infant's communication system. Interactions may be evaluated by using behavioral observation systems or interaction assessment checklists. Interventionists may examine broad behaviors such as responsivity or more specific behaviors such as vocalizations. The type of instrument used will depend on the type of information desired. Many of these instruments are professionally completed and thus are based on professional judgment about the quality of parent-child interactions and home environment which may differ across cultures. Therefore, this type of formal assessment should be considered only when families determine that this is a desired area of attention for intervention (Bailey, 1996).

Family information gathering ought to be designed to determine the family's perception of the child, the child's needs, and the family's desire for services or other kinds of support from professionals (Bailey, 1996). Interventionists should realize that the range of concerns families may have is considerable. If the child has extensive needs, the family may feel overwhelmed and unsure of where to begin. Professionals can provide information to help

them sort out their concerns and needs and make informal decisions about their priorities. It is likely that the priorities and concerns will change over time. The premise behind family information-gathering is that, with the right kind of resources, every family can support the development of a child with special needs, and services should assist, not supplant, the family (Raver, 1999).

Considerations for Gathering Information from Families

If conducted appropriately, family information gathering should help early intervention programs be consistent with a family-centered approach (Bailey, 1996). The process of identifying family strengths and needs must be done on an individual basis. These interactions can take place in the family home, at neighborhood gathering spots, or at schools as long as family is comfortable with the setting (Turnbull & Turnbull, 1997). In order to reduce the likelihood of family information-gathering being viewed as intrusive, Bailey (1991) offers the following suggestions:

- Emphasize the role of family choice in whether to participate in family assessment activities, as well as how they might participate.
- Use the least formal and most functional procedures necessary. Families will feel that assessment activities are helpful if they seem practical and directly related to their needs.
- Be sensitive to the importance of the precise way questions are stated. Straightforward, positively oriented terminology is preferable to jargon and a focus on problems.
- Be especially sensitive to cultural variation in preferences and expectations for appropriate and acceptable professional behavior.
- Assure confidentiality of responses, and tell families what information will be maintained in the records and who will have access to it.

Methods for Information-Gathering

The early interventionist always must view the family as a system and assess the different factors that influence it (Ostfeld & Gibbs, 1990). A variety of methods may be used to gather family information, including interviews, observation, self-report questionnaires, and instruments. The law does not mandate that formal surveys, indices, scales, and questionnaires be used (Slentz & Bricker, 1992). The method and the content area of the assessment should be chosen to fulfill the program's goals.

Interviews

Parent or caregiver interviews may be used either to gather or clarify information from other sources, such as the caregiver's perceptions about specific events and identification of priorities for services. The interview may be either nondirected or structured/focused. Nondirected interviews provide the opportunity to build rapport but make data gathering and goal setting difficult. Inexperienced staff may have difficulty with interpreting data from unstructured interviews. An informal or nonstructured interview might focus on topics pertaining to the family and child such as those listed in Table 2–2.

A structured or focused interview has specific questions or goals. The questions may have forced-choice responses or be open-ended. This type of interview may be helpful for families who are uncomfortable with a questionnaire (Ostfeld & Gibbs, 1990). Research has indicated that slightly over 50% of mothers surveyed preferred to share information through the written survey as opposed to personal interviews (Sexton, Snyder, Rheams, Barron-Sharp, & Perez, 1991). These results indicate that early interventionists should provide a variety of means for families to share information about their needs and strengths.

Eco-Mapping. Eco-mapping is the process of visually portraying family relationships and representations of the family's associations with informal (e.g., friends, extended family) and formal (e.g., early intervention, community services) supports (McBride & Brotherson, 1997). This is a strategy that interventionists can use to learn whom families consider in their membership and to identify whom and what resources they consider to be sources of support. A map is constructed by putting the immediate family in a large center circle and drawing connecting lines to other resources such as friends, school, healthcare providers, or religious institutions. The strength and quality of these relationships can be shown by using different types of connecting lines. For example, a stressful relationship could be symbolized by a hatched line; bold lines could represent strong, helpful relationships; dashed lines could represent weaker relationships; and arrows could be used to indicate the flow of resources (McBride & Brotherson, 1997).

Observations

Observations may also be structured or unstructured. Observations may be used to determine the rate, quality, or pattern of behavior (e.g., caregiver-child interactions) in natural or clinical settings. Structured observations are helpful when specific information is needed. For example, a coding system may be used to measure a predetermined behavior or category of behaviors (e.g., displays of affection, initiations of interactions by caregiver) (Benner, 1992). A running record of observation is another technique which might be useful. Running records are discussed further in Chapter 11 on Ecological Assessment. The professional should always remember that it is difficult to be natural when you're being observed. These techniques should be compatible with family functioning style and the types of information needed.

Questionnaires and Test Instruments

Standardized instruments as well as less formal self-report checklists and scales provide an efficient, uniform way of gathering information (Ostfeld & Gibbs, 1990). Some instruments are designed to identify family strengths, needs, resources, and sources of support. Other instruments are designed to determine family functioning in specific areas, such as stress, knowledge of infant development, or depression. Assessment of family functioning should only be used if specific areas of concern arise during the process of identifying strengths and needs. Professionals should remember that self-report questionnaires may have items that parents see as being intrusive, and they have the right to choose not to respond. When administering a questionnaire, the professional needs to provide a general statement of purpose and allow parents/caregivers not to answer. Staff members should be accessible for questions that aren't understood.

Many types of assessment are available which may or may not be appropriate for use in a particular early intervention program with a particular family. Some of the various instruments and strategies which might be used in assessing families are listed in Table 2–3. Bailey (1996) recommended that family assessment strategies should be evaluated rigorously with regard to their effects and usefulness. Ostfeld and Gibbs (1990) recommended that professionals (1) know what a test purports to measure, (2) avoid interpretations that go beyond the data, and (3) recognize and respect individual differences. These authors further recommend, when selecting and evaluating an assessment method, that a review of the literature on the selected instrument or method be conducted to ascertain the latest data on reliability and validity for the particular families with which it will be used. They also suggest that interpretation of findings and making appropriate recommendations based on these instruments should be directed to a mental health practitioner who has the clinical experience in the counseling of families with children with special needs. Henderson, Aydlett, and Bailey (1993) suggested two criteria that are fundamentally important to choosing assessments: (1) Does the assessment procedure result in useful information? and (2) Is the assessment process acceptable to families? Families should not only be allowed to decide whether they participate or not, but also be provided reasonable alternatives for strategies for sharing this information (Bailey, 1996). The decision to use an instrument for information-gathering should be based on whether this instrument will provide information related to the family's resources, priorities, and concerns about the care of their young child with a disability.

Simeonsson (1986) cautioned professionals to be aware of the subjectivity of their own philosophies and value systems in order to avoid imposing demands on families that are incompatible with the family's lifestyle and belief system. For example, instruments developed by and for the Western white population reflect a set of cultural norms and beliefs about children, parenting, and the role of the families. The cultural values of families from diverse backgrounds may differ from Western white middle-class standards (Hanson, Lynch, & Wayman, 1990).

Family Participation in Collecting Assessment Information

Turnbull and Turnbull (1997) suggested some options for creating a partnership with families in evaluation. They suggest inviting families to:

1. Share their family story
2. Express their preferences and great expectations and describe their child's strengths and needs
3. Assist professionals in administering assessments

TABLE 2–3
Instruments for Family Information Gathering

Family Resources, Priorities, and Concerns		
Instrument	**Purpose**	**Source**
Family Resource Scale (Dunst & Lee, 1994)	Identify a family's needs for social support and resources	*Supporting and strengthening families.* Cambridge, MA: Brookline.
Family Functioning Style Scale (Deal, Trivette, & Dunst, 1994)	Assess various kinds of family strengths and capabilities	*Supporting and strengthening families.* Cambridge, MA: Brookline.
Family Support Scale (Dunst, Jenkins, & Trivette, 1994)	Identify parents' perceptions of how helpful various supports are in raising young children	*Supporting and strengthening families.* Cambridge, MA: Brookline.
AEPS Family Interest Survey (Cripe & Bricker, 1992)	Provide specific items and open-ended questions to identify family interests, designate their priority and indicate the preferred method of service delivery	Baltimore: Paul H. Brookes
Family Needs Scale (Dunst, Jenkins, & Trivette, 1988)	Asks for extent that a need occurs	*Enabling and empowering families: Principles and guidelines for practice.* Cambridge, MA: Brookline.
Family Needs Survey (Bailey & Simeonsson, 1988)	Asks whether help is needed in particular domains (e.g., child care)	*Family assessment in early intervention.* Columbus, OH: Merrill; Frank Porter Graham Child Development Center, CB #8180, University of North Carolina, Chapel Hill, NC
How Can We Help? (Child Development Resources, 1989) (Johnson, McGonigel, & Kaufman)	Asks whether help is needed in particular domains (e.g., information)	Child Development Resources, Norge, VA
Family Information Preference Inventory (Turnbull & Turnbull, 1986)	Asks parents to rate the extent to which they need or want information in five areas and how they want to receive this information	*Families, professionals, and exceptionality: A special partnership* (2nd ed.). Englewood Cliffs, NJ: Merrill
Parent Needs Survey (Seligman & Darling, 1989)	Asks parents to identify extent of need for various areas	*Ordinary families, special children: A systems approach to childhood disability.* New York: Guilford.
Family Inventory of Resources for Management (McCubbin, Comeau, & Larsen, 1981)	Document the resources families feel they have available to them in everyday life	*Family assessment inventories for research and practice.* Madison, WI: University of Wisconsin-Madison Family Stress Coping and Health Project (McCubbin & Thompson, 1987)

TABLE 2–3
continued

Instrument	Purpose	Source
Family Crisis Oriented Personal Evaluation Scales (McCubbin, Olson, & Larsen, 1981)	Measure problem-solving strategies used by families	*Family assessment inventories for research and practice.* Madison, WI: University of Wisconsin-Madison Family Stress Coping and Health Project (McCubbin & Thompson, 1987)

Measures of Stress

Instrument	Purpose	Source
Parenting Stress Index (Abidin, 1990)	Measure the amount of stress in parent-child interactions	Pediatric Psychology Press, Charlottesville, VA
Questionnaire on Resources and Stress (Holroyd, 1974)	Identify parental/family stress	Clinical Psychology Publishers, Brandon, VT
Family Inventory of Life Events and Changes (McCubbin, Patterson, & Wilson, 1983)	Indicate life events likely to cause stress in families	*Family assessment inventories for research and practice.* Madison, WI: University of Wisconsin-Madison Family Stress Coping and Health Project (McCubbin & Thompson, 1987)

Parent/Caregiver-Child Interaction Measures

Instrument	Purpose	Source
Maternal Behavior Rating Scale (Mahoney, Powell, & Finger, 1986)	Identify dynamics of parent/child interactions [abbreviated form of MBRS (1985)]	*Topics in Early Childhood Special Education, 6,* 44–56
Infant-Parent Social Interaction Code (Baird, 1998)	Evaluate parent/child interactions from videotaped sample	Samera Baird, Auburn University, Department of Rehabilitation and Special Education, Auburn, AL 36849
Nursing Child Assessment Feeding Scale (NCAFS) (Barnard, 1978)	Rate extent to which parents and child interact in a mutually effective and synchronous fashion	NCAST Publications, University of Washington, WJ-10, Seattle, WA 98195
Nursing Child Assessment Teaching Scale (NCATS) (Barnard, 1978)	Rate extent to which parents and child interact in a mutually effective and synchronous fashion	NCAST Publications, University of Washington, WJ-10, Seattle, WA 98195
Maternal Behavior Rating Scale (Mahoney, Finger, Powell, 1985)	Assess parent's free play on such variables as expressiveness, warmth, sensitivity to child state, achievement orientation, social stimulation, etc.	*American Journal of Mental Deficiency, 90,* 296–302

Parent/Caregiver-Child Interaction Measures		
Instrument	**Purpose**	**Source**
Social Interaction Assessment/Intervention (McCollum & Stayton, 1985)	Assess dimensions of parent-child interactions	*Journal of the Division for Early Childhood, 9*(2), 125–135
Parent Behavior Progression (Bromwich, 1981)	Assess dimensions of parent-child interactions	The Center for Research Development and Services, Department of Educational Psychology, California State University, Northridge, CA 91330
Teaching Skills Inventory (Rosenberg, Robinson, & Beckman, 1984)	Assess infant-parent interaction for research and instructional programs for infants with established risk	Cordelia Robinson, JFK Center for Developmental Disabilities, University of Colorado Health Sciences Center, Campus Box C234, 4200 E Ninth St, Denver, CO 80262

Additional Instruments		
Instrument	**Purpose**	**Source**
The Coping Inventory (Zeitlin, Williamson, & Szczepanski, 1988)	Assess reactive and self-initiated behaviors of children	Scholastic Testing Service, Bensenville, IL
Home Observation for the Measurement of the Environment (Caldwell & Bradley, 1972)	Rate home environment and parental responsivity	Robert Bradley, University of Arkansas, Center for Child Development and Education, Little Rock, AR

4. Collaborate with professionals in constructing authentic assessments
5. Share their own priorities, resources, and concerns, especially in the case of infant and toddler evaluation

Sharing the Family Story

The first suggestion is to have the family share their story. This helps the interventionist get to know the family, and thus helps to create a positive relationship. The most relevant information comes from informal conversations in which families share in an open-ended way their hopes, worries, successes, and questions as a basis for planning the evaluation. Turnbull and Turnbull (1997) provided a number of topics in their Conversation Guide. A variety of open-ended questions which might be explored with families are given in this guide. The major topics include family characteristics, family interaction, family functions, and family life cycle. These topics may be used as probes for conversing with families and eliciting their story in ways consistent with the family system (Turnbull & Turnbull, 1997). A summary of this guide is provided in Table 2–4.

Expressing Preferences, Great Expectations, Strengths, and Needs

The second approach allows the family and child the opportunity to share their preferences, great expectations, strengths, and needs. Families can

TABLE 2–4
Conversation Guide for Early Childhood

Family Characteristics	
Characteristics of the family	Questions focus on family members, cultural characteristics, what's important to teach children, particular concerns and challenges, and the major strengths of the family.
Personal characteristics	Asks about the child's typical day, likes and dislikes, what's going well at home and school, particular challenges to be faced, effective and ineffective ways to deal with problems, particular health concerns, and people available to help.
Special challenges	Questions about particular challenges, issues or circumstances impacting time, energy, and resources.
Family Interaction	
Marital interactions	Questions pertain to current marital status, child's impact on your marriage, child's educational program and marital strain, strengths and interests of each person involved, and custody issues.
Parental interactions	Explores sharing of parental roles, preferences for participation, additional adults taking on parental responsibilities and their involvement, most and least enjoyable interactions with child, pattern of parental responsibilities over time, and basic parental needs staff could support.
Sibling interactions	Contains questions about most and least enjoyable ways children interact, ways siblings can provide educational support, challenges for other children, distributing time and attention across children and siblings attending conferences about child.
Extended family interactions	Explores who is in extended family, how often do you see them, support received from these family members, information that they would find helpful, and their attendance at conferences.

Source: Families, professionals and exceptionality: 3/e A special partnership by A. P. Turnbull & H. R. Turnbull III, © 1997. Adapted by permission of Prentice-Hall, Inc., Upper Saddle River, NJ.

express their concerns, their likes and dislikes, their future aspirations, and any other relevant information. Perceived control is a critically important family factor in the empowerment process. When information about family preferences is available at the beginning of the evaluation process, members of the multidisciplinary evaluation team can ensure that assessments take these preferences into account (Turnbull & Turnbull, 1997). Families can be encouraged to share this information by using probe questions and actively listening.

Administering Assessments

Another alternative is collaborating with families in administering assessments. Using more flexible assessment instruments which allow for more family participation encourages collaboration with the family. In recent years, several tools have been designed for completion by families themselves. One example of such a tool is the *Ages and Stages Questionnaires* (Bricker, Squires, Mounts, Potter, Nickel, & Farrell, 1995). *The Ages and Stages Questionnaires* are a multidomain developmental measure used to monitor at-risk children. Another example is the "Family Report" from the *Assessment, Evaluation, and Programming System* (Bricker, 1993). This informal questionnaire is to be completed by the parents regarding the development in the five primary domains: cognitive, communicative, social, motor, and adaptive. Parents can comment on their child's skills in these areas, any concerns they may have, and what they would like their child to be doing in these areas in 6 months to a year. The more the interventionist collaborates with families in collecting evaluation information, the more likely he is to have accurate information and to develop a reliable alliance with them (Turnbull & Turnbull, 1997).

Constructing Authentic Assessments

The fourth alternative is to rely more heavily on authentic assessment. Authentic assessments provide opportunities for children to demonstrate their mastery of skills and knowledge in real-life situations. Authentic assessments also assure a close link between typical experiences and school and thus a greater role for family partnership (Turnbull & Turnbull, 1997). An example of this would be encouraging parents to jot down notes and share information about their child's interests and activities.

Sharing Priorities, Resources, and Concerns

The final alternative discussed by Turnbull and Turnbull (2001) is the reminder that families of infants and toddlers have the option of discussing their resources, priorities, and concerns related to enhancing the development of their child. This alternative is good practice for children of any age. The purpose of the provision for sharing priorities, resources, and concerns is to plan services and supports that can promote family well-being related to the child's

development. This identification of resources, priorities, and concerns must be (1) voluntary; (2) carried out by personnel trained to use appropriate methods and procedures; (3) based on a personal interview; and (4) carried out by incorporating the family's own description of their resources, priorities, and concerns. This process should be customized to the particular child and family.

An Ecocultural Approach

Bernheimer and Keogh (1995) proposed that designing interventions for children with developmental problems requires an assessment that takes into account three kinds of information: the characteristics of the child, the physical/social context of the home and family, and the goals and beliefs of family members. An ecocultural approach to assessment provides a framework for gathering information on those three aspects of developmental problems.

The basis of this ecocultural approach is the idea that families actively and proactively respond to the circumstances in which they live, and that they build and organize environments that give meaning and direction to their lives (Bernheimer, Gallimore, & Weisner, 1990; Gallimore, Weisner, Kaufman, & Bernheimer, 1989; Weisner, 1984). This constructive activity is based in part on the nature and expression of the child's problems as well as on the actual material aspects of the family's conditions, such as income, level of education, physical characteristics, and so on. Family activities and responses to the child with developmental problems also are based on parents' beliefs, goals, and values. Therefore, the family's activities and responses are based on their perceptions of the problems, their sense of what can be done, and their sense of what is important to be done. Bernheimer and Keogh (1995) suggested that in order to plan interventions, it is necessary to build a picture of everyday life by gathering detailed information about the family's daily routine.

Daily Routines

All families construct daily routines which reflect the functional activities of family living. These family routines will vary but they provide a picture of the ways in which families organize their lives. The daily routines reflect a mix of personal and cultural values as well as the constraints, pressures, and resources in the environment. Therefore, information is gathered about the daily routine through interviews with the parents. Parents are asked to describe what a typical day is like. These stories describe everyday aspects of family life and provide the interviewer with the opportunity to ask about parent goals and values regarding their child with delays. Describing the daily routine provides clues to the practicality and feasibility of recommendations for interventions because successful intervention is usually dependent on how easily and effectively the activities can be incorporated into the daily lives of family members (Bernheimer & Keogh, 1995).

Accommodation

The parents' stories about their daily routines are then organized into 10 areas known as the accommodation domains. Accommodations are defined as the family's functional responses or adjustments to the demands of daily life with a child with delays. These accommodation domains provide a framework for gathering information that gives a comprehensive picture of family life (Table 2–5). Rather than following specific guidelines or relying on standard forms or questionnaires, all domains are touched on in the interview with parents (Bernheimer & Keogh, 1995). This information is then used as the foundation for planning with families the interventions that are likely to be incorporated and sustained into their daily routines over time.

Family-Centered Assessment and Intervention

In family-centered early intervention programs, services reflect the choices and preferences of families and are tailored to meet their needs. Goals on the IFSP and the IEP are selected by the family. Family members have the opportunity to be actively involved in all aspects of the child's program plan, selecting appropriate services and service providers, implementing the intervention, and evaluating the outcomes of the intervention. Parents are asked their ideas about how to accomplish targeted goals and about existing family resources for carrying out intervention activities. The interventionist works with parents to generate intervention options and lets the family members decide which options best fit their resources and desires (McWilliam & Winton, 1990).

A major concern of families is the development of individualized family service plans (Able-Boone, Goodwin, Sandall, Gordon, & Martin, 1992). Family-guided intervention practices can promote individualized plans of service that are appropriate and fit the lifestyle, priorities, and context of each family. A collaborative partnership between families and professionals will result in a better understanding of the child's strengths, great expectations, preferences, and needs. This understanding will become the foundation for the IFSP/IEP and assure long-term goals of independence, contribution, inclusion, and empowerment (Turnbull & Turnbull, 1997).

As explained in Chapter 1, Part C of the IDEA (PL 105–17) requires IFSPs for children from birth to age 3; Part B of the IDEA requires IEPs for children ages 3 to 21. IFSPs and IEPs are formal planning documents that must be developed in order for children to receive early intervention, special education, or related services. The development of and comparison of the IFSP/IEP are included in this section for

TABLE 2–5
Accommodation Domains and Examples

Domain	Examples
Family subsistence	Hours worked; flexibility of work schedule; adequacy of financial resources; amount of coverage provided by medical insurance
Services	Availability of services; eligibility for services; sources of transportation; amount of parent involvement required
Home/neighborhood safety and convenience	Safety and accessibility of play area; alterations in home (installation of locks and fences related to safety concerns); choice of particular neighborhood
Domestic workload	Amount of work that needs to be done; persons available to do it; amount of time spent by different family members
Childcare tasks	Complexity of childcare tasks; presence of extraordinary childcare demands (medical problems, behavior problems); number and availability of caregivers
Child peer groups	Child's play groups (children with disabilities and typically developing children); amount of parent supervision needed; role of siblings as playmates
Marital roles	Amount of shared decision making regarding child with delays; degree to which childcare and household tasks are shared
Instrumental/emotional support	Availability and use of formal (church, parent groups) and informal (friends, relatives) sources of support; costs of using support
Father/spouse role	Amount of involvement with child with delays; amount of emotional support provided
Parent information	Reliance on professional and nonprofessional sources of information; amount of time and effort spent accessing information
Family Functions	
Affection	In what ways does child appreciate affection, how important is it to children and people outside family upon whom child depends for affection?
Self-esteem	How does child see herself? Family beliefs about self-esteem, positive and negative school experiences, and how to support child's sense of capability?
Economics	Influences of family economics on support provided, child's requirements on economic resources, and special family responsibilities for dealing with insurance and reimbursement
Daily care	Questions about a typical day, most challenging parts of day, time for rest and relaxation, responsibility for daily tasks, and assistance which might be provided for teaching child skills to assist in daily routines
Recreation	What does family do for fun and what skills might child learn that would make recreation more enjoyable?

TABLE 2–5
continued

Family Functions	
Socialization	Who does child socialize with outside of educational agency or program, child's friendship network, influence of exceptionality on socialization and extent family friends support child?
Education	Questions about educators who have had good relationship with child, previous difficult educational situations, child's future, ways family enjoys participating in child's education and family preferences for school communications.

Family Life Cycle	
Early childhood	Asks about happiest and most problematic memories, how exceptionality was communicated, and views of child's early childhood program.

From "Weaving interventions into the fabric of everyday life: An approach fo family assessment," by L. P. Bernheimer & B. K. Keogh, 1995, *Topics in Early Childhood Special Education, 15*(4), pp. 415–433. Copyright 1995 by PRO-ED, Inc. Reprinted with permission.

two reasons: (1) the process of developing an IFSP or IEP begins with the assessment process, and (2) the literature indicates these documents are a major concern for families. The purposes, components, and processes involved in developing these plans are highlighted in this section.

Individualized Family Service Plan (IFSP)

IFSPs are written planning documents outlining services for families and infants and toddlers (birth to age 3) who are eligible for early intervention services. The IFSP is somewhat different from the IEP in that it relies heavily on a family-driven orientation to service delivery. IFSPs are based on the multidisciplinary assessment of the child and the identification of the concerns, priorities, and resources of the child's family. The IFSP is written by, or its writing is monitored by, the family, with assistance from members of a qualified multidisciplinary team of professionals. Parents or guardians serve as integral members of the team. As discussed previously in this chapter, the manner in which families are involved depends on the family's individual preferences. The IFSP should provide

a plan for services that enhance the development of the child and the capacity of the family to meet the special needs of the child.

The law provides some guidance with respect to the development and completion of the IFSP process. Information is included about the content, participants, meetings, and timelines of the process. The IFSP must include the following components:

✓ A statement of the child's present level of development in five domains: physical, cognitive, communication, social or emotional, and adaptive development;

✓ Family information, including a statement of the family's resources, priorities, and concerns related to enhancing the development of the child;

✓ Outcomes to be achieved for the child and family, as well as the criteria, procedures, and timelines used to monitor progress.

✓ Specific services the child and family will receive, including the frequency, intensity, and method of delivering services;

✓ A statement of the natural environments in which services are to be delivered, including a justification of the extent, if at all, to which the services will not be provided in a natural environment;

✓ The projected dates for initiation of services and the anticipated duration of services;

✓ The name of the service coordinator responsible for the IFSP;

✓ A plan to support the transition of the child at age 3 to preschool services or other appropriate services.

No specific format is required for the IFSP except that it must be a written plan. The emphasis is on the process, rather than the completion of a standardized form. The development and implementation of the IFSP is an ongoing supportive activity. The end result should be a set of identified outcomes on the IFSP that address the changes that families have identified for themselves and their children.

The service coordinator is the hub of communication and ongoing support for the family. The service coordinator guides the family through the referral and evaluation process and plays a significant role in the IFSP/IEP conference. Service coordinators also ensure that necessary intervention services and supports are coordinated for the benefit of all team members.

Individualized Education Program (IEP)

The IEP is an annual document developed for children with disabilities from ages 3 to 21 who are eligible for special education services. The IEP is a direct requirement of the IDEA, which mandates that all students with disabilities receive a free and appropriate public education. This requirement acknowledges that children with disabilities need a unique, specially designed instructional program.

The IEP is developed and signed by a team that must include the child's parent(s) or guardian(s), at least one special education teacher, a regular education teacher, if the child is or may be participating in regular education, an agency representative, an individual who can

interpret the instructional implications of evaluation results, and other representatives deemed necessary by the parents or school district, such as related service personnel. The IEP contains the following information:

✓ A statement of the child's present level of educational performance including (a) how the child's disability affects the child's involvement and progress in the general curriculum, or (b) for preschool children, as appropriate, how the disability affects the child's participation in appropriate activities;

✓ The child's measurable annual goals, including benchmarks or short-term objectives, related to (a) meeting the child's needs that result from the child's disability to enable the child to be involved in and progress in the general curriculum, and (b) meeting each of the child's other educational needs that result from the child's disability;

✓ The special education and related services and supplementary aids and services to be provided on behalf of the child, and a statement of the program modifications or supports for school personnel that will be provided;

✓ An explanation of the extent, if any, to which the child will not participate in the regular education program;

✓ A statement of any individual modifications in the administration of state or district-wide assessments of student achievement that are needed in order for the child to participate in such assessment; or if the IEP team determines that the child will not participate in such assessment, a statement of why that assessment is not appropriate and how the child will be assessed;

✓ The projected date for the beginning of services and modifications, the anticipated frequency, location, and duration of those services;

✓ The way in which the child's progress will be determined and how the parents will be informed of their child's progress, which must be at least as often as the progress of nondisabled children;

✓ An optional transition plan (if deemed appropriate by the IEP team).

The primary purpose of the IEP is to provide a written plan of the special education program designed to meet the needs of the child. In this way, the IEP provides direction for the teacher in meeting the needs of the child with a disability. There should be an integrated relationship among the child's needs, the IEP goals and objectives, and the instruction provided in the educational environment (Davis, Kilgo, & Gamel-McCormick, 1998). The IEP also serves as the basis for evaluation. The annual goals become the standards against which to judge student progress and instructional effectiveness. The final purpose is to function as a communication vehicle for team members in program planning and implementation (Davis, Kilgo, & Gamel-McCormick, 1998).

Comparison of the IFSP and IEP

The IFSP and IEP have several similarities. For example, they both require a statement of the child's level of performance. However, the domains included in the documents are different. The domains in the IFSP are cognitive, communication, social/emotional, and adaptive skill development. In the IEP, the domains include academic achievement, social adaptation, prevocational and vocational skills, psychomotor skills, and self-help skills.

The IFSP and IEP differ in other ways. The IEP does not require a statement of the family's resources, priorities, and concerns, nor does it require a service coordinator and a transition plan. However, the regulations state that nothing prevents the IEP from focusing on transition in the same manner as does the IFSP. Another difference is that the IEP contains a statement on the extent of a preschool-aged

child's regular classroom participation, whereas the IFSP requires a statement of the natural intervention environment.

The major underlying difference between the two documents is that the IFSP is based on a family-centered orientation in which the family is the focus of services, whereas the IEP is based more on a service delivery in which the needs of the child are the focus of services. Some states have determined that the family-centered orientation is so important that they have made efforts to extend the use of the IFSP to preschool special education. Another difference is that the IEP must be completed before programming can officially begin; therefore, the IEP may seem more like a product than a continuous process.

A collaborative partnership between families and professionals will result in a better understanding of the child's strengths, great expectations, preferences, and needs. This understanding will become the foundation for the IFSP/IEP and assure long-term goals of independence, contribution, inclusion, and empowerment. The Division for Early Childhood of the Council for Exceptional Children has compiled recommendations for practice in early childhood special education.

Summary

The evolution of family-centered services in early intervention represents a significant change in the way that services to young children and the involvement of families in these services are conceptualized. Family-centered practice could be defined as a friendly, respectful partnership with families that provides (1) emotional and educational supports; (2) opportunities to participate in service delivery and to make decisions; and (3) activities to enhance family members' capacities to carry out their self-determined roles (McWilliam, Tocci, & Harbin, 1998). Families must be involved as collaborators, and professionals must create an atmosphere that encourages active participation and engagement. Collaboration between caregivers and professionals is essential to meaningful assessment, program planning, and intervention. A critical aspect of effective family-practitioner collaboration is respect for family values, practices, and decisions, especially as these relate to the child.

An assessment of family strengths, concerns, cultural values, and preferences plays a significant role in the development and delivery of early childhood special education services. The assessment process should balance what a parent knows about such factors as a child's general health and mood with what the professional knows about a particular aspect of the child's development or her condition (Rocco, 1996). We are reminded that it is the team's job to identify supports that will enhance the quality of life and the relationship between the child and family rather than listing the child's deficits and how to fix them (Rocco, 1996). The information collected through assessment of child and family should assist in developing the IFSP objectives and enhance the effectiveness of intervention strategies for the child and family (Slentz & Bricker, 1992).

References

Able-Boone, H., Goodwin, L. D., Sandall, S. R., Gordon, N., & Martin, D. G. (1992). Consumer-based early intervention services. *Journal of Early Intervention*, 16, 201–209.

Aponte, H. (1986). "If I don't get simple, I cry." *Family Process*, 25(4), 531–548.

Aponte, H. (1976). Underorganization in the poor family. In P. Guerin (Ed.), *Family therapy: Theory and practice*, New York: Science Press.

Bailey, D. B. (1991). Issues and perspective on family assessment. *Infants and Young Children*, 4(1), 26–34.

Bailey, D. B. (1996). Assessing family resources, priorities, and concerns. In M. McLean, D. B. Bailey, & M. Wolery (Eds.), *Assessing infants and preschoolers with special needs* (pp. 202–233). Upper Saddle River, NJ: Merrill/Prentice Hall.

Bailey, D. B., & Simeonsson, R. J. (1988). *Family assessment in early intervention*. Columbus, OH: Merrill.

Bailey, D. B., Simeonsson, R., Isbell, P., Huntington, G., Winton, P., Comfort, M., & Helm, J. (1988). Inservice training in family assessment and goal-setting for early interventionists: Outcomes and issues. *Journal of the Division of Early Childhood*, 12(2), 126–136.

Benner, S. (1992). *Assessing young children with special needs: An ecological perspective*. New York: Longman.

Berger, M. (1986). Contributions of family therapy to the development of early childhood special education services that enhance individual and family development.

Training professionals to interact with families (Monograph 2). Parent/Family Support Series, University of Idaho, Moscow, ID 83843.

Berman, C., & Shaw, E. (1996). Family-directed child evaluation and assessment under the Individuals with Disabilities Education Act (IDEA). In S. J. Meisels & E. Fenichel (Eds.), *New visions for the developmental assessment of infants and young children*. Washington, DC: Zero to Three/National Center for Infants, Toddlers, and Families.

Bernheimer, L. P., Gallimore, R., & Weisner, T. S. (1990). Ecocultural theory as a context for the Individual Family Service Plan. *Journal of Early Intervention*, 14, 219–233.

Bernheimer, L. P., & Keogh, B. K. (1995). Weaving interventions into the fabric of everyday life: An approach to family assessment. *Topics in Early Childhood Special Education*, 15(4), 415–433.

Bernheimer, L., Young, M., & Winton, P. (1983). Stress over time: Parents with young handicapped children. *Journal of Developmental and Behavioral Pediatrics*, 4, 177–181.

Bricker, D. (1993). *Assessment, Evaluation, and Programming System (AEPS) for Infants and Children*. Baltimore: Paul H. Brookes.

Bricker, D., & Squires, J. (1989). The effectiveness of parental screening of at-risk infants: The Infant Monitoring Questionnaires. *Topics in Early Childhood Special Education*, 9, 67–85.

Bricker, D., Squires, J., Mounts, L., Potter, L., Nickel, B., & Farrell, J. (1995). *Ages and Stages Questionnaires*. Baltimore: Paul H. Brookes.

Bronfenbrenner, U. (1979). *The ecology of human development*. Cambridge, MA: Harvard University Press.

Bruns, D. A., & Fowler, S. A. (1999). Culturally sensitive transition plans for young children and their families. *Teaching Exceptional Children*, 31(5), 26–30.

Bryant, C. (1984). Working for families with dysfunctional children: An approach and structure for the first family therapy interview. *Child and Adolescent Social Work*, 1(2), 102–117.

Chan, S. (1998). Families with Asian roots. In E. W. Lynch & M. J. Hanson (Eds.), *Developing cross-cultural competence: A guide for working with young children and their families* (2nd ed., pp. 251–354). Baltimore: Paul H. Brookes.

Davis, M. D., Kilgo, J. L., & Gamel-McCormick, M. (1998). *Young children with special needs: A developmentally appropriate approach*. Needham Heights, MA: Allyn & Bacon.

Demers, S. T ., & Fiorello, C. (1999). Legal and ethical issues in preschool assessment and screening. In E. V. Nuttall, I. Romero, & J. Kalesnik (Eds.), *Assessing and screening preschoolers: Psychological and educational dimensions* (2nd ed., pp. 50–58). Needham Heights, MA: Allyn & Bacon.

Diamond, K., & Squires, J. (1993). The role of parental report in the screening and assessment of young children. *Journal of Early Intervention*, 17(2), 107–115.

Dunst, C. J., Johanson, C., Trivette, C. M., & Hamby, D. (1991). Family-oriented early intervention policies and practices: Family-centered or not? *Exceptional Children*, 58(2), 115–126.

Dunst, C., Trivette, C., & Deal, A. (1988). *Enabling and empowering families: Principles and guidelines for practice.* Cambridge, MA: Brookline.

Dunst, C. J., Trivette, C., & Deal, A. (1994). Enabling and empowering families. In C. J. Dunst, C. Trivette, & A. Deal (Eds.), *Supporting and strengthening families: Methods, strategies, and practices* (pp. 2–11). Cambridge, MA: Brookline Books.

Gallimore, R., Weisner, T. S., Kaufman, S. Z., & Bernheimer, L. P. (1989). The social construction of ecocultural niches: Family accommodation of developmentally delayed children. *American Journal on Mental Retardation, 94,* 216–230.

Glaser, B., & Strauss, A. (1967). *Discovery of grounded theory.* Chicago: Aldene.

Gorden, R. (1969). *Interviewing strategies, techniques and tactics.* Homewood, IL: Dorsey Press.

Hains, A. H., Rosenkoetter, S. E., & Fowler, S. A. (1991). Transition planning with families in early intervention programs. *Infants and Young Children, 3*(4), 38–47.

Hanson, M. J., Lynch, E. W., & Wayman, K. I. (1990). Honoring the cultural diversity of families when gathering data. *Topics in Early Childhood Special Education, 10*(1), 112–131.

Henderson, L. W., Aydlett, L. A., & Bailey, D. B. (1993). Evaluating family needs surveys: Do standard measures of reliability and validity tell us what we want to know? *Journal of Psychoeducational Assessment, 11,* 208–219.

Henderson, L., & Meisels, S. (1994). Parental involvement in the developmental screening of their young child: A multiple source perspective. *Journal of Early Intervention, 18*(2), 141–154.

Johnson, B. H., McGonigel, M. J., & Kaufmann, R. K. (Eds.). (1989). *Guidelines and recommended practices for the individualized family service plan.* Chapel Hill, NC: National Early Childhood Technical Assistance System and the Association for the Care of Children's Health.

Kaiser, A., & Hemmeter, M. (1989). Value-based approaches to family intervention. *Topics in Early Childhood Special Education, 8*(4), 72–86.

Kazak, A., & Wilcox, B. (1984). The structure and function of social support networks in families with handicapped children. *American Journal of Community Psychology, 12*(6), 645–661.

Linder, T. W. (1993). *Transdisciplinary play-based assessment: A functional approach to working with young children* (rev. ed.). Baltimore: Paul H. Brookes.

Mahoney, G., Finger, I., & Powell, A. (1985). Relationship of maternal behavior style to the development of organically impaired mentally retarded infants. *American Journal of Mental Deficiency, 90,* 296–302.

Mahoney, G., Powell, A., & Finger, I. (1986). The maternal behavior rating scale. *Topics in Early Childhood Special Education, 6,* 44–56.

McBride, S. L., & Brotherson, M. J. (1997). Guiding practitioners toward valuing and implementing family-centered practices. In P. J. Winton, J. A. McCollum, & C. Catlett (Eds.), *Reforming personnel preparation in early intervention* (pp. 253–276). Baltimore: Paul H. Brookes.

McCubbin, H., & Patterson, J. (1983a). The family stress process: The double ABCX model of family adjustment and adaptation. In H. McCubbin, M. Sussman, & J. Patterson (Eds.), *Advances and developments in family stress theory and research.* New York: Haworth.

McCubbin, H., & Patterson, J. (1983b). Family transitions: Adaptation to stress. In H. McCubbin & C. Figley (Eds.), *Stress and the family. Vol. 1: Coping with normative transitions* (pp. 5–25). New York: Brunner/Mazel.

McWilliam, R. A., Tocci, L., & Harbin, G. L. (1998). Family-centered services: Service providers discourse and behavior. *Topics in Early Childhood Special Education, 18*(4), 206–221.

McWilliam, R. A., & Winton, P. J. (1990). *Brass tacks: A self-rating of family-centered practices in early intervention.* Chapel Hill, NC: University of North Carolina at Chapel Hill, Frank Porter Graham Child Development Center.

Meisels, S. J., & Provence, S. (1989). *Screening and assessment: Guidelines for identifying young disabled and developmentally vulnerable children and their families.* Washington, DC: National Center for Clinical Infant Programs.

Noonan, M. J., & McCormick, L. (1993). *Early intervention in natural environments: Methods and procedures.* Pacific Grove, CA: Brooks/Cole.

Nuttall, E. V., Romero, I., & Kalesnik, J. (1999). *Assessing and screening preschoolers.* Needham Heights, MA: Allyn & Bacon.

Ostfeld, B. M., & Gibbs, E. D. (1990). Use of family assessment in early intervention. In E. D. Gibbs & D. M. Teti (Eds.), *Interdisciplinary assessment of infants: A guide for early intervention professionals* (pp. 249–271). Baltimore: Paul H. Brookes.

Parke, R. (1986). Fathers, families, and support systems: Their role in the development of at-risk and retarded infants and children. In J. Gallagher & P. Vietze (Eds.), *Families of handicapped persons* (pp. 101–114). Baltimore: Paul H. Brookes.

Raver, S. A. (1999). *Intervention strategies for infants and toddlers with special needs: A team approach* (2nd ed.). Upper Saddle River, NJ: Merrill/Prentice Hall.

Rocco, S. (1996). Toward shared commitment and responsibility: A parent's vision of developmental assessment. In S. J. Meisels & E. Fenichel (Eds.), *New visions for the developmental assessment of infants and young children.* Washington, DC: Zero to Three/National Center for Infants, Toddlers, and Families.

Sexton, D., Snyder, P., Rheams, T., Barron-Sharp, B., & Perez, J. (1991). Considerations in using written surveys to identify family strengths and needs during the IFSP process. *Topics in Early Childhood Special Education. 11*(3), 81–91.

Simeonsson, R. J. (1986). *Psychological and developmental assessment of special children.* Boston: Allyn & Bacon.

Simeonsson, R. J., & Bailey, D. B. (1986). Siblings of handicapped children. In J. Gallagher & P. Vietze (Eds.), *Families of handicapped persons* (pp. 67–80). Baltimore: Paul H. Brookes.

Slentz, K., & Bricker, D. (1992). Family-guided assessment for IFSP development: Jumping off the family assessment bandwagon. *Journal of Early Intervention*, 16(1), 11–19.

Slentz, K., Walker, B., & Bricker, D. (1989). Supporting involvement in early intervention: A role-taking model. In G. Singer & L. Irvin (Eds.), *Support for caregiving families: Enabling positive adaptations to disability* (pp. 221–238). Baltimore: Paul H. Brookes.

Stoneman, A., & Manders, J. E. (1998). Partnerships with families. In W. Umansky & S. R. Hooper, *Young children with special needs* (3rd ed.). Upper Saddle River, NJ: Merrill/Prentice Hall.

Summers, J. A., Dell'Oliver, C., Turnbull, A. P., Benson, H. A., Santelli, E., Campbell, M., & Siegel-Causey, E. (1990). Examining the Individualized Family Service Plan process: What are family and practitioners preferences? *Topics in Early Childhood Special Education*, 10(1), 78–99.

Turnbull, A. P., & Turnbull III, H. R. (1997). *Families, professionals and exceptionality: A special partnership*. Upper Saddle River, NJ: Merrill/Prentice-Hall.

Turnbull, A. P., & Turnbull III, H. R. (2001). *Families, professionals and exceptionality: A special partnership*. Upper Saddle River, NJ: Merrill/Prentice-Hall.

Turnbull, R., & Cilley, M. (1999). *Explanations and implications of the 1997 Amendments to IDEA*. Upper Saddle River, NJ: Merrill/Prentice Hall.

Vincent, L. J., & McLean, M. E. (1996). Family participation. In S. L. Odom & M. E. McLean. *Early intervention/early childhood special education: Recommended practices* (pp. 59–76). Austin, TX: PRO-ED.

Weisner, T. S. (1984). Ecocultural niches of middle childhood: A cross-cultural perspective. In W. A. Collins (Ed.), *Development during middle childhood: The years from six to twelve* (pp. 335–369). Washington, DC: National Academy of Sciences Press.

Wikler, L. (1981). Chronic stress of families of mentally retarded children. *Family Relations*, 30, 281–288.

Wilson, S. (1977). The use of ethnographic techniques in educational research. *Review of Educational Research*, 47(1), 245–265.

Winton, P. J., & Bailey, D. B. (1988). The family-focused interview: A collaborative mechanism for family assessment and goal-setting. *Journal of the Division for Early Childhood*, 12, 195–207.

3

Cultural and Linguistic Diversity

Two powerful forces have increased professional awareness of the importance of cross-cultural sensitivity. The first is the change in the population demographics of the United States, and the second is federal legislation which began with the Education of the Handicapped Act of 1986 (PL 99–457) and continued with the Individuals with Disabilities Education Acts of 1990 (PL 101–476) and 1997 (PL 105–17) (Hanson, 1998).

The first force is the fact that the number of children in our early childhood programs who come from culturally and linguistically diverse families is rapidly increasing. As of 1997, 30 percent of the population of the United States was of non-Anglo European ancestry. This percentage is expected to continue to increase. This projected increase is based on the higher birth rate among non-white, non-Anglo women, the greater numbers of women of childbearing age within these groups, and the increased immigration of non-Europeans (Hanson, 1998). It is estimated that 41 percent of the nation's children will be Latino and children of color by the year 2030 (Hanson, Lynch, & Wayman, 1990).

The number of people age 5 and older who spoke a language other than English in their homes increased between 1979 and 1989 by more than 40 percent (Waggoner, January, 1992). Within this increase in people of non-English language background there are important shifts in the language groups within this population (Cloud, 1993). The numbers of speakers of Arabic, Cambodian, Chinese, Creole, Farsi, Asian Indian, Korean, and Filipino languages are increasing substantially, whereas the number of speakers of European languages is declining (Cloud, 1993).

The United States is no longer considered a melting pot. Today the nation, not just our urban areas, reflects a wide range of groups who retain a primary identification with their native heritage. Although most members do participate and share in aspects of the dominant culture orientation of the United States, terms such as cultural diversity, cultural pluralism, and multiculturalism more clearly define our society today (Lynch & Hanson, 1996).

Children and families who are culturally and linguistically diverse will need services that are comprehensive, flexible, and family-focused. Service providers will need to see children in the context of their families and the families in the context of their communities. The process of assessment must be individualized for each child and family in order to maintain relevance and minimize bias. Individualized assessment and intervention are required for each child and family unit within a given cultural context. In order to meet the needs of these children and families from diverse backgrounds, professionals must familiarize themselves with the guidelines and questions that encourage an individualized, nonbiased perspective (Anderson & Goldberg, 1991).

This chapter explores the concerns raised in the assessment of young children who are culturally and linguistically diverse. The chapter begins with the legislative mandates for the assessment process, the role of culture and language in the assessment of children and families, a look at the cultural competence of the examiner, and the problems with test translations and interpretations. The second part of the chapter focuses on considerations for more effective assessment, assessment methods and instruments, and recommendations to make the assessment process more responsive to cultural and linguistic differences. It is hoped that this chapter will increase the reader's understanding of the influence of culture and language on the assessment process and provide some concrete methods for developing culturally and linguistically responsive assessment for young children and their families.

Legislative Mandates

PL 105–17 links nondiscriminatory evaluation to the child's program. The evaluation is the basis for determining not only whether the child has a disability but also, if that is the case, what the school must do about the disability. This means that the school must develop and carry out an appropriate education through the IEP and provide services in the least restrictive environment (Turnbull & Cilley, 1999).

Turnbull and Cilley (1999) have outlined the specific standards to which an evaluation team must adhere. Those standards as related to the student include:

- The test selected and administered must not be discriminatory on a racial or cultural basis;
- The test must be provided and administered in the child's native language or other mode of communication; and
- The student must be evaluated with two purposes which are to determine (1) whether the child has a disability; and (2) the content of the child's IEP, including information related to enabling the preschool child to participate in appropriate activities.

The tests to be used must:

- Have been validated for the specific purpose for which they are used;
- Be administered by trained and knowledgeable personnel; and
- Be administered in accordance with any instructions provided by the producer of such tests.

The evaluation process must:

- Include a variety of assessment tools and strategies to gather relevant functional and developmental information, including information provided by the parent which may assist in determining if the child has a disability and what the child's education should consist of;

- Not rely on any single procedure as the sole criterion for determining whether a disability exists and the educational program; and
- Use technically sound instruments.

A basic premise of special education is that of educating the whole child. Just as special educators understand that students with disabilities cannot be properly served unless educators respond to the nature and the extent of the disability characteristics, early childhood special educators also must understand and respond to language and culture, two other essential characteristics (Cloud, 1993). The focus in special education on nondiscriminatory assessment has made special educators aware of the cultural biases inherent in tests and the testing process (Chamberlain & Medinos-Landurand, 1991). Early interventionists/early childhood special educators must be extremely careful when assessing children who are culturally diverse, especially when identifying the need for special services. A biased assessment could result in the classification of a child as delayed or disabled when in fact the insensitivity of the test itself contributed to the low score attained by the child. Screening and assessment must be sensitive to the cultural biases that could lead to over- or underidentification of perceived deficits in children from various cultural and linguistic groups. These cultural differences are particularly important as early interventionists respond to the family focus of recent legislation. Sensitivity to and respect for the cultural values and customs of families, as well as actions demonstrating respect, are crucial to the success of the process as professionals and families enter into partnerships in the assessment, planning, and implementation activities (Hanson, Lynch, & Wayman, 1990). Therefore, the next section will consider the effect of culture on the family in relation to assessment activities.

Culture and the Family Perspective

A child's life is embedded within a cultural and family context. When assessing a child with possible developmental delays, it is essential to consider the family's culture. Culture can be conceptualized as the framework of meanings within which a population, individually and as a group, shapes its lifeways. This cultural framework provides a world view that influences our ways of perceiving the world around us and defines desirable attitudes, values, and behaviors, and influences how we evaluate our needs (J. Lynch, 1992). This framework is neither static nor absolute, but it is an ongoing process in which individuals are constantly trying out new ideas and behaviors. Individuals and families lie along different points of their cultural continua, ranging from traditional to fully bicultural. Each family and individual within a culture will not respond in the same way to the same or a similar situation (Anderson & Fenichel, 1989).

Assessment procedures must recognize the critical roles of the family within the cultural and linguistic background of each individual family. The parents/caregivers are the constants in their children's lives and the chief decision makers. Children must be viewed as having strengths, needs, and resources that are part of a larger family and social context. All relevant family members, as defined by the culture, need to be considered and encouraged to be full partners in the intervention process. The early interventionist must be sensitive to the effect of culture on family values, beliefs, and practices. For example, not all families are prepared for or feel comfortable with the degree of family participation expected in early intervention programs. However, one must not assume that they do not wish to be involved or that they are not involved from their own perspective.

The early interventionist or early childhood special educator needs to be aware of internal characteristics, such as values, thoughts, and cognitive orientations which vary from culture to culture and hidden aspects such as unspoken rules and norms (Garcia & Malkin, 1993). Culture influences variables such as language and communication, childrearing practices, the definition of family, and beliefs about wellness and disability. For example, different cultures have various rules for communication patterns, i.e., how an adult communicates with a child and how children communicate to each other. Other conditions, such as socioeconomic and educational status, are not characteristics of specific cultures but rather are cross-cultural. A combination of these factors may impact upon children and families and influence the assessment process (Anderson & Goldberg, 1991).

Language and Communication

Effective communication is essential to the family-professional relationship. Members of some cultures may be reticent to go to a facility without a speaker of the language with which they are more comfortable. Communication consists of verbal and nonverbal communication. Nonverbal communication has important and varied cultural meanings. Cultures rely differentially on situational cues, established hierarchies, and nonconfrontational responses. Thus, important information may not be adequately communicated through a translator who does not understand these differences.

Body language and other forms of communication are important considerations in the assessment process. Professionals must have an understanding of the different meanings attached to the body language they may use. For example, eye contact, personal space, and touching are forms of body language which have different meanings in different cultures. Effective assessment relies on sharing information through observation and written and spoken language. When language differences occur, the real meanings may not be understood even with translation.

Child-rearing Practices

Child-rearing ideologies vary among cultures, families, and family members. Ideas about the process of child-rearing are culturally defined. The pervasive theme across cultures is children's development, but the ways in which this development is supported and fostered differ across cultures. Children are raised in a way that socializes them for optimal adjustments and success in their own culture (Westby, 1986). Expectations of children may vary with respect to the types of competence and behaviors regarded as normal or ideal for a particular age or sex group. These expectations may require children to become competent in areas other than those needed in the mainstream society (Anderson & Fenichel, 1989). In Anglo-American society, children often are encouraged to be as independent as possible. Child-rearing practices reflect this perspective in the emphasis on early toilet training and self-reliance. Asian-American parents generally take very active roles in encouraging their children's learning activities at home (Anderson & Fenichel, 1989). African-American families have a strong belief in disciplining inappropriate behavior in children. Traditional Cuban cultures fear that, if too much independence is promoted, the children will be at risk for physical harm. Native American families traditionally have been permissive and accepting of their children and adults give the same respect to children as they do to one another (Bearcrane, Dodd, Nelson, & Ostwald, 1990).

Ideas about the ways in which children learn and the best ways to teach children also vary. Native American children tend to be treated with respect for their innate characteristics, which are believed to be permanent; there is a tolerance for mistakes with minimal punishment (Anderson & Fenichel, 1989). Some cultures rely heavily on adult-directed learning, whereas others strongly support child-directed learning. The effectiveness of an early interventionist in working with a family who is ethnolinguistically diverse will be influenced by the family's cultural values and practices regarding child-rearing. If the goal is to optimize early child development, then the early interventionist must select behavioral goals that are congruent with the family's values.

Family Membership

The view of what constitutes a family, including the structures and relationships, differs from culture to culture. Professionals need to understand these variations in family structure and roles. In many cultures, the family is extended in different ways. Various relatives and frequently nonrelatives or temporary relatives may make up the primary closely knit group. The family membership may be constant, with changes occurring only as a result of birth or death, or it may be somewhat fluid. The traditional Asian family tends to be extended, with tightly-knit families and many generations living under one roof.

Family roles and relationships vary from culture to culture and may change over time. Situations and relationships may vary among distant relatives or nonrelatives who are considered family members. Family members may or may not constitute an important support network for one another. There may be a strict hierarchy among family members or rigidly defined gender roles (Anderson & Fenichel, 1989). For example, cultures have varying ideas about the family member who cares for and educates children of various ages and sexes. In many cultures, children may be cared for, to a significant extent, by their mother and also by siblings, grandparents, other relatives, neighbors, entire families, or even entire communities. African-American families often have a system of shared child care and parenting arrangements. Mothers and grandmothers are traditionally central influences on young children. Asian-American families may function in a strict gender, sibling, and age hierarchy. In this hierarchy, fathers may hold a traditional leadership role, with mothers functioning as family nurturers and caretakers, in submission to their husbands. The younger male siblings are submissive to the older males, and the female siblings submissive to all. For example, in patriarchal Hispanic families, the ultimate responsibility for the care and well-being of the family falls to the husband/father. In the Native American cultures, the extended family may also be the primary source of support and identity. In a number of tribal cultures, grandparents and elders traditionally exert a powerful influence over their adult children and the raising of grandchildren (Anderson & Fenichel, 1989). Decision-making and caregiving patterns must be understood and recognized by professionals in order to provide effective intervention.

Wellness/Disability

Cultural groups differ greatly in their views of health, prevention of illness or disability, medicine, and health care. The occurrence of a disability is given different meaning by different cultures. Some cultures emphasize the role of fate. Others may place responsibility on the person with the disability or his family. Guilt or shame may result from the view that the disability is seen as a punishment for sins or resulting from some action by the mother or father during pregnancy or by a remote ancestor. Other cultures attribute the disability to a person's bad luck or misfortune. Among Asian-American populations, Nguyen (1987) reports that birth defects and other disabilities may be viewed as punishments for sins committed not only by parents but by more remote ancestors as well. Another belief is that unborn children can be harmed if a pregnant woman fails to avoid places and situations where evil spirits may be lurking. In Hispanic-American families, vitality and health are prized. An infant or a child with a disability may be hidden and deprived of

treatment. In most Native American cultures, health and religious beliefs are associated with parental behavior and are often seen as causally linked to birth defects or disease (Anderson & Fenichel, 1989). In African and Carribean societies, it is believed that witchcraft is the cause of the disability (Groce, 1990). An individual who is disabled is thought to be bewitched, and close association with a child with a disability is thought to put others at risk for the evil witchcraft. The affected child and family members are avoided by community members. The responsibility for the disability as well as its cure is placed on the child and the family (Chan, 1990).

Different disabilities may cause different levels of concern in different cultures. A disability that is common among a particular cultural group may be seen as little cause for concern. Such perceptions will influence the family's willingness to seek help or participate in the intervention program (Hanson, Lynch & Wayman, 1990).

Young children with disabilities may have serious medical problems that require intervention. A conflict may occur about the recommended course of action because medical practices are integrally linked to cultural traditions. For example, among some Native American tribes, the medicine man or shaman and the tribal community are considered essential to the healing process (Lynch, 1987). The physician or health worker who is advocating surgery, drug treatments, or other medical procedures needs to be aware of the family's beliefs and practices and the value and significance of these rituals to the family and community (Lynch & Hanson, 1998).

The Child's Language Competence

Sufficient information about the cultural and linguistic patterns in the home must be obtained prior to screening or assessment. The information that is most critical to appropriate individualization is actually which language is used in the home. How well does a child communicate through a particular language and for what purpose(s) does the child communicate (Barrera, 1993)? That is, it is important to know not only what language is spoken, but also the degree of bilingualism, and the nature and patterns of language practices. For example, a bilingual child may have been bilingual only a year or two; the family may speak one language at home, but the child may be with a sitter all day who speaks another language. The degree of proficiency in one or more languages must be assessed (Barrera Metz, 1991; Chamberlain & Medinos-Landurand, 1991). Language proficiency refers to the degree of control one has over the language in question (Hamayan & Damico, 1991).

The child must be assessed in the area of language prior to any other assessment. This assessment must include an assessment of competence in the child's home language as well as in English. This is also true for children who are nonverbal or severely disabled. Differences in affect and muscle tone have been noted in children who are nonverbal and severely disabled when using the child's home language (Barrera Metz, 1991). Scores obtained on assessment instruments for children who are language-minority are most often minimal indications of abilities. The child's level of proficiency in both the home language and in English must be made. Assessment of proficiency should include both receptive and expressive language. Assessment instruments should be carefully chosen. If no instruments exist to test proficiency in the child's home language, then an informal assessment should be made.

When assessing a child's ability to use language in interaction, it is too simplistic to look at language proficiency alone. Language competence is connected to the issue of cultural knowledge of the child and family, that is, how people interpret situations and guide their communicative behavior as a result. Research

has suggested that the successful functioning of Hispanic and other students who are ethnic-minority can be affected dramatically by the interactional competencies that extend beyond the knowledge of the structural features of the language (Goldman & Trueba, 1987). These interactional competencies involve such skills as knowing when and how to respond to a teacher's questions, how to ask for clarifications of information, and the appropriate demeanor for using language in the activities of the classroom. The communicative competence of a child is also affected by the communicative strategies used by other students, the teacher, and the differences in social relations among the speakers (Duran, 1989). Garcia and Ortiz (1988) have compiled a number of variables which should be considered when assessing communicative competence. These variables are shown in Figure 3–1 which has been adapted to young children.

The Cultural Competence of the Examiner

Cultural diversity is deemed present when there is a probability that within the interaction with the child or family, the assessor will attribute different meanings or values to the behaviors or events than would the family (Barrera, 1996). Cultural competence has been defined as "the ability to think, feel, and act in ways that acknowledge, respect, and build upon ethnic, [socio]cultural, and linguistic diversity" (Lynch & Hanson, 1993, p. 50). The culturally competent individual values diversity, is able to self-assess, is conscious of the dynamics involved when cultures interact, has acquired cultural knowledge, and has developed adaptations to diversity (Bazron, Dennis & Isaacs, 1989). Anderson and Fenichel (1989) state that cultural sensitivity cannot mean knowing everything about a culture. Cultural sensitivity is being aware that cultural differences and similarities

FIGURE 3–1
Child Variables

Experimental background

Are there any variables related to family history that may be affecting the child's performance?

- Lifestyle
- Length of residence in the United States
- Stress (e.g., poverty, lack of emotional support)

Are there any variables related to the child's medical history that may have affected performance?

- Vision
- Nutrition
- Illness
- Hearing
- Trauma or injury

Culture

How is the child's cultural background different from the culture of the school community she will enter and the larger society? (Mattes & Omark, 1984; Saville-Troike, 1978)

- Family (family size and structure, roles, responsibilities, expectations)
- Aspirations (success, goals)
- Language and communication (rules for adult, adult-child, child-child, child communication, language use at home, nonverbal communication)
- Religion (dietary restrictions, roles expectation)
- Traditions and history (contact with homeland, reason for immigration)
- Decorum and discipline (standards for acceptable behavior)

To what extent are the child's characteristics representative of the larger group?

- Continuum of culture (traditional, dualistic atraditional (Ramirez & Castaneda, 1974))
- Degree of acculturation or assimilation

Is the child able to function successfully in more than one cultural setting?
Is the child's behavior culturally appropriate?

Language proficiency

What is the child's dominant language? Which is the preferred?

- Settings (child care or preschool, playground, home, church)
- Topics (at child care or preschool, day-to-day interactions)
- Speakers (parents, teachers, siblings, peers)
- Aspects of each language (syntax, vocabulary, phonology, use)
- Expressive versus receptive

What is the child's level of proficiency in the primary language and in English? (Cummins, 1984)

- Interpersonal communcication skills
- Cognitive/preacademic-related skills

Are the styles of verbal interaction used in the primary language different from those most valued in English? (Heath, 1986)

- Label quests (e.g., What's this? Who?)
- Meaning quests (adult infers for child, interprets or asks for explanation)
- Accounts (generated by teller, information new to listener—e.g., show and tell)
- Stories

If so, has the child been exposed to those that are unfamiliar to her?
What is the extent and nature of exposure to each language?
What language(s) do the parents speak to each other?
What language(s) do the children use with each other?
What television programs are seen in each language?
Are stories read to the child? In what language(s)?
Are the child's behaviors characteristic of second-language acquisition?
What types of language intervention has the child received?

- Bilingual versus monolingual instruction.
- Language development, enrichment, remediation
- Additive versus subtractive bilingualism (transition versus maintenance)

Learning style

Does the child's learning style require instructional accommodation?

- Perceptual style differences (e.g., visual versus auditory learner)
- Cognitive style differences (e.g., inductive versus deductive thinking)
- Preferred style of participation (e.g., one-to-one versus small or large group)

If so, were these characteristics accommodated, or were alternative styles used?

Motivational influences

Is the child's self-concept enhanced by school experiences?

- Child care or preschool environment communicates respect for culture and language
- Child experiences preacademic and social success

Is education perceived as relevant and necessary for success in the child's family and community?

- Aspirations
- Realistic expectations based on community experience
- Culturally different criteria for success
- Education perceived by the community as a tool for assimilation

From "Student variables," in S. Garcia and A. Ortiz,1988, *Preventing inappropriate referrals of language minority students to special education. New Focus 5:7.* Copyright 1988 by the National Clearinghouse for Bilingual Education Occasional Papers in Bilingual Education. Adapted with Permission.

exist, learning about the cultures in your region, and realizing that cultural differences affect every family's participation in an intervention program because we are all influenced by the culture of our ancestors. All of us are members of social communities with cultural values that strongly influence what we believe, and how we respond to families (Brown & Barrera, 1999).

To become culturally competent early interventionists must:

- Clarify their own values and assumptions.
- Gather and analyze ethnographic information related to the community in which the family resides.
- Determine the degree to which the family operates transculturally.
- Examine the family's orientation to specific childrearing issues. (Hanson, Lynch & Wayman, 1990).

Cultural Awareness

Cultural self-awareness involves exploring one's own heritage. Learning about one's own roots is the first step in determining how one's own values, beliefs, customs, and behaviors have been shaped by culture. This new knowledge helps individuals separate the ways of thinking, believing, and behaving that have been assumed to be universal from those that are based on cultural beliefs and biases. The next step is to examine the values, behaviors, beliefs, and customs that are identified with one's own cultural heritage (Lynch, 1998).

Culture-Specific Awareness and Understanding

After interventionists become familiar with their own culture and its influence on them, the next step is to learn about other cultures through readings, interactions, and involvement. Lynch (1998) suggests the four most effective ways are:

1. learning through books, the arts, and technology

2. talking and working with individuals from the culture who can act as guides or mediators
3. participating in the daily life of another culture
4. learning the language of the other culture.

When addressing the issue of cultural diversity, caution must be exercised in trying to describe any group in a generalized sense. There are often as many and as wide variations within a group as between groups. In an attempt to better understand cultural difference and variability, we must always be careful not to perpetuate stereotypes (McAdoo, 1978).

Anderson and Fenichel (1989) described culture as the specific framework of meanings in which a population, individually and as a group, shapes its life. A cultural framework is not absolute, but it is an ongoing process. The cultural framework must be seen as a set of possible tendencies from which to choose. As Ortiz (1987) indicated, culture exists on a continuum. Early intervention must discern where on the continuum of assimilation into the majority culture a family functions, and recognize that this may change. Individual families may accept, deny, modify, or situationally exhibit various cultural tendencies.

Brown and Barrera (1999) suggested three elements of cultural competency to assist in the assessment process. The first is the use of multiple perceptual and conceptual lenses to see the range of perspectives, not just our own or those in the assessment materials, but also the perspectives of the child and family. The second element is "third space" thinking which respects and includes variables or values that differ from one's own. The final element is skilled dialogue which is based on the premise that all behavior and values have a positive intent.

In this chapter, no attempt is made to describe individual cultural groups. The content of this chapter applies to everyone regardless of culture or religious group, i.e., Hispanic, white, Asian, Native American, Jewish, or Islamic, and so on. References to additional informative resource materials are provided in order that the reader may begin to understand cultural differences that occur between individuals and groups. Emphasis is placed on general considerations for assessing individuals from culturally diverse backgrounds.

Problems with Test Translations and Using Interpreters

Translating Assessment Instruments

Hanson, Lynch, and Wayman (1990) pointed out that language is more than words. It is a way of thinking and viewing the world. Even in the most textbook-perfect translations, there is a great deal inherent in many languages that cannot be communicated adequately.

Cultures can be characterized by the forms of communication they use and prefer (Hall, 1976). High-context cultures rely on situational cues, established hierarchies, and nonconfrontational responses in their communication with others. Low-context cultures tend to prefer direct messages and rely more on what is said than what is left unsaid (Chan & Mahseredjian, 1989). The Anglo-American culture is a low-context culture that values direction, speed, and "getting the job done." Real exchanges of information can occur only after the relationship has been built, and this requires time (Hanson, Lynch, & Wayman, 1990).

Examiners often evaluate the child with the help of an interpreter. Effective interpreters should have proficiency in the languages spoken by the families and the service providers. They also must have knowledge of the cultures of both the families and the early interventionists, proficiency in cross-cultural communication, and the ability to keep information confidential (Lynch & Hanson, 1992).

The interpreter should have experience in administering tests. If using a standardized instrument, the examiner must remember that normed samples may not have included individuals from this child's population. In order to assess a child who is culturally diverse, the examiner must do more than simply translate the test into the child's dominant language. The problems inherent in test translations and using an interpreter are summarized below (Chamberlain & Medinos-Landurand, 1991; Nuttall, Landurand, & Goldman, 1984; Sattler, 1988):

- The interpreter may not be equally fluent in both languages, resulting in incorrect translations.
- Many concepts have either no equivalent in another language or are difficult to translate without causing ambiguity. Thus, the meaning of important phrases may be lost in translations.
- The interpreter may not use the particular dialectical or regional variation with which the child is familiar. Some words may have different meanings for Chinese-Americans who originate from the People's Republic of China, Hong Kong, or Taiwan.
- The language familiar to the child may be a combination of two languages, so a monolingual translation may be inappropriate.
- The level of difficulty of words may change as a result of translation. For example, the Spanish equivalent of the common English word "pet" is "animal domestico," which is not commonly used in conversational Spanish.
- Translation can alter the meanings of words. For example, seemingly harmless English words may translate into Spanish profanity. "Huevo" is the literal translation of the word "egg," but the Spanish term has more earthy connotations.
- The interpreter may inadvertently prompt the child through translation attempts, gestures, or intonations common to the language in question.
- Interpreters usually are not trained or familiar with administering tests.

The major concern with translations is to ensure that each translated phrase is equivalent to the phrase in the original language. The translator must be aware of the impact of translation on the context of the request. Merely choosing the exact phrasing without addressing the meaning and intent could be very harmful. An important rule in translating is that the translator must have a good acquaintance with the language as used by the prospective examinee.

An interpreter or culture-language mediator should be used by an intervention program to assist in the screening or assessment. A culture-language mediator is a person who is familiar with both the environment of the child and family and the assessment environment (Barrera, 1990). The culture-language mediator has two responsibilities: (1) to assist service providers in becoming aware of any unfamiliar values, behaviors, language, or rules that are part of the family's environment; and (2) to assist the family and child in becoming familiar with any unfamiliar values, beliefs, language, or rules that are part of the assessment environment (Barerra, 1996).

The culture-language mediators must be bilingual and be able to speak and understand the words used in the child's home and those used in the environment setting. They also must be competent in understanding and interpreting the contexts, values, and meanings underlying those words, for example, understanding that a missed appointment may mean something other than a lack of interest in a child's needs (Barrera, 1996).

The mediator or interpreter should meet with the assessor prior to the assessment to be shown the test to be used and trained in giving it. The mediator needs to be familiar with the purpose of the test items. Mediators may present the test items or simply watch. The mediator explains what is happening to the family. After the assessment, the family and mediator may add what the family has told them about their language or culture. The

mediator participates for the benefit of both the family and the intervention program.

If an interpreter is not familiar with the culture of the family, then a culture-language mediator should be used by the intervention program to assist in the screening or assessment. Intervention programs in a community should share resource lists of individuals who are able to serve as interpreters or culture-language mediators for families from a variety of language backgrounds.

In this section, the use of interpreters and culture-language mediators has been discussed. Important consideration in communication between families and intervention should also be given to the interview process. In the next section, some effective pointers are given for conducting interviews using interpreters. These guidelines will assist in improving the communication between families and intervenors.

Conducting an Interview

Each interaction with a family involves assessment (Bailey, 1991). Effective communication focuses assessors on forming hypotheses about the significance and meaning of data and examining the validity of these responses from a variety of perspectives (Brown & Barrera, 1999). Brown and Barrera (1999) referred to this type of communication as "skilled dialogue," which is described as reciprocal, engaging all parties, respectful, responsive, and treating all values or perspectives as legitimate. Skilled dialogue is based on the belief that all behaviors and values have a positive intent. The goal is to establish a context within which commonalities are generated in relation to concrete differences without needing to eliminate differences.

Conducting an interview with a family is more difficult when an interpreter is needed. E. W. Lynch (1992, pp. 55–56) has summarized the guidelines suggested by previous researchers for conducting an assessment or interview with the help of interpreters (Hagen,

1989; Randall-David, 1989; Schilling & Brannon, 1986). These guidelines are:

- Learn proper protocols and forms of address (including a few greetings and social phrases) in the family's primary language, the name they wish to be called, and the correct pronunciation.
- Introduce yourself and the interpreter, describe your respective roles, and clarify mutual expectations and the purpose of the encounter.
- Learn basic words and sentences in the family's language and become familiar with special terminology they may use so you can selectively attend to them during interpreter-family exchanges.
- During the interaction, address your remarks and questions directly to the family (not the interpreter); look at and listen to family members as they speak and observe their nonverbal communication.
- Avoid body language or gestures that may be offensive or misunderstood.
- Use a positive tone of voice and facial expressions that sincerely convey respect and your interest in the family; address them in a calm, unhurried manner.
- Speak clearly and somewhat more slowly, not more loudly.
- Limit your remarks and questions to a few sentences between translations and avoid giving too much information or long complex discussions of several topics in a single session.
- Avoid technical jargon, colloquialisms, idioms, slang, and abstractions.
- Avoid oversimplification and condensing important explanations.
- Give instructions in a clear, logical sequence; emphasize key words or points; and offer reasons for specific recommendations.
- Periodically check on the family's understanding and the accuracy of the translation by asking the family to repeat instructions or whatever has been communicated in their own words, with the interpreter facilitating, but avoid literally asking, "Do you understand?"
- When possible, reinforce verbal information with materials written in the family's language and visual aids or behavioral modeling if appropriate. Before introducing written materials, tactfully determine the client's literacy level through the interpreter.
- Be patient and prepared for the additional time that will inevitably be required for careful interpretation.

Considerations for More Effective Assessment

Considerations for conducting a more effective assessment include (a) the examiner, (b) establishing rapport and getting to know the family, (c) how to optimize the test situation, (d) the appropriate use of tests, and (e) interpreting test data. The following sections consider each of these variables and provide suggestions for conducting a more effective assessment and thus obtaining more accurate information.

The Examiner

The individual conducting the assessment is the most important variable in the process. This individual not only must possess the necessary skills, knowledge, and experience, but also be sensitive and open to working with families from another culture. This openness includes the willingness to acknowledge one's own limitations. Recognize any stereotypes that you may have about the child's ethnic group. Be sure that your own preconceived images or notions do not interfere with your work. Questions that an assessor might ask himself include: How do I feel about this (Asian, Hispanic) child? Will my attitude unfairly affect this child's performance? Can I evaluate this child fairly without positive or negative prejudice or preconceived notions? If I cannot, would I refer the child to someone else? (Illinois Resource Center, 1986; Leung, 1986).

Anderson and Goldberg (1991) provided a list of questions for professionals to ask themselves in order to ensure cultural competence. These questions are provided in Figure 3–2.

Learn as much as you can about the child's ethnic group and culture. Try to understand the ethnic group's viewpoint and accept the premise that each child must be given an equal opportunity to achieve to the limits of his capacity.

It is important to establish contact with diverse cultural groups before working with the children and families. A network needs to be established and programs need to get to know the cultural community and establish credibility before screening and assessment begin.

A transdisciplinary or multidisciplinary team approach to assessment can provide much needed assistance in order to conduct a non-biased assessment, especially between bilingual and early childhood special educators. The evaluator should rely on a multidisciplinary approach to assessment and gather relevant information about the child from a variety of sources. This will result in a more accurate assessment of the child's strengths and weaknesses. Providing an ongoing assessment of the child within the classroom using a method such as the Transdisciplinary Play-Based Assessment (TPBA) (Linder, 1993) will provide a more accurate picture of the child's strengths and needs.

Establishing Rapport and Getting to Know the Family

When developing the IFSP, a thorough assessment of the family's present needs and resources is essential. Information is gathered on family resources (family members, cultural values, beliefs about school), family interaction (reactions to the child with a disability, family activities, family interests and hobbies, family routines), family functions (division of family chores, home intervention activities, community activities) and family life cycle (information on past life events and future goals). The reader should refer to Chapter 2 on Family Involvement for more information on assessing families' concerns, priorities, and resources. For the professional working with culturally diverse families, it is also beneficial to expand the family assessment. The following variables should be considered part of any effective family assessment:

- The family's experiences in the native country, where applicable;
- The perception of the child and expectations for the child;
- Family coping strategies;
- The role of extended family members and siblings;
- The amount of community support available;
- Religious, spiritual, or cultural beliefs (including views of disabilities);
- Parenting and behavior management practices (discipline versus independence);
- Child-rearing beliefs and practices; and
- Communication styles. (Chan, 1983; Fradd & Weismantel, 1989)

These culture-specific issues are so essential in working with families that have a child with a disability that they merit special attention (E. W. Lynch, 1992). Wayman, Lynch and Hanson (1990) have designed a set of "Guidelines for the Home Visitor" that can be used to learn more about the family's cultural values and preferences (see Figure 3–3). These guidelines are not intended to be used as a checklist or an interview protocol, but they do include questions about family attitudes, beliefs, and practices that could influence the services and the approach to providing services. It is essential that no assumptions be made about their concerns, priorities, and resources based on a family's cultural background. This culture-specific information will help the interventionists in matching the interventions to the family's way of life (Wayman, Lynch, & Hanson, 1990).

FIGURE 3–2

Questions for Professionals to Ask When Conducting a Culturally Sensitive Screening and Assessment

1. With what cultural group was this screening or assessment tool normed? Is it the same culture as that of the child I am serving?

2. Have I examined this screening and assessment tool for cultural biases? Has it been reviewed by members of the cultural group being served?

3. If I have modified or adapted a standardized screening or assessment tool, have I received input on the changes to be certain it is culturally appropriate? If using a standardized tool, or one to which I have made changes, have I carefully scored and interpreted the results in consideration of cultural or linguistic variation? When interpreting and reporting screening and assessment results, have I made clear reference that the instrument was modified and how?

4. Have representatives from the cultural community met to create guidelines for culturally competent screening and assessment for children from that group? Has information about child-rearing practices and typical child development for children from that community been gathered and recorded for use by those serving the families?

5. What do I know about the child-rearing practices of this cultural group? How do these practices impact child development?

6. Am I aware of my own values and biases regarding child-rearing practices and the kind of information gathered in the screening and assessment process? Can I utilize nondiscriminatory and culturally competent skills and practices in my work with children and families?

7. Do I utilize parents and other family members in gathering information for the screening and assessment? Am I aware of the people with whom the child spends time, and the level of acculturation of these individuals?

8. Do I know where or how to find out about specific cultural or linguistic information that may be needed in order for me to be culturally competent in the screening and assessment process?

9. Do I have bilingual or bicultural skills, or do I have access to another person who can provide direct service or consultation? Do I know what skills are required of a quality interpreter or mediator?

10. Have I participated in training sessions on cultural competence in screening and assessment? Am I continuing to develop my knowledge base through additional formal training and by spending time with community members to learn the cultural attributes specific to the community and families I serve? Is there a network of peer and supervisory practitioners who are addressing these issues, and can I become a participating member?

From *Cultural Competence in Screening and Assessment: Implications for Services to Young Children with Special Needs Ages Birth Through Five.* Copyright 1991, by NECTAS and PACER Center, 4826 Chicago Ave. S., Minneapolis, MN 55417; (612) 827–2966. Reprinted with permission.

FIGURE 3–3
Guidelines for the Home Visitor

Part I—Family structure and child-rearing practices

Family structure

Family composition

- Who are the members of the family system?
- Who are the key decision makers?
- Is decision making related to specific situations?
- Is decision making individual or group oriented?
- Do family members all live in the same household?
- What is the relationship of friends to the family system?
- What is the hierarchy within the family? Is status related to gender or age?

Primary caregiver(s)

- Who is the primary caregiver?
- Who else participates in the caregiving?
- What is the amount of care given by the mother versus others?
- How much time does the infant spend away from the primary caregiver?
- Is there conflict between caregivers regarding appropriate practices?
- What ecological/environmental issues impinge on general caregiving (e.g., housing, jobs)?

Child-rearing practices

Family feeding practices

- What are the family feeding practices?
- What are the mealtime rules?
- What types of foods are eaten?
- What are the beliefs regarding breastfeeding and weaning?
- What are the beliefs regarding bottle-feeding?
- What are the family practices regarding transitioning to solid food?
- Which family members prepare food?
- Is food purchased or homemade?
- Are there any taboos related to food preparation or handling?
- Which family members feed the child?
- What is the configuration of the family mealtime?
- What are the family's views on independent feeding?
- Is there a discrepancy among family members regarding the beliefs and practices related to feeding an infant/toddler?

Family sleeping patterns

- Does the infant sleep in the same room/bed as the parents?
- At what age is the infant moved away from close proximity to the mother?
- Is there an established bedtime?
- What is the family response to an infant when he awakens at night?
- What practices surround daytime napping?

Family's response to disobedience and aggression

- What are the parameters of acceptable child behavior?
- What form does the discipline take?
- Who metes out the disciplinary action?

Family's response to a crying infant

- Temporal qualities—How long before the caregiver picks up a crying infant?
- How does the caregiver calm an upset infant?

Part II—Family perceptions and attitudes

Family perception of child's disability

- Are there cultural or religious factors that would shape family perceptions?
- To what/where/whom does the family assign responsibility for their child's disability?
- How does the family view the role of fate in their lives?
- How does the family view their role in intervening with their child? Do they feel they can make a difference or do they consider it hopeless?

Family's perception of health and healing

- What is the family's approach to medical needs?
    - Do they rely solely on Western medical services?
    - Do they rely solely on holistic approaches?
    - Do they utilize a combination of these approaches?
- Who is the primary medical provider or conveyer of medical information?
    - Family members? Elders? Friends? Folk healers? Family doctor? Medical specialists?
    - Do all members of the family agree on approaches to medical needs?

Family's perception of help-seeking and intervention

- From whom does the family seek help—family members or outside agencies/individuals?
- Does the family seek help directly or indirectly?
- What are the general feelings of the family when seeking assistance (ashamed, angry, demand as a right, view as unnecessary)?
- With which community systems does the family interact (educational/medical/social)?

FIGURE 3–3

Continued

- How are these interactions completed (face-to-face, telephone, letter)?
- Which family member interacts with other systems?
- Does that family member feel comfortable when interacting with other systems?

Part III—Language and communication styles

Language

- To what degree:
  - Is the home visitor proficient in the family's native language?
  - Is the family proficient in English?
- If an interpreter is used:
  - With which culture is the interpreter primarily affiliated?
  - Is the interpreter familiar with the colloquialisms of the family members' country or region of origin?
  - Is the family member comfortable with the interpreter? Would the family member feel more comfortable with an interpreter of the same sex?
- If written materials are used, are they in the family's native language?

Interaction styles

- Does the family communicate with each other in a direct or indirect style?
- Does the family tend to interact in a quiet manner or a loud manner?
- Do family members share feelings when discussing emotional issues?
- Does the family ask you direct questions?
- Does the family value a lengthy social time at each home visit unrelated to the early childhood services program goals?
- Is it important for the family to know about the home visitor's extended family? Is the home visitor comfortable sharing that information?

From "Home-based early childhood services: Cultural sensitivity in a family systems approach" by K. I. Wayman, E. W. Lynch, & M. J. Hanson, 1990, *Topics in Early Childhood Special Education, 10*, 65–66. Copyright 1990 by PRO-ED, Inc. Reprinted by permission.

Optimizing the Testing Situation

The assessment should always be arranged at a time and place that allows the individuals who are important to the family to be present. This may include not only the direct caregivers, but also any other individual who has respon-sibility for decision making in the family, e.g., a grandmother. The assessment should occur in the setting where the family feels most comfortable. This might be in the home, at the early intervention program site, or a neutral place. Explaining every part of the assessment and its purpose to the family also will make them more comfortable. These explanations should be made frequently and in a variety of ways.

Remember the child's behavior during a testing situation may be influenced by the way his culture defines learning, by past experiences with test taking, whether he is being raised in a cooperative or competitive environment, his cognitive style, and the cultural values of his family.

Take care to determine whether the child understands the verbal test instructions and questions. You may repeat the instructions and questions where permitted by the test manual. You may ask the child to repeat the instructions or questions to be sure that he understands them. On nonstandardized tests, you may also give the instructions in a different way to see if this enhances the child's responsiveness. If you suspect that language variations are interfering with a child's ability to repeat accurately, ask the child to repeat or elaborate upon his response.

Try to enhance the child's motivation and interest by helping him feel as comfortable as possible in the assessment situation. Take as much time as is needed to enlist the child's cooperation. If at all possible, the examiner should be someone who is familiar to the child.

Curriculum-based assessment and ongoing data collection within the classroom will provide a better picture of a child's abilities. Standardized tests should be supplemented with information obtained from observations, interviews, and anecdotal information from a variety of sources and contexts.

Using Tests Appropriately

In testing children who have learned a language other than English in the home, administer a language test in the dominant language spoken by the child and a nonlanguage performance scale. Never use a nonlanguage test or a language test exclusively. In testing a bilingual child, intelligence tests should be administered in both languages on the assumption that the

ability repertoires in the separate languages will rarely overlap completely.

After giving a test item according to the standardized procedures, try teaching a missed test item to see how quickly the child can learn and what kind of teaching is effective. This strategy will provide useful information for developing intervention plans.

Interpreting Data Appropriately

The examiner must understand the cultural background of the child. He must understand the composition of the family membership, who is considered part of the child's family, and the roles these individuals play in the child's life. Who are the decision makers? This information will allow the examiner to know who should be included in the interviews, in the gathering of assessment data, and in the interpreting of test information. Assessment should go beyond the test itself. It should take into account the child's entire learning environment.

The validity and reliability of tests may be reduced because of such factors as the child's limited language proficiency in the language of the test, lack of familiarity with the content of the test items, lack of social and cultural sensitivity on the part of the test administrator, and the child's lack of familiarity with test-taking strategies. Information from an assessment of the child's language competence will assist the examiner in more accurately interpreting test results.

Be flexible in your interpretations. The observer may be influenced by his experiences and value system, which then influence the potential for interpretive and cultural bias (Baird, Haas, McCormick, Carruth, & Turner, 1992). Know the research findings about how children from specific ethnic groups perform on the tests that you have selected. Recognize that principles of test interpretation that apply to the nonminority group may not be applicable to all minority groups. The examiner must be aware of any biases that he may have which may impact on his interpretation of test results.

Take into account the degree of acculturation in the child and the child's family. As discussed previously in this chapter, culture falls on a continuum. The examiner must determine where this family is in the acculturation process. Recognize that acculturation will take different forms among different individuals, ethnic groups, and subgroups. Cultural factors impact upon children and families and influence the entire assessment process.

Assessment Methods and Instruments

The attempt to select or develop a perfect test for every cultural or linguistic group is impossible. However, the use of standardized psychometric tests cannot be totally eliminated from the assessment process. Leung (1986) suggests the examiner (1) understand the limitations of tests in general, (2) know the technical limitations of commonly used tests and weight the results accordingly, (3) choose test measures based on the kinds of information needed, and (4) administer the test in a nonstandardized manner (e.g., use the test-teach-test technique and avoid applying inappropriate norms).

Li, Walton and Nuttall (1999) have provided an extensive review of specific instruments used for assessing preschoolers. In their chapter "Preschool evaluation of culturally diverse children," they summarized the research on instruments used for screening, cognition, language, social-emotional-adaptive skills, and curriculum-based assessment. The instruments provided in this text were selected because their standardization sample included populations of diverse preschoolers or they have specific translations (sometimes adaptations with norms) in languages other than English, or because reliability or validity studies have been conducted

with preschoolers from diverse backgrounds (Li, Walton, & Nuttall, 1999). Li and colleagues also discuss the research findings in regard to various populations who are culturally diverse.

Alternative Assessment Approaches

Various alternatives have been sought to create tests that are less culturally biased (Duran, 1989; Laosa, 1977; Nuttall, Landurand & Goldman, 1984). Some of these assessment alternatives are offered to provide a direct connection between assessment and instruction.

Criterion-Referenced or Curriculum-Based Tests. Criterion-referenced or curriculum-based tests, which measure the child against his own previous performance, rather than against the majority, may be less biased. However, criterion referenced tests must be evaluated as to who determines what the objective will be and who establishes the criterion. This type of test may also be culturally biased if the objectives and criteria reflect majority standards and values. The validity of the developmental sequence for groups who are culturally diverse has not been well researched (Li, Walton, & Nuttall, 1999). One advantage of the criterion-referenced test is that it yields specific information regarding skills the child can and cannot perform. This information is more useful for educational programming than the numerical score yielded by the standardized test.

The TPBA (Linder, 1993) seems to be a promising alternative approach for assessing preschoolers who are culturally diverse because it is a natural, holistic, functional, and dynamic approach that includes parents in the assessment process and allows cross-disciplinary analysis of developmental level, learning style, interaction patterns, and other factors (Li, Walton, & Nuttall, 1999). The TPBA is an arena assessment and involves the child in structured and unstructured play situations at various times with a facilitating adult, the parent(s), and another child or children. Developmental observations of the child's cognitive, social-emotional, communication and language, and sensorimotor domains are provided. Two particular advantages of the TPBA are its ease for children with language difficulties and its flexibility in testing (Li, Walton, & Nuttall, 1999). These advantages may decrease assessment bias against children who are less verbal or who come from a different cultural or linguistic background. Because the use of the TPBA with children who are culturally diverse was not an emphasis in the development of the assessment, it is important that the assessor review the cultural appropriateness of the items and interpret the child's behavior from a cultural perspective as developmental expectations of young children vary greatly from one culture to another (Li, Walton, & Nuttall, 1999).

Dynamic Assessment. Dynamic assessment is a specific way of eliciting information from children using Vygotsky's (1929; 1962; 1978) concept of the Zone of Proximal Development (ZPD). Instead of seeing a child's performance only as what the child can do independently, dynamic assessment probes emerging skills. These skills can be tapped as the early childhood special educator and the child interact. The early childhood special educator tries to identify learning strategies that the child already uses as well as the instructional processes most likely to promote future learning (Berk & Winsler, 1995). The hints, prompts, cues, and questions used by the early childhood special educator are recorded along with the child's responses. By examining the assistance that makes a difference in the child's ability to perform the task, the early childhood special educator learns about the child's current level of understanding and skill, thus providing direction for future teaching. For example, the teacher plans prompts or hints to provide more assistance as the child needs it. A teacher might provide a hint by giving the beginning letter of

a word to a child as he is trying to develop the beginning stages of learning about sound-symbol relationships while taking advantage of the child's ability to use picture cues to try to read. In this way, dynamic assessment provides information at the lower or unassisted level of the ZPD and at the upper or maximally assisted level.

Dynamic assessment employs a fundamental test-train-test cycle. In dynamic assessment there is a strong link between testing and teaching. The early childhood special educator is encouraged to use clinical judgment in the evaluation of the child's performance. The early childhood special educator observes the child's growth from assisted performance to unassisted performance. There can be great variation in the target skills and content areas for learning and in the testing and training procedures.

Two general approaches to conducting dynamic assessment can be seen. One of these emphasizes clinical probing of a child's readiness to master new skills. The early childhood special educator relies on clinical judgment in diagnosing the readiness of a child to learn and determines which hints and cues can promote new learning. A second approach relies on a pre-established set of hints and cues that represent skill levels in a problem-solving task. Each response of the child is matched against the learning hierarchy and the child is given an appropriate set of cues or hints.

These approaches can easily be used in the classroom every day. If a preordered set of cues is used which go from general to specific, the lower the number of hints and cues needed by the student, the greater the learning potential. Children can be compared on their readiness to learn on the same problem-solving tasks. Dynamic assessment can be used to teach general cognitive or thinking skills and specific content skills.

Neo-Piagetian Task Performance. The child may be tested on his ability to perform Piagetian tasks.

Stages associated with these tasks occur across cultures and, therefore, tests associated with them are less likely to contain bias. The Ordinal Scales of Psychological Development developed by Uzgiris and McV. Hunt (1975) is an appropriate example of such a test for young children. This assessment is comprised of six scales: visual pursuit and permanence of objects, means for obtaining desired environmental events, vocal and gestural imitation, operational causality, construction of object relations in space, and relation to objects. These scales are broken into steps or test items. The assessment includes an activity for eliciting the response, suggested location and materials, and criterion behaviors. Although no norms are provided, Dunst (1980) assigned for each scale step estimated developmental age placements that provide a reasonable estimate of current functioning (McCormick, 1996).

Another assessment of Piagetian task performance is the Concept Assessment Kit—Conservation (Goldschmid & Beatler, 1968). The Concept Assessment Kit is intended for 4- to 7-year-olds; it tests their ability to conserve. Conservation is the idea that the amount or quantity of matter stays the same regardless of any changes in an irrelevant dimension. For example, if a row of five pennies is moved further apart, there are still only five pennies. This test is individually administered. Using Piaget's research technique, the examiner demonstrates a phenomenon that the child is then asked to explain. The test is normed and provides validity and reliability data. Studies have revealed some positive correlations between performance on these Piagetian-based scales and more traditional tests of intelligence (Goodwin & Driscoll, 1980).

Li, Walton and Nuttall (1999) also suggest the Columbia Mental Maturity Scale (CMMS) (Burgemeister, Blum, & Lorge, 1972) and the Boehm Test of Basic Concepts—Preschool Version (Boehm, 1986) as other specific tests

of cognitive development. Several general tests of cognitive knowledge are reviewed in Chapter 9.

Observational Techniques. Informal observational techniques are recommended to assess the behavior of a child who is culturally or linguistically diverse. This approach is very appropriate for preschool children, because they are less inhibited by adult observers than are older children, and thus can provide much valuable information to the trained observer. Of course, the information from informal observation is only as biased as the observer who records it. The child's entire learning environment should be taken into account.

Observational techniques are discussed in Chapter 12 on behavioral assessment. The examiner should make qualitative observations as noted in Chapter 6 to provide a better understanding of the child. However, the examiner should be cautioned not to make value judgments about the behavior, but simply to observe to learn more about the child and his interactions with others around him.

Task Analysis Approach. The task analysis approach requires the teacher to analyze the skills and behaviors needed to accomplish the task and then determine why the child is not able to do the task. The child is then trained in the areas of weakness and retested (Kaufman, 1977). Children are treated as individuals, not compared with others. The method is a test-teach-test approach (Mercer & Ysseldyke, 1977). However, this approach becomes difficult when tasks become complex. See Chapters 7 and 12 for additional information on task analysis.

Because it is unlikely that a truly unbiased test will ever be developed, strategies have been recommended to ensure that assessments are as fair as possible. These recommendations that are shown in Figure 3–4 apply to the assessment of any child and family but are

FIGURE 3–4

Assessment Strategies for Professionals Working with Families from Various Cultural or Linguistic Groups

1. The examiner needs to use the skills of bilingual and bicultural staff, interpreters, or mediators effectively (Anderson & Goldberg, 1991).

2. The interpreter or mediator should be able to interpret both language and cultural cues.

3. The examiner should have a knowledge of cultural factors, and be aware of his own strengths and limitations by doing a self-assessment of his own cultural background, experiences, values, and biases (Anderson & Goldberg, 1991; Lynch & Hanson, 1992).

4. Use multiple measures and gather data in naturalistic contexts to ensure that the best representation of the child and his or her abilities has been obtained (Bailey, 1989).

5. Use a transdisciplinary or multidisciplinary team approach to evaluation so that one area of development is not the sole focus (Bailey, 1989).

6. Take time to establish the trust needed to fully involve the family in the assessment process (Anderson & Goldberg, 1991).

7. Try to maintain a consistency of providers to allow the family to establish trust and ongoing communication.

8. Involve parents as significant partners in the assessment process and focus intervention goals and objectives on those areas viewed as particularly important to parents. Gather information in the areas in which the family has expressed concern. This shows respect for all families (Bailey, 1989; Lynch & Hanson, 1992).

9. Individualize the assessment process for parents and children because children and families may be at various levels of acculturation, and this requires varying degrees of modifications, such as language interpretation (Anderson & Goldberg, 1991; Lynch & Hanson, 1992).

10. Allow for flexibility in the assessment process and procedures. Meet with parents where they feel most comfortable (e.g., child care center, job site, in the home) (Anderson & Goldberg, 1991; Lynch & Hanson, 1992).

11. Focus on skills, rather than on a label when describing a child's functioning (Bailey, 1989).

12. When commercially available assessment instruments are used, examine test manuals to determine if evidence is presented supporting the fair use of the test with children who are from a minority culture and with both boys and girls. Choose only those that are appropriate for the language and culture of the child and family (Lynch & Hanson, 1992).

13. Examine test items or questions to ensure that they are not biased against children of a certain gender or cultural background. Modify test items to ensure cultural competency except if using standardized tests which do not allow variations (Bailey, 1989).

14. Limit the number of forms, questionnaires and other paperwork. Gather only the data necessary to begin working with the child and family. Families who have minimal competence in English may be overwhelmed by these forms, etc. (Lynch & Hanson, 1992).

15. Participate in staff training on cultural competence skills in assessment and maintain ongoing discussions with practitioners, parents, policymakers, and members of the cultural community served (Anderson & Goldberg, 1991).

Adapted from *Cultural competence in screening and assessment: Implications for services to young children with special needs ages birth through five*, from P. P. Anderson, and P. F. Goldberg, 1991, Chapel Hill, NC: NECTAS & PACER. (Available from PACER Center, 4826 Chicago Ave. S., Minneapolis, MN 55417); "Assessment and its importance in early intervention" by D. B. Bailey, 1989. In D. B. Bailey & M. Wolery (Eds.), *Assessing infants and preschoolers with handicaps* (pp. 1–21). Columbus, OH: Copyright 1989 by Merrill Publishing; and *Developing cross-cultural competence*, by E. W. Lynch and M. J. Hanson, 1992, Baltimore: Brookes. Copyright 1992 by Paul H. Brookes.

emphasized here because they are even more crucial when assessing a child and family who are culturally or linguistically diverse. These recommended strategies are a result of interviews, a review of the literature, and individual experiences of individuals from diverse backgrounds. These suggestions will assist the professional to be more culturally competent in his assessment of the child and family.

Making the Assessment Process Culturally Responsive

A culturally responsive approach involves a transdisciplinary or multidisciplinary team assessment which would include at least one person who speaks the child's language and is familiar with the child's culture and one person experienced in bilingual education, preferably in the child's language. Barrera (1996) stated that the steps involved in making an assessment culturally responsive are not significantly different from those required by any assessment. The basic steps required in this process are to (1) gather background information, (2) formulate hypotheses, (3) actively assess, (4) analyze and interpret information, (5) report findings, and (6) develop intervention. However, there are key aspects of each assessment step that are critical when assessing young children from sociocultural backgrounds unfamiliar to the assessor (Barrera, 1996). The global approach advocated by Nuttall, Landurand, and Goldman (1984) to decrease test bias takes a similar view. Nonbiased assessment is viewed as a process, rather than a set of instruments. Both approaches value language dominance, adaptive behavior, and sociocultural background. The assessment process is evaluated at each stage for possible sources of bias. The key aspects of these two approaches will be summarized based on the six steps discussed by Barrera (1996).

Gathering Background Information

Typical assessment items and procedures reflect assumptions that apply to all children uniformly. These assumptions do not take into account the role of social groups in differentially reinforcing and valuing children for choices they may make. The child being assessed is only the "foreground" of a total picture (Barrera, 1996). The sociocultural context(s) also must be assessed. If the child's background is different from that of the assessor, then the assessor must learn as much as possible before starting to observe and judge the child's behavior. Barrera (1996) provided three dimensions of sociocultural context which are significant when assessing the needs and strengths of young children and their families. The three dimensions outlined by Barrera (1996) are:

- Personal-social: Rules and patterns for developing and expressing one's identity and for interacting with others.
- Communicative-linguistic: Rules and patterns for appropriate and valued communication which would include but not be limited to the specific language used.
- Sensory-cognitive: Preferred and valued ways of identifying and processing information about the world (i.e. learning strategies).

A culturally responsive assessment begins by gathering information about the structure of these three dimensions in the child's environment. The assessor must understand the child's experience in these dimensions to determine whether the behavior observed indicates a need or strength. A culture-language mediator will assist the assessor and the family to understand the cultural aspects relevant to the assessment.

Hypothesis Formation

Hypothesis formation involves formulating hypotheses about the changes in typical assessment procedures and materials that may be necessary (Barrera, 1996). The assessor should answer the following questions:

- What are the optimum communicative-linguistic ways that will elicit the child's strongest response? For example, what language (e.g., English, Spanish) should be used, as well as nonverbals such as touch and distance and use of questions or modeling, and so on?
- What should the content of the assessment include? For example, will manipulating blocks give a true picture of eye-hand coordination?
- What environmental, situational, temporal, or relational features will be most appropriate? For example, where should the assessment take place and at what time?

The answers to these questions will vary depending on the purpose of the assessment. If the purpose is to determine the child's basic abilities, then the communicative-linguistic approach, the content, and the context of the assessment should reflect aspects most familiar to the child. If the purpose is to determine the child's readiness for an early childhood setting, then features of the early childhood setting should be included in the assessment (Barrera, 1996). When reporting assessment results, the assessor should always identify the purpose of the assessment, the specific adaptations made, and the persons involved.

The team member who is knowledgeable about the child's culture and language should prepare a home survey after visiting the child in his home. This survey should determine the language the family normally speaks, what language(s) is spoken in the neighborhood, and the amount of exposure the child has had to English. This information about the child's history and experience is very important to cross-cultural assessment.

Active Assessment

After formulating hypotheses, more structured interactions with the child and family can begin.

These interactions are primarily aimed at identifying what the child knows and can do within his environment and identifying learning abilities and strengths as they pertain to new environments. Usually assessments do not distinguish between these types of information (Barrera, 1996).

Vincent, Salisbury, Strain, McCormick, and Tessier (1990) present a behavioral-ecological approach. This approach uses naturalistic observation in the full range of environments with the full range of people with whom the child usually interacts. This would, of course, necessitate the inclusion of parents as equal members of the assessment team.

The behavioral-ecological approach requires the early interventionist to evaluate the environments where the child functions daily to determine what skills he needs now and in the future in order to be successful. The direct observation of the environments in which the young child functions would be conducted based on an analysis with the family of what settings are most important to them (Vincent, et al., 1990). This analysis is based on the behavioral approach discussed in Chapter 12.

The ecological focus in this approach requires that assessment must also include a look at family concerns and priorities. A combination of methods is necessary to gather this information. These methods include family self-report, structured interviews, and direct observation (Vincent, et al., 1990) Chapters 2 and 11 provide information on assessing the family needs and resources and ecological assessment. The fundamental basis of the assessment is the concept that all families have needs and resources.

The assessor must be careful to distinguish observations of behavior from inferences about the meaning of behavior. Interpreting a child's reluctance to separate from his mother as inappropriate may or may not be valid for the sociocultural context of the child and family (Barrera, 1996). Observational data yield clues and lead to certain guesses about strengths and needs. The assessor then must find additional information to confirm or deny the validity of the guess. Barrera (1996) suggested several key questions throughout the active assessment:

1. Am I really communicating with this child and family in a way that will elicit desired responses?
2. Is my interpretation of the behavior of this child and family similar to the interpretation that a family member or other member of the child's community would make?
3. Do the child's and family's responses indicate their true abilities and potentials?
4. Do the child's responses suggest that he is unfamiliar with the tasks presented or that, in the child's experience, little value is assigned to these tasks?
5. To what degree is the child's behavior being influenced by stress resulting from being in a situation where, because of unfamiliar norms and mores, the behavior of others is difficult or impossible to predict. (pp. 79–80)

When conducting an interview, it is important to work and talk with specific personnel who have had contacts with the child and family. Some general guidelines which have been suggested by Leung (1986) for use with Asian families could apply to all interviews, regardless of cultural background:

- Give the family the option of where the interview should take place.
- Offer to bring an interpreter if unsure about the primary language.
- Accept hospitality. This conveys acceptance of the family.
- Spend time building rapport.
- State your purpose clearly and often, so that there are not misunderstandings about your visit.
- Be aware that nonverbal cues may be more important than verbal cues, especially if the parents are unfamiliar with English.

- When in doubt, adjust your communication style/body language to that of the family.
- Be sure to follow up the visit with updates of information and decisions.
- Most important, be patient. There are many potential barriers to cross-cultural communication. You may be an important link.

An additional area recommended by Nuttall, Landurand, and Goldman (1984) is an educational assessment. For infants, toddlers, and preschoolers an educational assessment would be the use of a criterion-based or curriculum-based assessment to determine what skills the child performs in the primary or second language.

All assessments should focus on determining how the child functions both socially and cognitively in both English and the home language. An integral part of this is the inclusion of a team member who is familiar with the child's culture and speaks the child's language. If no appropriately qualified professional is familiar with the child's home language, then an interpreter needs to be found and trained to work with the monolingual assessor (Nuttall, Landurand, & Goldman, 1984).

Analysis and Interpretation of Information

Informed judgments must be made about the observational data gathered in the previous step. Inferences made must be reviewed critically in light of the values, expectations, and experiences common to the child's most familiar environment. If the child's behavior is appropriate within that environment, then such behavior probably reflects intact learning abilities. If the behavior that is demonstrated is not appropriate within the child's most familiar environment, then there is a stronger probability of limited abilities to learn or adapt (Barrera, 1996).

Socioculturally responsive assessment requires specific attention to what the presence or absence of behaviors may reflect. Certain questions need to be asked in order to interpret the behavior in a nonbiased way. Barrera (1996) suggested the following questions:

1. Is the child's performance on par with that of peers even though it may be below that of the norms used by the assessor?
2. If the child is demonstrating age-expected behaviors for his community, to what degree are these behaviors adaptive for the environments the child will be entering as he leaves home?
3. If the child is not exhibiting behaviors and skills considered typical for child of his age in the community, has the child had the opportunities to learn these behaviors? Does this inability indicate a learning impairment or a "temporary" disability?
4. Is the child exhibiting behaviors and skills that extend beyond what can be explained by sociocultural adaptation or limited opportunity to learn? When this seems to be the case, the possibility of a delay or disability should be assessed.

Reporting Findings

Often the greatest bias lies in the way the data are reported, not in the actual assessment (Barrera, 1996). The assessor should report not only the child's performance, but also "how" the performance was elicited and measured. For example, the report should state what items were presented and how familiar these items were to the child. Information about community behavioral expectations is important. The assessor can then make judgments about what represents a behavior that is typical for a particular group and what represents an individual difference that may be considered limited. "In general, a child who is developmentally on a par with peers in his community has intact learning and language abilities, although he may need opportunities to learn and speak in ways that will be necessary to function well in other environments" (Barrera, 1996, p. 82).

Program Development

The assessment process is completed with the identification of a child's strengths, and the development of specific goals, objectives, and strategies for intervention. For a young child who is culturally diverse, the goal is to help children learn to function in as many settings as their developmental capacities allow. Because early childhood assessment may have life-changing implications for those assessed, early interventionists must be as competent as possible (Barrera, 1996).

Summary

Families and children served by early intervention and early childhood special education are diverse in culture, ethnicity, language, family structure, composition, and values. A genuine sensitivity to and appreciation for the uniqueness of each child and the child's family and their concerns and priorities must be established as an integral part of screening and assessment. This diversity requires that professionals develop cross-cultural competence.

The emphasis in assessment has shifted from the child-in-isolation to a broad contextual view, including collecting data from multiple sources using multiple methods and assessing children in the contexts within which they typically find themselves (Meisels & Fenichel, 1996). The context for conducting assessment has moved to more naturalistic, nonthreatening settings. Assessments are now made by teams relying more on clinical judgment than standardized instruments. The extensive use of clinical judgment is an attempt to overcome the limitation of more traditional psychometric approaches and provide information that is more directly useful in guiding appropriate intervention. For culturally competent assessment to become truly useful for intervention, both multiple lenses and skilled dialogue with families are necessary. Culturally competent assessment requires that personnel have knowledge of their own personal and professional contexts as well as experience in transdisciplinary strategies.

An important fact for the examiner to keep in mind is that the purpose of the assessment is to learn more about the child and family to determine if special assistance is needed in order for the child to develop to his full potential. Professionals in assessment should be advocates for children and families, rather than agents who legitimize the location of the problem within the child. If you are an advocate, you will examine the cultural and educational contexts in which the child has developed.

Cultural diversity should be viewed as a strength, not as a deficit. This stresses the use and importance of family interviews and observation procedures as sources of information for planning. If children who are culturally/linguistically diverse are to receive appropriate assessment, placements, and programs, then emphasis must be placed on administrative coordination, finding qualified personnel who speak minority languages, providing descriptive data, and clearly articulated guidelines and procedures.

References

Anderson, M., & Goldberg, P. F. (1991). *Cultural competence in screening and assessment: Implications for services to young children with special needs ages birth through five.* Chapel Hill, NC: NECTAS & PACER. [Available from PACER Center, 4826 Chicago Ave. South, Minneapolis, MN 55417, (612) 827–2966.]

Anderson, P. P., & Fenichel, E. S. (1989). *Serving culturally diverse families of infants and toddlers with disabilities.* Arlington, VA: The National Center for Clinical Infant Programs.

Bailey, D. B. (1989). Assessment and its importance in early intervention. In D. B. Bailey & M. Wolery (Eds.), *Assessing infants and preschoolers with handicaps* (pp. 1–21). Upper Saddle River, NJ: Merrill/Prentice Hall.

Bailey, D. B. (1991). Issues and perspectives on family assessment. *Infants and Young Children*, 4(1), 26–34.

Baird, S. M., Haas, L., McCormick, K., Carruth, C., & Turner, K. D. (1992). Approaching an objective system for observation and measurement: Infant-parent social interaction code. *Topics in Early Childhood Special Education*, 12(4), 544–571.

Barrera, I. (1990). *Honoring the differences: Six essential features of serving culturally/linguistically diverse children with special needs.* Unpublished monograph available from author: University of New Mexico; Special Education; MVH 3006; Albuquerque, NM 87131.

Barrera, I. (1993). Effective and appropriate instruction for all children: The challenge of cultural/linguistic diversity and young children with special needs. *Topics in Early Childhood Special Education*, 13(4), 461–487.

Barrera, I. (1996). Thoughts on the assessment of young children. In S. J. Meisels & E. Fenichel (Eds.), *New visions for the developmental assessment of infants and young children* (pp. 69–84). Washington, DC: Zero to Three/National Center for Infants, Toddlers, and Families.

Barrera Metz, I. (1991). Learning from personal experience. In M. Anderson & P. F. Goldberg, *Cultural competence in screening and assessment: Implications for services to young children with special needs ages birth through five.* Chapel Hill, NC: NECTAS & PACER.

Bazron, B. J., Dennis, K. W., & Isaacs, M. R. (1989). *Toward a culturally competent system of care: A monograpgh on effective services for minority children who are severely emotionally disturbed.* Washington, DC: The National Institutes of Health, Child, and Adolescent Service System Program (CASSP). [Available from CASSP Technical Assistance Center, Georgetown University Child Development Center, 3800 Reservoir Rd. NW, Washington, DC 20007; (202) 687–8635.]

Bearcrane, J., Dodd, J. M., Nelson, J. R., & Ostwald, S. W. (1990). Educational characteristics of Native Americans. *Rural Educator*, 11, 1–5.

Berk, L. E., & Winsler, A. (1995). *Scaffolding children's learning: Vygotsky and early childhood education.* Washington, DC: National Association for the Education of Young Children.

Boehm, A. E. (1986). *Boehm Test of Basic Concepts—Preschool.* San Antonio, TX: The Psychological Corporation.

Brown, W., & Barrera, I. (1999). Enduring problems in assessment: The persistent challenges of cultural dynamics and family issues. *Infants and Young Children*, 12(1), 34–42.

Burgemeister, B. B., Blum, L. H., & Lorge, I. (1972). *Columbia Mental Maturity Scale,* (3rd ed.). New York: The Psychological Corporation.

Chamberlain, P., & Medinos-Landurand, P. M. (1991). Practical considerations for the assessment of LEP students with special needs. In E. V. Manayan & J. S. Damico (Eds.), *Limiting bias in the assessment of bilingual students* (pp. 111–156). Austin, TX: PRO-ED.

Chan, S. (1983). *Assessment of Chinese-Americans: Cultural considerations.* Unpublished paper.

Chan, S. (1990). Early intervention with culturally diverse families of infants and toddlers with disabilities. *Infants and Young Children*, 3, 78–87.

Chan, S., & Mahseredjian, H. (1989). Cultural competence: Effectively serving ethnic minority children and families. Workshop presented at the Infant Conference 1989, Los Angeles.

Cloud, N. (1993). Language, culture, and disability: Implications for instruction and teacher preparation. *Teacher Education & Special Education*, 16(1), 60–72.

Cummins, J. (1984). *Bilingualism and special education: Issues in assessment and pedagogy.* Philadelphia: Multilingual Matters.

Dunst, C. J. (1980). *A clinical and educational manual for use with the Uzgiris and Hunt scales of infant psychological development.* Austin, TX: PRO-ED.

Duran, R. P. (1989). Assessment and instruction of at-risk Hispanic students, *Exceptional Children*, 56(2), 154–158.

Fradd, S. H., & Weismantel, M. J. (1989). *Meeting the needs of culturally and linguistically different students: A handbook for educators*. Boston: Little, Brown & Co.

Garcia, S. B., & Malkin, D. (1993). Toward defining programs and services for culturally and linguistically diverse learners in special education. *Teaching Exceptional Children*, Fall 1993, pp. 52–58.

Garcia, S., & Ortiz, A. (1988). Preventing referrals of language minority students to special education. *New Focus*, 5, 1–11.

Goldman, S. R., & Trueba, H. T. (Eds.) (1987). *Becoming literate in English as a second language*. Norwood, NJ: Ablex.

Goldschmid, M. L., & Beatler, P. M. (1968). *Manual: Concept assessment kit—conservation*. San Diego: Educational and Industrial Testing Service.

Goodwin, W. L., & Driscoll, L. A. (1980). *Handbook for measurement and evaluation in early childhood education*. San Francisco: Jossey-Bass.

Groce, N. (1990). Comparative and cross-cultural issues. *Disabilities Studies Quarterly*, 10, 1–39.

Hagen, E. (1989). *Communicating effectively with Southeast Asian patients*. Los Angeles: Immaculate Heart College Center.

Hall, E. T. (1976). *Beyond culture*. Garden City, NY: Anchor Press/Doubleday.

Hamayan, E. V., & Damico, J. S. (1991). Developing and using a second language. In E. V. Hamayan & J. S. Damico (Eds.), *Limiting bias in the assessment of bilingual students* (pp. 39–76). Austin, TX: PRO-ED.

Hanson, M. J. (1998). Ethnic, cultural, and language diversity in intervention settings. In E. W. Lynch & M. J. Hanson (Eds.), *Developing cross-cultural competence: A guide for working with children and their families* (4th ed.), (pp. 3–22). Baltimore: Brookes.

Hanson, M. J., Lynch, E. W., & Wayman, K.I. (1990). Honoring the cultural diversity of families when gathering data. *Topics in Early Childhood Special Education*, 10(1), 112–131.

Illinois Resource Center. (1986). *Meeting the needs of exceptional children of limited English proficiency*. Manual.

Kaufman, J. (1977). *Proceedings of a multicultural colloquium on non-biased pupil assessment*. Bureau of School Psychological and Social Services, New York State Department of Education.

Laosa, L. (1977). Nonbiased assessment of children's abilities: Historical antecedents and current issues. In T. Oakland (Ed.), *Psychological and educational assessment of minority children*. New York: Brunner/Mazel.

Leung, B. (1986). Psychoeducational assessment of Asian students. In M. K. Kitano & P. C. Chinn (Eds.), *Exceptional Asian children and youth*. Reston, VA: ERIC Clearinghouse on Handicapped and Gifted Children, Council for Exceptional Children.

Li, C., Walton, J. R., & Nuttall, E. V. (1999). Preschool evaluation of culturally and linguistically diverse children. In

E. V. Nuttall, I. Romero, & J. Kalesnik (Eds.), *Assessing and screening preschoolers: Psychological and educational dimensions* (pp. 296–317). Needham Heights, MA: Allyn & Bacon.

Linder, T. (1993). *Transdisciplinary play-based assessment* (rev. ed.). Baltimore: Brookes.

Lynch, E. W. (1987). Families from different cultures. In M. Bristol & C. Kasari (Eds.), *The Family Support Network Series: Monograph one* (pp. 80–88). Moscow, ID: Family Support Network Project, University of Idaho.

Lynch, E. W. (1992). Developing cross-cultural competence. In E. W. Lynch & M. J. Hanson (Eds.), *Developing cross-cultural competence: A guide for working with young children and their families* (pp. 35–62). Baltimore: Brookes.

Lynch, E. W. (1998). Developing cross cultural competence. In E. W. Lynch & M. J. Hanson (Eds.), *Developing cross-cultural competence* (2nd ed.) (pp. 47–86). Baltimore: Brookes.

Lynch, E. W., & Hanson, M. J. (Eds.). (1992). *Developing cross-cultural competence: A guide for working with young children and their families* Baltimore: Brookes.

Lynch, E. W., & Hanson, M. J. (1993). Changing demographics: Implications for training in early intervention. *Infants and Young Children*, 6(1), 50–55.

Lynch, E. W., & Hanson, M. J. (1996). Ensuring cultural competence in assessment. In M. E. McLean, D. B. Bailey, & M. Wolery (Eds.), *Assessing infants and preschoolers with handicaps* (pp. 69–95). Upper Saddle River, NJ: Merrill/Prentice Hall.

Lynch, E. W., & Hanson, M. J. (Eds.). (1998). *Developing cross-cultural competence: A guide for working with young children and their families* (2nd ed.). Baltimore: Brookes.

Lynch, J. (1992). *Educating for citizenship in a multicultural society*. New York: Cassell.

Mattes, L. J., & Omark, D. R. (1984). *Speech and language assessment for the bilingual handicapped*. San Diego, CA: College Hill Press.

McAdoo, H. (1978). Minority families. In J. H. Stevens & M. Matthews (Eds.), *Mother/child, father/child relationships* (pp. 177–195). Washington, DC: National Association for the Education of Young Children.

McCormick, K. (1996). Assessing cognitive development. In M. E. McLean, D. B. Bailey, & M. Wolery (Eds.), *Assessing infants and preschoolers with handicaps* (pp. 268–304). Upper Saddle River, NJ: Merrill/Prentice Hall.

Meisels, S. J., & Fenichel, E. (Eds.). (1996). *New visions for the developmental assessment of infants and young children*. Washington, DC: Zero to Three/National Center for Infants, Toddlers, and Families.

Mercer, J. R., & Ysseldyke, J. (1977). Designing diagnostic-intervention programs. In T. Oakland (Ed.), *Psychological and educational assessment of minority children*. New York: Brunner/Mazel.

Nguyen, Dao. (1987). Presentation at Multicultural Issues Track Session, Topical Conference of the Technical

Assistance for Parent Programs (TAPP) Project. Boston. (Conference in Crystal City, VA) December, 7–10.

Nuttall, E. V., Landurand, P. M., & Goldman, P. (1984). A critical look at testing and evaluation from a cross-cultural perspective. In P. C. Chinn (Ed.), *Education of culturally and linguistically different exceptional children* (pp. 42–62). Reston, VA: CEC.

Ortiz, A. A. (1987). The influence of locus of control and culture on learning styles of language minority students. In J. J. Johnson & B. A. Ramierez (Eds.), *American Indian exceptional children and youth* (pp. 9–16). Reston, VA: ERIC Clearinghouse on Handicapped and Gifted Children, Council for Exceptional Children.

Ramirez, M., & Castaneda, A. (1974). *Cultural democracy, bicognitive development and education.* New York: Academic Press.

Randall-David, E. (1989). *Strategies for working with culturally diverse communities and clients.* Washington, DC: Association for the Care of Children's Health.

Sattler, Jerome M. (1988). *Assessment of children.* San Diego: Jerome M. Sattler.

Saville-Troike, M. (1978). *A guide to culture in the classroom.* Rosslyn, VA: National Clearinghouse for Bilingual Education.

Schilling, B., & Brannon, E. (1986). *Cross-cultural counseling: A guide for nutrition and health counselors.* Washington, DC: United States Department of Agriculture/Department of Health and Human Services.

Turnbull, R., & Cilley, M. (1999). *Explanations and implications of the 1997 amendments to IDEA.* Upper Saddle River, NJ: Merrill/Prentice Hall.

Uzgiris, I. C., & McV. Hunt, J. (1975). *Assessment in infancy: Ordinal scales of psychological development.* Urbana, IL: University of Illinois Press.

Vincent, L. J., Salisbury, C. L., Strain, P., McCormick, C., & Tessier, A. (1990). A behavioral-ecological approach to early intervention: Focus on cultural diversity. In S. J. Meisels & J. P. Shonkoff (Eds.), *Handbook of early childhood intervention* (pp. 173–195). New York: Cambridge University Press.

Vygotsky, L. S. (1929). The problem of cultural development of the child. *Journal of Genetic Psychology, 36,* 515–534.

Vygotsky, L. S. (1962). *Thought and language.* Cambridge, MA: MIT Press.

Vygotsky, L. S. (1978). *Mind in society: The development of higher psychological processes.* M. Cole, V. John-Steiner, S. Scribner, & E. Soubermen (Eds. and Trans.). Cambridge, MA: Harvard University Press.

Waggoner, D. (January, 1992). Numbers of home speakers of non-English languages increasing. *Numbers and Needs: Ethnic and Linguistic Minorities in the United States, 2*(1), 2. [Available through Box G1H/B, 3900 Watshon Place, N.W., Washington, DC. 20016].

Wayman, K., Lynch. E. W., & Hanson, M. J. (1990). Home-based early childhood services: Cultural sensitivity in a family systems approach. *Topics in Early Childhood Special Education, 10*(4), 56–75.

Westby, C. E. (1986). Cultural differences in caregiver-child interaction: Implications for assessment and intervention. In L. Cole & V. Deal (Eds.), *Communication disorders in multicultural populations.* Rockville, MD: American Speech & Hearing Association.

4

The Team Process

The Team Approach

The provisions of PL 105–17 require that services include a multidisciplinary assessment and a written IFSP, which is to be developed by a multidisciplinary team that includes a family-directed identification of needs. The team approach reflects the early interventionists' view of human development as an integrated and interactive whole, not simply a collection of separate parts (Golin & Duncanis, 1981). This interrelated nature of the developmental domains is prompting early interventionists to recognize the need for professionals to work together as a team (Woodruff & McGonigel, 1988). The complexity of child and family issues requires teaming across disciplines. This chapter presents an overview of the various team members, their roles, and a review of the three prevalent models of team functioning. The greater the ability of the team to interact, to share roles, and to inform each other across disciplines, the more unified and complete a child's services are likely to be (Howard, Williams, Port, & Lepper, 2001). Therefore, this chapter emphasizes the transdisciplinary model because it requires the most interaction and sharing of roles across disciplines.

Team Members

Early intervention teams involve a variety of disciplines. Teams are composed of professionals representing disciplines including special education; social work; psychology; medicine; child development; and physical, occupational, and speech and language therapy. The family is also considered an equal member of the team. The areas of expertise and roles or functions of the disciplines involved in early intervention are summarized in Table 4–1. All of these disciplines have several common tasks or services. These common services include assessment of the child's developmental status and

the development and implementation of a program to meet identified needs. The way these services are carried out by a multidisciplinary team may differ based on the way the team functions.

The structure for interaction among team members distinguishes early intervention teams. Three service delivery models that structure interaction among team members have been identified and differentiated in the literature: multidisciplinary, interdisciplinary and transdisciplinary. These team approaches differ in philosophy and in the way they function. Table 4–2 outlines the differences in the multidisciplinary, interdisciplinary, and transdisciplinary team approaches to intervention. These three team models are discussed in the remainder of this chapter. Considerable discussion is given to the transdisciplinary model because it is often a recommended approach that minimizes disciplinary boundaries and promotes team consensus.

Multidisciplinary Model

The multidisciplinary approach is the most widely used model. This model uses several professionals who emphasize their own discipline in assessing particular developmental domains (Bagnato & Neisworth, 1991). Many individual consultations from different disciplines are obtained, but the various evaluations are carried out independently of each other with little opportunity for professional interaction. Each professional uses instrument(s) specifically designed to measure development in her own discipline. This style of assessment requires each professional to participate separately by using the procedures and outlook unique to her own discipline. Bagnato, Neisworth, and Munson (1997) have argued that this form of "teamwork" masquerades as a team approach but actually disregards the needs of young children and their families. The multidisciplinary model is a "team" model

TABLE 4–1

Expertise and Functions of Service Providers

Discipline	Areas of Expertise	Function
Early Interventionist Early Childhood Special Educator	Overall educational growth and development of child in all domains	Generally takes responsibility for child's overall educational growth and development. Planning and educational programming, educational assessment, child and family advocacy, and referral to related services.
Speech/Language Pathologist	Speech and language abilities; augmentative communication	Has primary responsibility for the child's development of communicative abilities. Concerned with oral-motor facilitation, feeding therapy, and development of preverbal communication.
Occupational Therapist	Motor abilities (gross motor and coordination); self-care skills; sensory and motor abilities	Takes primary responsibility for the child's sensory development and integration with emphasis on sensory information processing which distinguishes the functions of occupational therapist from speech/language therapist.
Physical Therapist	Neurologic functioning underlying gross motor development	Takes primary responsibility for the child's positioning, handling, and movement and the suppression of abnormal movement along with the occupational therapist.
Psychologist	Cognitive abilities and adaptive behavior; social-emotional abilities	Has primary responsibility for psychological assessment, child and family counseling, and consultation with other team members concerning the child's behavior and development.
Social Worker	Family and child functioning and emotional well-being	Provides link between home and program. Knowledge of family dynamics, information about siblings, extended family members, and understanding of family stresses.

TABLE 4–1
continued

Discipline	Areas of Expertise	Function
Developmental Pediatrician	Overall medical and developmental needs	Helps clarify relationships among the child's medical needs, developmental competencies, and endurance for program participation.
Nurse	Medical status including administration of specific procedures and drugs	Has responsibility for medical well-being of child and family. Involves general preventive physical exams and routine inoculations, as well as specific treatments of medical disorders such as seizure disorders.
Nutritionist	Nutritional status and nutritional counseling	Is responsible for ensuring optimal nutrition by providing guidance in food purchase, preservation, and preparation to help provide proper diet and treat dietary problems.

in a very loose sense. The minimal interaction of its members does not allow for the dynamics that lead to team cohesion and commitment and, therefore, there may be no team consensus.

The number of team members may be set or members may be selected to address the problems presented by the referral source. For example, the referral problem for one child may demand the presence of a physical therapist whereas another child's referral problem may not indicate the need for a physical therapist. Team members develop the part of the service plan related to their own discipline. Peterson (1987) compared the way multidisciplinary team members interact to parallel play. They work side by side but separately. Each professional on the team assesses the child and provides verbal and written feedback to the parent or referral source. These professionals do not necessarily discuss their findings with other team members.

Interaction among team members is minimal and, thus, does not foster services that reflect the child as an integrated and interactive whole (Linder, 1983). This approach omits the possibility of group synthesis and can result in fragmented or duplicated services for families and confusing or conflicting reports to parents. Even when a selected professional is responsible for presenting the results from all of the different disciplines involved, concerns may arise related to the comfort of that professional with all of the information being provided, and biases can emerge (Fewell, 1983a).

Another concern of this model is the lack of communication between team members that places the burden of coordination and case management on the family. Recommendations may be communicated via individual written reports or by talking directly to the family. In some cases, the information may be collected by or sent to one team member who then inter-

TABLE 4–2

Three Models for Early Intervention

Intervention	Multidisciplinary	Interdisciplinary	Transdisciplinary
Assessment	Separate assessments by team members	Separate assessments by team members	Team members and family conduct a comprehensive developmental assessment together
Parent Participation	Parents meet with individual team members	Parents meet with team or team representative	Parents are full, active, and participating members of the team
Service Plan Development	Team members develop separate plans for their discipline	Team members share their separate plans with one another	Team members and the parents develop a service plan based upon family priorities, needs, and resources
Service Plan Responsibility	Team members are responsible for implementing their section of the plan	Team members are responsible for sharing information with one another as well as for implementing their section of the plan	Team members are responsible and accountable for how the primary service provider implements the plan
Service Plan Implementation	Team members implement the part of the service plan related to their discipline	Team members implement their section of the plan and incorporate other sections where possible	A primary service provider is assigned to implement the plan with the family
Lines of Communication	Informal lines	Periodic case-specific team meetings	Regular team meeting where continuous transfer of information, knowledge, and skills are shared among team members
Guiding Philosophy	Team members recognize the importance of contributions from other disciplines	Team members are willing and able to develop, share, and be responsible for providing services that are a part of the total service plan	Team members make a commitment to teach, learn, and work together across discipline boundaries to implement unified service plan
Staff Development	Independent and within their discipline	Independent within as well as outside of their discipline	An integral component of team meetings for learning across disciplines and team building

From Woodruff, G., & Hanson, C. (1987). Project KAI, 77B Warren St., Brighton, MA 02135. Funded by U.S. Department of Education, Special Education Programs, Handicapped Children's Early Education Program. Copyright 1981 by Council for Exceptional Education. Reprinted with permission.

prets that information and presents the recommendations. Individual reports may also be presented at staff meetings, but the purpose of exchanging information is to present the goals and plans of each discipline, not to coordinate across disciplines (McCollum & Hughes, 1988).

A strength of the multidisciplinary model is that more than one discipline is involved. Therefore, there is more expertise available with which to make decisions and less chance for one person's mistakes or biases to determine the course of events.

Interdisciplinary Model

An interdisciplinary team is composed of both parents/caregivers and professionals representing several disciplines. The difference between multidisciplinary and interdisciplinary teams is in the interaction among team members. Professionals and parents/caregivers work together cooperatively to plan and deliver services to the child or parents/caregivers. Interdisciplinary teams have formal channels of communication that encourage team members to share their information and discuss individual results (Fewell, 1983b; Peterson, 1987). Separate assessments are conducted by individual disciplines, with each discipline specialist basically responsible for the part of the service plan in her area at scheduled therapy or consultation times. Typically, one team member is assigned to coordinate services. The interdisciplinary team attempts to conduct evaluations over a day or two, which may improve the information being provided to families and referral sources. Regular meetings are planned to discuss the results of individual assessments and to develop plans for intervention. This approach outlines a process in which professionals from different but related disciplines work together to assess and manage problems by actively participating in mutual decision making. The team

members share information with one another but independently implement their sections of a plan. Emphasis is on teamwork and interaction among the team members to provide well-coordinated, integrated services for the child and family. These efforts to share and coordinate information are a strength of the interdisciplinary model.

Garshelis and McConnell (1993) compared mothers' assessments of their own needs to assessments of family needs made by interagency early intervention teams and individual professionals on these teams. Interdisciplinary teams were found to be more accurate in assessing family needs than were individual professionals, but even teams did very poorly. The study found that a family needs survey and follow-up personal discussions with families would help ensure that services focus on those needs that are a direct concern to families and may ultimately lead to better outcomes for children. The researchers also found that the extent to which individual professionals or teams agreed with mothers was unrelated to the discipline represented or the amount of time an interdisciplinary team had worked together. In their study, Garshelis and McConnell found that only 67 percent of the mothers felt they had input into plans made for their family, and 25 percent were not sure if they felt part of the team. Hopefully, provisions for family involvement outlined in PL 105-17 have assured that families are actually part of the team.

Although the inclusion of ongoing communication in a single session or two may improve the information being provided to families and referral sources, concerns remain that one professional may take charge and dominate a team meeting. Team members generally advocate joint decision making and development of a unified intervention plan, but in practice there are often problems related to information sharing. Information often flows only one way from team members involved in assessment to a direct service provider. There is no provision for feedback from the service provider to those responsible for assessment and intervention recommendations. In addition, despite the fact that professionals may have the opportunities to talk to one another about their findings, this does not ensure that they will understand each other.

One way to address team-based concerns is to systematize the data collection process. The System to Plan Early Childhood Services (SPECS) (Bagnato & Neisworth, 1990) includes materials and procedures that assist the early intervention or early childhood special education team in reaching consensus in the assessment process. Parents and professionals independently rate a child on 19 developmental and functional dimensions. From these ratings, the dimensions of concern or disagreement are identified, and the discrepant ratings are then discussed until a consensus is reached for a rating on each dimension. The child's assessment profile then can be detailed and appropriate programming options can be recommended (Hooper & Edmondson, 1998).

An interdisciplinary model assumes a whole-child perspective and stresses the integral involvement of parents as partners on the team by a process of collaborative goal setting. Services are organized around functional skills or developmental domains, rather than by the discipline that provides those services. Curriculum-based assessments are most often used by interdisciplinary assessment teams to focus services and link assessment to program planning. Team members are encouraged to consult frequently so that a unified view about child and family needs is created. Intervention goals are designed so that common goals are integrated into each discipline's therapy. For example, language goals are included as central features of a child with language delay's activities within the early childhood setting. The interdisciplinary model

is a real team approach with members constantly working to reduce conflict and ensuring coordination of services (Bagnato & Neisworth, 1991).

Transdisciplinary Model

The transdisciplinary approach describes what many professionals believe to be the ideal type of interdisciplinary team functioning. Transdisciplinary teaming involves the mutual sharing of assessment results and dictates professional involvement and participation which crosses traditional discipline boundaries. Woodruff and McGonigel (1988) recommended the transdisciplinary approach as a sound, logical, and valid system for offering coordination and comprehensive services to young children and their families. The transdisciplinary model is of particular interest for identification and provision of services to infants and very young children, because these young children and their families often have needs that extend beyond the expertise of any single discipline.

Rationale

The basic rationale for the transdisciplinary approach is the desire for fewer people to work directly with the family and child, improved continuity in programming, maximum consistency of services in the home and center, and increased integration of parent participation (Raver, 1991). Both theoretically and philosophically there are very real differences between the transdisciplinary model and the other models, multidisciplinary and interdisciplinary. The most notable difference is the commitment to sharing information and skills among team members (Noonan & McCormick, 1993).

Two basic beliefs are integral to this approach. First, the child's development must be seen as integrated and interactive. Secondly, children must be served within the context of the family (Woodruff & McGonigel, 1988). The transdisciplinary approach attempts to meet the needs of the child and family without compartmentalization and fragmentation of planning and services. The interaction that takes place between team members allows professionals to obtain a more balanced and integrated picture of the whole child. Each discipline cannot be concerned solely with the needs in that particular professional area. For example, the physical therapist cannot just look at the motor needs of the child, but how motor status impacts on the child's functioning in other areas as well (i.e., educational performance, personal-social interactions, play skills, etc.). Team members accept and accentuate each other's knowledge and strengths to benefit the team, the child, and the family (Lyon & Lyon, 1980).

Lyon and Lyon (1980) defined the relevant characteristics of the transdisciplinary team model as (1) joint functioning, (2) continuous staff development, and (3) role release or sharing. Joint functioning means that team members perform required services together whenever possible. Arena assessment is an example of joint functioning. Staff development means that team members train one another on an ongoing basis so that the skills of all team members are always being expanded. This emphasis on continued opportunities for skill development is one of the greatest strengths of the transdisciplinary team model. Role release or sharing requires the distributing of responsibilities across disciplines and is possible owing to this continuous staff development. Key elements of the transdisciplinary approach are the arena assessment, integrated therapy, and collaboration.

Role of Transdisciplinary Team Members

Transdisciplinary teams are composed of parents and professionals from several disciplines. Professionals from any of the disciplines involved in early intervention and early childhood special education (e.g., nursing, nutrition, psychology, social work, special education, occupational and physical therapy, speech/language, hearing) may be included in a transdisciplinary team approach. The team members systematically cross traditional discipline boundaries to better understand other disciplines and thus provide services to families who require skills outside their own discipline when it is appropriate and necessary. The shared responsibilities of transdisciplinary teamwork are not easily achieved. The approach demands flexibility, tolerance, and understanding among those involved (Garland, Woodruff, & Buck, 1988).

Families are seen as part of the transdisciplinary team and participate in the assessment, goal setting, and program decisions because they have the greatest influence on the child's development. Using this approach, professionals work together with the direct guidance of the family to develop a unified and integrated plan for the child and the family. Although all team members share the responsibility for the development of the service plan, it is carried out by the family and one other team member who is designated as the primary service provider.

Team leadership depends on the child's and the family's strengths and preferences. If the program is part of an educational system, then the teacher is likely to be the team leader who coordinates the activities of all members in ways that best address the individual child and family needs (Campbell, 1989). If the child is under 3 years of age, then the service coordinator may be the team leader or the primary service provider. This depends on the family's choice. In most cases the direct service provider is the teacher for preschoolers (Noonan & McCormick, 1993). In either situation, the parents or caregivers are key team members.

It is essential for the implementation of the team plan that the primary service provider has a solid knowledge and understanding of all the domain areas and intervention strategies. The primary service provider does not try to replace the other specialists, but rather attempts to continually pool information and skills between specialists to better develop and implement a service plan. If direct "hands-on" interventions are needed, then the actual professional from the discipline of need will provide those services (McGonigel, Woodruff, & Roszmann-Millican, 1994).

Transdisciplinary team members have many responsibilities. They conduct assessments and develop service plans as a team with the direct collaboration of families and focusing on the families' priorities. A primary service provider is authorized by the team to work directly with the family and implement the plan with the family. Each team member is accountable for how the primary service provider implements the plan with the family. Many meetings are needed to discuss assessment, diagnosis and goal setting, planning and program implementation, and evaluation of the program and child. All decisions in the areas of assessment and program planning, implementation, and evaluation are made by team consensus.

To become a successful transdisciplinary team requires continual attention to team building to diminish professional turf issues. Positive team outcomes begin at the level of the individual team member. Positive team functioning is a reflection of individual involvement, commitment, and contribution. Therefore, there must be a commitment from the administrative staff to grant the necessary time, training, and support for team development (McGonigel, Woodruff, & Roszmann-Millican, 1994).

Team members are responsible for organizing regular staff development meetings for teaching their discipline skills to team members and sharing discipline-specific information. An integral part of the transdisciplinary approach is learning across discipline lines. The program is developed by the whole team and implemented by each team member, not just the service provider. Staff development as mutual training may occur at three different levels: (1) sharing general information, (2) teaching others to make specific judgments, and (3) teaching others to perform specific actions. The first two levels entail merely sharing information, whereas the third level involves sharing of roles.

Role Sharing

Role sharing is the distribution of responsibilities and roles across disciplines by more than one team member (Raver, 1999). This process of role sharing is what distinguishes transdisciplinary teaming from interdisciplinary teaming. The transdisciplinary model requires administrators and other professionals to commit themselves to teaching, learning, and working across discipline boundaries. Role sharing allows professionals to teach discipline-specific skills to other professionals on their team from different discipline backgrounds. Transdisciplinary teams must participate in role acceptance. Role acceptance requires accepting that one's role may include more than what one was specifically trained for (Raver, 1999).

Role sharing occurs when the team member assists the direct service provider in the performance of a function that is typically part of the assisting team member's role. For example, the team leader performing the assessment is assisted in choosing the skills to be assessed. At different times during intervention, team members role share to the direct service provider, who implements specific intervention recommendations. All team members at some point role share their direct service roles to function as consultants and facilitators for the direct service provider.

The process of role sharing demands continuous professional and personal change and continuous dialogue between team members. Role sharing can extend from team members sharing general information to teaching other team members to make specific judgments regarding intervention, and ultimately to training members to perform specific techniques for intervention. Each discipline has standards of professional responsibility that limit sharing of some disciplinary roles. It is the responsibility of each professional to state clearly when it is inadvisable to share professional skills (Drew & Turnbull, 1987). Any reservations of professional organizations about role sharing that their services could be supplanted by other professionals taking on their roles suggest a lack of understanding about the judicious nature of this model (Raver, 1999). Researchers found that fewer teams teach each other decision-making skills and judgment skills regarding specific treatments to children (Ryan-Vincek, Tuesday-Heathfield, & Lamorey, 1995). These researchers attributed this discrepancy as possibly owing to the tacit nature of professionals' knowledge and the subsequent difficulty inherent in both sharing and acquiring decision-making skills outside the realm of one's own professional experiences.

Components of the Transdisciplinary Model

Transdisciplinary procedures must be implemented throughout each phase of service delivery from intake to reassessment. Administrators and team members must be aware of how the model affects program operation in each phase of service delivery. The components of the transdisciplinary approach which must be implemented throughout the service delivery have been outlined by Woodruff and Hanson (1987) and are shown in Figure 4–1.

In the following section, the arena assessment is discussed. This approach to assessment is common to the transdisciplinary model but could be used in an interdisciplinary model or in programs wanting to become transdisciplinary.

Arena Assessment

Transdisciplinary teams often use an assessment process called an arena assessment. In an arena assessment, one professional does the testing while the other team members, including the family, observe. The professionals sit on the floor around the child and caregiver(s), and observe while one professional acts as the facilitator. The role of the facilitator is to engage the child in activities that demonstrate the child's developmental strengths and weaknesses.

Team members meet before an arena assessment and identify for the facilitator behaviors that they would like to see for their individual evaluations. If the professionals in the arena assessment did not observe all they needed during the assessment, then parent report items are used or another assessment time is arranged. Following the arena assessment, the team meets to discuss the assessment results and plan intervention. This sharing then becomes natural and continuous. Professionals who use arena assessment report that it saves time and, with training, they can see what they need for their discipline-specific evaluations while also observing the child's overall functioning.

Myers, McBride and Peterson (1996) compared multidisciplinary, standardized assessment to a transdisciplinary, play-based assessment. Data on parent perceptions, staff perceptions, time factors, functional utility of reports and parent and staff congruence in judgment-based ratings were evaluated. The play-based assessments resulted in favorable parent and staff perceptions, provided useful reports, and had high congruence in developmental ratings. This study provided empirical evidence supporting the social validity of transdisciplinary, play-based assessment methods. Prior to this study, the only published research was by Wolery and Dyk (1984), who published a comparative study examining the transdisciplinary model. These researchers evaluated children under 5 years of age using an interdisciplinary, standardized assessment model and then reevaluated the same children 8 to 10 months later using a transdisciplinary, arena assessment model. For each aspect questioned on the survey, most parents favored the transdisciplinary model.

FIGURE 4–1
Components of the Transdisciplinary Model

Intake

Responsibility rotated among team members.
Rapport established with family.
Family information and child data gathered.
Transdisciplinary model explained.

Pre-Arena Preparation

Facilitator and coach chosen for assessment.
Case presentation provided.
Team members coach facilitator.
Team members share information across disciplines.
Staff member chosen to lead post-arena feedback to parent.

Arena Assessment

Arena facilitator works with child and parents.
Team members observe all aspects of child's behavior and parent-child interaction.
Team members observe and record across all developmental areas.
Arena facilitator works to reassure parent and gain involvement.

Post-Arena Feedback to Family

Child's strengths and needs are established.
Family's goals and priorities are discussed.
Activities are recommended for home implementation.

Post-Arena Discussion of Team Process

Primary service provider (PSP) assignment is made.
Team evaluates assessment process and provides feedback to one another.

IFSP Development

Team develops goals, objectives, and activities.
Parents and PSP reach consensus on which IFSP goals, objectives, and activities will be initiated first.

Activity Planning

Team establishes regular meetings to monitor the implementation of the IFSP, to assign daily or weekly activities, and to make revisions in the plan.

Program Implementation

PSP implements the plan.
Team members monitor the implementation, maintain accountability for their discipline, provide role support, and when needed, supervision.

Reassessment

Team follows pre-arena, arena, and post-arena procedures.

Program Continues to Repeat Cycle

From Woodruff, G., & Hanson, C. (1987). Project KAI, 77B Warren Street, Brighton, MA 02135. Funded by the U.S. Department of Education, Special Education Programs, Handicapped Children's Early Education Program. Copyright 1987 by Council for Exceptional Education. Reprinted with permission.

Selection of Assessment Instruments. The use of instruments during the arena process varies dependent on the age and needs of the child. The team must choose the appropriate assessment instrument. Each professional must identify the essential information she wishes to learn from the evaluation and specify the sample of behavior that would allow him to draw such inferences. In addition to standardized assessment instruments, the use of informal assessment procedures and observations is essential. These may include instruments and procedures focusing on adult-child interactions and patterns, motor tasks, activities of daily living, and interviews (McAfee & Leong, 1994; Noonan & McCormick, 1993). The team then constructs a general outline of the categories of assessment (Foley, 1990). Foley (1990) provided an example of such an outline for an arena assessment of an infant as shown in Figure 4–2; he cautions that this list is not exhaustive.

Foley (1990) encouraged that the team should strive to identify a single arena instrument. This instrument should contain the broadest item pool and sample the most representative range of behaviors covering the most categories in the general outline. This is just one part of the multidimensional, multisource assessment process. This single instrument is then supplemented with more in-depth assessments in particular areas needing additional information.

Conducting an Arena Assessment. Arena assessments should be conducted in an ecological setting with which the child is familiar, such as the home (Noonan & McCormick, 1993; Wolery & Dyk, 1984). The logistics for arranging this for a number of professionals may be difficult. If a location outside the home is used during the arena process, these facilities should closely resemble an early intervention program with the necessary materials and child-size furnishings (Parette, Bryde, Hoge, & Hogan, 1995). Physical and temporal issues must be addressed such as

accommodating physical disabilities. Family members also may require interpreters or other services to ensure effective communication.

Family members must be contributing and active participants of the team and not just observers (Linder, 1993). The process of how the assessment is to be conducted should be clearly explained to the family and others, including the child when appropriate. Any family questions and concerns should be answered in a careful and sensitive manner. Professionals should be sensitive to the fact that this experience may be intimidating and uncomfortable for some families. Strategies that protect the integrity of the family unit and are sensitive to family cultural differences should be used (Division for Early Childhood, 1993). Whenever possible, arena facilitators should be from the same culture as the child being assessed (Figueroa, 1990).

Immediately following the assessment, family members or caregivers who observe the assessment should be provided the opportunity to discuss how typical the child's performance was in each assessment situation (Parette, Bryde, Hoge, & Hogan, 1995). Discussions with family members can serve to identify emerging and inconsistent behaviors not displayed in the assessment situation or items that were failed but have been observed in other settings. One assessment report that integrates the findings of all disciplines involved should be developed and one intervention plan across all domains.

There is no definite script for an arena assessment. The exact manner in which the assessment will be carried out varies according to the child and family needs. This process will develop for each team after the members work together for a time. Foley (1990) suggested a more structured sequence that might be followed with older toddlers. This sequence is summarized in Figure 4–3.

Pragmatic Considerations. The arena assessment is a major component of the transdisciplinary model, but occasionally this format may not be

FIGURE 4–2

Outline of Assessment (Observations to Be Made in Arena Evaluation)

Behavior and Style

Appearance
Temperament
State regulation
Rhythmicity
Reactivity
Attention
Frustration tolerance
Level of organization
Kinetics

Object Interaction/Cognition

Schema use
Symbolic object use
Discrimination
Object classification
Reality testing
Learning style
  Sensory assimilation
  Imitation
  Trial and error
  Planned problem solving
Learning modalities

Social/Emotional

Contact/cueing style
Reaction to strangers
Predominant affect/mood
Affective range
Attachment/separation behavior
Individuation/autonomy
Coping strategies
Defensive strategies
Play style
  Solitary
  Observer
  Parallel
  Associative
Adaptability
Social appropriateness

Communication

Mode of communication
Frequency/duration
Echolalia
Speech
  Respiration
  Voice
  Vocalization
  Intonation
  Word approximation
  Intelligibility
  Articulation
  Rate
  Fluency
Receptive language
  Receptive vocabulary
  Comprehension—
    direction/questions
  Comprehension—
    connected discourse
Expressive language
  Spontaneity
  Vocabulary/retrieval
  Knowledge level
  Length & quality of connected
    discourse
Pragmatics
  Communicative Intent
  Turn taking
  Topic maintenance/expansion
  Felicity
Syntax
  Grammatical form
  Overgeneralization

Sensorimotor

Sensory
  Tactile responsivity/sensitivity
  Auditory/visual perception
  Vestibular/proprioceptive
    responsivity
  Body image
Gross motor
  Primitive reflexes
  Postural tone
  Symmetry
  Components of movement
    Head control
    Trunk control
    Proximal joint control
    Weight shifting
    Dynamic equilibrium
    Rotation
    Antigravitational control
    Transitional postures
    Bilateral integration
    Locomotion
    Motor planning
Fine motor
  Prehension
  Tool use
  Visual-motor accuracy
Oral motor
  Infantile reflexes
  Sucking/drinking/chewing
  Tongue/jaw control
  Oral motor planning

Self-help

Feeding
Dressing
Toileting
Activities of daily living

From Portrait of the arena evaluation: Assessment in the transdisciplinary approach, by G. M. Foley. In Gibbs, E. D., & Teti, D. M. (Eds.) (1990). *Interdisciplinary assessment of infants: A guide for early intervention professionals* (p. 281). Baltimore: Paul H. Brookes Publishing Co. Reprinted with permission.

FIGURE 4–3
Sequence for Arena Assessment

Greeting and Warm-up

Family and team get-acquainted time. Child may explore area with guidance and interact with various team members. Team may observe child's coping strategies, style, and mood and may decide on preliminary strategies about space, sequence, style of interaction, instrumentation, and location of the team.

Formal Task-Centered Segment

Chosen instrument is administered by the chosen facilitator and scored by a colleague. Other professionals may be scoring discipline-specific instruments and making clinical notes and comments.

Snack Breaks and Refueling

Child has snacks with her caregivers. This is a good chance to observe self-help skills, oral motor functioning, spontaneous language, and social interaction.

Separation and Reunion

After the snack break, the facilitator takes the child for a bathroom break, which provides the team the opportunity to observe separation behavior and spontaneous movement.

Story Time or Teaching Samples

This time is used to collect additional samples or behavior as needed. Key assessment items that may have been failed earlier may be reintroduced. The length and content of this segment are dependent on the age and functional level of the child.

Free Play

During this segment the team observes spontaneous movement and interaction with toys. The physical and occupational therapists may enter the assessment at this time to assess the child.

Closing and Physical Examination

The facilitator and parents help the child unwind. If a physical examination is to be given, it may be completed at this time.

Brief Staffing and Feedback

Team meets to form impressions while the family worker collects the parents' comments about the encounter. This allows the parents to have some closure and feedback so they do not leave with unnecessary anxiety and ambiguity.

Formal Staffing and Interpretation

This segment occurs after the team has had time to analyze and reflect on the data collected. The results are reviewed at this time and a composite report and preliminary intervention plan are organized. If the caregivers are not present at this session, then a formal feedback session must be held with them.

From Portrait of the arena evaluation: Assessment in the transdisciplinary approach, by G. M. Foley. In Gibbs, E. D., & Teti, D. M. (Eds.) (1990). *Interdisciplinary assessment of infants: A guide for early intervention professionals* (pp. 282–285). Baltimore: Paul H. Brookes Publishing Co. Adapted with permission.

ideal for an individual child or family. Some families may be very uneasy in the presence of more than one person at a time, and they may not be willing to participate. A child may be so sensitive or distractible that she cannot perform well in an arena. Some preschool children might be too self-conscious to interact with a facilitator/leader in the presence of an audience (Linder, 1993). Although the arena assessment approach supports family participation, some children may interact favorably in the presence of family members whereas others may display greater cooperation when family members are not present or visible to the child (Parette, Bryde, Hoge, & Hogan, 1995). Programs should be sensitive to this possibility and alter assessment as needed (Woodruff & McGonigel, 1988). The use of one-way mirrors with caregiver knowledge and permission can address this problem.

A tremendous amount of planning is necessary in the arena assessment process (Summers, Lane, Collier, & Friedebach, 1993). The process requires coordination of family and professional schedules. The work schedules of family members as well as those of the professionals complicate the assessment process. Professionals who have heavy caseloads in addition to performing assessments increase the scheduling difficulties. It is often a tremendous challenge to arrange for all personnel to be present. In addition, appointments may be missed owing to the illness of the child, transportation problems, or inclement weather. Rescheduling assessments within legal timetables could be a problem.

Another area of potential concerns is billing providers. Billing procedures may vary markedly across disciplines and agencies involved in the arena assessment. Consideration should be given to billing procedures prior to conducting the assessment. Provisions for medicaid payments or reimbursements also will need to be made prior to the assessment.

Advantages. An arena assessment offers advantages for the child, the family and the whole team (Woodruff, 1980). Advantages for the family include: (1) communication to caregivers that they are fully functioning members of the team; (2) decreasing the possibility of service providers asking the same questions; and (3) communicating that efforts to assist the child are a series of problem-solving experiences. The arena assessment does not require multiple testing sessions which attempt to obtain important information across a wide range of developmental areas in a brief period of time. Only one assessment time may be needed, instead of separate domain-specific assessments. The child is able to demonstrate strengths in a natural, more global set of circumstances. Personnel from all disciplines are simultaneously available during the assessment session to ask specific questions about assessment strategies and observations (Parette, Bryde, Hoge, & Hogan, 1995). Arena assessment provides a unified approach to assessment and facilitates greater consistency in assessment findings among team members. The facilitator or leader with the best rapport is able to continue working with the child, allowing other team members to make suggestions and ask questions.

Advantages for the team include: (1) provision of comprehensive, integrated assessment of the child; (2) team sharing of knowledge of child's development based on the same observation of the child, leading to easier consensus; and (3) expansion of knowledge of all team members, because they are all able to see the child from the vantage of their own discipline and simultaneously receive a perception of the child from another discipline. Each team member can make immediate use of the information obtained by other professionals, rather than waiting for this information in a written report.

Examples of Transdisciplinary Assessments

Linder's *Transdisciplinary Play-Based Assessment Model* (TPBA) (1993) is designed to provide an arena assessment. A play-based assessment occurs in a child's natural environment and offers flexibility to meet a child's individual needs. Observation guidelines are outlined for cognitive, social-emotional, communication and language, and sensorimotor development. Linder has outlined a flexible six-phase process that may be used with a preschool child. Table 4–3 gives an overview of the format used in the TPBA.

Reed (1993) developed the Revised Arena Format (RAF) for use with relatively older and higher functioning children. The RAF was developed specifically for evaluating kindergarten children who were referred owing to significant difficulties they were experiencing in a specific area, such as speech and language. Traditional arena assessments involve three or more professionals, a parent, and possibly a teacher. The RAF seldom involves more than two professionals and a parent or caregiver. Two evaluators, whose diagnostic procedures complement one another, conduct the evaluation. Reed (1993) suggested that this coordination increases the likelihood that the testing session will contain variety, lack periods of inactivity (which occur when an examiner records a response or shifts to a different activity), and generally run more smoothly and quickly. Using two evaluators also

TABLE 4–3
TPBA Play Session

Phase	Session
I	Unstructured facilitation (20–25 mins.)
	Child takes lead. Facilitator interacts in response to the child. Attempts to move child to higher skill levels through modeling.
II	Structured facilitation (10–15 mins.)
	Involves the cognitive and language activities that did not occur in the first phase. Facilitator takes direct approach making specific requests to the child with play continuing to be the mode for assessment.
III	Child-child interaction (5–10 mins.)
	Child to child interactions are observed in an unstructured situation. A slightly older child without disabilities, familiar to the child being assessed and of the same sex, should be chosen.
IV	Parent-child interaction (10 mins.)
	Parent has opportunity to play with child as routinely done at home. After this unstructured play, the caregiver leaves the room for a few minutes and then returns. Team members note separation and greeting behaviors. When caregivers return, they are asked to teach child an unfamiliar task.
V	Motor play (10–20 mins.)
	Includes both structured and unstructured motor play.
VI	Snack (5–10 mins.)
	Facilitator may allow the other child used in the assessment to join in with the snack. This provides the opportunity to observe social interactions.

Adapted from: Linder, Toni W. (1993). *Transdisciplinary play-based assessment: A functional approach to working with young children* (p. 43). Baltimore: Paul H. Brookes Publishing Co.

eliminates the threat that a group of adults would pose to a higher functioning preschooler.

An "arena-style" transdisciplinary play-based assessment model was adapted for use across a televideo connection (Smith, 1997). A facilitator met a family at a remote site in the family's home community, and other team specialists remained at a local site to perform the arena-type assessment across the televideo screen. "Close simulation of the conventional 'in-person' assessment procedure was successfully attained, including successfully identifying a subtle anomaly and unexpectedly providing 'enhanced' transdisciplinary communication" (Smith, 1997, p. 58).

Integrated Therapy

Transdisciplinary teaming is enhanced through the use of integrated related services or integrated therapy (Gallivan-Fenlon, 1994). Integrated therapy refers to the incorporation of educational and therapeutic techniques employed cooperatively to assess, plan, implement, evaluate, and report progress on common needs and goals (Giangreco, 1986). Integrated therapy also has been defined as the delivery of related services in situations where skills will be functional and performance meaningful for an individual student (Sternat, Messina, Nietupski, Lyon, & Brown, 1977). When trans-disciplinary teams integrate related services into the home or classroom, they teach communication, motor, social skills, and so on, within the context of many typical home or preschool activities and routines that occur throughout the day. This provides the child with repeated opportunities to learn and practice the skills in natural environments where they will be needed and used. Implementing interventions during routines supports assessment in context, as well as addressing skills in context and increasing practice opportunities. Specialists, teachers, and families can monitor progress on a regular basis using rating forms with the

child's outcomes on them (Scott, McWilliam, & Mayhew, 1999).

Research indicates that the therapy approach most frequently used by transdisciplinary teams is a combination of direct and integrated therapy (Ryan-Vincek, Tuesday-Heathfield, & Lamorey, 1995). These researchers suggested that this finding may reflect the specialized needs of infants and very young children with disabilities that warrant an increase in direct therapy in contrast to children of school age.

Criteria for Effective Transdisciplinary Teams

Personal Characteristics. Hutchinson (1974), a primary advocate of this approach, stressed several criteria for working effectively in a trans-disciplinary team. These criteria have been summarized by Peterson (1987) as follows:

1. A team member must have depth and be particularly strong in his or her own discipline. Without this knowledge the member is in no position to make decisions or to pass on information in a form that another professional can implement.
2. Each team member's role must be continuously enriched by expanding his or her knowledge through training and supervision provided by other team members. For this to occur, the appropriate disciplinary representative must give "role sharing" and authorization of the designated team member to act as the direct service agent with a particular child in behalf of each discipline.
3. Team members must provide continuous consultative back-up to one another. Ongoing problem solving, information exchange, and feedback between the consulting discipline and the primary service agent of the team for a given child are critical. Procedures or new information may have to be tested by a disciplinary representative before being passed on to the overall team and prescribed as the

treatment strategy for the primary service agent to use.

4. Throughout the transdisciplinary process each team member must remain accountable for the information and directives delivered to others. Each disciplinary representative also must remain accountable for how well the primary service agent learns the service delivery strategy for that discipline and carries it out with the child. Finally, every discipline involved must remain accountable for the child's progress under their own prescriptions. (p. 487)

Variables that were identified as positive contributors to transdisciplinary team functioning were (1) a strong sense of involvement combined with effective communication skills; and (2) individual professional skill development within and across disciplines that appears to be supplemented by training from other disciplines (Ryan-Vincek, Tuesday-Heathfield, & Lamorey, 1995).

Administrative Considerations. Ryan-Vincek, Tuesday-Heathfield, and Lamorey (1995) investigated actual practice of transdisciplinary service delivery compared to theory on transdisciplinary teams. Surveys were sent to professionals in a variety of disciplines serving infants and toddlers with disabilities who identified themselves as members of transdisciplinary teams. Ryan-Vincek and colleagues summarized the perceived benefits and criticisms of transdisciplinary teaming. The perceived benefits include:

- More active parent participation in assessment, intervention, and team collaboration;
- Increased professional knowledge and skills through collaboration among team members;
- Facilitation of therapy and teaching skills through the child's natural environment;
- Increased mutual respect and professional growth among team members;
- Shared responsibility for problem solving and decision making; and

- More equal distribution of responsibilities among team members.

On the other hand, criticisms include:

- The lack of empirical research;
- Unclear role definitions;
- Liability questions concerning indirect integrated therapy;
- Inadequacies in professional training programs;
- Resistance of team members to change; and
- The use of specialized vocabularies or jargon by professionals that may hinder team communication.

Overall, it seems that the negative barriers most frequently reported by transdisciplinary team members reflect administrative factors (Ryan-Vincek, Tuesday-Heathfield, & Lamorey, 1995). The most significant negative factor cited was overworked staff. Other negative factors cited were lack of in-service training, questions of liability, inequitable distribution of work, and resistance to change. These factors exist at an administrative or program level and are perceived by team members as factors beyond their control. Administrators may provide support for teams by considering role reconceptualization, distribution of workload, and the provision of time for team collaboration. Researchers speculated that the report that 50 percent of the teams surveyed felt "significantly" overworked could reflect a general increase in infants and young children identified by child find, a lack of qualified personnel in the field of early intervention, or fiscal restraints.

In order for integrated transdisciplinary teaming to be successful, it is essential that administrators provide adequate time for teams to meet on a regularly scheduled basis. For example, the teacher would present the theme for the upcoming week along with various activities that have been planned for different lessons. Information and ideas then are gathered from other team members regarding therapeutic interventions, materials, or positioning that can be incorporated into activities to allow students to work on particular IEP goals and participate in thematic activities.

Administrators should also facilitate team functioning by closely monitoring team dynamics, assisting teams to periodically assess strengths and set future goals and providing various information and strategies that teams would find useful, such as cooperative goal structuring and conflict resolution (Gallivan-Fenlon, 1994).

Another important consideration for administrators is that related services staff, whether contracted or direct hire therapists, be paid for all relevant activities that involve transdisciplinary teaming as well as for direct therapy and evaluation of children. For example, consultation to team members, team meetings, and IEP planning must be reimbursed. Cost-effectiveness data appear to be focused on early intervention in general rather than comparing individual service delivery models. Specifically, data regarding the cost effectiveness of the transdisciplinary models are limited. These fiscal issues must be addressed in order to expand support for a specified delivery model.

A final element that is crucial for success of this approach is flexibility on the part of both related services personnel and educators. Related services staff may want to determine therapy schedules in coordination with the classroom schedule and routine activities. For example, physical therapy may be delivered in the context of daily gross motor time or directly outside the classroom setting. By indicating therapists on the daily schedule it is clear that direct or indirect therapy is being provided. The provision for direct therapy outside the classroom may be owing to the need for privacy (adjusting adaptive equipment for a particular child); conducting some types of formalized assessment; and teaching a highly individualized skill such as the use of an augmentative

communication system during its initial stages (Gallivan-Fenlon, 1994). Direct therapy should not be conducted outside of the classroom for an extended period of time.

Creating Collaborative Teams

A collaborative team should be made up of all those individuals who are essential in serving the young child with disabilities. Team members include the parents (any extended family members as appropriate), the teachers (both regular and special educators), the specialists and therapists who work directly with the child, a family advocate, an administrator or designee who can commit program services, and someone who can interpret evaluation results as needed. If the family is linguistically diverse, then an interpreter is needed. Other team members might include paraprofessionals who provided one-on-one aid to the child, and perhaps medical personnel such as the nurse or pediatrician (Howard, Williams, Port, & Lepper, 2001).

Although researchers disagree on the essential components of collaborative teaming, Howard and colleagues (2001) found at least five elements, or attributes, common to most models of collaborative, or cooperative, teaming:

1. A common goal or set of goals to which all parties agree. The team must agree on the primary goal and then all other decisions should be measured against this fundamental intent.

2. The team must agree on a strategy for achieving each goal or set of goals. Team members must determine the most effective method(s) for achieving the goal(s).

3. There is a commitment to meaningful and professional interactions, individual skill development, and task completion.

4. There is a commitment to dependence on each other. Each team member must carry out her responsibility.

5. Individuals must commit to a shared system of decision making and accountability.

Several other factors believed necessary for teams to function successfully are:

- A way of building and maintaining trust;
- Face-to-face interactions;
- Basic skills in small-group interpersonal interactions;
- Voluntary collaboration; and
- Equity among participants. (Howard, Williams, Port, & Lepper, 2001)

The team must bring together all relevant professionals from various disciplines to share their expertise, decision-making, and intervention skills with parents. This process requires that team members trust each other's competencies, opinions, and skills (Roberts-DeGennaro, 1996). Roberts-DeGennaro (1996) suggested a series of steps that teams can go through to bring them closer to working together. These progressive stages include:

Step 1—Unidisciplinary: Believing that one's own discipline can make an important contribution to the young child's intervention.

Step 2—Intradisciplinary: Recognizing that other disciplines also have important contributions.

Step 3—Multidisciplinary: Articulating a philosophy that coordinated and comprehensive services must be made available to all young children who are at-risk or have a disability.

Step 4—Interdisciplinary: Being willing and able to work with other disciplines in the development of jointly planned programs and being willing to assume responsibility for providing needed disciplinary services and treatment as part of the total program.

Step 5—Transdisciplinary: Committing oneself to teaching, learning, and working together with other service providers across traditional disciplinary boundaries. (Howard, Williams, Port, & Lepper, 2001)

In order to progress toward increased collaboration, a number of regular activities are required. These activities include:

1. Setting a clear team purpose and identifying what each individual brings to the team.
2. Establishing schedules for meeting times.
3. Conducting meetings with specific purposes and tasks.
4. Sharing workload and responsibilities.
5. Sharing expertise.
6. Following through with responsibilities.
7. Celebrating successes and shouldering failures together.
8. Keeping the lines of communication open. (Stump & Wilson, 1996)

Early intervention teams coordinate several important components necessary for serving young children with disabilities and their families. If early intervention systems are working well, then services will be individually matched to the needs of the child and family. Some families will require intensive, long-term programs, whereas others will require only minimal supports. Professionals must have a great deal of knowledge and the will to use it flexibly based on the needs of the individual families (Howard, Williams, Port, & Lepper, 2001).

Summary

This chapter has presented three models for multidisciplinary team assessment. The transdisciplinary approach is recommended as a reasonable, practical, and efficient method for providing services to young children with special needs and their families (Woodruff & McGonigel, 1988). However, Woodruff and McGonigel caution early interventionists that the transdisciplinary approach is not an easy process and may not be suitable for every program. The service delivery model that best meets the unique needs of a given child and family, in fact, may need to be chosen on an individual basis. This transdisciplinary process requires tremendous planning, effort, time, and expense at the beginning. The arena assessment model and integrated therapy are presented to demonstrate how the transdisciplinary approach may be incorporated into the assessment process.

More research needs to be conducted around this approach. In the "real world," assessment may be a combination of models such as the interdisciplinary and transdisciplinary. Mechanisms for reimbursement must be developed which will support this model. As this model of service delivery is expanded, refined, and applied by more early intervention programs, it is hoped that we will be better equipped to provide the integrated, family-driven services needed by infants, toddlers, and preschoolers with special needs and their families.

References

Bagnato, S. J., & Neisworth, J. T. (1990). *System to Plan Early Childhood Services* (SPECS). Circle Pines, MN: American Guidance Service.

Bagnato, S. J., & Neisworth, J. T. (1991). *Assessment for early intervention: Best practices for professionals.* New York: Guilford Press.

Bagnato, S. J., Neisworth, J. T., & Munson, S. M. (1997). *LINKing assessment and early intervention: An authentic curriculum-based approach.* Baltimore: Brookes.

Campbell, P. H. (1989). Students with physical disabilities. In R. Gaylord-Ross (Ed.), *Integration strategies for persons with handicaps* (pp. 53–76). Baltimore: Brookes.

Division for Early Childhood Task Force. (1993). *DEC recommended practices: Indicators of quality programs for infants and young children with special needs and their families.* Pittsburgh, PA: Council for Exceptional Children, Division for Early Childhood.

Drew, C. J., & Turnbull, H. R. (1987). Whose ethics, whose code: An analysis of problems in interdisciplinary intervention. *Mental Retardation, 25,* 113–117.

Fewell, R. R. (1983a). Assessing handicapped infants. In S. G. Garwood & R. R. Fewell (Eds.), *Educating handicapped infants: Issues in development and intervention* (pp. 257–297). Rockville, MD: Aspen.

Fewell, R. R. (1983b). The team approach to infant education. In S. G. Garwood & R. R. Fewell (Eds.), *Educating handicapped infants: Issues in development and intervention* (pp. 299–322). Rockville, MD: Aspen.

Figueroa, R. A. (1990). Assessment of linguistic minority group children. In C. R. Reynolds & R. W. Kamphaus (Eds.), *Handbook of psychological and educational assessment of children. Vol. 1: Intelligence and achievement* (pp. 671–696). New York: Guilford.

Foley, G. M. (1990). Portrait of the arena evaluation: Assessment in the transdisciplinary approach. In E. D. Gibbs & D. M. Teti (Eds.), *Interdisciplinary assessment of infants: A guide for early intervention professionals* (pp. 271–286). Baltimore: Brookes.

Gallivan-Fenlon, A. (1994). Integrated transdisciplinary teams. *Teaching Exceptional Children, 26*(3), 16–20.

Garland, C. W., Woodruff, G., & Buck, D. (1988). *Case management.* (Division for Early Childhood White Paper.) Reston, VA: The Council for Exceptional Children.

Garshelis, J. A., & McConnell, S. R. (1993). Comparison of family needs assessment by mothers, individual professionals, and interdisciplinary teams. *Journal of Early Intervention, 17*(1), 36–49.

Giangreco, M. F. (1986). Effects of integrated therapy: A pilot study. *Journal of the Association for Persons with Severe Handicaps, 11*(3), 205–208.

Golin, A. K., & Duncanis, A. J. (1981). *The interdisciplinary team.* Rockville, MD: Aspen.

Hooper, S. R., & Edmondson, R. (1998). Assessment of young children: Standards, stages, and approaches. In W. Umansky & S. R. Hooper (Eds.), *Young children with special needs* (pp. 340–371). Upper Saddle River, NJ: Merrill/Prentice Hall.

Howard, V. F., Williams, B. F., Port, P. D., & Lepper, C. (2001). *Very young children with special needs: A formative approach for the 21st century* (2nd ed.). Upper Saddle River, NJ: Merrill/Prentice Hall.

Hutchinson, D. A. (1974). *A model for transdisciplinary staff development: A nationally organized collaborative project to provide comprehensive services to atypical infants and their families.* (Technical Report #8.) New York: United Cerebral Palsy Association.

Linder, T. (1983). *Early childhood special education: Program development and administration.* Baltimore: Brookes.

Linder, T. W. (1993). *Transdisciplinary play-based assessment: A functional approach to working with young children.* Baltimore: Brookes.

Lyon, S., & Lyon, G. (1980). Team functioning and staff development: A role release approach to providing integrated educational services for the severely handicapped students. *The Journal of the Association for the Severely Handicapped, 5*(3), 250–263.

McAfee, O., & Leong, D. (1994). *Assessing and guiding young children's development and learning.* Boston: Allyn & Bacon.

McCollum, J. A., & Hughes, M. (1988). Staffing patterns and team models in infancy programs. In J. B. Jordan, J. J. Gallagher, P. L. Hutinger, & M. B. Karnes (Eds.), *Early childhood special education: Birth to three.* (pp. 129–146). Reston, VA: The Council for Exceptional Children.

McGonigel, M. J., Woodruff, G., & Roszmann-Millican, M. (1994). The transdisciplinary team: A model for family-centered early intervention. In L. J. Johnson, R. J. Gallagher, P. L. Hutinger, & M. B. Karnes (Eds.), *Meeting early intervention challenges: Issues from birth to three* (2nd ed.) (pp. 95–132). Baltimore: Brookes.

Mowder, B. A., Widerstrom, A. H., & Sandall, S. R. (1989). School psychologists serving at-risk and handicapped infants, toddlers and their families. *Professional School Psychology*, 4(3), 161.

Myers, C. L., McBride, S. L., & Peterson, C. A. (1996). Transdisciplinary play-based assessment in early childhood special education: An examination of social validity. *Topics in Early Childhood Special Education*, 16(1), 102–126.

Noonan, M. J., & McCormick, L. (1993). *Early intervention in natural environments: Methods and procedures*. Belmont, CA: Brooks/Cole.

Parette, H. P., Bryde, S., Hoge, D. R., & Hogan, A. (1995). Pragmatic issues regarding arena assessment in early intervention. *Infant-Toddler Intervention*, 5(3), 243–254.

Peterson, N. (1987). *Early intervention for handicapped and at-risk children: An introduction to early childhood special education*. Denver: Love.

Raver, S. A. (1991). *Strategies for teaching at-risk and handicapped infants and toddlers: A transdisciplinary approach*. Upper Saddle River, NJ: Merrill/Prentice Hall.

Raver, S. A. (1999). *Intervention strategies for infants and toddlers with special needs: A transdisciplinary approach* (2nd ed.). Upper Saddle River, NJ: Merrill/Prentice Hall.

Reed, M. L. (1993). The revised arena format (RAF): Adaptations of transdisciplinary evaluation procedures for young preschool children. *Education and Treatment of Children*, 16(2), 198–205.

Roberts-DeGennaro, M. (1996). An interdisciplinary training model in the field of early intervention. *Social Work in Education*, 18(1), 20–30.

Ryan-Vincek, S., Tuesday-Heathfield, L., & Lamorey, S. (1995). From theory to practice: A pilot study of team

perspectives on transdisciplinary service delivery. *Infant-Toddler Intervention*, 5(2), 153–175.

Scott, S. M., McWilliam, R. A., & Mayhew, L. (1999). Integrating therapies into the classroom. *Young Exceptional Children*, 2(3), 15–24.

Smith, D. (1997). Teleassessment: A model of team developmental assessment of high-rise infants using a televideo network. *Infants and Young Children*, 9(4), 58–61.

Sternat, J., Messina, R., Nietupski, J., Lyon, S., & Brown, L. (1977). Occupational and physical therapy services for severely handicapped students: Toward a naturalized public school service delivery model. In E. Sontag, J. Smith, & N. Certo (Eds.), *Educational programming for the severely and profoundly handicapped* (pp. 263–277). Reston, VA: The Council for Exceptional Children.

Stump, C. S., & Wilson, C. (1996). Collaboration: Making it happen. *Intervention in School & Clinic*, 31(5), 310–313.

Summers, J. A., Lane, V., Collier, T., & Friedebach, M. A. (1993). *Early intervention for infants and toddlers with special needs and their families: An interdisciplinary training curriculum*. Jefferson City, MO: Missouri Department of Elementary and Secondary Education.

Wolery, M., & Dyk, L. (1984). Arena assessment: Description and preliminary social validity data. *Journal of the Association for the Severely Handicapped*, 3, 231–235.

Woodruff, G. (1980). Transdisciplinary approach for preschool children and parents. *The Exceptional Parent*, 10(1), 13–16.

Woodruff, G., & Hanson, C. (1987). *Project KAI training packet*. Unpublished manuscript.

Woodruff, G., & McGonigel, M. J. (1988). Early intervention team approaches: The transdisciplinary model. In J. B. Jordan, J. J. Gallagher, P. L. Hutinger, & M. B. Karnes (Eds.), *Early childhood special education: Birth to three* (pp. 164–181). Reston, VA: The Council for Exceptional Children.

Basic Considerations for Assessment

5

The Assessment Experience

Christopher Lopata

Overview

Benefits of interventions for young children have been recognized at the individual (e.g., Bricker, 1989; Department of Health and Rehabilitative Services, State of Florida, 1990; Guralnick, 1998; Molfese, 1989), family, and societal levels (e.g., Interact, 1981; National Committee for Economic Development, 1987). Although the benefits have been identified, significant challenges face those charged with the task of assessing young children. The broad and diverse nature of the task of assessing infants, toddlers, and preschoolers requires careful attention and consideration.

In broad terms, assessment is defined as an information gathering process intended to facilitate decision making (Association for Advanced Training In the Behavioral Sciences, 1997). Assessments are generally conducted for four general purposes: screening; diagnosis and eligibility determination; intervention/program planning; and intervention/program monitoring (McLean, 1996; Taylor, 1993; Wallace, Larsen, & Elksnin, 1992). In this chapter, assessment will be discussed as it pertains to eligibility determination for special education services. Use of assessment results for intervention development and monitoring is essential but beyond the scope of the current discussion.

Although significant challenges are associated with the assessment of young children, several areas of assessment practice have achieved general acceptance owing to legal mandates as well as assessment expert consensus. Examples include the requirements that assessments be multidisciplinary and multidimensional (McLean, 1996; Sattler, 1992). Despite these requirements, significant disagreement and controversy surround the assessment of young children. Issues involving developmental variability and the adequacy of standardized tests are examples of the many concerns that confront assessment professionals. Chapter 6 examines the process of assessment of young children, whereas this chapter examines the components of assessment for young children, as well as factors that affect performance on assessment tasks.

Components of Assessment

Assessment of young children is done using a team approach (Taylor, 1993). Before beginning an assessment, team members identify specific questions to be answered based on the stated concerns of primary caregivers. Assessment questions then lead to identification of the areas to be assessed, as well as appropriate instruments (Bucy, Smith, & Landau, 1999). Data gathered during the assessment process are generally used to identify those "at-risk" because precise categorical diagnosis is problematic owing to the variability in development of young children (Wodrich, 1997). The potential inadequacies of standardized instruments have prompted many to view the assessment of young children as developmental. Developmental tasks in the assessment process allow for the comparison of the individual child's performance on certain tasks with skills typically demonstrated by age-peers (Wallace, Larsen, & Elksnin, 1992).

Methods of assessment often vary based on state requirements and the unique characteristics of the young child. Gathering comprehensive information from multiple informants and settings can be done using a variety of methods, including both formal (i.e., standardized instruments) and informal (e.g., observations, work samples) techniques. Difficulties inherent in the assessment of young children require that approaches be adaptable and flexible. The following section contains general descriptions of assessment procedures commonly used in the assessment of young children, including family interviews, individual assessment, observation, and play assessment.

Family Interviews

A critical source of information in the assessment process is the young child's parents/caregiver and family members (National Association of School Psychologists, 1999). Family members provide critical information related to longitudinal developmental progression as well as current functioning. Identification of developmental milestones can serve as markers reflecting accelerated, appropriate, or delayed development across a variety of areas (Miller & Robinson, 1996; National Association of School Psychologists, 1999). Several studies have found family members to be accurate and reliable reporters of daily performance, difficulties, and behaviors (Bricker & Squires, 1989; Dale, 1991).

Family interviews also provide information from a more naturalistic perspective (Miller & Robinson, 1996). This is considered essential because contrived testing situations sometimes result in discomfort, fatigue, and distress in young children, leading to results that do not represent typical functioning (Sattler, 1992). Information that accurately reflects the young child's functioning in naturalistic settings can be gathered using informal techniques, such as observations and unstructured interviews (Taylor, 1993), or formal techniques (e.g., structured checklists or inventories). These techniques sample various domains of performance, behavior, and development that the young child demonstrates in familiar and naturalistic environments. Information presented by parents/caregiver and family members can provide contextual validity to assessment results and increase precision in the assessment of skill levels, delays, and ultimately eligibility determination. Chapter 2 discusses the involvement of families in the assessment process.

Individual Assessment

The assessment of critical domains, including cognition, psychosocial development, physical development, speech and language development, and self-help, can be done using a variety of techniques. Individual assessment is one method that provides useful information about a child's current skills and abilities. In individual assessment, the young child performs assessment tasks designed to test specific areas of functioning.

Individual assessments are typically conducted within a pre-established time and space. According to Luciano (1994), this is generally done during a specified period in the young child's home, classroom, or other designated area. The purpose is to obtain information on the child's skills and abilities related to a set of tasks. The assessor attempts to "stimulate the performance of specific tasks or skill-behaviors by structuring or directing the activity" (Luciano, 1994, p. 18). Several methods can be utilized within the specified time and space.

The tasks selected by the evaluator often represent diverse assessment measures, including standardized tests, skills-based checklists, behavioral checklists, and observational techniques. Objective standardized instruments provide information about the young child's performance on specified tasks compared with other children in the standardization sample (Association for Advanced Training in the Behavioral Sciences, 1997; Sattler, 1992). This allows for identification of the individual's skills and abilities relative to those of other children of the same age. Examples of standardized instruments include the *Bayley Scales of Infant Development*-II (Bayley, 1993), *Battelle Developmental Inventory* (Newborg, Stock, Wnek, Guidubaldi, & Svinicki, 1984), and the *Stanford-Binet Intelligence Scale: Fourth Edition* (Thorndike, Hagen, & Sattler, 1986). These tests provide standard scores and standard deviations that are used by some states for eligibility determination. Normed tests are discussed in Chapter 9.

Although objective standardized tests provide valuable information, their use with young children has been challenged. The primary criticisms involve poor test-taking skills and rapidly changing development that weaken the technical adequacy of the instruments, i.e., reliability and validity (Katz, 1997; National Association of School Psychologists, 1999). A thorough exploration of the issues surrounding the use of standardized tests with young children is provided later in this section.

Other techniques for individual assessment can include criterion-referenced and curriculum-referenced measures. These measures assess the young child's skills and abilities relative to some predetermined objectives or curriculum (Bailey & Nabors, 1996). Scores obtained from criterion-referenced or curriculum-referenced measures identify the young child's skills along a skill/developmental continuum and provide a measure of mastery (Sattler, 1992). These assessment instruments are recognized for their ability to facilitate instructional decisions and monitor instructional progress (Bailey & Nabors, 1996). Examples of criterion-referenced measures include the Brigance Inventory of Early Development—Revised (Brigance, 1991) and Carolina Curriculum for Preschoolers with Special Needs (Johnson-Martin, Attermeier, & Hacker, 1990). Criterion-referenced, curriculum-referenced, and norm-referenced standardized tests are recognized as serving distinct roles that contribute to the understanding of young children's skills and abilities (Sattler, 1992).

In addition to norm-referenced standardized instruments and criterion-referenced and curriculum-referenced techniques, evaluators utilize behavioral observations. Although observation will be discussed in a separate section of this chapter, it plays an essential role during the individual assessment process. According to Luciano (1994), individual assessment allows for observation of close interpersonal interaction. Assessors also have the opportunity to directly observe the manner in which the young child responds to task demands, approaches problems, and engages in play activities. Obser-

vations can be conducted using unstructured recording of behavior, structured observations, or behavior rating scales/checklists. Careful attention should be given to observations during individual assessment as behavioral performance can support or invalidate results obtained from norm-referenced standardized and criterion-referenced and curriculum-referenced instruments (Sattler, 1992). In addition, behavior rating scales and checklists can provide quantitative support for assessment observations.

The use of standardized tests/instruments with young children is frequently challenged on the basis of technical issues. Few appropriate instruments have been developed for this population (McLean, 1996). According to the Association for Advanced Training in the Behavioral Sciences (1997), instruments are weaker for younger children owing to rapid changes in abilities and development. Young children are characterized by variable and rapid developmental growth (Hills, 1993; National Association of School Psychologists, 1999). The standardized nature of many instruments assumes the presence of specific skills/abilities at given ages and/or developmental stages that allow for the comparison of individuals against an absolute standard.

Legal mandates involving the assessment of young children require that tests be validated for the purposes for which they are used (McLean, 1996). In general, tests designed for this population have lower levels of reliability and validity (Association for Advanced Training in the Behavioral Sciences, 1997; Neisworth & Bagnato, 1992). Poor reliability indicates inadequate stability over time. For any instrument, this interferes with the establishment of validity. As a result, many instruments should not be utilized because they have not been adequately validated for that particular purpose or population. Because standardized tests are less accurate and predictive for young children, they should be used with great caution (National Association of School Psychologists, 1999).

In infants and toddlers, delays are often conceptualized from a global, rather than specific, standpoint of being "at-risk" (Wodrich, 1997). Despite widespread recognition that many instruments lack technical adequacy, standardized instruments have been found to be stronger predictors when severity is considered. Wodrich (1997) examined the extent to which test results and developmental delay correlated with future performance. From the standpoint of prediction, severity of delay served as a strong predictor of future delays. For example, very low scores on ability measures, especially for those with prenatal or perinatal risk factors, were more highly associated with future delays. For infants with less significant delays, prediction was not as reliable. Based on these findings, it has been suggested that future functioning cannot be reliably predicted, except in cases of very significant ability deficits.

Although limitations of traditional assessment instruments are widely acknowledged, Miller and Robinson (1996) believe that they should not be abandoned altogether. Instead, their weaknesses should be considered in light of the information obtained from all areas assessed. The integration of information from multiple assessment techniques, along with test scores, is more reliable in predicting delays than are results considered separately (Wodrich, 1997). Errors in interpretation can be greatly minimized if evaluators are aware of potential weaknesses and inadequacies inherent in instruments for infants, toddlers, and preschoolers (Katz, 1997). With critical consideration given to psychometric properties (i.e., reliability and validity), testing instruments can serve as an additional source of information in the evaluation of young children.

Observation

According to Hills (1993), observation is the most effective means of understanding the child.

Beyond the validation of individual assessment results, observation plays a seminal role in understanding young children's skills and abilities. Sattler (1992) identified several advantages of observations, including the opportunity to observe spontaneous behavior, interpersonal skills, and learning style. Observations can also provide information on the young child's developmental skills, temperament, and interactive style (Luciano, 1994). Of particular interest to assessors is the manner in which the young child interacts with others and objects in the environment, especially under naturalistic circumstances. This requires consideration of cultural demands and variability (Bronfenbrenner, 1989) as well as the conditions under which the young child has learned to gain desired attention and responses (Elliott & Gresham, 1993).

When using observational techniques, the information needed often directs the strategy, as various approaches produce differing information (Katz, 1997). Observational approaches are primarily categorized as quantitative or qualitative. A brief overview of each model is provided.

Qualitative methods of observation are generally characterized by the gathering of descriptive information of natural behavior using narrative recording techniques, such as anecdotal recording and running record (Sattler, 1992). Both of these procedures lead to in-depth understanding and describe the young child's behavior without the use of quantitative methods such as counting behaviors. For a more in-depth examination of qualitative methods of observation, see Chapter 6, "Qualitative Observations of Behavior," and Chapter 11, "Ecological Assessment."

In contrast, quantitative methods focus on specific behaviors during specified time periods. These methods track the occurrence of behaviors using one of several approaches. Two of the most commonly used quantitative methods are interval recording and event recording (i.e., event sampling). In interval recording, a predetermined time period is divided into a series of equal time intervals. The observer then notes whether or not the targeted behaviors were demonstrated during each of the time intervals (Sattler, 1992). Resulting data indicate the number of intervals in which the behavior did or did not occur, without data on the specific frequency of target behaviors. According to Sattler (1992), interval recording is useful for behaviors that do not have a clearly defined beginning and ending.

Event recording, on the other hand, produces quantifiable data using a frequency count of target behaviors. In this method, the observer records each occurrence of a specific behavior during a given time period. Data can also be gathered on the duration, intensity, or latency (i.e., length of time between request and onset of behavior) of specific behaviors. Sattler (1992) identified this approach as particularly useful for behaviors that have a clearly defined beginning and end, as well as behaviors that occur at lower rates. Additional information on quantitative observation techniques is contained in Chapter 12, "Behavioral Assessment."

Whether utilizing qualitative or quantitative methods, observation serves as a major source of information. Given the recognition of young children as inconsistent test-takers (Katz, 1997), as well as complications associated with some disabilities, observations sometimes serve as the only valid assessment tool. Regardless of the specific approach, Hills (1993) felt that observations should be done systematically and should answer specific questions. These answers will produce greater accuracy in the assessment process, useful information for intervention, and enhanced monitoring of intervention effectiveness.

Play Assessment

In the area of assessment for young children, play has gained increased importance. Current consensus acknowledges that play serves multiple purposes beyond that of enjoyment and entertainment for young children. It allows young children to explore their environment spontaneously and creatively (Buchanan & Cooney, 2000) as well as develop and practice new behaviors and skills (Association for Advanced Training in the Behavioral Sciences, 1997; Christie & Johnson, 1983). Developmental practitioners generally view play as an important contributor to growth in several areas including cognition, physical development, social development, and emotional development (e.g., Buchanan & Cooney, 2000; Fewell & Kaminski, 1988). Acquisition of these skills is considered essential for healthy development and future functioning.

Play has been found to follow a general developmental sequence. As such, it allows for establishment of where a child currently functions in the developmental acquisition of skills across various domains (Lifter, 1996). Although there is considerable overlap in the sequence of play development, a general pattern has been identified. Of particular interest in the assessment of young children is the manner in which play reflects cognitive and social development (Buchanan & Cooney, 2000; Lifter, 1996; Parten, 1932). Identifying a young child's skills in utilizing objects and interacting with others provides insight into these two critical areas of development. A brief review of the developmental sequence will provide a general framework from which to observe and assess play skills and development.

Most descriptions focus on two sequential aspects of play development, cognitive functions and social functions. Cognitive development is generally conceptualized as the manner in which young children utilize objects in play, that is, the forms of play (Buchanan & Cooney, 2000; Lifter, 1996). From the social perspective, play is examined using the child's interactions with others during play activities, such as with whom and in what form of interaction is the young child engaged (Lifter, 1996; Parten, 1932).

Cognitive and social aspects of play will be presented as they correspond to the developmental levels of infants, toddlers, and preschoolers.

Cognitively, infants are characterized by exploration and manipulation of objects (Lifter, 1996). This can be observed in behaviors such as mouthing, banging, and visual inspection of objects. Games such as tickling and peek-a-boo also have been noted as forms of play for infants. Socially, infants and young toddlers primarily engage in solitary play (Parten, 1932), which involves playing alone with objects or toys that differ from others in close proximity. In this way, infants and young toddlers focus on the object/toy without recognition and awareness of others. Progression to the toddler–late toddler stage represents a change in the form and social aspects of play.

Toddlers are characterized by functional use of objects, reflecting more advanced cognitive development (Buchanan & Cooney, 2000). In this stage, play primarily involves simultaneous use of two or more objects in which the toddler experiments with object functions. In terms of the social aspects of play, young toddlers move from solitary play to parallel play. Parallel play is more peer oriented and often observed as toddlers play beside one another with similar objects. Although these toddlers play alone, they are intensely interested in what other children are doing (Association for Advanced Training in the Behavioral Sciences, 1997; Parten, 1932).

At the end of the toddler stage and into the preschool stage, forms of play represent higher cognitive skills. In this stage, older toddlers and preschoolers engage in constructive and dramatic play (Buchanan & Cooney, 2000). Constructive play is described as play in which the young child uses representational objects to construct things (e.g., house, spaceship). These objects are then used to act out scenarios. Dramatic play incorporates elements of pretend into play scenarios, with attention focused on the role rather than on the materials (Lifter,

1996). Dramatic and cooperative play also characterizes social aspects of play among preschoolers. The cooperative and interactive nature of play scenarios represents a mutual exchange of ideas and advanced social skills (Buchanan & Cooney, 2000). Although this information represents a brief overview of play, it provides a general understanding of the cognitive and social aspects of play development for young children. Beyond social and cognitive development, play can be used to assess many areas of development by observing specific skills that occur during natural free play and structured play.

Inclusion of play in the assessment process has gained considerable recognition (Taylor, 1993). Emphasis on play assessment has increased because of its flexibility, including the ability to utilize free or semi-structured play (McLean, 1996), naturalistic or artificial settings (Buchanan & Cooney, 2000), and simultaneous cross-discipline assessors, as well as formal and informal techniques. Informal procedures often include observations of unstructured free play, whereas formal instruments evaluate play based on developmental theory (Lifter, 1996). Examples of assessment instruments include the *Play Assessment Scale* (Fewell & Rich, 1987), *Transdisciplinary Play-Based Assessment* (Linder, 1993), and *Developmental Play Assessment Instrument* (Lifter, Edwards, Avery, Anderson, & Sulzer-Azaroff, 1988). These instruments provide a structured approach to determining the young child's skills relative to developmental expectations.

Play serves as an indicator of progression through the developmental sequence of play. Along with its utility in determining eligibility for special services, many play assessment procedures provide valuable information for development of intervention strategies and goals (Lifter, 1996). As a result, play assessment is considered by many to be essential in the assessment of young children (see Chapter 14, "Assessing Cognition," and Chapter 16, "Assessing Emotional and Social Development).

Assessment of Young Children

The assessment of young children poses unique and significant challenges. As previously indicated, assessment is defined as an information gathering process intended to facilitate decision making, including eligibility determination (Association for Advanced Training in the Behavioral Sciences, 1997). Careful consideration should be given to the selection of assessment procedures as young children respond to the evaluation process in a multitude of ways.

Legal, as well as general, considerations require careful attention. Parts C and B of the IDEA mandate that all assessment procedures be nondiscriminatory. This includes administration of test/assessment procedures in the native language of the parents or other mode of communication, utilization of materials and procedures that are not racially or culturally discriminatory, assessment by qualified professionals, and the elimination of eligibility based on a single procedure. The following is a discussion of factors that impact assessment results including the child, setting, evaluator, and parent/caregiver support.

The Child

Assessors of young children recognize that each child enters the assessment process with a distinct and unique set of characteristics and experiences (Bucy, Smith, & Landau, 1999). These unique characteristics and needs warrant careful examination. Consideration should be given to the presence of medical needs or medication side effects, adaptive equipment, mode of communication, behavior (Bucy, Smith, & Landau, 1999), motor deficits, sensory needs (Miller & Robinson, 1996), and the ability to manipulate objects (Wodrich, 1997). The existence of one or more of these can significantly impact performance on assessment tasks.

Although each young child possesses unique and distinct abilities, several common characteristics have been identified in this population. According to Wallace, Larsen, and Elksnin (1992), assessors should expect inconsistent performance on assessment tasks, particularly if the child is assessed in an unfamiliar setting. Lack of comfort within the child often influences overall performance. Additional common characteristics include short attention span, distractibility, and mood variability (Hills, 1993; Sattler, 1992). Individual motivation also plays a significant role in overall performance.

Several other factors affect performance during an assessment. One of these includes the young child's behavioral state, defined as the individual's level of arousal/consciousness (Bucy, Smith, & Landau, 1999). According to Wallace, Larsen, and Elksnin (1992), behavioral state characteristics fall into six categories: drowsy, quiet awake, active awake, distress, quiet sleep, and active sleep. Accurately identifying the young child's behavioral state during the assessment is important because under- or over-arousal can have a detrimental impact on performance and weaken the overall validity of assessment results.

Developmental variables should always be considered when assessing young children. Behaviors observed or reported by others serve as markers reflecting progress through developmental stages. Individual and experiential variability play major roles in rate of development and can impact areas such as speech/language, cognition, motor, and social skills. Assessors must be mindful that this period of development (i.e., birth to 5 years) is characterized by rapid change (Hills, 1993).

Other developmentally appropriate reactions and responses that can influence assessment performance require brief mention. Some of these include the emergence of stranger anxiety between the ages of 7 to 10 months, assertion of autonomy in toddlers, and motor stamina limitations that affect length of testing sessions and activities (Luciano, 1994). Poor awareness of the developmental appropriateness of these elements can lead to inaccurate assessment results and interpretations. For example, an assessor might inaccurately perceive a toddler's pursuit of autonomy as defiance if developmental level is not considered. Thorough understanding of development and developmentally appropriate behavior fosters greater accuracy in the assessment of young children.

The Setting

Optimizing performance during the assessment process is essential for accurately identifying skills and abilities as well as determining eligibility for intervention services. This includes careful attention to the environment(s) in which assessment activities are conducted. As previously noted, assessments should include performance samples from multiple settings (Sattler, 1992). This is necessary for determining the young child's functional abilities. According to Miller and Robinson (1996), functional abilities reflect how the child carries out activities of daily living.

Assessment of functional abilities is often most accurate when conducted in the home setting. Buchanan and Cooney (2000) noted that young children display more advanced skills in familiar settings including the home. This is critical because young children have been found to demonstrate inconsistent performance in unfamiliar settings (Wallace, Larsen, & Elksnin, 1992). Use of familiar settings can also include familiar adults/caregivers. As such, assessors are encouraged to conduct naturalistic observations and procedures in the home or other familiar setting whenever possible (National Association of School Psychologists, 1999). Familiar comfortable settings strengthen the accuracy and validity of assessment results. According to Miller and Robinson (1996), familiar environments and typical structures provide support for contextual validity.

Although there is widespread acknowledgment that naturalistic environments can produce the most accurate findings, assessments are often conducted at assessment sites alone or in conjunction with naturalistic procedures. Important information can be gained, however, by observing the young child's response to the assessment setting and how the young child copes with new environmental demands. According to Williamson and Zeitlin (1990), this adjustment includes the manner in which the young child adapts and responds to environmental demands in order to meet his own needs. Responding to the demands of an unfamiliar setting provides some insight into the young child's coping skills.

Because comfort level has a significant impact on the young child's performance and results can be negatively "affected by temporary states of fatigue, anxiety, or stress" (Sattler, 1992, p. 5), the assessment environment should be made as nonthreatening, inviting, and comfortable as possible. Making the setting more conducive to the assessment process can foster greater assessment accuracy. Luciano (1994) provided several suggestions for creating an assessment environment that maximizes the young child's performance. The environment should be "cheerful and warm but not too distracting" (p. 22). This produces a setting that is comfortable and functional. The presence of too many toys or objects in the room can distract from primary assessment tasks. Noise level should also be considered because it can serve as a distraction. An environment that is consistently quiet is likely to be most conducive to maximal performance.

Furniture size is another environmental factor that requires consideration. According to Luciano (1994), chair size should allow the young child's feet to be flat on the floor with his back leaning on the rear of the chair. Table height should also be considered; a suggested height is waist-high to the young child (Bagnato & Neisworth, 1991). This allows the child to easily respond to assessment activities such as object manipulation, drawing, and building. The need for adaptive equipment or modified materials based on the needs of the young child should be considered and identified prior to the assessment. A carpeted room is also recommended, because floor play is natural for infants and young children. Larger furniture is appropriate when conducting family interviews and meeting with caregivers.

Luciano (1994) also identified lighting as an important environmental factor. Optimally, lighting should adequately illuminate pictures and testing materials but not be too harsh. Flickering or humming lights can serve as a significant distraction. For some young children, flickering or humming lights might have a self-stimulatory effect.

A general rule-of-thumb is to make the environment as "homelike" as possible (Bagnato & Neisworth, 1991), thus creating a sense of familiarity that fosters comfort and optimizes performance. The more similar the environment to that of the home, the greater the likelihood of obtaining accurate results. Patience and sensitivity can also help to create a conducive and inviting setting (Luciano, 1994).

The Assessors

As previously noted, assessments of young children are required to be multidisciplinary (Bagnato & Neisworth, 1991; McLean, 1996). Examples of multidisciplinary fields can include psychology, education, speech/language, audiology, physical therapy, occupational therapy, medicine, and social work, as well as parents/caregivers. Assessors of young children recognize parents/caregivers as critical members of the assessment team. Respecting their role has been described as effective, ethical, and legally required (Bagnato & Neisworth, 1991). Practitioners from each discipline are faced with similar challenges when working with this unique

population. (See Chapter 4 for further information on team assessment.)

Although the basic purpose of assessment with young children is the same as that of other age groups, often the techniques differ. According to Wallace, Larsen, and Elksnin (1992), many assessors are unfamiliar with this population, and thus they are unaware of the significant problems and barriers that interfere with the assessment process. Assessments of infants and young children require specialized skills and training beyond those used with older children.

The National Association of School Psychologists (1999) outlined four specific areas of training and procedural recommendations for assessors of infants and young children. First, assessors must possess adequate knowledge of typical and atypical developmental patterns. This includes awareness of development in multiple developmental domains. Second, assessors must possess knowledge of appropriate assessment techniques and instruments. Awareness of issues involving technical adequacy fosters selection of valid and useful techniques. Third, instruments and techniques should be selected based on their ability to provide information useful for development, implementation, and assessment of interventions as well as eligibility determination. Lastly, assessors are encouraged to use a noncategorical system of service delivery. Such an approach is advocated as specific categorical diagnosis is difficult with young children (Wodrich, 1997).

Several additional recommendations have been identified as useful for assessors of young children. Although flexibility is required in the assessment process, having a structured and organized sequence of activities facilitates more effective transitions (Luciano, 1994). This can include time allotments for structured testing, structured play, unstructured play, and social interaction. As previously noted, assessors should also prepare the assessment environment to minimize distractions (Bucy, Smith, & Landau, 1999). These organization and environmental preparations should be done prior to beginning the session in order to maximize active engagement with the young child.

Throughout the assessment, assessors must recognize that young children have had little exposure to assessments and often limited motivation to perform when prompted (Luciano, 1994). As a result, they are frequently reluctant to cooperate with unfamiliar adult-directed activities. Assessors are encouraged to present themselves in a confident, warm, and friendly manner to help prevent resistant reactions (Sattler, 1992). Less formal, comfortable clothes can also foster a more relaxed and inviting environment. The young child's responses and behaviors provide cues for initiating, continuing, and ending activities, as well as when support, encouragement, or reduced interaction is appropriate (Luciano, 1994).

According to Sattler (1992), assessors must "guide the child every step of the way, maintaining their attention and cooperation" (p. 90). In order to effectively guide the young child, careful attention to pace is needed, and whenever possible, assessors should work at the child's pace. Establishing and maintaining attention and cooperation can also be fostered through activities conducted at the beginning of the session. Specifically, it is advisable to begin the assessment with activities/items that ensure success (Bucy, Smith, & Landau, 1999). Early success can increase motivation, attention, and cooperation.

Parent/Caregiver Support

Among professionals in the area of young children's assessment, there is consensus that parents/caregivers are critical contributors to the assessment and intervention process (Bucy, Smith, & Landau, 1999). Beyond serving as a source of information, family members/caregivers provide security and stability for the young child in an unfamiliar setting. In addition,

Luciano (1994) claimed that parent/caregiver involvement fosters more accurate and productive intervention decisions and increases family investment. Parent involvement is also necessary because assessment of family strengths and needs is considered essential for family intervention development.

A family-centered approach provides parents/caregivers decision-making options in all phases of the assessment process, not merely input during the social history (McLean, 1996). Throughout the assessment, parents/caregivers provide critical information regarding skill and ability levels. Because parents/caregivers are recognized as accurate and reliable reporters of child behaviors and difficulties, they are viewed as partners in the assessment process, not merely passive participants (National Association of School Psychologists, 1999). Parent/caregiver involvement promotes better understanding of the assessment process and can facilitate more effective intervention development and implementation.

Bucy, Smith, and Landau (1999) recommended the inclusion of one or both parents/caregivers during assessment sessions. Benefits can accompany the inclusion of parents/caregivers in the assessment environment. Luciano (1994) identified several positive elements associated with parent/caregiver involvement. First, the young child's adaptation to the assessment environment can be enhanced by the presence of parents/caregivers. Mere presence or proximity can serve as a source of reassurance. Second, parent/caregiver encouragement conveys that participation in assessment activities is important. Informing parents/caregivers of the goals and assessment procedures can promote greater comfort, which is then conveyed to the child. Third, inclusion of parents/caregivers can sometimes prevent behavioral resistance resulting from separation. Infants and young children can be expected to be confronting issues of separation anxiety, separation tolerance, and independence (i.e., autonomy).

An additional benefit includes the opportunity to observe parent-child interactions. According to Wallace, Larsen, and Elksnin (1992), these interactions provide information on psychosocial development as well as elements of the parent-child relationship. Finally, assessors can gather information from parents/caregivers regarding the young child's performance during the assessment. Parents are able to assess the young child's performance as it relates to everyday functioning and developmental background (Bucy, Smith, & Landau, 1999). This information can serve to validate assessment results and increase assessor confidence in eligibility and intervention determination.

In early intervention programming (i.e., birth to 3 years), the family unit is viewed as the recipient of services, rather than the infant/toddler (McLean, 1996). Although preschoolers are viewed as the primary recipient of special education services, there is strong recognition that family involvement can enhance intervention outcomes. Because the family system has been recognized as a critical element in the assessment and intervention process, the system's strengths and weaknesses need to be assessed. Specifically, it is necessary to assess each family's specific and individualized needs (Winton & Bailey, 1988). Several aspects of the family system should be included in the family assessment.

Turnbull and Turnbull (1990) identified four elements that are useful in the assessment of family system functioning. First, family characteristics should be assessed. These include the characteristics of the young child's disability, as well as the individual characteristics of each family member, overall family, and family challenges or barriers. Second, assessors examine family interactions, including the quality of family member relationships, such as the marital relationship, parent-child relationships, and the presence of extended family. Third, attention is given to family member functions. These functions involve each member's roles and responsibilities (e.g., education, career/job, health care). Finally, assessors examine the family's life cycle. This entails identifying the developmental stages of family members, current functioning in those stages, and expected changes that are forthcoming. Identifying the family's current standing on these issues is beneficial because they can impact changes in parental responsibilities as the family addresses issues related to the young child's disability and progress. Additional information involving the role of the family in the assessment process, as well as identification of family concerns, resources, and priorities, is considered in Chapter 2.

Summary

The assessment of young children poses significant challenges to professionals and the field of early child education/intervention. Rapid changes in development, lack of exposure to test-taking experiences, issues involving technical adequacy of instruments, and insufficient training often hinder assessment accuracy with this unique population. As a result, professionals working with young children are forced to expand their repertoire of assessment techniques to gain needed information. Some of the techniques that can foster accuracy in the assessment process include family interviews, individually administered tasks, observation, and play assessment. Strong emphasis on family involvement and intervention is considered unique to special education services for infants and toddlers. Although significant challenges confront assessors of young children, accuracy is necessary for eligibility determinations. Correctly identifying those young children and families in need is essential as the merits of early intervention have been clearly demonstrated (Sattler, 1992).

References

Association for Advanced Training in the Behavioral Sciences (1997). *Psychology written licensure examination review*. Ventura, CA: Author.

Bagnato, S. J., & Neisworth, J. T. (1991). *Assessment for early intervention: Best practices for professionals.* New York: Guilford Press.

Bailey, D. B., & Nabors, L. A. (1996). Tests and test development. In M. McLean, D. B. Bailey, & M. Wolery (Eds.), *Assessing infants and preschoolers with special needs* (2nd ed.) (pp. 32–45). Upper Saddle River, NJ: Merrill/Prentice Hall.

Bayley, N. (1993). *Bayley scales of infant development* (2nd ed.). San Antonio, TX: The Psychological Corporation.

Bricker, D. D. (1989). *Early education of at-risk and handicapped infants, toddlers, and preschool children* (2nd ed.). Palo Alto, CA: VORT.

Bricker, D., & Squires, J. (1989). The effectiveness of parental screening of at-risk infants: The infant monitoring questionnaires. *Topics in Early Childhood Special Education, 9,* 67–85.

Brigance, A. H. (1991). *Brigance diagnostic inventory of early development.* North Billerica, MA: Curriculum Associates.

Bronfenbrenner, U. (1989). Ecological systems theory. *Annals of Child Development, 6,* 187–249.

Buchanan, M., & Cooney, M. (2000). Play at home, play in the classroom: Parent/professional partnerships in supporting child play. *Young Exceptional Children, 3*(4), 9–15.

Bucy, J. E., Smith, T., & Landau, A. (1999). Assessment of preschool children with developmental disabilities and at-risk conditions. In E. V. Nuttall, I. Romero, & J. Kalesnik (Eds.), *Assessing and screening preschoolers* (2nd ed.) (pp. 318–339). Boston: Allyn & Bacon.

Christie, J., & Johnson, J. (1983). The role of play in social-intellectual development. *Review of Educational Research, 53,* 93–115.

Dale, P. (1991). The validity of a parent report measure of vocabulary and syntax at 24 months. *Journal of Speech and Hearing Research, 34,* 565–571.

Department of Health and Rehabilitative Services, State of Florida (1990). *Quality early intervention linking research and practice.* Tallahassee, FL: Author.

Elliott, S. N., & Gresham, F. M. (1993). Social skills intervention for children. *Behavior Modification, 17,* 287–313.

Fewell, R. R., & Kaminski, R. (1988). Play skills development and instruction for young children with handicaps. In S. L. Odom & M. B. Karnes (Eds.), *Early intervention for infants and children with handicaps* (pp. 145–158). Baltimore: Brookes.

Fewell, R. R., & Rich, J. S. (1987). Play assessment as a procedure for examining cognitive, communication, and social skills in multihandicapped children. *Journal of Psychoeducational Assessment, 2,* 107–118.

Guralnick, M. J. (1998). Effectiveness of early intervention for vulnerable children: A developmental perspective. *American Journal of Mental Retardation, 102,* 319–345.

Hills, T. W. (1993). Reaching potentials through appropriate assessment. In S. Bredekamp & T. Rosengrant (Eds.), *Reaching potentials: Appropriate curriculum and assessment for young children,* Vol.1 (pp. 43–63). Washington, DC: National Association for the Education of Young Children.

Interact. (1981). *Early intervention for children with special needs and their families.* National Committee for Services to Very Young Children with Special Needs and Their Families. Seattle: WESPAK.

Johnson-Martin, N., Attermeier, S., & Hacker, B. (1990). *Carolina curriculum for preschoolers with special needs.* Baltimore: Brookes.

Katz, L. G. (1997). A developmental approach to assessment of young children. ERIC D*igest.* Urbana-Champaign, IL: ERIC Clearinghouse.

Lifter, K. (1996). Assessing play skills. In M. McLean, D. B. Bailey Jr., & M. Wolery (Eds.), *Assessing infants and preschoolers with special needs* (2nd ed.) (pp. 435–461). Upper Saddle River, NJ: Merrill/Prentice Hall.

Lifter, K., Edwards, G., Avery, D., Anderson, S. R., & Sulzer-Azaroff, B. (1988). *Developmental assessment of children's play: Implications for intervention.* Paper presented at Annual Convention of the American Speech-Language-Hearing Association. Boston.

Linder, T. W. (1993). *Transdisciplinary play-based assessment: A functional approach to working with young children* (Rev. ed.). Baltimore: Brookes.

Luciano, L. (1994). The assessment experience. In J. A. Bondurant-Utz & L. Luciano (Eds.), *A practical guide to infant and preschool assessment in special education* (pp. 17–26). Needham, MA: Allyn & Bacon.

McLean, M. (1996). Assessment and its importance in early intervention/early childhood special education. In M. McLean, D. B. Bailey Jr., & M. Wolery (Eds.), *Assessing infants and preschoolers with special needs* (2nd ed.) (pp. 1–22). Upper Saddle River, NJ: Merrill/ Prentice Hall.

Miller, L. J., & Robinson, C. C. (1996). Strategies for meaningful assessment of infants and toddlers with significant physical and sensory disabilities. In S. J. Meisels & E. Fenichel (Eds.), *New visions for the developmental assessment of infants and young children* (pp. 313–328). Washington, DC: National Center for Infants, Toddlers, and Families.

Molfese, V. J. (1989). *Perinatal risk and infant development.* New York: Guilford Press.

National Association of School Psychologists. (1999). Early childhood assessment. *Position Statement.*

National Committee for Economic Development. (1987). *Children in need: Investment strategies for the educationally disadvantaged.* Unpublished manuscript: Author.

Neisworth, J. G., & Bagnato, S. J. (1992). The case against intelligence testing in early intervention. *Topics in Early Childhood Special Education, 12*(1), 1–20.

Newborg, J., Stock, J., Wnek, L., Guidubaldi, J., & Svinicki, J. (1984). *Battelle developmental inventory.* Allen, TX: DLM Teaching Resources.

Parten, M. (1932). Social participation among preschool children. *Journal of Abnormal and Social Psychology, 27,* 243–269.

Sattler, J. M. (1992). *Assessment of children* (3rd ed.). San Diego: Author.

Taylor, R. T. (1993). *Assessment of exceptional students: Educational and psychological procedures* (3rd ed.). Needham Heights, MA: Allyn & Bacon.

Thorndike, R. L., Hagen, E. P., & Sattler, J. M. (1986). *Stanford-Binet intelligence scale* (4th ed.). Chicago: Riverside.

Turnbull, A. P., & Turnbull, R. H. III (1990). *Families, professionals, and exceptionality: A special partnership* (2nd ed.). Upper Saddle River, NJ: Merrill/Prentice Hall.

Wallace, G., Larsen, S. C., & Elksnin, L. K. (1992). *Educational assessment of learning problems: Testing for teaching* (2nd ed.). Needham Heights, MA: Allyn & Bacon.

Williamson, G. G., & Zeitlin, S. (1990). Assessment of coping and temperament. In E. D. Gibbs & D. M. Teti (Eds.), *Interdisciplinary assessment of infants* (pp. 215–226). Baltimore: Brookes.

Winton, P. J., & Bailey, D. B. Jr. (1988). The family-focused interview: A collaborative mechanism for assessment and goal setting. *Journal for the Division for Early Childhood, 12,* 195–207.

Wodrich, D. L. (1997). *Children's psychological testing: A guide for nonpsychologists* (3rd ed.). Baltimore: Brookes.

Qualitative Observations of Behavior

Christopher Lopata

Observation: Characteristics and Caveats

In all assessments, careful consideration needs to be given to the referral problem. Specific details involving areas of concern, developmental history, and current functioning lead to greater precision in the gathering of evaluation information (Wodrich, 1997). Greater understanding of these areas allows assessors to select appropriate assessment instruments and procedures prior to beginning an assessment. According to Bagnato, Neisworth, and Munson (1997), assessment materials and techniques must be established prior to an assessment.

The assessment of young children often involves both qualitative and quantitative methodology. Legal mandates prohibiting the use of a single test instrument as the basis for eligibility determination compel assessors to utilize a wide range of techniques for gathering information. Recognition of young children as poor test-takers (Katz, 1997) and issues of technical adequacy of current test instruments (McLean, 1996) force assessors to seek assessment techniques that accurately represent the young child's current level of functioning. The presence of other deficits, such as language, sensory, social skills, multiple disabilities, and behavior, can also limit performance on standardized instruments (Bagnato & Neisworth, 1994). These concerns and difficulties require techniques that extend beyond standardized tests.

One method often used is that of observation. According to Taylor (1993), "observation is undoubtedly the most pervasive and widely used method of assessment" (p. 79). Observational techniques assume even greater importance given concerns involving the technical inadequacies of standardized tests and lack of conformity to testing demands. Observation also represents a common mode of assessment that is utilized by the various disciplines that comprise assessment teams (e.g., speech/language, occupational therapy, physical therapy, psychology). Often, observation serves as a primary means of assessment for young children (Hills, 1993b).

The central issue in all assessments is the gathering of information that accurately reflects the young child's skills and abilities. Observation is frequently described as the most direct and effective means for gathering assessment data and understanding young children (Hills, 1993a; Taylor, 1993). Included among the many benefits of observation is the ability to view the child in multiple settings ranging from the artificial testing room to naturalistic environments in which the child is more likely to demonstrate typical behaviors. Sattler (1992) claimed that observations provide information related to settings, setting dynamics, and the manner in which the settings meet the needs of the child. Observational procedures recognize the critical role environment plays in the young child's behaviors (Bucy, Smith, & Landau, 1999).

Observations require identification of needed information and the manner in which information will be obtained. Methods can be informal or systematic but should be based on specific questions to be answered in the assessment process. This becomes critical because the information contributes to eligibility decisions (Hills, 1993a; McLean, 1996). Observations serve several additional purposes beyond that of eligibility determination. Some of these include identification of strengths and weaknesses, facilitation of decision making, intervention planning, progress monitoring, and longitudinal tracking (Bucy, Smith, & Landau, 1999; National Association of School Psychologists, 1999; Taylor, 1993).

Benefits

Observations have many benefits in the assessment process. For example, observations can include parents or familiar persons from multiple settings (Bucy, Smith, & Landau, 1999). In addition, observations can be conducted in naturalistic or staged settings, thereby providing information needed for convergence of results. Observations also serve to enhance testing results (i.e., support or invalidate results) or explain variability within results (Bracken, 1983). Fundamental to the use of observations is the assumption that behaviors demonstrated over time reflect the young child's patterns and skills. This assumption places even greater emphasis on the use of multiple sources and measures on multiple occasions.

Cautions

Although observations serve a primary and critical purpose in the assessment and intervention process, caution is necessary when examining observational data. Hills (1993a) claimed that young children are acutely sensitive to their surroundings. This sensitivity can sometimes lead to anomalies in behavior and assessment results in artificial testing environments. As such, it is necessary to observe the child across settings, including familiar settings, to obtain a more accurate understanding of the young child's behaviors. Examples of familiar settings can include the home, preschool, child care center, or play groups. Observations in an artificial testing environment have substantial limitations. According to Luciano (1994), observations obtained in the testing environment should not be generalized to other settings.

Assessors must also recognize that they can impact observation results. The mere presence of the assessor can alter the behavior of the child (Luciano, 1994). Positive or negative reactions might result in information that is inconsistent with typical behavior. The impact of the environment, including the presence of the assessor, must be considered when interpreting observational data.

Bracken (1991) provided four suggestions and caveats when utilizing observations in the assessment process. First, observations are identified as more subjective and vulnerable than are results of standardized test scores. Observational techniques, as well as individual assessors, vary in the type of data they produce. Second, the rapid rate of development that characterizes young children makes determination of "normalcy" or typical behavior difficult. This sentiment is echoed by the Association for Advanced Training in the Behavioral Sciences (1997), which described this age as a period of rapid growth and development. Third, Bracken (1991) recommended that behavioral observations be used to describe the young child's behavior as it relates to improving or inhibiting performance on assessment tasks. Finally, observational data are described as an effective method for enhancing assessment results. As previously noted, observational data can serve to support or refute results obtained through various assessment tasks.

Despite potential limitations, observations serve as a major assessment technique and source of information in the assessment of young children. Observations can be conducted using a variety of techniques. Two broad categories of methodology include quantitative and qualitative observation. The following section contains a detailed description of qualitative methods of observation.

Qualitative Methods

Qualitative methods of observation play a central role in the assessment of young children. They can be applied in a variety of ways to gather broad information. Before utilizing this method of observation, assessors must possess a solid understanding of qualitative methodology as well as the specific methods that comprise this approach.

Chapter 6

General Considerations of Qualitative Methods

The substantial information available through observation compels assessors to develop effective observation techniques. The qualitative approach uses descriptive information to gain insight into the young child's skills and abilities. This information can be interpreted alone or used to gather subsequent quantitative data. As an independent procedure, qualitative observations provide rich descriptive information that is sometimes described as more accurate than results of more formal and standardized procedures (Hills, 1993b). Qualitative observations produce valuable information involving assessment behavior as well as behavior across settings and observers.

Qualitative techniques are often recognized for their applicability in naturalistic and authentic environments. The importance of assessment in naturalistic environments has been clearly established for young children. Various qualitative techniques can be applied within the context of authentic assessment because authentic assessment "emphasizes the real-life nature of a task and the natural context in which the assessment occurs or the observational data gathered" (Bagnato, Neisworth, & Munson, 1997, p. 26).

Qualitative observations are also consistent with a functional approach to understanding young children's skills and abilities. The functional approach focuses on observable skills and deficits as they relate to typical performance. Although use of developmental milestones can be inappropriate at times, Bagnato, Neisworth, and Munson (1997) claimed that a functional sequence of development provides a reference point for determining the degree of impairment as well as intervention planning.

Flexibility and creativity are required in the assessment of young children (Bucy, Smith, & Landau, 1999). Qualitative methods are consistent with this requirement, as they are effective in producing information without intrusion or disruption of the child's daily routine. Specifically, information can be gathered without limiting or infringing on typical performance (Keller, 1986).

Guiding Principles

Regardless of the specific qualitative technique employed, several guiding principles can increase accuracy. Hills (1993a) provided several suggestions to enhance the process of qualitative observation. Assessors are encouraged to carefully determine needed information because systematic planning produces more useful information. Such planning includes specifically identifying the purpose of the observation, conducting the observation, compiling data on the child and the group, and analyzing data. Careful planning can also include delineation of the number of times needed to observe the child, length of observation periods, method of recording, and target areas of functioning (Sattler, 1992). Following this basic sequence can produce more accurate and useful information. Although qualitative observational techniques are often described in reference to naturalistic environments, they can also be utilized within the testing environment. The following section provides a description of several qualitative observation techniques.

Techniques for Qualitative Observation

Observations generally lead to descriptive statements of behavior, including low inference statements that simply describe the observed behavior, or high inference statements that reflect some degree of interpretation (Sattler, 1992). According to Bracken (1983), it is more informative to report on what the young child does and interpret the behavior in positive terms, rather than what the child is unable to do.

Qualitative observations can be conducted using two basic approaches. One approach utilizes specific categories of behaviors of interest. Using this approach, the assessor establishes predetermined areas of functioning to gather specific information. The second approach represents an open-ended procedure in which the assessor identifies no pre-set categories and instead focuses on diverse behaviors. Although the open-ended method reduces the chances of missing valuable information owing to limited target areas, the use of specific categories has been found to produce more reliable information (Keller, 1986).

Prior to beginning an observation, the observer should gather as much information as possible regarding the young child's current performance. Wodrich (1997) recommended identifying areas of concern, including factors such as time and place, frequency of behaviors, and environmental variables. This information helps to ensure attainment of more useful information.

Selecting a recording procedure also requires consideration, because these procedures vary significantly in terms of recording demands. For example, some qualitative recording procedures are labor intensive and require immediate recording of behaviors as they occur, which can limit the amount and degree of time the assessor will be able to interact with the young child. Other techniques maximize the amount and degree of interaction with the young child by allowing recording following the observation period. However, detailed descriptions may be forgotten during the time lapse between observation and recording. The strengths and weaknesses of each approach need to be considered in light of the referral concerns to ensure that an appropriate technique is selected.

The following recording techniques can be applied under varying circumstances, including naturalistic settings and assessment settings (i.e., testing environment). Despite the wide range of qualitative observation methods, Jones, Reid, and Patterson (1975) recommended using techniques that require minimal

inference. The following is a brief description of qualitative observation techniques commonly used during assessments, as well as in development and monitoring of interventions. These specific techniques generally fall under the heading of narrative methods.

Narrative recording is a broad heading encompassing multiple techniques designed "to formulate a rich and comprehensive description of the child's (or group's) natural behavior" (Sattler, 1992, p. 476). Narrative observation techniques focus on the young child's behavior in relation to the environment to gather information on skills, abilities, interaction style, and learning style. Specifically, this information is acquired by gathering as much information as possible about events in the observation setting (Beaty, 1990).

Narrative methods can be divided into two categories based on the timing of recording procedures: techniques that require immediate recording of behaviors as they occur, and techniques that require recording following the observation. Two commonly used techniques that require recording as the behavior occurs are running records and specimen descriptions. Common techniques that utilize recording following an observation include logs and journals (Hills, 1993a), anecdotal recording, and diary descriptions (Beaty, 1990; Gordon & Browne, 1985). Each of these approaches possesses strengths and weaknesses that impact the observer's selection of technique. (For additional information on narrative methods, see Chapter 11, "Ecological Assessment.")

Narratives often serve as the principal recording method in an assessment (Sattler, 1992). They have several advantages. One advantage is that they can preserve the original sequence of events, thereby fostering identification of antecedents, behaviors, and consequences for intervention development (Alessi, 1988). A second advantage involves flexibility. Observers can target specific behaviors or utilize an open-ended approach to gather information that might otherwise be missed (Beaty, 1990).

Although narrative techniques provide critical information in the assessment and intervention process, there are several disadvantages. One of the primary disadvantages involves the extent and intensity of recording demands. Advocates of narrative procedures frequently cite the time-consuming nature of the recording procedures as a disadvantage (e.g., Beaty, 1990; Gordon & Browne, 1985; Hills, 1993a). Interpreting the information can also be challenging if the observational data are too broad. Another area of difficulty involves the validation of results. According to Sattler (1992), narrative recordings are difficult to validate and are only as good as the observer. Despite these areas of concern, narrative recording plays a critical role in the assessment of young children, as well as a means for monitoring progress and intervention effectiveness.

Finally, the use of qualitative observations requires appropriate training and skill development, including observer competence and the ability to observe behavior in an impartial manner (Jones, Reid, & Patterson, 1975). In addition, observers "should develop objective, reliable, and valid observational skills" (Bracken, 1983, p. 64). These skills, however, typically develop over time and sometimes require guidance and structure in the initial stages. Luciano (1994) echoed these sentiments in her statement that, "Initially, however, the use of a structured observation system can assist the examiner/practitioner in gathering information for appropriate interventions" (p. 38). She continues that observers tend to become more spontaneous with increased experience.

Important Components of Observations

Although observation techniques vary considerably, several areas of development and functioning provide valuable information on the young child's skills and abilities. Assessment performance should be considered from a developmental perspective, with careful attention to the skills, abilities, and behaviors common to various developmental domains at given ages. This provides a framework for understanding development progress as well as for determining eligibility for support services. According to Bagnato, Neisworth, and Munson (1997), eligibility determinations often involve comparison of the child's behaviors with that of normative behavior. Close attention should also be given to the impact of disabilities on performance during assessment tasks as well as performance in naturalistic settings.

Obtaining an accurate and comprehensive understanding of a young child requires consideration of multiple areas of functioning. Luciano (1994) recommended assessment of several areas, including the young child's physical characteristics, temperament and behavioral style, interactive and communicative style, problem-solving and learning style, and adaptive behavior. The following provides a description of these areas and possible features to consider.

Physical Characteristics

Assessors attend to multiple areas of physical development and characteristics during the assessment process. These areas can provide valuable insights into the child's strengths, weaknesses, and current physical condition. Assessors often record information on general appearance, height and weight, anomalies in physical development (Bracken, 1983), clothing, and hygiene (Sattler, 1992). Luciano (1994) recommended careful attention to relative weight and size because these can reflect rate of development and health. These observations, however, must be considered in relation to family traits and features. Attention should also be given to additional features, such as redness around the nose or ears, dark circles under eyes, pale skin, tiredness, sleep pattern, and diet, because these signs might suggest areas in need of further assessment.

The ability to perceive stimuli should also be assessed. This is frequently observed in the young child's vision and hearing abilities (Bucy, Smith, & Landau, 1999). Information on vision and hearing can be obtained through observation of behavior as well as parental reports of vision and hearing assessments. Observations of behavior often provide insight into vision and hearing levels. For example, the assessor should note if the young child moves closer to materials, consistently turns the head in a specific direction when listening, squints, or relies on verbal repetition or visual cues/gestures (Luciano, 1994). The presence of such behaviors may suggest difficulty with reception of auditory or visual material.

Gross and fine motor skills must also be assessed (Sattler, 1992). Although these skills can be formally assessed using tests, qualitative observations often provide a great deal of information. Observations of gross and fine motor development can include areas such as coordination, gait, and posture (Luciano, 1994). The young child's skills and abilities in these areas are often compared with developmental expectations for that given age. Careful attention is warranted for the impact of physical disabilities on gross and fine motor skills as well as the impact on assessment performance.

The effect of medication requires special attention; specifically, the manner in which medication affects behavior and performance (Bucy, Smith, & Landau, 1999). The effect of medication across domains of assessment (e.g., speech/language, occupational therapy, psychology) should be considered prior to interpreting assessment results. This information can include substantial input from medical professionals or the parents.

Careful assessment of physical health and health issues leads to better understanding of assessment and naturalistic behaviors. Assessors must go beyond merely identifying the presence of physical features and examine their implications. According to Bracken (1991), describing the impact of physical features on assessment performance is more meaningful than simply noting the existence of the features.

In addition, the impact of environment must be considered in light of possible physical difficulties. Specifically, young children with physical disabilities sometimes have not had exposure to assessment type tasks. Luciano (1994) claimed that children with physical disabilities sometimes demonstrate higher level skills if the tasks or environment is more consistent with their natural environment.

The impact of physical difficulties on assessment performance must always be considered. Assessors recognize that severe disabilities can significantly interfere with performance in a way that potentially invalidates testing results. For example, poor performance on a test might reflect depressed performance rather than low ability/skills. Further in-depth assessment by a specialist may be warranted under such conditions.

Temperament and Behavioral Style

Qualitative observations provide a great deal of information on a young child's temperament and behavioral style. According to Bracken (1983), assessors should target and describe test and non-test behaviors as well as general behavioral trends. To the maximum extent possible, this should involve observations on several occasions in differing settings (Luciano, 1994). Behaviors should then be examined from a developmental perspective, including how the behaviors relate to those expected at various developmental levels. Behaviors warrant attention when manifest to a degree that is excessive, based on age and developmental level, and pose a threat to future development (Bagnato, Neisworth, & Munson, 1997).

One approach that provides broad information involves examination of the young child's behavioral states. Behavioral states are described as the individual's arousal level and consciousness (Bucy, Smith, & Landau, 1999). The manner in which a young child explores the environment, reacts to new persons, settings, and materials, and appears interested and motivated often reflects the behavioral state (Luciano, 1994). Additional areas implicated in behavioral state include energy level, activity, alertness, irritability, anxiety (Luciano, 1994), drowsiness, fatigue, withdrawal, frustration (Bracken, 1983), distractibility, and general mood (Sattler, 1992). Along with these negative elements, lack of familiarity can be detrimental because naturalistic environments frequently lead to more representative behaviors. Behavioral states often impact the young child's ability to self-regulate behavior. For example, excessive or depressed arousal might significantly interfere with task completion, cooperation, or interpersonal interactions, because the young child is unable to exercise age-appropriate self-control. The potential impact of medication on behavioral state and behavior must also be considered because side effects can substantially impact behavioral functioning. The possible negative effects of medication should be discussed as they relate to performance.

Qualitative observations provide in-depth information regarding temperament and behavioral style. Careful consideration needs to be given to the observed behaviors as they correspond to developmental and age expectations. The behaviors might reflect developmental delays or problems that require further assessment if deemed excessive or deficient in light of developmental expectations. The presence of additional disabilities can also challenge assessor conclusions. Of particular concern are physical disabilities that inhibit behavioral states and responses unrelated to the demands of the immediate environment and tasks. When physical limitations impact performance, assessment

results can be rendered invalid. Under these circumstances, alternative methods of assessment, including qualitative observations in naturalistic settings, can be more representative of the young child's skills and abilities.

Communication and Interaction

Communication and interaction are highly interrelated aspects of young children's development. More directly, communication is needed for human interaction, and human interaction requires modes of communication. As such, assessors often consider both aspects simultaneously during interpersonal exchanges. According to Luciano (1994), careful attention should be given to verbal and nonverbal communication skills. Valuable information can be obtained by observing how the young child describes himself, pursues desired information, responds to others, and negotiates social interactions. Hills (1993a) indicated that interpersonal relationships are most readily assessed using observations.

When assessing social reciprocity, assessors examine interpersonal skills, including facial expressions, body language, behavior, gestures (Sattler, 1992), turn-taking, eye contact, and topic maintenance. These skills can reflect accelerated, typical, or delayed social development and communication. The presence or absence of these skills at various ages and developmental levels provides insight into the young child's current skills and developmental progress.

Beyond the interactive style of a young child, issues of speech/language production are considered important. Specific skills associated with speech production can include fluency (e.g., stuttering and stammering), lisps, articulation, grammar, and vocabulary level (Heward, 2000). Assessment of receptive (i.e., ability to understand spoken language) and expressive (i.e., ability to express ideas) language skills is also considered essential. Assessors are especially attentive to the degree to which the young child exhibits distress in reaction to difficulties in these areas (Bracken, 1983). Difficulties with speech production or receptive or expressive language can have a detrimental effect on social development.

Assessment of speech/language skills often provides information related to other areas of functioning, including cognition, problem-solving style, and awareness of others and the environment (Bracken, 1983). According to Luciano (1994), the process of rapport establishment (i.e., quick or slow to warm up) and reaction to unfamiliar settings and individuals can represent keys to understanding the young child's social development and coping. She goes on to indicate that a young child's initiation of social interaction, as well as independence, can reflect trust, self-esteem, or attention span. For a young child with known verbal ability, apprehension to interact might be a product of anxiety or discomfort (Bracken, 1991).

Consideration should also be given to the young child's primary means of communication because developmental and physical disabilities sometimes require the use of augmentative devices and communication systems. The young child's interactions using an alternative system should be assessed. Although the presence of a developmental or physical disability will likely interfere with communication, skill levels must be assessed using the young child's primary mode of communication. As stated earlier, depressed performance should not necessarily be interpreted as a lack of skills or abilities.

Problem-Solving and Learning Style

Qualitative observations provide valuable insights into young children's problem-solving and learning styles (Sattler, 1992). Direct observations often reflect skill levels as well as strategies to solve various problem situations and tasks. Specifically, assessment tasks help the assessor determine the child's most effective means of problem-solving (e.g., visual, verbal). For example, does the young child seek verbal clarification and direction when confronted with a problem that requires visual skills (e.g., replicating a block design)? Conversely, a young child might request a visual model to solve a verbally based item. A need for repetition and modeling can also reflect current skills and ability levels (Luciano, 1994). To illustrate, the need for verbal repetition might be the product of a speech/language delay or low verbal ability. Behavioral observations during different types of tasks often provide insight into problem-solving and learning styles.

Young children often verbally express their thoughts while solving problems (Bracken, 1983). This provides access to information that is often unavailable in older children. Attention should be given to the approach used to solve various problems. This information is useful because certain problem-solving strategies reflect more highly developed skills and abilities. For instance, a young child who develops a strategy to solve a puzzle by beginning with the outside edge pieces has demonstrated more advanced skills than one who relies exclusively on trial-and-error insertion of individual pieces.

Several other aspects are important in assessing problem-solving and learning style. Levels of perseverance and persistence sometimes parallel skill level. According to Bracken (1983), young children often remain on-task until assessment tasks become too difficult. Just as perseverance and persistence may reflect the presence of skills, perseveration may sometimes reflect skill deficits. Perseverative play (i.e., repetitive play), for instance, sometimes indicates that the child has learned only one way to engage with a given object (Bagnato & Neisworth, 1991). For example, the need to play with all toys as if they were a train might reflect a perseverative pattern of play.

The manner in which a young child manipulates objects and responds to the challenges in an unfamiliar environment can also be an indication of cognitive ability (Luciano, 1994). Flexibility and coping skills often represent advanced problem-solving skills and learning. "The ability to transfer skills learned in one setting to another setting offers the strongest evidence that a child is generalizing and, therefore, learning" (Bagnato, Neisworth, & Munson, 1997, p. 19). Use of naturalistic observations helps assessors assess the generalization of skills across settings and tasks. Specifically, assessors can assess the degree to which the young child was able to use skills evident in the natural environment in the assessment setting. Finally, assessors must consider the impact of specific disabilities should they be present. These conditions can limit completion of tasks or interactions (Luciano, 1994), and depress scores on various assessment tasks. Results must be presented cautiously when disabilities are present.

Adaptive Behavior

Assessment of adaptive behavior provides a broad and in-depth view of the young child's functioning across daily tasks. Although adaptive behavior can be assessed using any number of formal adaptive behavior instruments, it can also be examined using qualitative observation. The American Psychiatric Association (1994) defines adaptive behavior as "how effectively individuals cope with common life demands and how well they meet the standards of personal independence expected of someone in their particular age group, sociocultural background, and community setting" (p. 40). This definition emphasizes behavior within contextual parameters (i.e., age, culture, community). As such, it is necessary to consider competence from the perspective of social demands (Grossman, 1983).

Another parameter to consider is the degree to which the child's behaviors are consistent with developmental expectations. According to Sattler (1992), adaptive behavior must be assessed within a developmental context. This provides assessors with benchmark skills commonly demonstrated by young children at given ages and developmental levels. It also allows assessors to view development longitudinally and provides valuable information for intervention development. Progress over time can be easily monitored through the young child's acquisition of skills.

Assessing adaptive behaviors often requires the use of several techniques, including observations and formal instruments. Currently, no single instrument adequately assesses all relevant domains of adaptive functioning (Sattler, 1992). The complex interaction of many factors such as social, cognitive, situational, and personal variables requires multiple modes of assessment.

Although a variety of assessment techniques are generally employed, several specific areas require consideration. Areas to assess often include physical development, language development, and independent functioning. (For an in-depth examination of adaptive assessment, see Chapter 18, "Adaptive Behavior.") Only the areas of independent functioning and self-help will be briefly discussed in this section because physical development, communication, and interaction were discussed previously in this chapter. Initially, assessors can observe the young child's adjustment to the assessment. Bucy, Smith, and Landau (1999) indicated that attention should be given to the degree to which the child adapts to changes in the environment. This can sometimes provide information on the young child's flexibility as well as development of autonomy and independence (Luciano, 1994).

Self-help and independence are two critical components in the assessment of adaptive behavior. According to Wallace, Larsen, and Elksnin (1992), self-help skills are readily assessed using observation. These skills generally reflect the young child's ability to independently complete activities of daily living (e.g., feeding, toileting, dressing, grooming, bathing; Luciano, 1999).

Again, these must be considered with regard to developmental expectations. In addition to self-help and independence skills, maladaptive behavior can be assessed. Maladaptive behaviors often interfere with the young child's development, acquisition of skills, and daily performance. Such behaviors may include self-stimulatory behaviors, stereotypic behaviors (i.e., repetitive nonfunctional behaviors), self-injurious behaviors, or aggression (Bucy, Smith, & Landau, 1999).

Much of this information can be obtained during observations, but observations are rarely sufficient; therefore, assessors regularly seek information from others who know the child more intimately. According to the American Psychiatric Association (1994), it is useful to gather information regarding adaptive behaviors from multiple reliable sources (e.g., parents, teachers, child care providers, relatives, or others who know the child intimately). Most often, parents/caregivers serve as the primary source of information regarding the young child's level of independence, skills, and behaviors (Luciano, 1994) and can provide an understanding of the contextual expectations for the child. Such insight is essential, because adaptive behavior is contingent upon the demands of a given social group.

In young children with additional physical disabilities assessment of adaptive behavior is often more challenging, and assessors must allow adequate time and opportunity for task completion. Luciano (1994) cautioned that young children with various disabilities can develop different strategies as they move toward greater independence. For example, young children with visual impairments may display greater reliance on auditory and tactile strategies, whereas those with hearing impairments may demonstrate more reliance on visual learning. A young child with motor-based difficulties may display alternate techniques for exploring the environment and manipulating objects. The alternative manner in which young children with physical disabilities demonstrates skills and independence can be considered adaptive, despite variation from how those without physical disabilities may display the skill.

Developmental Issues for Young Children

As indicated throughout this chapter, careful attention needs to be given to skills, abilities, and behaviors as they relate to developmental expectations. Behaviors reflecting a disability typically are those that are excessive or deficient based on what would be expected of a specific child at a given age. Of particular interest for eligibility determination is performance within and outside the assessment process, as well as behaviors that interfere with the young child's development of interpersonal skills (Luciano, 1994). Three areas are particularly relevant to the assessment of young children: separation, autonomy, and activity level and attention span. The following section examines these areas as they relate to the assessment of young children.

Separation Issues

Behaviors involving separation are important developmental markers for assessors of young children. For this reason it is critical to observe the young child's willingness to separate from caregivers, as well as adjustment to the assessment setting (Sattler, 1992). Assessors should recognize that young children often are apprehensive in unfamiliar settings and should avoid misinterpreting apprehension as significant separation difficulty.

Issues of separation can be largely developmental, making knowledge of developmentally appropriate behaviors essential for assessors. Two developmental periods generally are characterized by separation difficulties. The first period lasts from approximately 6 to 18 months of age when young children demonstrate wariness of strangers (Wallace, Larsen, & Elksnin, 1992). Assessors conducting an assessment with a young child of this age should recognize the developmental appropriateness of this separation difficulty. The second period generally extends from eighteen months until approximately 3 to $3\frac{1}{2}$ years of age. According to Luciano (1994), young children typically are able to separate from primary caregivers for brief periods by 3 to $3\frac{1}{2}$ years of age. Recognition that developmental phases are highly variable will help assessors avoid inaccurate conclusions.

Anticipating separation difficulty during specific developmental periods can assist assessors in preventing resistant reactions. One approach is to conduct the assessment in the young child's home when feasible. This technique is consistent with current assessment practices that focus on naturalistic settings, including home and school environments (Hills, 1993b; National Association of School Psychologists, 1999). Assessments conducted in these settings allow assessors to elicit behaviors and skills that might not be observed in an unfamiliar setting. Parental presence in the home environment has also been described as beneficial (Bucy, Smith, & Landau, 1999).

Although conducting an assessment in a young child's home may be advisable, it is not always feasible. As a result, assessment teams are sometimes required to utilize assessment sites. Several suggestions have been identified to reduce separation difficulty for young children in unfamiliar settings. Luciano (1994) provided some techniques that may assist with separation difficulty. First, assessors can promote comfort by allowing the young child to become familiar with the assessment setting; for example, a period of familiarization in the waiting area in which the young child is allowed to explore the environment. Second, assessors can interact with the young child and the parents/caregivers in the waiting room. Third,

assessors can describe assessment activities and "games" to be done in the testing room. If the young child is still unable to separate, the parents/caregivers can be invited into the assessment room. Luciano believes that caregiver inclusion is recommended for children under the age of 3.

Separation difficulty also can be reduced by assessing the young child over several occasions, thus allowing for the establishment of rapport and increased comfort level. If separation difficulties persist despite parental presence in the assessment room, parental support, and parental encouragement, then assessors should report the difficulty (Luciano, 1994). Observations in naturalistic environments often allow the assessor to gain a better understanding of the young child without triggering separation difficulty.

Autonomy Issues

Related to issues of separation is the development of autonomy. Generally, autonomy involves a young child's development of independence, with reduced reliance upon primary caregivers. Progressive movement toward increased independence and separation is typical among young children. Excessive struggles with issues of autonomy can lead to behavior that is unresponsive to adult direction, even during structured activities. According to Bagnato and Neisworth (1991), oppositional behavior can be expected at certain ages or developmental levels based on developing autonomy and independence, along with a lack of experience with assessment task demands. For example, a young child seeking to establish autonomy might tantrum, refuse assessor directives, or appear noncompliant toward assessment activities. In a less severe form, autonomy might be observed in self-directed exploration of the assessment environment (Luciano, 1994).

Assessors should exercise caution in immediately attributing noncompliant behavior to issues of autonomy. Although oppositional behavior might reflect difficulty with autonomy, it may also be a function of difficulty in one or more areas of functioning, such as attention span, memory deficits, speech/language deficits, anxiety, or other factors. Oppositional behavior should also be examined from a behavioral perspective to determine if the observed behavioral difficulty is merely a function of a behavior pattern in which the young child has been reinforced for noncompliant behavior. This can be assessed by comparing the young child's behavior (e.g., noncompliance) against developmental expectations (i.e., issues of autonomy). If the young child's behavior is not characteristic of a developmental period, then questions involving a behavior pattern will emerge. In addition to comparing behavior and developmental level, assessors can observe parent-child interactions. For example, if a child successfully avoids certain tasks (i.e., noncompliance) by seeking a parent/caregiver, and the parent/caregiver fosters the behavior by allowing the young child to refuse, then an avoidance pattern may be present. Pursuing these questions will assist the assessor to better understand challenging behavior and its likely underlying cause.

The impact of behaviors resulting from autonomy issues must also be described in terms of their impact on assessment results. Bracken (1991) cautioned that poor cooperation should not be assumed to represent lack of ability. Although behaviors associated with autonomy issues can negatively impact test performance, they provide valuable information on developmental progression and degree of independence. Should the young child demonstrate oppositional behavior and refuse to engage in assessment tasks, Luciano (1994) recommended focusing on spontaneous behaviors. Self-directed spontaneous behaviors, such as storytelling and block-building, can provide rich information regarding a number of areas of development (e.g., speech/language,

problem-solving, play skills, social skills, motor development, cognitive abilities).

Activity Level and Attention Span

Two areas of performance that impact assessment results include activity level and attention span. Although their impact on assessment results requires considerable attention, they can also be assessed within the context of developmental expectations and impact on daily functioning. Activity levels during assessment tasks as well as during naturalistic observations should be examined. Cross-setting comparisons are essential because assessors determine the degree to which activity level facilitates or inhibits daily performance (Wallace, Larsen, & Elksnin, 1992). Activity level is also important because it can reflect the young child's self-regulation skills. According to Luciano (1994), it "is important to distinguish between a naturally high activity level, which may not interfere with learning and task performance, and excessively high activity or impulsivity, which may suggest limited ability to inhibit a response that does interfere with task performance" (p. 38). Assessors may compare the individual child's task participation, amount of tasks completed, need for structure, and need for prompting with others of the same age/developmental level. This is sometimes complicated by the fact that high activity level and energy during learning and engagement are often developmentally appropriate.

Attention span can also enhance or inhibit daily functioning and assessment results. From a developmental perspective, young children's attention spans tend to be short. Although there is significant variability within and between individuals, it has been suggested that young children's attention span is generally less than 15 minutes (Luciano, 1994). As such, assessors should not interpret a developmentally appropriate attention span as inattention. Excessive inattention and impulsivity, however, can negatively impact assessment performance (Bracken, 1983) as well as reflect difficulty with self-regulation of behavior. Poor performance associated with limited attention span can lead to inaccurate results that fail to reflect the young child's actual ability and skill levels.

Qualitative observations provide extensive information on activity level and attention span. When assessing activity level and attention span, assessors should examine results across settings to ensure that levels of behavior are consistent. If not consistent, assessors are compelled to identify the nature of the environments or tasks that explain the variability. The young child's ability to self-regulate behavior in a developmentally appropriate manner has significant implications for intervention and future learning.

Summary

Qualitative observation techniques assume a critical role in the assessment of young children. One of the greatest assets of qualitative observation techniques involves flexibility. These procedures can serve as a primary assessment instrument for a given domain, or be used to validate and supplement information obtained by other testing instruments. The broad applicability of the techniques is well-recognized and useful for all settings in which assessment procedures are conducted. This can include naturalistic and formal assessment settings (McLean, 1996).

Qualitative observation represents a central assessment tool that is also useful across disciplines and is especially beneficial based on requirements for multidisciplinary and multidimensional assessment (McLean, 1996; Sattler, 1992). Qualitative observations can provide a rich and in-depth understanding of the young child. Young children's lack of conformity to typical test-taking procedures warrants the use of more appropriate techniques in the assessment process (Katz, 1997). Application of qualitative observations, however, requires that professionals have adequate education and training. As previously noted, Luciano (1994) has suggested that assessors may initially want to choose a more structured

qualitative observation method to obtain specific information. As the professional develops expertise over time, less structured and more spontaneous techniques will likely emerge. Qualitative methods of observation will continue to serve a primary role in the assessment of young children.

References

Alessi, G. (1988). Direct observation methods for emotional/behavioral problems. In E. S. Shapiro & T. R. Kratochwill (Eds.), *Behavioral assessment in schools* (pp. 14–75). New York: Guilford Press.

American Psychiatric Association (1994). *Diagnostic and statistical manual of mental disorders* (4th ed.) Washington, DC: Authors.

Association for Advanced Training in the Behavioral Sciences (1997). *Psychology written licensure examination review*. Ventura, CA: Author.

Bagnato, S. J., & Neisworth, J. T. (1991). *Assessment for early intervention: Best practice for professionals*. New York: Guilford Press.

Bagnato, S. J., & Neisworth, J. T. (1994). A national study of the social and treatment "invalidity" of intelligence testing for early intervention. *School Psychology Quarterly*, 9, 81–102.

Bagnato, S. J., Neisworth, J. T., & Munson, S. M. (1997). *Linking assessment and early intervention: An authentic curriculum-based approach*. Baltimore: Brookes.

Beaty, J. (1990). *Observing development of the young child*. Upper Saddle River, NJ: Merrill/Prentice Hall.

Bracken, B. A. (1983). Observing the assessment behavior of preschool children. In K. A. Paget & B. A. Bracken (Eds.), *The psychoeducational assessment of preschool children* (pp. 63–79). Orlando, FL: Grune & Stratton.

Bracken, B. A. (1991). The clinical observation of preschool assessment behavior. In B. A. Bracken (Ed.), *The psychoeducational assessment of preschool children* (pp. 40–52). Boston: Allyn & Bacon.

Bucy, J. E., Smith, T., & Landau, A. (1999). Assessment of preschool children with developmental disabilities and at-risk conditions. In I. V. Nuttall, I. Romero, & J. Kalesnik (Eds.), *Assessing and screening preschoolers*, (2nd ed.) (pp. 318–339). Boston: Allyn & Bacon.

Gordon, A. M., & Browne, K. W. (1985). *Beginnings and beyond: Foundations in early childhood education*. New York: Delmar.

Grossman, H. J. (1983). *Classification and mental retardation*. Washington, DC: American Association on Mental Deficiency.

Heward, W. L. (2000). *Exceptional children: An introduction to special education* (6th ed.). Upper Saddle River, NJ: Merrill/Prentice Hall.

Hills, T. W. (1993a). Reaching potentials through appropriate assessment. In S. Bredekamp & T. Rosengrant (Eds.), *Reaching potentials: Appropriate curriculum and assessment for young children*, Volume one (pp. 43–63). Washington, DC: National Association for the Education of Young Children.

Hills, T. W. (1993b). Assessment in context: Teachers and children at work. *Young Children*, 48(5), 20–28.

Jones, R. R., Reid, J. B., & Patterson, G. R. (1975). Naturalistic observation in clinical assessment. In P. McReynolds (Ed.), *Advances in psychological assessment, Volume three* (pp. 42–95). San Francisco: Jossey-Bass.

Katz, L. G. (1997). A developmental approach to assessment of young children. ERIC *Digest*. Urbana-Champaign, IL: ERIC Clearinghouse.

Keller, H. R. (1986). Behavioral observation approaches to personality assessment. In H. M. Knoff (Ed.), *The assessment of child and adolescent personality* (pp. 353–397). New York: Guilford Press.

Luciano, L. (1994). Qualitative observations of assessment behaviors. In J. A. Bondurant-Utz & L. Luciano (Eds.), A *practical guide to infant and preschool assessment in special education* (pp. 27–39). Needham, MA: Allyn & Bacon.

McLean, M. (1996). Assessment and its importance in early intervention/early childhood special education. In M. McLean, D. B. Bailey Jr., & M. Wolery (Eds.), *Assessing infants and preschoolers with special needs* (2nd ed.) (pp. 1–22). Upper Saddle River, NJ: Merrill/Prentice Hall.

National Association of School Psychologists (1999). Early childhood assessment. *Position Statement*.

Sattler, J. M. (1992). *Assessment of children* (3rd ed.). San Diego, CA: Author.

Taylor, R. T. (1993). *Assessment of exceptional students: Educational and psychological procedures* (3rd ed.). Needham Heights, MA: Allyn & Bacon.

Wallace, G., Larsen, S. C., & Elksnin, L. K. (1992). *Educational assessment of learning problems: Testing for teaching* (2nd ed.). Needham Heights, MA: Allyn & Bacon.

Wodrich, D. L. (1997). *Children's psychological testing: A guide for nonpsychologists* (3rd ed.). Baltimore: Brookes.

Assessing Young Children with Severe Disabilities

Catherine Cook-Cottone

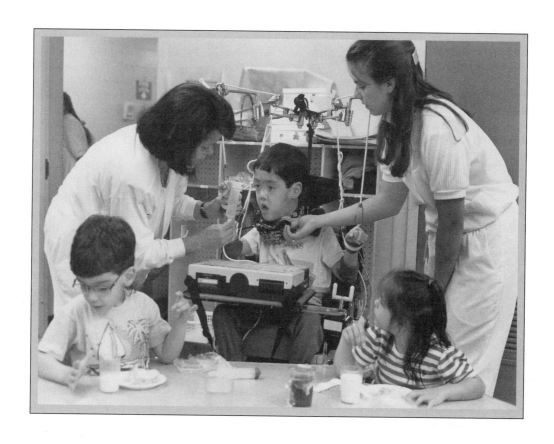

Overview

Children with severe disabilities constitute an extremely diverse and heterogeneous group. This category includes children with visual and hearing impairments, motor delays, affective/behavioral impairments, overall developmental delay, and severe childhood illnesses. Although they are very different in many ways, they all share severe functional impairment; that is, owing to the intensity of their physical, mental, health, or emotional problems, they require highly specialized education, social, psychological, and medical services to maximize their full potential for useful and meaningful participation in society and for self-fulfillment (Heward, 2000). For these children, effective educational program implementation must build on existing functional and intellectual skills. However, owing to the complexity and variability inherent in each child with a severe disability, educators cannot rely on functional prescriptions based on the type of disorder. Consequently, best practices are guided by appropriate and valid assessment.

Unique Assessment Issues

Individualized assessment is a key component of successful service provision for children with severe disabilities (McConnell, 2000). For example, both Nicole and Jacob have cerebral palsy and visual impairment. Although their diagnoses are the same, their needs are quite different. Nicole needs one-on-one instruction to provide the intensive, behaviorally-based instructional methods and positioning assistance that she requires to learn. Conversely, Jacob learns best in a small-group setting, with ongoing physical therapy and orientation and mobility consultation support for his teacher. As illustrated by Nicole's and Jacob's very different educational needs, a highly individualized assessment and description of current functional levels is required (McConnell, 2000).

Once functional strengths and weakness are identified, prescriptive services can be defined. In sum, successful educational intervention must be assessment driven and specific to the child's strengths and weaknesses.

There are problems inherent to the assessment of infants and preschoolers who are severely disabled. The child with severe disabilities often presents with limitations that can result in less reliable standardized assessment procedures. Specifically, the characteristics of the child's severe disability may lead to significant underestimation of such characteristics as intellectual functioning and problem-solving ability. The child may have the capacity to perform the thought process the item was designed to measure, yet response demands mask these abilities. To illustrate, the child may have the intellectual capacity to perform multistep directions, understand color concepts, and conceptualize sorting, yet receive a score indicating "no credit" on the Bayley-2 (a standardized developmental assessment tool). Unfortunately for this child, the item measuring these skills requires the child to sort colored pegs into cups using his fingers to grasp the pegs, arm and trunk control to move the pegs to the cups, and fine motor control and visual/motor integration to release the pegs into the cups. Although cognitively capable of the task, he cannot motorically manipulate colored pegs. Consequently, he cannot show his receptive language skills, color knowledge, or sorting capabilities. The inexperienced observer may assume the child lacks these intellectual skills when, in fact, he lacks the ability to express these skills in this modality.

This chapter discusses issues germane to assessment of infants and preschoolers with severe disabilities. First, assessment of children with severe disabilities should be completed with an understanding of the use and capacity of the standardized assessment tools, as well as an ability to capitalize on observations, incorporate task analysis, and utilize a team approach for convergent assessment. These techniques are described and explained. Next, each aspect of the assessment process should be implemented within the context of a full understanding of the impact of the known disability on overall functioning (Luciano, 1994). To address this need, important assessment guidelines and tools for use with young children with severe disabilities are presented according to type of deficit or disorder.

Standardized Assessment

Historically, standardized assessments have been required to document need and access services (Neisworth & Bagnato, 1992; Preator & McAllister, 1995; McConnell, 2000). It has been accepted that they provide a reliable measure of ability and maintain predictive validity. However, researchers argue that utilization of standardized tools with young children does not fill these needs (Neisworth & Bagnato, 1992; Preator & McAllister, 1995; McConnell, 2000). Reliability and predictive validity studies yield disappointing results (Neisworth & Bagnato, 1992; McConnell, 2000). As discussed earlier, such findings are amplified among those with severe disabilities. Use of standardized measures with this population must be supplemented with a more qualitative assessment process (Preator & McAllister, 1995; McConnell, 2000). A more meaningful assessment can be accomplished by adapting materials, the environment, or the approach (Luciano, 1994; McConnell, 2000). Luciano (1994) noted that adaptations may alter the validity of some measures, thus precluding use of standardized scores. A careful and descriptive reporting style is required. Such effort results in the rich and informative convergence of qualitative and quantitative data (Preator & McAllister, 1995) and a highly useful assessment.

In choosing a test, it is important to consider response modality and expectations. Best results come from a careful match of test response mode with the child's capacity to respond. The goal is to find the most reliable means of assessing a child's skills with minimal penalty for the child's specific disability (Luciano, 1994). Again, it is very important that any changes in standardized procedures be described and justified. Of note, responses to altered items should be interpreted as estimates of functioning (Gerken, 1991). Further, a qualitative description should be included for all items attempted. This provides valuable information about the child's functioning. Consequently, the assessment yields a report of successful versus unsuccessful item completion when given in standardized form, a description of altered procedures and consequent success or failure, and a qualitative description of the child's processes as she attempted the item in all conditions. It is important to include qualitative information such as how much scaffolding, or support, did the child require for successful completion of the item? Ultimately, when assessing infants and preschoolers with severe disabilities, assessors will find that the less formal assessment procedures (e.g., Observation, Play Assessment, Interview, and Task Analysis) will provide the bulk of the assessment information. Preator and McAllister (1995) recommended searching for trends in multiple measures, from multiple sources, in multiple settings, on multiple occasions. The resulting report, then, capitalizes on standardized and qualitative assessment by describing trends.

Team Approach and Convergent Assessment

Infants and preschoolers are typically assessed using a team approach (Vinson, 1996). Because of the problems with standardized testing, the transdisciplinary approach is invaluable with the population who is severely disabled. Transdisciplinary assessment allows for convergent assessment. Specifically, convergent assessment follows a qualitative model and finds its validity and utility in convergence, rather than in standardized measures. Convergent assessment refers to the synthesis of information from several sources, such as instruments, settings, observations, interviews, and occasions, to appraise developmental status and complete assessment purposes, which are identification, prescription, progress evaluation, and prediction (Bagnato, Neisworth, & Munson, 1997). Although it is generally accepted that traditional psychometrics or norm referenced tests do not work for children with severe disabilities, convergent assessment provides a robust and natural sampling of the child's skills and an integrated composite of the family's needs (Bagnato, Neisworth, & Munson, 1997). By utilizing the knowledge and experience of each of the specialists (ranging from the parents to the developmental pediatrician), transdisciplinary assessment targets program development on the child's authentic developmental progress and functional performance and does not make inferential prescriptions based on invalid standardized scores.

Task Analysis

Task analysis can be extremely useful in the assessment of the child with a severe disability (Luciano, 1994). Task analysis can answer the question, "How accurately or completely can a child perform a task?" (Berg, Wacker, & Steege, 1995). In this approach, the task is broken down into smaller subskills that are requisite to the skill being assessed (Berg, Wacker, & Steege, 1995; Hallahan & Kauffman, 2000). The child is scored on performance of each subskill, earning either a plus for successful demonstration of a subskill or a minus for an unsuccessful attempt (Berg, Wacker, & Steege, 1995). Consequently, task analysis translates quite nicely to intervention. The assessor is able to determine the extent to which a child demonstrates portions of a skill and at which point assistance or intervention should be implemented (Luciano, 1994).

Berg and colleagues (1995) suggested that an alternative method for assessing a performance

by task analysis is to describe the level of assistance required to complete each task step completely. Assistance level can range from no assistance to complete physical guidance, as in hand-over-hand guidance (Berg, Wacker, & Steege, 1995). In these cases, levels of assistance can be categorized and numbered. The number rather than the plus or minus, is placed next to the task step (Berg, Wacker, & Steege, 1995). Berg and colleagues (1995) reported this technique is also a useful way to monitor progress as the assessor documents the child's movement to more independent functioning (Steege, Wacker, & McMahon, 1987).

Luciano (1994) suggested that through task analysis the assessor is better able to identify aspects of the child's difficulty in performing a task and the effect of specific disabilities. Berg and colleagues (1995) reported that task analysis is especially useful in educational settings because it provides information regarding types of errors as well as the child's overall level of accuracy. Further, task analysis allows the assessor to explore motivation and skill issues (Berg, Wacker, & Steege, 1995). For example, if the child attempts each of the task steps and cannot successfully complete some of the steps owing to error, then it is clear that the child has demonstrated a skill deficit; conversely, if the child does not attempt the task steps, then motivation may be part of the difficulty (Berg, Wacker, & Steege, 1995). Motivational issues can be further explored using contingent reinforcers (Berg, Wacker, & Steege, 1995).

Task analysis often involves skill sequencing and changing of responses (Luciano, 1994). In skill sequencing, the task is explicated through a sequence of skills that lead to mastery of the more advanced skills (Benner, 1992; Luciano, 1994). For example, Benner (1992) explained that subskills of independent toileting include muscle control, anticipation of need, dressing and undressing, standing or sitting balance, general hygiene concepts, and an ability to follow a multistep process. In chaining, the assessor identifies specific behaviors as they occur during the completion of a task (Benner, 1992; Luciano, 1994). Luciano (1994) explained that the assessor describes, in detail, the skill steps needed in sequence (as links in a chain), and describes the exact point (or link) at which the chain breaks. For example, in order to transition in circle time, the child must complete the following chain of skills: (a) attends to teacher's verbal prompts to move to circle time, (b) stops current activity, (c) walks to the circle area, (d) finds place in circle, (e) sits on place in circle, and (f) attends to circle time instruction. Through sequencing or chaining, the task analysis provides instruction-ready information.

Accommodations for Specific Disorders

The assessment of children with severe disabilities requires attention to the unique needs and sensitivities of a very heterogeneous group of children. Depending on the type of disorder or disability the child has, the assessment recommendations may vary significantly. Although many of the assessment accommodations can be applied to various disabilities, each specific disability presents with its own unique set of characteristic needs. For example, although both are considered severely disabled, the child with deaf-blindness and the child with autism present with very different assessment needs. The remainder of this chapter describes the specific needs and sensitivities of infants and preschoolers with various disorders or disabilities including neuromotor impairment, visual impairment, hearing impairment, deaf-blindness, social/emotional disorder, autism, human immunodeficiency virus (HIV) and acquired immunodeficiency syndrome (AIDS), childhood cancer, and prematurity. This guide is designed to provide practical tips for parents and educators. Table 7–1 on pages 163–164 lists assessment tools by the area of disability they address.

Motor (or Neuromotor) Impairments

Children use movement to organize their environment, to communicate and interact physically, to change postures and adjust positions, to respond to the demands of the environment, and to meet their own needs (Campbell, Kolobe, Osten, Lenke, & Girolami, 1995; Cowden & Torrey, 1995). Consequently, the neuromotor development of children is extremely important to overall development and learning (Shine, 1998). For example, a study of children with spina bifida found that they spent more time on simple manipulation behaviors, such as taking blocks out of the box, and less time engaging in task-orientated behaviors, such as using blocks to build a house (Landry, Robinson, Copeland, & Garner, 1993). As illustrated, owing to neuromotor impairments, more time is spent on basic motor control. Specifically, children with neuromotor impairments have difficulty with postural control (control of the body's position in space for stability, balance, and orientation), stability (the ability to maintain the center of body mass within the base of support), and orientation (the alignment of the body's segments with respect to one another as needed for the task) (Campbell, et al., 1995; Shumway-Cook & Woollacott, 1993). Meaningful developmental assessment of a child with motor impairment must minimize the effects of this motor involvement and maximize conceptual understanding, problem solving, and social communication (Bagnato & Neisworth, 1991; Luciano, 1994).

It is very easy to underestimate the child's functional level because neuromotor restrictions severely limit response modality. It is important to address positioning, adaptive equipment needs, and response limitations, and assess reliable modes of response (Bagnato & Neisworth, 1991). When positioning cannot adequately reduce neuromotor complications, alternative modes of response should be considered (Luciano, 1994). Of note, a child's attempts may not yield successful task completion, yet a clear intent was demonstrated. To fully capture intellectual functioning, recognition, acknowledgment, and reporting of intent are important. Further, affective responses may be an indicator or cognitive awareness and awareness of desired responses (Luciano, 1994). As such, this should also be recorded.

Authentic Criterial Competencies. Bagnato and colleagues (1997) suggested authentic criterial competencies as the most equitable modification in childhood assessment. Using this assessment method, functional skills are hierarchically sequenced, described, and defined according to the function achieved rather than by the topography of the behavior to be assessed (Bagnato, Neisworth, & Munson, 1997). These researchers stress standardization of the behavior being assessed, and not standardization of the situations (administration) or response. Bagnato and colleagues (1997) suggested competencies such as "get across the room by self." In this case, the child must be able to get across the room; however, he can do so using a wheelchair, a walker, or by walking. Another example is "initiated social interaction." The child can initiate social interaction through computer-assisted communication, a communication board, or with a verbal "hello."

Process Approach. Assessment typically focuses on the child's current developmental status. Adaptive assessment allows exploration of the child's learning process (Luciano, 1994). The process or child-referenced approach is different in that the child's learning process is explored and documented. Although the child's developmental status remains important, the process of gaining skills is emphasized. The assessor assesses how the child learns, under what conditions the child can perform a task, and what portions of the tasks are most readily performed (Luciano, 1994). Rosenberg and Robinson (1990) suggested that the process approach can also be a meaningful way to assess the strengths and weakness of young children.

The OBSERVE Method. The OBSERVE method (Wachs & Sheehan, 1988) integrates authentic assessment and the process approach by examining the child's ability to learn new behaviors within the context of various learning conditions. Within this model, the child is observed in a variety of contexts (i.e., circle time, free play, group time, meals, outside play, bathroom). As the child moves through his daily routine, developmental interactions are observed and identified (Luciano, 1994). Five levels of interaction, based on Piaget's sequence of sensorimotor cognitive development, are utilized to describe the child's learning processes.

First, attentional interactions, or the capacity to attend to and discriminate between stimuli, are assessed, such as looking at a caregiver when talking or singing, smiling when talked to, or orienting toward the voice when the child's name is called (Wachs & Sheehan, 1988). Second, contingency interactions, or the use of simple, undifferentiated forms of behavior to initiate and sustain control over reinforcing consequences, are observed (i.e., smiles to get an adult to continue an activity, reaches to initiate interaction, picks up a toy to examine it). At the third level, differentiated interactions are assessed; that is, the coordination and regulation of behavior that reflects elaboration and progress toward conventionalization (i.e., uses head shake or facial expression to indicate yes or no, imitates actions of other children, shows the ability to feed a doll with a bottle). Level four addresses encoded interactions or the use of conventionalized forms of behavior that are context bound and that depend on referents as a basis for evoking the behaviors (Wachs & Sheehan, 1988). Encoded behaviors include using a symbol board to select the food she wants, putting dolls in appropriate situations when playing house, or using a communication board to indicate a desired activity. The last level is symbolic interaction, which is the use of conventionalized forms of behavior to communicate a message in the absence of reference-giving clues

(Wachs & Sheehan, 1988). The assessor observes the child communicating using the communication board, generating his own ideas and comments, and initiating communicative behaviors.

The assessment provides a context-based description of the child's interactional capabilities and describes the developmental processes that are present during the period of the assessment observation. An authentic observational assessment allows for a qualitative description of the child's current learning processes not bound by the typical standardized assessment. As described, this type of assessment may be less likely to underestimate the child's actual functioning because it is based on authentic, environmental data.

The ROADMAP. Cowden and Torrey (1995) provided the ROADMAP (Role of Assessment Directed Movements, Actions, and Patterns) model to assess the motor actions of young children. The model defines and describes assessment inputs, processes, products, outputs, and outcomes (Cowden & Torrey, 1995). This method recommends the combined use of formal and informal measures. Informal observation, free-play, standardized assessment, need identification, and objective planning are included (Cowden & Torrey, 1995). These researchers also provided an overview of recommended assessment instruments utilized for motor assessment purposes.

Examiner Skills. Wilhelm, Johnson, and Eisert (1986) indicated the importance of experience, skills, collaboration, and consultation. For children with neuromotor impairments, examiner skills must include the ability to incorporate traditional standardized, quantitative assessment and less formal, sometimes observational and collateral qualitative assessment. The assessor must collaborate well with other professions, such as occupational therapists, nurses, speech and language pathologists, and physical therapists.

The examiner must be capable of reporting findings in a manner that accurately reflects successful standardized responses as well as observed and reported developmental progress. Wilhelm and colleagues (1986) suggested that it is easy both to underestimate and overestimate the skills of a child with severe disabilities. Relying too heavily on standardized assessment procedures, lack of awareness of biases and prejudice, and low expectations can result in an assessment that underreports skills. Conversely, skills may be overreported owing to inaccurate use or reporting of supports, inappropriate assistance, or lack of acknowledgment of a wish for the child to do well. The assessor must be able to integrate a qualitative, supportive, and sensitive approach and maintain objectivity.

Positioning. Proper positioning and seating are critically important for children with neuromotor disabilities (Heward, 2000). Proper positioning affords greater access to and more independent interaction with the environment (Luciano, 1994). Neuromotor impairments place the additional demands of posture maintenance on the child. As indicated previously, the child's attentional system and energy are directed primarily at accomplishing stability. Consequently other tasks such as learning and social engagement receive only peripheral attention and focus. Single task demands become multitask. The child becomes more quickly fatigued and frustrated. Proper positioning can alleviate added systemic demands freeing the child to apply full effort and attention to the assessment.

Proper positioning is tailored to meet individual needs. If the child needs assistance maintaining an upright posture, then use of supportive seating devices, inserts, wedges, and strapping should be considered (Luciano, 1994). Stability positively affects use of the upper body and allows the child to expend energy on visual and other behaviors associated with the task (Amerson, 1999). When addressing positioning and seating, the feet should be stabilized, level, and supported on the floor, a stool, or on wheelchair peddles (Heller, Alberto, Forney, & Schwartzman, 1996). Second, the hips should be back toward the chair and weight should be evenly distributed on both sides of the buttocks (Heller, et al., 1996). Third, the shoulders and upper trunk should be supported in the upright position using a seat belt, leg separator, shoulder straps, and chest straps (Heller, et al., 1996). Fourth, a normal curvature of the spine should be facilitated by positioning the trunk in the midline position (Heller, et al., 1996). Fifth, the shoulders should be positioned in the midline position, pulled back, and prone (Heller, et al., 1996). Finally, the neck, head, and face should be positioned so that the child is facing forward and in the midline position.

In general, a variety of working positions should be used to help reinforce basic stability and movement (Amerson, 1999). Caution is recommended when manipulating the child's head to direct gaze. Amerson (1999) warned that abrupt changes in positions can influence overall muscle tone. It may be helpful to encourage the child to work with his arms extended or to stabilize the upper body by bearing weight on one arm while completing the test item with the other arm (Amerson, 1999). Be sure to place target items within an arc that is within the child's reach (Amerson, 1999).

For children who need help bringing their hands to midline, corner chairs and side-lying devices are useful (Luciano, 1994). Work should be placed at a height generally midway between waist and shoulder level (Amerson, 1999). Be careful to determine the child's optimal working distance from the work surface (Amerson, 1999). Children in wheelchairs sometimes prefer a lap board to a tabletop, finding it more accessible (Bagnato & Neisworth, 1991; Luciano, 1994). For some, standing or prone boards, allowing for attachment of table surfaces, provide the most comfortable and stable positioning (Bagnato & Neisworth, 1991; Luciano, 1994). Supine or side-lying positions may be helpful

for some tasks (Amerson, 1999). Amerson (1999) suggested that when utilizing the former, the child should be placed supine on the edge of a wedge, allowing the arms and hands to reach the floor. Materials intended for manipulation should be placed on the floor. This positioning allows the child to watch his hands while manipulating items (Amerson, 1999).

Assistive Technology. Assistive technology is often used to facilitate response and communication. Assistive technology devices vary from the very simplistic pencil holder (low-tech) to a sophisticated or high-tech communication board (Lane & Mistrett, 1996). According to the IDEA, assistive technology is "any item, piece of equipment, or product system, whether acquired commercially off the shelf, modified, or customized, that is used to increase, maintain, or improve functional capabilities of individuals with disabilities." Lane and Mistrett (1996) suggested that low-tech applications (i.e., simple tools, commercially available devices and solutions) can be readily available, inexpensive, and require minimal training for the user. They recommend low-tech solutions such as adjusting the seating of a child with a rolled towel or a beveled phone book or using a picture board for communication (Lane & Mistrett, 1996). Both high-tech and low-tech devices can facilitate communication, adapt test stimuli, or modify the testing environment.

Modification of the response modes available to the child can be helpful (Bagnato, Neisworth, & Munson, 1997). Children with neuromotor impairments often have difficulty in effectively expressing themselves verbally, motorically, or both. The levels of impairment can vary significantly. The goal is to maximize opportunity to demonstrate understanding, intent, or mastery of the assessment task (Luciano, 1994).

Carefully adapt the response mode to each child's expressive strengths and weaknesses. Children with severe disabilities can utilize computers, communication boards, light wands, head pointers (Bagnato, Neisworth, & Munson, 1997). A head-mounted pointer stick and a keyboard guard will enable a child with limited fine-motor control to respond using a computer (Heward, 2000). Lane and Mistrett (1996) suggested low-tech, commercially available options, including picture boards, Big Mack, tape recorder, Dynafox, AlphaTalker, and Macaw. Soft-tip pens, which require less pressure, can be used when writing is required. Children with poor grasp can utilize switches, peg-like handles on puzzle pieces, hand splints and straps, and modified utensils (Bagnato & Neisworth, 1991; Luciano, 1994). Robinson and Fieber (1988) suggested the use of eye gaze or eye pointing as a response mode so long as no ocular-motor problems exist.

Modification of stimulus characteristics is sometimes necessary to facilitate assessment (Bagnato, Neisworth, & Munson, 1997); for example, it may be helpful to increase the size of an object. To illustrate, a test item may require the child to stack a tower of six blocks. You may utilize six larger blocks that are more easily grasped by the child with neuromotor impairment. If the test requires the child to place small colored discs on matching color spots, then enlarge the discs and the spots; the item is measuring color-matching skills, not the manipulations of small colored discs. If the task requires the child to assemble a puzzle, then add hook-and-loop tape or felt to the bottom of the pieces to eliminate sliding and displacement. A puzzle board that assesses shape discrimination (circle, square, and triangle) can be replaced by larger shape puzzles with grasping pegs on each shape. Using these modifications, shape discrimination is assessed, without the added assessment of the child's ability to grasp thin, flat, plastic shapes. Lane and Mistrett (1996) recommended the use of low-tech options, such as extenders/stabilizers, larger knobs, switches, and magnifiers.

Environmental accommodations can also be very useful during the assessment process.

Bagnato and Neisworth (1991) suggested adapting the tabletop with a nonslip substance (i.e., Dycem) that will help keep toys and manipulatives from sliding around. Some children perform best when utilizing a slanted work surface, such as easels, wedges, or reading stands (Amerson, 1999). Dycem matting also helps stabilize materials on slanted surfaces (Amerson, 1999). Environmental accommodations can be coupled with stabilizing positioning to achieve optimal effect.

Assisted Movement. Assisted movement can help to minimize the effects of the disability. The examiner provides hand/arms stability, strength, or improved grasp (Robinson & Fieber, 1988). The child is able to demonstrate his cognitive awareness and problem-solving skills, which typically can be inhibited by impaired motor dexterity (Luciano, 1994). When documenting tasks are completed in this manner, the assessor should tentatively report responses and clearly explicate supports given. Luciano (1994) suggested that even the most skilled and experienced practitioners can unintentionally guide a response not intended by the child, and warned that anticipated responses, assumption of estimated skills, and reaction to involuntary muscle movement can lead the child's response.

Visual Impairments

The American Foundation for the Blind (AFB) (2000) explains that the majority of learning in infants and young children takes place through vision and the effects of visual impairments are far-reaching. Soon after birth, infants who are visually impaired respond differently to their parents and their world (AFB, 2000; Hallahan & Kauffman, 2000). Early bonding experiences, emotional growth, and developmental gains depend on effective early intervention (AFB, 2000). Further, most traditional educational strategies are based on vision as the primary modality of sensory input (AFB, 2000). As the child with visual impairment grows, the absence or reduction of vision significantly and sometimes dramatically limits the child's understanding of the world (AFB, 2000). According to the AFB (2000), no other sense stimulates curiosity, helps to combine information, or invites exploration as effectively or efficiently as does vision. The AFB (2000) stresses that children with visual impairments can learn and even succeed academically, but they require specific interventions and modifications of their education program.

Adapted Techniques. Assessment of the educational needs of the child with visual impairment can be difficult in light of the impact of the disability on the child's experiences, opportunity to learn, and information processing (Davidson & Legouri, 1986). Serial assessments at short intervals (every 3 months) are recommended to monitor the child's development during the infant and preschool years (Davidson & Legouri, 1986). Suggestions are as follows:

1. Adjust the work surface so it is at a height midway between the child's waist and shoulder level (Amerson, 1999).
2. Be careful to determine the child's optimal working distance from the work surface (Amerson, 1999).
3. For students with impaired vision, present tasks that require visual attention when the child's energy level is highest (Amerson, 1999).
4. Use a slanted work surface (i.e., easel, wedge, or reading stand) with Dycem to help stabilize materials (Amerson, 1999).
5. Determine the most effective visual adaptations required by the child, such as color, size, contrast, lighting, simplicity of design, location, and distant (Amerson, 1999; Luciano, 1994).
6. Place target items in varied locations within an arm's-length arc (Amerson, 1999).
7. To increase the child's focus of energy on the visual skills required for task completion, reduce interfering sensory variables (Amerson, 1999; Luciano, 1994).

8. Give the infant or preschooler additional time to identify and attend to events (Luciano, 1994).
9. Observe and record how the child positions himself in the environment (Luciano, 1994).

Materials. Luciano (1994) suggested several important assessment material characteristics that are important to consider. First, materials should be bright and protected from glare (Luciano, 1994). Second, materials should utilize contrasting color combinations, that is, black on white or buff, or yellow on black, blue, or purple (Luciano, 1994). When conducting a play-based assessment, the assessor should use materials that offer more than just visual appeal (Luciano, 1994); for example, spinning toys, pinwheels, brightly colored yarn, pop beads, and slinky toys (Luciano, 1994). Finally, Luciano (1994) suggested that materials specifically designed for those with visual impairments may be useful (i.e., magnifying lenses and audio recordings).

Exploration. Infants and young children with visual impairments often experience delays in motor development or mobility (Hallahan & Kauffman, 2000). This appears to be due to the lack of visual stimuli experienced. Apparently, infants and preschoolers with visual impairments have not learned that there are items in their environment to pursue (Hallahan & Kauffman, 2000). This is further complicated by protective parents reluctant to allow the children to risk injury (Hallahan & Kauffman, 2000). It is believed that without specific training, some infants will not reach out for things they hear until well into their first year (Hallahan & Kauffman, 2000). Therefore, it is crucial to assess the motor development of the infant or preschooler with visual impairments to address risk of delay and to plan appropriate mobility training. This can be done through consultation with a mobility and orientation specialist or with the collaboration of a physical therapist.

Limited Research. Kundert, Kuhn, and Brown (1998) indicated that visual impairment is considered a low-incidence disability. Consequently, as with many other low-incidence disabilities, published research on best-practices for assessment has been limited (Luciano, 1994). Luciano (1994) cautioned that assessment efforts should proceed with caution and global generalizations regarding developmental level and potential of a particular child based on a short-term assessment should be avoided.

Selected Measures. When standardized assessment tools are necessary, infants and preschoolers with visual impairments should be assessed utilizing tests that provide specific adaptation instructions or normative data for children with visual impairments, Several assessment tools have been adapted or standardized for use with children with visual impairments, (Luciano, 1994); the level of instruction for the assessor and modifications for the child vary. Some tests are developed specifically for children with visual impairments, whereas others are modified for use with the specific populations. Tests described include tests of cognitive development, orientation and mobility, language development, and behavioral presentation. For an annotated list, please refer to Luciano (1994), Moore and McLaughlin (1992), or Bagnato and colleagues (1997).

First, the standardized assessment of intellectual ability or development can be completed using a variety of tools and methods. The tools developed specifically for the child with visual improvements include *The Informal Assessment of Developmental Skills for Visually Handicapped Students* (Swallow, Mangold, & Mangold, 1978) for ages birth to 16 years. This scale provides a compilation of criterion-referenced checklists and inventories (Moore & McLaughlin, 1992; Nuttall, Romero, & Kalesnik, 1992). *The Reynell-Zinkin Developmental Scales-Visually Impaired* (Reynell & Zinkin, 1979) includes ages birth to 5 years and specifies developmental expectation for the child with visual impairments

in seven domains: social adaptation, sensorimotor understanding, exploration of environment, response to sound and verbal comprehension, vocalization and expressive language (structure), expressive language (vocabulary and content), and communication (Bagnato, Neisworth, & Munson, 1997). Bagnato and colleagues (1997) reported that this assessment is particularly compatible with the Oregon Project Curriculum (described below). *The Tactile Test of Basic Concepts* (Caton, 1986) assesses the mastery of infant and preschool curriculum and concepts essential to understanding oral communication from kindergarten to second grade (Nuttall, Romero, & Kalesnik, 1992). This test includes raised drawings and detailed instructions (Nuttall, et al., 1992).

The Oregon Project Curriculum for Visually Impaired and Blind Preschooler Children (Brown, Simmons, & Methvin, 1994) provides a sequence commensurate with that for typically developing infants and preschoolers from birth to 5 years (Bagnato, Neisworth, & Munson, 1997). Development is emphasized in the following areas: cognition, language, self-help, socialization, fine motor, and gross motor. The assessment provides a unique coding system that notes skills that are appropriate for an infant or preschooler with a particular vision problem or whose development may be occurring at a rate slower than other children. Bagnato and colleagues (1997) reported that this instrument is sensitive enough to track progress.

Several other tests have been developed specifically for the child with visual impairment. The *Perkins-Binet Tests of Intelligence for the Blind* (Davis, 1980) were specifically designed for children with visual impairments from ages 3 to 18 years. According to Moore and McLaughlin (1992), other inventories designed specifically for children with visual impairments mentioned include the *Tactile Test of Basic Concepts* (Caton, 1986) covering ages 5 to 9 years. For a more complete list of other inventories designed specifically for children with visual impairments, see Moore and McLaughlin (1992).

When specialized assessment tools are not available, more commonly used tests of cognitive development are modified. For example, Moore and McLaughlin (1992) and Nuttall and colleagues (1992) suggested using selected subtests of the *Kaufman Assessment Battery for Children* (Kaufman & Kaufman, 1983) for children ages 2½ to 12½ years. Number Recall and Riddles are recommended specifically for children who are blind, because the receptive and expressive qualities of the items are auditory and verbal (Moore & McLaughlin, 1992; Nuttall, Romero, & Kalesnik, 1992). For those children with low-vision these researchers recommend Hand Movements, Number Recall, Riddles, Triangles, Word Order, Expressive Vocabulary, Faces & Places, and Arithmetic. To illustrate further, the *Stanford-Binet Intelligence Scale (4th ed.)* (Thorndike, Hagen, & Sattler, 1986) provides general adaptations for children with visual impairments, ages 2 years to adult; and modifications are recommended for the use of braille (Moore & McLaughlin, 1992; Nuttall, Romero, & Kalesnik, 1992); these researchers caution that often preschoolers have not learned braille. Other scales recommended by Moore and McLaughlin (1992) for adaptation include the *Battelle Developmental Inventory* (Newborg, Stock, Wnek, Guidubaldi, & Svinicki, 1988) for children ages birth to 8 years; *Brigance Diagnostic Inventory of Early Development-Revised Edition* (Brigance, 1991), ages birth to 6 years, 11 months; *The Callier-Azusa Scale: Assessment of Deaf-Blind Children* (Stillman, 1974), ages birth to 9 years; and *Southern California Ordinal Scales of Development* (Ashhurst, et al., 1985) for children ages birth to 13 years.

Orientation and mobility of children from birth to 5 years can be assessed utilizing the *Preschool Orientation and Mobility Screening* (Dodson-Burk & Hill, 1989), which is a criterion-referenced inventory of orientation and mobility skills (Nuttall, Romero, & Kalesnik, 1992). This screening assesses many aspects of orientation and mobility, including positional concepts, current level of visual functioning, body parts, tactile skills, mobility skills, and orientation skills (Nuttall, Romero, & Kalesnik, 1992).

Anderson and Smith (1979) developed the *Receptive Expressive Language Scale: Assessment for the Visually Impaired* for children ages birth to 5 years. The scales adapt the *Preschool Language Scale* (Zimmerman, Steiner, & Evatt, 1969) and the *Maxfield-Buchholz Scale of Social Maturity for Preschool Blind Children* (Maxfield-Buchholz, 1957) to measure receptive and expressive language skills through predominantly auditory and tactile responses (Nuttall, Romero, & Kalesnik, 1992). Nuttall and colleagues (1992) warned that limited field testing dictates judicious interpretation.

To evaluate social-emotional and behavioral presentation, the *Child Behavior Checklist* (Achenbach & Edelbrock, 1981) provides normative data for preschool-aged children. Further standardized assessment of social-emotional or behavioral functioning would utilize tests designed for nondisabled age-mates. For the infant and preschool populations, assessment of this domain is typically conducted using checklists and observation. It will be important to note that children with visual impairments are being compared to normative data on peers without disabilities.

Hearing Impairments

Hearing plays a key role in the innate, effortless development of typical acquisition of speech and language (Heward, 2000). By listening to others, children are repetitively exposed to proper articulation and patterns, develop an exponentially growing meaning vocabulary, and hear communication of ideas and thought. Speech and language development is closely linked with the development of relationships and cognitive development. As children develop language, they learn the verbal means of interacting with peers and adults. They learn how to meet their needs using words, allowing for an efficient interaction with their world. The tantrums of the 2-year-old are replaced by the growing language of the 3- and 4-year old. Language organizes their ideas in connected meaning units or schemata. Children can communicate their own ideas and understanding with others and listen to the responses and arguments of others. The Socratic method of understanding is based on verbal banter. This interconnected developmental progress is built on hearing and experiencing the verbal world. The child with a hearing impairment lacks this integrating and facilitating experience.

Hearing impairments manifest most significantly in expressive and receptive language. Mullen (1992) suggested that the degree of impairment depends on: (1) the amount of hearing impairment, (2) age at hearing loss (prelingual or postlingual), (3) age at identification, (4) initiation of intervention, and (5) the type of intervention provided. These factors influence how effectively the child can communicate his wants, needs, and ideas to others (Luciano, 1994). As a consequence of the collective effects of these factors, the child's preferred mode and efficiency of communication are developed (Mullen, 1992).

Assessment Considerations. Understanding the effects of hearing impairments helps to determine assessment considerations. As verbal communication difficulties manifest in expressive and receptive language, assessment strategies should reduce emphasis on this modality. These considerations should include verbal instructions, questions, auditory cues and models, and language concepts (Luciano, 1994). Because of verbal communication difficulties, tests that emphasize verbal responses penalize a child who is deaf (DuBose, 1981). Consequently, assessment techniques that emphasize nonverbal tasks are essential (Luciano, 1994). Evaluators should consider the following:

1. Consult with sensory specialists (Bagnato & Neisworth, 1991).
2. Provide a distraction-free, well-defined work area (Bagnato & Neisworth, 1991).

3. Select brightly colored, moveable, multisensory, multifunctional materials (Bagnato & Neisworth, 1991).
4. Be demonstrative in gesture and facial expressions (Bagnato & Neisworth, 1991).
5. Stress the total communication approach, which is described later in this chapter (Bagnato & Neisworth, 1991).
6. Provide demonstrations and manually guide the child through practice items to teach the desired response mode (Bagnato & Neisworth, 1991).
7. Physically prompt the child to look at and orient toward the task (Bagnato & Neisworth, 1991).
8. Include smiles, touch, and clapping in your rewards for the child's efforts (Bagnato & Neisworth, 1991).
9. Spend additional time building rapport to address shyness, hesitance, and social withdrawal that are not uncommon behaviors for children who are deaf (Bagnato & Neisworth, 1991).
10. Take time during rapport building to become accustomed to the child's speech. Understanding of the child's speech can improve with exposure (Heward, 2000).
11. Write down any words that the child is having difficulty understanding (Heward, 2000).

Total Communication Approach. The total communication approach, or simultaneous communication, advocates the use of simultaneous presentation of manual communication (by signs and finger spelling) and speech through speech reading and residual hearing (Heward, 2000). Total communication is the instructional method of choice for many schools (Heward, 2000). When assessing a child with a hearing impairment, the total communication approach can be achieved by collaborating with an interpreter. As the assessor speaks any verbal instructions, the interpreter signs and finger spells the message. Properly trained interpreters can be reached through the Registry of

Interpreters for the Deaf (RID). Heward (2000) suggested the following when facilitating speech reading:

1. Face the child and sit no more than 4 feet away.
2. Adequately illuminate the room.
3. Do not sit in front of a strong or glaring light.
4. Try to keep your whole face visible.
5. Speak clearly and naturally maintaining a slow, even pace.
6. Do not over-exaggerate mouth movements.
7. Do not raise the level of your voice.
8. If the child is having difficulty understanding certain words (some words are harder to speech read), try substituting different words (if standardization allows).

Heward (2000) suggested the following considerations to keep in mind when using an interpreter to facilitate communication with sign language:

1. The interpreter's role is to facilitate communication between the evaluator and the child. The interpreter should not be required to give opinions or advice.
2. Eye contact should be maintained with the hearing-impaired person, not the interpreter.
3. The assessor should remain face-to-face with the child; the interpreter should sit a little to the side and behind the assessor.

Heward (2000) suggested that written messages may be helpful in communicating, and recommended that the following be considered:

1. Write out words in full, avoiding abbreviations.
2. Use simple and direct language.
3. Keep in mind that responses written by a student with severe hearing impairment may be grammatically incorrect, yet contain the key information needed to verify understanding.
4. Consider that written responses will reflect a lack of experience with spoken English and often do not accurately reflect the child's full intellectual capacity.

5. Supplement with visual aids (i.e., pictures, diagrams, flow charts).
6. Supplement written messages with nonlinguistic cues (i.e., gestures and facial expressions).

Multiple Measures. As indicated previously, children with hearing impairments have reduced exposure to verbal language and consequently often present with weak or delayed verbal skills. Assessment of cognitive development or achievement competencies can be complicated by confounding verbal factors. Further, the verbal expressions of a child with a hearing impairment, either oral or written, often misrepresent understanding and competencies in that they reflect lack of exposure to language. Consequently, Rogers and Soper (1982) suggested using more than one test to assess the skills of the child with hearing impairment. Multiple measures provide a greater opportunity to become familiar with the child and his skills (Luciano, 1994). The child also has the opportunity to become familiar with the assessment procedures and test expectations (Luciano, 1994). Utilizing multiple assessments allows for measurement of a broader sample of skills and behavior throughout exposure to different task demands (Luciano, 1994). Analysis of test performance may yield a greater understanding of the child's strengths and weaknesses than might be identified using only one measure (Luciano, 1994).

Naturalistic observations can be used as additional measures of the child's functioning. Luciano (1994) recommended observation of the child's play, social interactions, familial interactions with parents and siblings, and peer interactions. Information about the child's communication skills, self-concept, and self-esteem can be gleaned. These observations can provide a rich supplement to standardized assessment. Such data provide additional convergent validity to standardized findings.

Multidisciplinary Importance. As is the case for all children with severe disabilities, a comprehensive, multidisciplinary assessment is critical for determining the functional strengths and weaknesses of the infant or preschooler with a disability (Luciano, 1994). It is important to record a detailed medical history documenting otologically related pathology. Crucial information to document is the age of onset, duration, treatment, and recovery from any ear infections. For example, it is important to note that Sarah, a child born with sensory neural hearing impairment, also had chronic otitis media (middle-ear infection) at age 4 months and received pressure equalizing (PE) tubes at 11 months, which cleared her ears by age 12 months. This medical history suggests that Sarah's hearing probably was further complicated by ear infection during a key developmental period for phonological development (a crucial building block for speaking and reading skills).

Multidisciplinary assessment should also include a full audiological assessment to document the current status of the hearing impairment (Mullen, 1992). A comprehensive speech and language assessment should follow to document phonological processes, articulation skills, receptive and expressive language, and pragmatics. A psychologist, school psychologist, developmental specialist, or education specialist should document cognitive functioning, social-emotional development, adaptive functioning, and academic skills.

Selected Measures. Children with hearing impairments may require standardized assessment as a requirement for service implementation. Generally, the assessor should utilize nonverbal measures whenever possible to capitalize on the child's nonverbal capabilities and avoid measuring disability-related weaknesses which can lead to underestimation of development in areas such as intellectual functioning and problem solving. There are not many scales specifically designed for the infant or preschooler with hearing impairment. Consequently, assessors utilize standard measures with modifications, or modified forms of standardized scales.

Assessment of cognitive development, intellectual capacity or problem-solving ability can be done through standardized measures developed for the hearing impaired as well as through the use of adapted measures. The *Scales of Early Communication Skills for Hearing-Impaired Children* (SECS) (Moog & Geers, 1975) are curriculum-compatible, norm-based assessment tools designed specifically for the individuals with hearing impairments from ages 24 to 96 months (Bagnato, Neisworth, & Munson, 1997). The content covers domains of receptive language skills, expressive language skills, nonverbal receptive skills, and nonverbal expressive skills and includes nonverbal skill samples and criteria for utilization of prompts and demonstrations in order to observe learning (Bagnato, Neisworth, & Munson, 1997). The scales are authentic because they rely on natural communication skills observed in typical everyday environments and contexts (Bagnato, Neisworth, & Munson, 1997). In addition, the *Central Institute for the Deaf* (CID) *Preschool Performance Scale* (Geers & Lane, 1984) provides another option as a test specifically designed for the hearing-impaired preschooler age 2 years to 5 years, 5 months. Subtest groupings are Manual Planning, Manual Dexterity, Form Perception, Perceptual Motor, and Preschool. The test is completely nonverbal both in instructions and response requirements. It is a totally nonverbal measure of general cognitive functioning, with norms for the child with hearing impairment provided (Mullen, 1992).

The *Columbia Mental Maturity Scale* (3rd ed.) (Burgemeister, Blum, & Lorge, 1972) is a totally nonverbal test of reasoning abilities with sample items and a brief administration time (Mullen, 1992). The test is designed for children ages $3\frac{1}{2}$ years to 9 years, 11 months. Other tests that can be utilized for cognitive assessment of the infant or preschooler with a hearing impairment include the *Hiskey-Nebraska Test of Learning Aptitude* (Hiskey, 1966) (ages 3 years to 18 years, 6 months); *Kaufman Assessment Battery for Children-Nonverbal Scale* (Kaufman & Kaufman, 1983) (ages 4 years to $12\frac{1}{2}$ years); and the *Leiter International Performance Scale-Arthur Adaptation* (Arthur, 1952) (ages 3 to 8 years). The *Smith-Johnson Nonverbal Performance Scale* (Smith & Johnson, 1977) (ages 2 to 4 years) and *Adaptation of the WPPSI for Deaf Children* (Ray & Ulissi, 1982) (ages 4 to $6\frac{1}{2}$ years) are additional examples of assessment tools specifically designed for toddlers and preschoolers with hearing impairments (Simeonsson, 1986).

Social/emotional assessment measures include the *Joseph Pre-School and Primary Self-Concept Screening Test* (Joseph, 1979) which provides a general measure of self-concept for children from age $3\frac{1}{2}$ years to 9 years, 11 months (Mullen, 1992). The child chooses between two pictures, indicating which is most like himself (Mullen, 1992). The instructions can be pantomimed; however, the nonverbal presentation format is not standardized (Mullen, 1992). The *Meadow/Kendall Social-Emotional Assessment Inventories for Deaf and Hearing Impaired Students—Preschool Form* (Meadow, 1983) was normed on preschoolers with hearing impairment and provides a rating scale of observable behavior, including some specific to hearing loss for ages 3 years to 6 years, 11 months (Mullen, 1992). Other scales that are useful for the social-emotional assessment of infants and preschoolers with hearing impairments include the *Scales of Independent Behavior* (Bruininks, Woodcock, Weatherman, & Hill, 1984) and the *Vineland Adaptive Behavior Scales Revised-Survey Form* (Sparrow, Balla, & Cicchetti, 1984).

Language assessment measures include the *Carolina Picture Vocabulary Test for Deaf and Hearing Impaired* (Layton & Holmes, 1985), designed to measure receptive sign vocabulary for children ages $2\frac{1}{2}$ to 16 years (Mullen, 1992). The assessor signs a word and the child points to one of four presented pictures (Mullen, 1992). The *Grammatical Analysis of Elicited Language Pre-Sentence Level, Simple Sentence Level, and Complex Sentence Level* (Moog & Geers, 1983) was standardized on orally educated children, children

with profound hearing impairment, and children using total communication, ages $2\frac{1}{2}$ years to 11 years, 11 months (Mullen, 1992). According to Mullen (1992), this measure provides a good communication baseline for young children, allowing comparisons to other hearing and hearing-impaired children. The *SECS* (Moog & Geers, 1975) are designed to measure speech and language development in hearing impaired children ages 2 to 8 years, 11 months, and include receptive language, expressive language, nonverbal receptive, and nonverbal expressive skills (Mullen, 1992). Mullen (1992) recommended that this is a useful and easily administered screening tool.

Deaf-Blindness

The U.S. Department of Education defined deaf-blindness as "children and youth having auditory and visual impairments, the combination of which creates such severe communication and other developmental and learning needs that they cannot be appropriately educated without social education related services . . ." (Baldwin, 1992, p. 1). The effect of the loss of both hearing and vision often produces disability far greater than the summation of these disabilities separately (Arnold, 1998). The loss of both senses creates a restriction to only proximal senses (i.e., touch, olfaction, gestation, and kinesthetic perceptions) and a loss of the ability to acquire information about the more distant environment (Arnold, 1998). Consequently, the impact on development is exponential, rather than additive, because these children are deprived of the two most stimulating sources of information (Arnold, 1998). Every aspect of development is affected, and ongoing developmental assessment is required to provide consistently informed intervention.

Assessment Implications. Arnold (1998) suggested that assessment begin with the completion of a complete medical history. In addition, a detailed documentation of ophthalmological and audio-logical assessments should also be included. Such documentation will inform both assessment and intervention. Arnold (1998) recommended a team approach to assessment of children with deaf-blindness. The assessment team should include a behavioral audiologist, an occupational therapist, a vision specialist, and an orientation and mobility specialist. Educational assessment should provide a functional assessment of residual hearing and visual sensations, as well as a developmental profile.

Use of standardized tests is not appropriate for these children (Arnold, 1998). Arnold (1998) indicated that standardized tests lack normative data and rely on auditory as well as visual stimuli and responses for assessment. Instead, assessment should focus on communication skills. According to Arnold (1998), assessment should include (1) the capacity to receive information through the various sensory modes, (2) the capacity to develop associations between objects and other symbols, (3) the capacity to express choices, (4) the manner in which choices are communicated, and (5) the ability to learn behaviorally the sequence of a daily routine. Functional assessment should be utilized to develop a behavioral curriculum based on the ability of the infant or young child to respond to the demands of the environment (Arnold, 1998). Task analysis also is recommended in order to provide prescriptive intervention plans designed to meet the child's need for ongoing physical or technological assistance (Arnold, 1998).

For some children with deaf-blindness, severe sensory deprivation leads to difficulty communicating, further complicated by the experience of significant frustration. This combination can result in a tendency to engage in a behavioral repertoire marked with self-injurious behavior, which maladaptively serves the purpose of communication (Arnold, 1998). Assessment should rule out medical cause for self-injurious behavior. Further, once medical cause is excluded, a functional assessment should be conducted to identify antecedent environmental conditions, the child's behaviors, and consequent experiences and behaviors. Such assessment will lead to systematic behavioral intervention. A full description of functional behavioral assessment is included in the section on emotional and behavioral disabilities discussed later in this chapter.

Selected Measures. Currently, specialists in infant and preschool assessment recommend the *Callier-Azusa Scale: Assessment of Deaf-Blind Children* (Stillman, 1974). This scale provides authenticity with observations conducted in natural settings as the children participate in everyday play activities (Bagnato, Neisworth, & Munson, 1997). Data are collected through multiple sources with a focus on functional skills (Bagnato, Neisworth, & Munson, 1997). These authors report that the scale is dedicated to the multiple needs of children with deaf-blindness, ages birth to 8 years, and that it emphasizes tactile modes of learning (Bagnato, Neisworth, & Munson, 1997; Stillman, 1974).

Affective/Behavioral Impairments

Researchers have suggested that one of the most serious issues facing education is the presence of affective/behavioral difficulties (Foster-Johnson & Dunlap, 1993). Assessing a child with delayed or disordered emotional and behavioral responses demands significant flexibility on the part of the assessor (Luciano, 1994). Children with affective/behavioral impairments can be quite unpredictable (Luciano, 1994). Luciano (1994) proposed that assessor readiness to modify testing procedures and methods will facilitate a broad reflection of the child's range and pattern of responsiveness. A school psychologist or a licensed psychologist should serve as a member of the assessment team (McConaughy & Ritter, 1995).

General Considerations. Assessment of the infant or preschooler with emotional disabilities requires careful attention to the child's levels of comfort and rapport building. Preparation must begin prior to the assessment. Phone contact with the parents should be completed to inform them of the assessment expectations and format. This allows the parents to prepare the child for the assessment process. During the presession phone contact, careful consideration with the parents should ascertain whether the assessment would be completed most successfully in a familiar setting or a clinical setting. Some children with emotional difficulties perform much better when permitted to complete the assessment in their home setting, whereas other children respond better to the less stimulating, structured office setting. Parents can help choose the most appropriate setting.

It may be helpful to begin the assessment with a nonverbal, structured play session. Familiar construction toys (e.g., Mr. Potato Head or Legos) can be a fun way to build rapport and begin noting early concept knowledge (i.e., body parts, early language concepts, and counting skills). The examiner can move from play to assessment using a nonverbal assessment tool. Generally, infants and preschoolers are often reluctant to engage in spontaneous and reciprocal verbalizations with an unfamiliar adult. A nonverbal tool can allow for immediate participation without the pressure to verbalize. The assessor can celebrate the child's participation without selectively reinforcing correct or incorrect responses. The remaining assessment procedures can follow the nonverbal assessment. The session should be carefully structured, allowing for bathroom and play breaks between procedures.

After standardized assessment is completed, a free-play session should be conducted. This will allow for spontaneous exploration of the test materials and an opportunity to observe the child's spontaneous play (Waterman, 1982). If attempts at standardized assessment are not successful, then the assessor should gather needed information from parents and supplement this information with observations in the home,

child care, or clinic setting (Waterman, 1982). Standardized checklists can be used to provide convergent validity for observations and parents' reports.

Multiple Measures. When assessing children with behavioral or emotional disorders, data should be gathered utilizing multiple measures. Bagnato and Neisworth (1991) alerted us to the need for reducing ambiguity and inaccurate interpretation of measurements by conducting "a multisource, multidimensional survey that synthesizes information from parent interview, observation of parent-child interaction, ratings of atypical and functional characteristics, and appraisal of verbal and nonverbal concept development and problems solving" (p. 52).

Standardized Behavioral Rating Scales. Standardized behavioral rating scales are an efficient method of assessing children's emotional and behavioral difficulties (McConaughy & Ritter, 1995). Some standardized behavioral rating scales utilize parent and teacher reports of children's behavior (i.e., the *Achenbach Child Behavior Checklist*). Others utilize the assessor's perceptions of the infant's or preschooler's behavior. Using scales with empirically-based problem scales, large normative samples, and sound psychometric properties offers many advantages (McConaughy & Ritter, 1995). These scales yield information that is organized systematically (McConaughy & Ritter, 1995). Normative data also allow for comparison of individual behaviors with age expectations based on large samples of nonreferred children (McConaughy & Ritter, 1995). Behavior rating scales are also time efficient, taking about 10 to 15 minutes to complete, and can be computer scored (McConaughy & Ritter, 1995). Rating scales that offer parallel forms for data gathering from multiple sources allow for comparison among environments (McConaughy & Ritter, 1995).

It is important to remember that rating scales are not objective measures of children's behavior and problems (McConaughy & Ritter,

1995). These ratings reflect the perceptions of the informants. Extremely stressed parents may rate their child with emotional disabilities within the clinical range across the board, reflecting their frustration rather than the child's actual behavioral presentation. It is important to clinically assess the validity of checklists on which the informant has responded. Questionable validity should be indicated in cases in which extremes in every behavioral domain are noted and supportive data are not found in other sources or measures. A good way to validate behavioral rating scale findings is to look for convergent validity. Ratings should be supported by others in the child's life. To do this, multiple sources should be used in each environment (i.e., both parents, a grandparent, several day care teachers).

Bagnato and colleagues (1997) recommended the *Preschool and Kindergarten Behavior Scales* (PKBS) (Merrell, 1994). These scales are norm-referenced, standardized, curriculum compatible scales of behavior and social skills (Bagnato, Neisworth, & Munson, 1997). The scales are a hybrid instrument used to assess children ages 3 to 6 years in a variety of settings utilizing multiple informants (Bagnato, Neisworth, & Munson, 1997). The social skills domain reflects cooperation, interaction, and independence, and the behavior domain reflects self-centered/ explosive, attention problems/overactive, antisocial/aggressive, social withdrawal, and anxiety/ somatic problems (Bagnato, Neisworth, & Munson, 1997). The scales provide strong authentic features and opportunity for convergent validity (Bagnato, et al., 1997). Bagnato and colleagues (1997) reported that the scales are excellent for determining eligibility for services, planning goals, and monitoring progress.

The *Parenting Stress Index* (PSI) (Abidin, 1995) offers valuable perspective in the assessment of the child's behaviors. The PSI is an interactive, norm-based diagnostic profile of perceived child and parent stress, focusing on ages 1 to 60 months (Bagnato, Neisworth, & Munson, 1997).

The PSI covers 13 subdomains within four major domains: total stress, child domain, parent domain, and life stress. The scores are based on parental perceptions and report, and individual items directly assess the degree of life stress and disruption in the parent-child interaction (Bagnato, Neisworth, & Munson, 1997). Researchers suggest that the scale effectively phrases items in "self-statements" capitalizing on parental emotions (Bagnato, Neisworth, & Munson, 1997). The scale can be effectively utilized with parents of children with learning and affective/behavioral difficulties (Bagnato, Neisworth, & Munson, 1997).

Behavioral Observation. Observation is an essential component of effective assessment; this is especially true for the child with emotional/behavioral disorders (Luciano, 1994). McConaughy and Ritter (1995) strongly recommended direct observations for children with such disorders. Luciano (1994) pointed out that observing the child over time, in a variety of settings, under varying conditions, and with different individuals is recommended. It is important to observe the child in both problematic situations and settings and in nonproblematic situations and settings (McConaughy & Ritter, 1995). Because children with emotional/behavioral disorders can be quite labile and demonstrate variable behavioral patterns, multiple observations in each setting are recommended. McConaughy and Ritter (1995) suggested making several observations of short duration (i.e., 10-minute samples on several different days).

The context of the observations alters observation recommendations. If the assessor is observing an infant or preschooler in a child care or preschool setting, it may be helpful to select one or two typical children to provide a peer comparison in the same setting (McConaughy & Ritter, 1995). It is helpful to focus on problem behaviors, noting antecedent and consequent events (McConaughy & Ritter, 1995). When observing the child within the context of the parent-child dyad, it is important to note parent behaviors and responses. Indications of the child's self-concept, self-esteem, and dependence-independence tendencies also may be demonstrated through parent-child observations (Luciano, 1994).

Sattler (1988) provided a series of well-organized questions about the nature and appropriateness of child's play. These questions serve to structure the play-based observation. Each phase of the child's play is documented, including play room entrance, initial engagement, direct play, and discontinuation of play. Sattler (1988) recommended carefully noting how the child responds to the play assessment initiation. First, does the child enter the play room easily or does he hold the assessor's or parent's hand on the way? Is the child able to move directly to play with the toys or does he cling to the caretaker?

Once the child is engaged in play, there are many aspects of play that are important to observe. When the child initiates play, how is that done? Sattler (1988) advocated noting the pace of the child's initiation of play, the amount of assistance the child requires to engage in play, the need for approval and encouragement, the level of self-directed or other-directed play, the degree of initiative and curiosity, the severity of impulsivity, and the length of engagement in activities. The amount of energy expended in play is also important (Sattler, 1988). It is important to observe the pace of energy expense, degree of fatigue, direction of momentum, and overall level of energy (Sattler, 1988). How does the child conduct manipulative actions in play? It is important to observe type of movements (sweeping or precise), manner of handling (free or tense), smoothness and efficiency of movements, and conventionality of toy use (Sattler, 1988).

A play observation also can document verbal behaviors and development as well as creativity, attitudes, and attempts at social interaction. Assessors should note type and quality of verbalizations in play. For example, does the child speak in phrases, sing, or use jargon with play (Sattler, 1988)? In addition, the assessor should note content, tone, purpose, and style of the child's verbalizations (Sattler, 1988). Quality of play should be recorded. Sattler (1988) suggested reviewing the tone, integration, creativity, and products of play. Finally, the age appropriateness of play and attitudes toward adults in play should be recorded (Sattler, 1988). A rich description of play can provide convergent validity for standardized rating scales as well as anecdotal data for assessment team discussions and intervention planning.

Linder's *Transdisciplinary Play-Based Assessment* (TPBA) (1993) provides a more structured way to assess the child's affective as well as overall development. The TPBA provides guidelines for the observer to assess the child's actions and interactions and was designed for children in infancy to age 6 years (Bagnato, Neisworth, & Munson, 1997). The TPBA provides an excellent format that links observation, analysis of findings, and program development in a functional way (Luciano, 1994). By utilizing observation guides and age charts along with summary worksheets, assessors can identify the child's strengths and weaknesses (Bagnato, Neisworth, & Munson, 1997). The scale provides a jargon-free curriculum guide to assist with intervention planning (Bagnato, Neisworth, & Munson, 1997).

The Interview-Based Functional Behavioral Assessment. Functional behavioral assessment is critical to effective intervention planning for the infant or preschooler with emotional or behavioral difficulties. This can be completed through a parent interview as a supplement to behavioral observation, standardized measures, and rating scale completion. Functional assessments are based on the assumption that challenging behavior is related to the context within which it occurs and that the behavior serves a function for the student (Foster-Johnson & Dunlap, 1993). A functional assessment is "a process whereby informed hypothesis statements are developed about relationships between events in the environment and the occurrence of a [child's] challenging behavior" (Foster-Johnson & Dunlap, 1993, p. 46). The functional assessment examines the circumstances involved in the occurrence or nonoccurrence of the behavior, and identifies variables and events consistently present in those situations and the function of the behavior for the child (Foster-Johnson & Dunlap, 1993). A functional assessment should be completed individually for each challenging behavior identified by the parents. Functional behavioral assessments are discussed in Chapter 12 on behavioral assessment.

First, ask the parents to identify the challenging behaviors presented by their child. With the parents, prioritize the list and begin the assessment, starting with the most challenging behavior. For infants and preschoolers, this is often tantrumming behavior or hitting. Note the frequency (how many times per hour, per day, per week), chronicity (how long this behavior has been problematic), intensity (how severe the tantrum is), and duration (how long the tantrum lasts). It is important to clearly define the behavior, including each of these dimensions.

Next, identify events and variables that are typically associated with the behavior (Foster-Johnson & Dunlap, 1993). Foster-Johnson and Dunlap (1993) found that there are three domains of possibilities that are frequently reported: sociological factors, the environment, and demands of the task. Physiological factors include sickness, allergies, side effects of medication, fatigue, hunger, thirst, and increased arousal owing to a fight or disrupted routine. Environmental factors include high noise levels, uncomfortable temperature, overstimulation, understimulation, frequent routine disruptions, visitors, and lack of organization and structure. The demands of the task variables include few opportunities for making choices, lack of predictability in the schedule, inadequate level of assistance with frustrating tasks, tasks that are too simple or too difficult for the child's developmental levels, unclear verbal instructions, few opportunities to communicate, activities that are too difficult or take a long time to complete, and activities that the child dislikes.

The next step is to determine the potential functions of the child's behavior. Often this involves identifying the consequences of the behavior (Foster-Johnson & Dunlap, 1993). Behavior frequently serves several possible functions: to gain attention from others, to gain a tangible, to experience internal or external stimulation, to avoid interaction, or to avoid a task. Foster-Johnson and Dunlap (1993) suggested that behavior may only serve two basic functions: to get something or to escape from something.

For example, the child experiences tantrums several times throughout the day. The interview reveals that these tantrums are relatively short and end with the child cuddling with his blanket and sitting alone. The tantrums often occur at meal time, when changing, when playing, and when trying to talk to his mother. A discussion may reveal that the child frequently becomes frustrated with such behaviors as using utensils independently, pulling his own shirt over his head, memorizing letters, and talking. Through the process of functional behavioral assessment, it becomes clear that the child's mother does not have a good understanding of age expectations and is requiring the child to attempt many tasks that are well above the child's expected developmental level. The result is a tantrum. The function of the tantrum is to escape the frustration that he feels every time she asks him to do something that he is not developmentally prepared to complete successfully. After escaping, the child attempts to calm himself by cuddling with his blanket. Through the functional behavioral assessment interview, intervention becomes readily apparent.

Autism

Autism is a severe disability marked by significant impairments in communication, social skills, and emotional function (Cole & Arndt,

1998; Heward, 2000). Since autism was first defined nearly 50 years ago, the diagnostic criteria have changed several times (New York State Department of Health Early Intervention Program [NYSEIP], 1999). Autism as defined by the IDEA:

> A developmental disability affecting verbal and nonverbal communication and social interaction, generally evident before age 3, that affects a child's performance. Other characteristics often associated with autism are engagement in repetitive activities and stereotyped movements, resistance to environmental change or change in daily routines, and unusual responses to sensory experiences. The term does not apply if a child's educational performance is adversely affected primarily because the child has a serious emotional disturbance. (34 C.F.R., § 3000.7[b][1])

The entire spectrum of autistic disorders includes qualitative impairments in social interaction; qualitative impairments in communication; and restricted, repetitive, and stereotyped patterns of behavior, interest, and activities. Diagnosis can be difficult (NYSEIP, 1999). Volmer (1995) noted that impaired language and socialization can be found in children with other disorders or disabilities. However, children with autism distinctively demonstrate significant repetitive stereotypical routines (Volmer, 1995). Those assessing a child with autism must be able to conceptualize each of the three characteristic aspects. When assessing children with autism, it is important to understand and strategically address each of the three areas of deficit or atypical functioning. Each area will be described and explained. Following the descriptions, implications for assessment and evaluation strategies will be addressed.

Description and Evaluation Implications for Social Impairments. Difficulties with social interactions play a key role in the manifestation of autism. It is generally accepted that children with autism show marked impairment, compared with their age-peers in the area of reciprocal social interactions. Research suggests that young children with

autism interact quite similarly with strangers, their teacher, and their parents (Volmer, 1995). The social impairments presented by a child can range quite significantly, from a lack of awareness of others to egocentric interactions with others based on their own obsessive interests (Volmer, 1995). Interestingly, this indifference toward others contrasts notably with the hypersensitivity to small alterations in their routine or environment (Volmer, 1995). The inability to meet needs socially and interpersonally, social isolation, and inability to modify social behaviors in order to respond to environmental demands are of most concern (Gillberg, 1990; Volmer, 1995).

Rogers (1999) reported that recent research indicates that children with autism may show more socially reciprocal behaviors than was previously suspected. It appears that the main difference between children with autism and their nondisabled peers is that the former require much more scaffolding through prompting, cueing, physical contact, initiations, redirection, and imitation (Rogers, 1999). When given this additional stimulation, children with autism can demonstrate positive social behavior commensurate with their age-peers (Rogers, 1999).

Attention to social impairments of children with autism is critical for successful assessment. Scaffolding issues are extremely important because these children will respond better when the assessor takes on a more active role (Rogers, 1999). It is important to initiate and structure interactions (Rogers, 1999). The scaffolding should be done carefully and actively, rather than in an overly directive manner (Rogers, 1999). There are several different ways that this can be done:

1. Include the child's parents and other family members in the assessment process in order to capitalize on established relationships (Cole & Arndt, 1998).
2. Allow time for familiarity. Assessing a child with autism as a novel individual may yield results that significantly underestimate the

child's developmental level and potential. The child's performance can vary significantly depending on familiarity with the assessor (NYSEIP, 1999).

3. Use tests requiring minimal social interactions (Marcus & Baker, 1986).

4. Utilize structure and routines that are not dependent on social cues (Marcus & Baker, 1986).

5. Use simple social interactions during test administration (Marcus & Baker, 1986).

6. Keep demands for response from child low (Marcus & Baker, 1986).

7. Maintain a constant awareness of the infant's or preschooler's difficulties in relating (Marcus & Baker, 1986).

8. Utilize physical prompts which include actively assisting the child through the motions of the task (Volmer, 1995).

9. It is crucial that the assessor gain the child's attention prior to giving verbal instructions (Volmer, 1995).

10. It is important to remember that a child with autism may not establish eye contact, but rather signals attention through body orientation, verbal response, or by ceasing other activities (Volmer, 1995).

11. Multiple assessment sessions are recommended because the child's comfort level with the assessor may increase over time (NYSEIP, 1999).

Definition and Evaluation Implications for Impaired Communication. Children with autism show significant delay and disorder in communication skill development. Specifically, although many of their skills are developing below expected rates (delay), there are also communicative behaviors present that would not be expected at any point in typical development (disorder). Communication problems can vary significantly, ranging from mild to severe. Some children with autism never develop language, whereas other children learn to communicate quite effectively (Paul, 1987). Kanner (1943), the pioneer of

research in children with autism, described the stereotypical linguistic markers as echoic repetition of whole phrases (repeating their own phrases and phrases of others), pronoun reversals (i.e., referring to self as "you" or self-referring by name, "Bobby hungry,"), and a literalness in interpretation (continuing beyond preschool years). In higher functioning children with autism, or Asperger's syndrome (those with average intelligence), language is described as lacking inflection, tangential, off the point, circumstantial, and concrete (Volmer, 1995).

According to Rogers (1999), research has indicated that pragmatics is the most impaired area in language development. A child developing pragmatic skills is learning how to use conversational skills effectively, responding to others by adapting their message, starting and ending conversations, and taking turns when speaking (Heward, 2000). Failure or delay in the development of pragmatic language is a marker of the development of autism. Some children with autism become verbally fluent, but they continue to show significant delay in the pragmatic use of language. Assessors need to carefully document the overall delay of language development as well as specifically report on the delay of pragmatic language development. Researchers suggest that this deficit can be apparent quite early, even in the preverbal infant. Specifically, researchers report that preverbal children with autism fail to demonstrate joint attention or the "capacity to knowingly share a common focus of attention, and to lead another's attentional focus" (Carpenter, Nagell, & Tomasello, 1998, p. 1). In verbal children with autism, the behaviors presenting as deficit include using gesture, prosody, organization of narrative, correction of breakdowns, and conversation skills (Rogers, 1999).

The following suggestions are recommended for the assessment process to address communication difficulties:

1. Visual cues can be provided at several different levels and can vary from complex to

basic. Visual cues help the child organize his understanding of the task to be completed and can increase focus.

2. High-functioning, older children can be given a written list or outline as a visual cue (Volmer, 1995).

3. A pictorial sequence can also be provided for the younger or lower-functioning child (Volmer, 1995).

4. The assessor should utilize clear, concise language, visual cues, gestures, and prompts when giving verbal directions (Volmer, 1995).

5. Potentially confusing words should be minimized (Volmer, 1995). For example, rather than saying, "I want you to finish coloring the picture, and then when you finish, you can select a game to play on the computer," state "First finish picture, then computer" (Volmer, 1995, p. 1035).

6. To add gestures, Volmer (1995) recommended that the assessor point to the colors and paper and then to the computer.

7. The assessor should use tests with limited language demands (Marcus & Baker, 1986).

8. Nonverbal assessment tools should be used when possible (Marcus & Baker, 1986).

9. Verbal and nonverbal instructions can be alternated (Marcus & Baker, 1986).

10. Visual cues such as tokens can be used (Marcus & Baker, 1986).

Definition and Assessment Implications for Restricted Repertoire of Activities and Interests. Children with autism present with a restricted repertoire of activities and interests. This restriction manifests in three ways: (1) adherence to and need for routine, (2) demonstration of compulsive rituals, and (3) restricted range of interests and stereotypical behavioral patterns. This section will describe each of the manifestations of the restrictions, and then provide a list of related assessment recommendations.

The first restriction is manifested in the dependence on daily routine. Children with autism are often rigidly dependent on personal and daily routines (Volmer, 1995). This dependence is manifested in distress over even small changes in their environment or routine (Volmer, 1995). For example, Sarah, a child with autism, may become excessively distressed because the child care teacher forgets to do the daily news routine before morning snack. This characteristic need for routine is especially important to the assessor because assessment typically alters routine and creates added distress.

The second manifestation appears in patterns of behavior or compulsive rituals. Children with autism also adhere to their own routines and may present with compulsive rituals or patterns of behaviors exhibited in repetitive and consistent sequences (Volmer, 1995). Young children are often described as lining up their toys in a particular order or playing with objects in a specific sequence. Older children demonstrate adherence to highly personalized behavioral routines that have developed over time in addition to engaging in repetitive activities.

The third manifestation reveals itself in extreme and narrow interests. According to Volmer (1995), these interests can often resemble those in normal children (i.e., rock music videos, astronomy, rocks). However, children with autism do not engage in these activities in order to socialize with others; they do so in a solitary manner.

This restricted repertoire of activities and interests is difficult to understand. Children with autism may have impairment in executive function or the ability to keep in mind a problem-solving set in order to attain a future goal (Rogers, 1999). The child with autism has difficulty holding sets, abstractions, and concepts in mind. Typically, as children learn, the ability to conceptualize events, relationships, and objects provides a sense of personal mastery, automizes thinking thereby allowing for efficiency, and facilitates the development of goal-driven behavior. Without the ability to conceptualize and plan abstractly, children with autism rely on their routines, repetition, and narrow interests to feel mastery, to facilitate efficient daily living, and to sublimate goal-directed drives. Consequently, interruption of routines can result in significant levels of discomfort and anxiety.

Volmer (1995) emphasized that the symptoms of autism exist on a continuum. Some children with autism exhibit many of the behaviors listed to the extreme, whereas others show only mild manifestations. In other words, autism is a spectrum disorder, ranging from mild to severe, and "the number and types of symptoms in children can differ" (Mayes & Calhoun, 1999, p. 95). Diagnostic and developmental assessments should assess and note the intensity, frequency, and duration of observed behaviors in order to properly reflect the degree of autistic tendency.

Implications for assessment are:

1. Children with autism may need assessors to highlight the use of objects, making expectations explicit (Rogers, 1999).
2. Those working with children with autism should label and demonstrate actions (Rogers, 1999).
3. Assessors should use materials that are interesting, yet not overly distracting (Marcus & Baker, 1986).
4. The room and work areas should be uncluttered (Marcus & Baker, 1986).
5. Visually distinct work and play areas will help structure the evaluation area (Marcus & Baker, 1986).
6. Materials should be presented in a clear and simple manner (Marcus & Baker, 1986).
7. Assessors should allow for short evaluation sessions and frequent breaks (Marcus & Baker, 1986).
8. Assessors should allow for behavior as a tension-relieving break (Marcus & Baker, 1986).
9. Assessors should be prepared to offer reward, to distract, to interrupt, and to further structure the assessment session (Marcus & Baker, 1986).
10. The assessment setting should be familiar and comfortable (NYSEIP, 1999).
11. To ensure familiarity and comfort, some assessments are conducted in the child's home.
12. Early sessions should consist of observations and unstructured play, leaving structured or standardized assessments for latter sessions. This will capitalize on the child's increasing familiarity and ease.

Health Assessment. Children suspected of having autism should have a complete health assessment to rule out medical conditions or developmental problems that can be mistaken for autism and to identify associated genetic syndromes or medical conditions often seen in children with autism (NYSEIP, 1999). This assessment should include food and environmental allergies, mental retardation, and neurological conditions.

Developmental Surveillance and Assessment. Developmental surveillance is the flexible, continuous process in which professionals monitor a child's developmental status during the provision of health services (NYSEIP, 1999). Early signs of autism are often identified during well child visits and pediatric developmental review. Practitioners watch for developmental signs between 15 months and 36 months; the average age of reported symptoms is 18 months (Cole & Arndt, 1998). Generally, these developmental milestones are in the area of language, social, and emotional development. Complete developmental assessments should be requested for children who fail to achieve key developmental milestones.

It is very important that the developmental assessment of children with autism be considered an ongoing process (NYSEIP, 1999). Definitively, autism is a developmental disorder. Consequently, an ongoing review of the child's development must be conducted in order to document disordered development and exclude other possible causes for disordered behavior. Early diagnosis of autism can have a dramatic effect on outcomes for many children (Cole & Arndt, 1998).

As with other severe developmental disabilities, the full developmental assessment of autism should address each aspect of functioning. Volmer (1995) suggested that behavioral assessment is the "cornerstone" of assessment when working with children with autism (p. 1033). The recommended assessment tools provide behavioral assessment options, as well as measures for specific diagnostic features including social skills, social/emotional development, speech and language skills, and cognitive development. Adaptive behavior should be measured in order to appropriately lead intervention. *The Scales of Independent Behavior-Revised* (SIB) (Bruininks, Woodcock, Weatherman, & Hill, 1984) can be completed with parents or caretakers as respondents. The SIB assesses adaptive and problem behaviors, providing prompts for discussing training objectives allowing for a structured discussion of goals and objectives (Volmer, 1995).

Facilitated Communication. Facilitated communication "involves a facilitator supporting hand, wrist, elbow or shoulder of the child while she selects a letter on a letter board, computer keyboard, or typewriter" (Volmer, 1995, p. 1037). The facilitator can help isolate the index finger and assist with stabilization of the hand, but the facilitator should not assist with letter or word selection (Volmer, 1995). Volmer (1995) reported that the research has concluded that some facilitators unknowingly influence the child's communications. Consequently, facilitated communication has become one of the most controversial topics in the field of autism (Volmer, 1995).

Selected Measures. Bagnato and colleagues (1997) reported that "the structured and comprehensive appraisal of the functional capabilities of young children with autism or self-regulatory disorders is one of the most difficult challenges faced by professionals" (p. 100). *The Autism Screening Instrument for Educational Planning (2nd ed.)*

(ASIEP-2) (Krug, Arick, & Almond, 1993) is a curriculum-compatible scale for diagnosis, placement, educational program planning, and progress analysis of infants and young children with autism (Bagnato, Neisworth, & Munson, 1997). The ASIEP-2 consists of five instruments: Autism Behavior Checklist (ABC); Sample of Oral Behavior (repetitiveness, noncommunication, intelligibility, and babbling); Interaction Assessment (spontaneous social interactions and responses to requests); Educational Assessment (staying seated, receptive language, expressive language, body concept, and speech imitation); and Prognosis for Learning Rate (Bagnato, Neisworth, & Munson, 1997). The scale utilizes a multisource approach and capitalizes on natural samples of behaviors in multiple contexts increasing authenticity. Bagnato and colleagues (1997) describe it as "the best noncurricular developmental scale for autism and related disorders" (p. 99).

The *Individualized Assessment and Treatment for Autistic and Developmentally Disabled Children* (IATA) (Schopler, Reichler, Bashford, Lansing, & Marcus, 1979) is a curriculum-imbedded assessment tool designed for children, ages 1 to 12 years, functioning at the preschool level (Bagnato, Neisworth, & Munson, 1997). The assessment includes Individualized Assessment and Treatment for Autistic and Developmentally Disabled Children Tracking Progress Chart and Weekly Home Log. Domains covered include imitation, perception, fine and gross motor, eye-hand coordination, cognitive performance, and cognitive verbal skills. Authenticity is maximized with an emphasis on real-life settings, activities, and methods (Bagnato, Neisworth, & Munson, 1997). In total, the assessment incorporates 250 teaching activities and goals.

Another scale developed for the assessment of autism is the *Behavior Observation Scale for Autism* (Freeman, Tonick, Ritvo, Guthrie, & Schroth, 1979) for children ages 30 to 60 months. The instrument utilizes structured and unstructured checklists addressing language, attending, response to help, response to play, response to pain, and motility disturbances to stimuli (Marcus & Baker, 1986). The *Childhood Autism Rating Scale* (CARS) (Schopler, Reichler, & Renner, 1988) is completed while directly observing a child. The child's behavior is rated in 14 different areas, including relationships with people, imitation, affect, use of body, relation to nonhuman objects, adaptation to environmental change, visual responsiveness, auditory responsiveness, near receptor responsiveness, anxiety reaction, verbal communications, nonverbal communication, activity level, and intellectual functioning. In addition the evaluator provides an overall general clinical impression. For further description of assessment tools, see Marcus and Baker (1986) and Bracken (1991). For a convenient listing of assessment tools by disability area see Table 7–1.

Developmental/Mental Retardation

The American Association of Mental Retardation (AAMR) identifies two areas of deficit for the classification of a child as mentally retarded: intellectual functioning and adaptive behavior. First, the child must be found to have significant subaverage intellectual functioning (Grossman, 1983). This is typically quantified utilizing a test of cognitive development or a standardized test of intelligence (IQ test). It is generally accepted that those scoring at or below 70 on an IQ test are considered to be functioning at the significantly subaverage level. According to the *Diagnostic and Statistical Manual of Mental Disorders* (DSM-IV-TR), IQ scores from 50–55 to 70 reflect mild mental retardation, 35–40 to 50–55 indicate moderate mental retardation, 20–25 to 35–40 indicate severe mental retardation, and below 20–25 suggest profound mental retardation (American Psychiatric Association [APA], 2000).

In addition to the significant intellectual deficit, children with mental retardation also demonstrate significant lags in adaptive functioning. That is, they have not developed age-appropriate skills in the areas of effective communication, self-care, social/interpersonal skills, home living, use of community resources, functional academic skills, self-direction, and leisure activities (APA, 2000). In addition to deficits in intellectual functioning and adaptive behavior, children who demonstrate moderate to severe mental retardation often manifest the characteristics of variable attention and mood, atypical muscle tone, articulation difficulties, limited and concrete/functional vocabulary, limited overall language development, underdeveloped social communication skills, passive behavior, little or no imitation of activity or interaction, self-stimulatory behavior, and underdeveloped play behaviors, that is, nonpurposeful play with or manipulation of objects (Luciano, 1994).

Although many children with mild mental retardation are now being educated in regular education classrooms, those with moderate to severe mental retardation require individualized support at varying levels throughout their school years. Infants and preschoolers in the mild to moderate ranges often do not fall developmentally behind their age mates until they approach their elementary school years (Heward, 2000). However, for those children who fall within the severe and profound ranges, significant developmental lags are typically evident from infancy (Heward, 2000). Currently, most schools have integration and inclusion programs which are highly individualized based on functional level and need for all children, including those with severe disability. Consequently, assessment is crucial for effective placement and objective planning.

The techniques and guidelines described for other developmental disabilities can be utilized for the assessment of infants and preschoolers with significant cognitive deficits (Bagnato & Neisworth, 1991). As with all severe disabilities, it is important to document trends and patterns through convergent assessment. Further, methods such as task analysis and functional behavioral assessment can be very useful for intervention-based referral questions. For specific developmental assessment tools, Bagnato and colleagues (1997) offered a wonderfully explicated overview of tests appropriate for the infant and preschool population.

It is important to remember that children with moderate to severe mental retardation will likely show delays in all aspects of development. Consequently, they will require complete assessments from trained specialists in each developmental area. The multidisciplinary assessment team should include a speech and language pathologist (articulation and language skills), physical therapist (gross motor functioning), licensed or school psychologist (cognitive/intellectual functioning and social/emotional functioning), occupational therapist (fine motor skills and adaptive behavior), educational specialist (play, social history, and pre-academic skills), and pediatrician (medical needs). Each specialist should perform a full assessment in his respective area to fully document developmental delay and make specific recommendations for intervention. (Team assessment is discussed further in Chapter 4.)

The following recommendations should be considered when assessing infants and preschoolers with severe mental retardation:

1. Utilize appropriate body positions as recommended for neuromotor impairments when assessing the infant's or preschooler's responsiveness to the environment.
2. Choose stimulating toys to increase responsiveness (Bagnato & Neisworth, 1991).
3. Ask teachers or parents to join in the assessment process to maximize performance through familiar interaction.
4. When possible, utilize existing augmentative communication systems.
5. Model required responses and give feedback for preferred responses.
6. Break down more complex test items into component parts, as in task analysis, and document partial completion of tasks.

7. Assess infants and preschoolers with mental retardation in short intervals, intermingling structured assessment with stimulating play and reward.
8. When necessary, use primary reinforcers (i.e., food) to elicit behavioral response (for example, rather than look for a bear under a cup, the child looks for an animal cracker).
9. Allow for many attempts providing support to reduce frustration.
10. End testing sessions with less frustrating, more basic tasks to allow the infant or preschooler to leave with a feeling of success and accomplishment.

Health Impairments

Health impairments affect the infant's or preschooler's strength, vitality, attention, and alertness. Effects on development range from inhibition of age-expected developmental gains to significant degeneration of skills. Ongoing developmental assessment is an integral part of educational intervention as well as medical treatment and symptom management. Health impairments not only affect ongoing development, but also the ability of the infant or preschooler to perform during developmental assessment (Luciano, 1994). Alertness, consciousness, and overall behavior can be affected by the illness or the medication during the assessment session (Martin, 1982). It is important to be aware of the effects of the child's particular medical difficulty as well as the potential side effects of medication. The following sections address general considerations for the assessment of infants and preschoolers with health impairments. In addition, prematurity, HIV and AIDS, and cancer are addressed directly.

Working with the Medical Community. Many referrals for infant and preschool assessment of children with severe disabilities come from family physicians and pediatricians (Preator & McAllister, 1995). Advances in medical technology have

TABLE 7–1
Assessment by Disability Areas

Disability	Test/Author	Age Range
Hearing	Carolina Picture Vocabulary Test for Deaf and Hearing Impaired (Layton & Holmes, 1985)	$2\frac{1}{2}$ years–16 years
	Columbia Mental Maturity Scale Third Edition (Burgemeister, Blum, & Lorge, 1972)	3 years, 9 months–9 years, 11 months
	Grammatical Analysis of Elicited Language Pre-Sentence Level (Moog & Geers,1983)	$2\frac{1}{2}$ years–11 years, 11 months
	Hiskey-Nebraska Test of Learning Aptitude (Hiskey, 1966)	3 years–18 years
	Joseph Pre-school and Primary Self-Concept Screening Test (Joseph,1979)	$3\frac{1}{2}$ years– 9 years, 11 months
	Kaufman Assessment Battery for Children— Nonverbal Scale (Kaufman & Kaufman, 1983)	4 years–$12\frac{1}{2}$ years
	Leiter International Performance Scale Arthur Adaptation (Arthur, 1952)	3 years–8 years
	Meadow/Kendall Social-Emotional Assessment Inventories for Deaf and Hearing-Impaired Students Preschool Form (Meadow,1983)	3 years–6 years, 11 months
	Scales of Independent Behavior (Bruininks, Woodcock, Weatherman, & Hill, 1984)	Infants and Preschoolers
	Smith-Johnson Nonverbal Performance Scale (Smith & Johnson, 1977)	2 years–4 years
	Vineland Adaptive Behavior Scales Revised Survey Form (Sparrow, Balla, & Cicchetti, 1984)	Infants and Preschoolers
Deaf-Blindness	Callier-Azusa Scale: Assessment of Deaf-Blind Children (Stillman, 1974)	Birth–8 years
Visual	Adaptation of the WPPSI for Deaf Children (Ray & Ulissi,1982)	4 years–6 years, 5 months
	Battelle Developmental Inventory (Newborg, Stock, Wnek, Guidubaldi, & Svinicki, 1988)	Birth–8 years

TABLE 7–1
continued

Disability	Test/Author	Age Range
Visual	Brigance Diagnostic Inventory for Early Development (Rev. ed.) (Brigance, 1991)	Birth–6 years, 11 months
	Informal Assessment of Developmental Skills for Visually Handicapped Students (Swallow, Mangold, & Mangold, 1978)	Birth–16 years
	Perkins-Binet Tests of Intelligence for the Blind (Davis, 1980)	3 years–18 years
	Preschool Orientation and Mobility Screening (Dodson-Burk & Hill, 1989)	Birth–5 years
	Receptive Expressive Language Assessment for the Visually Impaired (Anderson & Smith, 1979)	Birth–5 years
	Reynell-Zinkin Developmental Scales— Visually Impaired (Reynell & Zinkin, 1979)	Birth–5 years
	Stanford-Binet Intelligence Scale (4th ed.) (Thorndike, Hagen, & Sattler, 1986)	2 years–adult
	Tactile Test of Basic Concepts (Caton, 1986)	5 years–9 years
Behavioral Assessment	CID Preschool Performance Scale (Moog & Lane, 1984)	2 years–5 years, 5 months
	Parenting Stress Index (Abidin, 1995)	1 month–60 months
	Preschool and Kindergarten Behavior Scales (Merrell, 1994)	Preschool and Kindergarten
	Transdisciplinary Play-Based Assessment (Linder, 1993)	Infancy–6 years
Autism	Autism Screening Instrument for Educational Planning (2nd ed.) (Krug, Arick, & Almond, 1993)	Infants and Young Children
	Behavior Rating Instrument for Autistic and Atypical Children (Marcus & Baker, 1986)	Children up to 54 months
	Individualized Assessment and Treatment for Autistic and Developmentally Disabled Children (Schopler, Reichler, Bashford, Lansing, & Marcus, 1979).	1 year–12 years

resulted in survival of low-birth-weight children and those with medically complex conditions (Preator & McAllister, 1995). Often, these children are in need of early intervention and preschool services (Preator & McAllister, 1995). Assessments should include medical input and initiate an ongoing discourse with medical personnel.

General Considerations. Luciano (1994) suggested that even short-term illness can have an effect on a child's functioning or performance during an assessment. The following guidelines are important to keep in mind when working with infants and preschoolers with health impairments:

1. Ask the infant's or preschooler's caregiver about recent and current health status (Luciano, 1994).
2. Document current medications and potential side effects (Luciano, 1994).
3. Ask the caregiver if assessment behavior differs from typical behavioral presentation (Luciano, 1994).
4. Document allergies (Luciano, 1994).
5. Record any recent seizures or staring spells (Luciano, 1994).
6. Schedule the assessment during the child's optimal functioning hours as indicated by the caregiver (Luciano, 1994).
7. Be sensitive to intensive treatment (i.e., chemotherapy) and schedule the assessment after sufficient recovery time has lapsed.
8. Conduct the assessment in an accessible part of the school building or in an office where medical supplies are readily available.
9. Provide soft-tip pens that require less pressure when writing (Heward, 2000).
10. Ensure appropriate positioning and stability.
11. Continuously monitor for signs of fatigue and take breaks or reschedule if necessary.

HIV *and* AIDS. According to the Centers for Disease Control and Prevention (CDC, 1995), infants born to infected mothers are one of the fastest growing groups testing positive for HIV.

Specifically, HIV infection refers to "infection with the immunodeficiency virus regardless of the presence of overt illness or clinical manifestations" (Mangione, Landau, & Pryor, 1998, p. 328). Following the presence of the HIV infection, life threatening HIV-related diseases can manifest (Mangione, Landau, & Pryor, 1998). AIDS occurs in the later stages of the disease following a breakdown of the immune system (Hallahan & Kauffman, 2000; Mangione, Landau, & Pryor, 1998). The weakened immune system leaves infants and children with AIDS vulnerable to opportunistic infections that rarely affect healthy children (Mangione, Landau, & Pryor, 1998). Because children with HIV and AIDS now live longer owing to medical developments, there is an increasing need for special education services for these children (Hallahan & Kauffman, 2000).

Children with HIV/AIDS are susceptible to affective disturbance. It appears that the effects of the illness are further confounded by the effects of related risk-factors such as poverty, parental loss and grief, social stigma, and minority status (Mangione, Landau, & Pryor, 1998). Consequently, it is important to include family history, medical history, developmental history, neurodevelopment status, current cognitive functioning, psychosocial status, physical impairments, receptive and expressive language, attention, memory, perceptual-motor skills, pre-academic skills, and adaptive behavior in assessment and developmental reports (Mangione, Landau, & Pryor, 1998; Wolters, Brouwers, & Moss, 1995).

Ongoing assessment is very important for children with HIV/AIDS. Mangione and colleagues (1998) reported that most parentally infected children will manifest an advanced stage of HIV by school age. According to Mangione and colleagues (1998) and Meyers (1994), pediatric cases present with complex, individual differences in central nervous system (CNS) compromise and significant changes over time. Areas of impairment will vary from child to child, depending on the area of the brain affected (Mangione, Landau, & Pryor, 1998).

Because of the deteriorating effects on the CNS over time and significant variation, a longitudinal approach to assessment of HIV-infected children is recommended (Mangione, Landau, & Pryor, 1998). Mangione and colleagues (1998) suggested that regular, comprehensive assessments are important to detect possible global or specific neuropsychological changes. Monitoring changes will help inform the multidisciplinary service provision team (Mangione, Landau, & Pryor, 1998). HIV-positive infants should be assessed by 2 months of age and re-evaluated every 6 months thereafter (Batshaw & Perret, 1992; Mangione, Landau, & Pryor, 1998). Mangione and colleagues (1998) advocated yearly assessments for those children who plateau or remit by age 2 and more frequent assessments for those who show deterioration of health.

Cancer. Chronic illness can manifest in many ways during development and can result in significant psychoeducational impairment (Thies, 1999). Children with cancer require specialized educational planning and ongoing assessment (Thies, 1999). According to the American Cancer Society (ACS, 2001), cancer is a group of diseases characterized by the spread and uncontrolled growth of abnormal cells. It is believed that various internal (i.e., hormones, immune conditions, and inherited mutations) and/or external (i.e., radiation and viruses) may act collectively or sequentially in carcinogenesis (ACS, 2001). Cancer is a very general term that includes a heterogeneous group of diseases, including leukemia (the most common form of childhood cancer), Wilm's tumor (a cancer of the kidney), neuroblastoma (a malignant tumor of the autonomic nervous system), rhabdomyosarcoma (malignant tumors involving striated muscle), osteogenic sarcoma (bone cancers), and retinoblastoma (eye cancer) (Li & Wendt, 1998). According to the American Cancer Society (2001), cancer is one of the leading causes of disease-related death among children 1 to 14 years of age. However, owing to medical advances,

childhood cancer has evolved from a fatal illness to a life-threatening, chronic condition (Thies, 1999). Since 1973, mortality rates have declined 50 percent (ACS, 2001). Childhood cancers are treated by a combination of therapies selected based on the specified cancer type and stage of the disease (ACS, 2001). A treatment team approach is utilized with members including: oncological physicians, pediatric nurses, social workers, psychologists, and other child specialists (ACS, 2001). For a succinct description of childhood cancer and the psychoeducational implications, see Li and Wendt's (1998) chapter in A *Guidebook for Understanding and Educating Health-Related Disorders in Children and Adolescents: A Compilation of 96 Rare and Common Disorders* (LeAdelle Phelps, ed.).

Assessment of children with cancer is sometimes necessary to document the effects of the cancer or the treatment on overall development. At initial diagnosis, a full arena assessment is recommended regarding cognitive, social-emotional, gross and fine motor, adaptive, and language development skills to provide a baseline for future comparison. When possible, standardized measures and rating scales should be used in order to record easily comparable standard scores. As always with infants and preschoolers, standardized testing should be supplemented with rich qualitative assessment and description. Assessment should be conducted approximately every six months to provide a running record of disease and medication effects.

Each assessment should include a full medical update. The update should document medications, noting possible and observed side effects. In addition, the latest medical interventions should be noted, including chemotherapy, surgery, and dietary manipulations. Social emotional changes should be noted, including the family's response to diagnosis and treatment progress. The child's alertness and medical state are very important to document. Assessment should be scheduled at peak performance hours. For example, if the child responds best an hour after taking medication and just after eating, then a mid-morning appointment would capitalize on peak performance hours. A statement should be included in regard to the validity of the day's assessment based on the child's ability to respond to testing. For example, a child who appears to be experiencing fatigue and nausea may not perform as well as she might normally.

Prematurity. Premature infants are assessed according to their adjusted age (Preator & McAllister, 1995). This is done either by using their due date or their age post-conception (Preator & McAllister, 1995). Consequently, the 6-month-old child who was born 3 months early is compared with 3-month-old children and developmental guidelines rather than 6-month-old children and developmental guidelines (Preator & McAllister, 1995). Premature infants often lag behind developmental expectation even for their adjusted ages (Preator & McAllister, 1995).

Preator and McAllister (1995) reported that motor skills tend to lag behind other skills. The premature infant's shoulders are often retracted and the "infants keep their arms and hands pulled back in line with or behind their shoulders rather than relaxed at the midline" (Preator & McAllister, 1995, p. 780). A physical therapist should be consulted to properly assess the effects of this possible birth outcome. Further, positioning and supports may be helpful (as described under neuromotor impairments).

Preator and McAllister (1995) found that most premature infants do not have long-lasting medical or developmental problems, with the exception of very-low-birth-weight babies (<3 lbs., 5 oz.) and those who experienced severe perinatal complications. With the more involved children, developmental problems include those discussed in this chapter (e.g., neuromotor impairments, mental retardation). Preator and McAllister (1995) found that babies born prematurely present with several medical needs and complications, including neurological difficulties (intraventricular hemorrhages or cysts, seizures, and sensory impairment), chronic lung disease (bronchopulmonary dysplasia, hyaline membrane disease or respiratory distress syndrome), apnea (lack of breathing for longer than 15 to 20 seconds), bradycardia (slower than normal heartbeat), and visual impairments (retinopathy of prematurity).

Summary

The assessment of a child with severe disabilities requires the assessor to be cognizant of the specialized methods and techniques that are generally most effective with this population, as well as the needs of each specific disability. Assessor flexibility and creativity are key to successful assessment. However, the creativity required for a successful and informative assessment must be accompanied by a descriptive narrative of supports, scaffolds, and accommodations utilized during the assessment session. Specialized procedures such as convergent assessment, task analysis, functional behavioral assessment, play assessment, and parent interview will provide the qualitative data needed to supplement the quantitative, standardized assessment tools when they are invalid in specific cases. Such an integration of technique and standardization requires additional assessment competencies, knowledge, and experience in the realm of adaptive materials and procedures (Luciano, 1994). Ultimately, a highly descriptive and informative assessment performed by a well-trained and sensitive assessor will serve to lead highly effective intervention planning.

References

Abidin, R. (1995). *Parenting Stress Index* (PSI). Odessa, FL: Psychological Assessment Resources.

Achenbach, T. M., & Edelbrock, C. S. (1981). Behaviorial problems and competencies reported to parents of normal and disturbed children aged 14 through 16. *Monographs of the Society for Research in Child Development*, 46 (Serial nos. 1 & 188).

American Cancer Society (2001). *Cancer facts and figures–2001*. Atlanta, GA: Author.

American Foundation for the Blind (2000). Home Page. Available at: *www.afb.org.*

American Psychiatric Association. (2000). *Diagnostic and statistical manual of mental disorders* (4th ed.- Text Revised). Washington, DC: Author.

Amerson, M. J. (1999). Helping children with visual and motor impairments make the most of their visual abilities. RE: -*View*, 31, 17–21.

Anderson, G., & Smith, A. (1979). *Receptive Expressive Language Assessment for the Visually Impaired.* Mason, MI: Ingham Intermediate School District.

Arnold, K. D. (1998). Deaf-blindness. In L. Phelps (Ed.), *A guidebook for understanding and educating health-related disorders in children and adolescents: A compilation of 96 rare and common disorders* (pp. 224–232). Washington, DC: American Psychological Association.

Arthur, G. (1952). The Arthur Adaptation of the Leiter International Performance Scale. *Journal of Clincial Psychology,* 5, 345–349.

Ashhurst, D., Bamberg, E., Barrett, J., Bisno, A., Burke, A., Chambers, D., Fentiman, J., Kadish, R., Mitchell, M., Neely, L., Thorne, T., & Wents, D. (1985). *California Ordinal Scales of Development.* Los Angeles, CA: Western Psychological Services.

Bagnato, S. J., & Neisworth, J. T. (1991). *Assessment for early intervention: Best practices for professionals.* New York: Guilford Press.

Bagnato, S. J., Neisworth, J. T., & Munson, S. M. (1997). *Linking assessment and early intervention: An authentic curriculum-based approach.* Baltimore: Brookes.

Baldwin, V. (1992, December). *Population/demographics: Presentations.* Paper presented at the National Symposium on Children and Youth Who Are Deaf-Blind, Tysons Corner, VA.

Batshaw, M. L., & Perret, Y. M. (1992). *Children with disabilities: A medical primer* (3rd ed.). Baltimore: Brookes.

Benner, S. M. (1992). *Assessing young children with special needs: An ecological perspective.* New York: Longman.

Berg, W. K., Wacker, D. P., & Steege, M. W. (1995). Best practices in assessment with persons who have severe and profound handicaps. In A. Thomas & J. Grimes (Eds.), *Best practices in school psychology–III* (pp. 805–816). Washington, DC: The National Association of School Psychologists.

Bracken, B. A. (1991). *The psychological assessment of preschool children* (2nd ed.). Boston: Allyn & Bacon.

Brigance, A. H. (1991). BRIGANCE *Diagnostic Inventory for Early Development-Revised* (BDIED-R). N. Billerica, MA: Curriculum Associates.

Brown, L. B., Simmons, J. C., & Methvin, E. (1994). *Oregon project curriculum for visually impaired and blind preschool children.* Medford, OR: Jackson County Education Service District.

Bruininks, R. H., Woodcock, R. W., Weatherman, R. F., & Hill, B. K. (1984). *Scales of Independent Behavior* (SIB). Allen, TX: DLM Teaching Resources.

Burgemeister, B. B., Blum, L. H., & Lorge, I. (1972). *Columbia Mental Maturity Scale* (3rd ed.). San Antonio: The Psychological Corporation.

Campbell, S. K., Kolobe, T., Osten, E. T., Lenke, M., & Girolami, G. L. (1995). Construct validity of the test of infant motor performance. *Physical Therapy,* 75, 585–596.

Carpenter, M., Nagell, K., & Tomasello, M. (1998). Social cognition, joint attention and communication competence from 9 to 15 months of age. In Clifton, R. K., Daehler, M. W., & McCall, D. (Eds.), *Monographs of the Society for Research in Child Development* (225th ed.) (p. 1). Chicago: University of Chicago Press.

Caton, H. (1986). *Tactile Test of Basic Concepts.* Louisville, KY: American Printing House for the Blind.

Centers for Disease Control. (1994). 1994 revised classification system for human immunodeficiency virus infection in children less than 13 years of age. *Morbidity and Mortality Weekly Report,* 43, 2–8.

Centers for Disease Control (1995). First 500,000 AIDS cases—United States, 1995. *Journal of the American Medical Association,* 274, 1827–1828.

Cole, C. L., & Arndt, K. (1998). Autism. In L. Phelps (Ed.), *A guidebook for understanding and educating health-related disorders in children and adolescents: A compilation of 96 rare and common disorders* (pp. 82–92). Washington, DC: American Psychological Association.

Cowden, J. E., & Torrey, C. C. (1995). A ROADMAP for assessing infants, toddlers, and preschoolers: The role of the adapted motor developmentalist. *Adapted Physical Activity Quarterly,* 12, 1–11.

Davidson, P., & Legouri, S. A. (1986). Assessment of visually impaired children. In R. J. Simeonson (Ed.), *Psychological and developmental assessment of special children* (pp. 217–239). Boston: Allyn & Bacon.

Davis, C. (1980). *Perkins-Binet Tests of Intelligence for the Blind.* Watertown, MA: Perkins School for the Blind.

Dodson-Burk, B., & Hill, E. (1989). *Preschool Orientation and Mobility Screening.* Alexandria, VA: Association for Education and Rehabilitation of the Blind and Visually Impaired.

DuBose, R. F. (1981). Assessment of severely impaired young children: Problems and recommendations. *Topics in Early Childhood Special Education,* 1, 9–21.

Foster-Johnson, L., & Dunlap, G. (1993). Using functional assessment to develop effective, individualized interventions for challenging behaviors. *Teaching Exceptional Children,* Spring, 44–50.

Freeman, B. J., Tonick, L., Ritvo, E. R., Guthrie, D., & Schroth, P. (1979). *The Behavior Observation Scale for Autism: Frequency analysis.* Paper presented at a meeting of the American Psychological Association, New York (ERIC Document Reproduction Services No. ED181 702).

Geers, A. E., & Lane, H. S. (1984). *Central Institute for the Deaf Preschool Performance Scale* (CID). Wood Dale, IL: Stoelting.

Gerken, K. C. (1991). Assessment of preschool children with severe handicaps. In B. A. Bracken (Ed.), *Psychoeducational assessment of preschool children* (pp. 392–429). Boston: Allyn & Bacon.

Gillberg, C. (1990). Infantile autism: Diagnosis and treatment. *Acta Psychiatrica Scandinavica*, 81, 209–215.

Grossman, H. J. (1983). *Classification in mental retardation*. Washington, DC: American Association of Mental Deficiency.

Hallahan, D. P., & Kauffman, J. M. (2000). *Exceptional learners: Introduction to special education* (8th ed.). Boston: Allyn & Bacon.

Heller, K. W., Alberto, P. A., Forney, P. E., & Schwartzman, M. N. (1996). *Understanding physical, sensory, and health impairments*. Pacific Grove, CA: Brooks/Cole.

Heward, W. L. (2000). *Exceptional children: An introduction to special education* (6th ed.). Upper Saddle River, NJ: Merrill/Prentice Hall.

Hiskey, M. S. (1966). *Manual for the Hiskey-Nebraska Test of Learning Aptitude*. Lincoln, NE: Union College Press.

Joseph, J. (1979). *Joseph Pre-School and Primary Self-Concept Screening Test*. Wood Dale, IL: Stoelting.

Kanner, L. (1943). Autistic disturbances of affective contact. *Nervous Child*, 2, 217–250.

Kaufman, A. S., & Kaufman, N. L. (1983). K-ABC: *Kaufman Assessment Battery for Children*. Circle Pines, MN: American Guidance Services.

Krug, D., Arick, J., & Almond, P. (1993). *Autism Screening Instrument for Educational Planning* (2nd ed.) (ASIEP-2). Austin, TX: PRO-ED.

Kundert, D. K., Kuhn, J. M., & Brown, M. B. (1998). Visual impairments: Amblyopia, nystagmus, and strabismus. In L. Phelps (Ed.), *A guidebook for understanding and educating health-related disorders in children and adolescents: A compilation of 96 rare and common disorders* (pp. 701–711). Washington, DC: American Psychological Association.

Landry, S. H., Robinson, S. S., Copeland, D., & Garner, P. (1993). Goal-directed behavior and perception of self-competence in children with spina bifida. *Journal of Pediatric Psychology*, 18, 389–396.

Lane, S. J., & Mistrett, S. G. (1996). Play and assistive technology issues for infants and young children with disabilities: A preliminary examination. *Focus on Autism and Other Developmental Disabilities*, 11, 96–105.

Layton, T., & Holmes, D. (1985). *Carolina Picture Vocabulary Test for Deaf and Hearing Impaired*. Austin, TX: PRO-ED.

Li, C. Y., & Wendt, R. N. (1998). Cancer (childhood). In L. Phelps (Ed.), *A guidebook for understanding and educating health-related disorders in children and adolescents: A compilation of 96 rare and common disorders* (pp. 114–120). Washington, DC: American Psychological Association.

Linder, T. W. (1993). *Transdisciplinary play-based assessment: A functional approach to working with young children* (Rev. ed.). Baltimore: Brookes.

Luciano, L. B. (1994). Children with severe disabilities. In J. A. Bondurant-Utz & L. Luciano (Eds.), *A practical guide to infant and preschool assessment in special education*. (pp. 99–140). Needham, MA: Allyn & Bacon.

Mangione, C., Landau, S., & Pryor, J. B. (1998). HIV and AIDS (Pediatric and adolescent). In L. Phelps (Ed.), *A guidebook for understanding and educating health-related disorders in children and adolescents: A compilation of 96 rare and common disorders*. (pp. 328–336). Washington, DC: American Psychological Association.

Marcus, L. M., & Baker, A. (1986). Assessment of autistic children. In R. J. Simeonsson (Ed.), *Psychological and developmental assessment of special children* (pp. 279–304). Boston: Allyn & Bacon.

Martin, H. P. (1982). Neurological and medical factors affecting assessment. In G. Ulrey & S. J. Rogers (Eds.), *Psychological assessment of handicapped infants and young children* (pp. 86–94). New York: Thieme-Stratton.

Maxfield-Buchholz, K. (1957). *Maxfield-Buchholz Scale of Social Maturity for Preschool Blind Children*. New York: American Foundation for the Blind.

Mayes, S. D., & Calhoun, S. L. (1999). Symptoms of autism in young children and correspondence with the DSM. *Infants and Young Children*, 12, 90–97.

McConaughy, S. H., & Ritter, D. R. (1995). Best practices in multidimensional assessment of emotional or behavioral disorders. In A. Thomas & J. Gries (Eds.), *Best practices in school psychology–III* (pp. 865–876). Washington, DC: The National Association of School Psychologists.

McConnell, S. R. (2000). Assessment in early intervention and early childhood special education: Building on the past to project into our future. *Topics in Early Childhood Special Education*, 20, 43–49.

Meadow, K. P. (1983). An instrument for assessment of social-emotional adjustment in hearing-impaired preschoolers. *American Annals of the Deaf*, 128, 826–884.

Merrell, K. W. (1994). *Preschool and Kindergarten Behavior Scales* (PKBS). Austin, TX: PRO-ED.

Meyers, A. (1994). Natural history of congenital HIV infection. *Journal of School Health*, 64, 9–10.

Moog, J., & Geers, A. (1975). *Scales of Early Communication Skills for Hearing-Impaired Children* (SECS). St. Louis, MO: Central Institute for the Deaf.

Moog, J., & Geers, A. (1983). *Grammatical analysis of elicited language* (GAEL). St. Louis, MO: Central Institute for the Deaf.

Moore, M. S., & McLaughlin, L. (1992). Assessment of the preschool child with visual impairment. In E. V. Nuttall, I. Romero, & J. Kalesnik (Eds.), *Assessing and screening preschoolers: Psychological and educational dimensions* (pp. 345–368). Boston: Allyn & Bacon.

Mullen, Y. (1992). Assessment of the preschool child with hearing impairment. In E. V. Nuttall, I. Romero, & J. Kalesnik (Eds.), *Assessing and screening preschoolers:*

Psychological and educational dimensions (pp. 327–343). Boston: Allyn & Bacon.

Neisworth, J. T., & Bagnato, S. J. (1992). The case against intelligence testing in early intervention. *Topics in Early Childhood Special Education, 12,* 1–20.

New York State Department of Health Early Intervention Program (1999). *Clinical practice guideline: Report of the recommendations.* Autism/pervasive developmental disorders, assessment and intervention for young children (age 0–3 years). Albany, NY: Author.

Newborg, J., Stock, J. R., Wnek, L., Guidubaldi, J., & Svinicki, J. S. (1988). *Battelle Developmental Inventory (BDI).* Chicago: Riverside.

Nuttall, E. V., Romero, I., & Kalesnik, J. (1992). *Assessing and screening preschoolers: Psychological and educational dimensions.* Boston: Allyn & Bacon.

Paul, R. (1987). Communication. In D. J. Cohen & A. M. Donnellan (Eds.), *Handbook of autism and pervasive developmental delays.* New York: Wiley.

Preator, K. K., & McAllister, J. R. (1995). Best practices assessing infants and toddlers. In A. Thomas & J. Grimes (Eds.), *Best practices in school psychology* (pp. 775–788). Washington, DC: National Association of School Psychologists.

Ray, S., & Ulissi, S. M. (1982). *Adaptation of the Weschler Preschool and Primary Scales of Intelligence for Deaf Children.* Natchitoches, LA: Steven Ray.

Reynell, J., & Zinkin, K. (1979). *Reynell-Zinkin Developmental Scales for Young Visually Handicapped Children (RZS).* Wood Dale, IL: Stoelting Company.

Robinson, C., & Fieber, N. (1988). Cognitive assessment with motorically impaired infants and preschoolers. In T. Wachs & R. Sheehan (Eds.), *Assessment of developmentally disabled children.* New York: Plenum.

Rogers, S. J. (1999). Intervention for young children with autism, from research to practice. *Infants & Young Children, 12,* 1–16.

Rogers, S. J., & Soper, E. (1982). Assessment considerations with hearing impaired preschoolers. In G. Ulrey & S. Rogers (Eds.), *Psychological assessment of handicapped infants and young children* (pp. 115–122). New York: Thieme-Stratton.

Rosenberg, S. A., & Robinson, C. (1990). Assessment of the infant with multiple handicaps. In E. Gibbs & D. Teti (Eds.), *Interdisciplinary assessment of infants: A guide for early intervention professionals* (pp. 177–188). Baltimore: Brookes.

Sattler, J. M. (1988). *Assessment of children.* San Diego: Author.

Schopler, E., Reichler, R., Bashford, A., Lansing, M., & Marcus, L. (1979). *Individualized Assessment and Treatment for Autistic and Developmentally Disabled Children (IATA).* Austin, TX: PRO-ED.

Schopler, E., Reichler, R. J., & Renner, B. R. (1988). *Childhood Autism Rating Scale (CARS).* Los Angeles: Western Psychological Services.

Shine, A. E. (1998). Spina bifida. In L. Phelps (Ed), A *guidebook for understanding and educating health-related disorders in children and adolescents: A compilation of 96 rare and common disorders.* (pp. 616–623). Washington, DC: American Psychological Association.

Shumway-Cook, A., & Woollacott, M. (1993). Theoretical issues in assessing postural control. In I. J. Wilhelm (Ed.), *Physical therapy assessment in early infancy* (pp. 161–171). New York: Churchill Livingston.

Simeonsson, R. J. (1986). *Psychological and developmental assessment of special children.* Boston: Allyn & Bacon.

Smith, A., & Johnson, R. E. (1977). *Smith-Johnson Nonverbal Performance Scale.* Los Angeles: Western Psychological Services.

Sparrow, S. S., Balla, D. A., & Cicchetti, D. V. (1984). *Vineland Adaptive Behavior Scales–Interview Edition.* Circle Pines, MN: American Guidance Services.

Steege, M., Wacker, D., & McMahon, C. (1987). Evaluation of the effectiveness and efficiency of two stimulus prompt strategies with severely handicapped students. *Journal of Applied Behavior Analysis, 20,* 293–299.

Stillman, R. (1974). *Callier-Azusa Scale: Assessment of Deaf-Blind Children (CAS).* Reston, VA: Council for Exceptional Children.

Swallow, R., Mangold, S., & Mangold, P. (1978). *Informal Assessment of Developmental Skills for Visually Handicapped Students.* New York: American Foundation for the Blind.

Thies, K. M. (1999). Identifying the educational implications of chronic illness in school children. *Journal of School Health, 69,* 392–405.

Thorndike, R. L., Hagen, E. P., & Sattler, J. M. (1986). *Guide for administering and scoring the Stanford-Binet Intelligence Scale:* (4th ed.). Chicago: Riverside.

Vinson, B. (1996). A team approach to preschool assessment. *Contemporary Education, 1,* 28–30.

Volmer, L. (1995). Best practices in working with students with autism. In A. Thomas & J. Grimes (Eds.), *Best practices in school psychology–III.* Washington, DC: The National Association of School Psychologists.

Wachs, T. D., & Sheehan, R. (1988). *Assessment of young developmentally disabled children.* New York: Plenum.

Waterman, J. (1982). Assessment considerations with the emotionally disturbed child. In G. Urley & S. J. Rogers (Eds.), *Psychological assessment of handicapped infants and young children* (pp. 142–148). New York: Thieme-Stratton.

Wilhelm, C., Johnson, M., & Eisert, D. (1986). Assessment of motor-impaired children. In R. J. Simeonsson (Ed.), *Psychological and developmental assessment of special children* (pp. 241–278). Newton, MA: Allyn & Bacon.

Wolters, P. L., Brouwers, P., & Moss, H. A. (1995). Pediatric HIV disease: Effects on cognition, learning, and behavior. *School Psychology Quarterly, 10,* 305–328.

Zimmerman, I. L., Steiner, V. G., & Evatt, R. L. (1969). *Preschool Language Scale.* Columbus, OH: Merrill.

III

Stages in the Assessment Process

8

Child Find, Screening, and Identification

Because infants, toddlers, and preschoolers are not required to participate in publicly supported educational programs, simply having a program available for young children with special needs does not ensure that the children who need these services will find them (McLean, 1996). Unlike older children who are conveniently grouped and observed in schools, infants, toddlers, and preschoolers typically are not encountered in one place. Parents and professionals who come into contact with these young children must be alerted to any indications of a child's need for early intervention services. This chapter describes the process of finding the young children who are in need of special services and the tracking and screening processes for determining if these young children are eligible for special services.

Child Find

Child Find is a systematic process of identifying infants and young children who are eligible or potentially eligible for enrollment in intervention programs (McLean, 1996, p. 97). These activities are intended to inform the general public about typical and atypical child development and inform parents of referral procedures if assessment or intervention is thought to be necessary.

Activities in the Child Find process alert parents and professionals to warning signs. Warning signs are developmental conditions which are considered to be disabling or which may lead to abnormal growth and development. The purpose of the Child Find stage is to alert families and professionals to signs which might indicate the need for early intervention, why early intervention is important, and where parents can find professionals who can help them to determine if the child needs to be screened for possible developmental delays. Child Find should be a systematic process of identifying

infants and children who are eligible or potentially eligible for enrollment in early intervention programs.

Legal Mandates for Child Find

PL 94–142 established Child Find programs in each state for children ages birth through 21 years (McLean, 1996). Child Find programs continued to be required for infants, toddlers, and preschoolers under PL 99–457 and PL 105–17. The Child Find system is to be comprehensive and include a system for making referrals to service providers and timelines for referrals and services. Each state must have a coordinated public awareness program that focuses on early identification of infants, toddlers, and preschoolers with disabilities. The Child Find system must be coordinated with all other state efforts to identify children for various education, health, and social service programs. This coordination of the Child Find system should ensure that there will not be duplication of efforts, existing resources will be used, and there are no gaps in services.

Child Find Strategies

Because every community is unique, many states have established local coordinating groups and formalized agreements to assist in coordination of Child Find efforts. One strategy for linking referrals to services is a collaborative community team composed of representatives from each of the agencies that provide services to infants, toddlers, and preschoolers who are at-risk or disabled and their families. Children who are suspected of being at-risk or disabled are referred, with parental permission, to the team to determine their eligibility for services. For example, for infants and toddlers, the service coordinator should be a part of this coordinating group and support the child and family throughout the assessment process.

Consolidating the forms for referral and using a single point of contact for families reduces the duplication of services and assures that the family is made aware of all services, as well as increases the likelihood that services will be coordinated (Hanson & Lynch, 1995).

Peterson (1987) described four strategies that may be used to gain referrals and recruit children for screening. Table 8–1 describes each of the recommended approaches for recruiting children. The first approach or strategy is building community awareness. Community awareness is increased by public announcements of screening clinics, presentations to community groups, and the formation of an advocacy group designed to increase visibility and local support

TABLE 8–1
Strategies for Casefinding

Task	Description	Strategies
Building community awareness	Purpose is to (a) educate the public about importance of early identification and intervention with handicapped and high-risk children, (b) alert the public of the availability of screening services and special early intervention programs, and (c) enlist assistance of public agencies, organizations, and local citizens in making referrals and in supporting services for young children with special needs.	1. Announcements alerting public about screening clinics and the importance of identifying children who need special help, through newspaper features, radio/TV spots, posters, or distribution of brochures/letters/ information sheets to community leaders, service agencies, and professional practitioners 2. Presentations to PTAs and other parent groups, church and civic groups, local professional organizations, special interest groups, and staffs of local service agencies. 3. Creation of an advocacy group among influential citizens and personnel in key positions within organizations who can bring visibility and local support to recruitment efforts.
Setting up system for referral and eliciting referrals	Purpose is to establish network of informed agencies and individuals who come into contact with a large number of children and who will take initiative to refer appropriate children for screening. Task is to (a) provide these persons or agencies with information on screening clinics and service programs for handi-capped/high-risk children, (b) provide information and written literature on contact person and procedure for making referrals, and (c) establish working relationships between referral agents and intake/screening contact person.	1. Direct contacts with officials of key community agencies to establish formal linkages for sending and receiving referrals (e.g., public schools, local preschool and care programs, churches, mental health clinics, social service and welfare offices, health clinics, and agencies serving the handicapped—such as Easter Seal, United Cerebral Palsy, Association for Retarded Citizens). 2. Direct contacts with private practitioners who serve young children and their parents and who are in a prime position to make referrals (e.g., pediatricians and other medical professionals, dentists, psychologists and family counselors, psychiatrists, social workers, and therapists in private clinics, such as speech-language-hearing clinics or mental health clinics).

TABLE 8–1
continued

Task	Description	Strategies
Canvassing community for children who need screening	Purpose is to conduct a systematic survey of children in the designated age range and geographical area to identify those for whom screening is needed and who may not be referred through other sources (often the mildly handicapped or developmentally delayed). The task is not only one of systematically canvassing the community to gain direct or indirect contact with the target population of children, but also to offer guides for helping parents and others identify child characteristics that suggest referral for a screening evaluation.	1. Direct observation of children or consultation with staff and parents associated with local preschool or day-care centers, local churches, parents' and women's groups, or any other major organization through which a large group of community members is brought together. 2. Direct door-to-door canvassing of community to share information on how to make referrals and to offer checklist guides for helping parents discern situations when a child should be referred for screening. 3. Distribution of information on screening services and referral procedures by sending materials home with school-age students or under-school-age youngsters enrolled in local preschool, day-care, and Head Start programs.
Maintaining local publicity and contacts with referral sources	Purpose is to maintain a continual flow of referrals from various sources by (a) keeping the network of individuals and agencies continually informed about the screening system and the current contact person(s), (b) sharing information on the ongoing activities of the screening placement system, and (c) providing yearly reports on the number of children identified for early intervention, and on the success of the screening system in linking children with community services.	1. Yearly renewal of official contacts with key citizens, agencies, and organizations in referral network, to provide updated information on referral procedures for new persons who may become involved as a result of normal turnover in agency personnel and organization membership. 2. Replenishment of written materials disseminated to the network of referral agencies and citizens so that casefinding activities are continued and do not fizzle out over time. 3. Dissemination of year-end written reports summarizing data on the number of children referred, number screened, and percentage of children subsequently placed in special service programs, to allow referral sources to see the outcomes of their efforts.

Source: From *Early Intervention for Handicapped and At-risk Children: An Introduction to Early Childhood-Special Education* (pp. 288–289), by Nancy L. Peterson, 1987. Denver: Love. Copyright 1987 by Love Publishing. Reprinted with permission.

of early intervention activities. Suggested methods to be used to inform the public include television, radio, and newspaper releases; pamphlets and posters in doctors' offices; and the use of a toll-free telephone service.

Once a system for referrals and eliciting referrals is established, the second strategy is initiated. Contact is made with community agencies such as health clinics, social services and welfare offices, local preschools and child care programs, agencies serving children with disabilities, and private practitioners serving families and young children with special needs. A central referral system, mandated in PL 99–457 and PL 105–17, can ease the confusion that parents often experience when they begin the search for appropriate community services.

The third strategy is canvassing the community for children who need screening. Peterson suggested direct observation of children in community programs, door-to-door canvassing to provide information and seek referrals, and distribution of informational flyers about screening clinics or other early intervention services to children.

The final approach is maintenance of local publicity and contacts with referral sources. The emphasis in this approach is on continuing contacts and relationships that have been established with various sources or agencies.

Tracking

Part C of PL 105–17 requires that states have a system for compiling data on the number of eligible infants and toddlers who are in need of early intervention services, the number actually served, and the types of services provided. Many states have included in their Child Find program a system for following or tracking infants or young children who are at-risk due to biological or environmental factors. A tracking program can help to ensure that children who are in need of early intervention will receive services as soon as possible (McLean, 1996).

Part C of the IDEA defines infants and toddlers as being "at-risk" if they are at risk of experiencing a substantial developmental delay if early intervention services were not provided to the individual (20 U.S.C. Chapter 33, Section 1432). The concept of risk is extremely broad. For example, some individuals would include all children from low-income families in a high-risk group. For others, a specific medical condition is the determiner of risk. (Eligibility criteria are discussed in Chapter 1.) Tjossem (1976) proposed definitions and descriptions of three major types of risk: established, environmental, and biological. These definitions have become standard across many professional disciplines. The category of at-risk pertains primarily to biological and environmental risk (McLean, 1996). An example of a biological risk would be a premature infant. An environmental risk would be the lack of health care. Children who are at-risk may receive early intervention services at the state's discretion; however, the majority of states do not provide intervention services to this group of children. A state that decides to serve this group must develop guidelines for determining which children would be eligible under this category. These guidelines may vary considerably based on how many risk factors the child must have to be at a higher probability of difficulties in child development and, therefore, in need of early intervention services (McLean, 1996).

States that offer a tracking system must decide which risk factors will qualify a child for tracking. Often a single risk factor, either biological or environmental, will qualify a child for tracking. Some children experience multiple or cumulative risks that combine to interfere with healthy development. Simeonsson (1991) suggested that simply counting the number of factors demonstrated by a child may not be most predictive because it may be the interaction *between* factors that is most important.

Many states have developed tracking systems to follow children who are at-risk for developmental delay but do not qualify for early intervention services. Referrals can be made by medical, social service, or education professionals or by parents or family members. The system of registry may be tied to the birth certificate process. With a birth review system, information about the newborn's birth can make the child eligible for tracking. The parents are offered tracking services if they desire. Information also may be provided about the potential effect on their child's development as well as available resources (McLean, 1996). It should be remembered that sensitivity to cultural variations and differences among families is critical for a successful tracking program. (Chapter 3 provides information on cultural diversity.)

An instrument developed specifically for monitoring child development is the Ages and Stages Questionnaires (ASQ) (Bricker, Squires, Mounts, Potter, Nickel, & Farrell, 1995). This questionnaire is designed to be completed by the family. Five sections are included: gross motor, fine motor, communication, personal-social, and adaptive development. Items are scored by checking "yes," "sometimes," and "not yet." Illustrations are provided to assist parents in assessing their child's behavior. The ASQ also can be used as an interview tool with families. Cutoff scores can be set at 1.0, l.5, or 2.0 SD below the mean. A lower SD will result in identifying more children. The user's guide includes procedures for establishing a monitoring system for prompting the mailing of questionnaires to families at appropriate times.

Children who have been identified as being at-risk for developmental delay must be assessed or screened to determine if any delays are present. The next step in the process is the screening stage. In this stage, a brief assessment of a child's overall development is administered to determine whether further testing is needed. This process is described in the next section of this chapter.

Screening

Screening is an important part of Child Find programs. Screening is a brief examination aimed at identifying those infants or young children who may be demonstrating developmental delays or differences, compared with standard expectations. This process allows the early detection of any developmental, sensory, or health problems. For example, early intervention specialists can survey multiple developmental domains, such as cognition, language, motor, adaptive, and social, in order to detect or identify abnormal development. Thorough screening can alert professionals, service providers, and parents to the need for further or fuller assessment of the child. Early intervention services may then be recommended as a result of this complete assessment. These early intervention services may lessen the impact of a disability on the child's development. Screening is a detection process that highlights possible problems in development which warrant more detailed assessment. The process locates areas of suspected difficulty but does not provide specifics.

Not all children should be screened. Children who have an established risk are clearly eligible for early intervention services as a result of a diagnosed condition or a substantial developmental delay. An established risk describes those children with a definite medical disorder or disease, such as Down's syndrome, which is known to result in developmental delay. These children should be referred directly for a complete assessment (McLean, 1996).

Optimal screening models rely on interagency efforts that provide periodic checks of children who appear to be developing normally and continuous follow-up watching infants, toddlers, and young children who are at-risk developmentally. A combination of screening settings, such as hospital health fairs, neighborhood health clinics, and mobile screening units that go to grocery stores, malls, community recreation centers, churches, and other places where people gather, can be used to reach families who do not seek routine health care (Hanson & Lynch, 1995). Some general considerations should be mentioned which will assist in developing effective screening programs.

General Guidelines for Screening

A number of factors must be considered when planning the screening of a particular population. Planners must determine the age of the group to be screened, how to access that population, the geographical location of the population to be served, and the likely range and prevalence of the developmental condition(s) for which screening is to be done. Meisels and Provence (1989) have summarized the key steps in developing a sound screening program:

1. Define the population for whom the screening and assessment model is intended.
2. Collect prevalence data for defined conditions.
3. Identify the origins of the defined conditions.
4. Identify standardized and nonstandardized measures that reflect the key etiological factors.
5. Develop an inventory of all existing screening and assessment programs and state-wide resources.
6. Devise a screening and assessment process.
7. Ascertain need for training and technical assistance.
8. Develop evaluation/research design, including provisions for longitudinal follow-up (p. 27).

Just as in any part of the developmental assessment process, screening information always should be considered in the context of the child's experience. Any assessment approach is a sampling process or a "snapshot" or series of snapshots of the child (Greenspan & Meisels, 1996).

The National Center for Infants, Toddlers, and Families has published a list of recommended guidelines for screening and assessment (Meisels & Provence, 1989). Including these considerations and recommendations in the planning of a screening program will increase the precision and effectiveness of the individual child screening program. This list is provided in Figure 8–1. Several aspects of the screening process should be emphasized and are discussed in the sections which follow (McLean, 1996).

Multiple Sources of Information. Although screening should be done quickly and economically, one must recognize that development is a complex process and multiple factors influence its course. In addition to the interdependence of developmental domains, both biological and environmental factors influence the development of infants and young children. These factors may support, facilitate, or impede the child's development (Greenspan & Meisels, 1996). When screening infants and young children who are at-risk, professionals should use an approach which allows for an overall scan of the child's functioning across a variety of domains and provides a view of family and environmental factors.

A comprehensive screening should include information from a variety of sources. Caregiving and environmental information should be combined with data about the child's biological status and environmental information (Meisels & Wasik, 1990). In the past, screening efforts have included developmental, sensory, and health factors (McLean, 1996). More recent research has shown that the presence of multiple risk factors, such as environmental and caregiving factors, results in a higher probability of difficulties in child development and thus is more predictive of developmental delay than merely looking at biological or health factors (Dunst, 1993; Greenbaum & Auerbach, 1992; Henderson & Meisels, 1994; Sameroff, Seifer, Barocas, Zax, & Greenspan, 1987). Because developmental disorders generally are attributable to multiple factors or causes, assessments should include multiple sources of information (Meisels & Provence, 1989). Such an approach could involve a pediatric examination, a family-responded developmental inventory, an overall look at the development of motor, language, cognitive, social, and self-help skills and a

FIGURE 8–1

Guidelines for Screening and Assessment

1. Screening and assessment should be viewed as services—as part of the intervention process—and not only as means of identification and measurement.
2. Processes, procedures, and instruments intended for screening and assessment should only be used for their specified purposes.
3. Multiple sources of information should be included in screening and assessment.
4. Developmental screening should take place on a recurrent or periodic basis. It is inappropriate to screen young children only once during their early years. Similarly, provisions should be made for reevaluation or reassessment after services have been initiated.
5. Developmental screening should be viewed as only one path to more in-depth assessment. Failure to qualify for services based on a single source of screening information should not become a barrier to further evaluation for intervention services if other risk factors (e.g., environmental, medical, familial) are present.
6. Screening and assessment procedures should be reliable and valid.
7. Family members should be an integral part of the screening and assessment process. Information provided by family members is critically important for determining whether or not to initiate more in-depth assessment and for designing appropriate intervention strategies. Parents should be accorded complete informed consent at all stages of the screening and assessment process.
8. During screening or assessment of developmental strengths and problems, the more relevant and familiar the tasks and setting are to the child and the child's family, the more likely it is that the results will be valid.
9. All tests, procedures, and processes intended for screening or assessment must be culturally sensitive.
10. Extensive and comprehensive training is needed by those who screen and assess very young children.

Source: From *Screening and Assessment: Guidelines for Identifying Young Disabled and Developmentally Vulnerable Children and Their Families*, p. 24 by S. J. Meisels and S. Provence, 1989, Arlington, VA: *Zero to Three*. Copyright 1989 by National Center for Clinical Infant Programs. Reprinted with permission.

review of environmental status. The screening process should also include teacher judgments of the developmental readiness of children in their preschool classes.

McLean (1996) cited a multivariate screening model developed for the state of Rhode Island as being an exemplary screening approach (Kochanek, 1988). This model uses a two-tiered approach with different levels of specificity. The first level identifies a large number of children as being at-risk. The first level of screening focuses on a review of available data regarding demographic variables (maternal age, education, marital status), child characteristics (neonatal and postnatal status, any known disabilities), and parental characteristics (performance of routine child care functions, reports of previous abuse or neglect, record of prenatal and preventive care). Based on the results obtained in the first level, children are referred to the second level of screening.

The second level of screening is completed in the home using established screening devices to review the child's developmental characteristics, family resources and supports, and parent-child interaction. Depending on the results of the second level, a child and family may be referred for an intensive multidisciplinary assessment or to an appropriate community-based resource that provides periodic monitoring. If no risk is observed, then the family may not be seen again until the next time that the first level of screening is scheduled (Kochanek, 1988). In this way, this approach combines information on child characteristics, parental traits, and mother-child interaction. Kochanek (1988) advised that any decision regarding the need for additional diagnostic testing should be made based on three sources of information: child characteristics, parental traits, and maternal-child interaction.

Family-Centered. Greenspan and Meisels (1996) emphasized "the child's relationship and interactions with his most trusted caregiver should form the cornerstone of an assessment" (p. 19). Screening, which is part of the developmental assessment process, should be family-centered. Chapter 2 provides a strong rationale for family involvement in the assessment process. Meisels and Provence (1989) emphasized that no screening should take place without the active participation of the child's parents. The parents are the most expert about the child. The task of those conducting the screening is to enable parents to transmit the information productively.

Screening is often the first experience a family has with the educational or human service system (Meisels & Provence, 1989). Involving families collaboratively at the very beginning will promote the formation of a stronger alliance with the family throughout the assessment and intervention process (McLean, 1996). Before beginning any part of the screening process, parents and caregivers should be informed about the entire process. They should be encouraged to participate in the screening process as fully as they feel comfortable. Adequate information about the screening's purpose, procedures, and possible outcomes must be given to ensure their full participation in the process. If necessary, the next step in the assessment process, referral for a diagnostic assessment, must be explained. The scope and limitations of screening should be described to establish appropriate expectations regarding the possible outcome of screening.

Parent information may be gathered in two ways. Parents may be asked in a general fashion if they have any particular concerns about their child's development. This question may be part of a structured interview or an item on a developmental screening questionnaire or instrument (Diamond & Squires, 1993). Another approach is to have parents complete a developmental questionnaire. Parent-completed developmental questionnaires for Child Find and screening can be a low-cost means of obtaining information about the child's current functioning levels (Squires, Nickel, & Bricker, 1990). Some tools that have been recommended for parent completion are: (1) Communication Development Inventory (short form) (Dale, Bates, Reznick, & Morisset, 1989); (2) Language Development Survey (Rescorla, 1989); (3) Denver II screening manual (Frankenburg & Dodds, 1990; and (4) Revised Parent Developmental Questionnaire (Knobloch, Stevens, Malone, Ellison, & Risemberg, 1979). Research has demonstrated that combining parent measures with another screening instrument increases the predictive accuracy of the developmental screening process (Henderson & Meisels, 1994). Parent knowledge of a child's functioning can be balanced with a professional's awareness of warning signs and risk factors.

Conducting a Screening

Greenspan and Meisels (1996) reminded us that assessment is the process of obtaining information in order to make evaluative decisions. The approach to be used or the choice of assessment tools depends on the type of decision that will be required as a result of the assessment.

The purpose of screening is to provide general information about the child's development and to identify children who are likely to be members of groups at-risk for health or developmental problems. The results of the developmental screening are not intended to be used for diagnostic purposes, placement decisions, or providing labels of disabilities.

Professionals involved in the screening must be well-qualified and experienced to perform such tasks. Some screening procedures require specially trained professionals and expensive assessment materials. Others can be conducted by volunteers after a brief training period. Expense versus benefit is always a consideration. The tests used for developmental screening of large groups of children should be brief, inexpensive, and have an objective scoring system (Lerner, Lowenthal, & Egan, 1998).

All methods, instruments and procedures used must be culturally sensitive. The accuracy of the screening will be increased by providing screening that is:

- Carried out in a manner that is consistent with family beliefs, values, and language preferences;
- Conducted in settings that families frequent and in which they are comfortable; and
- Performed by people that families trust.

Ascertaining that these provisions are followed will also increase the chances that families will pursue more in-depth assessment if necessary. Scales should be selected that are similar in content to the skills expected to be learned and taught in early childhood programs. These screening batteries should contain multiple skills at each age level. Alberts, Davis, and Prentice (1995) recommended indirect screening for a diverse population of preschoolers. Indirect screening methods include teacher rating scales and checklists. This allows for observation of the child in a familiar context by culturally sensitive observers over a period of time. Alberts and colleagues (1995) used the Davis Observation Checklist for Texas (DOCT) to screen preschool children for communication disorders in Head Start programs in Texas. Results of the study showed the DOCT to be adequately sensitive and specific, compared with criterion measures used in identifying children with communication disorders.

Professionals planning screening programs must be careful that the screening procedures used are adequate in separating infants and preschoolers with disabilities or potentially disabling conditions from those with no potential problems. However, the failure to qualify for services based on one source of information should not prevent further assessment if other risk factors are evident.

"Screening models must be periodic and multivariate in design, and reflect an ongoing 'process' which discriminates between transient and permanent problems and takes into account child/environment transactions" (Kochanek, 1988, p. 18). All screening programs should incorporate a follow-up component to track those children who present with significant risks for developmental delay. Screening is an initial step and cannot result in diagnosing or classifying the child until further assessment is completed. If follow-up services are not available to infants who are at-risk, then screening programs have little or no impact. Effective screening programs have a high rate of follow-up or follow-through. Screening programs can be only one part of the services and interventions available to a population. Although identifying children with potential problems is the first step, encouraging families to seek further assessment for their child is the next step. The partnership which can be established between parents and screeners is important to the follow-through effort (Hanson & Lynch, 1995). Hanson and Lynch (1995) pointed out that asking family members to share information about their child as a valued part of the screening program and giving information about the findings of the screening in a clear yet supportive manner increase the chances that parents and caregivers will feel concerned and confident enough to obtain a more in-depth assessment.

The guidelines recommended in this chapter and the suggestions for conducting a screening are essential for providing effective screening programs. Another key factor is the accuracy of the instruments used to make these decisions. Careful consideration must also be given to finding accurate screening instruments.

Accuracy of Instruments

Typically, screening brings to mind the use of psychometric instruments. However, the guidelines recommended by Meisels and Provence (1989) demonstrate that such instruments must be embedded within a process that incorporates multiple variables reviewed on several occasions, in a variety of settings, by a number of trained individuals who are informed by clinical insights obtained from children and their families. The screening instruments that are chosen should be "brief, norm-referenced, inexpensive, standardized in administration, objectively scored" (Meisels & Wasik, 1990, p. 613). Screening tests must be nondiscriminatory, and they should be as reliable and valid as possible (Meisels, 1991; Meisels & Wasik, 1990).

Reliability. Reliability refers to the consistency and stability of measurement. This is a critical dimension for tests (McLean, 1996). Reliability estimates are provided for norm-referenced tests. This concept is discussed in detail in Chapter 9 on norm-referenced assessment.

Before an assessment measure is chosen for a screening program, the test manual should be reviewed and research articles examined that have measured the reliability of the particular assessment chosen. It is assumed that all members of the screening team would be fully trained in administering and scoring this

assessment and that periodic checks are conducted in the administration and scoring of the assessment (McLean, 1996).

Validity. Validity involves the extent to which measures can be used for specific purposes. Screening measures should provide for two types of criterion validity: concurrent and predictive (McLean, 1996). Concurrent validity refers to the extent to which the screening test agrees with more thorough measures such as diagnostic tests. Predictive validity refers to the extent to which the screening test agrees with children's performance on outcome measures later in time. In other words, the screening measure given to a young child accurately predicts her performance on an instrument administered in the first grade (McLean, 1996). Validity is discussed more fully in Chapter 9 on norm-referenced assessment.

When choosing an assessment instrument for a screening program, the test manual should be examined for information on the validity of the instrument. The instrument should be free from bias regarding age, sex, geographic region, economic background, and racial or ethnic status. The test manual should include information about the standardization population to ensure that this population is similar to those for whom the measure is being considered (McLean, 1996).

Sensitivity and Specificity. Sensitivity refers to the ability of the test to identify a high proportion of the children who are actually developmentally delayed or have a disability. Specificity refers to the ability of the test to not identify children who do not have a disability or developmental delay (McLean, 1996). The test should identify those who should be referred and those who should not be referred for further assessment. The level of sensitivity and specificity can be adjusted to the screening program. If fewer children need to be identified, then the standard deviation below the mean would be larger, possibly 2.0 SD. Requiring a smaller standard deviation, such as 1.0 SD, would result in more children being identified. Any of the standardized screening instruments would allow the examiner to choose the cutoff score for identifying children for referral for further assessment. Standard deviation is discussed in Chapter 9 on norm-based assessment.

Possible Screening Errors. Two possible errors that can occur in the screening process are the identification of false positives and false negatives. False positives identify children as needing referral for further assessment and possible intervention when they are actually progressing normally. Screenings that result in high numbers of false positives create an overidentification of children who need follow-up diagnostic examinations. On the other hand, screenings that result in high numbers of false negatives lead to the underidentification of children needing diagnostic follow-up and possible intervention. False negatives occur when children who were not targeted for follow-up at a screening have future developmental progress indicating that they should have been. Ensuring and facilitating follow-up services will help to minimize false positives and false negatives.

Selecting a Screening Instrument

In order to select the appropriate screening instrument for a specific population, the Meisels and Provence (1989) guidelines outlined in this chapter must be followed. If these guidelines and rationale for screening are followed, then measurement activities in early childhood can be used to help children and families receive services and assist states in meeting the mandates of PL 105–17. McLean (1996) provided extensive information on seven currently used screening instruments, including reliability and validity data, administration information, materials provided in the test kit, and examples of items from some of the assessments. Information

about these instruments is summarized in Table 8–2 (McLean, 1996).

Another screening instrument not included in this table is the *Early Screening Inventory-Revised* (ESI-R) (Meisels, Marsden, Wiske, & Henderson, 1997). This is a developmental screening instrument for 3- to 6-year-olds. The inventory comprises two sample scoring sheets, one for preschool (ages 3 to 4) and one for kindergarten (ages 4 to 6), and a parent questionnaire. The inventory is designed to be individually administered for the purpose of identifying children who may need special education services. The measure covers the developmental areas of visual motor/adaptive, language and cognition, and gross motor skills. Important features are the ease of learning and administration, the 15- to 20-minute time requirement, and the ease with which administrators can interpret and parents can understand results.

Evaluation of Screening Programs

McLean (1996) recommended screening programs be evaluated on a regular basis to ensure effectiveness. The following general questions are provided to guide evaluation efforts:

- Are there children who passed the screening and later are found to need special education services?
- Are there children referred for assessment who are found to not be eligible for services?
- Are the families who participate in screening satisfied with the experience?
- Is assessment being completed in a timely fashion for those children who are referred for evaluation as a result of screening? (p. 108)

It is suggested that the first two questions be answered by completing a follow-up of the children and comparing the children who were eventually identified as needing services with those who were not. An effective screening program would identify only those children

TABLE 8–2
Selected Screening Instruments

Instrument	Publisher	Age Range	Domains	Outcomes	Norms
AGS Early Screening Instrument (Harrison et al., 1990)	American Guidance Service, Inc., Circle Pines, MN	2 years to 6 years, 11 months	Profiles: Cognitive/ Language Motor Self-Help/Social Surveys: Articulation Home Survey Health History Survey Behavior Survey	Level I: Above Average Average Below Average Level II Profiles: Standard scores Normal curve equivalents Percentile scores Stanines Age equivalents	1149 children stratified by age, geographic region, race, gender, parent education, and size of school district
Battelle Developmental Screening Test (Newborg, Stock, Wnek, Guidubaldi & Svinicki, 1988)	Riverside Publishing Company, Chicago, IL	Birth to 8 years	Personal/Social Adaptive Motor Communication Cognition	Pass/Fail based on −1.0, −1.5, or −2.0 cut-off; age equivalents	800 children stratified by age, race, and gender
Brigance Preschool Screen (Brigance, 1985); Brigance Early Preschool Screen (Brigance, 1990)	Curriculum Associates, N. Billerica, MA	2 years, 9 months to 5 years; 21–36 months	Not divided into domains	Referral for further evaluation or no referral	None reported
Denver II (Frankenburg & Dodds, 1990)	Denver Develop-mental Materials, Denver, CO	Birth to 6 years	Personal/Social Fine Motor/ Adaptive Language Gross Motor	Normal Abnormal Questionable Untestable	2096 children stratified by age, maternal education, ethnicity, and urban or rural residence

TABLE 8-2
continued

Instrument	Publisher	Age Range	Domains	Outcomes	Norms
Developmental Activities Screening Inventory–II (Fewell & Langley, 1984)	Pro-Ed Publishing Company, Austin, TX	1 month to 60 months	Not divided into domains	Developmental age scores	None reported
Developmental Indicators for the Assessment of Learning–Revised (DIAL–R) (Mardell-Czudnowski & Goldenberg, 1990)	American Guidance Service, Circle Pines, MN	2 years to 5 years, 11 months	Motor Concepts Language Social-Emotional Checklist	Potential Problem; OK; Potential Advanced; based on ±1.0, ±1.5, or ±2.0 cutoff	1983 standardization reanalyzed; 2227 children stratified by age, geographic region, sex, size of community, and race; White sample, Minority sample, or Census sample may be chosen
FirstSTEP (Miller, 1993)	Psychological Corporation, San Antonio, TX	2 years, 9 months to 6 years, 2 months	Cognition Communication Motor Social/Emotional Adaptive Parent/Teacher Scale	Scaled scores; normal, borderline, delayed outcomes	1433 children stratified by age, sex, geographic region, race/ethnicity, and parent education

Source: From *Assessing Infants and Preschoolers with Special Needs*, 2/e by McLean/Bailey/Wolery, © 1996. Reprinted by permission of Pearson Education, Inc., Upper Saddle River, NJ.

needing services (McLean, 1996). Families also should be given the opportunity to evaluate their experience with the screening program. Families may be surveyed immediately after the screening or by being mailed a questionnaire or a telephone contact. This follow-up also will provide information as to how quickly assessment is completed after the screening so that any time lags can be corrected as soon as possible (McLean, 1996).

Some additional questions to consider for evaluating identification and screening programs have been provided by Hanson and Lynch (1995):

1. Does the screening lead to more extensive diagnostic assessment and intervention services when appropriate?
2. Are the existing screening and identification programs reaching all members of the community?
3. Are Child Find and screening efforts well-publicized, nonthreatening, and positive in their approach?
4. Does the screening program follow through with agencies and families to determine the outcome of referrals?
5. Do referral and assessment processes and procedures honor family preferences and comply with state regulations?
6. Do procedures exist for including families in the screening process and do professionals value and use their input?

Summary

The ways in which Child Find and screening programs are conducted may vary from state to state, but they all should share a common set of characteristics. All screening programs should be simple to implement, accurate, comprehensive, cost-effective, and conducted in partnership with family members and caregivers who know the most about the child's development (Hanson & Lynch, 1995). A collection or battery of developmental measures is needed from a multidisciplinary team. Assessors must

remember that not every child has the same pattern of strengths and weaknesses; there are variations in the development of children. Single screening sessions will not reliably capture these qualitative and quantitative changes. Optimal screening models rely on interagency efforts that provide periodic checks of children who appear to be developing normally and continuous follow-up watching young children who are at-risk for developmental delays.

References

Alberts, F. M., Davis, B. L., & Prentice, L. (1995). Validity of an observation screening instrument in a multicultural population. *Journal of Early Intervention,* 19(2), 168–177.

Bricker, D., Squires, J., Mounts, L., Potter, L., Nickel, B., & Farrell, J. (1995). *Ages and Stages Questionnaires.* Baltimore: Brookes.

Dale, P. S., Bates, E., Reznick, J. S., & Morisset, C. (1989). The validity of a parent report instrument of child language at twenty months. *Journal of Child Language,* 16, 239–249.

Diamond, K. E., & Squires, J. (1993). The role of the parental report in the screening and assessment of young children. *Journal of Early Intervention,* 17(2), 107–115.

Dunst, C. J. (1993). Issues related to "at risk": Implications of risk and opportunity for assessment and intervention practice. *Topics in Early Childhood Special Education,* 13(2), 143–153.

Frankenburg, W. K., & Dodds, J. B. (1990). Denver II screening manual. Denver: Denver Developmental Materials.

Greenbaum, C., & Auerbach, J. (Eds.). (1992). *Longitudinal studies of children at psychological risk: Cross national perspectives.* Denver: Colorado Department of Education.

Greenspan, S. I., & Meisels, S. J. (1996). Toward a new vision for the developmental assessment of infants and young children. In S. J. Meisels & E. Fenichel (Eds.), *New visions for the developmental assessment of infants and young children* (pp. 11–26). Washington, DC: Zero to Three: National Center for Infants, Toddlers, and Families.

Hanson, M. J., & Lynch, E. W. (1995). *Early intervention: Implementing child and family services for infants and toddlers who are at risk or disabled.* Austin, TX: PRO-ED.

Henderson, L. W., & Meisels, S. (1994). Parental involvement in the developmental screening of their young children: A multiple-source perspective. *Journal of Early Intervention,* 18(2), 141–154.

Knobloch, H., Stevens, F., Malone, A., Ellison, P., & Risemberg, H. (1979). The validity of parental reporting of infant development. *Pediatrics,* 63, 873–878.

Kochanek, T. T. (1988). Conceptualizing screening models for developmentally disabled high risk children and their families. *Zero to Three,* 9(2), 16–20.

Lerner, J. W., Lowenthal, B., & Egan, R. (1998). *Preschool children with special needs*. Needham Heights, MA: Allyn & Bacon.

McLean, M. (1996). Child Find, tracking, and screening. In M. McLean, D. B. Bailey, & M. Wolery (Eds.), *Assessing infants and preschoolers with special needs* (2nd ed.) (pp. 96–122). Upper Saddle River, NJ: Merrill/Prentice Hall.

Meisels, S. J. (1991). Dimensions of early identification. *Journal of Early Intervention*, 15, 26–35.

Meisels, S. J., Marsden, D. B., Wiske, M. S., & Henderson, L. W. (1997). *Early Screening Inventory-Revised*. Ann Arbor, MI: Rebus.

Meisels, S. J., & Provence, S. (1989). *Screening and assessment: Guidelines for identifying young disabled and developmentally vulnerable children and their families*, Washington, DC: National Center for Clinical Infant Programs.

Meisels, S. J., & Wasik, B. A. (1990). Who should be served? Identifying children in need of early intervention. In S. J. Meisels & J. P. Shonkoff (Eds.), *Handbook of early childhood intervention* (pp. 605–632). New York: Cambridge University Press.

Peterson, N. (1987). *Early intervention for handicapped and at-risk children: An introduction to early childhood-special education*. Denver: Love.

Rescorla, L. (1989). The Language Development Survey: A screening tool for delayed language in toddlers. *Journal of Speech and Hearing Disorders*, 54, 587–599.

Sameroff, A. J., Seifer, R., Barocas, R. M., Zax, M., & Greenspan, S. (1987). Intelligence quotient scores of 4-year-old children: Social-emotional risk factors. *Pediatrics*, 79, 343–350.

Simeonsson, R. (1991). Primary, secondary, and tertiary prevention in early intervention. *Journal of Early Intervention*, 15(2), 124–134.

Squires, J. K., Nickel, R., & Bricker, D. (1990). Use of parent-completed developmental questionnaires for child-find and screening. *Infants and Young Children*, 3(2), 46–57.

Tjossem, T. D. (1976). Early intervention: Issues and approaches. In T. D. Tjossem (Ed.), *Intervention strategies for high risk infants and young children* (pp. 3–33). Baltimore: University Park Press.

Norm-Based Assessment

When a developmental screening indicates an area or areas of suspected delay for a child, a fuller assessment is warranted. In order to determine the nature and extent of a child's potential need for special assistance, the family is now directed to pursue a multidisciplinary assessment of the child's functioning, including strengths and weaknesses. The information gathered during such an assessment will be the basis for determining eligibility for special educational services.

Bagnato, Neisworth, and Munson (1997) pointed out that parents who suspect that their child may have a problem will ask, "What's wrong with [our] child?" (p. 1). The question of what is wrong with the child asks the professional to make a diagnosis of which syndrome or clinical category the child best fits. Making such a diagnosis often involves comparing the child's characteristics and performance with the typical or normative performance of children of the same age (Bagnato, Neisworth, & Munson, 1997). This comparison is often required to determine eligibility for early intervention. "Norm-based assessment, therefore, plays a primary role in diagnosing or categorizing childhood disorders . . ." (Bagnato, Neisworth, & Munson, 1997, p. 1). This chapter attempts to provide a basic understanding of the role of norm-based testing in the assessment process, its purpose, and the basic concepts and principles of norm-referenced assessment.

Diagnostic Process

The second stage in the assessment process goes beyond the level of a screening and involves a more in-depth or "diagnostic" look at the child than does a screening. The diagnostic process is designed to confirm or disconfirm the existence of a developmental delay or disability severe enough to require remediation. According to PL 105–17, each state must set forth guidelines and eligibility criteria by which to determine the severity of delay which qualifies a child for the provision of early intervention services in that state. The diagnostic stage also serves to provide more information about the suspected problem. For example, it must be determined whether the delay is global, affecting all aspects of the child's development, or specific, affecting one particular aspect of development, such as speech or motor skills. The gathered data also provide useful information to be utilized in the development of an intervention program. Additional examination of a child's mastery of specific developmental and educational skills is needed as well.

Entitlement to Full Assessment

As provided by the 1997 Amendments of the IDEA (PL 105–17), a review of pertinent records related to the child's current health status and medical history should be conducted. The child should be assessed in all areas related to the suspected disability, that is, cognitive development; physical development, including vision and hearing; social or emotional development; and adaptive development. For an infant or toddler, this assessment must incorporate the family's description of its resources, priorities, and concerns related to enhancing the child's development. The law provides that the assessment of the child must (a) be conducted by trained personnel who utilize appropriate methods and procedures; (b) be based on informed clinical opinion; and (c) provide that no single procedure is to be used for determining a child's eligibility for special educational services.

Definitions of Eligibility

Each state or territory has established criteria for determining whether a measurable developmental delay exists. Shackelford (1992) found that some states use a quantitative measure of developmental delay; for example, two standard deviations below the mean (−2 SD) or a 25 percent delay in a developmental area. The specific criteria vary considerably among states in terms of the type of measure used and also in terms of the level of delay required. Three different types of quantitative definitions are in use (McLean, 1996; Shackelford, 1992):

1. The difference between chronological age and actual performance level as determined through an age-equivalent measure of performance in the specified developmental domains.
2. A delay in performance as expressed in a certain number of months below chronological age.
3. A delay in performance as indicated by standard deviation below the mean which requires a standardized instrument. Standard scores will be discussed later in this chapter.

Some states use a qualitative definition. McLean (1996) pointed out that Hawaii uses a multidisciplinary team consensus. No level of standard deviation or percentage delay is specified. This type of eligibility does not require a quantitative measure. Determining eligibility based on team consensus has come about as a result of the lack of reliable and valid instruments for this age group (Neisworth & Bagnato, 1992; Shonkoff & Meisels, 1991). The use of qualitative criteria for assessing eligibility is referred to as "professional judgment" or "informed clinical opinion." In fact, under the 1997 Amendments to the IDEA, assessment must be based on "informed clinical opinion" and should not be limited to the use of test scores. Because there is an insufficient number of reliable and valid instruments for the birth-to-3-years age group and questionable predictive validity for available instruments, determining delay by traditional assessment can be problematic (Benn, 1994; Shonkoff & Meisels, 1991). This is also a problem for preschoolers. Informed clinical opinion relies on qualitative and quantitative information to determine the need for early intervention services, and typically is derived from the consensus of a multidisciplinary team that includes parents and information from multiple sources (Benn, 1994; Biro, Daulton, & Szanton, 1991; Harbin, Gallagher, & Terry, 1991).

Purpose and Description

Bagnato and Neisworth (1991) gave two purposes for using norm-based measures: (1) to describe the child's functional skills in comparative terms, and (2) to classify the degree of the child's deficits in terms of a preexisting diagnostic category. The former purpose for using norm-referenced or norm-based tests is to indicate a child's developmental level in relation to that of other children. In order to compare children, norm-based assessments have undergone standardization on a carefully chosen reference group, which then becomes the normative group. The norm-based test is used to compare a child's performance with that of a normative group consisting of children who match the norm group or have similar characteristics (i.e., age, sex). Measures of cognitive and conceptual abilities are the most well-known kinds of norm-based measures (Bagnato & Neisworth, 1991).

Norm-referenced tests are generally appropriate in situations requiring selectivity, such as determining whether a child demonstrates significant enough developmental delay to be eligible for special education or early intervention services. Norm-based scales provide comparisons between children, and thus, can screen, diagnose, and gauge the relative extent of problems (Bagnato & Neisworth, 1991). Norm-based assessment may be a required component in determining the degree or severity of a child's disability and, subsequently, determining eligibility for special educational services.

A norm-based assessment should be only one of the procedures utilized in assessing and planning for needed services for young children. If a quantitative score is required as an outcome of assessment, the team might use a norm-referenced measure that can be supplemented with procedures that require less structure. The purpose of this chapter is to explain norm-based assessment and provide guidelines for its use in early childhood special education.

Test Standardization

A norm-based test is a set of standardized tasks presented to a child. The purpose of the testing is to determine how well a child performs on the tasks presented. In designing a standardized test, test developers must first determine its rationale and purpose. Second, the developers must explain what the test will measure. There are many types of standardized tests, such as achievement, readiness, developmental screening, diagnostic, and intelligence tests. The test developers must also explain to whom the test will be given and how the test results will be used. Standardization of a test includes several components: standard materials, administrative procedures, scoring procedures, and score interpretation. The purpose of standardization is to ensure uniformity and objectivity. This means that all children taking the test receive essentially the same experience, perform the same tasks with the same set of materials, receive the same amount of assistance and number of directions from the evaluator, and are assessed according to a standard set of criteria (Bailey & Nabors, 1996). If all of these factors are not the same, then the results cannot be compared among children.

For example, standardized tests supply all of the materials needed such as puzzles, blocks, or any other toys. Directions are provided for each of the test items so that each item is administered in exactly the same way, using the same

size or complexity of item(s), and allowing the same amount of time to complete the item(s).

Bailey and Nabors (1996) gave an example of a nonstandardized test item for assembling a three-piece puzzle. If no specific instructions were given, it would be up to the examiner to determine how to administer the item and what type of three-piece puzzle to use. Even a simple item such as a three-piece puzzle can vary a great deal in size and complexity. This task could be an interlocking puzzle or merely placing three shapes into slots. What directions would be given to the child for assembling the puzzle? The time allowed for constructing the puzzle could vary greatly depending upon the examiner. Therefore, this simple item could test a wide range of skills in assembling a puzzle.

The Normative Group

Standardized tests undergo a research and development phase before they are released for use. As part of this phase, a prospective test is administered to many children. The scores from these children form a norm group or standardization sample. The population, or group of individuals, on which the test is normed is very important. Creation of a norm group is a key distinguishing characteristic of standardized tests. The norm group helps assessors keep tabs on what normal is. Each child's score can be compared with the norm group to determine the child's standing in relation to peers.

Three factors should be considered when an examiner is matching a test's norm group to a particular child: (1) the representativeness of the group, (2) the number of cases in the group, and (3) the relevance of the group (Salvia & Ysseldyke, 1995; Sattler, 1988). Test constructors must develop some method of selecting individuals who are representative. Representativeness is the extent to which the characteristics of the norm group correspond with those of the child to be tested. The norm group also must be sufficiently large. The size of the norm group influences the stability and accuracy of the test scoring. Norms are the scores obtained from testing the normative sample. The larger the norm group is, the more stable the norms are. Relevance, the final factor, is critical in the appropriate unbiased testing of children with special needs. Many tests that are primarily used to assess children with disabilities had norm groups which specifically excluded such children. The rationale is that norms should provide an indication of normal developmental sequences and milestones. It is assumed that the purpose of testing is to determine the nature and extent of deviation from the norm. However, there are some valid arguments suggesting that there is some degree of unfairness inherent in comparing the development of a child with a disability to children without disabilities (Bailey & Nabors, 1996). Children with significant motor and sensory impairments typically are excluded when populations are recruited for standardization of developmental assessment instruments. A task such as putting shapes in a formboard, which is designed to measure cognitive development, may be physically impossible for a child with motor disabilities to perform; thus, the child would fail this item and be judged to lack ability (Miller & Robinson, 1996). Therefore, many of the norm-referenced tests used in special education may not be valid with a population with special needs. The assessor must examine the test carefully to determine how valid the child's score would be.

Using a norm-referenced test assumes that the child being assessed has had life experiences and opportunities for learning that are comparable to those of children in the standardization sample. Infants and toddlers with significant physical disabilities are unlikely to have had opportunities for experiences with the content and tasks of formal assessment instruments that are comparable to the experiences of children in a standardization sample. Thus, the competencies of children with disabilities may be underrated (Miller & Robinson, 1996).

The norm-based measure which is being considered for use should be examined carefully to determine the basis from which norm-referenced scores are derived. If the test was administered to a normative sample, then the process used for norming the test should be evaluated, and the year that the testing was done should be noted. The older the norms, the less likely the sample is representative of children today. Characteristics of the normative group should be examined. The reference group from which the norms are derived should be large and stratified with proportionate representation of various cultures, geographic regions, gender, socioeconomic status, and urban-rural distribution. The norm group should be demographically representative of the population to be tested. Mindes, Ireton, and Mardell-Czudnowski (1996) summarized criteria for evaluating the technical adequacy of norms as follows:

1. Norms should be available in the manual or in an accompanying technical publication in the form of standard scores.
2. The test manual needs to define the standardization of the normative sample clearly so that the test user can determine the suitability for a particular population. Such defining characteristics should include five or more of the following variables: ages, grade levels, gender, geographic areas, race, socioeconomic status, ethnicity, parental education, or other relevant variables.
3. The norm-sampling method should be well-defined. If the norm sample is based on convenience or readily available populations, it is not acceptable.
4. For each subgroup examined, an adequate sample size should be used with 100 subjects per age or grade considered the lower limit. In addition, there should be 1,000 or more subjects in the total sample.
5. The test's norms should not be more than fifteen years old. (pp. 93–94)

Kubiszyn and Borich (1990) recommended that assessors specify the reason for testing and the type of information needed prior to deciding whether to use a norm-referenced type of test. Their recommendation highlights the importance of considering the information needed prior to testing to ensure that the resulting data will be helpful. A standardized test may be required to determine the severity of the delay to establish eligibility for special education services. It should be pointed out that some tests allow for accommodations for children with various disabilities. For example, the Vineland Adaptive Behavior Scales offer regular norms plus supplementary norms derived from samples from children with mental retardation, emotional disabilities, visual impairments, and hearing impairments. Assessors should attempt to find a test which allows for these accommodations.

Types of Scores from Norm-Based Tests

Norm-based tests are generally quantifiable, which means that they yield numerical scores. At the simplest level, a numerical score may be the tabulation of the number of items correct, or the raw score. The raw score must be compared with the performance of a group of children of known characteristics that are described in the test manual. These comparison scores are called derived scores. Derived scores are arrived at by first calculating a raw score. The raw scores are transformed into standard or derived scores based on the distribution tables of the normative sample found in the administrative manual. A derived score is a single score that shows how a child's performance compares with the norm group. These distribution tables allow assessors to produce a derived score. Four types of scores may be derived that can be used to compare a child's performance with that of a normative group: developmental age equivalents (year and month); developmental quotients (DQ) or intelligence quotients (IQ); standard scores (i.e., T-scores, z-scores); and percentile ranks.

The purpose of derived scores is to convert an otherwise meaningless raw score into a score

that makes sense (Wodrich, 1997). "Standard" scores allow for comparison between scores; such scores are comparable from test to test. One may compare a child's scores with those of another child or to those of the normative group. The score reflects whether the child demonstrates average, below average, or above average assessed skills relative to the group. One may compare a child's score in one assessed area to that in another domain, yielding a pattern of strengths and weaknesses. The confidence with which one makes those comparisons is, of course, dependent upon the reliability and validity established for the given test. Reliability and validity are discussed later in this chapter.

Developmental Age Scores. A developmental age or age-equivalent score is derived based on the average performance of a certain age group. An example of a developmental age equivalent score is 3–5 years, which means that the child's performance on the test is considered to be the same as an average child who is 3 years, 5 months old. The developmental age score tells the average age at which 50 percent of the normative sample achieved a particular raw score. A developmental age score may be reported for an entire measure or for individual subscales. One advantage of developmental age scores is that they are easy for parents and professionals to interpret. To state that a child is functioning at the 36-month level is easy to understand. Another advantage of developmental age scores is that they usually do reflect positive growth or change (Fewell & Sandall, 1986). For parents of children with disabilities who are often informed of their child's slow progress, information provided by developmental age scores may confirm developmental gains where other measures may not.

However, potential problems occur when using and interpreting developmental age scores. Two children with the same score may perform very differently. Because the developmental age score depends solely on the raw score and is a global summary of performance, the developmental age score does not show patterns of performance. Another problem is that most developmental age scores are extrapolated, which means that children of a particular age may not actually have been tested as part of the normative process. Another possibility is that the child's raw scores may be too low for the range of scores covered by the specific test. Rather than simply reporting that the child's performance was below the lowest obtainable score on the instrument, the test developer used a statistical procedure to extrapolate such scores. For example, the Battelle Developmental Inventory provides a formula by which extreme scores may be calculated. Because development is uneven, this poses a potential problem (Bailey & Nabors, 1996; Keogh & Sheehan, 1981).

There are additional concerns related to age-equivalent scores. A summary score can be misleading. Stating that a child functions like a 3-year-old provides a wide range because 3-year-olds are quite varied in their abilities. A developmental score is best interpreted as an estimate within a range of performance. Finally, the differences between developmental ages are not necessarily equal. At younger ages, a 1-year delay may be more significant than at older ages, when 1 year is not as great a proportion of the child's total age (Bailey & Nabors, 1996).

Developmental Quotient (DQ) Scores. A developmental quotient is a ratio of developmental to chronological age, which takes into account the child's age at the time of the test. This quotient is computed by dividing a child's developmental age by his chronological age and multiplying the result by 100. The average child who is progressing at an average rate would receive a DQ score of 100. The developmental quotient is usually a relatively stable score. Therefore, developmental quotients are seen by some as a more desirable unit of measurement than developmental age scores in assessing the

effects of intervention (Bailey & Nabors, 1996; Snyder-McLean, 1987).

The major limitation of the developmental quotient is that as children get older, equal increases in developmental age represent smaller proportions of chronological age, and thus result in smaller DQ changes. For example, a developmental quotient of 90 at one age is not directly comparable to a DQ of 90 at another age. Because of these small changes, DQ scores are rarely used (Bailey & Nabors, 1996).

Percentile Ranks. A percentile rank is another score that provides information regarding an individual's performance relative to the rest of the population. Percentile ranks are derived scores which indicate the percentage of individuals in the normative group whose test scores fall at or below a given raw score. Specifically, percentile ranks tell what percentage of the norm group obtained the same number of correct answers. Thus, a percentile rank of 75 indicates that this individual's score exceeded 75 out of every 100 children in the norm group and was exceeded by only 25 children in the norm group.

These scores offer a means to explain a given individual's performance compared with those of his peers. The major limitation of percentile ranks is that they are not on an equal interval scale. The difference between percentile ranks at the extremes is more significant than the difference between percentile ranks closer to the mean. There is a big difference between being in the 98th percentile as opposed to the 99th percentile, whereas there is a very small difference between the 50th percentile and the 51st percentile. Percentile ranks should never be used to determine the success of an intervention (Bailey & Nabors, 1996).

Standard Scores. A standard score is the general name for any derived score that has been transformed or changed in some way so that the mean and standard deviation have predetermined values. Standard scores are derived scores that offer a precise method of pinpointing an individual's performance, compared with a defined peer group. A standard score is a score that has been transformed to fit a normal curve, with a mean and standard deviation that remain the same across the ages. The normal curve is a theoretical distribution of scores that is the model against which actual performance is interpreted. The normal curve is bell-shaped and provides the statistical basis for both percentiles and standard scores. An illustration of the relationship among these scores and the normal, bell-shaped curve appears in Figure 9–1. It assumes that on any given variable, most individuals will score at or near the mean. As scores deviate from the mean, fewer instances of those scores will be observed.

Standard deviation is a statistic that measures a distribution's amount of dispersion or variance and is calculated from the scores of the norm group. A standard deviation is a number that helps explain an individual's performance by describing how many standard deviations above or below the mean an individual's score is. Within the normal curve model, it is assumed that one standard deviation on either side of the mean (±1 SD) encompasses approximately 34 percent of the individuals in a group, whereas two standard deviations on either side of the mean (±2 SD) would encompass 48 percent of the individuals in a group. A standard deviation is always reported as being above or below the mean. Thus, to say that a child's score was one standard deviation below the mean

FIGURE 9–1

Relationship Among Scores and the Normal Curve

Source: From *Assessing Students with Special Needs* (2nd ed.) (p. 101), by J. J. Venn, © 2000. Reprinted by permission of Pearson Education, Inc. Upper Saddle River, NJ 07458.

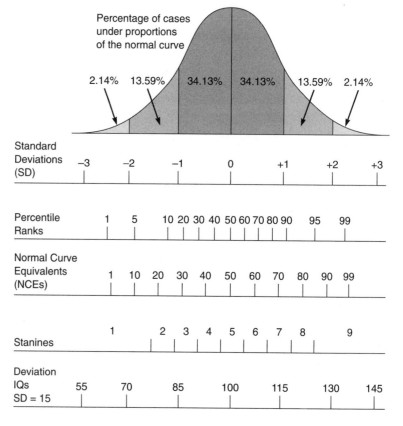

would be interpreted to mean the child's performance was better than 16 percent of the total population (Bailey & Nabors, 1996). Unlike percentiles, derived scores are equal distances on the normal curve. A standard score is expressed in terms of the score's distance from the mean of a normal distribution.

There are five commonly used standard score distributions: z-scores, T-scores, deviation IQs, normal-curve equivalents, and stanines. The most commonly used standard scores are z-scores or T-scores. These scores are interpreted in exactly the same fashion as any other standard score, the only difference being in the defined parameters of the score. A z-score is a standard score distribution with a mean of zero and a standard deviation of one. A T-score is a standard deviation of 10. Stanines are standard scores that divide the distribution into nine parts. As a rule, the first, second, and third stanines represent below-average performance; the fourth, fifth, and sixth are average performance; and the seventh, eighth, and ninth stanines represent above-average performance. Although a stanine is not as precise as other standard scores, the single-digit score is easily understood.

Test Reliability

Test reliability is the consistency, dependability, or stability of test performance. Reliability is concerned with how much error is involved in measurement or how far observed scores depart from the true score. If a child took a test over and over again and no practice effect occurred, what would be the variability in the child's performance? If several children were administered the same test and each received a different score, how much of that variability would be attributable to true differences in the children's abilities? The less error variance in the answer to either of these questions, the greater the test's reliability.

Errors in measurement may result from several sources. The most common error can be in the characteristics of the test itself. Variation in administrative conditions, child characteristics, and aspects of the examiner also will result in errors of measurement. Items on a test should be clear in terms of the materials required and administration procedures. Otherwise, an examiner might use different procedures. Scoring procedures also should be clear or else one examiner might score an answer as a pass and another examiner might score it as a failure. If the test is too short or too long, then the test is less likely to be reliable. Usually, the longer the test or the more items that it contains, the more reliable it will be. That is one of the main reasons that diagnostic tests are more reliable than screening tests. However, if a test is too long, the child may become tired or bored, resulting in inaccurate scores. Any of these test characteristics can result in a lack of reliability.

Differences in administrative and subject conditions can result in a lack of reliability. Aspects of a particular test administration may also affect a child's performance and result in score variation. Examples of these aspects are a room that is hot or stuffy, poorly lighted, or very noisy. The child may not interact well with the adult administering the test owing to unfamiliarity or characteristics of the adult such as personality, style, culture, or gender. Characteristics of the individual child that might result in score variance on a test include the child's general ability to comprehend instructions, test-taking skills, health, fatigue, motivation, emotional strain, or fluctuations in attention.

The skill of the examiner influences the reliability of administration. The examiner must be aware of and follow the administrative and scoring procedures. Mistakes can be made in score calculations and transformations. The examiner or scorer can influence test scores by giving extra help, pointing out errors, and allowing additional time. The more complex the scoring procedures required and the more calculations necessary, the greater the likelihood of error (see Figure 9–2).

Assessing Test Reliability

The administrative manual of the particular instrument should provide detailed reliability data. The reliability studies of particular measures often are published in the professional literature. There are several ways to document test reliability, including procedural and scoring reliability, test-retest reliability, alternate forms reliability, the standard error of measurement,

FIGURE 9–2
Sources of Errors in Measurement

Characteristics of the test

Unclear materials required
Unclear administration procedures
Unclear scoring procedures
Too many or too few items

Administrative conditions

Room too hot or stuffy
Room poorly lighted
High noise level

Child characteristics

Child's ability to comprehend instructions
Test-taking skills
Health
Fatigue
Motivation
Emotional strain
Fluctuations in attention
Not able to relate to examiner

Aspects of the examiner

Awareness of and ability to follow
   administrative and scoring procedures
Mistakes in calculations and transformations
Giving extra help
Pointing out error
Allowing additional time
Not establishing good rapport with child

and internal consistency reliability. The reliability measure used varies according to the question of interest (Bailey & Nabors, 1996). Figure 9–3 summarizes ways to assess reliability.

Procedural and Scoring Reliability. Procedural or scoring reliability is the extent to which the examiner follows the administrative procedures required by a test. Scoring reliability refers to the extent to which the score calculations and summaries are accurate. Both of these types of reliability could be assessed by having one person watch another examiner administering the test. Scoring reliability consists of determining if the examiner gave the proper credit for the child's response and if the examiner calculated the correct score for the child. Observing the test administration would be required to determine the reliability of the administration. Whether the score was calculated correctly can be ascertained by having two individuals independently scoring a test. If a test can generalize to other examiners, then it has inter-rater or interscorer reliability.

Test-Retest Reliability. Test-retest reliability yields a stability coefficient that indicates the consistency of a test over time. It is determined by administering the same test to a group of children on two different occasions and assessing the extent to which their scores are stable over

FIGURE 9–3
Assessment of Test Reliability

Procedural and scoring	Extent administrative procedures are followed
Test-retest	Test consistency over time
Alternate forms	Parallel forms of the same test
Internal consistency	Variability of performance across items on the same test

time. The correlation between total test scores in first and second administration gives the reliability of the test. If factors such as fatigue, motivation, and rapport with the examiner are producing errors, then repeated measurements should allow these factors to negate each other.

Alternate Forms. Alternate or equivalent forms reliability is provided when parallel forms of the same test are developed. Alternate or parallel forms of reliability assess the extent to which a child's performance on one measure is consistent with his performance on the other. It requires that the same child be administered both forms of the test. Scores on both of the test forms are then compared to provide the reliability.

Internal Consistency. Internal consistency or split-half is another form of reliability. This form of reliability tries to determine whether a child's response on a specified administration of a test is internally consistent. Was there variability in performance across items or was the child's performance relatively consistent? This type of question can be assessed only on a single construct. Items are divided into two comparable halves and a Spearman Brown correlation is calculated. This correlation is simply a measure of how things are related to one another. It is a measure of whether there is an association between two variables and if so, how much. The degree of relationship is called a correlation coefficient, which can range from +1.00 to −1.00; no relationship at all is .00. The number of the correlation coefficient tells us the strength of the relationship, and the sign (+ or −) tells us the direction of the relationship. In a positive relationship, as one variable goes up, so does the other. However, correlations do not indicate causality—just because two variables are correlated does not mean that one causes the other. Another variable actually may cause either or both results. For example, a child's performance across different domains cannot be compared.

Performance may be expected to vary across domains.

Internal consistency can be assessed by different procedures. One of the simplest procedures is split-half reliability. This procedure divides the test into two parts, and the reliability measure is the correlation between the two parts. More complex procedures for computing internal consistency are the formulae of Kuder-Richardson or Cronbach's Alpha in which all possible splits are assessed.

Standard Error of Measurement. It is commonly acknowledged that no test is free from error. The standard error of measurement tries to assess the reliability of a test by answering the hypothetical question of how stable a child's performance on a test would be if the child took the test over and over again. The standard error of measurement is produced by testing, retesting, and then calculating how closely the two scores agree. If this was completed and resulted in a large number of scores for the same child, then that set of scores would have a mean and standard deviation. The standard error of measurement is the estimate of the amount of variation that can be expected in test scores as a result of reliability correlations. It is then reported in the test manual. A large standard error implies that scores varied widely on repeated administrations. A small standard error implies that each measurement must be fairly close to the true score and thus without error.

Test reliability is an important concern in selecting a measure. The reliability coefficient is a general index of reliability. The reliability coefficient can be calculated by using the same test-retest data that are used to calculate the standard error of measurement. Instruments should be selected that have reliability coefficients greater than .80, preferably greater than .90, and for which there is a small error of measurement. Assessors should be familiar with test administration and scoring procedures. Any unclear items should have local standards adopted to which each staff person can adhere. If reports are provided to other agencies, then these standards should be fully explained (Bailey & Nabors, 1996).

Eight criteria summarized by Mindes, Ireton, and Mardell-Czudnowski (1996) from their review of the literature on guides and recommendations for technical adequacy of reliability include:

1. The test manual should supply an estimate of test-retest reliability for relevant subgroups. A correlation coefficient of .60, .80, or .90 or better for group tests, screening tests, and diagnostic tests, respectively, is a current best practice criterion.
2. The test manual should report empirical evidence of internal consistency with a correlation coefficient of .90 or better.
3. Reliability coefficients as well as standard errors of measurement (Sems) should be presented in tabular format.
4. Reliability procedures and samples of at least 25 subjects should be described.
5. Quantitative methods used to study and control item difficulty and other systematic item analyses should be reported in the manual.
6. Measures of central tendency and variability (means and standard deviations for the total raw scores) should be reported for relevant subgroups during the norming procedures.
7. Empirical evidence of interrater reliability at .85 or better should be reported in the manual.
8. The steepness of the test items should be controlled by having a minimum of three raw score items per standard deviation. The range of items for the youngest children should span two or more standard deviations below the mean score for each subtest and for the total score of the test. (p. 94)

Test Validity

Although test reliability is important, professionals also must be concerned about test validity. Validity is the most important consideration in the construction and use of tests. Test validity refers to the extent to which a test performs the functions for which it was intended. Validity answers the question, "Does the test measure what it claims to measure?" For example, a test claiming to measure intelligence can be quite reliable; that is, it may measure some trait consistently, but that trait may have absolutely nothing to do with intelligence. Tests must be both reliable and valid. Four types of validity to be considered are content, instructional, criterion, and construct (Table 9–1).

Content Validity

Content validity refers to the subjective analysis of how well the content of the test represents the domain tested. It is concerned with how well the items on a test represent all of the items that could be covered in that particular domain. Content validity is established by evaluating three factors: how appropriate the items are; how complete the item samples are; and the way in which the items assess the content (Salvia & Ysseldyke, 1995; Sattler, 1988). This method of assessing validity consists of examining test items and making a judgment about whether the items are measuring what they claim. For example, a test of motor skills should reflect current theories on motor development. An initial test of content validity would be the extent to which the test developer convinces you that a thorough and systematic process has occurred in the selection of test content. The test manual should contain a discussion of the theoretical basis for item selection, the source of items, and any data to support the extent to which test content reflects the domain assessed. Content validity is assessed through a logical analysis of the item development process and of the actual items (Bailey & Nabors, 1996).

Instructional Utility

Instructional utility is a type of validity that is closely related to content validity. Instructional

TABLE 9–1
Types of Validity

Type	Description
Content	Subjective analysis of how well the test content represents domain tested
Instructional Utility	Extent to which test provides useful information for planning intervention
Criterion	Extent to which test corresponds to another test • concurrent (test administered at same time) • predictive (current test scores predict an independent criterion in the future)
Construct	Relationship between test scores and a theoretical construct or trait (e.g., intelligence)

utility is the extent to which an instrument provides useful information for planning intervention programs for young children with disabilities. Instructional utility can be assessed by asking users to rate the appropriateness of the items for instruction.

Criterion Validity

Criterion validity is the relationship between the scores on a test and another (criterion) measure. It assesses the extent to which a test corresponds to some other independent measure. It is established by comparing test scores with an external variable that is a direct measure of the characteristic or behavior that the test claims to measure. This type of validity is usually expressed as a correlation coefficient. There are two categories or types of criterion validity, concurrent and predictive validity. These differ only on the basis of time.

Concurrent validity refers to the extent to which a test correlates with another measure administered at approximately the same time. For example, when a test is developed, the children in the normative sample are administered a well-established test at the same time. The new test is said to have concurrent validity with the well-established test. This type of validity

is useful for instruments that are designed to assess an individual's present status.

Predictive validity refers to how accurately the child's current test score can be used to estimate performance on some variable or criterion in the future or the extent to which a test relates to some future measure of performance. The higher the correlation, the greater the test's predictive power, and the greater its validity. The essence of predictive validity is that current test scores foretell some independent criterion in the future. Predictive validity strongly suggests that if a child currently has a score that indicates a developmental delay, it is likely that the child is at-risk for future school failure.

Concurrent and predictive validity are particularly important considerations for screening tests. Screening tests that lack concurrent validity are likely to result in children being referred for assessment who will not be diagnosed as delayed. Concurrent validity also is important for tests used in diagnosing delays.

Construct Validity

Construct validity is similar to content validity. It is concerned with the relationship between test scores and a theoretical construct or trait that underlies performance, such as personality, intelligence, or creativity. These traits are considered theoretical because they are not observable behaviors that can be measured directly. Construct validity is a hypothetical attribute that is designed to account for variability in behavior (Bailey & Nabors, 1996). Construct validity renders a judgment but relies on more sophisticated logic and observations, rather than on simple item inspection. Construct validity begins with an explanatory variable designed to explain behavior. Judgments of construct validity are based on the accumulation of research results (American Psychological Association, 1985). An example of a construct validity question would be to ask whether a particular instrument is actually a measure of intelligence.

Questions about validity are very important for early childhood special educators and related service personnel because they ask whether an instrument fulfills the purpose for which it was intended. Validity is separate from and tied to reliability. It is well-accepted that test validity can be no higher than the test's reliability, and usually is considerably lower (Bailey & Nabors, 1996). How could an unreliable test be accurate? The fact that a test is reliable does not mean that it has any validity for certain purposes. A screening test may be reliable but have no value in planning instructional programs. Bailey and Nabors (1996) pointed out that the vast majority of validity studies conducted on norm-based measures have failed to examine the validity of these instruments for use with individuals with disabilities.

Assessing Validity

Validity coefficients are correlation coefficients that give information about the strength and direction of relationships between a test and other related tests or measures of relevant criteria. Factors which influence validity coefficients are the length of time between test administrations, the range of the trait being measured, and the examinees themselves. Test-related factors include anxiety, motivation, understanding of directions, rapport between the examiner and examinee, degree of bilingualism, unfamiliarity with the test materials, and other differences from the norm group. Validity also is affected by factors related to the criterion used in establishing criterion-related validity. These statistics should not be automatically accepted at face value. The size of the sample, existing group differences, and the nature of the external criteria that are used to establish criterion-related validity should be considered. Test manuals should report more than one type of validity study. Many test manuals report multiple validity studies addressing various types of validity.

Tests are valid for specific purposes. An important consideration in evaluating validity is the use the examiner intends to make of the test. If the purpose is prediction, then predictive validity needs to be demonstrated. Content validity is important if achievement is the goal.

Criteria for evaluating the validity of a standardized test are:

1. The test manual must define what the test measures and what the test should be used for.
2. Evidence of at least one type of validity should be provided for the major types of inferences for which the use of a test is recommended (i.e., content; criterion-related; concurrent or predictive construct).
3. For content validity, the manual should define the content area(s) and explain how the content and skills to be tested were selected. Tests that are based on content validity should update content on revised forms.
4. For both types of criterion-related validity, that is, concurrent and predictive, (a) the criteria should be clearly defined; (b) validity of the criteria should be reported; (c) samples should be completely described; (d) correlation coefficients with other tests should be reported; and (e) for predictive validity, a statement concerning the length of time for which predictions can be made should be included.

5. For construct validity, the manual should clearly define the ability or aptitude measured. For tests for which there is a time limit, the manual should state how speed affects scores. (Mindes, Ireton, & Mardell-Czudnowski, 1996, pp. 94–95)

Commonly Used Norm-Referenced Tests

The psychologist on the team often administers norm-referenced tests which address intellectual or overall development during initial phases of assessment. Often, diagnostic concerns and issues of program eligibility are in question at this point. The *Bayley Scales of Infant Development* II (BSID-II) (Bayley, 1993) is the most widely used norm-referenced test for infants and toddlers (Meisels, 1996). Although the primary purpose of the BSID-II is to rank the mental and motor performance of young children, the manual claims that the primary value of the test is to diagnose developmental delay and plan appropriate intervention strategies. Meisels (1996) questioned the instrument's ability to plan intervention strategies. He pointed out that although the BSID-II may tell us that a child can discriminate patterns, sort pegs by color, and so on, this information does not provide the basis for an intervention strategy. Much more information is needed, such as context, family factors, socio-emotional characteristics, and other qualitative information about children's preferences, approaches to learning, and styles of response.

Other commonly used standardized instruments are the *Kaufman Assessment Battery for Children* (Kaufman & Kaufman, 1983), the *Stanford-Binet Intelligence Scale (4th Ed.)* (Thorndike, Hagen, & Sattler, 1986), the *Wechsler Preschool and Primary Scale of Intelligence-Revised* (Wechsler, 1989), and the *Battelle Developmental Inventory* (Newborg, Stock, Wnek, Guidubaldi, & Svinicki, 1988). Some features of these and other measures are shown in the table in Appendix 9–1 on page 211.

Other professionals on the team (i.e., speech/language pathologists, occupational and physical therapists) also employ norm-referenced tools relevant to their areas of expertise when assessing a child's abilities and skills and determining the need for special educational related services. (These will be referred to in the appropriate chapters in Part IV of this book.)

Norm-referenced measures are designed to verify, through extensive direct assessment, the nature and extent of a child's developmental delay. Bagnato and Neisworth (1991) recommended an approach which requires the agreement of at least two independent sources of diagnostic information before affirming developmental delay. One source should always involve the caregivers and the other the early intervention team or diagnostic specialist. Professionals are cautioned to remember that tests provide only an indication of a child's abilities and skills exhibited at a given time. Some of the advantages and cautions in using norm-based assessment are presented in the next section.

Using Norm-Based Tests in Early Childhood

Advantages of Norm-Based Tests

As stated previously in this chapter, the primary purpose in giving norm-based tests is to indicate a child's developmental level in relation to that of other children. Standardized tests are also given to classify the degree of the child's deficits in terms of a preexisting diagnostic category. In summary, some advantages of administering norm-referenced tests include:

1. Test results are expressed in terms of a child's standing among a group of peers of the same age and other characteristics (i.e., sex).
2. The child's performance can be compared with the performance of a normed, representative population, allowing for greater generalizability of findings.

3. Norms provide an indication of average or expected performance for age.
4. The derived scores of norm-referenced tests allow us to compare the child's performance on one test with his performance on other tests (i.e., help identify strengths and weaknesses), as well as compare the performance on different scales or domains.
5. Test results can be expressed in the form of a developmental score, an age equivalent, a percentile, a standard score, or other derived scores, allowing for flexible and relevant use of the results, as needed.
6. Norm-referenced assessments tap broader capabilities, (e.g., personality measures, intelligence).
7. Norm-referenced instruments provide some continuity in assessment when children move to other programs where they may not employ similar curricula.

The changeable and inconsistent nature of many developmental and behavioral characteristics of preschool children makes reliable assessment inherently more difficult than assessing school-aged children. Individuals working with young children understand that they typically are quite active and their ability to maintain attention and stay on task is limited. Young children are highly inquisitive and enjoy exploring their surroundings (Bagnato & Neisworth, 1991). Paget and Nagle (1986) noted the unique characteristics of the preschool child and suggested that assessment strategies with preschoolers should focus on situational differences in order to develop and prioritize interventions, rather than assuming that unreliability is something to be minimized or eliminated (Romero, 1999). These characteristics are discussed further in Chapter 5.

Preschoolers show qualitatively different patterns of cognitive development than do older children (Bagnato & Neisworth, 1991; Piaget, 1952). Their preoperational thought is idiosyncratic and highly intuitive. Concept development is limited. Young children assimilate new experiences into existing patterns of thinking

much more readily than they can accommodate or change these patterns to meet external demands. Therefore, a play-based assessment is more informative than conforming to structure or rules.

Although many individuals may understand that young children are qualitatively different from older children, this concept is typically overlooked in the design and construction of tests for preschool children (Bagnato & Neisworth, 1991). When using norm-based tests that have been developed with standardized procedures, the child's performance is judged according to set criteria, and then the raw scores are translated into standard scores based on a normative group. Emphasis is placed on control of the child and on compliance to standard procedures. Materials are supplied which may or may not be of interest to the child. The manner and sequence of eliciting responses are fixed. Verbal instructions may be quite formal and the complexity of instructions may often exceed the concept development of the child.

Norm-based tests serve a purpose in early childhood assessment. It is often important to compare a child's abilities with those of age peers. This helps to determine the child's relative standing with respect to expected performance for age. Although norm-based measures have a place in early childhood special education assessment, they may be overused and misused (Garwood, 1982; Shonkoff, 1983). As with any measure, one should take care to avoid misuse of or overreliance on this one type of assessment. Some caution should be exercised when using norm-based assessments. The next section discusses some cautions and limitations of using this type of assessment.

Cautions and Limitations

Norm-referenced assessment often carries an assumption that it is objective and valid. The assumption is that it can be observed and documented in a reliable fashion. Barrera (1996) pointed out that every observer has a particular lens or way of seeing the world through which he views and evaluates what is observed. This subjective aspect of observation is especially relevant to socioculturally competent assessment. The assessor must acknowledge his own professional community's subjectivity and thus recognize and respect the way a family's subjective world affects the behavior and development of the child. (See Chapter 3 on cultural diversity.)

When selecting a norm-referenced measure for potential use, professionals should carefully examine the test manual for a variety of features. It is important to note how the test was normed and to determine whether the characteristics of the sample population are representative of the child or children with whom the measure is to be used. It also is important to note that children with disabilities are rarely included in a normative, sample group, because norms typically provide an indication of normal developmental sequences and milestones. The purpose of testing is to determine the nature and extent of deviation from the norm.

One should also examine the basis from which the norm-referenced scores were derived. Some instruments allow the generation of developmental age scores, but the instrument itself was never normed. Rather, the developmental age equivalent is assigned to each item, or clusters of items, based on norm-based sources such as the Bayley Scales (1993) or the Gesell Developmental Schedules (Knoblock, Stevens, & Malone, 1980). Professionals should not rely on the accuracy of "age levels" drawn from non-normed measures.

A major problem inherent with standardized tests is that the examiner is confined to specific materials and procedures, thereby limiting his freedom to adapt to a child's particular interests and preferred materials. Tasks are selected which will demonstrate specific skills. The child's performance is assessed according to set criteria and then translated into a score which provides an indication of standing in the normative group. Some norm-referenced tests such as the Battelle Developmental Inventory (Newborg, Stock, Wnek, Guidubaldi, & Svinicki, 1988) also allow the use of observation and family report.

Although it is important to follow standard procedures to maintain reliability and validity, procedures that emphasize control, uniformity, and direction are incompatible with the characteristics of young children. Rigid adherence to standard procedures can be in direct conflict with the characteristics, style, and performance needs of the young child. The very nature of infants, toddlers, and preschoolers defies the notion of "performance on demand." Shyness, separation difficulties, or oppositional features frequently seen in young children also may make it difficult to assess young children, especially if they are at-risk or have a disability. Meisels (1996) warned that assessment methodology devised for older children is highly limited in its usefulness, results in meaningless scores, and may lead to inappropriate recommendations for services, educational placements, and programs. (See Chapter 5 for considerations in accommodating the needs of young children.)

The task of assessing a young child with a disability is even more difficult than assessing a young child who is developing normally. Specific disabilities in areas of vision, hearing, language, or motor development will hamper a child's performance on most standardized tests. The child's ability to receive information and make responses may be impaired by limitations of vision or hearing, language problems, and difficulty with motor skills. Administering a test with strict standardization procedures can result in erroneous conclusions about children with disabilities. For example, a child with cerebral palsy may not be able to perform motor or verbal components of those tasks even though the child has the cognitive skills needed to do so. The directions or questions through which the examiner must elicit responses are fixed. These fixed directions or questions may include verbalizations that exceed the child's language development or differ from the usual context within which the child may have experienced similar activities. In such cases, "failure" of an item may reflect misunderstanding of directions, rather than inability to perform a given task.

The use of standardized procedures and materials makes it very difficult to use appropriate adaptations in materials, manner of presentation, or in criteria for assessing to accommodate special needs. Rigid adherence to standard procedures will prevent an examiner from making adaptations to circumvent the child's impairments (Bagnato & Neisworth, 1991). If these impairments are not taken into account when testing, then the child's score may not reflect an accurate representation of the child's abilities. The skilled and experienced examiner must administer tests and interpret results with utmost caution when assessing young children with disabilities.

Many norm-based assessments do not sample skills that are emphasized in early childhood settings or in kindergarten curricula. Bagnato and Neisworth (1991) emphasized choosing only those norm-referenced instruments that sample skills required in the early childhood setting and that one should be cautious when interpreting early childhood measures. Their effectiveness in the realm of early childhood education is ensured only when they are used as part of a comprehensive assessment of a child's skills and needs. Some tools also strive for curricular relevance as well as the comparative benefits of norm-referencing. If the program's curriculum and the normative instrument are both based on developmental milestones, then a high correlation between these measures is shown (MacTurk & Neisworth, 1978). Typically, developmentally based normative assessments are likely to be program related (Bagnato & Neisworth, 1991). Bagnato and Neisworth (1991) recommended

the use of an instrument such as the BDI (Newborg, Stock, Wnek, Guidubaldi, & Svinicki, 1988). This tool is an excellent example of a developmental scale that provides curricular objectives that are norm-referenced. When a program's curriculum is based on an instrument such as the BDI, a child's progress can be assessed in terms of response to the program's interventions, as well as compared with peers in the national norm group.

Although the BDI was not normed on children with disabilities, much of the early development of the instrument took place with children with disabilities prior to the normative work described in the manual (Boyd, Welge, Sexton, & Miller, 1989). The test manual also describes some of the uses of the inventory with young children with disabilities and demonstrates a sensitivity toward this population that is reflected in the recommended adaptations when assessing children with sensory and motor disabilities. The skilled and experienced examiner must administer tests and interpret results with utmost caution when assessing young children with disabilities.

Miller and Robinson (1996) proposed two questions that should be answered before using any test with a child with a particular disability: (1) What questions about the child's development can this test be expected to answer? and (2) How do other children with this child's type of disability perform on this test? The second question must be answered through research studies which include large groups of children with the specific disability in question.

Discussing Assessment Results with Parents

Parents should be involved in each step of the assessment process. Involving parents in the initial assessment activities builds relationships with them so that they become equal team members. To promote this involvement, professionals should:

- Schedule meetings at times and in locations convenient for the parents.
- Be flexible in terms of the modes of communication (by telephone or in face-to-face meetings).
- Listen to and address parents' concerns.
- Present parents with choices when open-ended questions result in deferral to professionals.
- Provide parents with information about the content of meetings well before the meetings occur.
- Use jargon-free language.
- Conduct meetings in an informal but efficient manner, rather than in an officious manner.
- Limit the number of professionals at meetings to avoid overwhelming families.
- Be prepared for meetings.

Under the IDEA, the assessment team typically (as individuals or collaboratively) scores each assessment instrument or procedure and synthesizes the separate assessment to obtain an overall understanding of the child. This synthesis of information typically takes place at a meeting. Many professionals assume that the scoring, analysis, and synthesis of assessments require technical expertise beyond that of most families. Although some assessment procedures such as an IQ test are standardized and may be administered and scored only by people with special training, many assessment procedures can be carried out collaboratively with family members and should be discussed thoroughly at each step of the process.

Although some families participate in the analysis of assessment information, others prefer not to be involved. Some families appreciate being present at any discussion related to their child. They may perceive that the best way to ensure that their perspective is considered is to be part of the decision-making process from its very beginning (Turnbull & Turnbull, 2001). Family members may have unique information

about their child that is not known to professionals. They can verify the validity of the conclusions made by professionals about the child's abilities and needs. They can provide information about what they believe the child needs to learn, which goals are most important for their child, which intervention strategies are acceptable to them, and which intervention strategies are likely to be used in various settings. This involvement provides them with opportunities to engage in collaborative problem solving with professionals. Regardless of whether family members participate in the synthesis of assessment data, interpretations of assessment data should not be considered final until they are reviewed and commented on by the families. If families are not present, then assessment data should lead to only tentative interpretations. The family's perspective and insights must be respected to create a true partnership.

Families have a variety of responses to assessment results. Information must be conveyed very sensitively. Families want hopeful information, and will be sorely disappointed by the confirmation of a disability (Turnbull & Turnbull, 2001). Other families will feel justified and relieved (Mallow & Bechtel, 1999) because they believed all along that their child had real needs and because now there will be an effective intervention (Turnbull & Turnbull, 2001).

A reliable alliance can be built with families by responding to parents' questions with clear descriptions and concrete examples of their child's performance. Professionals should demonstrate genuine interest and commitment to the child's success and highlight the child's strengths and abilities. The importance of listening, expressing empathy, and empathetic communication cannot be overemphasized (Turnbull & Turnbull, 2001).

Agenda for Discussing Results

A suggested agenda for discussing results has at least three goals for the meeting (Teglasi, 1985; Turnbull & Turnbull, 2001). These goals are:

1. Ensuring a clear understanding of the child's strengths, preferences, great expectations, and needs;
2. Empathetic support of the family and child in the emotional adjustment to the assessment information; and
3. Interpretation and communication of information to facilitate an appropriate education for the child and empowerment for the child, family and team members.

Four components are suggested to be included in this meeting: (1) initial proceedings, (2) presentation of findings, (3) recommendations, and (4) summary (Turnbull & Turnbull, 2001). In the initial proceedings, the family should have the opportunity to provide input, react to, and reflect on the others' input according to their preferences. The family's perspectives and comments about the child's functioning will provide information about their current level of understanding about their child. When presenting findings, professionals should be as concrete and specific as possible (Hirsch, 1981). First, the domain being discussed should be introduced with examples of this area. In the next step, the child's current level of functioning within that domain is discussed as well as how it compares with chronological age peers. Examples of skills within the domain that the child can and cannot perform should be given. Finally, the importance of that discrepancy between age and achievement and how the discrepancy may affect the child's development now or in the future should be discussed. Again, good communication skills should be employed. Communication should be direct but sensitive and jargon-free, and should clearly convey the message that the child and family's interests are of concern. Suggestions for follow-up reading material should be provided. The assessment team should present a composite of the child's strengths, preferences, expectations, and needs. The conference should stimulate a discussion and assist in addressing the priorities and concerns of the family and other team members.

At the end of the conference, recommendations must be made. The more that parents have been involved in the assessment process, the more likely they are to follow through on these recommendations. In this partnership, families and professionals reflect collaboratively about the assessment data and generate recommendations for action. The IDEA requires that these recommendations should describe the specially designed instruction, related services, and assistive technology to be provided for the child. Detailed information must be provided about the child's participation and progress in the least restrictive environment. These recommendations should build on strengths and remediate needs. It is helpful to recommend a specific plan of action, specifying who is responsible for following through on each recommendation, when those people will begin and finish their duties, the necessary resources for the job, and how people will know the work has been done. Subsequent IFSP/IEP conferences should provide continuous reflection about the extent to which a reliable alliance has been developed.

It is essential that the professional remember that the parents' expectations for the child's future may be largely determined by the words and messages that they receive at this crucial time. The professional can be a catalyst for the long-term positive outcomes that this parent experienced through the reliable alliances that were built with families in the referral and assessment process (Turnbull & Turnbull, 2001).

Summary

Norm-based measures constitute an important part of the assessment process, particularly in relation to the diagnostic criteria used in determining a child's special service needs. Norm-based assessments can provide information that may be useful when making diagnostic assessments, placement decisions, and assessments of a child's progress. Professional judgment, as well as additional information from caregivers, health professionals, teachers, and so on, should be used when making eligibility or placement decisions, as well as when developing intervention programs. Norm-based assessment should be only one part of a comprehensive assessment battery. Multidimensional assessment or using multiple types of assessment instruments will provide a broader, more valid and useful profile of a child's abilities and needs.

References

American Psychological Association. (1985). *Standards for educational and psychological tests*. Washington, DC: APA.

Bagnato, S. J., & Neisworth, J. T. (1991). *Assessment for early intervention: Best practices for professionals*. New York: Guilford Press.

Bagnato, S. J., Neisworth, J. T., & Munson, S. M. (1997). *Linking developmental assessment and early intervention: An authentic approach*. Baltimore: Brookes.

Bailey, D. B., & Nabors, L. A. (1996). Tests and test development. In M. McLean, D. B. Bailey, & M. Wolery (Eds.), *Assessing infants and preschoolers with special needs* (2nd ed., pp. 24–25). Upper Saddle River, NJ: Merrill/Prentice Hall.

Barrera, I. (1996). Thoughts on the assessment of young children whose sociocultural background is unfamiliar to the assessor. In S. J. Meisels & E. Fenichel (Eds.), *New visions for the developmental assessment of infants and young children* (pp. 69–84). Washington, DC: National Center for Infants, Toddlers, and Families.

Bayley, N. (1993). *Manual for the Bayley Scales of Infant Development* (2nd ed.). San Antonio: The Psychological Corporation.

Benn, R. (1994). Conceptualizing eligibility for early intervention services. In D. M. Bryant & M. A. Graham (Eds.), *Implementing early intervention* (pp. 18–45). New York: Guilford Press.

Biro, P., Daulton, D., & Szanton, E. (1991, December 30). *Informed clinical opinion* (NEC*TAS Notes No. 4). Chapel Hill, NC: NEC*TAS.

Boyd, R. D., Welge, P., Sexton, D., & Miller, J. H. (1989). Concurrent validity of the Battelle Developmental Inventory with the Bayley Scales in young children with known or suspected disabilities. *Journal of Early Intervention, 13*(1), 14–23.

Fewell, R. R., & Sandall, S. R. (1986). Developmental testing of handicapped infants: A measurement dilemma. *Topics in Early Childhood Special Education, 6*, 86–99.

Garwood, S. G. (1982). (Mis)use of developmental scales in program evaluation. *Topics in Early Childhood Special Education, 6*(3), 72–86.

Harbin, G. L., Gallagher, J. J., & Terry, D. V. (1991). Defining the eligible population: Policy issues and challenges. *Journal of Early Intervention, 15*(1), 13–20.

Hirsch, G. P. (1981). *Training developmental disability specialists in parent conference skills*. Unpublished doctoral dissertation, University of Kansas, Lawrence.

Kaufman, A. S., & Kaufman, N. L. (1983). *Kaufman Assessment Battery for Children*. Circle Pines, MN: American Guidance Service.

Keogh, B. K., & Sheehan, R. (1981). The use of developmental test data for documenting handicapped children's progress: Problems and recommendations. *Journal of the Division for Early Childhood, 3*, 42–47.

Knoblock, H., Stevens, F., & Malone, A. F. (1980). *Manual of developmental diagnosis*. New York: Harper & Row.

Kubiszyn, T., & Borich, G. (1990). *Educational testing and measurement: Classroom applications* (3rd ed.). Glenview, IL: Scott, Foresman.

MacTurk, R., & Neisworth, J. T. (1978). Norm-referenced and criterion-based measures with preschoolers. *Exceptional Children, 45*(1), 34–39.

Mallow, G. E., & Bechtel, G. A. (1999). Chronic sorrow: The experience of parents with children who are developmentally disabled. *Journal of Psychosocial Nursing, 37*(7), 31–35.

McLean, M. (1996). Assessment and its importance in early intervention/early childhood education. In M. McLean, D. B. Bailey, & M. Wolery (Eds.), *Assessing infants and preschoolers with special needs* (2nd ed., pp. 1–22). Upper Saddle River, NJ: Merrill/Prentice Hall.

Meisels, S. J. (1996). Charting the continuum of assessment and intervention. In S. J. Meisels & E. Fenichel (Eds.), *New visions for the developmental assessment of infants and young children* (pp. 27–52). Washington, DC: National Center for Infants, Toddlers, and Families.

Miller, L. J., & Robinson, C. C. (1996). Strategies for meaningful assessment of infants and toddlers with significant physical and sensory disabilities. In S. J. Meisels & E. Fenichel (Eds.), *New visions for the developmental assessment of infants and young children* (pp. 313–328). Washington, DC: National Center for Infants, Toddlers, and Families.

Mindes, G., Ireton, H., & Mardell-Czudnowski, C. (1996). *Assessing young children*. Albany, NY: Delmar.

Neisworth, J. T., & Bagnato, S. J. (1992). The case against intelligence testing in early intervention. *Topics in Early Childhood Special Education, 12*(1), 1–20.

Newborg, J., Stock, J., Wnek, L., Guidubaldi, J., & Svinicki, J. S. (1988). *Battelle Developmental Inventory*. Chicago: Riverside.

Paget, K. D., & Nagle, R. J. (1986). A conceptual model of preschool assessment. *School Psychology Review, 15*(2), 154–165.

Piaget, J. (1952). *The origins of intelligence in children*. New York: International Universities Press.

Romero, I. (1999). Individual assessment procedures with preschool children. In E. V. Nuttall, I. Romero, & J. Kalesnik (Eds.), *Assessing and screening preschoolers: Psychological and educational dimensions* (2nd ed., pp. 59–71). Needham Heights, MA: Allyn & Bacon.

Salvia, J., & Ysseldyke, J. (1995). *Assessment* (6th ed.). Boston: Houghton, Mifflin.

Sattler, J. M. (1988). *Assessment of children*. San Diego: Sattler.

Shackelford, J. (1992, October). State/jurisdiction eligibility definitions for Part H. NECTAS *Notes*, 5.

Shonkoff, J. (1983). The limitations of normative assessments of high-risk infants. *Topics in Early Childhood Special Education*, 2(1), 29–41.

Shonkoff, J., & Meisels, S. (1991). Defining eligibility for services under Public Law 99–457. *Journal of Early Intervention*, 15(1), 21–25.

Snyder-McLean, L. (1987). Reporting norm-referenced program evaluation data: Some considerations. *Journal of the Division for Early Childhood*, 11, 254–264.

Teglasi, H. (1985). Best practices in interpreting psychological assessment data to parents. In A. Thomas & J. Grimes (Eds.), *Best practices in school psychology* (pp. 415–430). Kent, OH: National Association of School Psychologists.

Thorndike, R. L., Hagen, E. P., & Sattler, J. M. (1986). *Guide for administering and scoring the Stanford-Binet Intelligence Scale* (4th ed.). Chicago: Riverside.

Turnbull, A., & Turnbull, R. (2001). *Families, professionals and exceptionality: Collaborating for empowerment* (4th ed.). Upper Saddle River, NJ: Merrill/Prentice Hall.

Venn, J. J. (2000). *Assessing students with special needs* (2nd ed.). Upper Saddle River, NJ: Merrill/Prentice Hall.

Wechsler, D. (1989). *Manual for the Wechsler Preschool and Primary Scale of Intelligence—Revised*. San Antonio: The Psychological Corporation.

Wodrich, D. L. (1997). *Children's psychological testing* (3rd ed.). Baltimore: Brookes.

APPENDIX 9–1
Norm-Referenced Assessments

Test Name	Target Population and Age Range/Purpose	Domains Covered	Outcomes	Publisher/ Vendor	Administration Time (min.)
Battelle Developmental Inventory (BDI) (Newborg, Stock, Wnek, Guidubaldi, & Svinicki 1988)	0 to 95 mos; norm-/curriculum-based; diagnosis, linkage, and progress evaluation	Personal-social, adaptive, motor, communication, cognitive	Developmental age, z-score, developmental rate, normal curve equivalent, percentile	DLM, Allen, TX	Screening: 10–30; Entire BDI: 60–120 depending on child's age
Bayley Scales of Infant Development (BSID-II, 1993)	Infants, 2 to 30 mos; comprehensive analysis of infant developmental skills	Mental, psychomotor	Developmental quotient, developmental age	Psychological Corporation, San Antonio, TX	25–30 (Mental)
Kaufman Assessment Battery for Children (Kaufman & Kaufman, 1983)	2–6 to 12–0 yrs	Verbal and nonverbal intelligence, mental processing, sequential simultaneous processing, achievement	Achievement; mental processing index; standard scores and scaled scores; percentile ranks; stanines	American Guidance Service, Circle Pines, MN	60

211

APPENDIX 9–1
continued

Test Name	Target Population and Age Range/Purpose	Domains Covered	Outcomes	Publisher/ Vendor	Administration Time (min.)
Leiter International Performance Scale– Revised (Roid & Miller, 1996)	2 to 20 yrs	Nonverbal: Reasoning Visualization Memory Attention	Weighted scores, percentile ranges, composite IQ	Roid & Stoelting Co., Woodale, IL	Depends on age and ability level
Stanford-Binet Intelligence Scale (Thorndike, Hagen, & Sattler, 1986)	2 yrs to Adult	General intelligence (verbal & nonverbal)	Mental age: IQ	Riverside Publishing, Chicago	60–90
Wechsler Preschool and Primary Scale of Intelligence Revised (Wechsler, 1989)	3 to 7–3 yrs	General intelligence (verbal & nonverbal)	Scaled scores for 6 verbal & 5 performance subtests; verbal performance and full scale IQs	Psychological Corporation, New York	45

10

Curriculum-Based Assessment
for Instructional Planning

$\mathbf{C}$riterion-referenced tests measure a child's mastery or performance of a skill or sequence of skills, rather than comparing the child with other children. Curriculum-based assessment is a form of criterion-referenced measurement in which the curricular objectives act as the criteria for the identification of instructional targets and for the assessment of the child's status and progress. Curriculum-based assessment is the most prominent form of assessment within early childhood special education (Bagnato, Neisworth, & Munson, 1997). This prominence is based on the direct relationship among testing, teaching, and progress evaluation which is provided by curriculum-based assessment.

Curriculum-based assessments are criterion-referenced tests that are organized into a developmentally sequenced curriculum. This type of assessment typically addresses several areas of development, such as gross and fine motor skills, cognition, language proficiency, self help, and social-emotional functioning. The developmental sequences of skills within each domain of the curriculum-based assessment are task-analyzed or broken down into subskills which then form the foundation and content for the curriculum-based assessment. The child's achievement is followed based on these developmental skills which then become the instructional targets or objectives for the child within the sequenced curriculum. The objectives within these areas may vary from major goals to finely graded sequences of prerequisite behaviors that constitute a given skill-objective. The child's performance is compared with past performance to monitor progress within the curriculum. Many curriculum-based assessments also include suggested teaching activities for each item on the scale.

This chapter will explain the purpose, types, and uses of curriculum-based assessment. Guidelines for choosing a curriculum-based assessment and evaluating these assessments will be provided. Helpful tips for conducting curriculum-based assessment and writing reports based on these assessments will also be discussed.

Purpose of Curriculum-Based Assessment

The purpose of curriculum-based assessment is to provide a direct link to the intervention goals and expected outcomes. This type of criterion-referenced measurement uses curricular objectives as the criteria for identification of instructional targets and for the assessment of status and progress along a continuum of objectives within a developmentally sequenced curriculum. Bagnato, Neisworth, and Munson (1997) listed the following five important purposes of curriculum-based assessment:

- Analyzing and profiling developmental competencies
- Offering adaptations for use with children who have disabilities
- Targeting integrated IFSP or IEP goals
- Monitoring incremental gains
- Facilitating teamwork

PL 105–17 stipulates that the evaluation and assessment of the child must include the child's level of functioning in each of the following developmental areas: cognitive, physical, communication, social-emotional, and adaptive. The assessment must include the unique needs of the child in terms of each developmental area and identification of services to meet those needs. Curriculum-based assessment facilitates this process by providing examination in these areas. The early interventionist using a curriculum-based assessment is able to identify where the child falls within the range of objectives of the program's curriculum in each domain. The curriculum-based assessment scale will also provide a profile of the child's specific strengths and weaknesses, and thus offer direct information for writing instructional objectives.

Bagnato and Neisworth (1991) compared curriculum-based assessment to a "map." The curriculum-based assessment is a way of finding specific directions for beginning a trip. The curriculum is the map which includes critical landmarks, possible destinations, and clear routes toward the destinations. This curriculum map should be detailed enough to permit progress checks, accommodations for various disabilities, and comprehensive and balanced objectives. This map will provide a more comprehensive and thorough view for writing the IEP or IFSP as well as pacing and altering the instruction. Curriculum-based assessment offers a way to track the child's progress throughout the year and, therefore, yields both formative and summative information about the efficacy of the program. In summary, developmental curriculum-based assessment can provide the major approach for (1) identifying curricular entry points, (2) prescribing the child's individual program planning, (3) progress monitoring, and (4) program evaluation (Neisworth & Bagnato, 1988). The information obtained from the curriculum-based assessment is directly relevant to the child's program. Two types of curriculum-based assessments are available; they are discussed in the next section.

Types of Curriculum-Based Assessments

Curriculum-Referenced Scales

Curriculum-based assessments can be categorized into two types. Curriculum-referenced scales sample objectives that are commonly emphasized in most developmental curricula but are not integral to any particular curriculum. They are composites of curriculum sequences (Neisworth & Bagnato, 1988). Although the assessment and curricular items are not identical, they should be similar enough to place a child within a curriculum. The BRIGANCE

Diagnostic Inventory of Early Development-Revised (Brigance, 1991) is a well-known example of a curriculum-referenced scale. Another example is the *Battelle Developmental Inventory* (BDI) (Newborg, Stock, Wnek, Guidubaldi, & Svinicki, 1988) which is a standardized developmental scale. It is the only norm-referenced diagnostic measure that also integrates criterion-referenced features into its structure but is not a curriculum. These curriculum-referenced assessments provide a means for assessing specific skills that are common to most developmental task curricula. The results provide a bridge or common base that is applicable across program-specific curricula. Curriculum-referenced scales should be selected for linkage with many curriculum types (Bagnato & Neisworth, 1991). Because the curriculum is the basis for curriculum-based assessment, it is essential that the type of curriculum assessment used matches the curriculum and the needs of the children to be assessed.

Curriculum-Embedded Scales

Curriculum-embedded scales are those in which the assessment items and the curricular objectives are one and the same. The curriculum itself is the source for both testing and teaching. The assessment items are taken directly from the program's curriculum. The teacher can track the child's progress through the curriculum by noting when mastery of specific objectives is achieved. One example of a curriculum-embedded measure is the *Hawaii Early Learning Profile* (HELP) (VORT, 1995), which is a widely used, comprehensive curriculum for both infants and preschoolers. The *Learning Accomplishments Profile-Revised* (LAP-R) (Glover, Preminger, Sanford, & Zelman, 1995) is another curriculum-embedded scale that is often used in early childhood special education programs. Curriculum-embedded scales provide direct linkage with a specific curriculum (Bagnato & Neisworth, 1991). An overview of four different types of curricular models is presented in the next section of this chapter.

Curricular Models

The content and methods presented in published curricula reflect a range of philosophies concerning appropriate practice. The curricular outcomes will vary according to the underlying philosophy or approach of the curriculum. The nature and extent of the special needs of the children for whom the curricula are designed are crucial factors that dictate the kind of curriculum content and how it is best offered. Philosophies regarding child development and the special needs of children enrolled in various programs are two major considerations in the design and content of curricular materials. Bagnato, Neisworth, and Munson (1997) identified four major curricular models: (1) developmental milestones, (2) functional/adaptive, (3) cognitive-constructivist, and (4) interactive/transactional. The early interventionist or early childhood special educator must examine the curriculum-based assessment to determine if the curricular approach of this assessment is appropriate for the children in the program.

Developmental Milestones Model

The developmental milestones approach is based on the empirical research and observation of normal child development. The developmental milestones evidenced by children at various ages (Bayley, 1969; Gesell, 1923; Knobloch, Stevens, & Malone, 1980) provide the basis of the curriculum. The content of the curriculum is the direction, sequence, and onset of major developmental milestones or capabilities. Curricula based on developmental milestones usually also include objectives that are precursors to each milestone. The milestones are broken down through task analysis into simpler components, subskills, or readiness skills. If the child

is not able to perform a skill, then the early childhood special educator must keep moving down the hierarchy until an objective that the child has mastered is reached. Instruction would begin at this skill. The hierarchies of objectives, progressing from easiest to most difficult, are provided in the developmental milestones approach. One example of a curriculum based on developmental milestones is the BRIGANCE *Prescriptive Readiness: Strategies and Practice* (Brigance, 1985). This assessment measures preacademic skills based on developmental milestones for children from prekindergarten into first grade. The results identify a child's pattern of strengths and areas of concern in a number of developmental domains and preacademic skills.

Developmental milestones curricula are often used in programs for children with special needs because they are highly structured and sequenced and allow the use of informal assessment measures. These developmental hierarchies provide diagnostic profiles of a child's capabilities or developmental status, compared with normally developing peers. Although the research is based on normal development and children with special needs often are delayed in these milestones, the sequence and pattern of development are the same for all children. However, this approach is often inappropriate for children with severe sensory or neurophysical difficulties who must use alternative sensory or response modes. A functional or adaptive curriculum would be more appropriate for meeting these children's needs.

Functional/Adaptive Model

The functional/adaptive model has two major characteristics. This model emphasizes the learning of skills that have immediate use and motivation for the child. Real-life outcomes are listed as suggested goals and are relevant for future success in predictable environments. Major life skills and adaptive behaviors are analyzed to identify components and sequences that can be taught and have immediate relevance. Task analysis is used to identify readiness or precursive skills, rather than developmental prerequisites. Another characteristic of the functional/adaptive curriculum approach is its emphasis on the function of a behavior, rather than on the form and shape of the behavior. The concept of form and function will be discussed later in this chapter.

This type of curriculum is especially suited for children with severe disabilities because it provides immediate success, motivation, and mastery. However, the child may not be prepared to succeed in future settings because broad developmental milestones and prerequisites are not emphasized. An example of functional/adaptive assessment is OBSERVE (Dunst & McWilliam, 1988), a system that enables interventionists to facilitate children's development of response-contingent skills by identifying each child's response capabilities and matching those capabilities with appropriate learning opportunities (Bagnato, Neisworth, & Munson, 1997). Further consideration of the OBSERVE system is included in Chapter 7.

Cognitive-Constructivist Model

The cognitive-constructivist approach is based on the research of Jean Piaget (Piaget, 1952; 1987). Piaget's observations have been used as a basis for devising developmental goals and objectives (Brazelton, 1973; Bricker, 1993; Dunst, 1981; Uzgiris & Hunt, 1975). A cognitive-constructivist curriculum contains Piaget's six concepts through the stages of the sensorimotor period that are assumed to be the foundation for later learning. These concepts are: (1) object permanence, (2) means-end relations, (3) operational causality, (4) imitation, (5) spatial awareness, and (6) object function. The hierarchies in these concepts become a guide for assessing and teaching conceptual skills during the developmental period. The *Uzgiris and Hunt Infant Psychological Development Scale* (IPDS): *Dunst Revision* (Dunst, 1980) is an example of this type

of assessment. Developmental competencies across several developmental processes in cognition, social communication, and motor exploration are sampled by the IPDS.

The cognitive-constructivist approach uses developmental stage, rather than age attainment. The teacher attempts to help each child progress through steps in the predicted stage. This model specifies the sequence of steps for teaching a stage level and provides clear instructional goals for what must be taught. The cognitive-constructivist approach provides guidelines for the areas of language and social development but does not adequately address fine and gross motor development, adaptive skills, and affective development to become a comprehensive curriculum (Bagnato, Neisworth, & Munson, 1997). Objectives for these areas would need to be added.

Interactive/Transactional Model

The interactive/transactional approach focuses on examining and facilitating caregiver-child interaction as a primary method for promoting child development. This approach is based on the premise that the quality of parent-child interaction during infancy may set the stage for subsequent cognitive and social development. There must be a match among the parents'/caregiver's actions, environmental events, and the child's capabilities, interests, and behavioral style in order for teaching efforts to be productive. The *Parent Behavior Progression* (Bromwich, 1981) is an example of an interactive or transactional approach. This assessment is helpful for identifying degrees or levels of skills along a hierarchy or task analysis of important parent/caregiver skills. It can be used as a curriculum for the parents/caregiver. The objectives are for the parents/caregiver and are designed to promote constructive adult-child interactions or transactions. These constructive interactions should produce optimal attainment of the developmental milestones.

This model is most congruent with a family-systems approach, which focuses on improving parent as well as child capabilities. A major disadvantage of this model is that promoting desirable interaction does not guarantee selection of child objectives. Another consideration for this approach is that many parents may not be ready, willing, or able to interact (Bagnato, Neisworth, & Munson, 1997).

The curricular choice should be based on the needs of the children and families in the program. Additional considerations for the decision are discussed in the next section.

Considerations for Implementing a Curriculum-Based Assessment

No single curriculum-based assessment is appropriate for all children and all programs. Curricula are usually designed for use with certain age ranges, special needs, and particular settings. Teachers, program supervisors, and other professionals involved in implementing a curriculum-based assessment should be aware of the weaknesses inherent in these tests. A number of considerations should be weighed before deciding on a curriculum-based assessment for a particular child or group of children. These considerations are discussed in the next sections and summarized in Figure 10–1.

Compatibility with Program

The assessment instrument chosen should be compatible with the philosophy and theoretical orientation of the program. The curriculum-based assessment should reflect the staff's philosophy of how children develop and how staff should facilitate learning. As previously discussed in this chapter, a program may choose a model based on a developmental milestones, cognitive-constructivist, functional, or an interactive/transactional model. Does the

FIGURE 10–1
Considerations for Implementing
Curriculum-Based Assessments

Compatibility with program
Family-focused
Multidimensional
Team approach
Developmental age of child
Developmental areas included
Size of steps
Age-appropriate, functional
Adaptive to disability
Form versus function
Results translatable to program planning
Profile of strengths and needs
Recordkeeping system
Feasibility and cost-effectiveness

curriculum-based assessment chosen reflect the program's content and approach to child development? If the curriculum-based assessment is not compatible with the theoretical orientation of the program, then it will not provide a fair assessment of the child's progress.

Family-Focused Assessment

The family, rather than solely the child, is the focus of the assessment and intervention. Curricula that support family participation are more effective in helping the child generalize and maintain the skills taught in the intervention program, which will minimize the variability between at-school and at-home performance and behavior. Teachers will better understand the conditions under which a skill is demonstrated if the child is observed at home as well as at school. Also in keeping with family-focused intervention, all findings and implications should be clearly presented so that they are easily interpreted by family members. Chapter 2 provides a more comprehensive discussion of family involvement in the assessment process.

Multidimensional Assessment

Interventionists should not rely solely on one observation by one professional, nor should they rely solely on one assessment instrument as the source of information. In order to obtain a truly accurate assessment, several different types of instruments should be used over a period of time to determine what a child can and cannot do. Instruments that examine different settings (e.g., preschool, home) and can be completed by different respondents (e.g., caregiver, teacher, speech/language pathologist) should be selected. Multisession assessments conducted by more than one professional in a variety of settings will provide a more representative picture of the child's abilities and skills.

Team Assessment

Curriculum-based assessment may also assist in organizing team assessment activities. Two features of curriculum-based assessment facilitate teamwork. These features are the domain structure within the curriculum-based assessment and the flexibility that curriculum-based assessment allows. Skill sequences are organized into domains and subdomains. These domains accommodate input from parents and various professionals involved with the child. The flexible procedures allow tasks to be administered differently for individual children, data to be gathered through observations and reports, and the team to use the style of interaction that best fits each child and family. The style used by the team may be multidisciplinary, interdisciplinary, or transdisciplinary. (Team assessment is discussed in Chapter 4.) All members of the multidisciplinary professional team need information typically obtained from curriculum-based assessments. Planning should occur within the team as to how the assessment can be conducted to avoid duplication. With a transdisciplinary approach, the arena assessment allows the team to observe the curriculum-based assessment being administered by one or two of its members. The observing team members may offer input through comments or suggestions during the session(s). The team then discusses the results based on a common ground. Additional assessment information can then be obtained in further testing that is specific to a domain or discipline as needed.

Developmental Age of Child

It is essential to choose a curriculum-based assessment appropriate to the developmental level of the child. However, the child's developmental age may be different from her chronological age. A child's development may also be variable across domains, being much lower in one area than another. If the curriculum chosen does not examine a wide enough age range, then it may be necessary to use two curricula. If a child is functioning considerably below her chronological age, then the examiner may need to adapt activities in order to maintain a more age-appropriate appeal of the curricular tasks. For example, a child with motor disabilities may need to be presented with motor skills at a much lower level. Thus, a curriculum at the infant level might need to be used along with skills at this lower level. However, it is important that the materials used are age appropriate to engage the child's interest. For example, the toys recommended within the assessment may not be interesting to an older child. Therefore, toys that are interesting to the child would need to be substituted for those that are recommended in the lower-level curriculum.

Developmental Areas Assessed

The curriculum-based assessment selected must include developmental areas appropriate to the child. A relevant sampling of skills and behaviors must be obtained which relate to the curricular needs of the child. A crucial factor in using curriculum-based assessment is choosing an appropriate curriculum. For example, children with social-emotional problems should be assessed with a curriculum-based assessment which includes items relating to social interactions, self-esteem, and so on. McAllister (1991) noted several inherent problems with curriculum-based assessments in the social skills domain. He proposed that social skills are sometimes underrepresented, may not reflect the complexity of social skill intervention, and may not adequately reflect the social development of children with certain disabilities. (See Chapter 16 for assessment of social-emotional development.)

Small Steps

The steps between the assessment items of the curriculum-based assessment must be small enough to measure progress, especially for those children with more severe deficits. Skills should be related to one another and provide for the emergence of more complex skills. The items should be sequential and relevant for children with disabilities. Tasks should be organized in a logical and sequential order. Easy tasks should precede more difficult tasks.

Age-Appropriate, Functional Norms

Curriculum-based assessment should provide objectives that are as normal and age-appropriate as possible. Early interventionists should identify functional skills that are needed across environments and that will have immediate and long-term, positive impact. These skills are functional or authentic in that they address true capabilities expressed in genuine daily activities. The benefits of these functional skills are more likely to be seen when children are integrated, mainstreamed, or included with normal children.

Adaptive to Disability

If the child has a sensory, neuromotor, or behavioral disability, then a curriculum-based assessment which allows for a variety of responses is necessary. For example, a child with autistic characteristics may not be able to provide a verbal response but could respond nonverbally by pointing. A disability may be circumvented by using alternate response modes, such as a light wand, eye localization, or computer, to accommodate for the disability. The way in which the stimulus is presented also may be varied using color contrast, magnifications, handles on form boards, or textures. Some curricula provide adaptive modifications, such as the *Battelle Developmental Inventory* (BDI) (Newborg, Stock, Wnek, Guidubaldi, & Svinicki, 1988). An example of an adaptation on the BDI is allowing credit for a child with severe motor disabilities, who is not physically able to move three cubes by picking up one cube at a time, to identify whether the examiner has three cubes in her hand. A child with a severe visual impairment is allowed to feel the cubes before giving them to the examiner. These are examples of adaptations which are suggested on the BDI for items which would be difficult for children with motor, sensory, or behavioral disabilities to perform. Both the *Carolina Curriculum for Infants and Toddlers with Special Needs, Second Edition* (Johnson-Martin, Jens, Attermeier, & Hacker, 1991) and the *Carolina Curriculum for Preschoolers with Special Needs* (Johnson-Martin, Attermeier, & Hacker, 1990) provide modifications for assessing young children with sensory, neural, or behavioral disabilities. Assessments that provide suggestions for making these accommodations yield a more valid appraisal of the child's capabilities and provide information about the types of instructional modifications necessary to help the child learn. Curricula that were developed for specific disabilities or that employ functional objectives are especially helpful for children with more serious sensory or response disabilities. The curriculum-based assessment that is chosen should be easily adaptable to various disabilities (Bagnato & Neisworth, 1991).

Form Versus Function

Many important skills, such as cognitive, communication, and social skills, needed by infants and young children can be performed by multiple behaviors. For example, initiating social interactions can be performed by speaking to other people, touching them, giving them an object, or making eye contact. Each of these behaviors may result in starting an interaction. Often, the more important goal is to initiate the interaction. Other skills should be performed by a relatively limited range of behaviors, such as self-care skills. For example, a child could use her fingers or a spoon to feed herself. She could also get the food into her mouth by lifting the plate and letting it slide in. Usually the most acceptable behavior is using a spoon.

In each of these examples there is a behavior and an effect of the behavior. White (1980) referred to this relationship as the "form versus function" issue. Forms are the observable behaviors of the child; functions are the effects of these forms on the environment. Assessment should provide information on the child's behavior and on the effects of the child's behavior. For example, a child might try to initiate an interaction with a teacher by tapping the teacher's hand. The teacher then turns to the child and acknowledges her tap. The hand tap is the form of the behavior, and the function or effect is the teacher acknowledging the child's request for attention. Various forms of behaviors may exist which accomplish the same function. Another form for initiating an interaction with the teacher might be the child saying the teacher's name. The same result could occur with the teacher's recognition of the child's

verbalization, and thus the function remains the same. Many different behaviors can produce the same effect. Each behavior or form is thought to produce some effect or function.

Curriculum-based assessments tend to emphasize form over function, but it is crucial for the examiner to realize the importance of both forms and functions. The examiner must identify the functions needed for adaptive performance. Can the child impact upon the environment effectively? For example, verbally asking for help is a form; the function is to indicate in some way that help is needed. This could be communicated in a variety of ways, even by simply making eye contact, a gesture, or a tap on the shoulder. If developing language is a goal for the child, then a one-word verbal request might be required for the child. For another child, the expected form might be the use of sign language or a picture card. The teacher or examiner must determine what functions exist, which functions are most important, how the functions are related to one another, and which forms are most useful (Wolery, 1991). In addition to identifying the forms and functions that are needed for adaptive performance, the long-term benefits of the skills and the values assigned by the families must be determined. The high priority skills are then established as objectives on the IFSP or IEP. Functional behavioral assessment is essential for children with severe disabilities. Therefore, this assessment model is described in the Chapter 12.

Results Translatable to Program Planning

Can the results obtained from the curriculum-based assessment be easily translated into information used in program planning? Are the skills assessed important for learning? For example, learning that actions cause effects sets the stage for meaningful exchanges with the physical and social environment. Identifying that a child is aware of cause-effect relationships (as a result of items in the curriculum-based assessment) should allow for the development of goals and objectives in which the child learns how actions impact upon an activity, game, or social interaction.

Profile of Strengths and Needs

Do the curriculum-based assessment results express both strengths and needs which can become the focus of program planning? Many curriculum-based assessments include a format for developing a profile of subscales of the test so that scores may be compared across skill areas. The profile is a visual representation of the child's relative strengths and weaknesses and is helpful in communicating this information with parents and other professionals. The profile provides a way of setting priorities for teaching skills. Areas of weakness may be given a higher priority than areas of strength and identified strengths may be used strategically to remediate weaknesses.

Recordkeeping System

Most curricula offer mastery checklists or a way of keeping track of the objectives that have or have not been mastered. Progress can be noted by (+) objective achieved, (−) not achieved, and (±) emerging. Ongoing assessments should be completed at regular intervals after the initial assessment. This method provides formative assessment information as the year progresses. Overall developmental age ranges can also provide summative information for program evaluation at the end of the year.

Feasibility and Cost-Effectiveness

The curriculum-based assessment that is chosen must be both feasible and cost-effective to implement. Early interventionists must have the time and skill to actually use the instrument,

and its cost should not be excessive. More expensive curriculum-based assessments usually include materials which can be easily found in a classroom. Useful questions to consider in determining the appropriateness of a curriculum-based assessment should include:

- How long does it take to administer?
- Who is qualified to administer the assessment?
- How much staff training time is necessary?
- What equipment or materials are needed to administer it?
- Can these items be found in the classroom?
- Is the recording system practical?

Systems for Curriculum-Based Assessment for Intervention

Curriculum-based developmental assessment is the primary technique used to plan instructional programs for young children who are exceptional. Among all other forms of assessment, curriculum-based assessment is unique in that assessment items are also curricular objectives based on developmental norms. This offers a way to pinpoint specific strengths and weaknesses, track curricular progress, synchronize team efforts, and provide comparisons to normal developmental milestones. In this section, three excellent examples of the curriculum-based assessment process are described.

Activity-Based Assessment and Intervention

The *Assessment, Evaluation, and Programming System* (AEPS) *for Infants and Children* (Bricker & Cripe, 1992) is a comprehensive system that facilitates linking assessment, intervention, and evaluation components. The basis of this system is the AEPS test (Bricker, 1993), which is a criterion-referenced instrument designed to measure the skills and abilities of infants and young children with disabilities up to age 6. This test was developed for use by direct service personnel, such as classroom teachers, home visitors, speech/language pathologists, and others. The AEPS test is available in four spiral-bound volumes: (1) AEPS *Measurement for Birth to Three Years* (Bricker, 1993); (2) AEPS *Curriculum for Birth to Three Years* (Cripe, Slentz, & Bricker, 1993); (3) AEPS *Measurement for Three to Six Years* (Bricker & Pretti-Frontczak, 1996); and (4) AEPS *Curriculum for Three to Six Years* (Bricker & Waddell, 1996).

The AEPS has many strengths, one of which is the use of routine activities that occur in the natural learning environment of the child as the context for assessment. The AEPS uses play as the medium for setting up play centers within the classroom to facilitate the assessment process. Assessing in this context avoids disrupting the ongoing program activities and the results are more likely to reflect a child's functional repertoire. Another strength of this system is the focus on functional skills and abilities which are essential for young children to function independently and to cope with environmental demands. A third advantage of this system is the presentation of items that reflect conceptual or response classes, rather than single, specific responses. This presentation facilitates adaptation for children with disabilities. Specific suggestions are given for adapting the presentation format or the criteria for children with disabilities, particularly those with sensory or motor disabilities. By providing the curriculum volumes for both age ranges (birth to 3 years and 3 to 6 years), the assessment results can be directly linked with curriculum materials. There is also a family assessment evaluation which enables caregivers to be a part of the process. Bagnato, Neisworth, and Munson (1997) cited the AEPS as perhaps the clearest and most outstanding example of assessment for intervention in which assessment and instruction are linked and reciprocal. The materials and strategies permit sensitive planning

and tracking of a child's progress toward family-centered goals.

Play-Based Assessment

Observing and interacting with a child or children during play time can provide much information in a variety of domains. Play-based assessment strategies are considered the most natural and developmentally appropriate way to assess young children. A child's social or emotional status may often be determined by observing her at play. The interaction of the child's growing self-awareness, her cognitive understanding of objects in the environment, and attachment to and investment in caregivers allow the child to begin playing (Benner, 1992).

Several types of play have been identified by researchers. These types of play have focused on interactions with people and with the exploration or use of objects. Parten (1932) developed a category system for social play which is often used to classify social play. Parten identified six categories of play in which children typically engage: unoccupied behavior, onlooker behavior, solitary independent play, parallel activity, associative play, and cooperative or organized supplementary play. Although this classification system was seen as sequential, it has been suggested that it is more useful when considered as a description of various types of social participation in young children, rather than as a developmental continuum (Benner, 1992; Rogers, 1982).

Play-based assessment varies from traditional assessments. The child is observed doing whatever she typically does in the environment. In some play-based assessments, certain toys or materials may be provided based on the child's developmental level. The examiner may observe and interact with the child as she plays, noting specific behaviors or skills that were outlined for observation prior to the session. The *Play Assessment Scale* (Fewell, 1986) is an example of how an examiner may assess multiple areas systematically through structured play routines.

The examiner who wants to assess play skills should directly observe play sessions to find out the types of social interaction and toy or object play demonstrated by the child. The assessment of toy play should focus on at least three goals: (1) describing children's general contact with toys; (2) identifying children's reactions to and preferences for specific toys; and (3) assessing children's levels and types of play (Wolery & Bailey, 1989). The examiner should also assess the types of play displayed, the complexity of that play and any themes that exist in the play (Wolery & Bailey, 1989).

Guidelines for Setting Up a Play Session. Wolery and Bailey (1989) provided a number of factors which should be considered when setting up a play assessment session. These factors are:

1. Children should be free to select various toys, have adequate space to play, and have peers available if social play is being assessed.
2. When assessing peer interactions, the familiarity of the peers chosen, their sex, the toys chosen, and the competence of the peers will influence the type and amount of play.
3. The type of activities will influence the amount of positive social interactions or play. To assess social play, the space should be small, peers should be available, and structured free-play activities should occur.
4. The type and number of toys and materials influence the type and nature of play. When assessing children's social play, a limited number of social materials should be available. The examiner should use toys that will produce certain types of play, such as constructive or pretend, when assessing the nature of play.
5. Observation over a few days will provide a more representative sample of children's play skills.
6. Children who seem to have few play skills may need to be prompted to play and the level of

assistance needed should be noted by the examiner. Children with motor disabilities may need to be provided with battery-operated toys and computer-activated switches. The examiner should observe the positions that allow the child to make movements, switches that are easily and efficiently activated, and children's toy preferences.

Transdisciplinary Play-Based Assessment. One of the most widely used play-based assessments is the *Transdisciplinary Play-Based Assessment* (TPBA) (Linder, 1993a), which provides both an assessment and intervention process, *Transdisciplinary Play-Based Intervention* (TPBI) (Linder, 1993b). Information is gathered from the family concerning the developmental status of the child. This information is then used to design the play session. Toys and materials are provided which are appropriate to the child's level of development. The content and sequence of the play session are structured so that the examiner may observe the child across developmental domains. One of the members of the transdisciplinary team facilitates the play, and the caregivers are included in certain phases of the session. The TPBA guidelines provide a structure for the observation of cognitive, social-emotional, communication and language, and sensorimotor development. The TPBA process allows the child to lead the play, while the facilitator keeps the child interested and motivated by joining in the play. The facilitator alternates between observing free play and attempting to elicit the child's highest levels of performance. It is recommended that the play session be videotaped for analysis and documentation of the child's progress.

The observation and summary worksheets which are provided include more detailed subcategories of abilities in each developmental domain. The observation and age charts in each developmental area are used in conjunction with the observation and summary worksheets. By using all of these forms, the team members are able to identify child strengths, areas of concern, and areas of readiness for intervention.

The curriculum for the TPBA, *Transdisciplinary Play-Based Intervention: Guidelines for Developing a Meaningful Curriculum for Young Children* (TPBI) (Linder, 1993b), links to the assessment and helps team members determine the child's goals and behavioral objectives based on the TPBA summary sheets. Parents and facilitators—the team members who are providing the intervention—learn how to plan the play environment, the play materials, and the overall structure of the day to facilitate enjoyable child-parent interactions. Play-based assessment is discussed in Chapter 4.

LINKing Assessment and Intervention

The LINK system proposed by Bagnato, Neisworth, and Munson (1997) is a process that helps special educators teaching young children implement curriculum-based assessments. The LINK approach is a philosophical perspective and a way to apply a set of guidelines for combining assessment and intervention. This approach addresses the purpose, content, methods, and applications for linking authentic curriculum-based assessment to instruction. In the LINK approach, the assessment is not a single event but a combination of qualitative and quantitative information. Parents and professionals reach a collaborative decision based on value judgments and interpretations from multidimensional information collected continuously over time. Therefore, no single curriculum-based assessment is recommended and then additional assessment instruments are used to provide a multidimensional approach and further information about the child's functioning. This process emphasizes (1) natural and functional developmental competencies or goals that are displayed by children in everyday play; (2) a developmentally appropriate style with adaptive modifications to accommodate special needs; (3) an individualized and longitudinal assessment

of children's developmental progress on a curricular sequence; and (4) parent-professional collaborative intervention. The LINK process and procedures help to put into practice the important relationships among assessment, intervention, child progress, and program evaluation. This system provides a mix of rigor and individualized options (Bagnato, Neisworth, & Munson, 1997).

Regardless of which curriculum-based assessment is chosen by a program or early interventionist, following the process and procedures outlined in the LINK system will provide a sound basis for assessment.

Examples of Curriculum-Based Assessments

A number of assessment instruments have been developed specifically for instructional planning with young children with disabilities. An overview of some of the most commonly used assessments is provided in Appendix 10–1 on page 237. This overview is not comprehensive and is simply a starting point for decision-making. Individual early interventionists and program supervisors must examine the curriculum-based instrument in relation to the needs of the children and families in their settings to determine the suitability of a particular curriculum-based assessment. The domains, age ranges, and a description of each of the assessments are included in this chart. In addition to the considerations provided earlier in this chapter, six criteria for evaluation of curriculum-based assessments are presented in the following sections.

Evaluation of Curriculum-Based Assessments

Deciding on a curriculum-based assessment for an early childhood program is a major decision. Bagnato, Neisworth, and Munson (1997) have suggested the following six standards and provided a rating scale for evaluating curriculum-based assessments: (1) authenticity, (2) collaboration, (3) convergence, (4) equity, (5) sensitivity, and (6) congruence. A summary of the characteristics of each of these standards follows.

Authenticity

Authentic assessments should sample direct examples of real-life skills in everyday situations. Authentic assessment refers to assessment based on student efforts in actual performance situations, rather than on the results of group tests such as achievement tests. Five factors are considered for judging the authenticity of an assessment. The assessment is considered authentic (1) if it is conducted in natural, everyday settings that are typical for a given child and family; (2) methods of collecting functional information are flexible, acceptable to the family, socially valid, and from multiple sources; (3) naturally occurring samples of real-life behavior using toys and activities that are a normal part of the family's daily life are emphasized; and (4) functional levels are readily translated into natural, activity-based goals that are useful for instruction and functional skills for the child's daily life. An authentic assessment should also require little inference about the skills being assessed. In other words, both the skill and the criterion level for achievement should be clearly stated. Putting on socks, going up steps, and using a telephone are examples of authentic activities that can be taught and used to assess cognitive, social, communication, motor, and other skills. Assessment and instructional materials should focus on functional, interesting, useful, authentic activities. An example of an authentic assessment is the collection of a child's work into a portfolio. Curriculum-based and authentic assessment models are closely and fundamentally compatible.

Portfolios. A portfolio is an ongoing account of what a child knows, compiled by the child herself and augmented by information from a teacher and others where appropriate. Portfolio assessments are compilations of children's permanent products over time that show both progress and the richness of their work (Graves & Sunstein, 1992; Hills, 1992). The performance activities of the portfolio should contain the skills a child will need to be successful when encountering future academic tasks. The authentic nature of portfolios is enhanced when (1) they allow children to demonstrate what they know relative to the objectives of a unit, (2) they give children ample opportunities to express the skills they know and the processes they use that relate the skills to concepts, (3) they have indicators that are reliable and valid, and (4) children themselves understand the purpose of the portfolio and the expectations that teachers have about what should be included (Scarpati & Silver, 1999).

Collaboration

Parent and professional partnerships are integral to family-centered early intervention. The parent-professional team must share purposes, aims, and methods in order to reach consensus about the needs of the child, the family, and the child's program. Collaborative decision making results in more accurate, complete assessments that are linked to intervention.

Convergence

A multidimensional perspective must be used when assessing young children. Convergence is the process of collecting and synthesizing data from multiple sources, measures, settings, domains, and occasions. The instrument should support a collaborative approach within the assessment process.

Equity

Assessment materials and practices must be adjusted to the unique needs of each child and family. These accommodations must be made when children have sensory, neuromotor, linguistic, affective, or behavioral disabilities. Adjustments may be made by (1) modifying the stimulus characteristics of toys and objects used to perform the assessment; (2) accepting a variety of functional responses; (3) being flexible when performing assessments and gathering information; (4) using responsive strategies to elicit child behaviors and examining the impact of those behaviors on learning; and (5) encouraging families to set priorities, ask questions, and suggest activities to obtain the best assessment information in areas of concern.

Sensitivity

The most effective curriculum-based assessment is sensitive in its ability to detect a child's current functional capabilities and to denote progress within the curriculum. A sensitive instrument contains sufficient, clearly written, prerequisite competencies in the functional hierarchy so that the assessor is able to identify the current status of the child and any change as a result of intervention, even for a child with the most severe disabilities and the least progress.

Congruence

Congruence refers to the suitability, developmental appropriateness, and field-tested validity of an assessment instrument. The selection of an instrument by a program or professional should be based on the extent to which the instrument is congruent with the expectations and the aims of early childhood intervention and the variability of typical and atypical early childhood development.

Advantages and Cautions

The use of a curriculum-based assessment is an integral part of the developmental assessment process. Curriculum-based assessment provides certain advantages for early childhood programs serving young children with disabilities and their families. However, certain cautions also need to be mentioned.

Advantages

Using a multidomain curriculum-based assessment has become very popular in programs for young children with disabilities. Although the use of only one tool in the assessment process is not advocated, the advantages of including a multidomain assessment include:

1. An agency can purchase one test and have subtests in all domains.
2. Single-domain tests can be purchased which enhance the information provided by the curriculum-based assessment. Individual therapists can provide further information through evaluations in their own domains such as speech and language.
3. Extensive training and experience are not needed for basic administrative purposes.
4. The tests items are sequenced or grouped by domain and age; they are easily translated into instructional objectives and activities are suggested.
5. The assessment can be administered repeatedly to the same child and thus provide formative assessment information.
6. Many curriculum-based assessments provide a developmental profile for each domain; thus it is possible to compare progress in one domain to that in another.
7. Some of the curriculum-based tests have items clustered as a screening test.
8. The tests often span several ages and thus can provide continuity and evaluation over a period of years.
9. Developmental scores expressed in months make possible the measurement of even small gains. (Fewell, 1991)

Cautions

When using a curriculum-based assessment, some cautions need to be considered. A curriculum-based assessment is only as good as the curriculum from which it is derived. Individuals using curriculum-based assessment should be careful to avoid the following possibilities:

1. Age equivalents were taken from developmental schedules, not from normative samples. Therefore, this renders them less reliable than those obtained through standardized or norm-referenced measures.
2. In some tests, age equivalents are not consistent within or across domains. The number of items needed to progress by 6 months in one section or part of a scale may not be comparable to that needed to indicate a similar gain in another section of the scale. Again, this may be a function of the lack of normative data in designing the scales.
3. Requirements in one domain on one age level may be far less demanding than at the same age in another domain.
4. Because only a few of these tests are standardized, it is difficult to compare scores on one test with those of another test.
5. Some of these tests offer several scoring options which may decrease the potential validity of the test results if interpreted carelessly. An example of this is the developmental quotient on the *Battelle Developmental Inventory* (Newborg, Stock, Wnek, Guidubaldi, & Svinicki, 1988). When testing a child with severe disabilities, a negative developmental quotient can be derived. Beware of "derived" scores on a non-normed test.
6. Because the tests are curriculum-referenced, the early interventionist may tend to teach to the test and thus severely limit the facilitation of many other appropriate, developmentally relevant skills which may not be specifically represented in the instrument utilized (Fewell, 1991).

Use of a multidimensional approach such as LINK will help to avoid the pitfalls described above. The process of beginning to use a curriculum-based assessment can be difficult for a team until each member is very familiar with all of the items on the test. Some helpful tips for initial use of a curriculum-based assessment are provided in the following section to facilitate the process.

Helpful Tips in Conducting the Assessment

Curriculum-based assessments should, for the most part, be carried out while the child is in the home or classroom. Assessments conducted in a familiar setting and over a period of time are much more valid than those allowing only a one-time session for the entire assessment battery. Using methods, such as a play-based assessment, will also provide a much more accurate picture of the child.

Curriculum-based assessment provides a match between the assessment items and the curriculum. The daily teaching activities should have assessment components within them and assessment should be viewed as an integral part of the intervention program. Ongoing, daily assessment provides program monitoring and is an essential part of the instructional program.

An example of how assessment and intervention are linked is found in the *Carolina Curriculum for Infants and Toddlers with Special Needs* (Johnson-Martin, et al., 1991). The "Curriculum Sequences" section expands the curriculum item in the Assessment Log. This section gives a description of the materials needed, procedures for encouraging the skill in the child's daily routines, adaptations for children with disabilities, and the criterion for mastery. These items can be condensed into a few words and then conveniently located where the intervention normally takes place, e.g., a list of snack-time activities placed by the table where snack time occurs or self-care activities placed by the door. Simple forms may be made for use at home and more complex ones for use at school. The Carolina Curriculum (Johnson-Martin, et al., 1991) also suggests having each item written on an individual activity sheet (see Figure 10–2) as an example of a form that can be helpful in assessing and monitoring child progress.

The Shopping List Approach

To ease the burden of completing the comprehensive lists of skills contained in most curriculum-based assessment's, Bagnato and Neisworth (1991) suggested preparing a "shopping list." The "shopper" or examiner prepares an initial list of skills in a particular area which provides a systematic sampling of behavior. A sample shopping list of communication skills is given in Table 10–1.

It should be noted that this is not a one-time look at the child. The assessor can start at any point, pick up any items, and then come back to get what may have been missed. The examiner would compare the results of this initial list with the curriculum-based assessment and prepare another list of behaviors to sample. This process would continue until the examiner is certain that a thorough and accurate assessment of skills had been completed.

This shopping list approach emphasizes the essential skills that need to be sampled, rather than the order or techniques for sampling. The examiner must be very knowledgeable in typical and atypical child development stages and patterns in order to choose the most appropriate skills to be assessed. Inventories or surveys of developmental skills can serve as appropriate models for the design of the shopping lists. The BRIGANCE *Diagnostic Inventory of Early Development-Revised* (Brigance, 1991), the *Early Intervention Developmental Profile* (Rogers, et al., 1981) and the *Developmental*

Programming for Infants and Young Children (Rogers & D'Eugenio, 1981) also provide listings of developmental skills in cognitive, language, gross motor, perceptual/fine motor, social-emotional and self-care domains which may be used to develop shopping lists.

Cue Card Approach

When conducting a curriculum-based assessment, early interventionists who are less familiar with a particular curriculum-based assessment often meticulously administer each item of the curriculum-based assessment in the sequence in which it is presented. To avoid this long and tedious experience, both for the examiner and the child, the examiner should familiarize herself with the instrument and its items prior to any assessment attempts. Then a "cue card" might be developed which will enable the examiner to keep track of the behaviors being assessed and the results. The cue card for using the *Learning Accomplishment Profile-Revised* (Glover, Preminger, Sanford & Zelman, 1995) might appear as shown in Figure 10–3. The listing of skills within each area will enable the examiner to note the child's success or failure with the items and make brief behavioral observations at the same time. The examiner must be familiar enough with the test items to judge success or failure at a variety of developmental levels without referring to the manual. For example, the examiner must know how long a child must balance on one foot in order to receive credit.

Figure 10–4 shows another example of the way a cue card or planning sheet might be organized for a 3-month-old infant using the *Early Learning Accomplishment Profile* (ELAP) (Glover, Preminger, & Sanford, 1995). This example provides much more detailed information than in the previous example. The ELAP example is organized around the position of the infant as opposed to the domain.

FIGURE 10–2

Sample Weekly Record for Child Learning Objectives of the IFSP

Name: _____ Week: _____

Location: _____

Situation for activities	Opportunity to observe					Mastered (date)
	M	T	W	Th	F	
Child on back (e.g., diapering, playing) Visually tracks in circle						
Turns head to search for sound						
Feet in air for play						
Child on back or sitting supported Glance from toy to toy when one in each hand						
Plays with toys placed in hand(s)						
Places both hands on toy at midline						
Looks or reaches for object that touches body out of sight						
Reacts to tactile stimulation with movement						
Repeats activities that get interesting results						
Social interactions, including meals Anticipates frequently occurring events in familiar games						
Responds differently to stranger and family members						
Laughs						
Repeats sounds when imitated						
Turns to name being called						
Repeats vocalizations that get reactions						
Smiles reciprocally						
Mealtime Munches food						
Vocalizes 5 or more consonant-vowel combinations						
Bathing and dressing Holds trunk steady when held at hips						

Source: From Johnson-Martin, N. M., Jens, K. G., Attermeier, S. M., and Hacker, B. J., © 1991. *The Carolina Curriculum for Infants and Toddlers with Special Needs* (p. 43). Baltimore: Paul H. Brookes Publishing Co. Reprinted with permission.

TABLE 10–1

Shopping List for Communication Skills

Developmental Area	Skills to Be Sampled
Pre-speech	
Orienting	Orients to sound
	Orients to voice
Responding	Responds selectively
	to voice
	Responds to name
Gesturing	Gives greetings
	Indicates needs
Vocalizing	Makes cooing, babbling-
	imitates sounds
Receptive language	
Identifying	Identifies body parts
	Identifies common objects
	Identifies colors
Following directions	Follows one-step direction
	Follows two-step direction
	Follows complex directions
Developmental areas	Skills samples
Expressive language	
Naming	Names people
	Names body parts
	Names common objects
Stating needs	States need to eat, drink
Describing action	Describes own actions
	Describes action of others
Speaking socially	Responds to questions
	Initiates discussion

Source: From *Assessment for Early Intervention: Best Practices for Professionals* (p. 77), by S. J. Bagnato and J. T. Neisworth, 1991, New York: Guilford. Copyright 1991 by Guilford Press. Reprinted with permission.

FIGURE 10–3

Common Items by Domain on the Learning Accomplishment Profile

Gross motor
- Balance
- Walk
- Jump
- Ball (catch, throw)
- Step (alternate, which foot)

Fine motor
- Tower
- Lid
- Book pages
- Pegboard
- Beads
  Pincer
  String
- Scissors
- Fold paper
- Puzzle

Pre-writing
- $-1 + 0$
- Draw body

Self-help
- Button
- Tie
- Zip
- Snap
- Buckle

Personal social
(parents report also)
- Imitates
- Turn taking
- Attentive to story
- Separates
- Make believe
- Age/name/address/family

Cognition
- Sort cubes
- Repeat digits
- Count
- Give objects
- Big/little
- Match (objects, pictures)
- Body parts
- Stack ring
- Missing object

Language
- Points-body parts
- 1-2-3 word phrases
- Plurals
- Pronouns
- Verbs
- Preps
- Telephone
- Names objects
- How/where/when/who
- If/then
- Retell story

Language samples
- Examiner should record examples of language obtained during assessment—both verbal and nonverbal

FIGURE 10–4
Early Learning Accomplishments Profile Cue Card

Supine activities
- Dangling toy   *Lean over and dangle toy over baby.*
    - Responses: Excitable (legs and arms react)
        Head position midline
        Legs kick in sequence/cycles
        Reaches for toy with both arms
        Move toy 180° arc from one side to other 4–6 inches.
    - Response: Child follows visually
- Rolling   *Prompt to roll to one side with toy.*
- Sounds   *Lean over baby 10 inches from face. Talk in quiet voice.*
    - Responses: Babbles/coos
        Localizes eyes of speaker
        Lean over baby. Play peek-a-boo.
    - Response: Child laughs
- Rattle   *Touch handle of rattle to child's fisted fingers.*
    - Response: Child holds it briefly.
        Place rattle in hands. Observe exploration.
    - Response: Brings to mouth, rubs, throws.
- Pull to sit   *Hold child's hands and pull to sit.*
    - Response: Head lags
        Hold sitting supported.
    - Response: Head forward

Standing activities
        Hold standing under arms across chest.
    - Responses: Extends legs, rises on toes
        Head unsteady, bobbing
        Sustains weight briefly, legs extend

Prone activities
        Place child across your arms on stomach. Lower child to floor.
    - Response: Head level/raised
        Observe in prone position.
    - Responses: Head lifts
        Hips lowered to floor at rest
        Raises chest 2 inches using arms
        Legs extend, one arm flexed

Sitting activities
- Sit baby on lap facing parent
    Approach baby from behind saying baby's name in low, quiet voice.
    - Response: Turns toward voice
        Show rattle to baby briefly. When baby looking at parent, shake rattle 8–10 inches opposite each ear out of range of vision.
    - Response: Head turns toward sound

These are some examples of ways to organize an assessment session. The examiner may also develop a cue card based on the practical use of the materials (i.e., list together all block items, pencil tasks, shape concepts, table vs. floor activities, or skill sequences). The idea is to conduct meaningful, smooth-flowing assessments. This enhances the child's performance and minimizes the distractions and transitions which will occur. Following the session with the child, the examiner may record the information on the appropriate assessment forms. If additional items need to be assessed, this can then take place at a later time(s).

Group Assessment

Because curriculum-based assessments do not have to follow rigid procedures, many of the skills assessed in such assessments may be conducted in group settings that are much more natural than a very structured one-to-one test situation. Often, curriculum-based assessments offer suggestions for group administration procedures. The BRIGANCE (1991) suggested ways to assess skills in group settings. For example, children may be observed in outdoor activities to see if they are able to perform many gross motor skills, such as running, hopping, or skipping.

Assessment Results

A curriculum-based assessment measures a child's performance in terms of curricular objectives. The purpose of curriculum-based assessment is to provide a direct link to the intervention goals and expected outcomes. Therefore, curriculum-based assessment is conducted to plan intervention programs for the child. The results are then communicated to the family and other professionals, both orally and in writing. Chapter 9 discussed presenting the results of the assessment to parents and caregivers. The remainder of this chapter focuses on the written report of assessment results.

The intervention program is derived from the written assessment. It also communicates with other team members, specifies the best estimation of a child's abilities at the time of the evaluation, and can be used to compare later performance. The report should be accurate, clear, objective, and detailed. The assessment report should include identifying information about the child and family, the assessment, background information, methods of assessment, results of the assessment, and recommendations (Wolery, 1996). The following sections of this chapter address the components of the written assessment report. An example of an assessment report is included in Appendix 10–2 on page 240.

Identifying Information. The first section of the report should include information about who was assessed, who conducted the assessment,

and when and where it occurred. This section should include demographic information about the child, such as age, sex, date of birth, and current placement, if any. The person who initiated the referral and the reason for the referral should be stated. The assessor's name and title, the setting in which the assessment activities took place, and the reference information for the tests that were used should be noted.

Background Information. This section should be a relatively brief summary presenting the historical information about the child. The background information should include the child's birth and medical history, developmental history, and educational experiences. The examiner should note the source of the information, whether it was from the parents or medical records. The developmental history should state the age at which the child achieved important developmental milestones and when the parents suspected that difficulties might exist. The educational history should be a record of the child's intervention contacts since birth and should include a listing and brief description of the services she has received (Wolery, 1996).

Methods. This section is a narrative and should include several subsections. All of the tests and scales used during the assessment should be listed, including when and by whom they were administered and the purpose of each. The report should state who conducted the observations, when they occurred, and what domains were observed, as well as a brief description of the setting, where the assessment took place, and who was present. Information should be included about the interviews with others. The assessor should state who was interviewed and the topic of the interview. Any environmental assessments should be described. This description should state which environments were assessed, what measures were used, when they occurred, who conducted them, and the purpose of the assessments (Wolery, 1996).

Assessment Results. Curriculum-based assessment activities assist with instructional program planning by identifying environmental factors and developmental skills which are relevant targets for instruction. Information directly relevant to the program planning should be noted. For example, the examiner should record the following information:

- Skills the child demonstrates independently;
- Skills the child performs with support, adaptation, or assistance;
- Instructional strategies that will be effective and efficient in teaching the infant or child; and
- Variables that may influence the way intervention is implemented.

The teacher or examiner should consider variables that may enhance or interfere with a child's performance. When a child does not successfully complete a task, the examiner should ask: Why didn't the child succeed? What factor(s) may have interfered with the child's performance? Factors which should be considered are:

- The place in which assessment occurred;
- The materials or tasks used;
- The level of task comprehension required;
- The mode of response expected;
- The rate of response needed;
- The mode of response needed;
- The quality of response given; and
- The efficiency of the child's skill acquisition.

The item or task is then modified to help determine the conditions under which the child performs best. This information is then used to provide a more meaningful, relevant instructional program for the child.

When compiling and reporting assessment information, it is important to include the following information in the assessment report:

- Observations of the child's behavior in interacting with the examiner and others;
- Strategies used which enhanced the child's attention and on-task performance;
- Patterns of strengths and weaknesses;
- Developmental age (DA) equivalents for each measured domain (i.e., cognitive, language, personal-social);
- A narrative of the specific skills demonstrated within the developmental domains; and
- Specific findings that address a description of the areas of weaknesses noted, which become the instructional targets when planning the child's intervention program.

Including this information in the report of results provides information that is relevant and practical and, therefore, has direct relevance to the design of a sound, effective intervention plan. It is helpful to organize this section by curricular area. This must be an accurate, objective description of the child's performance.

Recommendations. This section should be a summary of the primary abilities of the child and the areas of need. Suggestions should be included about (1) the need for additional assessment activities, (2) potential long-term goals, and (3) potential intervention strategies along with a list of any variables that would influence how the intervention should be implemented (Wolery, 1996).

The examiner should remember when writing the report that it must communicate with multiple audiences, the other team members, the child's parents, and future caregivers. Therefore, the report must be clear, objective, and free of jargon, yet sensitive. This means that conclusions should be described, qualified, and supported by the information gathered during the assessment. Any assumptions or inferences should be noted as such (Wolery, 1996).

Summary

The use of curriculum-based assessment is fundamental to the creation of a new vision for developmental assessment, an assessment process that is child- and family-centered and yields substantive information that is directly relevant to intervention (Bricker, 1996). This new vision emphasizes that children must be observed in their usual environments where they negotiate daily demands, problem-solve, and communicate with those around them. Family members must be included in the process in a variety of ways. The processes and strategies presented in this chapter will yield relevant and practical information about children and families. The result of this information will be the development of sound, appropriate, and effective intervention plans.

References

Bagnato, S. J., & Neisworth, J. T. (1991). *Assessment for early intervention: Best practices for professionals*. New York: Guilford Press.

Bagnato, S. J., Neisworth, J. T., & Munson, S. M. (1997). *LINKing assessment and early intervention: An authentic curriculum-based approach*. Baltimore: Brookes.

Bayley, N. (1969). *Bayley Scales of Infant Development*. San Antonio: The Psychological Corp.

Benner, S. M. (1992). *Assessing young children with special needs: An ecological approach*. New York: Longman.

Brazelton, T. B. (1973). *Neonatal Behavioral Assessment Scale*. London: Spastics International Medical Publications.

Bricker, D. (Ed.). (1993). *Assessment, Evaluation, and Programming System (AEPS) for infants and children* (Vol. 1). *AEPS measurement for birth to three years*. Baltimore: Brookes.

Bricker, D. (1996). Assessment for IFSP development and intervention planning. In S. J. Meisels & E. Fenichel (Eds.), *New visions for the developmental assessment of infants and young children* (pp. 169–192). Washington, DC: Zero to Three/National Center for Infants, Toddlers, and Families.

Bricker, D., & Cripe, J. J. W. (1992). *An activity-based approach to early intervention*. Baltimore: Brookes.

Bricker, D., Gentry, D., & Bailey, E. (1992). Assessment, Evaluation, and Programming System Test. In D. Bricker (Ed.). *Assessment, Evaluation, and Programming System (AEPS) for infants and children* (Vol. 1): *AEPS measurement for birth to three years*. Baltimore: Brookes.

Bricker, D., & Pretti-Frontczak, K. (Eds.). (1996). *Assessment, Evaluation, and Programming System (AEPS) for infants and children* (Vol. 3): *AEPS measurement for three to six years*. Baltimore: Brookes.

Bricker, D., & Waddell, M. (Eds.). (1996). *Assessment, Evaluation, and Programming Sytem (AEPS) for infants and children* (Vol. 4): *AEPS curriculum for three to six years*. Baltimore: Brookes.

Brigance, A. H. (1985). BRIGANCE *prescriptive readiness: Strategies and practice*. North Billerica, MA: Curriculum Associates.

Brigance, A. H. (1991). BRIGANCE *Diagnostic Inventory of Early Development (Revised)*. North Billerica, MA: Curriculum Associates.

Bromwich, A. J. (1981). *Working with parents and infants: An interactional approach*. Baltimore: University Park Press.

Brown, S. L., D'Eugenio, D. B., Drews, J. E., Haskin, B. S., Lynch, E. W., Moersch, M. S., & Rogers, S. J. (1981). *Preschool Developmental Profile*. Ann Arbor: University of Michigan Press.

Cripe, J., Slentz, K., & Bricker, D. (1993). AEPS *curriculum for birth to three years* (Vol. 2). Baltimore: Brookes.

Dunst, C. J. (1980). A *clinical and educational manual for use with the Uzgiris and Hunt scales of infant psychological development*. Austin, TX: PRO-ED.

Dunst, C. (1981). *Infant learning: A cognitive-linguistic intervention strategy*. Austin, TX: PRO-ED.

Dunst, C., & McWilliam, R. A. (1988). Cognitive assessment of multiply handicapped young children. In T. D. Wachs & R. Sheehan (Eds.), *Assessment of developmentally disabled children* (pp. 213–238). New York: Plenum.

Fewell, R. R. (1986). *Play Assessment Scale (PAS) Research Edition*. New Orleans, LA: Tulane University.

Fewell, R. R. (1991). Trends in the assessment of infants and toddlers with disabilities. *Exceptional Children, 58*(2), 166–173.

Gesell, A. (1923). *The preschool child: From the standpoint of public hygiene and education*. Boston: Houghton Mifflin.

Glover, E. M., Preminger, J., & Sanford, A. R. (1995). *Early Learning Accomplishment Profile (ELAP)*. Chapel Hill, NC: Chapel Hill Training-Outreach Project.

Glover, E. M., Preminger, J., Sanford, A. R., & Zelman, J. G. (1995). *Learning Accomplishment Profile-Revised*. Chapel Hill, NC: Chapel Hill Training-Outreach Project.

Graves, D., & Sunstein, B. S. (1992). *Portfolio portraits*. Portsmouth, NH: Heinmann.

Hills, T. W. (1992). Reaching potentials through appropriate assessment. In S. Bredekamp & T. Rosegrant (Eds.), *Reaching potentials: Appropriate curriculum and assessment for young children* (Vol. 1) (pp. 43–63). Washington, DC: National Association for the Education of Young Children.

Johnson-Martin, N. M., Attermeier, S. M., & Hacker, B. J. (1990). *The Carolina Curriculum for Preschoolers with Special Needs* (2nd ed.). Baltimore: Brookes.

Johnson-Martin, N. M., Jens, K. G., Attermeier, S. M., & Hacker, B. J. (1991). *The Carolina Curriculum for Infants and Toddlers with Special Needs* (2nd ed.). Baltimore: Brookes.

Knobloch, H., Stevens, F., & Malone, A. F. (1980). *Gesell Developmental Schedules: Manual of developmental diagnosis* (Rev. ed.). New York: Harper & Row.

Linder, T. W. (1993a). *Transdisciplinary Play-Based Assessment: A functional approach to working with young children.* (Rev. ed.). Baltimore: Brookes.

Linder, T. W. (1993b). *Transdisciplinary Play-Based Intervention: Guidelines for developing a meaningful curriculum for young children.* Baltimore: Brookes.

McAllister, J. R. (1991). Curriculum-based behavioral intervention for preschool children with handicaps. *Topics in Early Childhood Special Education,* 11(2), 48–58.

Nehring, A. D., Nehring, E. F., Bruni, J. R., & Randolph, P. L. (1992). *Learning Accomplishment Profile-Diagnostic Standardized Assessment (LAP-D).* Lewisville, NC: Kaplan School Supply & Chapel Hill Training-Outreach Project.

Neisworth, J. T., & Bagnato, S. J. (1988). Assessment in early childhood special education: A typology of dependent measures. In S. L. Odom and M. B. Karnes (Eds.), *Early intervention for infants and children with handicaps: An empirical approach* (pp. 23–49). Baltimore: Brookes.

Newborg, J., Stock, J., Wnek, L., Guildubaldi, J., & Svinicki, J. S. (1988). *Battelle Developmental Inventory (BDI).* Chicago: Riverside.

Parks, S., Furono, S., O'Reilly, K., Inatsuka, T., Hoska, C. M., & Zeisloft-Falbey, B. (1994). *Hawaii Early Learning Profile (HELP): HELP (Birth to 3).* Palo Alto, CA: VORT Corp.

Parten, M. B. (1932). Social participation among preschool children. *Journal of Abnormal and Social Psychology,* 27, 243–269.

Piaget, J. (1952). *The origins of intelligence in children.* New York: International Universities Press.

Piaget, J. (1987). *Possibility and necessity: The role of necessity in cognitive development.* Minneapolis: University of Minnesota Press.

Rogers, S. J. (1982). Techniques of infant assessment. In G. Ulrey & S. J. Rogers (Eds.), *Psychological assessment of handicapped infants and young children* (pp. 45–53). New York: Thieme-Stratton.

Rogers, S. J., & D'Eugenio, D. B. (1981). *Developmental Programming for Infants and Young Children (DPIYC) (Vol. 2): Early Intervention Developmental Profile (EIDP).* Ann Arbor: University of Michigan Press.

Rogers, S. J., Donovan, C. M., D'Eugenio, D. B., Brown, S. L., Lynch, E. W., Moersch, M. S., & Schafer, D. S. (1981). *Early Intervention Developmental Profile.* Ann Arbor: University of Michigan Press.

Scarpati, S., & Silver, P. G. (1999). Readiness for academic achievement in preschool children. In E. Vazquez Nuttall, I. Romero, & J. Kalesnik (Eds.), *Assessing and screening preschoolers: Psychological and educational dimensions* (pp. 262–280). Needham Heights, MA: Allyn & Bacon.

Uzgiris, I., & Hunt, J. (1975). *Assessment in infancy: Ordinal scales of psychological development.* Urbana: University of Illinois Press.

VORT Corporation. (1995). HELP *for preschoolers.* Palo Alto, CA: Author.

White, O. R. (1980). Adaptive performance objectives: Form versus function. In W. Sailor, G. Wilcox, & L. Brown (Eds.), *Methods of instruction for severely handicapped students* (pp. 47–69). Baltimore: Brookes.

Wolery, M. (1991). Instruction in early childhood special education: "Seeing through a glass darkly . . . knowing in part." *Exceptional Children,* 58(2), 127–134.

Wolery, M. (1996). Using assessment information to plan intervention programs. In M. McLean, D. B. Bailey, & M. Wolery (Eds.), *Assessing infants and preschoolers with special needs* (2nd ed., pp. 491–518). Upper Saddle River, NJ: Merrill/Prentice Hall.

Wolery, M., & Bailey, D. B. (1989). Assessing play skills. In D. B. Bailey and M. Wolery (Eds.), *Assessing infants and preschoolers with handicaps* (pp. 428–446). Upper Saddle River, NJ: Merrill/Prentice Hall.

Test/Source	Age Range	Domains Assessed	Descriptions
Assessment, Evaluation, and Programming System (AEPS) for Infants and Children (Bricker, Vol. 1, 1993; Cripe, Slentz, & Bricker, Vol. 2, 1993) Brookes	Birth to 3 yrs	Fine motor, gross motor, adaptive, cognitive, social-communication, social	Have strong family involvement; easy transition to curriculum goals and objectives from assessment items; has periodic assessments of child's progress, sensitive tracking; activity-based, developmentally appropriate instruction
Assessment, Evaluation, and Programming System (AEPS) for Infants and Children (Bricker & Pretti-Frontczak, Vol. 3, 1996; Bricker & Waddell, Vol. 4, 1996) Brookes	3 to 6 yrs	Fine motor, gross motor, adaptive, cognitive, social-communication, social	
Battelle Developmental Inventory (BDI) (Newborg, Stock, Wnek, Guildubaldi, & Svinicki, 1988) Riverside Publishing Co.	Birth to 95 mos	Personal-social adaptive, motor, communication, cognitive	Is a curriculum-referenced test; merges norm-based and curriculum-based assessment; has adaptive features; requires family input
BRIGANCE Diagnostic Inventory of Early Development (Revised Ed.) (BDIED-R) (Brigance, 1991) Curriculum Associates	Birth to 7 yrs	Preambulatory motor, gross motor, fine motor, self-help, speech and language, general knowledge and comprehension, social-emotional development, readiness, basic reading skills, manuscript writing, basic math	Is frequently used owing to ease of use; blends assessment with selection of objectives and evaluation of progress; appropriate only for children who are at-risk or have mild disabilities; lacks field validation with children with special needs
Carolina Curriculum for Infants and Toddlers with Special Needs (2nd Ed.) (CCITSN) (Johnson-Martin, Jens, Attermeier, & Hacker, 1991) Brookes	Birth to 2 yrs	Cognition, communication, social/adaptation, fine motor, gross motor	Has specific adaptations to accommodate sensory and motor needs; items are ordered by logical teaching sequence; family involvement; easy to implement with good data collection system; functional activities with good details and suggestions

Test/Source	Age Range	Domains Assessed	Descriptions
Carolina Curriculum for Preschoolers with Special Needs (CCPSN) (Johnson-Martin, Attermeier, & Hacker, 1990) Brookes	2 to 5 yrs	Cognition, communication, social adaptation, fine motor, gross motor	Is easy to implement with good data collection system; notes characteristics of specific disabilities and the effects of these disabilities in the classroom; functional activities; family involvement; provides task analyses and alternative activities
Developmental Programming for Infants and Young Children (Revised Ed.) (DPIYC) (Rogers & D'Eugenio, 1981) Univ. of Michigan	Birth to 36 mos	Perceptual/fine motor, cognition, language, social-emotional, adaptive, gross motor	Note adaptations; focuses on parents for intervention program; provides short-term goals and suggested activities; designed especially for interdisciplinary teams
Developmental Programming for Infants and Young Children (Brown, et al., 1981) Univ. of Michigan	3 to 6 yrs	Perceptual/fine motor, cognition, language, social-emotional, adaptive, gross motor	
Hawaii Early Learning Profile (HELP) (Parks, et al., 1994) VORT	Birth to 3 yrs	Gross motor, fine motor, cognition, expressive language, social-emotional development, adaptive	Has clearly written plans and a variety of activities; provides suggestions for intervention with particular special needs; has family guides for additional parent information and record keeping; computer software for planning and reporting
Hawaii Early Learning Profile (HELP) (VORT, 1995)	3 to 6 yrs	Gross motor, fine motor, cognition, expressive language, social-emotional development, adaptive	

Instrument	Age Range	Domains	Features/Comments
Infant-Toddler Developmental Assessment (IDA) (Provence, Erikson, Vater, & Palmeri, 1995) Riverside	Birth to 42 mos	Motor, language, cognitive-adaptive, feelings, social adaptation, personality	Facilitates integrated approach to assessment and decision making; provides link between assessment and intervention; ensures parent participation
Early Learning Accomplishment Profile (ELAP) (Glover, Preminger, & Sanford, 1995) Chapel Hill Training-Outreach Project	Birth to 3 yrs	Fine and gross motor, language, self-help, social-emotional, cognitive	Easy to use but have fewer number of items; some items lack teachability; do not provide adaptations for special needs; encourage multidisciplinary use; include supplemental materials and audiovisual aids
Learning Accomplishment Profile-Revised (LAP-R) (Glover, Preminger, Sanford, & Zelman, 1995) Chapel Hill Training-Outreach Project	3 to 6 yrs	Fine and gross motor, language, prewriting, self-help, personal-social, cognitive	
Learning Accomplishment Profile-Diagnostic Standardized Assessment (LAP-D) (Revised 1992) (Nehring, Nehring, Bruni, & Randolph, 1992) Chapel Hill Training-Outreach Project & Kaplan School Supply	30 to 72 mos	Fine motor, gross motor, language, cognition	Was normed externally for LAP developmental sequence; facilitates linking assessment and curriculum; contains traditional, contrived tasks, not natural, activity-based assessment; appropriate only for children who are at-risk or who have mild disabilities
Transdisciplinary Play-Based Assessment (TPBA) (Linder, 1993) Brookes	Infancy to 6 yrs	Cognitive, social-emotional, communication and language, sensorimotor	Provides good foundation for program planning; highly individualized; natural and functional; encourages transdisciplinary assessment

APPENDIX 10–2
Example of a Curriculum-Based Assessment Report

Identifying Information:

Child tested: Jared	Examiner: Early childhood special educator
Sex: Male	Placement: Early Steps Head Start
Birthdate: 9/12/1996	Assessment location: Preschool and home
Date of test: 12/20/2000	Assessment used: *The Carolina Curriculum for*
Age at testing: 4 yrs, 3 mos	*Preschoolers with Special Needs* (Johnson-Martin, Attermeier, & Hacker, 1990).

A mental health referral has currently been completed by Jared's education staff on his mother's request. Earlier in the school year concerns were brought to the parents. Jared had been displaying many difficult behaviors in class, such as aggressiveness towards peers and staff, biting, a very low frustration level, and inappropriate vocalizations. Jared also had been noted as having a very short attention span and difficulty following directions. After the referral, Jared was moved from the afternoon class to the morning collaboration program where a five-member staff team is present daily. Staff had hoped that with more adults available to work with Jared, there would be more improvements with his coping skills and aggressive behaviors. At the present time, small improvements have been seen but nothing consistent.

Background Information

Jared, a 4-year, 3-month-old African-American boy, was assessed by the early childhood special educator in the Head Start collaboration classroom and in his grandmother's home. Jared attends a half-day Head Start collaboration program in the mornings and afternoons are spent at his grandmother's home. Jared has a younger sister who is 2 years old and spends the entire day at the grandmother's home.

Since Jared's mother was at work, his grandmother was interviewed by the assessor. Jared's grandmother reported that his birth was normal and there have been no medical problems to date. She reported that the family had not had any concerns related to Jared's developmental milestones. However, both Jared's mother and his grandmother have described him as being uncontrollable and easily influenced by the behaviors of others. She reported that Jared's mother is very frustrated and feels overwhelmed. Jared's mother recently told staff that she did not know what to do with him anymore.

The Head Start classroom staff from the afternoon class reported that Jared likes classroom activities but usually needs a staff member close by to help him stay on task. He also has a hard time controlling his frustration levels when an activity does not go exactly as he chooses. Jared is very affectionate with his teacher and often seeks her attention during circle or small-group times. If he is unable to obtain immediate attention, he will display a behavior such as hitting a peer or running out of the room, which demands the attention he wants.

There have been reports from Jared's teachers that his mother is in an abusive relationship. This has led to a referral and the recommendation for family counseling. Counseling has not begun as of this date. Jared has not been referred for any special services to date. The purpose of this assessment is to determine if he may need special services.

Methods

The examiner observed Jared in his classroom approximately 1 hour before pulling him for direct testing. Approximately 15 other children were present in the classroom and a variety of play activities

APPENDIX 10–2

were available. Within that hour of observation, the examiner was able to observe Jared's behavior and abilities in the classroom, which staff had said was a typical day for him. In the classroom, Jared was very outgoing, sought attention from favorite adults in the room, did not stay at one activity for more than a few minutes without support, and interacted with peers during playtime. Jared needed instructions repeated more than once for him and often had a tantrum or became aggressive if activities were not to his liking.

The *Carolina Curriculum for Preschoolers with Special Needs* (CCPSN) (Johnson-Martin, Attermeier, & Hacker, 1990) was used for the observation and direct testing in the classroom. Jared also was observed in the afternoon at his grandmother's house. His younger sister was present in the same room, but they did not play with the same toys. Items from the CCPSN were also the basis for observing him in the grandmother's home later in the afternoon and for discussing his developmental skills with his grandmother

Assessment Results

The following are the numerical results from Jared's assessment:

Cognition	3 to 3.5 years
Communication	3.5 to 4 years
Social Adaptation-Social	3 to 3.5 years
Self-Help	3.5 to 4 years
Fine Motor	3.5 to 4 years
Gross Motor	4 to 4.5 years

Jared was displaying the greatest delays in the Cognition and Social Adaptation-Social domains. He was showing approximately a 1-year to 1-year, 3-months delay. He was also below age level in Communication, Self-Help, and Fine Motor. He demonstrated approximately a 4- to 9-month delay in these areas. Jared was age-appropriate in the Gross Motor section. Jared's overall performance on the CCPSN was below his chronological age of 4 years, 3 months.

The Cognition domain on the CCPSN includes the following curriculum sequences: attention and memory, concepts, symbolic play, reasoning, and visual perception. Jared showed deficits in the areas of concepts and visual perception. He was just beginning to demonstrate emerging skills in the 3- to 3.5-year age level. Some examples of activities in which he has emerging skills are understanding "under," "over," and "next to," understanding "fast" and "slow," copying a horizontal bridge using blocks, and matching geometric forms. Jared's strength in the cognitive domain was symbolic play, where he was displaying skills at the 4-year-old level. Cognitive skills fluctuated but overall performance was at the 3- to 3.5-year age level.

The Communication domain contained the following sequences: expressive vocabulary, interest in sounds and language functions, receptive skills, conversation skills, and sentence construction. Jared was showing delays in expressive vocabulary and conversation skills. Both of these sequences had emerging skills in the 3.5- to 4-year age level, with the majority of skills lying in the 3- to 3.5-year age level. Jared is just beginning to work on defining two or more simple words and increasing conversation skills by correctly responding to "what do you do" and "why do we" questions. For the most part, Jared showed skills at the 3.5- to 4-year-old level.

The Social Adaptation domain combines social and self-help skills. Jared demonstrated below-average skills in the social section while showing almost age-appropriate skills in the self-help section. Jared was delayed considerably in the responsibility and interpersonal skills sequences. Skills were only emerging in his knowledge of appropriate use of toys (a 3-year age level skill), and he did not

APPENDIX 10–2

continued

have the skill of expressing regret when another child was hurt or experiencing unpleasantness (a 3-year level skill). Overall performance in the social domain was 3 to 3.5 years, and the overall performance in the self-help domain was at the 3.5- to 4-year age level with some skills emerging in the 4- to 4.5-year age level.

The Fine Motor domain consisted of the following curriculum sequences: hand use, manipulation, bilateral skills, tool use, and visual-motor skills. Jared's strength was tool use (using a wooden hammer with pegs, transferring material with different utensils), where he was age-appropriate when tested. However, Jared was showing obvious weakness in the visual-motor sequence (pencil control and copying). He was at a 3- to 3.5-year age level, with emerging skills into the 3.5- to 4-year age level. The Gross Motor domain was age-appropriate, with some skills above average into the 4.5- to 5-year age level (locomotion and outdoor equipment).

Through observation and formal testing, the examiner saw that Jared had problems attending and was very self-directed. When testing on a one-to-one basis, Jared was much better at attending and following through on a task he was given. He was very eager to please the examiner and was able to be redirected back to a task if he began to disengage.

Jared had difficulties understanding general concepts, such as colors, shapes, numbers, and prepositions (in, on, under, next to). Lack of these general concepts may be contributing to Jared's lack of motivation in the classroom and his frustration level. Jared also seemed to do better whenever a visual prompt was used in testing. Although Jared was very outgoing and talkative, he had problems defining simple words; for example, when asked "what is a pencil?" Jared seemed confused and could not answer the question even with verbal and visual prompts. He immediately tried to get the examiner to stop questioning by asking his own question, "Do you want to meet my sister?" Jared also used some great conversation skills during testing. He used greetings, asked questions, requested assistance from the examiner, used turn-taking, and was able to sustain conversation. He did have difficulties describing items by color, shape, texture, or spatial relationship. This is obvious from his lack of these concepts in the cognitive section. Because Jared could not describe an item by its attributes, he could not move further in the conversation skills sequence. Therefore, this gave him a score of only 3 to 3.5 years, with some emerging skills in the 3.5- to 4-year age level. Jared did use good sentence structure throughout testing and did not seem to have any problems with his hearing.

The examiner was able to build rapport with Jared very quickly, and he immediately tried to seek her attention. He used consistent eye contact and cooperated enthusiastically throughout the formal assessment. Unlike in the classroom, Jared did not show any behaviors, such as aggressiveness or a low frustration level. Jared appeared to use age-appropriate self-help skills within the classroom setting. Jared seemed to favor his right hand when using a utensil or writing tool. He seemed to have no problems crossing midline and used a proper grasp when using a writing instrument. Jared appeared to have difficulty with his eye-hand coordination. He needed a lot of verbal and physical prompts to be redirected back to the task. It was not obvious to the examiner if this was from lack of interest or lack of ability. Jared appeared age-appropriate in all gross motor activities, such as climbing stairs, sitting position, jumping, and maintaining balance.

Recommendations

In the time spent with Jared, it was obvious to the examiner that he performed much better on a one-to-one basis. He seemed less distracted in a room in which no visual or auditory stimulation was present and was able to sit for a very long time while formal testing was going on. It would appear that Jared may do better in a smaller classroom with fewer children and where more staff are available to

APPENDIX 10–2

give individualized attention. A structured setting with a consistent routine would help Jared know what was expected of him and help him be successful.

Two major areas for learning targets are cognition and social skills. Both of these domains are affecting Jared's performance in other areas, such as language and behavior. Jared's lack of knowledge is contributing to his below-average scores in expressive and receptive language and conversation skills. Not knowing general concepts in a preschool class will lead to a child being frustrated and contribute to poor attending skills and lack of task follow-through. Not knowing appropriate social skills would also contribute to his responses to peers and adults, aggressiveness and inappropriate language.

Jared's overall poor performance in cognition indicates he is having the most difficulty with general concepts and concepts involving size and number. Program planning should begin with these concepts. The classroom staff would like to see Jared at least at a 3.5- to 4-year age level, with the other teaching sequences in the cognitive domain ideally at age level, 4 to 4.5 years. These learning targets are very important, because knowing general concepts of color, size, number, and shape will help Jared be able to participate more in classroom activities and help his tolerance and attending levels both in and outside the classroom and as he moves into kindergarten.

Some learning targets in the social domain would be responsibility, self-concept, and interpersonal skills. All of these were considerably low for his age level. These would all be important targets because of the behaviors Jared has been displaying in and outside of class. Because these targets are also a great concern for Jared's mother, intervention should begin at once in these areas. Inappropriate social skills and lack of self-concept would contribute to Jared's aggressiveness and noncompliance with adults and peers. Targeting this area will also help Jared to be able to interact with peers during small-group activities and playtime. It is important for Jared to feel valued by caregivers, teachers, and peers in order for him to value himself. Good feelings about himself give him enthusiasm for trying and the ability to cope with failure. These skills are also very important as Jared moves into kindergarten.

It is also recommended that further assessment information be obtained on Jared's social-emotional abilities. Without further testing, it is not possible to determine the extent of delay Jared is displaying in his social-emotional skills. If Jared does have social-emotional concerns, these could affect his demeanor and his lack of motivation in learning new concepts and maintaining old skills. This is especially important because of the referral for family counseling and based on the behaviors Jared is displaying in the classroom. Even though the CCPSN is showing deficits in Jared's social skills, more information should be obtained to substantiate if Jared has social-emotional problems or deficits and to provide more information about the skills he needs to develop.

11

Ecological Assessment

Careful assessment of a child in isolation might produce very accurate and informative details about a child's current functioning under specific conditions in a particular setting. However, it will not tell the examiner whether the child can perform similar tasks in different settings or why a child is unable to perform certain tasks in various settings. It is important to assess children across a variety of settings in which they are expected to function. Analysis of how settings influence behavior must also be addressed to assess the performance of a child in a variety of settings.

Ecological and behavioral assessments recognize the significant influence of the environment on behavior and development. Both the ecological and behavioral approaches provide an analysis of how the environment is influencing the child's behavior. The value of these approaches is that they provide a means whereby the contextual and functional influences of the environment can be assessed (Simeonsson, 1986). The major objective of ecological and behavioral assessment is to define the environmental influences on behavior. This recognition of the influence of the environment on behavior is a commonality between the ecological and the behavioral approaches. However, there are basic differences in their viewpoints.

This chapter will present the ecological approach and Chapter 12 will present the behavioral approach. Both of these approaches are important to the assessment process but have differences in their views of the interaction between the environment and the child. This chapter begins by discussing the major differences between these two approaches. The theoretical basis of ecological assessment is then presented as well as the methods used in conducting an ecological assessment. Examples of published environmental assessment measures for conducting this type of assessment will also be presented. In the final section of the chapter, a framework for incorporating ecological factors into the entire assessment process is presented.

An Ecological Versus Behavioral Viewpoint

Both ecological and behavioral psychologists recognize the important influence environment has on behavior. However, a major difference between the ecological and behavioral approaches resides in the manner in which the environmental influence is defined and assessed. The ecological approach views the child's behavior as an interdependent part of the total setting (Barker, 1965). The relationship between the child and the environment is interactive. The behavioral position expressed by Bijou and Baer (1961) views behavior as a function of eliciting or reinforcing stimuli. The behavioral approach is defined by specific environmental stimuli that elicit or reinforce behavior. A behavioral viewpoint focuses on how the environment influences or controls the child's behavior. The major difference between the two approaches is an interactive role versus a functional role.

Although there are major differences between ecological and behavioral approaches to assessment, they do have certain commonalities. Common features relevant to assessment include: (1) both strategies rely on systematic observation of the child; (2) both approaches can be used to assess children of any age; and (3) each approach tries to define the role of the environment relative to a specific child (Simeonsson, 1986). Both approaches are relevant to the assessment process, and both may be used on a daily basis in the "real world" when assessing young children with disabilities.

What Is Ecological Assessment?

Ecological psychology views a child's behavior as an interdependent part of the total setting (Barker, 1965). The relationship between the child and the environment is interactive. Ecological assessment characterizes the social and physical qualities of the child's natural environment at home and in child care or preschool settings. Observations are made in as nonintrusive a manner as possible, patterns and sequences of behavior are analyzed, and a systematic method for examining the direct influence of the environment on behavior is provided by the ecological assessment. In addition to examining the current environments of the child, this type of assessment has also been applied to the preparation of children for other environments through the use of ecological inventories (Noonan & McCormick, 1993), which assess the skills required in other current and future environments as a basis for program planning.

Importance of an Ecological Framework

The ecological approach provides a means whereby the contextual and functional influences of the environment can be assessed. Consideration of the influences of environmental and situational factors on an individual or a group (i.e., family, group of children) is an essential component of any effective assessment (Thurman & Widerstrom, 1985). The screening, diagnostic, and assessment stages presented in previous chapters can provide important information about the child's functioning under specific conditions in a specific setting with specific individuals. However, assessment results from one situation cannot be assumed to be generalizable across a variety of situations. The success with which assessment information can be used

to prescribe intervention is very dependent on the degree to which environmental factors are taken into account. This means that the assessment data must accurately describe as many aspects of the child's functioning as possible in the home, school, and community. The information provided by these assessment data will enable the assessors to have the information necessary to plan an intervention program that will affect as much of the child's life as possible.

Simeonsson (1986) stated that the value of the ecological approach is that it provides a way to assess the influences of the environment on the performance of the child. The information obtained from an ecological assessment perspective enhances and expands that which is obtained from other assessment strategies. Information is obtained about the context within which a child's behavior is exhibited. The ecological approach is an important addition to a good assessment program. This approach can help the team to better understand the range of responses that a child and family may exhibit under a variety of conditions. This approach should be integral to the daily, ongoing assessment process. All environmental factors which contribute to the child's status should be considered. Using this approach will enable the examiner to be fair to children from diverse cultures and provide data that are useful for planning a meaningful and realistic intervention program, which is individualized for each child and ongoing so that teaching strategies can be adjusted daily if necessary to provide effective intervention.

Theoretical Basis of Ecological Assessment

The ecological approach views the child as interacting with the environment. According to Bronfenbrenner (1976, 1986), experimentation using an ecological structure must reflect the natural environment, including the microsystems, mesosystems, exosystems, and macrosystems affecting subjects involved in the experiment. Bronfenbrenner (1977) noted the nested arrangement of structures that constitute an ecological system. He stated that the smallest element in this context is the *microsystem*, which is the complex relationship between the developing person and the environment in an immediate setting containing that person. A setting is defined as a place with particular physical features in which participants engage in particular roles for a particular period of time. The elements of the setting are the factors of place, time, physical features, activity, participant, and role (Bronfenbrenner, 1977). A child's home environment and the preschool he attends are two examples of microsystems.

Above the microsystem level is the *mesosystem*, which comprises the interrelationships among the major settings containing a person at any given point in time. The mesosystems incorporate all of the major settings of a particular learner and the interrelationships or interactions of the settings. Thus, a child's mesosystem may include his home, preschool, church, doctor's office, park, and relationships across each of them. For example, events in the home influence behavior in the preschool, which in turn influences behavior in the home.

The concepts of the exosystem and macrosystem are also included. The *exosystem* includes social structures (such as the public school system and health care system). When the exosystem is incorporated into the ecological assessment, features of the community and surrounding environment must be taken into account. The final level of expansion is the *macrosystem*, which addresses global institutions and ideologies. The macrosystems are defined as the overarching institutional patterns of the culture or subculture that generally carry information and endow the meaning and motivation to institutions and activities (e.g., regional or ethnic customs and values) (Vazquez Nuttall,

Nuttall-Vazquez, & Hampel, 1999). The importance of macrosystem influences is demonstrated through the observable differences in child development seen in cross-cultural studies. For example, 2-year-olds in China are able to sit quietly for extended periods of time, whereas in America we would never expect this behavior of a 2-year-old (Benner, 1992).

Figure 11–1 presents a version of the Bronfenbrenner model adapted to the preschool child and his family. The innermost circle of the model addresses the individual child and the domains of behavior that are important to include in assessment: cognitive, social-emotional, language, gross and fine motor skills, academic readiness, and adaptability. Most of the assessment done at this level focuses on the child.

The second circle of the model is the immediate family and focuses on those people who are in direct charge of the child, including parents, step-parents, foster parents, relatives, or other primary caregivers.

The extended family and friends of both parents are included in the third circle. The literature on family support systems (Lynch & Hanson, 1992) emphasizes the importance of relatives, especially with families of culturally and linguistically diverse backgrounds, in helping deal with the stresses and demands of caring for a child with special needs. Other individuals who should be included for consideration are friends, neighbors, and coworkers because they often play an important role in helping parents cope with a child with disabilities.

The next level of focus is the agencies, which are extremely important because of the need children with disabilities and their families have for services. Services must be available for infants and toddlers with special needs, and public education must be available for young children with disabilities. The assessment process should include information about the location of the family and the presence and nature of services and preschools available in the city or town where the child lives.

FIGURE 11–1

The Ecomap of Child and Family Functioning

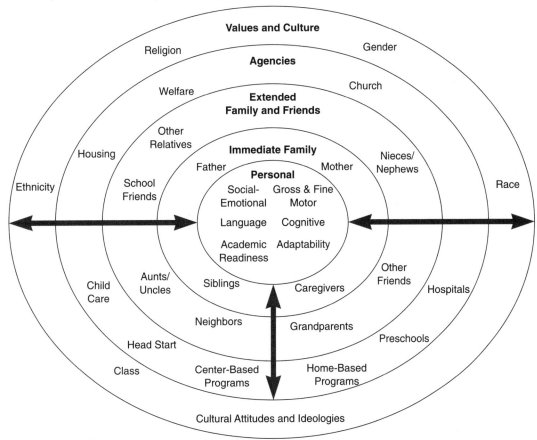

Source: From Introduction (pp. 1–8) by E. Vazquez Nuttall, K. Nuttall-Vazquez, and A. Hempel, in *Assessing and screening preschoolers: Psychological and educational dimensions*, E. Vazquez Nuttall, I. Romero, and J. Kalesnik (Eds.), 1999, Needham Heights, MA: Allyn & Bacon. Copyright 1999 by Allyn & Bacon. Adapted from H. Knopf, (1986). *The Assessment of Child and Adolescent Personality,* figure 1.1, p. 16. New York: Guilford Press.

The outermost circle of the model is concerned with values and culture. Infants and young children are more purely products of their particular culture than children who have been socialized for several years into American culture by the schools. Because most of the developmental norms have been obtained on children of the mainstream culture only, assessors must be careful in their assessments. It is important to understand the family structure and dynamics of different cultural groups as well as their child rearing patterns (Hanson & Lynch, 1992).

Ecological assessment probes the child's developmental context, including preschool and home environments, peer interactions, caregiver responsiveness, child management techniques, safety features, parent/family participation, and even the toys with which a child plays. Ecological assessment promotes a transactional view of child development (Bagnato & Neisworth, 1991).

Conducting Ecological Assessments

Ecological assessment measures can be properly used to accomplish two major purposes: (1) to describe the nature and qualities of child and environmental interactions, and (2) to identify specific child and milieu dimensions that can be added or rearranged to improve interactions (Bagnato & Neisworth, 1991). The ecological approach sees the child as interacting with the environment. Observation of the young child in the home, child care center, or any other environment in which the child is a part becomes more important as a source of information. The nature of the setting is determined by the type of information needed. For example, if an assessment has shown that a child has the competency to perform a particular task, but observation of the child reveals that he rarely performs this task in the preschool setting, then an ecological assessment may determine what environmental factor(s) increase the child's tendency to perform this task. To find the answer to this question, the child must be observed in all settings in which he is a part, such as the home and preschool.

The major characteristics of ecological methods include: (1) the focus on naturalistic observation, (2) documentation of behavior obtained with minimal predetermination of criteria for recording observations, (3) observations made in as nonintrusive a manner as possible, and (4) making inferences about the interplay of behavior and environment after the recording is completed. The goal of the observer is then to identify patterns and sequences of behaviors.

Naturalness

The concept of naturalness is translated into assessment practice by requiring that documentation of behavior settings be done with the least degree of predetermined criteria by which observations are recorded. The observer records events in as unbiased and noninferential a manner as possible. Only after all recording has been completed is an attempt made to analyze the records to determine what patterns and sequences may emerge (Simeonsson, 1986).

Another important issue of the ecological approach pertains to the methodology of assessment. Because naturalness is emphasized, observations are to be made in as nonintrusive a manner as possible and should be comprehensive rather than selective in scope, resulting in data that are extremely complex and rich in information. As data are divided into categories, however, they can provide a great deal of information, such as the structure of behavior in children, the effectiveness of teachers, and the pattern of activities of child advocates (Scott, 1980). The ecological approach provides a systematic means for examining the direct influence of the environment on behavior, which has particular relevance for children with special needs. Observational methods for conducting ecological assessment are discussed in the next section.

Observational Recording Methods

Narrative Descriptions

Narrative descriptions are possibly the easiest and least structured form of informal observation. Anecdotal and running records are examples of narrative descriptions. Checklists and rating scales are more structured forms of observational data. Narratives seem best suited for assessing a child's social or emotional development, and the checklist is useful for assessing academic needs (Thurman & Widerstrom, 1985). Irwin and Bushnell (1980) organized observations into three types: narrative descriptions (anecdotal records, running records, specimen descriptions), sampling techniques (time and event sampling), and checklists and rating scales. Another type of recording is jottings

(McAfee & Leong, 1997). Two of the types of observation (narratives; checklists and rating scales) will be discussed in the next section. Sampling techniques will be discussed in Chapter 12.

Anecdotal Records

Anecdotal records have been used by classroom teachers for many years to record the behavior of children. This record requires no particular length, time, or structure of recording. It is simply a collection of descriptions about one child made intermittently whenever there is something of interest to record. For example, a child who has never talked in class begins speaking. The teacher writes down what the child said and under what circumstances this event has occurred. Although it reflects the observer's own biases, this description can help the observer gain information concerning a child's behavior and what conditions might be reinforcing it. Another example is an aggressive child who may react more to certain other children or to certain kinds of statements from other children.

Brandt (1972) developed the following guidelines for researchers using anecdotal records (the guidelines are also useful for teachers):

1. Write down the anecdote as soon as possible after it occurs. Although this may be difficult for busy teachers, it is important to have as accurate information as possible.
2. Identify the basic action of the key person and what was said. Try to record verbatim what was said by the child and the response. It may be necessary to paraphrase what other individuals involved have said, but the basic flavor of the conversation should be preserved.
3. Include a statement that identifies the setting, time of day, and the basic activity at the beginning of the anecdote. Record what should have been happening if it is different from what is expected.
4. Preserve the sequence of the episode. The anecdote should have a beginning, middle, and an end.
5. Three levels of action should be included in the anecdote: (1) the molar level describes the main activity described in the anecdote; (2) the subordinate molar level records more specific information about the main activity; and (3) the molecular level gives a qualitative description of the activity. (Adapted from Thurman & Widerstrom, 1985)

It is important that the method used be convenient. The recorder may wish to develop his own abbreviations and symbols to help in writing quickly. For example, a T for teacher, first initials for children's names, and shorthand for objects, such as "hse" for house, "blk" for block, and so on. The most important factor is to make the system easy. Keep pens and pencils handy in your pocket, around your neck, in magnetic boxes attached to furniture, etc. Notebooks and papers of various kinds should be readily available. Sticky back notes are handy and can be kept in key areas around the room or in pockets; afterward they can be placed on paper for filing. Clipboards placed in strategic centers around the room can be helpful for keeping anecdotal records. Various-sized cards can be arranged and rearranged with notes for the summarization process. Another strategy is to divide a letter-sized piece of paper into sections for four to six children. After observations are entered, the paper can be cut into pieces for filing. Chapter 12 provides further information and guidelines for keeping anecdotal records. An example of an anecdotal record is also provided in Chapter 12.

Running Records

The running record provides more complete information than does the anecdotal record because it continues over a period of time. The writer of the running record must record behavior at scheduled, predetermined intervals. In a running record, an observer records everything that occurs within a given time period by taking notes or videotaping. It is a useful technique for the teacher to get a general idea of what is happening and the sequence of events. The running record may be used at any point in the assessment process, whether it is to make a placement decision, identify areas of child functioning that need further assessment, or for program evaluation.

Once the observation is complete, the observer has a large volume of information that is not organized into a meaningful way. The observer must convert the information into another form for analysis and interpretation. The way the information is organized can have significant influence on the meanings of the information. The observer can study the data in order to form categories, or the data can be studied using previously identified categories. The Behavioral Coding System (BCS) (Jones, Reid, & Patterson, 1975) is an example of a psychometrically validated and reliable coding system that can reduce the likelihood of misinterpretation. The BCS contains 28 observable categories which can be noted during an observation. Two examples of behavior categories are verbal and nonverbal. These categories are further defined into more specific categories such as a command (an immediate or clearly stated request) and command negative (a command which is very different in attitude from a reasonable command or request).

Specimen Descriptions

The specimen description is a more formal way of recording behavior. This method requires that the subject, setting, time, and episode be identified at the beginning of each narrative. It is limited to a series of episodes, and each description must contain only one episode or event. The observer must sit uninterrupted and record events during an entire episode. This is an impossible task for a classroom teacher who is

working with a group of children. If an outside observer, who is presumably less involved with the children, is available, he would provide for more objective reporting and make fewer inferences regarding their feelings, thoughts, and intentions than do writers of anecdotal or running records.

Jottings

Jottings are condensed accounts or short notes about significant aspects or characteristics of a behavior. They contain the same important details but take less time to write than descriptive narratives and anecdotal records. Jottings document relevant aspects of a behavior or skill by writing in phrases, leaving out unimportant words and using abbreviations; for example, "Lvs. hskpng. ctr. aft. 5 min." The same format used in writing anecdotal records can also be used with jottings.

Jottings are a flexible recording technique. They can be made quickly and preserve detailed information in a small space. Jottings are often added to products from the classroom to provide supplemental information. However, if jottings are too brief, they can be unreliable. If the teacher is unfamiliar with a behavior, then significant elements may be missed. A teacher must be familiar with the behavior or skill being assessed so that significant elements are identified (McAfee & Leong, 1997).

It is recommended that jottings be used to supplement other information by placing them in a specific place on the record. They may be written directly on the child's product or attached to a sketch of the design. Jottings should be kept in chronological order so that the recorder can distinguish the order of events.

Checklists and Rating Scales

Checklists. This method is a more structured form of observational data. These are useful for gathering information concerning development of specific skill areas. The teacher may use a formal or informal developmental checklist to record a child's progress in mastering developmental milestones or skills and to track a child's progress in comparison to age level expectations. The checklist is informal in that there is no prescribed way in which tasks must be presented. Items on checklists may be assessed by observing the child during his daily routine, or specific tasks may be presented to the child to perform, and the observer merely records whatever the child happens to do. Examples of items from a checklist may include using a pincer grasp, one-word utterances, or initiating interactions with other children.

A checklist is simply a list of skills that are usually arranged in a developmental sequence. The child either passes or fails an item, without consideration for the quality of his performance. However, a clear criterion must be stated so that the observer can decide on an objective basis whether or not the child can perform the task. A good checklist should clearly spell out the criteria for mastery. This increases the ease with which the tool can be used as well as the reliability of the data recorded. Some developmental curricula may be used as developmental checklists. Curriculum-based or norm-based assessments provide skill checklists in each developmental area. The checklist is meant to be part of an ongoing process rather than to be administered only once or twice as are formal tests. New information is then constantly available for incorporating into individual daily planning.

Many early childhood educators feel that commercially available checklists do not break skills down into small enough components to be useful for lesson planning. For that reason, they often prefer to develop their own checklists. The teacher or early interventionist may design his own checklist by compiling tasks or skills examined by a variety of instruments.

In developing one's own checklist, a task analysis may be used to break down the skill into smaller components. The task analysis approach is very useful for children with severe or multiple disabilities who may display gain in smaller increments or be able to perform only part of a skill in some cases. This method is discussed more fully in Chapter 12. Thurman and Widerstrom (1985) presented an example of this process in Figure 11–2. The teacher may record the date on which the child demonstrates the skill as well as the level of proficiency displayed. Factors such as whether the child performs independently, with teacher-assistance or with physical or verbal prompts, may be noted.

Behavior Rating Scales. A rating scale or checklist may be used to make judgments about a child's behavior or the environment. The checklist or rating scale may be used at regular intervals by the teacher or caregiver. This checklist notes the absence or occurrence of specific behaviors or skills. The list may include appropriate or inappropriate behaviors to be recorded. The rating may consist of a simple yes-no response, a continuum ranging from "always" to "never," or a qualitative judgment from "excellent" to "poor." Although highly subjective, using the rating scale at regular intervals and having more than one individual rate the behavior will increase the amount and reliability of information obtained from the rating scale.

This type of judgment-based assessment provides an excellent means for input from the family and a variety of professionals who come into contact with the child. This input can challenge or support the information obtained from more formal assessment. This method also allows for more qualitative observation of a child's overall functioning than the specific items of direct testing methods typically allow. Rating scales may also be used to assess the environment of the child. An example of such a rating scale is shown in Table 11–1.

FIGURE 11–2
Steps in Developing Skills Checklist

Guideline

1. Choose a developmental area in which the child needs special instruction. Pick a skill from this area to assess.

Self-help skills: feeding self

2. Observe several older children to find out what the specific components of the skill are. Use a commercial checklist to get you started. List the developmental steps in sequence.

Steps to self-feeding as presented in Learning Accomplishment Profile	Observed
1.	a. b.
2.	a. b.
3.	a. b.
4.	a. b.

3. Transfer your skill sequence to a checklist format with room for recording date first assessed, date of mastery, and comments.

Skill	Date Assessed	Date Mastered	Comments
1.			
a.			
b.			
2.			
a.			
b.			

Source: From S. K. Thurman and A. H. Widerstrom, *Young Children with Special Needs: A Developmental Ecological Approach.* Copyright © 1985 by Allyn & Bacon. Reprinted by permission.

Contexts for Assessment

The context or setting is defined by the tangible factors in the environment, such as the physical space or people (Bentzen, 1992; Boehm & Weinberg, 1987). It has a powerful effect on children and adults. Variations in these factors affect the outcome of assessment and influence the type of behavior and interaction that occurs (Barker, 1968). The context or setting must be examined to provide further information for determining the influence of the setting on the child.

Categories of Static and Dynamic Features of the Environment

Scott (1980) defined a behavior setting not only by time, place, and object characteristics but

TABLE 11–1
Infant/Toddler Environment Rating Scale

	Inadequate 1	2	Minimal 3	4	Good 5	6	Excellent 7
Personal grooming	Little attention paid to child's personal grooming (Ex: no hand or face washing, wet clothes not changed quickly). Same towel or washcloth used for different children.		Children's hands washed as needed (Ex: after diapering/toileting, before and after meals, after messy play). Own towel/washcloth (paper or cloth) used for each child. Extra clothes available and children changed when needed.		Care given to children's apperance (Ex: faces washed, cleaned up after messy play, hair combed with own comb, bibs used if needed). Self-help encouraged in personal grooming as children are able (Ex: child cooperates in changing clothes, encouraged to wash own hands). Personal care activities made more acceptable to children (Ex: caregiver sings songs, gently washes baby's face and avoids making baby cry).		Personal grooming used as learning experience (Ex: learning names for body parts and clothing, letting child look in mirror). Individual toothbrushes properly stored and used for each toddler at least once during the day. Easy place for toddlers to wash hands (Ex: steps near sink).
Listening and talking Informal use of language	Little or no talking to infants and toddlers. Little or no response to children's attempts to communicate through gestures, sounds, or words.		Talking used mainly to control child's behavior (Ex: "come here," "take this," "don't touch"). Some social talking to children (Ex: "What a pretty baby"). Some response to children's attempts to communicate.		Caregiver frequently responds verbally to infants'/toddlers' crying, gestures, sounds, words, and questions. Caregiver usually maintains eye contact while talking to child. Caregiver names and talks about many objects and actions for infants/toddlers. Caregiver takes part in verbal play.		Caregiver talks to each infant and toddler during play and routines about child's activities. Caregiver repeats what toddlers say, adding words and ideas when appropriate. Caregiver adds to children's understanding of language all day (Ex: gives clear directions, repeats new words often). Caregiver maintains a good balance between listening and talking (Ex: does not overwhelm child with constant talk).

Source: Reprinted by permission of the publisher from Harms, T., Cryer, D., Clifford, R. M., *Infant/Toddler Environment Rating Scale,* (New York: Teachers College Press, © 1990 by Teachers College, Columbia University. All rights reserved.), Instructor's Manual.

also by a specified pattern of behavior. Both of the elements of the definition are essential to describe a behavior setting. Neisworth and Bagnato (1988) supported this theory in their model of ecological assessment as an interactive model which stresses that behavior is a function of personal variables interacting with environmental variables. Their categories for these variables or features in ecological assessment are listed by variable in Figure 11–3. These features can be categorized as static or dynamic. Both static and dynamic features are described in the next section. Consider these factors when choosing a context for assessment.

Static Features. The static aspects of the preschool classroom environments which are fairly stable and relatively unaffected by student behavior include the types of materials present and their arrangement, the spatial configuration, the student-teacher ratio, the number of peers present, and their level of functioning. The static variables may set the stage for students to respond. For example, the arrangement

FIGURE 11–3
Static and Dynamic Features of the Environment

Static or physical elements

Organization and arrangement of the
  classroom
Number and arrangement of materials
  available
Lighting
Temperature control
Number, properties, and arrangement of toys
Number of children present
Physical arrangement of children
Teacher-student ratio and staffing pattern

Dynamic or social features

Extent of peer interaction
Caregiver sensitivity and responsiveness
Provision for rewards and punishment

---

of tables and chairs in the room will influence the kind of interaction between children and teachers. The static variable which has received the most attention in the literature is the effect of materials on student behavior. Naturalistic studies document that children's behavior in preschools varies as a result of the type, the number, and the arrangement of materials in classrooms. Children will attend and interact with certain toys for longer periods of time than with other toys. Among these play objects are blocks and sand, art materials, and role play materials (Carta, Sainato, & Greenwood, 1988). Shure (1963) found differences in play behaviors depending on the type of play area that was made available to children. Subjects engaged in social interaction most frequently and at most complex levels when they played in the doll play area. The lowest degree of social interaction was noted when they played in the art area. Quilitch and Risley (1973) found that children engaged in social play 78 percent of the time when they were involved with social toys (e.g., games that involved competition such as checkers, playing cards, Pick-Up Stix, and board games). The same children engaged in social play only 16 percent of the time when isolate toys (e.g., puzzles, crayons, play dough) were made available. The arrangement and number of toys simultaneously available are other aspects of materials that influence specific behaviors of preschoolers. Arranging toys on shelves rather than in toy boxes increases the amount of time children will engage in manipulating toys (Montes & Risley, 1975). The number of materials made available affects a variety of children's behaviors during play. When the number of toys available to a group of children falls below a certain critical point, the children tend to engage in more social contacts, teasing, crying, and quarreling, and more aggression and rough-and-tumble play. When half the group needed to wait for materials, disruptions were most frequent within the group, especially among children who had no materials.

Spatial arrangements are another aspect of the ecology which has received attention in the literature. Several aspects of classroom space have been shown to affect students' behavior in numerous ways. For example, the actual physical location of children in relationship to other children in the classroom may affect the way they behave. The arrangement or organization of the classroom is another spatial variable related to preschool environments. Children tend to play more cooperatively in enclosed spaces and tend to be less restrained and run around more in large open spaces (Eck, 1975; Krantz & Risley, 1977). The number of children is another variable. It appears that spatial density has some effect on preschoolers' behavior in educational settings, but the effects are very likely mediated by the amount of direction employed by the teacher (Carta, Sainato, & Greenwood, 1988).

The number of adults present and the general staffing patterns in the classroom have been examined. Mixed results have been found in studies which examined the teacher-child ratio, the number of child-teacher contacts, and the length of engagement in activities by children (Carta, Sainato, & Greenwood, 1988). Consider the physical space, materials, activities, people, and amount of teacher structure when choosing a context for assessment.

Dynamic Features. The best examples of dynamic, interdependent features of the classroom environment include teacher behaviors and peer behaviors (Carta, Sainato, & Greenwood, 1988). Dynamic variables, such as teacher or parent behaviors, may affect the ways in which students behave but may themselves be affected by student behavior (Carta, Sainato, & Greenwood, 1988). For example, the number of children and teachers in the room affects both the children's and the teacher's behavior. The greater the number of adults in the room, the greater the likelihood of interaction between adults and children. The findings from the observational studies

suggest that less directive teachers encourage more task engagement in their students (Carta, Sainato, & Greenwood, 1988).

Both static and dynamic features or variables affect preschoolers' behavior. The interaction between these features is examined using learning or behavioral variables. These variables consist of setting events (what is occurring within the setting), discriminative stimuli (stimuli which signal a particular response), child's behavior, consequences (what follows the behavior), and contingencies among all of the psychological or learning variables. Assessment of these static variables is discussed in greater depth in Chapter 12.

Examples of Published Environmental Assessment Measures

Considerable attention has focused on the importance of the physical environment and its effects on the child's situation and progress (Bronfenbrenner, 1979). Home and intervention settings are equally important to include in ecological assessment. Participation of the parents in the assessment of the child's environment may result in beneficial effects. The parents may become aware of the need for a structured yet stimulating home environment. Early interventionists or early childhood special educators may become aware of factors in the child's environment that encourage or discourage the establishment of certain behaviors which would help the child to function more effectively in the environment.

Environmental assessment measures are available to examine the home and classroom environments. Some measures often used in the formative stages of development vary in the amount of field-testing conducted and in their demonstrated technical adequacy. These scales use different types of assessment formats to obtain information, such as clinical rating scales, anecdotal records, criterion checklists, and normative assessments. Examples of reliable and valid tools are discussed below. Parents may participate in the completion of these scales.

The *Home Observation for Measurement of the Environment* (HOME) (Caldwell & Bradley, 1978) test measures the content, quality, and responsiveness of a young child's home environment. It is very widely used and is appropriate for use with children from birth to 5 years of age.

Another example of an ecological assessment is the *Early Childhood Environmental Rating Scale* (ECERS) (Harms & Clifford, 1980). The quality of the classroom setting is rated across a number of variables using a seven-point scale. The authors of the ECERS have developed two additional measures that incorporate the same approach and framework for environmental assessment but focus on two types of environments, *The Infant/Toddler Environment Rating Scale* (ITERS) (Harms, Cryer, & Clifford, 1990) and the *Family Day Care Rating Scale* (FDCRS) (Harms & Clifford, 1990). The ITERS is designed to assess the quality of care provided for children under age 30 months. The FDCRS is designed to assess the quality of care in a child care setting. Although the ECERS, ITERS, and FDCRS focus on different settings, some subscales included on each are personal or basic care routines, furnishings and display for children, language-reasoning experiences, social development or interaction, creative or learning activities, and adult needs. These environmental inventories may be used to identify specific child and milieu dimensions that can be added or rearranged to improve interactions.

Incorporating Ecological Assessment into the Assessment Process

Thurman (1977) suggested an ecological congruence model for providing special education services. This model suggests that educational interventions must be concerned not only with changing the child to fit the environment but also with changing the environment to fit the child. When the child and environment are in harmony, a state of ecological congruence exists.

To create this state of ecological congruence, the child must be assessed within his ecological system. The assessment of an individual child within an ecological system is dependent on adequate knowledge of a child's developmental progress and the various factors that account for it. A child's ability to perform a certain task or behavior is based on the interrelationship of his developmental status, degree of competency, and the setting's reaction to this behavior. A nine-step process to assess ecological congruence has been suggested (Thurman, 1977; Thurman & Widerstrom, 1985). This nine-step sequence demonstrates how ecological assessment can be involved in the entire intervention process. These steps are summarized in Figure 11–4 and discussed in the following sections.

Identification of Major Environmental Settings. The first step is to identify the major environmental settings in which a child functions, such as the home and preschool. According to Barker (1968), behavior settings have a standing pattern of behavior and a specific milieu. The standing pattern of behavior and milieu remain constant. For example, meals tend to have a standing pattern of behavior. To identify the behavior settings, parents and primary caregivers must be interviewed. Parents can be asked to describe a typical day in their family. Interviews can also include asking questions about the frequency of certain activities and keeping simple logs or diaries for a week or so to gain additional insights into the behavior settings of the target child.

Inventory of Critical Tasks. Each behavioral setting is defined in part by a series of behavioral tasks. After identifying the most important settings,

FIGURE 11–4

Steps for Assessing Ecological Congruence

1. Identify major environmental settings in child's life.
2. Develop an inventory of critical tasks in those settings.
3. Assess child's competence to perform tasks.
4. Assess motivational variables and other factors affecting child's ability to perform tasks.
5. Determine correctness of fit between child and environmental or social context.
6. Determine child's behaviors or characteristics not developed sufficiently for child to perform necessary tasks.
7. Identify objectives for each component of ecology which will provide increased ecological congruence.
8. Identify strategies for accomplishment of objectives.
9. Establish means by which interventions are to be monitored and effectiveness assessed.

Source: Adapted from "The congruence of behavioral ecologies: A model for special education programming," by S. K. Thurman, 1977, *Journal of Special Education, 11*, pp. 329–333. Copyright 1977 by *Journal of Special Education* and *Young children with special needs: A developmental ecological approach*, by S. K. Thurman and A. H. Widerstrom, 1985, Boston: Allyn & Bacon. Copyright 1985 by Allyn & Bacon.

further analysis of these settings may be necessary to identify the competencies required for independent functioning of the child within this setting. Critical competencies exist in most settings. Interviews with parents and caregivers as well as systematic observations of behavior settings can be useful for identifying critical tasks for independent functioning (Thurman, 1977).

Assessing the Child's Competencies. There are a number of standardized and informal instruments which can be used to assess the competency of young children with disabilities. These instruments may be used to get a general picture of the child's ability. However, these assessments are not tied directly to competencies required in specific behavior settings. A task analysis is a way to assess children's competence to perform specific tasks in a given setting. Task analysis is discussed further in Chapter 12.

Assessing Motivational Variables. An assessment may show that a child has the competency to perform a particular task, but observation of

the child may reveal that he rarely performs the task spontaneously and independently. Motivational variables may account for the child's lack of performance. The child may simply lack the motivation to perform competently (Thurman, 1977).

An understanding of motivational factors is necessary for establishing ecological congruence. These motivational variables may be extrinsic or intrinsic. Although almost no one is totally intrinsically or extrinsically motivated, children tend to perform tasks because their behavior results in certain consequences in the external environment. These consequences may be arranged so that children are more likely to behave in one way or another. Arranging the learning environments in certain ways can increase the motivation and thus increases task performance and learning.

It is important to assess how a child is best motivated. What environment or arrangement of the environment increases the child's tendency to perform critical tasks? In order to do this, both the child and the environment must be observed. Observation should be structured to determine what consequences children receive for their behavior. This type of observation is called a functional behavioral assessment and is discussed in Chapter 12.

Assessing the Child's Tolerance of the Environment. The child should be observed systematically to assess his tolerance of his environment (Thurman, 1977). These observations should be carried out in a number of different settings and during various activities within each setting. The purpose of this observation is to determine to what degree the child spontaneously interacts with people and objects. How frequently and with whom are these contacts made?

Another factor for determining a child's tolerance of a particular environment is to examine how easily a child enters the setting. A child who protests when entering a room suggests a low level of tolerance for this environment. Another child may enter the room freely but protest when a certain activity occurs or when entering a certain area of the room. Observation of these factors will increase the information about the level of ecological congruence within the child's environment.

Assessing Tolerance in the Environment. The degree of tolerance in any environmental setting is defined by the people in that setting (Thurman, 1977). It is important to assess the degree of tolerance in the social system for the child. For example, one parent may tolerate a child's inability to toilet himself independently, whereas the other parent may not. Do individuals approach the child and under what circumstances? Does a child's behavior result in negative consequences from an adult?

An individual's expectations also determine the tolerance level for a child's behavior. If expectations are too high, then the tolerance level may be lower. An understanding of expectations and limits of tolerance is important for establishing ecological congruence and developing long-term

objectives. Observations of individuals interacting with the child and interviews with these individuals will help to determine their level of tolerance and expectations for the child.

Identifying Program Objectives. The sources of incongruence and the specific settings or situations where incongruence exists must be discovered (Thurman, 1977). These data and the characteristics of the child are the basis for the objectives. The objectives must state what behaviors and physical modifications must be brought about to establish ecological congruence. These objectives should be established by a team of parents and professionals and should identify which areas of incongruence are most important and thus must be made a priority. When developing these objectives, changes in the individual child, the child's environment, and the social system should be considered.

Identifying Strategies for Accomplishing Objectives. The individual's or system's particular characteristics and the conditions accounting for the incongruence in the ecology must be understood in order to identify strategies for change (Thurman, 1977). The following aspects are important to consider in establishing an effective learning environment: (1) physical structure, (2) affective structure, (3) materials, and (4) human resources (Thurman & Widerstrom, 1985). Having considered each of these aspects, strategies should be selected for accomplishing the objectives identified to establish ecological congruence.

Identifying Means for Monitoring Progress. The planning process should include a way of monitoring progress toward congruence (Thurman, 1977). This planning should establish the frequency of and guidelines for monitoring activities. Well-constructed objectives should provide a means of program monitoring by clearly specifying the behavior, the conditions under which the behavior will occur, and the criterion level for acceptable performance. If the objective has been met, then progress is being made.

Establishing timelines is another aspect that is helpful for program monitoring. Certain objectives may take 2 months to achieve, whereas others may take longer. These time targets can be useful, but they should be flexible because many factors affect how quickly objectives are met.

This ecological congruence model provides a framework for conducting ecological assessment. This assessment characterizes the social and physical qualities of the child's natural environment at home and in the child care or preschool setting. Various observational recording methods and published environmental assessments that have been presented in this chapter may be used to determine the interaction between the child and the environment.

Summary

Ecological assessment refers to examination of the physical, social, and psychological aspects of behavior settings in which a child functions. This type of assessment provides a means for assessing the contextual and functional influences of the environment. The child's environment begins with the child in his own immediate setting and expands to the outermost circle which is concerned with values and culture of society. Ecological assessment describes the nature and qualities of the child and environmental interactions and identifies specific child and milieu dimensions that can be added or rearranged to improve interactions. The primary elements of ecologically valid assessment should be kept in mind when assessing young children:

- Young children should be assessed in their natural environment which provides information that can be used to determine actual functioning level of the child.
- Analysis of the settings in which behavior occurs provides essential information when interpreting assessment results.
- The settings in which child assessments are conducted directly and indirectly influence the behaviors of all persons involved in the setting.
- The examiner should remember that each person's perspective of the child's functioning is a reality regardless of discrepancies between these perspectives and the child's actual behavior.
- Each child represents a unique set of mesosystems of which he is a participant and, therefore, the analysis and synthesis of information from all of the mesosystems will provide a complete picture of the child who is operating across systems (Benner, 1992).

The ecological assessment will provide the information necessary to plan and implement environmental changes which promote effective intervention with young children with disabilities.

References

Bagnato, S.J., & Neisworth, J. T. (1991). *Assessment for early intervention: Best practices for professionals*. New York: Guilford Press.

Bailey, D. B. (1989). Assessing environments. In D. B. Bailey & M. Wolery (Eds.), *Assessing infants and preschoolers with handicaps* (pp. 97–118). Upper Saddle River, NJ: Merrill/Prentice Hall.

Barker, R. G. (1965). Explorations in ecological psychology. *American Psychologist, 20*, 1–14.

Barker, R. G. (1968). *Ecological psychology*. Stanford, CA: Stanford University Press.

Benner, S. (1992). *Assessing young children with special needs: An ecological perspective*. New York: Longman.

Bentzen, W. R. (1992). *Seeing young children: A guide to observing and recording behavior* (2nd ed.). New York: Delmar.

Bijou, S. W., & Baer, D. M. (1961). *Child development: Vol. A. A sytematic and empirical theory*. New York: Appleton-Century-Crofts.

Boehm, A. E., & Weinberg, R. A. (1987). *The classroom observer: A guide for developing observation skills*. New York: Teachers College Press.

Brandt, R. M. (1972). *Studying behavior in natural settings*. New York: Holt, Rinehart, & Winston.

Bronfenbrenner, U. (1976). The experimental ecology of education. *Educational Research, 5*(9), 5–15.

Bronfenbrenner, U. (1977). Toward an experimental ecology of human development. *American Psychologist, 32*, 513–531.

Bronfenbrenner, U. (1979). *The ecology of human development: Experiments by nature and design*. Cambridge, MA: Harvard University Press.

Bronfenbrenner, U. (1986). Ecology of the family as a context for human development research perspectives. *Developmental Psychology, 22*, 723–742.

Caldwell, B., & Bradley, R. (1978). *Home Observation for Measurement of the Environment* (HOME). Little Rock, AR: University of Arkansas, Human Development.

Carta, J. J., Sainato, D. M., & Greenwood, C. R. (1988). Advances in the ecological assessment of classroom instruction for young children with handicaps. In S. L. Odom and M. B. Karnes (Eds.), *Early intervention for infants & children with handicaps: An empirical base* (pp. 217–240). Baltimore: Brookes.

Eck, R. (1975). *Removing the time-wasting aspects of nap time for young children.* Unpublished master's thesis, University of Kansas, Lawrence.

Hanson, M. J., & Lynch, E. W. (1992). Family diversity: Implications for policy and practice. *Topics in Early Childhood Special Education, 12*(3), 283–306.

Harms, T., & Clifford, R. M. (1980). *Early Childhood Environment Rating Scale* (ECERS). New York: Teacher's College Press.

Harms, T., & Clifford, R. M. (1990). *The Family Day Care Rating Scale.* New York: Teacher's College Press.

Harms, T., Cryer, D., & Clifford, R. M. (1990). *Infant/Toddler Environment Rating Scale.* New York: Teacher's College Press.

Irwin, J. V., & Bushnell, M. (1980). *Observational strategies for child study.* New York: Holt, Rinehart, & Winston.

Jones, R. R., Reid, J. B., & Patterson, G. R. (1975). Naturalistic observation in clinical assessment. In P. McReynolds (Ed.), *Advances in psychological assessment* (Vol. 3). San Francisco: Jossey-Bass.

Krantz, P., & Risley, T. R. (1977). Behavior ecology in the classroom. In K. D. O'Leary & S. G. O'Leary (Eds.), *Classroom management: The successful use of behavior modification* (pp. 349–366). New York: Pergamon Press.

Lynch, E. W., & Hanson, M. J. (1992). *Developing cross-cultural competence: A guide for working with young children and their families.* Baltimore: Brookes.

McAfee, O., & Leong, D. (1997). *Assessing and guiding young children's development and learning* (2nd ed.). Needham Heights, MA: Allyn & Bacon.

Montes, F., & Risley, T. R. (1975). Evaluating traditional day care practices: An empirical approach. *Child Care Quarterly, 4,* 208–215.

Neisworth, J. T., & Bagnato, S. J. (1988). Assessment in early childhood special education: A typology of dependent measures. In S. L. Odom & M. B. Karnes (Eds.), *Early intervention for infants & children with handicaps: An empirical base* (pp. 23–50). Baltimore: Brookes.

Noonan, M. J., & McCormick, L. (1993). *Early intervention in natural environments: Methods and procedures.* Pacific Grove, CA: Brooks/Cole.

Quilitch, H. R., & Risley, T. R. (1973). The effects of play materials on social play. *Journal of Applied Behavior Analysis, 6,* 575–578.

Scott, M. (1980). Ecological theory and methods for research in special education. *Journal of Special Education. 14*(3), 279–294.

Shure, M. B. (1963). The psychological ecology of the nursery school. *Child Development, 34,* 979–992.

Simeonsson, R. J. (1986). *Psychological and developmental assessment of special children.* Boston: Allyn & Bacon.

Thurman, S. K. (1977). The congruence of behavioral ecologies: A model for special education programming. *Journal of Special Education, 11,* 329–333.

Thurman, S. K., & Widerstrom, A. H. (1985). *Young children with special needs: A developmental ecological approach.* Boston: Allyn & Bacon.

Vazquez Nuttall, E., & Nuttall, R. L. (1979, March). *Families as support systems and psychological helpers.* Paper presented at the annual convention of the American Personnel and Guidance Association, Atlanta, GA.

Vazquez Nuttall, E., Nuttall-Vazquez, K., & Hampel, A. (1999). Introduction. In E. Vazquez Nuttall, I. Romero, & J. Kalesnik (Eds.), *Assessing and screening preschoolers: Psychological and educational dimensions* (p. 1–8). Needham Heights, MA: Allyn & Bacon.

12

Behavioral Assessment

Behavioral approaches have been applied to effect change in children of all ages, dealing with a wide range of problems and in a variety of settings. Behavioral assessments are often used when a child has severe disabilities or is demonstrating very challenging behaviors. This type of assessment provides an analysis of how the environment is influencing the child's behavior. A functional analysis of behavior model links assessment and intervention procedures.

The purpose of this chapter is to provide further information for assessing children across a variety of settings in which they are expected to function. The focus will be placed on the identification of strategies that are uniquely suited to assess the behavior of children and on the relationship of behavior with environmental contexts. An overview of the theoretical basis of the strategy will be provided. Development of a functional assessment and analysis mandated by IDEA 1997 Amendments to Part B, for use with children with challenging behaviors, will be offered.

Importance of a Behavioral Framework

Simeonsson (1986) stated that the value of the behavioral approach is that it provides a way to assess the influences of the environment on the performance of the child. The behavioral approach yields an assessment of the contextual and functional influences of the environment. The data obtained from the behavioral assessment perspective enhance and expand the information from other assessment strategies. The result of a behavioral assessment is a functional analysis which allows the examiner to make inferences about the causal relationships between stimuli in the environment and behavior.

Consideration of the influences of environmental and situational factors on an individual or a group (i.e., family, group of children) is an essential component of any effective assessment (Thurman & Widerstrom, 1985). This approach can help the team to better understand the range of responses a child and family may exhibit under a variety of conditions. Behavioral assessment should be integral to the daily, ongoing assessment process, especially with young children with severe disabilities in whom progress is very slow and with young children with challenging behavioral disabilities (see Chapter 7). All environmental factors that contribute to the child's status should be considered. A child with disabilities may lack some of the skills needed to participate and may need special assistance to develop or use needed skills in the context of the typical preschool classroom. An ongoing assessment of the child's ability in relation to the activity demands, routines, and interactional patterns (both peer and adult) of the preschool setting and the development of daily inclusion plans based on these assessment results are critical to achieving such inclusion. Questions that concern how specific intervention strategies alter the emergence of a new behavior or skill or how a particular treatment variable influences the performance of a specific observable behavior may be best addressed through quantitative or behavioral assessment (Schwartz & Olswang, 1996). Using this approach to assessment will enable the examiner to be fair to children from diverse cultures; will provide data that are useful for planning a meaningful and realistic intervention program that is specifically designed for each child so that learning may be individualized and ongoing; and allows for teaching strategies to be adjusted daily, if necessary, to provide effective intervention.

Theoretical Basis of Behavioral Assessment

The basis of behaviorism is the learning principles suggested by proponents of an operant conditioning model for explaining, predicting, and changing human behavior. The best known operant conditioner was B. F. Skinner (1904–1988), who was the first individual to distinguish operant from respondent conditioning (Alberto & Troutman, 1999). Respondent conditioning deals with behaviors elicited by the stimuli that precede them. Most of these behaviors are reflexive; that is, they are not under voluntary control. Operant conditioning, on the other hand, deals with behaviors usually thought of as voluntary rather than reflexive. Operant conditioning is concerned primarily with the consequences of behavior and the establishment of functional relationships between behavior and consequences.

The application of operant conditioning techniques to human beings was directed toward establishing that the principles governing animal behavior also govern human behavior. The use of these principles to change human behavior was called behavior modification (Alberto & Troutman, 1990). The application of behavior modification in real life settings became so prevalent that a new journal, the *Journal of Applied Behavior Analysis*, was founded to publish the results of research. Baer, Wolf, and Risley (1968) defined applied behavior analysis in the first volume as the "process of applying sometimes tentative principles of behavior to the improvement of specific behaviors, and simultaneously evaluating whether or not any changes noted are indeed attributed to the process of application" (p. 91). These researchers suggested that for research to qualify as applied behavior analysis it must change socially important behavior. The behavior must be chosen because it needs change, not because it is convenient to the researcher. The research must deal with observable and quantifiable behavior, objectively defined or defined in terms of examples. Clear evidence of a functional relationship between the behavior to be changed and the experimenter's intervention must exist (Alberto & Troutman, 1990).

Behavioral Assessment

A behavioral approach views the child's behavior as a function of the antecedents and consequences. What factors in the immediate environment have a functional relationship to the behaviors in question? Which environmental factors increase, decrease, or maintain the rate of occurrence of the specific behaviors? Behavioral assessment provides information about the setting or context within which a child's behavior occurs by using a functional analysis. This analysis permits inferences about the relationships between stimuli and behavior. Two issues should be considered when a behavioral strategy is used in assessment, one of which involves operationalizing behavior and the other the selection of observation methodology (Simeonsson, 1986).

Behavioral or functional analysis requires that the target(s) of observation be defined in operational terms before the observation occurs. To qualify as a behavior, something must be observable and quantifiable (Baer, Wolf, & Risley, 1968). The observer must be able to see, hear, feel, or possibly even smell the behavior. To make such direct observation meaningful, some way of measuring the behavior in quantitative terms must be established (How much? How long? How often?) (Alberto & Troutman, 1990). The method for collecting and recording data is also determined beforehand. Behavior is then observed and recorded under controlled conditions. The frequency, intensity, and duration of a particular behavior are examples of dimensions or characteristics that can be measured.

The second issue in the adoption of a behavioral strategy of assessment is the selection of a methodology of observation. Direct or systematic observation and recording of behavior have been the fundamental procedures for behavioral assessment. The observation of behavior may occur under a variety of circumstances or formats, including:

1. In vivo or naturalistic, e.g., in the home or classroom;

2. Simulated or staged, where a situation and materials are provided to permit or occasion the target behavior, e.g., certain toys are pre-arranged; and

3. Role play or prompted circumstances, wherein the child is asked what she would do in a certain situation.

Behavioral Methods of Data Collection

Many different types and methods of data-recording systems can be used to gather information about a child's performance or behavior. Observation is an essential technique which involves gathering qualitative and quantitative data about a child's behavior. Some observation systems are more formal and structured than others. In any case, the examiner needs to focus on the actual events and behaviors and to be as objective as possible in the interpretations of those behaviors. The various types of data gathering systems to use and when to use them will be discussed in the next section.

Behavioral Observation Recording Methods

The first step in the process of behavioral observation is to select a system of data collection. The system selected must be appropriate to the behavior being observed. Behavior may be measured across a number of dimensions, which include rate (how often a behavior occurs within a specific time period), duration (how long a behavior lasts), latency (how long it takes before a child starts performing a behavior), topography (what the behavior looks like, e.g., verbal or nonverbal), force (how strongly a behavior is performed), or the locus (where the behavior occurs).

The decision to use a specific recording method is made based on the dimension of behavior that is to be observed. There are four general approaches for collecting data: (1) analyzing written records (anecdotal reports), (2) observing tangible products (permanent product recording), (3) task analysis, and (4) observing a sample of behavior (event, interval, time sampling, duration, and latency recording) (Schloss & Smith, 1998).

Anecdotal Reports

Anecdotal reports are written to provide as complete a description as possible of a child's behavior in a particular setting or at a particular time. Notes are made by the teacher, assistant, therapist, psychologist, or caregiver with respect to significant observations of a child's behavior or activities. Anecdotal records do not identify a pre-defined target behavior. It is anticipated that after writing and analyzing the anecdotal data, a specific behavior may be identified as the source of a general disturbance or the reason the child is not progressing developmentally. The individual recording the information should indicate the nature of the data (i.e., fact, judgment, interpretation). Specific circumstances may be recorded which might include events that preceded or followed a behavior. The recorder may include specific words used by the child. Conditions under which the child exhibited certain behaviors might be noted. Specific occurrences of a temper tantrum, seizure, or a notable social interaction might be recorded.

Schloss and Smith (1998) cited four major purposes for keeping anecdotal records. First, these records can confirm the existence of a hypothesized problem. Second, they can reveal conditions that provoke or cause the problem behavior. Third, the narrative may indicate events that reinforce or punish the problem behavior. Finally, the anecdotal record may help identify alternative positive social behaviors that may be used to replace disruptive responses. This description may then assist the professional or caregiver in identifying the relationship between the child's behavior and that which occurs just prior to or following that behavior. Anecdotal reports or records can assist teachers, parents, or other early intervention professionals to determine what factors are eliciting or maintaining behaviors.

An anecdotal record may be developed by first identifying and defining the behavior to be observed. A notebook or pad is kept handy and a narrative is written whenever the behavior occurs. The narrative includes an objective description of the child's reaction, the time and place, professionals and peers involved, and significant events. It is important that the recording be accomplished during or immediately after the event. Wright (1960) suggested the following guidelines for writing anecdotal reports:

1. Before beginning to write anecdotal data, describe the setting as you see it. In writing, describe the individuals in the setting, their relationships to one another, and the activity occurring as you are about to begin recording (e.g., snack time, free play).
2. Include in your description everything the target child says and does, indicating to whom or to what.
3. Include in your description everything said and done to the target child and by whom.
4. As you are writing, clearly differentiate fact from your impressions or interpretations of cause and reaction.
5. Provide some time indications so you can judge how long particular responses or interactions are occurring.

After observations have been made, anecdotal reports are analyzed to determine the behavior(s), if any, that may be the subject of a behavior change program. The anecdotal record usually concentrates on the content or style of behavior, rather than on precise measurement of its frequency or duration. Because the observations in the initial anecdotal format may be difficult to separate into individual behaviors and relationships, Bijou, Peterson, and Ault

(1968) offered a system for sequence analysis in which they rewrite an anecdotal report into a form that reflects a behavioral view of environmental interactions. This "A-B-C" (i.e., antecedent-behavior-consequence) analysis approach can be most helpful in seeing functional relationships that may exist (Alberto & Troutman, 1990) (Table 12–1). This information will serve as the basis for making decisions about possible changes in the environment or in behavior management strategies. Anecdotal observation may also be a first step in a longer process for dealing with persistent or seriously harmful behaviors. This process, known as functional assessment, is dealt with later in this chapter.

Permanent Product Samples

Another method of data collection involves the gathering of samples of the child's work at regular intervals for comparisons of earlier works with later products. Permanent products may include arts and crafts work, pencil and crayon drawings, audiotapes of vocalizations, or videotapes of social behavior or task performance. This method of data collection is very useful in demonstrating changes and progress in a child's skills or behavior to caregivers and professionals alike. These samples give concrete evidence of the child's progress over time and may assist with program evaluation as well.

Task Analysis Recording

Task analysis is a procedure for reducing complex behaviors into component parts or skills for the purpose of systematizing instruction. Learning is facilitated by breaking large goals, which are too large to be learned, into smaller objectives which are sequenced for instruction. Task analysis is a means of analyzing curriculum content so that the child is able to acquire and chain together component skills that comprise the more complex skill. Teaching begins by

TABLE 12–1
Structuring of an Anecdotal Record

Time	Antecedent	Response	Consequence
5:15 PM	1. Mother (M.) working at sink.		
		2. Chris (C.) throws pans on floor.	
			3. M. picks up pans; tells C. to stop.
		4. C. spins lid.	
			5. M. restacks pans; closes cabinet.
	6. M. returns to sink.		
		7. C. throws lid across room; spills salt shaker.	
			8. M. stops cooking; cleans salt.
		9. C. spins pan lid.	
	10. M. opens refrigerator.		
		11. C. pulls refrigerator door.	
			12. M. holds door.
		13. C. screams.	
			14. M. slams door; talks to C.

Source: From *Applied behavior analysis for teachers* (3rd ed.) (p. 101), by P. A. Alberto and A. C. Troutman, © 1990. Reprinted by permission of Prentice-Hall, Inc. Upper Saddle River, NJ.

developing the first component skill or step, followed by beginning instruction on the second step, and so on, until all component skills are mastered and the complex skill can be performed without hesitation. For example, learning to put on a jacket can be broken down into smaller steps which are taught one at a time and then chained together so that the child is eventually able to put on her jacket by herself. This "chaining" process may also be reversed, with instruction beginning with the last step and moving backwards to the next to last step, and so on. As mentioned in Chapter 10, curriculum-based assessments often have skills which need to be broken down in order for the child to reach the next major skill or step on the assessment. Task analysis provides the means for helping the young child acquire developmental skills.

The early childhood special educator must be able to break the complex skill into its component steps and assess when mastery of each component skill is achieved prior to moving to the next component step. A simple form that may be used for collecting task analysis data is shown in Figure 12–1. Four major elements of

task analysis recording should be included on this form (Schloss & Smith, 1998):

1. The overall objective or complex skill is identified at the top of the form. The objective statement should include the child's name, the complex skill, the conditions under which the skill will be performed, and the criterion for successful performance.
2. The component skills are listed sequentially from first to last or from last to first. These skills should be described in clear and complete terms so that all observers are able to agree on their acceptable performance.

FIGURE 12–1
Form for Collecting Task Analysis Data

Child: _____ Date Began: _____
Teacher/Observer: _____ Setting: _____
Developmental Skill: _____
Criterion Level for Success: _____

Skill	Trials				
	1	2	3	4	5
1.					
2.					
3.					
4.					
5.					
6.					
7.					
8.					

Prompt Key: S = self-initiate (+) = skill performed to criteria
V = verbal (−) = skill not performed to criteria
M = modeling
P = physical guidance

3. Spaces are provided for recording a series of trials for each component skill. The child should be provided with several opportunities to perform the skill. These recording opportunities should reveal progress toward mastery.

4. Each component skill in each trial is recorded using the prompt key, the level of prompt used for successful performance. These prompts may include self-initiating (performs the skill without the teacher's assistance), verbal prompt (performs the skill following verbal instruction), modeling prompt (performs following demonstration), and physical prompting (manually guides the child through the skill).

Task analysis data can be summarized in a number of ways depending on the actual recording method. If prompt levels are indicated, then the average prompt level for each session or on the final trial of a session is recorded. If only independent performance is noted, then the early childhood special educator may report the average number of subskills performed successfully each day.

Observational Recording Systems

Observational recording systems are used to record samples of behavior as they are actually occurring. Data collection procedures which may be used to gather information on ongoing performance include event or interval recording, duration, and latency.

Event or Frequency Recording. A behavior is monitored and recorded in terms of the number of its occurrences. The observer tallies every time the child engages in the target behavior over a specified period of time. The teacher or caregiver is then able to count the number of discrete instances of a particular behavior as it occurs during a specified length of time. Frequency recording is appropriate when the beginning and end of the behavior are easily identifiable. Examples of behaviors which lend themselves to event

recording are the number of tantrums occurring daily, the number of times a child talks to another child during free play time, and the number of times a child requests assistance. The frequency of a behavior is documented by recording the number of times it occurs during a specified time period. An example of a data sheet for recording the frequency of occurrence of a child's behavior is shown in Figure 12–2.

When the observational time is variable, frequency of response should be converted to rate of response. Response rate is established from frequency data by dividing the number of occurrences (frequency) by the duration of the observation. For example, if a child initiates five verbal interactions with another child in 5 hours, the rate of response would be one initiation per hour (five initiations divided by 5 hours).

Interval Recording. Interval recording is a data collection system for recording an estimate of the actual number of times behavior occurs. Instead of counting each occurrence, the observer counts the number of intervals of time within an observational period during which the behavior occurs. The specific observation period is divided into a number of predetermined intervals (e.g., 15 or 30 seconds). Behavior is observed in terms of whether a defined behavior occurs within a specified time interval. The presence or absence of a behavior is noted during each interval using a stopwatch or prerecorded tape with interval times recorded. The number of intervals in which the behavior occurred is counted and divided by the total number of intervals observed to obtain a ratio of total intervals. This is then reported as a percentage. Behaviors that may be recorded using interval recording are often behaviors which do not have a discrete beginning or end, such as time on-task or off-task. These methods allow continuous and high frequency behaviors to be counted. Figure 12–3 is an example of a sample data sheet.

Two approaches may be used to record interval data. The approach selected is based on

FIGURE 12–2

Sample Data Sheet for Event Recording

Child: _____

Observer: _____

Date: _____

Target behavior: _____

Date	Time Start	Stop	Notations of occurrences	Total occurrences

FIGURE 12–3

Sample Data Sheet for Recording Interval Observations of a Child

Child: _____ Date: _____

Observer: _____

Behavior: _____

Time Start: _____

Time Stop: _____

Note occurrence within the 15-second interval.

X = occurrence

0 = nonoccurrence

15-second interval

	1	2	3	4
Min 1				
Min 2				
Min 3				
Min 4				

the instructional conditions and the nature of the target behavior. *Whole-interval recording* is conducted by noting if the target response occurs throughout the interval. *Partial-interval recording* is conducted by scoring the target response if it occurs at any time during the interval.

Time Sampling. Time sampling is similar to interval recording, but the intervals in time sampling are often minutes rather than seconds. Behavior is monitored by observing a child at designated time intervals to record the presence or absence of a specific behavior. The observer predetermines the length of time between observations (e.g., 5 minutes, 30 minutes) and observations are taken exactly at the defined time intervals. At the end of the observation the teacher counts the number of intervals in which the child exhibited the behavior and divides this count by the total number of intervals to obtain a percentage measure. Time sampling can be adapted to allow for observations of multiple students or multiple behaviors of one student. A time sampling procedure referred to as "mapping" has proved useful (Ruggles, 1982). Mapping may be used to learn more about children's interactions with others or with particular areas of the classroom. The data sheet in Figure 12–4 might be used to record a child's behavior in a playground setting. Using this "map," a time sampling of the amount of time six children spend in the various areas of the playground could be recorded.

Duration and Latency Data. Duration recording is used when the primary concern is the length of time a child engages in a particular behavior. The observer records how long a behavior lasts. A stopwatch is used to measure the total time a child engages in the targeted appropriate or inappropriate behavior. Event recording provides information about the number of times a behavior occurs, but duration tells how long it occurs. Duration recording is effective only when the target behavior has a discrete and easily definable beginning and end. An example

of behavior that is appropriate for duration recording includes how long a child plays with a toy or with another child. A duration recording sheet should note the time the student began the response and the time the response ended.

Latency recording data measure how long a child takes to begin performing a behavior once its performance has been requested. The observer records the time that elapses before a child exhibits a particular behavior. A stopwatch is used to measure the elapsed time. The length of time that it takes a child to begin to respond to a direction or command after instructions are given is appropriate to latency data collection. Recording the amount of time it takes for a child to begin playing once she is allowed to go to a center is another example in which latency data may be recorded. A latency recording sheet should note the time the student was given the cue to begin the response and the time the response actually began.

Functional Behavioral Assessment

Goals of a Functional Behavioral Assessment

Young children who display serious behavior problems require comprehensive multidisciplinary services. To select appropriate services and develop interventions, members of the multidisciplinary team need to gather and evaluate assessment data. Functional assessment provides one of the most valid methods for assessing challenging behaviors. The purpose of functional assessment is to identify variables that may be associated with the target behavior (e.g., curricular or instructional variables) as well as the consequences that may be maintaining the target behavior. A functional behavioral assessment identifies those clusters of behaviors that have the greatest likelihood of increasing a child's ability to interact with people and objects in the environment.

FIGURE 12–4

Sample Data Sheet for Time Sampling Procedure of Mapping

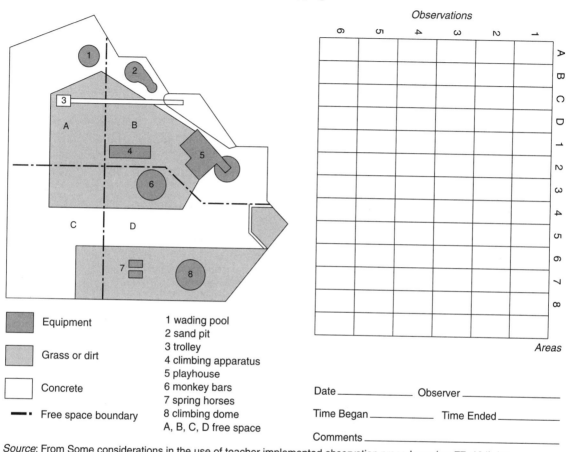

Equipment

Grass or dirt

Concrete

Free space boundary

1 wading pool
2 sand pit
3 trolley
4 climbing apparatus
5 playhouse
6 monkey bars
7 spring horses
8 climbing dome
A, B, C, D free space

Observations

Areas

Date _____ Observer _____

Time Began _____ Time Ended _____

Comments _____

Source: From Some considerations in the use of teacher implemented observation procedures (pp. 77–104), by T. R. Ruggles, in *Early childhood education: Special problems, special solutions*, K. E. Allen and E. M. Goetz (Eds.), 1982, Rockville, MD: Aspen Systems. Copyright 1982 by Aspen Systems. Reprinted with permission.

Functional assessment follows a multistage, multiinformant approach using a variety of assessment sources such as interviews, direct observations, and behavior checklists and ratings from significant others in the child's environment, including teachers, parents, and therapists (Wehby, Symon, & Hollo, 1997). Performing a functional assessment should enable the professional to achieve several goals (Smith, 2001). First, the professional can identify factors that are contributing to the occurrence of the behavior. Second, she can establish a strong link between assessment and intervention. Having knowledge of any factors which are contributing to the occurrence of the behavior will have direct implications for intervention. Third, the professional can identify the current status of excess and deficit behaviors. The results of a functional assessment will document the frequency, duration, and intensity of inappropriate behavior. The results of the functional assessment will allow the professional to determine just how much the behavior of the individual varies from that of her peers or the expectations of others in her educational or community environment. Fourth, results from a subsequent assessment can be used to measure the effects of intervention on the behavior. If the results are positive, then the program should continue; if negative, then additional modifications are needed.

Legal Mandate for Functional Behavioral Assessment

The IDEA 1997 Amendments to Part B, and the subsequent regulations issued by the U.S. Department of Education, mandate specific interventions for students ages 3 to 21 years who demonstrate behavior problems in school. These interventions include conducting a functional behavioral assessment (FBA) and developing and implementing a behavior intervention plan (BIP). Figure 12–5 summarizes the major points for an FBA. A BIP is developed from the information gathered during the FBA. These interventions are designed to reduce problem behavior and teach alternative methods for addressing the function of the behavior. Although FBAs and BIPs are not specifically defined in the law, Congress has determined that they are necessary in order to ensure a free appropriate public education for children with behavioral disorders and requires school districts to use these strategies. Although FBAs and BIPs are not specifically mandated for young children served under Part C, interpretations of the standards developed under Part B have been applied to Part C unless contrary to other standards or rules in Part C (LaRocque, Brown, & Johnson, 2001).

FIGURE 12–5
Functional Behavioral Assessment (FBA)

What is it?

Set of processes that help to identify environmental events that reliably predict and maintain behavior

How is it developed?

Interviews, direct observations, rating scales, and experimental manipulations of environments

Why is it carried out?

Provides information about why, when, and where problem behavior occurs in order to draw inferences about the relationships between stimuli and behavior. Behavior intervention plans are developed on the basis of this information.

What are the outcomes?

1. Description of the problem behavior.
2. Identification of the times and situations that predict when the behavior is likely to occur.
3. Identification of consequences that maintain the behavior.
4. Development of hypotheses that describe the behavior (when it occurs and the consequences maintaining it).
5. Direct observation data that support the summary statements.

According to LaRocque, Brown, and Johnson (2001), the specific regulations of Part C support the use of both FBAs and BIPs in developing appropriate interventions for young children.

Finding the Function of a Behavior

Two assumptions underlie a functional assessment (Foster-Johnson & Dunlap, 1993). The first assumption is that challenging behaviors are influenced by the events or consequences that follow them. In other words, inappropriate behavior will increase if rewarded and decrease if punished. Challenging behavior is also influenced by the circumstances or content in which it occurs. Content can include a variety of factors, such as specific directions from authority figures, peer interactions, and the individual's physiological and emotional status. The second assumption is that challenging behavior serves a function for the individual. The child uses inappropriate behavior either because she does not know what else to do or because it is easier to do than the appropriate alternative and more effective in producing the desired outcomes. The challenging behaviors usually allow an individual to obtain something, such as adult or peer attention, an object, or sensory stimulation. Another possibility is that the challenging behaviors may enable the individual to avoid something unpleasant or difficult. The applied behavior analyst tries to answer the following questions (Lennox & Miltenberger, 1989):

1. What antecedent is occasioning the behavior?
2. What consequence is maintaining the behavior?
3. Can the child be taught an alternative, appropriate behavior to accomplish the same function as the inappropriate behavior?

Information may be gathered by direct or indirect observation. Data collection procedures requiring direct observation include event or interval, duration, and latency recording. These direct observational recording methods were described in the previous section and are used to gather the information needed to form a hypothesis as to variables occasioning or maintaining a behavior. The type of data collection method to be used would depend on the dimension of the behavior to be observed (e.g., rate, duration, latency). Indirect or informant observation may also be used to gather information. These indirect methods will be discussed in the next section. Based on the results of the functional assessment, the early childhood special educator may then manipulate the identified variables to verify their effect on the behavior and thus determine any functional relationship between the identified variables and the problem behavior. This process is known as functional analysis.

Functional Assessment Techniques

Information must be gathered from a variety of sources. These sources include checklists and rating scales, interviews, and direct observation. Most researchers have used a combination of assessment procedures that included structured interviews or teacher rating scales; direct observation of antecedents, target behaviors and consequences; and hypothesis development and validation (Heckaman, Conroy, Fox, & Chait, 2000). Each of these sources which are appropriate for young children will be discussed separately. A flow chart is provided in Figure 12–6 to assist the reader in following the sequence in a functional assessment.

Behavioral Interview. The purpose of a behavioral interview is to get as complete a picture as possible of the problem behavior and the environmental conditions and events surrounding it. An early childhood special educator may interview a parent about a behavior occurring at home or a child care provider about a behavior occurring in a child care center.

When working with family members, the interviewer should explain how the meeting was

FIGURE 12–6
Flow Chart of Functional Assessment Techniques

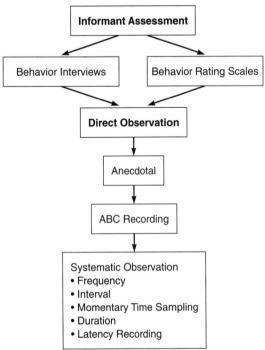

arranged, how she became involved in the situation, what she already knows, and what the purpose of the interview is (Morgenstern, 1988). General interviewing strategies, including open-ended questions, should be used (Berdine & Meyer, 1987; Gross, 1984; Smith, 2001). Suggested questions to ask include: "What can you tell me about your child's behavior?", "What happens just before?", "What happens after?", "Does the behavior occur more in the morning or in the afternoon?", and "What do you want your child to do instead?" (Smith, 2001). The professional can use the interview as a way of obtaining ideas for incentives and deterrents. The professional can also use the interview to obtain consent for assessment, share information about the assessment process, and get a sense of the willingness of significant others to assist in the development and implementation of an intervention.

Similar questions can be asked of early childhood educators and other professionals involved with the young child. Alberto and Troutman (1990) suggested obtaining the following preliminary information, which may be helpful in structuring the direct observation and data collection:

- The topography (form) of the behavior to pinpoint a description of it
- At what times of day the behavior occurs
- During what activity(s) the behavior often or always occurs
- In what setting(s) the behavior often or always occurs
- With what materials the child is engaged
- Who is present
- What often or always happens right before the behavior occurs
- What the child does immediately after the behavior occurs
- What other people do immediately after the behavior occurs
- What medication the child is being given
- What efforts have already been made to reduce the behavior

In addition, the professional can ask about interactions with peers, how the child functions in large and small groups, the length of the child's attention span, and how the child compares with other peers developmentally. The interview enables the professional to gather information about the parents' and early childhood educators' concerns and the reasons they are seeking assistance. The goals of any subsequent interventions can also be discussed at this time.

The Functional Assessment Interview (FAI) (O'Neill, Horner, Albin, Sprague, Storey, & Newton, 1997) provides for more structured informant interviews. Alberto and Troutman (1999) have summarized the 10 sections of the FAI:

- Describing the behavior (i.e., topography, frequency, duration)
- Defining potential ecological or setting events (i.e., room arrangements, staffing patterns, daily schedule)

- Defining antecedents (i.e., time of day, people present, activity)
- Identifying outcomes (access to attention or reinforcement, escape, sensory consequences, or how changes in routine affect behavior)
- Defining the efficiency of the behavior (i.e., slapping is very effective in getting attention)
- Determining what functional alternative behavior the child already knows
- Determining the primary ways the child uses to communicate (i.e., saying, "No")
- Deciding what things should be done or avoided when working with this child (i.e., avoiding touch or positive vocal tone)
- Determining what potential reinforcers might be used
- Finding out what previous attempts have been made at behavior reduction

At times the interview may be the only source of information available before forming a hypothesis and making suggestions. However, it is hoped that the interview is only the beginning in a series of information-gathering steps (Alberto & Troutman, 1990). In the next section, behavior rating scales are discussed. These scales are an additional means of gathering information in the functional assessment interview.

Behavior Rating Scales. Rating scales and checklists are easy and inexpensive ways to obtain quantitative information. These instruments allow the professional to gather some tentative information regarding the nature and seriousness of the problem behavior. The professional completes the scale using a Likert scale that ranges from "never" to "always." The items are related to several possible functions that behavior might serve. The function(s) whose items receive the highest cumulative rating is hypothesized to be the variable maintaining the child's inappropriate behavior. Responses on checklists are often categorized according to four types of motivation: sensory, escape, attention, and tangible.

Examples of checklists include the Child Behavior Problem Checklist (Achenbach, 1978), Connors Behavior Checklist (Connors, 1969), The Motivation Assessment Scale (Durand, 1990), the Walker Problem Behavior Identification Checklist (Walker, 1983), the Functional Analysis Screening Tool (Iwata & DeLeon, 1996), and the Problem Behavior Questionnaire (Lewis, Scott, & Sugai, 1994).

Checklists and rating scales can be used during assessment and after intervention so the professional can obtain global measures of the nature and severity of the individual's behavior as it is perceived by significant others. A note of caution: Checklists and rating scales are indirect forms of assessment and can produce rater bias. The respondent can make an individual's behavior seem very inappropriate to justify treatment or more normal to avoid perceptions of deviancy. Another problem is that checklists and rating scales may not provide the information needed to determine the inappropriate behavior (Gross & Wixted, 1988).

Direct Observations

Direct observation is more reliable than rating scales or checklists. Observing the problem behavior directly will offer a more accurate measure of potential antecedent and consequent stimuli maintaining the behavior. According to Smith (2001), there are several advantages to using direct observations:

- They are nonbiased because they require the development of objective definitions of behavior, rather than relying on subjective impressions.
- They can be conducted in the setting(s) where the problem behavior is occurring.
- They link assessment to treatment by focusing directly on the behavior of concern and environmental events that directly precede or follow the behavior. An intervention program can be developed by identifying these events.

- Direct intervention techniques can be used daily to assess the effects of the intervention.
- Observational data are more sensitive to the types of progress individuals with challenging behaviors display over time. Small improvements in behavior can be documented.

There are two major categories of observation within functional assessment (Smith, 2001). These categories will be described in the next sections.

Anecdotal Observation. An anecdotal observation allows the professional to become acquainted with the child and her behavior in the natural environment (Gelfand & Hartmann, 1984). The anecdotal observation is useful when what is happening in the situation is not exactly clear. The observation can verify the accuracy of another person's observations and be used to develop and refine all aspects of a definition of a challenging behavior. The anecdotal report written after the observation can confirm the existence of the hypothesized problem and its relationship to the environmental events of behavior.

The initial anecdotal report can have a narrative format. A narrative report describes critical events that occurred during the observation period. The individual who is conducting the observation and writing the report should have no preconceived notions about exactly what is going on. Permission from the parents should be obtained before conducting any anecdotal observation.

During the anecdotal observation, the professional who is conducting the observation should be as unobtrusive as possible. Every attempt should be made to minimize the child's awareness that she is being observed. The observer should note the date, the number of people in the setting and their relationship to each other, the flow of activities and conversation, the beginning and ending times of important events, and environmental events that precede and follow each event. At least two observations

should be conducted to verify that critical events are typical rather than unique.

The narrative report should be written as soon after the observation as possible. The narrative report can confirm that a problem is present, help the individual target a specific behavior in need of changing, and suggest conditions that are contributing to the problem and factors that could be reinforcing the behavior. The observer then conducts a more structured anecdotal report using an A-B-C recording.

A-B-C Recording. Bijou, Peterson, and Ault (1968) first described the Antecedent-Behavior-Consequence (A-B-C) recording method. The A-B-C assessment attempts to describe and assess the stimuli surrounding a behavior. The professional uses this method to generate a hypothesis about the relationship between each inappropriate behavior and the environmental events surrounding its occurrence. The child may be using this problem behavior to escape task demands, obtain attention, communicate physical status, entertain herself, receive sensory stimulation, or gain access to desired objects (Smith, 2001).

Antecedents are visual, auditory, or tactile cues that are present in a situation which determine the occurrence and direction of a particular behavior (Berdine & Meyer, 1987). Three categories of antecedents have been identified: physiological factors (e.g., illness, allergies, medication, hunger); factors related to the setting (e.g., noise, temperature, furniture arrangement, schedule); and the curriculum (e.g., the child's preference for the activities in the classroom, level of assistance needed from teachers, time to participate in classroom activities). An antecedent can cue an appropriate behavior; for example, a young child may go immediately to the block area when she enters the room. An antecedent may also cue an inappropriate behavior; for example, when it is time to transition to another activity, the child has a tantrum because she is not ready to stop her favorite activity in which she is involved.

A consequence is usually a staff or peer response to the child's challenging behavior. These responses can strengthen, weaken, or maintain the behavior. Events that increase or maintain a behavior are called reinforcers. A positive event occurring after a behavior increases the future probability of that behavior because it is perceived as pleasant by that child.

Negative reinforcement can also increase or maintain an inappropriate behavior. Negative reinforcement is described as an event occurring after a behavior that increases the future probability because it allows the child to escape or avoid something unpleasant. An example of negative reinforcement is the early childhood educator allowing a child to continue an activity, rather than transitioning to another activity that is less desirable to the child.

Punishment is a third type of consequence. Punishment is an event that follows a behavior and decreases the probability of future occurrences because the child finds it unpleasant. Responses to inappropriate behavior often are not truly punishing. If they were, then there would be no need to conduct functional assessments. What is intended to be a punisher actually may not be punishing for the child.

An A-B-C analysis may then be developed from an anecdotal record after it has been recorded. The A-B-C structure can also be used during the observation period by collecting data on a predesigned data collection sheet (Alberto & Troutman, 1990). The professional can use the A-B-C recording form presented in Figure 12–7.

The professional reviews the information from the A-B-C analysis, the procedures for producing a narrative report, and the information from checklists, rating scales, interviews, and narrative reports. At this time, the professional should have a clear idea of the behavior of concern and, therefore, directs her attention to see if there is a relationship between the occurrence of the behavior and the presence of specific antecedents or consequences. The A-B-C recording should be conducted on several occasions. Observing at the same time each day will help the professional decide if the behavior is consistently occurring under the same set of circumstances. On the other hand, observing at different times each day will help the observer know if the same pattern of behavior is occurring in other settings with other people.

Systematic Observation. After the professional has conducted anecdotal observations using an A-B-C recording, she has a better understanding of the behavior and how to go about gathering more information. Therefore, the next step in the assessment process involves the use of systematic observation. Systematic observation requires assessment of the child in the particular setting where the behavior is occurring. There are several different techniques for conducting systematic observation. They have different purposes, complexity, and the degree of effort involved. Professionals who are trained in their use should have no difficulty, and parents can be instructed in how to gather systematic observation data. Professionals and parents who are working with the child will be able to use only those procedures that will allow them to collect data efficiently while doing other things. There are five systematic observation techniques (described earlier in this chapter): frequency, interval, momentary time sampling, duration, and latency recording. The examples provided may be modified to meet the particular needs of the situation.

Smith (2001) offered some general suggestions that can enhance the accuracy and usefulness of data gathered from systematic observations.

1. Develop a definition of the behavior of interest. Anecdotal observation data can be very helpful in this effort.
2. Careful consideration of the nature of the challenging behavior being measured is essential, as is matching these characteristics to the

FIGURE 12–7
Antecedent-Behavior-Consequence (A-B-C) Recording Form

Child: _____	Date: _____
Observer: _____	Time: _____
Setting: _____	
Others present: _____	

Antecedent	Behavior	Consequence

requirements of the systematic data collection method.

3. Provide adequate training so that everyone who will be observing is thoroughly familiar with the definition and data collection procedures.
4. Practice collecting data to ensure its reliability before using it to make programmatic decisions.
5. Conduct systematic observations on a regular basis to ensure that an accurate and comprehensive picture of the child's behavior emerges.

Although there are no exact guidelines for how long data should be gathered (Foster, Bell-Dolan, & Burge, 1988), an average of six data points is needed for gathering data with children with severe to profound disabilities (Farlow & Snell, 1989). Data from systematic observations are most usable when they are graphed.

Functional Analysis

Once the functional assessment is completed, it is time to conduct a functional analysis.

The purpose of the functional analysis is to determine whether the occurrence of a target behavior changes as a function of the variable that is hypothesized to be occasioning or maintaining it during the functional assessment (Axelrod, 1987; Iwata, Dorsey, Slifer, Bauman, & Richman, 1982). The process of conducting functional analysis involves placing the child in a situation in which the variable can be manipulated. The goal is to examine in a systematic way the effect of the variable's presence, absence, increase, or decrease.

To conduct a functional analysis, the professional examines all of the data gathered during the functional assessment and generates a hypothesis. Hypotheses that describe the relationship between the challenging behavior and environmental variables must be developed. These hypotheses should be specific, connected to observations, and stated so that the environmental variables can be manipulated in the setting to create changes in the behavior (Dunlap, et al., 1993). For example, if the results of the functional assessment indicate a hypothesis that the child's inappropriate behavior is being maintained by the teacher's attention, then the child is placed in a condition where teacher attention is present (the teacher pays attention to each instance of the behavior) and in a condition where teacher attention is absent. Data must be collected during each condition to measure and verify changes in the occurrence of the behavior (Alberto & Troutman, 1990).

The next step is to develop the intervention program. The condition that seems to be associated with high levels of inappropriate behavior is now identified. Now the professional should put into place the condition that is hypothesized to produce low levels of undesirable behaviors. In other words, the professional can select and teach an appropriate replacement skill that will allow the child to satisfy needs and wants. The child will no longer have to rely on the challenging behaviors to have her demands met.

Assessments of the individual behavior and program effectiveness should be conducted. An A-B-C recording may be used to assess the effectiveness of the program as well as to gather systematic observation data. If the intervention is effective, then the program should be continued; if not effective, then an effective program must be identified. If the goal has been met, then it is time to address other areas of concern.

Intervention priorities must be established. If the child is displaying more than one challenging behavior that must be addressed, then the professional or parent must choose which to address first. Behaviors that pose the greatest risk to the safety of the child or those around her should be addressed first. These behaviors are very likely to draw the most negative attention and undermine the potential for success in inclusive settings. The next behaviors to target are those that interfere with the child's learning and are a concern to significant others.

An example of the use of functional assessment and analysis is given by Blair, Umbreit, and Bos (1999). These researchers conducted a study with four young children identified with behavioral disorders who demonstrated aggressive, disruptive, off-task, and noncompliant behaviors. Based on the information from the functional assessment, the authors hypothesized that student preferences and interests were the variables associated with all four of the youngsters' problem behaviors. In addition, one child's problem behaviors appeared to function to gain teacher attention and also were hypothesized to occur owing to poor social interaction skills. The interventions involved incorporating preferred activities into targeted preacademic curricular activities with the four children and, for the one child, providing frequent attention and prompting of appropriate social behavior. The teachers also included student preferences in the other activities throughout the class day, and generalization was assessed in a nontargeted activity. Results indicated that the children's problem behaviors were nearly eliminated during intervention, with similar outcomes in other settings in which they participated.

Summary

Behavioral assessment provides a supplement to norm-referenced and criterion-referenced testing and offers a direct link between assessment and intervention. Direct observation of children's behavior is most useful for describing and analyzing behavioral-environmental relationships or contingencies. Appropriate uses for direct observation include:

1. Documenting if a perception concerning a child is factual or representative of actual behavior
2. Determining how a child behaves in a given setting under specified conditions
3. Clarifying the child's presenting problem
4. Selecting instructional materials and techniques
5. Providing a clearer analysis or close-up of curricular skill attainment
6. Evaluating progress (change) in specific aspects of development
7. Providing concurrent validity measures of other forms of assessment
8. Determining local or situational norms to provide the parameters of "normality" and "abnormality"
9. Assessing low-functioning, nonverbal children who cannot or will not respond to traditional assessment situations (Adapted from Neisworth & Bagnato, 1988, p. 44)

Collecting data and documenting that programs are providing services that are educationally beneficial will always be a part of early intervention. As the face of early childhood special education programs changes, the challenge becomes one of maintaining rigor and accountability of data collection systems while providing services that are naturalistic, developmentally appropriate, and effective. Behavioral assessment provides a means for monitoring child progress as well as how the intervention strategies and practices are being used.

References

Achenbach, T. M. (1978). The child behavior profile: I. Boys aged 6–11. *Journal of Consulting and Clinical Psychology, 4*, 478–488.

Alberto, P. A., & Troutman, A. C. (1990). *Applied behavior analysis for teachers.* Upper Saddle River, NJ: Merrill/ Prentice Hall.

Alberto, P. A., & Troutman, A. C. (1999). *Applied behavior analysis for teachers* (5th ed.). Upper Saddle River, NJ: Merrill/ Prentice Hall.

Axelrod, S. (1987). Functional and structural analyses of behavior: Approaches leading to reduced use of punishment procedures? *Research in Developmental Disabilities, 8*, 165–178.

Baer, D., Wolf, M., & Risley, T. (1968). Some current dimensions of applied behavior analysis. *Journal of Applied Behavior Analysis, 1*, 91–97.

Berdine, W. H., & Meyer, S. A. (1987). *Assessment in special education.* Boston: Little, Brown.

Bijou, S. W., Peterson, R. F., & Ault, M. H. (1968). A method to integrate descriptive and experimental field studies at the level of data and empirical concepts. *Journal of Applied Behavior Analysis, 1*, 175–191.

Blair, K. C., Umbreit, J., & Bos, C. S. (1999). Using functional assessment and children's preferences to improve the behavior of young children with behavioral disorders. *Behavioral Disorders, 24*, 151–166.

Connors, C. K. (1969). A teacher rating scale for use in drug studies with children. *American Journal of Psychiatry, 126*, 884–888.

Dunlap, G., Kern, L., dePerczel, M., Clarke, S., Wilson, D., Childs, K. E., White, R., & Falk, G. D. (1993). Functional analysis of classroom variables for students with emotional and behavioral disorders. *Behavioral Disorders, 18*, 275–291.

Durand, V. M. (1990). *Severe behavior problems: A functional communication training approach.* New York: Guilford Press.

Farlow, L. J., & Snell, M. E. (1989). Teacher use of student performance data to make instructional decisions: Practices in programs for students with moderate to profound disabilities. *Journal of the Association for Persons with Severe Handicaps, 14*, 13–22.

Foster, S. L., Bell-Dolan, D. J., & Burge, D. A. (1988). Behavioral observation. In A. S. Bellack & M. Hersen (Eds.), *Behavioral assessment: A practical handbook* (3rd ed., pp. 119–160). New York: Pergamon Press.

Foster-Johnson, L., & Dunlap, G. (1993). Using functional assessment to develop effective, individualized interventions for challenging behaviors. *Teaching Exceptional Children, 25*(3), 44–50.

Gelfand, D. M., & Hartmann, D. P. (1984). *Child behavior analysis and therapy* (2nd ed.). New York: Pergamon Press.

Gross, A. M. (1984). Behavioral interviewing. In T. H. Ollendick & M. Hersen (Eds.), *Child behavioral assessment: Principles and procedures* (pp. 61–81). New York: Pergamon Press.

Gross, A. M., & Wixted, J. T. (1988). Assessment of child behavior problems. In A. S. Bellack & M. Hersen (Eds.),

Behavior assessment: A practical handbook (3rd ed., pp. 578–608). New York: Pergamon Press.

Heckaman, K., Conroy, M., Fox, J., & Chait, A. (2000). Functional assessment-based intervention research on students with or at risk for emotional and behavioral disorders in school settings. *Behavioral Disorders*, 25(3), 196–210.

Iwata, B., & DeLeon, I. (1996). *The Functional Analysis Screening Tool.* Gainesville, FL: The University of Florida, The Florida Center on Self-Injury.

Iwata, B., Dorsey, M., Slifer, K., Bauman, K., & Richman, G. (1982). Toward a functional analysis of self-injury. *Analysis and Intervention in Developmental Disabilities*, 2, 3–20.

LaRocque, M., Brown, S. E., & Johnson, K. L. (2001). Functional behavioral assessments and intervention plans in early intervention settings. *Infants and Young Children*, 13(3), 59–68.

Lennox, L. D., & Miltenberger, R. (1989). Conducting a functional assessment of problem behavior in applied settings. *Journal of the Association for Persons with Severe Handicaps*, 14, 304–331.

Lewis, T., Scott, T., & Sugai, G. (1994). The Problem Behavior Questionnaire: A teacher-based instrument to develop functional hypotheses of problem behavior in general education classrooms. *Diagnostique*, 19(2–3), 103–115.

Morgenstern, K. P. (1988). Behavioral interviewing. In A. S. Bellack & M. Hersen (Eds.), *Behavioral assessment: A practical handbook* (3rd ed., pp. 86–118). New York: Pergamon Press.

Neisworth, J. T., & Bagnato, S. J. (1988). Assessment in early childhood special education: A typology of dependent measures. In S. L. Odom & M. B. Karnes. *Early intervention for infants & children with handicaps: An empirical base* (pp. 23–50). Baltimore: Brookes.

O'Neill, R., Horner, R., Albin, R., Sprague, J., Storey, K., & Newton, J. S. (1997). *Functional assessment and program development for problem behavior* (2nd ed.). Pacific Grove, CA: Brooks/Cole.

Ruggles, T. R. (1982). Some considerations in the use of teacher implemented observation procedures. In K. E. Allen & E. M. Goetz (Eds.), *Early childhood education: Special problems, special solutions* (pp. 77–104). Rockville, MD: Aspen Systems.

Schloss, P. J., & Smith, M. A. (1998). *Applied behavior analysis in the classroom.* Boston: Allyn & Bacon.

Schwartz, I. S., & Olswang, L. B. (1996). Evaluating child behavior change in natural settings: Exploring alternative strategies for data collection. *Topics in Early Childhood Special Education*, 16(1), 82–101.

Simeonsson, R. J. (1986). *Psychological and developmental assessment of special children*, Boston: Allyn & Bacon.

Smith, M. A. (2001). Functional assessment of challenging behaviors in school and community settings. In S. Alper, D. Ryndak, & C. Schloss (Eds.), *Alternate assessment of students with disabilities in inclusive settings* (pp. 256–272). Needham Heights, MA: Allyn & Bacon.

Thurman, S. K., & Widerstrom, A. H. (1985). *Young children with special needs: A developmental ecological approach.* Boston: Allyn & Bacon.

Walker, H. (1983). *Walker Problem Behavior Identification Checklist* (rev.). Los Angeles: Western Psychological Services.

Wehby, J. H., Symon, F. J., & Hollo, A. (1997). Promote appropriate assessment. *Journal of Emotional and Behavioral Disorders*, 5, 45–54.

Wright, H. (1960). Observational study. In P. J. Mussen (Ed.), *Handbook of research methods in child development.* New York: Wiley.

≈13≈

Program Evaluation

Program evaluation is the final link in the model presented by Bagnato, Neisworth and Munson (1989). It is not a collection of a series of pre- or post-measures that are separate from intervention. There should be a strong link between programming and evaluation (Bricker & Littman, 1982; Johnson & LaMontagne, 1994). Program evaluation data should provide the basis for intervention and help determine the value of the intervention for groups of children and their families.

Program evaluation in early intervention and early childhood special education settings consists of systematically collecting, synthesizing, and interpreting information about programs for the purpose of assisting with decision making (Snyder & Sheehan, 1996). The quality of the overall intervention program must be evaluated and its impact on the children and families it serves must be documented. Program evaluation is the process of determining the progress of children and the efficacy of the total intervention program. Did the program achieve its stated goals? Did the program do what it set out to do? If the program is not accomplishing what it started out to do, then changes can be made which lead to improvements in its effectiveness. Program evaluation provides a means for early childhood practitioners to collect information, make informed judgments and decisions based on the evaluation data, and make any changes indicated by the evaluation data to improve the effectiveness of the program (Cohen & Spenciner, 1994; Johnson & LaMontagne, 1994).

This chapter will discuss the purpose and levels of program evaluation. Various models of program evaluation will be presented, including a comprehensive three-phase model developed by Johnson and LaMontagne (1994). This triphase model provides a framework for developing program evaluations. A practical how-to approach can assist program planners in the initial stages of program evaluation.

Purpose of Program Evaluation

Although evaluation may seem far removed from the daily responsibilities of program management, it is an integral part of intervention. Service providers are faced with a critical need for quality data to guide important decisions. These decisions are multilevel and affect both the quantity and quality of services provided (Cohen & Spenciner, 1994; Johnson & LaMontagne, 1994). Program evaluation serves a number of purposes:

1. Guiding development and implementation of individual programming (Bricker & Littman, 1982; LaMontagne & Russell, 1998);
2. Providing monitoring and feedback about success of individual programming and progress toward individual goals and objectives (Bricker & Littman, 1982; LaMontagne & Russell, 1998);
3. Providing a system for determining the value of an intervention system for groups of children (Bricker & Littman, 1982);
4. Demonstrating program accountability and effectiveness (Harrison, 1995; Linder, 1983);
5. Influencing and developing policy and procedures within the program and the community (Bricker & Littman, 1982; Harrison, 1995; Johnson, 1988; Johnson & LaMontagne, 1994; Takanishi & Feshbach, 1982; Wolery & Bailey, 1984);
6. Acquiring feedback from consumers (e.g., children, families, program administrators, teachers, related-services professionals, community agency personnel) related to program outcomes (LaMontagne & Russell, 1998); and
7. Enabling program administrators to make a wide range of decisions about program operations and allocation of resources (Harrison, 1995; Johnson & LaMontagne, 1994).

Almost every decision that is made in programs is based on some sort of appraisal or evaluation of the situation. From the daily decisions about intervention to the larger programmatic decisions, such as how to present the budget to the board, some evaluation is conducted. For example, are the children in the program meeting their IEP objectives? If not, then should changes be made in the intervention approach? Are children and families meeting their outcomes on their IFSPs? Does the program meet the state regulations for adult-child ratios? Have consumers (families) been surveyed to determine if they are satisfied with the program?

Judgments must be made about three aspects of a program: (1) overall child outcomes, (2) the efficiency and quality of program operations (e.g., staff performance), and (3) consumer satisfaction (Peterson, 1987). Peterson (1987) has offered an extensive list of questions and alternative strategies for evaluating the effectiveness of early childhood special education programs (Table 13–1). This list of questions and evaluation strategies evaluates child outcomes, efficiency of program operation, and consumer and staff satisfaction with programs.

Child Outcomes

The main reason we evaluate is to show that the child is progressing as a result of special services. Program evaluation documents overall child outcomes by assessing the impact the program had on children and families. Were the defined goals and objectives met? Programs need to demonstrate that the intervention provided was effective. It is important to verify that the gains and progress made were greater than would be attributable to maturation alone; that is, if the child and family had not participated in the program.

Efficiency and Quality of Program Operations

Did the children show sufficient gain based on the cost of the special services? Did the program

run smoothly and staff perform effectively? For example, are individual staff members performing their jobs effectively and based upon objective evaluation information. Programs need to provide evidence that money is well spent. Positive program evaluation data will justify requests for funds. These data also provide the basis for improvements and changes in services for the children and families.

Consumer Satisfaction

What do parents of children enrolled think about the program? Do they feel the program is beneficial to their child? Caregivers should be asked to rate the program, services they received, and the way in which the staff deals with them and their children (Peterson, 1987).

Feedback should be obtained from individuals who are intrinsic and extrinsic to the program. Internal feedback is collected from participants and staff within a program. External feedback is obtained from individuals who are not directly associated with the program.

Approaches to Evaluation

Two types of evaluation information are often described in the literature: formative and summative (Fitz-Gibbon & Morris, 1987). Program evaluation should include both formative and summative evaluation. Such evaluations provide the basis for selecting evaluation tools and deciding when evaluation will occur.

Formative Evaluation

Formative evaluation includes activities that provide feedback as a program is being developed. This type of feedback is used to provide information about the program's progress, and the information is used to make midcourse corrections and adjustments as needed. Periodic evaluation occurs on a daily, weekly, or monthly basis. Results of individual assessments are examined to determine if each child has made progress in relationship to the goals of the program. A purpose of formative evaluation is to help program planners keep on target. The information obtained is used to make changes as the need arises and as the program is being developed. If program planners want to know how quickly the children are progressing on their IEP goals so that timely revisions can be made, then they would want frequent evaluations so that they can make immediate changes in the program. This may be done on a monthly, weekly, or daily basis, depending on the child and the particular objective.

Summative Evaluation

Summative evaluation examines the final results of a program or project and assesses overall gains at the end of a longer period of time. To evaluate how much progress the children make over the course of a year, one would want to evaluate at least twice—at the beginning of the year and at the end of the year. The product or outcome scores summarize the performance of participants in a program and allow judgments as to whether or not gain has been significant, thereby reflecting on the efficacy of the program.

Although a distinction is usually made between formative and summative evaluation, the strategies used to collect the data are often the same. The difference is in how the results or findings are used and sometimes in who collects the information. Typically, members of the program staff collect formative evaluation data, making the process more internal, and external evaluators are more likely to be recruited to collect summative data (Harrison, 1995). Researchers have suggested that greater emphasis should be placed on formative evaluation during the first two years of program operation (Anastasiow, 1981; Caldwell, 1977). For example, measure-

ments of child progress may be made to plan appropriate curriculum, develop effective instructional techniques, and give feedback to teachers, aides, and parents. The second year should continue to stress formative evaluation and further refine, modify, and adapt instructional methodology and curriculum. In the third year, summative evaluation can validate a clear intervention approach when the program is clearly developed (Peterson, 1987).

Evaluation Models

Wolery (1994) pointed out that many different evaluation models have been used in early intervention and early childhood special education, because the field of early intervention is dealing with such complex research and evaluation questions as well as with many new and diverse measurement methods. Five classes of educational evaluation models were developed by Popham (1988). Each of these models is described briefly in the next section.

Goal-Attainment Models

These models focus on the extent to which a program's goals are being accomplished, and they rely on clearly specified behavioral objectives against which the program's progress is measured. For example, programs may focus on child-related goals, family attainment of outcomes, numbers of children served, or interagency collaboration. Using a goal-attainment model of evaluation, the program's effectiveness is based on the extent to which the prespecified goals and objectives were achieved (Harrison, 1995).

Input-Based Judgmental Evaluation

Input-based judgmental evaluation models rely on professional judgment of what is required to

TABLE 13–1
Examples of Strategies for Evaluating Program Effectiveness

Evaluation Task	Possible Questions to Be Asked	Potential Data Collection/ Evaluation Strategies
	Formative and Summative Questions	*Internal Review Strategies*
Evaluation of Efficiency and Quality of Program Operations	• Are program purposes, goals and philosophy clearly defined and understood by all staff members?	• Regular staff business meetings to address issues and review progress
	• Are operational procedures clearly defined and followed by staff?	• Regular consultations and interviews with individual staff by program director or coordinator
	• Are staff activities organized and well-coordinated?	• Formal review procedure for giving individual staff feedback on job performance at least once or twice a year
	• Are individual staff members performing their jobs effectively and showing continuous growth in their own professional skills?	• Formal staff evaluation of program operations via
	• Are programs planned for individual children and based upon objective evaluation information?	—round table discussions —checklist or questionnaire evaluation on program —questionnaire or checklist for self-evaluation of job role and performance
	• Does daily curriculum reflect children's IEP objectives, and are individualized programs carried out according to plan?	• Informal staff or client feedback via —personal conferences —suggestion box —presentations by individual staff on activities or procedures, with discussion and reactions
	• Does staff have objective means for assessing how well children are doing?	
	• Are records up-to-date, readily available, well-organized, and used in effective ways?	*External Review Strategies*
	• Do staff members communicate on program matters in a timely way and work together effectively as a team with children and in solving program issues?	• Observations and review by outside evaluation team • Comparison of program operations with those of other similar programs staff may visit
	• Are things staff members say are important reflected in daily operations and services?	• Review of program by state and local officials to determine compliance with regulations
	• Is the program in compliance with local and state regulations for education and for early childhood programs?	• Examination of program documents, records, and operational procedures by a consultant, advisory board members, representatives of funding agency, colleagues from other similar programs, or experts in the field
Evaluation of Child Progress and Developmental Outcomes	*Formative and Summative Questions*	*Formative Evaluation Strategies*
	• What is the rate of progress shown by each child in learning activities? Is this below what the child is capable of doing?	• Collection of performance data during learning activities with graphing/charting of data daily or weekly

Evaluation Task	Possible Questions to Be Asked	Potential Data Collection/ Evaluation Strategies
Evaluation of Child Progress and Developmental Outcomes	*Formative and Summative Questions* • Are each child's needs being met within the program, and is each child being responsive to the activities/therapy given? • Is each child progressing steadily toward learning objectives and mastery of new skills under current teaching methods? • Are children meeting IEP goals and objectives as defined, and in the projected timeline? • What are the overall gains made by children who participate in the program? • Are children maintaining new skills and generalizing them to new situations and settings? • What other benefits are occurring for the child and parents as a result of their participation in the program? • Is the program producing the expected outcomes for children and parents that are considered important?	*Formative Evaluation Strategies* • Weekly or biweekly review of child's progress on learning objectives • Recording of child's behavior or incidents via direct observation and data collection, anecdotal records, rating scales, or checklists *Summative Evaluation Strategies* • Individual child and group data on standardized tests, developmental checklists, or other objective measures or progress collected as part of a pre-test–post-test design or post-test only design for comparison with a control group • Feedback from parents and others familiar with child on progress as reported by formal or informal checklists or assessment instruments • Summarized observational data showing cumulative change over time for individual children and for group of children in program • Samples of children's work before and after intervention, such as drawings, worksheets, videotapes of behavior, or audiotapes of speech/language performance
Evaluation of Consumer and Staff Satisfaction with Program	*Formative and Summative Questions* • How do parents view the program, its staff, and its methods of operating? How do staff members view themselves and their own activities? • How do parents rate the program, the services they receive, and the manner in which staff deals with them and their child? Are they satisfied with the program? How do staff members rate themselves on the same variables?	*Formative Evaluation Strategies* • Appointment of parent advisory council with intermittent meetings with staff for purposes of input and program review • Suggestion box for staff and parent input or feedback • Requests to individuals or groups for input on program practices at begining of year or as need arises, via questionnaires, checklists, or roundtable discussions

TABLE 13–1
continued

Evaluation Task	Possible Questions to Be Asked	Potential Data Collection/ Evaluation Strategies
Evaluation of Consumer and Staff Satisfaction with Program	*Formative and Summative Questions* • Do parents feel welcome, feel fairly treated by the program, and view their role as an important member of the intervention team? How do staff members view their relationships with parents? • Do parents understand the program and have sufficient information about its operations? Does staff think parents are given enough information and understand what the program is about? • Do parents have suggestions on how the program can be improved? What do parents view as strengths and weaknesses in the program? • Do staff members have suggestions on how the program can be improved? What do they view as program strengths and weaknesses? • How do other agencies who refer children to the program view its services and relationships with parents and with the community at large?	*Formative Evaluation Strategies* • Formal and informal meetings between parents and staff, among staff members, or between staff and administrative personnel, for purposes of program review and problem solving *Summative Evaluation Strategies* • Formal evaluation/feedback questionnaires or rating scales for parents and for staff • Formal interviews with parents or staff concerning perceptions of program and their own role in program • Formal feedback via rating form from referring agencies • Review and data collection by outside party via observations, interviews, or questionnaires

Source: From *Early intervention for handicapped and at-risk children: An introduction to early childhood special education* (pp. 316–317), N. L. Peterson, 1987, Denver: Love. Copyright 1987 by Love Publishing Co. Reprinted with permission.

operate an adequate to exemplary program. For example, a state interagency task force may develop a list of input criteria that an early intervention program must meet to receive state funds. Input criteria usually refer to things that a program must have, such as a 1-to-3 adult-to-child ratio, a specified number of square feet, professional staff from a certain number of disciplines who hold appropriate certification or licensure, and so on. The evaluator reviews the program based on whether it meets those criteria or possesses these internal characteristics (Harrison, 1995).

Output-Based Judgmental Evaluation

In output-based judgmental evaluation, or goal-free evaluation, both the appropriateness of goals and objectives and the attainment of them are evaluated. These models emphasize that the worthiness of the goals is an important part of the evaluation. An outside evaluator, who has little knowledge of the program, is employed to determine the actual impact of the program, regardless of stated objectives, the premise being that preknowledge of program goals interferes with the evaluator's unbiased identification of program effects (Scriven, 1974). The evaluator does not need to know what the objectives are, but rather is concerned with identifying the actual impact of the program, whether or not this impact is intended. The advantages to this approach are: (1) the evaluator is in a discovery role and is not limited to simply determining whether goals were reached; (2) the person with a new perspective does not have tunnel vision and may be open to seeing more results; and (3) the evaluation is more critical. The disadvantages include: (1) the lack of structure; (2) no standard to use consistently; and (3) this model does not include interveners and is conducted after the fact, and thus is not an integral part of the program (Johnson, 1988).

Decision-Facilitation Evaluation

This model is designed to reduce or eliminate personal judgment. There are three steps in this process: (1) delineating the information to be collected; (2) obtaining the information, and (3) providing information to decision makers (Stufflebeam, 1971, 1974). The evaluator gathers data which are then presented to the program's decision makers for action. The decision makers are then responsible for continuing, terminating, or modifying the program. This model is expensive and time-consuming and few programs could carry it out. Johnson and LaMontagne (1994) have proposed a three-phase evaluation plan based on this model, which is discussed later in this chapter. Program evaluators may use Johnson and LaMontagne (1994) as a model in planning their own evaluation, even if their own plan is much simpler.

Naturalistic or Qualitative Evaluation

This model is based on an ethnographic approach to data gathering. Data gathering includes case studies, observations, interviews, and participant surveys. A running record is kept of the individual child's behavior and a description of the context in which the behaviors occur. Through the analysis of patterns of individual

behaviors, interactions can be discovered. These analyses can focus on specific goals of units and thus provide information on the child's attainment of goals (Benner, 1992). Focus groups are another qualitative evaluation strategy. A focus group is a way to solicit opinions about a service or product from a group of people in an informal setting through a semi-structured interview.

Each type of evaluation model has its strengths and weaknesses and each is more appropriate for some evaluation questions than for others. Any comprehensive evaluation plan should be developed jointly by the program staff and a professional in evaluation. The next section outlines a thorough evaluation plan which was developed by Johnson and LaMontagne (1994) and based primarily on Stufflebeam's Decision Making Model.

Triphase Evaluation

Current thinking on evaluation suggests that there should be a strong link between programming and evaluation (Johnson & LaMontagne, 1994). Evaluation data should provide the basis for intervention and help determine the value of the intervention on groups of children (Bricker & Littman, 1982). Johnson and LaMontagne (1994) proposed a triphase evaluation process based primarily on Stufflebeam's Decision Making Model. The three phases are input, process, and outcome. Each of the three phases is interwoven into a single process that begins with program planning, continues through implementation, and then looks at program impact. This triphase evaluation model is a decision-making process that (1) delineates the information to be collected, (2) obtains the information, and (3) provides the information to decision makers (Stufflebeam, 1971, 1974) (Figure 13–1).

This process is comprehensive and concerns itself with all aspects of the program. In the input phase, the focus is on determining child, family, or community needs and developing a program to meet these needs. In the process

FIGURE 13–1
Triphase Model of Evaluation

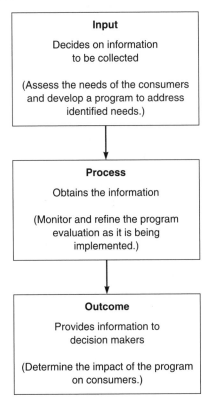

phase, attention is given to monitoring progress toward objectives and determining if there are any discrepancies between what was proposed and what is being implemented. In the outcome phase, attention is directed at evaluating the effectiveness of the program in meeting the identified needs of the child, family, or community. The phases build on each other, with the input and process phases being the most critical to the implementation of a good program (Johnson & LaMontagne, 1994). This program evaluation design encompasses four basic steps, which are summarized in Table 13–2.

Input Evaluation

The input phase focuses on assessing the needs of children and their families and developing a plan to meet those needs. Services that currently exist must be examined and compared with the services being proposed to meet identified needs. The input and process phases are considered to be part of formative evaluation, which is the collection of evaluation data to aid in program planning and implementation. Examples of data that might be collected during the input phase of the evaluation plan are needs assessments that collect information from administrators, service providers, and families to help determine early intervention service delivery schedules, essential components of programming, and expectations. This phase examines a program based on the extent to which it is designed according to "recommended practices," as documented in the literature. The emphasis is on elements of planning and program structure (e.g., ratio of adults to children).

Input evaluation is a concern for service providers and program planners. Every time a new child and his family enters a program, the service provider must assess the child and family needs and then develop a plan to meet those needs. Input evaluation is also important when a new program or a new component of an existing program is being developed. One of the first steps is to conduct a simple needs assessment. The needs assessment is a comprehensive plan by which data are collected from several sources to determine what is needed to serve the children and families entering the program, or if the new program component is really needed. Johnson and LaMontagne (1994) outlined a series of steps that will help to ensure the systematic collection of needs assessment data (Figure 13–2). These same steps are equally useful in collecting outcome evaluation data. The steps are outlined in the following sections.

Determine Key Elements. The first step is to determine the purpose of and the clients and audiences for the needs assessment. A set of goals or questions to be addressed is developed and prioritized. For example, questions

TABLE 13–2
Steps to Program Evaluation

Steps	Description	Focus
I	Identify the purpose and issues: Program evaluation must have an articulated purpose in order to be systematically implemented in a rigorous manner.	What are the goals of your program? Who are the stakeholders? Primary consumers? Secondary consumers? What are the needs of the stakeholders? What are the key features that make your program unique?
II	Identify the best way to collect information: Keep it simple and manageable.	Unobtrusive measures? Existing data such as test scores, IFSP/IEP goals, parent-teacher conference notes Observations? Child, staff, interactions Interviews? Professionals, family members, community staff Tests? Pre–post measurements Questionnaires? Rating scales for consumers and stakeholders
III	Design your plan: Program evaluation is a "team sport" and needs all of its members to be successful.	What are you going to do (i.e., action plan)? Rationale for doing it as designed Who is responsible for what part of the action plan? Time line for accomplishing each part of the action plan
IV	Implement, evaluate, and reimplement: Program evaluation is cyclical and builds on past efforts and information.	Implement action plan Identify expected outcomes and unintended outcomes Identify problems and solutions Refine the action plan needed

Source: From Informal and formal assessment (p. 226), by M. J. LaMontagne and G. W. Russell, in *Early childhood education: Blending theory, blending practice*, L. J. Johnson, M. J. LaMontagne, P. M. Elgas, and A. M. Bauer (Eds.), 1998, Baltimore: Brookes. Copyright 1998 by Paul H. Brookes Publishing. Reprinted with permission.

might include such information as how many families who have young children with special needs are in need of services, what the characteristics of the children and their families are, and so on.

Identify Information Sources. The next step is to determine the sources of information from which to answer the questions identified in the needs assessment. Sources of information can include stakeholders (e.g., parents, professionals, community agency personnel) or permanent products (e.g., records, reports, program plans). A data collection method must be developed

that will efficiently and accurately obtain the needed information. Typical data collection methods include unobtrusive measures, observation, interviews, focus groups, questionnaires, and tests. Because these methods are equally useful in the outcome phase of the evaluation plan, they will be discussed more fully later in the outcome phase presented later in this chapter.

Develop a Management Plan. Johnson and LaMontagne (1994) suggested the development of an evaluation matrix which delineates the issues or goals to be examined and the sources of

FIGURE 13–2
Input Evaluation Steps

- Determine key elements
- Identify information sources
- Develop a management plan
- Collect data
- Analyze and interpret data
- Develop the program

data that are to be used in making judgments about the identified issues or goals. This matrix serves as a simple way to organize an evaluation plan and ensure that the appropriate sets of data are collected for issues and goals to be addressed by the program. A plan for collecting data from the identified sources must be developed along with a schedule for data-gathering procedures and synthesis and analysis of the data, as well as a staff loading chart indicating who is responsible for each of the data collection procedures.

Collect Data. Data should be collected according to the steps delineated in the management plan. The schedule or time line should be referred to often in order to keep data collection on schedule. These methods are discussed in greater detail in the outcome phase.

Analyze and Interpret Data. The purpose of this step is to analyze the data and interpret the analysis. Analysis is the process of bringing order to the data by grouping data into meaningful units, examining the trends within units, and making comparisons among units. Interpretation involves attaching meaning to data trends within and among descriptive units. Quantitative and qualitative data are equally useful in determining the needs and program impact. Johnson and LaMontagne (1994) suggest Borg and Gall (1983) for a more complete discussion of data analysis techniques. Miles and Huberman (1984) or Patton

(1980) is suggested for analysis of qualitative data (Johnson & LaMontagne, 1994).

Develop the Program. The final step is to develop an intervention program that will meet the identified needs of the community. This is an ongoing process. As plans are being developed, they are revised as new data are obtained and summarized. The tentative plans are refined into goals, which are provided on two different levels. These different levels include goals that are program-oriented and look at program outcomes and goals that are child-oriented and provide the teacher with a way to view child progress.

Process Evaluation

In the process evaluation phase, the focus is on movement toward the goals and objectives of the proposed plan. The formative evaluation data that are collected in this phase provide feedback to service providers on progress being made by specific children and their families as well as information on the overall progress of the program. These data shape, mold, and form the structure from which early intervention is provided. For example, if program objectives have not been met, it is likely that the intervention used in the program was ineffective or may indicate the inadequacy of the implementation of the program. This may be the most important aspect of the process evaluation phase, because data collected in this phase may be the first indication of intervention plans that need modification and they create a template for following the effect of the program on children and their families throughout intervention. Monitoring program goals and family needs provides service providers and families with the information necessary to make changes and adaptations that allow for continued progress toward anticipated outcomes of early intervention programming.

Outcome Evaluation

The outcome phase is a summative evaluation component, and the purpose of data collection shifts to providing information on the impact of the program. The focus of the outcome evaluation is to determine the impact of the program on children, their families, and the community. Research methods are used to establish that the program is the most likely explanation for family and child outcomes. Interpretation of the data means determining the causal effect of the program on outcomes. Outcome evaluation eliminates any other rival explanations for child and family changes. The stronger the research design, the more readily other explanations for findings can be discarded (Johnson & LaMontagne, 1994).

Implementing Outcome Evaluation. As indicated in the input phase, the steps delineated in the input evaluation for determining needs are equally useful to the implementation of a good outcome evaluation. The steps are: (1) determine key elements, (2) identify information sources, (3) develop a management plan, (4) collect data, and (5) analyze and interpret data.

The key elements must be determined. The purpose and audience of the outcome evaluation must be decided. The questions that need to be answered also must be determined. The sources of information needed to answer the evaluation questions must be identified. A research design must be selected that will give the greatest control possible over any internal threats to validity. The data collection methods are essentially the same as in the input phase. These data collection methods are described below and listed in Figure 13–3.

Data Collection Methods. A data collection method must be developed that will obtain the needed information in as easy and accurate a way as possible. Data should be collected from a variety of sources using a variety of methods.

FIGURE 13–3
Data Collecton Methods for Outcome Evaluation

- Unobtrusive measures
- Observations
- Interviews
- Focus groups
- Questionnaires

Typical data collection methods include unobtrusive measures, observation, interviews, and questionnaires. Johnson and LaMontagne (1994) provided an excellent overview of these data collection methods.

Unobtrusive Measures. These sources are nonreactive because children and families are not required to change their routine and may not even be aware of the data gathering. Examples of unobtrusive measures would be finding out how many books parents checked out of the resource library or the number of toys checked out of the toy-lending library (Casto, 1988).

Observations. Systematic recordings of operationally defined behaviors are made by teachers or other professionals in the setting. Definitions are based on observable, measurable characteristics of the behavior (see Chapter 11).

Interviews. Interviews can be extremely powerful tools for collecting data (Johnson & LaMontagne, 1994). Interviews are simply asking questions and recording responses. Interviews may be unstructured, semistructured, or structured (Patton, 1980). The unstructured interview has a general objective, but respondents are allowed to respond in their own words and time. An unstructured interview is very useful in helping to identify issues that were previously unknown or in collecting potentially damaging information. This type of interview is vulnerable to bias and can provide uninterpretable information.

The semistructured interview provides a list of questions that all respondents are asked. However, the interviewer is allowed to branch off and pursue responses in greater depth if needed. This structure helps to ensure that information of interest is collected from the respondents and, at the same time, provides the opportunity to uncover issues or relationships that were unanticipated or too complex to be identified by simple questions. This also allows for subjective biases, because the interviewer can lead the respondent to desired responses.

The structured interview is similar to an objective questionnaire. A specific set of questions is asked and respondents may even be given a set of specific responses from which to choose. Responses are limited so that the interviewer cannot lead the respondent. Structured interviews have the potential for becoming intrusive and creating a defensive atmosphere.

The following guidelines for engaging in the structured interview have been adapted by Johnson (1988) from Udinsky, Osterlind, and Lynch (1981):

1. Word questions clearly and encourage effective communication between the interviewer and the respondent.
2. Make respondents aware of the purpose of each question they are asked.
3. Be sure that the population from which the respondents have been selected actually has the information being sought and that the interview questions permit the reasonable recovery of this information.
4. Avoid leading questions; that is, questions that suggest a desirable or preferred answer.
5. Ensure that a clear frame of reference is provided for each question, so that all respondents hear questions in the same way. (p. 191).

Focus Groups. Focus groups are group, rather than one-to-one, interviews. The interviewer holds a large meeting with a group of individuals from whom information is sought. These groups may consist of parents, service providers, or administrators. The interviewer explains the purpose of the meeting, breaks the group into several small work groups, and has each group address a specific issue or question. After some time, the small groups are brought together to present the responses of their groups to the larger group. Responses are discussed and refined until there is a group consensus.

Questionnaires. Questionnaires are often used for data collection. It is important to keep the purpose of the questionnaire in mind and limit the length of the questionnaire. It is also imperative to state questions as simply and unambiguously as possible.

Questions should be objective and provide a set of alternative responses. Open-ended questions may be asked, and these allow the respondent to explain answers and thus provide more information. Specific statements may be rated on a scale of "strongly agree" to "strongly disagree." It is recommended to provide an even-numbered scale, which forces the individual to make an affirmative or negative decision about the statement (Udinsky, Osterlind, & Lynch, 1981).

Many questionnaires covering a variety of areas from child development to family dynamics are available for purchase. Examples of these include such instruments as the Family Satisfaction Scale (Olson, McCubbin, Barnes, Larsen, Muxen, & Wilson, 1982), the Parenting Stress Index (Abdin, 1983), and the Family-Centered Program Rating Scale (Murphy & Lee, 1991). Dunst, Trivette, and Deal (1994) have developed a number of scales for assessing family concerns and needs. Although these are valuable instruments, evaluation planners must be certain that the questionnaire that is developed or adopted is reflective of their program goals and child or family needs. Any newly developed questionnaire should be piloted before it is actually used.

The purpose of this phase is to determine the impact of the program on children, their families, and the community. Even the best-designed program, appropriately implemented, would be of little value if it did not have the desired impact on children and their families. Program evaluation verifies the impact of the program on everyone.

Indicators of a Quality Evaluation Plan

Early intervention programs are extremely diverse in their characteristics, the children and families served by such programs, and the contexts of such programs. Practices appropriate for program evaluation in early intervention will vary according to the nature of the evaluation and the characteristics of the program.

The framework for discussing recommended practices of program evaluation follows the outline of the *Program Evaluation Standards* prepared by the Joint Committee on Standards for Educational Evaluation (1994). The framework categorizes the practices according to four fundamental attributes of evaluation: utility, feasibility, propriety, and technical adequacy.

Utility

Useful practices are those that support the ability of an evaluation to serve the needs of evaluation stakeholders (program staff, administrators, parents, funding agents) in a manner that is credible, informative, timely, and influential. Snyder & Sheehan (1996) purported that evaluations are more useful when the following conditions are met:

- The evaluator is qualified;
- Stakeholders are actively involved;
- Evaluation questions are clearly articulated to assist with decision making;
- Appropriate information is gathered;
- The results are disseminated in a manner that maximizes opportunities for successful decision making; and

- Program evaluation is an integral part of service delivery.

Past research shows that program evaluation has not been an integral, valued, or influential component of most special education programs (George, George, & Grosenick, 1990). Much of the program evaluation has simply been compliance monitoring for federal and state mandates. Evidence suggests that programs can and do benefit when program evaluation is made a routine component of operations (Sechrest & Figueredo, 1993; George, George, & Grosenick, 1990). Obtaining information that is useful for the program and its stakeholders is a key factor in evaluation.

Feasibility

Evaluation practices are feasible when they support the conduct of program evaluation within the constraints imposed by limited resources, time, and the political subtext of early intervention programs. How plausible is the evaluation plan for implementation? These practices should minimize the disruptions to stakeholders (Snyder & Sheehan, 1996).

The evaluation should acknowledge the diversity of families, respecting their values, cultures, coping styles, and priorities. All data collection tools should be reviewed to ensure that language usage is respectful to families. Evaluators should seek to identify the strengths of parents and families as well as their needs (McGonigel, 1988).

Program evaluators should always keep in mind that the success of program evaluation is frequently determined by the goodwill and support of the staff and families involved. The evaluation should not disrupt delivery of services. Disruptions can be minimized by involving staff and families in the planning of a program evaluation. Using existent data such as assessment results, IEPs, and staff logs or gathering data that can also be used to assist individual intervention planning (supplemental assessment data) can also reduce disruptions. It is better to implement a simple program evaluation successfully, even if it evaluates only one goal, than to try to implement a complex program evaluation unsuccessfully. The evaluator and program director must determine whether the anticipated benefits (e.g., efforts to improve staff performance) of the evaluation outweigh the expected costs (e.g., staff time, expense).

Propriety

Proprietary evaluation practices are ethical and protect the constitutional rights of participants in and audiences of program evaluation. It is the responsibility of evaluators to protect such rights (Snyder & Sheehan, 1996). These standards apply to treatment of families, staff, and children as data sources; treatment of data that have been gathered; and reporting of data once they have been gathered. Confidentiality of data is critical in establishing an atmosphere in which consumers feel safe to provide honest responses without fear of retribution.

Before collecting data, families and staff should be allowed to ask about the kind of information they will share and be reassured that their participation is confidential and voluntary and can stop at the request of the family member, staff member, or child without any recrimination. After collecting data, it should be coded to protect informant identity and should not be used for any other purpose without permission. Evaluation data should be kept for 7 years to allow the retrieval of the data to perform follow-up analyses for the program being evaluated.

Technical Adequacy

Technical adequacy is assured when evaluation practices support the gathering, analysis, and interpretation of information in ways that are valid, reliable, accurate, fair, and replicable (Snyder & Sheehan, 1996). Evaluation practices become technically adequate when the following conditions are followed:

- Descriptions of programs and contexts are precise;
- Methodology and analyses are clearly described, justified, systematically monitored, and understood by decision makers;
- Multiple appropriate sources of information are accessed;
- Instruments and measurement procedures are appropriate for the respondents and generate information that is reliable and valid for decision making; and
- Objective findings are clearly reported.

In order for program evaluation to be effective, there must be a high degree of faith that the information gathered was collected from consumers with their appropriate knowledge related to the goals of the early childhood program and that the data were collected, analyzed, and interpreted using procedures and methods to ensure objectivity. Keeping in mind the recommended practices previously outlined can help stakeholders and evaluators plan and conduct the best evaluations possible, given the needs, constraints, and compromises unique to a specific evaluation.

General Considerations in Planning Program Evaluations

Several general guidelines for planning and implementing program evaluation should be considered:

1. The program philosophy, objectives, and evaluation should all relate to each other. The objectives of the program should define the kind of content to be evaluated. The factors to be evaluated define the kind of documentation needed.
2. Evaluation for early intervention programs should be multidimensional. A variety of types of assessment should be used and

these should involve all of the professionals across disciplines who are involved in the program.

3. The evaluation design must be carefully planned. Instruments should be selected that assess the major thrust of the program and the population being served. Measurement of program effectiveness should match the specific goals of each child's intervention. For example, if social interaction is a major component, then assessment instrument(s) must be chosen which will measure the gains made as a result of the intervention.

4. Assessment and evaluation strategies should be feasible and practical. Will the staff have time to implement these strategies? Can the program afford the cost of internal and external reviews?

5. The program evaluation should overlap the entire assessment process used in the intervention program. Evaluation should be both formative (during the program) and summative (at the end of the services). Diagnosis of individual children's capabilities and deficits at the beginning of the program also may serve as baseline performance monitoring data or formative evaluation.

6. Programs should also measure the outcomes of various family variables, such as the use of support networks or the family's ability to manage resources.

Beginning Program Evaluation

Many programs operate without any consistent and well-planned system of evaluation. If program evaluation is most likely to be implemented, it should be the least intrusive and burdensome to program deliverers. Programs that are new to evaluation might proceed in stages: start with some simple indicators, provide feedback to staff, and then continue.

One way to develop a system of program evaluation is to form a committee to decide how the evaluation will be conducted. Representatives from the groups that are most affected by program policies should be included, such as administrators, teachers, and families. Effective program evaluation must have staff cooperation and people to implement the program evaluation.

The next step would be for the committee to look at the program's philosophy, goals, and objectives to determine what the program is trying to accomplish. The committee will also have to determine how to decide whether the program is adhering to its philosophy, goals, and objectives. Other factors to consider are what evaluation tools will be used and how often evaluation will occur. It should be noted that individuals who are collecting data should receive feedback about the data emerging from the process or they will lose interest. After considering how the program will be evaluated and implementing these procedures, the committee can determine the weak and strong points of the program and thus would know if the program is effective.

As mentioned previously, Peterson's chart for program evaluation (Table 13–1) provides an excellent guide for questions and alternative strategies for evaluating the effectiveness of an early intervention program. DeStefano, Howe, Horn, and Smith (1991) provided an example of a simple program assessment that might be used to begin program evaluation (Figure 13–4). This program assessment includes six components: (1) curriculum programming, (2) organization of the learning environment, (3) social skills, (4) using support services, (5) family involvement, and (6) transition. The team members check the appropriate response for questions in each section. The responses that may be checked are: (1) This is an important part of my program; (2) I'd like my program to improve in this area; (3) I'm not sure why this is important; and (4) I'd like more information on this. This questionnaire may be distributed to the intervention team members which, of course, include

FIGURE 13–4
Self-Assessment Form—Communication Skill Builders

Best Practices
Evaluating Early Childhood Special Education Programs
Self-Assessment Form

Completed by _____ Date _____

Component 1: Curriculum Programming

This is an important part of my program. *I'd like my program to improve in this area.* *I'm not sure why this is important.* *I'd like more information on this.* *

Child-Centered Assessments

☐ ☐ ☐ ☐ Do assessments consider the child's:
- needs in the current environment?
- current level of functioning?
- potential needs in future environments?

Curriculum Content

☐ ☐ ☐ ☐ Are skills chosen for training:
- useful for the child now?
- appropriate for the child's developmental age?
- teachable during various activities?
- intended to increase the child's ability to interact with people and things?
- taught during times in which using the skill is appropriate and makes sense?

☐ ☐ ☐ ☐ Are goals and objectives embedded into both naturally occurring daily activities and planned activities?

IEPs and IFSPs

☐ ☐ ☐ ☐ Do the IEPs and IFSPs you write—
1. Reflect family concerns, strengths, and needs?
2. Set objectives based on an analysis of the child assessments and the ecological inventory?
3. Identify training needs that are:
   - useful?
   - immediately applicable?
   - appropriate to the child?
   - appropriate to the family?
4. Allow the child to join in an activity even though unable to perform the skills without help?

Component 2: Organization of the Learning Environment

This is an important part of my program. *I'd like my program to improve in this area.* *I'm not sure why this is important.* *I'd like more information on this.*

Settings

☐ ☐ ☐ ☐ Are settings based upon the individual needs of the child and family?

☐ ☐ ☐ ☐ Settings should be flexible, because those needs change over time. Are yours?

☐ ☐ ☐ ☐ Is your use of space efficient and safe? Do you have:
- clearly posted general safety guidelines?
- clearly delineated areas (listening/reading area, academic area, art area ...)?
- adequate space to move about?
- appropriate modifications in place (door closed to reduce noise, adequate lighting, carpeted area)?

Organization of Instruction

☐ ☐ ☐ ☐ Does the schedule:
- assign staff responsibilities?
- assign children to activities and classroom areas?
- allow adequate time for each activity?
- allow the use of appropriate equipment and materials?

☐ ☐ ☐ ☐ Are activities organized to:
- reflect the educational needs of each child?
- address appropriate educational objectives throughout the day?
- provide a balance of 1-to-1, small-group, and large-group instruction?
- promote integration with typical peers?

☐ ☐ ☐ ☐ Are activities:
- appropriate to the needs of the child and family?
- useful to the child?
- making use of naturally occurring cues?

*The responses that may be checked are: (1) This is an important part of my program; (2) I'd like to improve in this area; (3) I'm not sure why this is important; and (4) I'd like more information on this.

FIGURE 13–4
continued

This is an important part of my program.	I'd like my program to improve in this area.	I'm not sure why this is important.	I'd like more information on this.	
☐	☐	☐	☐	**Are activities and materials within the settings:** • challenging but not too difficult? • encouraging child responses? • encouraging social interactions at home and school? • using appropriate adaptive equipment?
☐	☐	☐	☐	**Are some materials accessible, so the child can explore independently? Are other materials hard to reach, so the child has to request them?**

Monitoring Child Progress

☐	☐	☐	☐	**Are procedures for collecting data clearly understood?**
☐	☐	☐	☐	**Are data analyzed on a regular basis?**
☐	☐	☐	☐	**Is progress reported to the family on a regular basis?**
☐	☐	☐	☐	**After the data are analyzed, are changes made by team consensus?**

Component 3: Social Skills

Assessing Social Skills

☐	☐	☐	☐	**Do assessments take place in home and/or preschool settings, such as at play or at meals?**
☐	☐	☐	☐	**Do you use scales that measure functional social interaction, such as:** • the *Maternal Behavior Rating Scale*? • the *SCIP Checklist*? • one designed by preschool staff?
☐	☐	☐	☐	**Do your assessments determine the:** • frequency (how often) of social interactions? • quality (positive/negative) of social interactions? • appropriateness (to the situation) of social interactions?
☐	☐	☐	☐	**Do your assessments analyze the level of continued interactions between children and/or between children and adults?**

This is an important part of my program.	I'd like my program to improve in this area.	I'm not sure why this is important.	I'd like more information on this.	

Training Social Skills

☐	☐	☐	☐	**Are the social skills you target for training:** • based upon results of child-centered assessments done within natural settings? • skills the child needs in the current environment and/or in future environments?
☐	☐	☐	☐	**Are your training activities:** • done during naturally occurring times throughout the day? (Are they done during wake up, at meals, when getting ready to go outside, when saying hello or goodbye, and when the child needs assistance?) • appropriate to the child's chronological age? (Do infants interact mostly with adults? Do toddlers interact more with other children?) • encouraging generalization of skills by providing a variety of interactions with different people? (For infants, this may include parents, aunts, uncles, siblings, grandparents, baby sitters. Toddlers might also interact with other toddlers and nonrelatives.) • designed to encourage continued interactions between the child and others? (Do they encourage the parents and the child to play together? Do they encourage modeling by parents and teachers, and tutoring by peers? Is the environment structured to encourage interactions?)

Arranging for Interaction

☐	☐	☐	☐	**Are materials, activities, and space arranged to encourage social interactions between the child and others, both children and adults?**
☐	☐	☐	☐	**Is physical space arranged so that the child is near others?**
☐	☐	☐	☐	**Do materials and activities encourage interactions between children? Are materials arranged so that several children can play together with them?**

FIGURE 13-4

Component 4: Using Support Services

Using Support Services

☐ ☐ ☐ ☐ Does your use and coordination of support services take into account:
- the family's needs (as identified in the IFSP)?
- the child's needs (as identified in the IEP or IFSP)?
- the teacher's skill level?
- the specialists' knowledge?
- the team model (multidisciplinary, inter-disciplinary, or transdisciplinary)?

Using Support Services—Within the Preschool/Home-Based Program

☐ ☐ ☐ ☐ Do the instructional goals reflect the child's needs across all disciplines?

☐ ☐ ☐ ☐ Are specialists' recommendations incorporated within the child's daily routine, such as those of the:
- physical therapist (crawling to a snack)?
- vision therapist (object location—locating a chair)?
- nutritionist (orange juice for vitamin C)?

☐ ☐ ☐ ☐ Do parents, teachers, and specialists share information?

☐ ☐ ☐ ☐ Do the specialists and the preschool teacher share information in order to expand their own learning?

☐ ☐ ☐ ☐ Do activities promote generalization of skills?

Using Support Services— Among Agencies

☐ ☐ ☐ ☐ Do you use support services from many different agencies, such as the:
- child's preschool?
- Department of Health?
- Department of Human Services?
- hospital?
- elementary school?
- university speech and hearing services department?

☐ ☐ ☐ ☐ To coordinate services among agencies, do you:
- identify a case manager from the "lead" agency?
- encourage case managers to gather the information that helps them identify services appropriate for the child and family?
- share information with the family so the family can make decisions about the child's program?
- locate, obtain, and use community resources according to the needs of the individual child and family?

Component 5: Family Involvement

Family Assessment

☐ ☐ ☐ ☐ Are your family assessments individualized? Do they reflect family priorities?

☐ ☐ ☐ ☐ To achieve that, do you use:
- direct assessments (such as the *Family Needs Survey* [Bailey and Simeonsson] or the *Family Needs Scale* [Dunst, Trivette, and Deal])?
- reports from parents?
- professional observations?
- assessment?
- setting goals (via the IFSP)?
- intervention?
- program evaluation?

Family-Professional Partnership

☐ ☐ ☐ ☐ Do professionals work with the family, so that family members become partners in making decisions? Do families know about:
- their child's disabilities?
- how to solve problems?
- how to become effective advocates?
- relevant laws and their own rights?
- available community resources (such as day care, preschools, respite care . . .)?

FIGURE 13–4
continued

This is an important part of my program.	I'd like my program to improve in this area.	I'm not sure why this is important.	I'd like more information on this.	Communication Strategies
☐	☐	☐	☐	**Does the case manager make sure that the family and the service personnel (such as the social worker and the physician) communicate with each other?**
☐	☐	☐	☐	**Does the case manager use progress notes and other written messages, personal contact, and telephone calls to keep communication channels open?**

Component 6: Transition

Transition Planning

☐ ☐ ☐ ☐ **When planning to move the child to a new setting, do you:**

1. Select a transition coordinator from each setting?
2. Set a general timeline for transition?
3. Convene a family meeting to:
   - determine transition needs for child, family, and staff in the current setting?
   - develop and write transition goals for the current setting?
   - identify options for placement?
   - obtain the parents' consent to release the child's name to the future program?
4. Arrange for family and staff to visit and evaluate possible future programs?
5. Convene a family meeting to:
   - determine transition needs for child, family, and staff in the future setting?
   - develop and write transition goals for the future setting?
   - determine placement?
6. Update the child's file and send it to the next program staff?
7. Have parents and both staffs evaluate transition procedures?

This is an important part of my program.	I'd like my program to improve in this area.	I'm not sure why this is important.	I'd like more information on this.	Transition from Home or Other "Noneducational" Setting
☐	☐	☐	☐	**To build interagency cooperation and communication, do you:** • try to coordinate services with agencies that screen and serve children? • identify a case manager(s) or transition coordinator? • organize a referral system and share records and information between agencies? • begin the transition process?

Transition Between Programs

☐ ☐ ☐ ☐ **When you prepare to move the child to a new setting, do you organize a transdisciplinary team that includes various members, such as:**
- family members?
- the baby sitter?
- the transition coordinator?
- the current teacher?
- the future teacher?

☐ ☐ ☐ ☐ **Do assessments and curricula in current and future programs focus upon the current and future needs of the child and the family?**

Is the child's individual transition plan:
- part of the IEP or IFSP?
- written and implemented by the transition team?

☐ ☐ ☐ ☐ **Do you have a strategy for follow-up and evaluation to assess the success of the transition?**

☐ ☐ ☐ ☐ **Do you keep communication lines open through personal contact, telephone calls, and/or written messages, in case problems arise?**

Communication Skill Builders, Inc.
3830 E. Bellevue/P.O. Box 42050
Tucson, Arizona 85733
(602) 323-7500

Item #8055

ISBN 0-88450-379-8
Catalog No. 7749
Printed in the U.S.A.

Source: From *Best Practices: Evaluating Early Childhood Special Education Programs.* Copyright © 1991 by Communication Skill Builders, a Harcourt Health Sciences Company. Reproduced by permission. All rights reserved.

the family. Each team member should complete the questionnaire and then discuss his or her evaluation responses in a team meeting. Areas of concern, or where there are inconsistent responses, would then be examined more critically to determine if changes need to be made or why these discrepancies exist.

Linking Intervention and Program Evaluation

Bricker (1986) suggested a three-level framework (shown in Figure 13–5) which can provide a useful system for measuring child/family change and program impact. This system offers a comprehensive approach to link assessment, intervention, and evaluation. The three levels offer a plan for evaluating program impact based on information from specific child data collection systems to overall program impact. Using this system provides both formative and summative evaluation data.

Measuring Progress Toward Weekly Training Targets

The first level is devising specific data collection formats which must be related to the child's objectives. Data might be collected on social interactions, language, and so on. Data collection procedures for monitoring child progress would include ongoing performance data (e.g., frequency, percentage, rate, duration) and might be collected by trial, probes, or observational samples. Permanent product samples or anecdotal recording or diaries might also be used. This type of data collection is discussed at length in Chapter 11.

The data collection on progress can be accomplished at the same time as the instructional program. The interventionist can record the behavior and teach a new response at the same time. The use of a grid format to record data has been suggested by Bricker (1986). This grid allows the teacher to target several different skills for each child across activity groups. The antecedent, response, and consequence written on the data grids are taken from the child's individual program plan.

Some form of weekly information should be collected and then systematically compared with the data collected each week. The data could be plotted on individual graphs to show percent, proportion, frequency, or rate of change over time. Program personnel should choose a simple and useful way to examine and display the weekly data to monitor progress and make sound educational decisions. Figure 13–6 provides an example of a form for monitoring the progress of three children on several targets. An activity is targeted with the individual objectives listed in six major domains. The number of trials or opportunities can be indicated at the bottom of each box. The children's progress can be compared over time based on the objectives that are reached and the number of trials required for achieving the skill.

Measuring Progress Toward Long-Range Goals and Training Objectives

At the second level, data are collected on child and family progress toward long-range goals and objectives. These data need to be analyzed in terms of total or subgroup scores if they are to be used in program evaluation. Bricker (1986) suggested published instruments with norms or reliability and validity information as being the most useful. These instruments should be the same ones used during the initial assessment when the child entered the program and when developing the IEP and IFSP. In addition, developmental checklists or behavior rating scales might also be used to provide information on child progress.

The predicted progress of each child and the group as a whole can be compared with actual progress by analyzing the progress toward long-range goals. Pre-test data can be compared with

FIGURE 13–5
Three-level Measurement Framework for Monitoring Weekly, Quarterly, and Annual Child Progress

---

Level One Activities—Weekly Child Progress

Purpose: Monitor and evaluate child progress toward prioritized IEP/IFSP goals and objectives.

Procedure: Collect weekly data.

Level Two Activities—Quarterly Child Progress

Purpose: Monitor and evaluate child progress toward prioritized IEP/IFSP goals and objectives, global curricular goals, and overall development.

Procedure: Administer quarterly program-relevant, criterion-referenced test.

Level Three Activities—Annual Child Progress

Purpose: Evaluate general program effect.

Procedure: Administer pre- and poststandardized or criterion-referenced test.

Source: From *An activity-based approach to intervention* (2nd ed., p. 152), by D. Bricker, K. Pretti-Frontezak, and N. McComas, 1998, Baltimore: Brookes. Copyright 1998 by Paul H. Brookes Publishing. Adapted with permission.

post-test data. Another method might be to establish timelines for goal attainment for the family and child and then compare the actual progress with these expectations. The outcome data would be used to determine program effectiveness as well as to modify goals and expected rate of attainment as appropriate.

Measuring Progress Toward Program Goals

The third and final level is assessment of progress toward program goals which can be used to evaluate child/family change but is usually more useful for assessing the total impact of the program on the children. Norm-referenced or criterion-based tests generally are most desirable. However, the interventionist should take into consideration the problems of using such tests in determining progress toward specific

program objectives (Chapters 9 and 10). The measure chosen should be sensitive enough to detect change in children's performance and should be compatible with the program philosophy and goals.

Published Assessment-Intervention-Evaluation Systems

The AEPS *System*. Bricker and Cripe (1992) proposed a system for linking intervention and evaluation activities in early intervention. The *Assessment, Evaluation and Programming System* (AEPS) *for Infants and Children* (Bricker, Gentry, & Bailey, 1992) is the basis for intervention in this model. The information obtained during the assessment phase for developing IEPs and IFSPs guides the selection of intervention content and strategies. The linked system described previously is illustrated in Figure 13–7.

FIGURE 13-6
Child Progress Monitoring Form for Use with Several Children and Several Targets

Activity: Cars   Date: Feb. 20, 1991   Recorder: Ms. Jones

Activity description:
1. Lean a board against a cupboard, box, or wall.
2. Use masking tape to make tracks or "lanes" on it.
3. Let small car roll up and down the hill.
4. Put blocks on board as barriers.

Materials needed: board, tape, cars, blocks

Training Targets by Domain

Children	Fine motor	Gross motor	Self-care	Cognitive	Social communication	Social
Joe	Reaches for car; grasps car 1 2 3 4 5	Stands with support 1 2 3 4 5	N/A	Visually tracks movement of car 1 2 3 4 5	Vocalizes; auditory attention 1 2 3 4 5	Plays near peers 1 2 3 4 5
Sally	Reaches, holds, grasps, releases car, transfers from hand to hand 1 2 3 4 5	Stands unsupported 1 2 3 4 5	N/A	Plays functionally with car 1 2 3 4 5	Labels car; makes noise for car 1 2 3 4 5	Observes peers; imitates peers 1 2 3 4 5
Bart	Maneuvers car along a course; avoids barriers 1 2 3 4 5	Stoops and recovers; stands and leans, maintaining balance 1 2 3 4 5	N/A	Drives car on track, around barriers; concept of up and down, stop and go 1 2 3 4 5	Two-word utterance (e.g., "car go") 1 2 3 4 5	Interacts with peers; initiates and/or responds 1 2 3 4 5

Source: From Bricker, D., and Cripe, J. W. (1992). *An activity-based approach to early intervention* (p. 155). Baltimore: Paul H. Brookes Publishing Co. Used with permission.

The first box is the assessment component that provides the information for developing the child's IEP and IFSP and forms the roots or foundation of the tree. The second box is the IEP and IFSP which outline the intervention content by providing the goals and objectives for the child and family. The actual intervention is the third box. Bricker and Cripe (1992) suggested an activity-based approach to guide children's goals and objectives. Evaluation is the final step that provides systematic feedback on program effects. Because the initial assessment is used to develop the IEP/IFSP and then forms the content of the intervention, it is extremely important that initial and follow-up assessments provide interventionists and caregivers with an accurate and comprehensive profile of the child. The link among assessment, goal development, intervention, and evaluation is a cyclical process and should continue as shown in Figure 13–7. It is recommended that curriculum-based assessments be used to develop these intervention plans (Notari, Slentz, & Bricker, 1991).

The AEPS covers six curricular areas: fine motor, gross motor, self-care, cognitive, social-communicative, and social. The particular sets of skills or behaviors in each domain are sequenced developmentally and are divided into strands, which organize related groups of behaviors under a common category. Items on the AEPS are sequenced to facilitate the assessment of a child's ability to perform a particular skill within a developmental sequence. Each strand contains a series of test items called goals and objectives. Based on a child's abilities and needs, the AEPS goals can be used to develop annual goals on a child's IEP and IFSP. The goals are arranged in hierarchical skill sequence.

Three methods of data collection are allowed, but the preferred method is observation. The examiner is able to view the topography or the form of the behavior, when and how frequently the behavior occurs, and the environmental events that may influence the infant's or child's performance. If the examiner does not have the

FIGURE 13–7
Illustration of a Linked Systems Framework

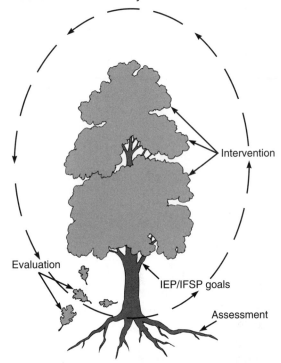

Source: From *An activity-based approach to intervention* (2nd ed., p. 25), by D. Bricker, K. Pretti-Frontczak, and N. McComas, 1998, Baltimore: Brookes. Copyright 1998 by Paul H. Brookes Publishing. Reprinted with permission.

opportunity to observe the behavior during classroom activities, then a situation may be created to elicit the behavior. Sources of reported information from the examiner, family, therapists, or written documentation from medical reports may also be used for data collection.

Work Sampling System. Meisels (1993) developed a performance assessment system for use in early childhood and early elementary grades called the Work Sampling System. This system contains three components: (1) developmental checklists, (2) portfolios, and (3) summary reports (Meisels, 1993). The checklists are completed by teachers based on their observations and knowledge of the child and are not designed to be used as tests. The portfolios include "core" items and "other" items. The core items are products of the child's work that are collected in several areas at least three times per year. The "other" items that are collected vary by child and date of collection. Photographs of achievements are recommended for children's key activities which do not result in permanent products (Poster, Jons, Abrams, & Freund, 1994). Video or audio recordings also can be used. The summary reports are narratives completed by the teacher based on observations that describe the child's performance in each domain. These summary reports are conducted three times per year.

Although performance assessments through direct observation in naturalistic contexts have been used a great deal in early childhood special education, the use of portfolio assessments and procedures such as the Work Sampling System (Meisels, 1993) remains relatively unstudied (Wolery, 1996). It has been suggested that this question is best answered when notions of validity are framed from the relationship between curricular expectations and the utility of the knowledge acquired. This can only be accomplished when teachers use a multitude of sources for evidence or when the indicators of knowledge existing in the portfolio are linked to the construct or intent of the unit around which the portfolio is developed (Wolery, 1996). Serious consideration also needs to be given to how the portfolios are to be used. Because they are essentially a "within student" assessment (i.e., a child's performance is sequentially developed and compared to himself), can accurate "between student" and eventually "between school" comparisons be made (Scarpati & Silver, 1999)?

Summary

Many factors complicate program evaluation practices in early intervention and early childhood special education, including the great diversity of response repertoires of children being served, the cultural diversity of families, competing demands for limited resources, ambiguities in some programs about goals service models, shortages of valid and reliable measures of program impact, and ethical and logistic constraints on evaluation designs (Snyder and Sheehan, 1996). The recommended practices outlined in this chapter can help service providers, evaluators, and families plan and conduct the best evaluation possible. An effective evaluation plan must consider information from the perspectives of input, process, and outcome (Johnson & LaMontagne, 1994). In the input stage, the needs of the consumers are assessed and a program to address the identified needs is developed. The process stage monitors and refines the program evaluation as it is being implemented. The last stage in the evaluation process is the outcome phase, which determines the impact of the program on consumers. A comprehensive evaluation plan can greatly enhance the ability to meet the needs of infants, toddlers, and preschoolers with disabilities and their families, help establish accountability, and provide data to convince policymakers of the need for and benefits of early intervention. Program evaluation is an integral aspect of all early intervention programs.

Program evaluation is not a simple procedure that occurs all at once. Ongoing assessment is a crucial part of program evaluation and is at the heart of effective decision making (Peterson, 1987).

References

Abidin, R. R. (1983). *Parenting Stress Index*. Charlottesville, VA: Pediatric Psychology Press.

Anastasiow, N. J. (1981). Early childhood education for the handicapped in the 1980s: Recommendations. *Exceptional Children, 47*, 276–284.

Bagnato, S. J., Neisworth, J. T., & Munson, S. M. (1989). *Linking developmental assessment and early intervention: Curriculum-based prescriptions* (2nd ed.) Rockville, MD: Aspen.

Benner, S. M. (1992). *Assessing young children with special needs: An ecological perspective*. New York: Longman.

Borg, W. R., & Gall, M. D. (1983). *Educational research*. New York: Longman.

Bricker, D. D. (1986). *Early education of at-risk and handicapped infants, toddlers, and preschool children*, Glenview, IL: Scott, Foresman.

Bricker, D., & Cripe, J. J. W. (1992). *An activity-based approach to early intervention*. Baltimore: Brookes.

Bricker, D., Gentry, D., & Bailey, E. J. (1992). AEPS Test. In D. Bricker (Ed.), *Assessment, Evaluation, and Programming System (AEPS) for Infants and Children: Vol. 1. AEPS measurement for birth to three years.* Baltimore: Brookes.

Bricker, D., Janko, S., Cripe, J., Bailey, E., & Kaminski, R. (1989, August). *Evaluation and programming system: For infants and young children.* Eugene: University of Oregon.

Bricker, D. D., & Littman, D. (1982). Intervention and evaluation: The inseparable mix. *Topics in Early Childhood Special Education, 1*(4), 23–33.

Caldwell, B. M. (1977). Evaluating program effectiveness. In B. M. Caldwell & D. J. Stedman (Eds.), *Infant education: A guide for helping handicapped children in the first three years.* New York: Walker.

Casto, G. (1988). Research and program evaluation in early childhood special education. In S. L. Odom and M. B. Karnes (Eds.), *Early intervention for infants and children with handicaps: An empirical base.* Baltimore: Brookes.

Cohen, L. G., & Spenciner, L. J. (1994). *Assessment of young children.* Reading, MA: Addison Wesley Longman.

DeStefano, D. M., Howe, A. G., Horn, E. M., & Smith, B. A. (1991). *Best practices: Evaluating early childhood special education programs.* Tucson, AZ: Communication Skill Builders.

Dunst, C. J., Trivette, C. M., & Deal, A. G. (Eds.) (1994). *Supporting and strengthening families: Methods, strategies and practices.* Cambridge, MA: Brookline Books.

Fitz-Gibbon, C. T., & Morris, L. L. (1987). *How to design a program evaluation.* Beverly Hills, CA: Sage.

George, M. P., George, N. L., & Grosenick, J. K. (1990). Features of program evaluation in special education. *Remedial and Special Education, 11,* 23–30.

Harrison, P. J. (1995). Evaluating programs. In M. J. Hanson & E. W. Lynch (Eds.), *Early intervention: Implementing child and family services for infants and toddlers who are at risk or disabled* (pp. 288–322). Austin, TX: PRO-ED.

Johnson, L. J. (1988). Program evaluation: The key to quality programming. In J. B. Jordan, J. J. Gallagher, P. L. Hutinger, & M. B. Karnes (Eds.), *Early childhood special education: Birth to three.* Reston, VA: The ERIC Clearinghouse on Handicapped and Gifted Children, The Council for Exceptional Children.

Johnson, L. J., & LaMontagne, M. J. (1994). Program evaluation: The key to quality programming. In L. J. Johnson, et al. (Eds.), *Meeting early intervention challenges: Issues from birth to three* (2nd ed., pp. 186–216). Baltimore: Brookes.

Joint Committee on Standards for Educational Evaluation. (1994). *The Program Evaluation Standards: How to assess evaluations of educational programs.* Thousand Oaks, CA: Sage.

LaMontagne, M. J., & Russell, G. W. (1998). Informal and formal assessment. In L. J. Johnson, M. J. LaMontagne, P. M. Elgas, & A. M. Bauer (Eds.), *Early childhood education: Blending theory, blending practice* (pp. 201–230). Baltimore: Brookes.

Linder, T. W. (1983). *Early childhood special education: Program development and administration.* Baltimore: Brookes.

McGonigel, M. (1988). *Guidelines for family-centered research.* Washington, DC: Association for the Care of Children's Health.

Meisels, S. (1993). Remaking classroom assessment with the Work Sampling System. *Young Children, 49,* 34–40.

Miles, M. B., & Huberman, A. M. (1984). Drawing valid meaning from qualitative data: Toward shared craft. *Educational Researcher, 13,* 20–30.

Murphy, D., & Lee, I. (1991). *Family-Centered Program Rating Scale: User's manual.* Lawrence, KS: Beach Center on Families and Disability, University of Kansas.

Notari, A., Slentz, K., & Bricker, D. (1991). Assessment-curriculum systems for early childhood/special education. In D. Mitchell & R. Brown (Eds.), *Early intervention studies for young children with special needs* (pp. 160–205). London: Chapman & Hall.

Olson, D. H., McCubbin, H. I., Barnes, H., Larsen, A., Muxen, M., & Wilson, M. (1982). *Family inventories.* St. Paul: University of Minnesota.

Patton, M. Q. (1980). *Qualitative evaluation methods.* Beverly Hills, CA: Sage.

Peterson, N. L. (1987). *Early intervention for handicapped and at-risk children: An introduction to early childhood–special education* (pp. 275–326). Denver: Love.

Popham, W. J. (1988). *Educational evaluation* (2nd ed.). Upper Saddle River, NJ: Prentice Hall.

Poster, M., Johns, S., Abrams, J., & Freund, C. (1994). The work sampling system implementation at Carnegie Mellon University Child Care Center: Year one reflections. *Pittsburgh Association for the Education of Young Children Newsletter.*

Scarpati, S., & Silver, P. G. (1999). Readiness for academic achievement in preschool children. In E. Vazquez Nuttall, I. Romero, & J. Kalesnik (Eds.), *Assessing and screening preschoolers: Psychological and educational dimensions* (pp. 262–280). Needham Heights, MA: Allyn & Bacon.

Scriven, M. (1974). Evaluation perspectives and procedures. In W. J. Popham (Ed.), *Evaluation in education: Current applications* (pp. 1–93). Berkeley, CA: McCutchan.

Sechrest, L., & Figueredo, A. J. (1993). Program evaluation. *Annual Review of Psychology, 44,* 645–674.

Snyder, S., & Sheehan, R. (1996). Program evaluation. In S. L. Odom & M. E. McLean (Eds.), *Early intervention/early childhood special education: Recommended practices* (pp. 359–378). Austin, TX: PRO-ED.

Stufflebeam, D. L. (1971). The relevance of the CIPP evaluation model for educational accountability. *Journal of Research and Development in Education, 5*(1), 19–23.

Stufflebeam, D. L. (1974). Alternative approaches to educational evaluation: A self-study guide for educators. In W. J. Popham (Ed.), *Evaluation in education: Current applications* (pp. 95–143). Berkeley, CA: McCutchan.

Takanishi, R., & Feshbach, N. D. (1982). Early childhood special education programs, evaluation, and social policies. *Topics in Early Childhood Special Education,* 1, 1–9.

Udinsky, F. F., Osterlind, S. J., & Lynch, S. W. (1981). *Evaluation resource handbook: Gathering, analyzing, reporting data.* San Diego: EDITS.

Wolery, M. (Ed.). (1994). Methodological issues and advances [Special issue]. *Topics in Early Childhood Special Education,* 14.

Wolery, M. (1996). Monitoring child progress. In M. McLean, D. B. Bailey, & M. Wolery (Eds.), *Assessing infants and preschoolers with special needs,* (2nd ed., pp. 519–560). Upper Saddle River, NJ: Merrill/Prentice Hall.

Wolery, M., & Bailey, D. B. (1984). Alternatives to impact evaluations: Suggestions for program evaluation in early intervention. *Journal of the Division for Early Childhood,* 9(1), 27–37.

Assessment Within Domains

14

Assessment of Cognitive Development

What Is Cognition?

Cognition has been defined as the processes by which sensory input is transformed, reduced, elaborated, stored, recovered and used (Neisser, 1967). In the infant, cognition is seen as sensori-motor intelligence. Sensorimotor intelligence is the integration and refinement of sensory and motor behaviors to produce adaptive responses to the environment in the child's first 2 years. Sensorimotor intelligence enables the child to solve problems through the integration of perception, postural adjustments, and movement. These sensorimotor skills begin with the simplest reflexive behaviors and provide the basis for acquiring increasingly more complex mental behaviors as children respond and adapt to sensory information through motoric interactions with the environment (Langley, 1989); sensorimotor skills are thought to be precursors to basic thinking and conceptual development.

Studies of infant perception, which is defined as the ability to learn or receive environmental information by using the senses of sight, hearing, smell, or touch, indicate that the senses are the starting point for the infant's expanding understanding of the world (Lockman, 1983). Normal infants experience a steady refinement of their perceptual and cognitive capabilities through early childhood (Yarrow, Rubenstein, & Pedersen, 1975). The heart of cognitive development is the infant's ability to organize and make sense of the environment to which she is exposed. The attainment of maximum cognitive skills requires that the child take advantage of basic sensory input as she explores her environment. In order for the child to attain cognitive skills, three basic psychological processes need to be operating: attention, perception, and memory.

Cognitive development has been described as the progressive change in internal mental processes, such as thinking, reasoning, and remembering, or as the ability to function adaptively in the world by receiving information from the environment, understanding the meaning of this information, and using it to plan appropriate actions (Dunst, 1981; Piaget, 1952; Raver, 1991). The term "cognition" has traditionally been used to refer to symbolic and representational thought processes that do not necessarily depend on immediate perceptual input (Rossetti, 1990). Cognitive development, intelligence and the ability to learn are all related concepts. Definitions of intelligence have three basic components in common: (1) the capacity to learn; (2) the sum total of knowledge an individual has acquired; and (3) the ability to adjust to various environments, particularly new situations (Robinson & Robinson, 1976). Experts have agreed on three behavioral descriptions for cognition or intelligence: abstract thinking or reasoning, the capacity to acquire knowledge, and problem-solving ability (Sattler, 1990).

The cognitive domain comprises a multitude of skills and abilities which are associated with intelligence. These skills are related to attention, discrimination, imitation, spatial relationships, temporal relationships, causality, reasoning, classification, sorting, sequencing, and problem solving (Benner, 1992). The feature that most distinguishes the cognitive competencies of the developing child from those of older children and adults is the close association between children's activity and their cognitive capabilities (Dunst, Mahoney, & Buchan, 1996). Older children engage in cognitive behaviors primarily through the use of symbolic rule systems and verbal mediators; that is, cognitive behaviors such as problem solving, reasoning, and judgment are carried out as mental operations that can be conducted independently of actual experiences (Dunst, Mahoney, & Buchan, 1996). Cognitive behavior in young children is intricately tied to their interactions with people and objects. The kinds of activities that children engage in while interacting with objects and people provide insight into their understanding and reasoning (Dunst, Mahoney, & Buchan, 1996). Early cognitive development is expressed by skills in communication, social, and motor development

(Bayley, 1969; Dunst, 1981). For example, children's repeated use of behaviors such as throwing and banging with a variety of objects and materials suggests that their interest in and understanding of their world is closely tied to the kinds of actions they perform with different objects, materials, and people. Children learn about objects and people in terms of the behavior they perform in interactions with these objects and people. Children's behaviors reflect their efforts to make sense of the world about them.

Cognition is an area of development that is particularly difficult to isolate from other domains in assessment. Although it can be conceptualized as separate from other domains, such as motor or language functioning, the outward manifestation of cognition usually necessitates motor or language output. Cognition is expressed through motor and language actions and behaviors that provide evidence of cognitive understanding. The separation of motor and language is critical to the assessment process.

Tests for very young children, which purport to measure ability, intelligence, mental developmental age, and preacademic skills, are all considered measures of cognition. They are often based on the assumption that motor skills or language skills reflect cognitive ability. Cognition is much broader than the preacademic skills found on developmental instruments. Cognition cannot be directly observed or measured but is inferred from the behavior of an individual within a specified context. Changes in behavior in similar contexts over time are assumed to reflect changes in cognitive functioning or structuring (Rossetti, 1990). The theories of cognitive development provide the bases for assessment instruments.

Theories of Cognitive Development

The basic perspectives regarding the cognitive development of young children are the models of developmental theory, behavioral/functional theory, information processing, social learning, and cognitive stages theory. Each of these theories has contributed to understanding the process of cognitive development. They have become the basis for assessment instruments, been used to describe children's current developmental skills, and laid the foundation for intervention planning. In 1997, the publication of the revised edition of *Developmentally Appropriate Practice in Early Childhood Programs* by Bredekamp and Copple emphasized the current understanding of cognitive development in young children by early childhood educators as being grounded in three broad theoretical perspectives: Piaget's theory describing these years as preoperational (1952); Vygotsky's socio-cultural theory (1978a); and the information-processing theorists studying short-term and long-term memory ability and use of cognitive strategies in young children (Siegler, 1983; Seifert, 1993). Therefore, these theories are presented in this section, but emphasis is given to theories of information processing, social learning, and cognitive stages.

Developmental Theory

The developmental or maturational theory is structured around the child's natural patterns of growth and development. Gesell and colleagues at the Yale Clinic for Child Development postulated that development and growth were biologically predetermined (McCormick, 1996). Maturation of the nervous system governs a child's physical, psychological, cognitive, and social development. The child's capabilities, behaviors, and cognitive development change as she matures. Qualitative change occurs at certain times as the young child ages (McCormick, 1996).

Developmentalists describe, explain, and predict how individuals at different stages typically think, feel, and behave (Horowitz, 1990). Universal norms suggest that development unfolds through a series of sequences or patterns and provide estimates for when certain levels of development will be reached. Sequences and rates of development of universal norms are often summarized into developmental charts. Developmental data on normal infants and children were used by Gesell (1925) and Knobloch and Pasamanick (1974) to identify motor, language, adaptive, and personal-social milestones or universal norms. Children who are unable to perform such tasks at certain developmental ages are considered developmentally delayed (Benner, 1992).

Behavioral or Functional Theory

The behaviorist or functional theory has an underlying foundation that all behavior is learned. The behaviorist model incorporates both classical conditioning, in which the child has no control over her response, and instrumental conditioning, in which the child's response to stimuli determines consequences. Skinner's explanation of learning is based on the premise that the consequences of behavior determine the probability that the behavior will occur again (Lefrancois, 1995). In this model, living organisms repeat behavior that is satisfying and avoid behavior that is not. The functional model is derived from the notion that the most critical and functional behaviors for the developing child are those that produce pleasant, positive interactions with people, objects, and environments (McCormick, 1996). The most important principle associated with this approach is reinforcement, which is an event that follows a response and changes the probability of whether a response will occur again. Behaviorists believe that behavior is controlled by stimuli and that development progresses as behaviors are modified to the demands of stimuli. The child must be observed carefully to determine what she is doing, what conditions trigger certain responses, and how the child's behavior can be

changed or modified through changes in the learning environment. This theory is discussed further in Chapter 12.

Information-Processing Theory

Information-processing models of cognitive development are grounded in the functioning of the psychological processes of perception, attention, and memory. This approach concentrates on the manner in which a child receives, interprets, and transmits information.

Perception involves the ability to make sense of information provided to the brain from the sense organs for seeing, tasting, touching, hearing, smelling, and physical movement of one's body. Everyone processes and interprets sensory information differently. Therefore, each person experiences unique reactions to the environment based on varying perceptions (Gibson & Spelke, 1983). Knowledge about early perceptual abilities is used to develop environments that enhance learning. Infants are born with perceptual abilities that allow them to begin learning immediately. These abilities allow children to learn from active exploration of their environment.

For children to learn, they must be able to focus their attention on the most relevant information and learn to ignore less relevant information (Dunlap, 1997). This ability to focus is known as selective attention. Young children typically have difficulty focusing on details, are easily distracted, and do not engage in one activity for long periods of time (Stodolsky, 1974). As children mature, however, they gradually become more purposeful in their activities. Attention becomes more sustained and planned during these years (Cocking & Copple, 1987), at least when their interest is engaged.

Memory is another important area related to cognitive development. The memory process involves the ability to store and retrieve information (Schneider & Pressley, 1989). Memory is complex and depends on the processes of attention and perception. Information that is perceived and remembered only momentarily is stored in short-term memory. Short-term memory storage lasts less than 60 seconds (Lipsitt, 1990). Information generally is not placed into short-term memory unless it is interesting or important and the individual is purposely attentive (Dunlap, 1997). Long-term memory may store information permanently and is limitless in capacity. Information is stored in long-term memory after being processed by short-term memory. Intent to remember is often aided by rehearsal (repetition). Presenting information repeatedly, providing rehearsal strategies, and encouraging rehearsals may help children to remember certain information (Dunlap, 1997). Young children have relatively poor recall of lists that are not embedded in meaningful contexts (Istomina, 1975; Murphy & Brown, 1975). Concreteness and egocentrism make children more likely to understand and remember relationships, concepts, and strategies acquired firsthand through meaningful experience (Bredekamp & Copple, 1997).

Information processing theorists look at developmental differences in cognitive performance in terms of children's changing abilities, such as attending to stimuli, holding information in short-term memory, storing it and retrieving it from long-term memory, and other aspects of processing information. Differences in capacity are related to the age of the child (Bredekamp & Copple, 1997).

Campione and Brown (1978) developed their theory of intelligence using two basic components: an architectural system (structural component) and an executive system (control component). The architectural system acts as a scaffold composed of capacity, durability or retention, and efficiency or speed of information encoded. The executive system operates as the learned components which include knowledge, schemes, control processes, and metacognition (Sattler, 1990). Schemes are used to describe the active construction of the rules of thinking

(McCormick, 1996). The mind is seen as a complex cognitive system such as a computer. Information processing explains decision making, knowing, and remembering as processes. Cognition becomes what the computer must know in order to produce a behavior.

Researchers have stated that the information processing models of intelligence have been greatly influenced by Vygotsky and Luria (Hoy & Gregg, 1994; McCormick, 1996). Vygotsky suggests that memory, attention, and conceptualizations are the products of the child's organization of object and social interaction (McCormick, 1996). Parents guide and mark or signal certain activities and objects for their child's attention and thus mediate their child's learning. Cognition develops through the child's internalization of social interactions and experiences (Hoy & Gregg, 1994). Although developmental constraints limit children's capacity to process information, appropriate adult guidance and support can strengthen children's processing skills.

The information processing approach links assessment directly with intervention (Lerner, Mardell-Czudnowski, & Goldenberg, 1987). Revealing the child's problem-solving strategies or styles of response may account for her failures and may be modifiable once they are identified. The emphasis here is not on what the child knows or can do but rather on how problems are approached and resolved. The analysis of testing and teaching tasks can indicate the child's preferred modes of functioning and where strengths and weaknesses in learning occur. Campione and Brown (1987) employed a test-train-retest model in which pre-test and post-test comparisons and the number of hints required to accomplish the task during training provide quantitative measures of cognitive development.

Social Learning

Soviet psychologists have also conceptualized cognitive development in a social context.

Vygotsky (1978b) contributed significant ideas about cognitive development in children. He suggests that memory, attention, and conceptualizations are the products of the child's organization of object and social interactions (McCormick, 1996). Vygotsky recognized that children learn within a social context and that the role of the significant adult is a critical element in guiding the learning. The adult serves as a mediator, assisting in making the environmental events meaningful to the child. An example of this may be a child sorting buttons by the basic colors of red, blue, green, and so on. When the child encounters some buttons that are shiny but not any one of these colors, the adult creates a new classification of "sparkly," and the child then puts all of these buttons together in a pile (Lerner, Lowenthal, & Egan, 1998). The adult mediates the situation, but the child solves the problem and makes the decision. The concept of mediated learning is important in early concept acquisition. Parents bring certain activities and objects to the child's attention. Cognition develops through the child's internalization of social interactions and experiences with others (Hoy & Gregg, 1994).

Another important aspect of Vygotsky's theories is known as the *zone of proximal development* (ZPD). This theory notes that a range of difficulty levels exists for any task. The lower end is a level that is very easy for the child, and the upper end is a level beyond the child's capacity. The ZPD refers to the midpoint and is the appropriate level for learning. This level provides a challenge but can be accomplished with the assistance of the adult in the environment. The role of the adult is to guide learning by finding the appropriate level for the child. A child who is learning to put on her coat is given assistance to put her arms in the coat and then to zip it up. The adult provides only the amount of guidance needed. The concept of a ZPD suggests that there is a zone that reflects the distance between the actual developmental level and the level of potential development. In other words, development occurs when a problem is presented that is just beyond the child's ability, and an adult or peer is able to mediate the experience to move the child to a new level of understanding (Anastasiow, 1986).

Social interaction plays a significant role in children's cognitive development (Bredekamp & Copple, 1997). Children construct their understanding of a concept by interacting with others. This process is known as social construction of knowledge (Shantz, 1975, 1982; Vygotsky, 1978a). Experiences and interactions with other people provide children with different points of view which challenge and begin to break down their egocentric perspectives (Bredekamp & Copple, 1997).

A social learning model was also proposed by Bandura (1978). He describes development as "reciprocal determinism," in which learning develops through the interaction of socialization, developmental status, environmental factors, and the child's motivation. In other words, the characteristics and properties of the environment in interaction with one another and with the child's thinking and judgment about her behavior account for the learning of new behavior and understanding of past and present behavior (Gage & Berliner, 1991).

Cognitive Stages Theory

Cognitive stages theory focuses on a child's progression to higher cognitive functions in sequential stages. The most comprehensive theory of cognitive development has been put forth by Jean Piaget (Umansky & Hooper, 1998). Piaget's theory of cognitive development laid the groundwork for much of our current understanding of infant cognition (Lerner, et al., 1998). He proposed that cognition is integrated into the overall functioning of humans. As children mature, the cognitive system changes and develops in an organized way in response to environmental stimuli. Piaget (1952, 1954, 1962) emphasized the sequential development of thinking that young children gradually acquire through concrete experiences. His theory emphasizes activities that will develop cognitive abilities, such as perception, discrimination, memory, concept formation, problem solving, and decision making.

According to Piaget, reasoning and problem solving develop through sequential stages. Movement from one stage to another results from environmental interactions characterized by assimilation and accommodation of the child's schemes, or understandings, of the world. *Assimilation* is the process by which children take into their models of thinking the awareness of aspects of the environment. Through the process of assimilation, children build a knowledge base by adding new information gained through experience. A child assimilates information from the environment to fit her own schemes or cognitive structures of the world.

As the child becomes aware that contradictions exist within her views of the world, disequilibrium occurs, and the child accommodates her thinking to alleviate the contradiction. In *accommodation*, children revise their internal schemata to fit their observations when confronted with something they cannot understand. Piaget proposed that disequilibration is a motivating process that drives an individual to make things fit or establish equilibrium. Through the process of accommodation, children integrate new information by reorganizing their current cognitive structure. The child focuses on the new features of the situation and changes the internal schemata or cognitive structure accordingly. Cognitive maturity and development are seen as a need to understand and fit the new with the old.

Piaget classified cognitive behaviors into four stages of development: sensorimotor, preoperational, concrete operational, and formal operational. Piagetian approaches to cognitive development attempt to measure qualitative differences in a child's reasoning rather than quantitative differences. Tests are constructed by age levels, with item clusters that attempt to measure multiple aspects of cognition such as seriation, conservation, number and spatial concepts, object permanence, deductive logic, classification and decentration. Piaget's cognitive stages from birth to 7 years are discussed in the next section. A summary of these beginning stages is provided in Table 14–1.

Sensorimotor Stage. The sensorimotor stage is the first of four major cognitive stages in Piaget's cognitive development theory. This stage focuses on infant cognitive development during the first 24 months of life and consists of six substages, each of which is characterized by significant cognitive events that provide the basis for adult thinking. Piaget believed that during the sensorimotor stage, infants use adaptive responses to the environment to develop the ability to engage in increasingly complex mental operations. The child begins to reflect on sensory information and selects a response from a number of alternatives. She can categorize many stimuli appropriately. The first five of these stages lay the foundation for the beginning of representational thought or the mental representation of objects and events. The sixth stage, with its full achievement of object permanence, marks the transition from sensorimotor "knowing" through patterns of action to mental knowledge and symbolic activity.

Substage 1 (0–1 Month). Infants in this stage are predominantly reflexive. They look at objects and people and hear sounds but do not relate the sounds to a particular person or thing. Most of their responses to the world are protective. Sudden loud sounds or the loss of support elicits a startle response. An infant withdraws her foot from a pinprick or closes her eyes to bright lights. Although infants at this stage have not learned to separate means from ends and do not understand that objects exist apart from them, external stimulation helps

TABLE 14–1
Piaget's Stages of Development from Birth to 7 Years

Stage	Ages	Description of Characteristics
Sensorimotor	Birth to 2 years	Children learn through sense and movement and by interacting with the physical environment. Primitive reflex activity progresses to repetitive activity, and later, to imitation. By moving, touching, and physically manipulating objects, the child learns about the properties of space, time, location, permanence, and causality. They develop the ability to imitate others and a sense of object permanence. Actions move from reflexive or automatic to purposeful.
Preoperational	2 to 7 years	During this period, children view the world only in direct relationship to themselves. Their thinking processes are generally concrete. Expressive language begins during this period and rapid progress is made in learning the names of objects and using speech to communicate ideas. The child masters an increasingly larger set of concepts. Learning is accomplished through imitation, symbolic play, drawings, mental mages, and verbal expression of events. Thinking is egocentric and often illogical.

their sensory and motor systems organize and get ready for learning (Wyly, 1997). These experiences provide the foundation for building more complex cognitive structures and prepare the child to become more directed in her actions.

Substage 2 (1–4 Months). Infants in this stage begin to coordinate sensory input with their motor actions. These sequences are called "primary circular reactions" because they are

limited to the infant's own body and are circular because they are usually repeated. An example of a primary circular reaction is a baby turning her head to sounds or repeatedly kicking, grasping, and releasing objects. In this stage, the infant gradually gains more voluntary control over her responses to the world. The infant's reflexive behavior leads to new experiences. For example, the infant discovers her thumb and assimilates her existing nipple-sucking schema. She accommodates to the new object (her thumb) and thus learns to suck her thumb, and may now suck her thumb when placed in a position that she associates with feeding. By 4 months, infants become more skilled at adapting their actions to a variety of events and objects. However, they are still unable to distinguish themselves from objects.

Substage 3 (4–8 Months). In this stage, infants learn that they can affect their environment. The infant becomes increasingly interactive with events and objects outside her body. Intentionality is the distinctive feature, with infants intentionally repeating actions that produce pleasurable results. An example of this is an infant banging different objects against a table to produce different sounds or accidentally hitting a mobile hanging above her crib. This action provides the visual experience of seeing the mobile move. The infant then tries to hit the mobile again to recreate this experience. These repetitive actions are called "secondary circular reactions." They are termed secondary because infants not only use their own bodies but also use objects around them to produce desired results. Infants visually and tactually explore objects. They learn to anticipate interactive game sequences, then respond, and finally initiate games, such as "peekabo." Important features of this stage are imitating adult actions and initial efforts to search for disappearing objects. This activity indicates the beginning concept of object permanence, that is, the understanding that objects exist separately in time and space.

Substage 4 (8–12 Months). In this stage, infants begin to use and coordinate their secondary circular reactions to achieve a specific goal. This stage is marked by three important characteristics: intention, imitation, and anticipation. Infants learn to put several behaviors together to accomplish a desired

goal. The infant can now look at the mobile and intentionally activate it. She now has the goal in mind before she engages in the behavior. She has discovered the means-end relationship. An infant will learn to push one object aside to get another object. Infants' problem-solving abilities also become more refined in this stage. Babies at this stage try out existing behavior schemes to solve a problem. They do not generate new behaviors to accomplish goals.

The child begins to refine her verbal imitation skills through approximations of her own sounds and the sounds she hears. This ability to imitate is also seen in gestures. After repeating her own movements, she then approximates those of someone else. An example of this is waving bye-bye.

Children in this stage show rather sophisticated anticipatory behavior. They may begin to cry when adults put on their coats to leave or when food they do not like is placed before them. They do not have to see the parents leave or taste the food in order to cry; they can anticipate the outcome (Umansky & Hooper, 1998).

In this stage infants come to recognize that objects have permanence and continue to exist in time and space even when the objects are not visible. Infants will continue to look for an object where it was last found, even if they see it being hidden in another location.

Substage 5 (12–18 Months). In this stage, infants learn new behaviors through trial and error. The infant searches for novelty through "tertiary circular reactions." Activities are repeated, but these actions become tertiary because the infant will deliberately vary the action to produce new and interesting results. She systematically changes her behavior and observes the effect. An example of this is a child dropping a piece of food on the floor from her highchair and then continuing to drop pieces from one side and then the other to observe what happens. Infants now have a wider range of behaviors, and their play becomes more complex.

Substage 6 (18–24 Months). This is the final substage in the sensorimotor period. Symbolic representation is the characteristic feature of this substage. An important cognitive leap is language acquisition. She can think through solutions to simple problems without the need for acting them out. An infant can now imagine where an object is hidden, rather than having to watch it being hidden. By the end of this substage, the infant has mastered the full concept of object permanence. This important cognitive capacity now frees the infant from her dependence on sensorimotor actions for understanding the world. This understanding frees the infant from the "here and now" world and enables her to develop memory skills.

The child has the capacity for mental representation or the ability to think. Two types of observed behavior show mental representation, deferred imitation and pretend play. An infant can imitate an action that has occurred previously. An example of this is a child talking on a play phone using the same tone of voice as her mother. Infants can now think of different ways to reach goals, rather than being limited to immediate sensorimotor actions to solve problems. Play involves pretending and symbolism. This internal symbolic representation is also expressed in her understanding that pictures represent objects. The child enjoys looking through a storybook and touching pictures of familiar objects. The end of this substage is the end of infancy.

Preoperational Stage. Following the sensorimotor period, young children continue to acquire a great deal of knowledge about how the animate and inanimate world is structured and operates. Piaget's second major stage of cognitive development is called the preoperational stage. Cognition

in children between ages 3 and 6 years is qualitatively different from that of infants and toddlers because children have acquired the ability to use language and mental representation. Although they are clearly more capable than sensorimotor infants, they are not yet able to perform the mental operations required of logical thinking and reasoning.

The Preconceptual Period (2–4 Years). A major accomplishment during this period is the development of symbolic activity. The child learns that one thing can represent another thing. This symbolic play is evidenced both in her pretend play and in increasing language development. A block can be used as a car or an airplane. Language is freed from the immediate context. Words as symbols can now be used to describe and share experiences that occurred in the past. During this time, children begin to develop mental templates that tell them how specific routines and repeatedly occurring events should work. Preschool children can think about events that happened weeks ago or those that have not yet happened.

The Intuitive Period (4–7 Years). During this period, the child makes an important transition into the period of concrete operations. She learns to categorize objects based on certain features. The child appears to learn that many things in the world can be classified and that some classifications are broader than others. For example, dogs and cats are animals, but beans are not animals. Although birds and butterflies both fly, butterflies are not birds. Toward the end of this period, the child begins to be able to decenter; that is, she is no longer only able to focus on one feature of an object at a time but will begin to demonstrate the ability to consider more than one characteristic simultaneously, as well as some reversibility in her thinking. By age 4 or 5, children sort and classify using more than one attribute of an object, such as color and size.

Preschool children have a more refined sense of causality than infants, and their perceptions of objects in space appear to be based on relationships between objects, as adults think, rather than in relation to themselves, as infants appear to think. Preschool children have more complex representational skills than infants. This is observed in their improved language skills, their drawings and pretend play, their initial use of language to control their own behavior, and their understanding of how the world is quantified and can be counted. Dramatic play episodes become much more elaborate and complex. These episodes provide opportunities for practicing social routines and solving problems.

Young children typically reason that one specific example applies to all examples. For instance, if a child's dog is friendly, then another dog is friendly. They also tend to presume a causal relationship if two events are closely associated in time or in some other way. For example, a child in a plane flying to grandma's house may ask another passenger if he is flying to her grandma's house (Bredekamp & Copple, 1997). Although the child cannot think logically at this stage, she clearly recognizes that events have causes and perceives the need for explanations.

Considerations for Choosing Techniques and Instruments

The techniques used in the assessment of cognition vary depending on the age and characteristics of the child (Benner, 1992). This section begins by discussing techniques which should be considered when assessing neonates, infants and toddlers, and preschoolers. In addition to the age of the child, characteristics such as the child's sensory and motor abilities need to be weighed as well as whether the test is multiple or single domain. Each of these factors needs to be

considered when choosing the techniques and instruments for assessing cognition. Examples of appropriate instruments are also included.

Age Differences

Techniques that are appropriate for neonates are different from those used with 1-year-olds. The same is true for assessing infants, compared with preschoolers who have well-developed receptive and expressive language skills. Preschool-aged children may be engaged in traditional preacademic activities and have well-developed receptive and expressive language skills. The assessment of cognitive abilities presents different challenges as the neonate develops into the preschooler.

Neonates. Infants are considered to be neonates during the first 28 days of extrauterine life. The Apgar score is used for assessment of neonates 1 minute and 5 minutes after birth (Apgar, 1953). The Apgar scoring system rates the infant on a scale of 0 to 2 on five signs: heart rate, respiratory effort, reflex irritability, muscle tone, and color. Infants who receive very low Apgar scores are considered to be at high risk for future complications. The research on the predictive validity of the Apgar rating noted the clearest findings are a strong relationship between low Apgar ratings and infant mortality (Francis, Self, & Horowitz, 1987). The findings are inconsistent regarding developmental progress.

Two instruments frequently used to assess neonates are the *Graham/Rosenblith Scales* (Rosenblith, 1974a, 1975) and the *Brazelton Neonatal Behavioral Assessment Scale* (NBAS) (Brazelton, 1973, 1984). The Graham/Rosenblith contains a motor scale, tactile-adaptive, visual responsiveness, auditory responsiveness, and muscle tone. The examiner can also include an irritability rating, which is assigned based on the infant's behavior throughout the entire examination. The NBAS measures both reflexive and elicited behavioral characteristics of the neonate and, therefore, is more widely used. The NBAS has been demonstrated to be an effective intervention device in the support of parenting with mothers of low socioeconomic status and adolescent mothers (Worobey & Brazelton, 1990). *The Neurological Assessment of the Preterm and Full-term Newborn Infant* (Dubowitz & Dubowitz, 1981) is an instrument that can be used by untrained staff in neonatal neurology on preterm neonates. There are four major areas of concern in the assessment: habituation (the ability to manage environmental input), muscle tone and movement patterns, testing of reflexes (primitive reflexes and tendon reflexes), and several neurobehavioral items. The neurobehavioral items are very similar to the state organization and orientation items on the NBAS. This instrument appears to be of potential use in the longitudinal study of at-risk neonates (Benner, 1992).

Infants and Toddlers. A variety of approaches are used in infant and toddler assessment, including traditional tests, Piagetian-based criterion-referenced tests, and perceptual-cognitive processing tests, and the observation and analysis of behavior during perceptual-cognitive processing tasks.

Traditional tests include norm-referenced tests and scales used to produce scores such as developmental quotient, developmental index, intelligence quotient (IQ), developmental age, and mental age. Criterion-referenced tests have also been developed that are similar in content to norm-referenced scales. The items on these traditional tests represent developmental landmarks in the child's maturation. The test items are generally derived from test items found on the *Gesell Developmental Schedules* (Gesell & Amatruda, 1947) and the more recent revision of the Gesell scales by Knobloch and Pasamanick (1974). The developmental schedules were developed by Gesell to be used as tools for determining the present condition of infants and

toddlers, not in predicting future performance or establishing a child's IQ (Benner, 1992).

Piagetian-based criterion-referenced instruments are also used to determine cognitive development in infants and toddlers. The purpose of these instruments is to identify a child's level of functioning in sensorimotor development. Examples of these instruments are discussed in the section on approaches to assessment.

Perceptual-cognitive processing tests are used to assess many infants with disabilities for whom traditional measures and Piagetian-based measures are unsatisfactory determinants of cognitive functioning. The prerequisite motor competence and dependence on cooperative behavior make these instruments inappropriate for infants with sensory or motor impairments. Zelazo (1979, 1982a, 1982b) developed a procedure to explore infants' capacity to process information during sequential visual and auditory events. The procedure he developed includes five events (two visual, three auditory) and is appropriate for infants between $3\frac{1}{2}$ and 36 months. This approach involves the presentation of an engagement visual or auditory event that is repeated until the child begins to expect it. Before the child loses interest, the event is presented three times with some modification. The original is then reintroduced for three additional presentations. The child's ability to create an expectation and her recognition of the return to the original event are noted.

Preschoolers. As toddlers mature, develop language, and improve in gross and fine motor skills, cognitive functioning may be assessed in more standard ways. Standard approaches for assessment of cognitive functioning include screening and readiness tests, traditional intelligence tests, behavioral checklists, and tests of basic concepts. Children with disabilities may also be assessed using alternative procedures, such as assessment of cognition through play, Piagetian-based tasks, and dynamic assessment paradigms.

Child Characteristics

Appropriate techniques also vary according to certain child characteristics. Techniques that are appropriate for children with intact hearing or vision often are not suitable for the child who is deaf or blind. Children with motor impairments and who may be nonoral present tremendous challenges to persons interested in assessing their cognitive functioning. Standard testing procedures do not work, are very unfair, and should be replaced with adaptive approaches (Benner, 1992). (See Chapter 7 for adaptive approaches to assessment.)

Age Ranges

The age ranges for which instruments are intended vary widely. For example, the *Bayley Scales of Infant Development* (2nd Ed.) (Bayley, 1993) are standardized on infants and toddlers from 1 to 42 months. The *McCarthy Scales of Children's Abilities* (McCarthy, 1972) can be used with children ages 2½ years to 8½ years. Instruments with wide age ranges can be used with many children and offer consistency for longitudinal studies. However, such instruments tend to be less accurate and have fewer skills. The number of items that can be included at each age level is often very limited on tests that cover a broad age span.

Multiple or Single Domain

Some instruments are designed exclusively for assessing cognitive functioning, whereas others include multiple domains. Selected instruments that are primarily associated with cognitive assessment are discussed in the next section. A summary of these instruments is provided in Table 14–2 on page 331. The *Bayley Scales* (Bayley, 1993), the *Battelle Developmental Inventory* (Newborg, Stock, Wnek, Guidubaldi, &

Svinicki, 1988) the *Vulpe Assessment Battery (Revised)* (Vulpe, 1994), and the *Infant Psychological Development Scales* (Uzgiris & Hunt, 1975) are commonly used to evaluate the cognitive functioning of infants and toddlers with disabilities.

Approaches to Assessment

In the past, researchers attempted to use traditional measures of infant development to predict a child's ability at school age (Kopp & McCall, 1982). The measures of infant development were poor at predicting later school performance (Shonkoff, 1983). The majority of instruments used to assess cognitive functioning are based on the traditional psychometric methodology or the more recent developmental theory approach. (See Chapter 9 for norm-based assessment and Chapter 10 for curriculum-based assessment.) Each of these approaches can be helpful in assessing current functioning, detecting delayed or abnormal development, planning an intervention program, or evaluating the effectiveness of an intervention. Early intervention team members should be cautious in the selection and interpretation of tools to measure cognitive development. The limitations of the instruments being used must be shared with all team members, especially the family members.

Accurate evaluation and assessment of young children are critical to appropriate interventions (McCormick, 1996). These terms connote two different processes. Evaluation may be defined as the procedures to determine a child's eligibility for services; assessment is the ongoing process used by qualified personnel throughout the time of a child's eligibility to identify the family's resources, priorities, and concerns as well as the child's unique needs (McLean & McCormick, 1993). The instruments chosen by the examiner must be appropriate to fulfill the requirements of each of these processes.

Traditional Methodology

Traditional scales include norm-referenced and criterion-referenced instruments which outline a sample of behaviors considered characteristic of a specific age range. Most traditional infant scales are norm-referenced. This means that a normative sample of children is established that is made up of representative ethnic, sex, income levels, and geographic areas. The average performance of this group is the standard against which the performance of individual children is compared. Traditional tests produce scores such as a developmental quotient, developmental index, IQ, developmental age, and mental age. Criterion-referenced tests have also been developed which have similar content to the norm-referenced instruments. The items on both types of tests represent developmental milestones in the child's maturation. These are primarily used for screening and diagnosis of cognitive ability.

Norm-Referenced Measures. Norm-referenced or standardized infant tests encompass more than cognitive skills measures. They include measures of social skills, gross and fine motor behaviors, language, and certain perceptual skills. More recently, studies of specific cognitive abilities such as habituation and visual recognition memory have been found to be more predictive of later IQ than traditional infant assessments (McCall & Carriger, 1993; McCall, 1994).

One of the first instruments to provide a well-standardized methodology for assessing infant mental development was the *Bayley Scales of Infant Development* (Bayley, 1969). The 1993 revision of these scales, *Bayley Scales of Infant Development* II, provides a comprehensive assessment of the development of children ages 1 through 42 months. The revised scales are similar to the first edition. Three scales are included: (1) a mental scale with the assessment of perceptual acuity, discrimination, object constancy and memory, learning and problem solving,

verbal ability, generalization, and classification; (2) a motor scale assessing muscle control and coordination; and (3) a behavior rating scale with four subscales of orientation/engagement, attention, motor quality, and emotional regulation. The Bayley scales have well-respected standardization qualities, have proven effectiveness in measuring skills of children with disabilities, and test a large number and variety of behaviors at each age level (Alfonso & Flanagan, 1999).

The *Griffiths Mental Development Scales* (Griffiths, 1954, 1979) were designed specifically for use with children with delays and deficits of various natures. The scales extend from birth to 8 years, with a separate instrument (*The Abilities of Babies*) for the measurement of abilities during the first 2 years. The Griffiths is British in origin and thus the applicability of the norms has been questioned on today's American children. It is suggested that the Griffiths' scales be used interchangeably with the Bayley scales (Beail, 1985). Some research has also suggested that scores obtained on the Griffiths are somewhat inflated (McLean, McCormick, & Baird, 1991).

The BDI (Newborg, et al., 1988) assesses all domains of development and allows observations, interviews, and direct testing to be used for evaluation. McCormick (1996) noted three distinct advantages of the Battelle: (1) it is a multidomain assessment (cognitive, communication, motor, personal-social, and adaptive); (2) it has a three-point scoring system that allows for the crediting of emerging abilities; and (3) three procedures are allowed for obtaining information (traditional administration, observation, and interview). Langley (1989) suggested the most attractive features of the BDI are the suggested adaptations of items for specific disabilities, the excellent and extremely comprehensive standardization data, and the provision for three methods of assessment. These researchers note the primary shortcomings to be the sparsity of items provided in each age range and the lack of items providing comprehensive assessment of the full range of sensorimotor

TABLE 14–2

Norm-Referenced Instruments for Assessing Cognitive Functioning

Measure	Age Range	Areas Assessed	Use with Children with Special Needs
Bayley Scales of Infant Development (Bayley, 1993)	1 to 42 mos	Mental, motor, and infant behavior recording	Yields youthful information on current developmental status; used in identifying infants with mild cognitive delay; not useful for children with visual, hearing, or motor deficits (Langley, 1989); clinical sample within normative sample included children with autism and developmental delay, and children born prematurely, HIV positive, prenatally exposed to drugs, or asphyxiated at birth.
Cattell Infant Intelligence Scale (Cattell, 1980)	2 to 30 mos	Single-factor model, including items from Gesell Schedules	Task modifications through increasing size and number of dimensions and changing the texture, brightness, or color of some items has been shown to improve scores of children who are deaf-blind (Kiernan & Dubose, 1974); correlates with Stanford-Binet (Benner, 1992).
Columbia Mental Maturity Scale (Burgemeister, Blum, & Lorge, 1972)	3-6 to 10-0 yrs	Only global score determined	No verbal response required from child; flexible directions; only requires 15–20 mins to administer.
Differential Ability Scales (Elliott, 1990)	2-6 to 17 yrs	Cognitive battery: preschool and school-age; academic achievement tests for school age	Adequate internal consistency and test-retest reliability; varied, colorful manipulatives and pictures for maintaining interest and participation; opportunities to ensure child has understood task and alternative stopping rules; may overestimate child's abilities
Griffiths Scales of Development (Griffiths, 1979)	0 to 8 yrs	Locomotor, personal-social, hearing and speech, eye-hand coordination performance	Measures wide range of functioning; enticing, childlike materials; yields useful information from nonverbal children (Langley, 1989).
Infant Mullen Scales of Early Learning (Mullen, 1991)	Birth to 38 mos	Gross motor base, visual receptive organization, visual expressive organization, language receptive organization, language expressive organization	Can use individual scales to assess competencies and areas of weakness; useful with children at-risk or with disabilities in assessing and setting intervention goals.

TABLE 14–2

continued

Measure	Age Range	Areas Assessed	Use with Children with Special Needs
Kaufman Assessment Battery for Children (Kaufman & Kaufman, 1983)	2-6 to 12-5 yrs	Sequential processing, simultaneous processing, achievement, and nonverbal	Test materials are colorful and use colorful photographs; subtests are used with younger children to accommodate shorter attention spans; nonverbal scale may provide supporting information about cognitive abilities of children who have limited English proficiency and children with hearing disabilities; limitations include few manipulative tasks; too few easy items; heavy emphasis on visual stimuli (difficult for children with visual disabilities), and little opportunity to sample verbal reasoning and spontaneous expression (Kamphaus & Kaufman, 1991).
Learning Accomplishment Profile-Diagnostic Standardized Assessment (Nehring, Nehring, Bruni, & Randolph, 1992)	30 to 72 mos	Fine motor (writing & manipulation), cognitive (matching & counting), language (naming & comprehension), gross motor (body & object movement)	Each domain has its own manual with materials; subtest floors and total test floor appear adequate; item gradient problems were noted for the lowest age range (30–35 mos); general authenticity is low because they contain traditional, contrived developmental tasks; appropriate only for children who are at-risk or have mild disabilities (Bagnato, Neisworth, & Munson, 1997).
McCarthy Scales of Children's Abilities (McCarthy, 1972)	2-6 to 8-6 yrs	Verbal, perceptual-performance, quantitative, memory, and motor	Has a limited floor (easy items) for children who are young or developmentally delayed.
Stanford-Binet Intelligence Scale (4th Ed.) (Thorndike, Hagen, & Sattler, 1985)	2 to 23 yrs	Verbal reasoning, abstract/visual reasoning, quantitative reasoning, short term memory	Technical properties are less strong for preschoolers; limited subtest floors fail to discriminate among children less than 3 years, 6 months (McCallum, 1991).
Wechsler Preschool and Primary Scale of Intelligence (Wechsler, 1989)	3-0 to 7-3 yrs	Verbal: information, comprehension, vocabulary, similarities; Performance: object assembly, geometric design, block design, mazes, picture completion	Has inadequate floor at beginning age level of test; adequate floor around age 3-8 years; test administration too long for children with mental retardation, autism, and behavioral disorders; receptive and expressive language demands are excessive; no nonverbal scale for linguistically diverse (Alfonso & Flanagan, 1999).

TABLE 14–2
continued

Measure	Age Range	Areas Assessed	Use with Children with Special Needs
Woodcock-Johnson Psycho-Educational Battery-Revised Tests of Cognitive Ability (Woodcock & Johnson, 1989)	24 months to 95+ yrs	21 tests of cognitive ability	Does not include manipulatives; attractive, well-organized test materials; all tests require verbal response; designed for educational decision making; few preschool children in normative sample; discontinue criteria may be too stringent, and thus frustrating for children with delays or behavioral difficulties.
Vulpe Assessment Battery-Revised (Vulpe, 1994)	0 to 8 yrs	Gross motor, fine motor, language, cognitive processes, adaptive behaviors, activities of daily living	Process-oriented, curriculum-compatible, developmental assessment, emphasizing children's functional abilities; more dense task analysis than most developmental scales; clear and often detailed curricular links; excellent for assessing low functional levels (Bagnato, Neisworth, & Munson, 1997).

cognitive abilities. Because the Battelle is an example of a norm-referenced and criterion-based assessment, it can be used for eligibility determination and program planning. However, McCormick (1996) cautioned examiners when using this instrument for both purposes. The Battelle is widely used for meeting psychometric standards for children 2 years and older with mild to moderate disabilities (McCormick, 1996).

Additional norm-referenced assessment measures are summarized in Table 14–2. A more detailed discussion of norm-referenced assessment is provided in Chapter 9. It must be stressed that not all children can be successfully assessed using traditional assessment instruments. The child with profound sensory, motor, social, or intellectual deficits may exhibit insufficient behavior to be measured by traditional assessment tools. Such a child warrants the use of nontraditional, process-oriented assessments to gain meaningful information for program planning (see Chapter 7).

Developmental Scales and Checklists. There is a multitude of criterion-referenced measures for

assessing the abilities of young children. A number of assessment tools have evolved from programs serving young children with disabilities and these instruments are available commercially. Generally, these instruments are recapitulations and reorganizations of the items from other scales deemed inappropriate by the developers of the new instrument, with some adaptations provided to compensate for the nature of the disability (Langley, 1989). Several attempts to provide more efficient and effective assessments have resulted, however, in tools that have merit for use with children with disabilities. Some of the developmental scales and checklists which are used in programs for young children with disabilities are included in the following discussion. A summary of developmental scales and checklists is provided in Table 14–3 with comments regarding their use with children with special needs.

The Gesell Developmental Schedules were revised by Knobloch and Pasamanick in 1974 and in 1980 by Knobloch, Stevens, and Malone. These schedules describe development across motor, communication, personal-social, and adaptive behavior for children between the ages of 4

TABLE 14–3
Developmental Checklists and Scales for Assessment of Cognitive Functioning

Measure	Age Range	Areas Assessed	Use with Children with Special Needs
Boehm Test of Basic Concepts-Preschool Version (Boehm, 1986)	3 to 5 yrs	26 basic relational concepts	Brief (10–15 mins); easy to administer; requires only a pointing response; limited in usefulness for children with visual impairments; designed to plan intervention and be indicator of school readiness.
Bracken Concept Development Series (Bracken, 1986)	2½ to 8 yrs	Measure 285 basic concepts in 11 subtest categories: color, letter identification, numbers/counting; comparison; shapes; textual/material; quantity	Pointing response appropriate for children with motor disabilities; provides colorful creative materials with lesson plans and suggestions for parents; limited usefulness for children with visual disabilities.
Developmental Diagnosis (Knobloch, Stevens, & Malone, 1980)	Birth to 3 yrs	Adaptive, gross motor, fine motor, language and personal-social behaviors	Manual provides excellent description of developmental skills (Langley, 1989).
Gesell Developmental Scales (Revised) (Knobloch, Stevens, & Malone, 1980)	4 wks to 72 mos	Fine motor, gross motor, adaptive, language, personal-social	Designed for clinical use as a diagnostic tool.

weeks and 72 months. The Gesell schedules were designed for clinical use, primarily as diagnostic tools (Lewis & Sullivan, 1985). Therefore, the schedules have been used extensively in clinical settings to assess young children's developmental status. Although the scale has been criticized for inadequate standardization validity and inadequate reliability tests, it nevertheless is a useful tool for assessing development because it incorporates naturally occurring activities into assessment. These schedules provided clinicians with a rich source of information about behavior and became the prototype for later assessments.

The *Vulpe Assessment Battery* (*Revised*) (Vulpe, 1994) is a process-oriented, curriculum-compatible developmental assessment emphasizing children's functional abilities (Bagnato, Neisworth, & Munson, 1997). This assessment may be used to gather information for early intervention and is appropriate for children who have atypical developmental patterns related to medical or social conditions (Bagnato, Neisworth, & Munson, 1997). The scoring is graduated enabling recording of the degree of instructional or behavioral assistance required and performance under various conditions. The Vulpe is a diagnostic-prescriptive assessment tool for instructional planning. The items on the Vulpe are all grouped within categories of behavior and a pattern of strengths and weaknesses may be derived. The Vulpe is very comprehensive and may be used for informal assessment over a period of time. Bagnato, Neisworth, and Munson (1997) praised the Vulpe as a welcome addition for programs that enroll young children with more severe disabilities. These researchers cited the Vulpe's adaptive qualities, use of sensory and response modifications, team-oriented approach, reliance on convergent data sources, and flexible procedures as incorporating most principles of recommended practice.

Curriculum-Based Scales

Curriculum-referenced scales such as the *Hawaii Early Learning Profile* (*Birth to 3*) (Parks, Furuno, O'Reilly, Inatsuka, Hoska, & Zeisloft-Falbey, 1994) and the *Hawaii Early Learning Profile for Preschoolers* (3–6) (VORT, 1995) have Piagetian-based cognitive sections. The *Carolina Curriculum for Infants and Toddlers with Special Needs, Second Edition* (Johnson-Martin, Jens, Attermeier, & Hacker, 1991) covers all developmental domains through 24 months and offers a comprehensive assessment of cognitive skills. This tool has a number of well-organized subsections for assessing Piaget's sensorimotor concepts. The purpose of curriculum-based assessment is to determine the child's level of functioning so that input to the child changes as the child's abilities change. The *Assessment, Evaluation, and Programming System* (AEPS) (Bricker, 1993; Cripe, Slentz, & Bricker, 1993) is a comprehensive system for obtaining information and planning intervention. The cognitive domain of the AEPS contains seven strands based primarily on Piagetian theory. These strands include sensory stimuli, object permanence, causality, imitation, problem solving, preacademic skills, and interaction with objects. Goals and specific objectives are included in each strand of the cognitive domain. These cognitive objectives can be incorporated into the child's daily activities. The system allows for easy transition from the assessment sequences to identification of goals and objectives and then to intervention strategies. The AEPS provides an opportunity to assess

young children within naturally occurring routines and environments. (See Chapter 10 for further information on the curriculum-based assessment.)

Ordinal Scales

Ordinal scales select cognitive items based on their hierarchical relationship to one another. The items within a cognitive domain are selected and sequentially ordered based on their level of difficulty. The acquisition of an item or competency is dependent on the mastery of a prior item. For instance, such items are designated as follows: looks at object, follows moving object with eyes, uncovers hidden object. Traditional assessments typically sample a range of behaviors judged to be typical for given chronological age groups. These behaviors measure responses involving social interaction, receptive and expressive language, object play, problem solving, and responses to auditory and visual stimuli. Ordinal scales can provide more descriptive information about an infant's specific cognitive capabilities. Traditional assessments gather data on an overall developmental profile, whereas ordinal scales gather data on an infant's performance within a particular cognitive domain. An ordinal scale makes it possible to identify the highest cognitive benchmark obtained by an infant.

Piaget (1952) described the theoretical framework for sensorimotor and symbolic development during a child's first 24 months. This framework details the changing approaches infants use to solve problems as development proceeds. This Piagetian framework used extensively in early intervention programs is the *Infant Psychological Development Scales* (Uzgiris & Hunt, 1975). These scales represent an approach toward cognitive assessment from the developmental theory framework. The scales are ordinal, which means they are based on the assumption that early cognitive abilities involve movement from lower to higher levels of functioning. The acquisition of competencies is dependent on the mastery of prior competencies at a lower level of functioning. Learning is hierarchical, with increasing expansion of previous learning (McCormick, 1996). Developmental status is obtained by noting the highest item passed on the scale, and most often do not include age ranges or equivalents.

Application of these scales for use with infants with disabilities has been expanded by the development of A *Clinical and Educational Manual for Use with the Uzgiris and Hunt Scales of Infant Psychological Development* by Dunst (1980). Dunst's protocol (1980) assists interventionists in successfully developing programs from these scales. Test items were selected to represent an ordinal sequencing of cognitive development within each of six major concept areas: (1) object permanence, (2) means-end relationships, (3) imitation (vocal and gestural), (4) causality, (5) construction of object relations in space, and (6) development of schemes for relating to objects. Although the scales are based on Piagetian theory, they are not designed to assign an infant to a specific sensorimotor stage. Infant performance on the scales provides a measure of current cognitive functioning. The scales make it possible to look for differences in rates of development in the six areas mentioned. Dunst (1980) provided a strategy which enables the assessor to obtain more standardized data following the administration of the scales. The procedures outlined by Dunst provide the assessor with additional insights concerning the child's sensorimotor capabilities and aid in the design of intervention strategies. Ordinal scales have a distinct advantage for testing children with disabilities. Test procedures are much more flexible and permit the examiner to vary materials and create situations that elicit the required response (McCormick, 1996).

The Observation of Behavior in Socially and Ecologically Relevant and Valid Environments (OBSERVE) (Dunst & McWilliam, 1988) provides an observational method of evaluation based on Piagetian stage theory that is particularly useful for children with multiple disabilities (Benner, 1992). The OBSERVE assesses interactive competencies in social and nonsocial environments, using a hierarchical system comprised of five levels of behavior capabilities: attentional interactions, contingency interactions, differentiated interactions, encoded interactions, and symbolic interactions. By closely matching learning conditions to the child's ability to interact with the environment and response capabilities, a more accurate measure of her ability to learn new behaviors may be obtained (McLean, Bruder, Baird, & Dunst, 1991). In other words, the response demands of the assessment are designed to match the response capabilities of the child, rather than the reverse.

McCune and colleagues (1990) cautioned examiners in the repeated use of Piagetian-based measures to assess cognitive development. If ordinal scales are used with little variation in procedure, the infant may learn how to solve a particular problem (e.g., pulling a string brings an object) rather than learn a general principle. This is especially important if these tasks are also used for intervention.

Play as an Alternative Approach

Play and cognitive development interact. Play leads to more complex, cognitive behavior which then affects the content of play (Athey, 1984; Piaget, 1962). Play assessment is very useful for observing a child's ability to organize her interactions with toys and play partners, and thus for assessing cognitive functioning (McCune, et al., 1990). Research on play has contributed enormously to the understanding of early cognitive competence of children with disabilities (Dunst, Mahoney, & Buchan, 1996). Three specific developmental transitions in a child's ability to play are: (1) decentration, (2) decontextualization, and (3) integration (Bond, Creasey, & Abrams, 1990). Decentration is the infant's transition to freedom from her own body to engage in symbolic actions. The child's ability to pretend in play beyond the immediate environment is decontextualization, and the transition to sequential organized play is integration (Benner, 1992).

Play is vital to and reflects a child's development in the cognitive, communicative, social-emotional, and motor domains. A child's play opportunities and experiences influence cognitive understanding, emotional development, social skills, language usage, and physical and motor development (Linder, 1993). A large body of research relates certain cognitive skills to various features of language development. Certain behaviors in a child's play express cognitive skills necessary for the development of language. Observing the child's play skills can give interventionists an insight into the child's communicative, social-emotional, and cognitive performance. Interventionists should be familiar with play and play assessment as it relates to cognitive, social-emotional, and language development. Although play assessment is introduced in this section, further consideration will be given when discussing language and social emotional development in Chapters 15 and 16.

Delays, defects, and deviations can be seen in a child's play that may reflect problems in one of these domains. A child who is nonverbal or has multiple disabilities may be observed during free or structured play to provide assessment information on cognitive functioning. The examiner may observe the child as she organizes her interactions with toys and playmates. The manner in which children interact with objects is a reflection of their cognitive development. When using play assessments, the examiner primarily observes and scores the actions of the child. The examiner may also observe the complexity and variety of play behaviors.

Play Assessment Procedures. A variety of nonstandardized assessment procedures and guides for the observation of children's play with objects or toys is available. The advantages of naturalistic environments and behavioral response sets such as play in the assessment of cognition are obvious. Children are free to interact with objects and environments that are interesting and motivating to them. Examiners are free to observe, to model, and to expand infant and child behaviors to more accurately ascertain the child's level of engagement with and understanding of familiar and novel physical and social environments. The choice of setting and environments for conducting assessments is discussed further in Chapters 5 and 10.

Some suggestions for free-play and structured or elicited assessments are listed below:

Elicited and Structured Play

Assessing performance, competence, and capacity in infant play: Relations to home environment and security of attachment (Belsky, Garduque, & Hrncir, 1984)

Play Assessment Scale (5th revision) (includes both free play and structured play) (Fewell, 1986)

A developmental sequence of agent use in late infancy (Watson & Fischer, 1977)

Free-Play Assessments

From exploration to play: A cross-sectional study of infant free play behavior (Belsky & Most, 1981)

Play Assessment Checklist for Infants (Bromwich, 1981)

The systematic observation of children's play. Unpublished scoring manual (Kearsley, 1984)

Manual for the Symbolic Play Test (Lowe & Costello, 1976)

A manual for analyzing free play (McCune-Nicolich, 1983)

The effects of peers on toddler interaction with mothers and toys (Rubenstein & Howes, 1976)

McCune (1986) described a format for collecting a sample of play with the caregiver or examiner using a standard set of toys. The play behavior is observed and assigned to developmental levels based on Piaget (1962). Table 14–4 describes the play levels that have been identified.

The *Manual for Analyzing Free Play* (MAFP) developed by McCune-Nicolich (1980) uses a play sequence initially suggested by Piaget (1962). The MAFP includes strategies for viewing symbolic play, relational play, and manipulative play. A series of discrete judgments may be made concerning the child's play behavior by categorizing the different types of play. Linder's (1993)

Transdisciplinary Play-Based Assessment (TPBA) is a developmental profile which assesses all major domains using structured and free play situations. The TPBA uses a transdisciplinary team to conduct a play-based assessment that can be adapted to various abilities. This assessment is process oriented and includes ecological and interactive variables and provides relevant information for intervention (Linder, 1993). The TPBA is discussed further in Chapter 10.

The advantages of the use of play-assessment data over traditional testing are provided by Fewell and Rich (1987). These include: (1) the testing environment is nonthreatening and elicits

TABLE 14–4
Structure of Pretend Play, 10–24 Months

Levels and Criteria	Examples
Sensorimotor period	
Level 1. Presymbolic scheme: The child shows understanding of object use or meaning by brief recognitory gestures. No pretending. Properties of present object are the stimulus. Child appears serious rather than playful.	The child picks up a comb, touches it to his or her hair, drops it. The child picks up the telephone receiver, puts it into ritual conversation position, sets it aside. The child gives the mop a swish on the floor.
Level 2. Auto-symbolic scheme: The child pretends at self-related activities. Pretending. Symbolism is directly involved with the child's body. Child appears playful, seems aware of pretending.	The child simulates drinking from a toy baby bottle. The child eats from an empty spoon. The child closes his or her eyes, pretending to sleep.
Symbolic Stage 1	
Level 3. Single scheme symbolic games: Child extends symbolism beyond his or her own actions by: Level 3.1. Including other actors or receivers of action, such as a doll. Level 3.2. Pretending at activities of other people or objects such as dogs, trucks, and trains.	Child feeds mother or doll. Child grooms mother or doll. Child pretends to read a book. Child pretends to mop floor. Child moves a block or toy car with appropriate sounds of vehicle.
Level 4. Combinatorial symbolic games: Level 4.1. Single scheme combinations: One pretend scheme is related to several actors or receivers of action.	Child combs own, then mother's hair. Child drinks from the bottle, feeds doll from bottle. Child puts an empty cup to mother's mouth, then experimenter, and self.

TABLE 14–4

continued

Levels and Criteria	Examples
Level 4.2 Multi-scheme combinations: Several schemes are related to one another in sequence.	Child holds phone to ear, dials. Child kisses doll, puts it to bed, puts spoon to its mouth. Child stirs in the pot, feeds doll, pours food into dish.
Level 5. Planned symbolic games: Child indicates verbally or nonverbally that pretend acts are planned ahead. Level 5.1. Planned single scheme symbolic acts—transitional type. Activities from levels 2 and 3 that are planned. Type A: Symbolic identification of one object with another. Type B: Symbolic identification of the child's body with some other person or object.	Child finds the iron, sets it down, searches for the cloth, tossing aside several objects. When cloth is found, he or she irons it. Child picks up play screwdriver, says "toothbrush" and makes the motions of toothbrushing. Child picks up the bottle, says "baby," then feeds the doll and covers it with a cloth.
Level 5.2 Combinations with planned elements: These are constructed of activities from levels 2 to 5.1, but always include some planned element. They tend toward realistic scenes.	Child puts play foods in a pot, stirs them. Then says "soup" or "Mommy" before feeding the mother. He or she waits, then says "more?" offering the spoon to the mother.

Source: From An interdisciplinary model of infant assessment (pp. 234–235), by McCune, et al., in *Handbook of Early Childhood Intervention,* S. J. Meisels & J. P. Shonkoff (Eds.), 1990, New York: Cambridge Univ. Press. Copyright 1990 by Cambridge University Press. Reprinted with the permission of Cambridge University Press.

better cooperation from the children; (2) the procedures are flexible enough to allow for the exchange of toys a child might find more appealing; (3) the procedures are easy to administer, with very few directions and no definite order of item presentation and freedom from time constraints; (4) the examiner may observe a child's preferred learning strategies and toy preferences; and (5) both accomplished and emerging skills can be noted.

Linking Assessment Information to Intervention

Assessment must be a comprehensive process of collecting information about a young child (Bagnato, Neisworth, & Munson, 1997). The information collected should permit the analysis of a child's language, personal-social, motor, cognitive, and interactive development. Developmental problems are rarely specific to one domain. A child with motor problems may not be able to move around her environment or initiate social interactions as well as another child. This restricted mobility may affect other areas of development, such as cognition, language, and social skills. Diagnostic specialists can no longer test only intelligence and believe that a child's behavior and skills were sampled representatively (Bagnato, Neisworth, & Munson, 1997). Assessment must include all areas of development to provide the whole picture of a child's functional development (Bagnato, Neisworth, & Munson, 1997). Alternative assessment methods, such as authentic, dynamic, portfolio, curriculum-based, process and performance assessments, and task analysis, are used to provide a more comprehensive picture of the child's developmental skills.

Summary

Because cognition is a composite of skills across developmental domains, the assessor must be familiar with normal developmental skill mastery across all domains. When considering the assessment of cognitive development, the assessor is examining processes that cannot be directly measured but only assumed on the basis of observed behaviors. Most cognitive assessment instruments attempt to assess the efficiency with which the child uses motor and sensory skills to solve problems (Langley, 1989). Assessment instruments must include behaviors that allow the child an opportunity to display behaviors across domains. Early interventionists should always search for innovative ways to elicit behaviors to which significance may be attached concerning developmental skill mastery (Rossetti, 1990). Once a wide sampling of behaviors is obtained, the assessor can judge how well an individual child displays behaviors that reflect appropriate cognitive functioning. When assessing children, interventionists must consider children's developmental histories, their cultural uniqueness, and the impact of their disabilities.

The assessment of cognition can be viewed from a number of perspectives, including traditional psychometrics, cognitive stage or Piagetian, information processing, social learning, maturation/developmental, and functional. Early interventionists should be familiar with norm-referenced instruments, developmental scales and checklists, ordinal scales, and play-based assessments.

Although a number of assessment instruments are available, it is ultimately the assessor's observational skill and integrating ability that will allow accurate and reliable judgments of cognitive functioning. Assessment instruments and strategies are only as good as the person using them. An awareness of the theoretical models of cognitive development allows early interventionists to be more knowledgeable consumers of assessment instruments. Both formal and curriculum-based measures may be used to assess the effectiveness of intervention choices and thus evaluate the efficacy of the intervention program for the child.

References

Alfonso, V. C., & Flanagan, D. P. (1999). Assessment of cognitive functioning in preschoolers. In E. Vazquez Nuttall, I. Romero, & J. Kalesnik (Eds.), *Assessing and screening preschoolers: Psychological and educational dimensions* (pp. 186–217). Needham Heights, MA: Allyn & Bacon.

Anastasiow, N. (1986). *Development and disability.* Baltimore: Brookes.

Apgar, V. (1953). A proposal for a new method of evaluation of the newborn infant. *Current Researches in Anesthesia and Analgesia, 32,* 260–267.

Athey, I. (1984). Contributions of play to development. In T. D. Yawkey & A. D. Pellegrine (Eds.), *Child's play: Developmental and applied* (pp. 9–28). Hillsdale, NJ: Lawrence Erlbaum Associates.

Bagnato, S. J., Neisworth, J. T., & Munson, S. M. (1997). *LINKing assessment and early intervention: An authentic curriculum-based approach.* Baltimore: Brookes.

Bandura, A. (1978). The self system in reciprocal determinism. *American Psychologist, 33,* 344–358.

Bayley, N. (1969). *Bayley Scales of Infant Development.* New York: Psychological Corporation.

Bayley, N. (1993). *Manual for the Bayley Scales of Infant Development* (2nd ed.). San Antonio: The Psychological Corporation.

Beail, N. (1985). A comparative study of profoundly multiply handicapped children's scores on the Bayley and the Griffiths' developmental scales. *Child: Care, Health and Development, 11(1),* 31–36.

Belsky, J., Garduque, L., & Hrncir, E. (1984). Assessing performance, competence, and capacity in infant play: Relations to home environment and security of attachment. *Developmental Psychology, 20,* 406–417.

Belsky, J., & Most, R. K. (1981). From exploration to play: A cross-sectional study of infant free play behavior. *Developmental Psychology, 17,* 630–639.

Benner, S. M. (1992). *Assessing young children with special needs: An ecological perspective.* New York: Longman.

Boehm, A. E. (1986). *Boehm Test of Basic Concepts-Preschool version.* San Antonio, TX: The Psychological Corp.

Bond, L. A., Creasey, G. L., & Abrams, C. L. (1990). Play assessment: Reflecting and promoting cognitive competence. In E. D. Gibbs & D. M. Teti (Eds.), *Interdisciplinary assessment of infants: A guide for early intervention professionals.* Baltimore: Brookes.

Bracken, B. A. (1986). *Bracken Basic Concept Scale.* San Antonio, TX: The Psychological Corp.

Brazelton, T. B. (1973). *Neonatal Behavioral Assessment Scale: National Spastics Society monograph.* Philadelphia: Lippincott.

Brazelton, T. B. (1984). *Neonatal Behavioral Assessment Scale.* Philadelphia: Lippincott.

Bredekamp, S., & Copple, C. (Eds.). (1997). *Developmentally appropriate practice in early childhood programs.* Washington, DC: National Association for the Education of Young Children.

Bricker, D. (Ed.). (1993). *Assessment, Evaluation, and Programming System for infants and children* (Vol. 1): *AEPS measurement for birth to three years.* Baltimore: Brookes.

Bromwich, R. M. (1981). *Play Assessment Checklist for Infants.* (Available from author, Department of Educational

Psychology, School of Education, California State University, Northridge.)

Burgemeister, B., Blum, L., & Lorge, I. (1972). *Columbia Mental Maturity Scale*. San Antonio, TX: Psychological Corp.

Campione, J. C., & Brown, A. L. (1978). Toward a theory of intelligence: Contributions from research with retarded children. *Intelligence, 2*, 279–304.

Campione, J. C., & Brown, A. L. (1987). Linking dynamic assessment with school achievement. In C. S. Lidz (Ed.), *Dynamic assessment: An interactional approach to evaluating learning potential*. New York: Guilford.

Cattell, P. (1980). *The measurement of intelligence of infants and young children* (5th reprint). San Antonio, TX: The Psychological Corporation.

Cocking, R. R., & Copple, C. E. (1987). Social influences on representational awareness: Plans for representing and plans as representation. In S. L. Friedman, E. K. Scholnick, & R. R. Cocking (Eds.), *Blueprints for thinking: The role of planning in cognitive development* (pp. 428–465). New York: Cambridge University Press.

Cripe, J., Slentz, K., & Bricker, D. (1993). *Assessment, Evaluation, and Programming System (AEPS) for infants and children* (Vol. 2): *AEPS curriculum for birth to three years*. Baltimore: Brookes.

Dubowitz, L., & Dubowitz, V. (1981). *The Neurological assessment of the preterm and full term newborn infant*. (Clinics in Developmental Medicine No. 79). London: Heinemann.

Dunlap, L. L. (1997). *An introduction to early childhood special education*. Needham Heights, MA: Allyn & Bacon.

Dunst, C. J. (1980). *A clinical and educational manual for use with the Uzgiris and Hunt Scales of Infant Psychological Development*. Austin, TX: PRO-ED.

Dunst, C. J. (1981). *Infant learning: A cognitive-linguistic intervention strategy*. Hingham, MA: Teaching Resources Corporation.

Dunst, C. J., Mahoney, G., & Buchan, K. (1996). Promoting the cognitive competence of young children with or at risk for developmental disabilities. In S. L. Odom and M. E. McLean (Eds.), *Early intervention/early childhood special education: Recommended practices* (pp. 159–196). Austin, TX: PRO-ED.

Dunst, C. J., & McWilliam, R. A. (1988). Cognitive assessment and multiply handicapped young children. In T. D. Wachs & R. Sheehan (Eds.), *Assessment of developmentally disabled children* (pp. 213–238). New York: Plenum Press.

Elliott, C. D. (1990). *The Differential Ability Scales*. San Antonio, TX: The Psychological Corp.

Fewell, R. R. (1986). *Play Assessment Scale* (5th rev.). Unpublished manuscript. University of Washington, Seattle.

Fewell, R. R., & Rich, J. S. (1987). Play assessment as a procedure for examining cognitive, communication, and social skills in multihandicapped children. *Journal of Psychoeducational Assessment, 2*, 107–118.

Francis, P. L., Self, P. A., & Horowitz, F. D. (1987). The behavioral assessment of the neonate: An overview. In J. D. Osofsky (Ed.), *Handbook of infant development*. New York: Wiley.

Gage, N. L., & Berliner, D. C. (1991). *Educational psychology*. Boston: Houghton Mifflin.

Gesell, A. (1925). *The mental growth of the preschool child*. New York: Macmillan.

Gesell, A., & Amatruda, C. S. (1947). *Developmental diagnosis*. New York: Hoeber.

Gibson, E. S., & Spelke, E. S. (1983). The development of perception. In J. H. Flavell & E. M. Markman (Eds.), *Handbook of child psychology* (Vol. 3): *Cognitive development* (4th ed., pp. 1–76). New York: Wiley.

Griffiths, R. (1954). *The Abilities of Babies*. London: University of London Press.

Griffiths, R. (1979). *The nature of human intelligence*. London: Child Development Research Center.

Horowitz, F. D. (1990). Developmental model of individual differences. In J. Colombo & J. Fagen (Eds.), *Individual differences in infancy: Reliability, stability; prediction* (pp. 3–18). Hillsdale, NJ: Erlbaum.

Hoy, C., & Gregg, N. (1994). *Assessment: The special educator's role*. Pacific Grove, CA: Brooks-Cole.

Istomina, Z. M. (1975). The development of voluntary memory in preschool-age children. *Soviet Psychology, 13* (Summer), 5–64.

Johnson-Martin, N. M., Jens, K. G., Attermeier, S. M., & Hacker, B. J. (1991). *The Carolina Curriculum for Infants and Toddlers with Special Needs* (2nd ed.). Baltimore: Brookes.

Kamphaus, R. W., & Kaufman, A. S. (1991). The assessment of preschool children with the Kaufman Assessment Battery for Children. In B. Bracken (Ed.), *The psycho-educational assessment of preschool children* (2nd ed.) (pp. 154–167). Boston: Allyn & Bacon.

Kaufman, A. S., & Kaufman, N. L. (1983). *Kaufman Assessment Battery for Children*. Circle Pines, MN: American Guidance Service.

Kearsley, R. B. (1984). *The systematic observation of children's play*. Unpublished scoring manual. (Available from the author, Child Health Services, Manchester, NH.)

Kiernan, D. W., & Dubose, R. F. (1974). Assessing the cognitive development of preschool deaf-blind children. *Education of the visually handicapped, 6*, 103–105.

Knobloch, H., & Pasamanick, B. (1974). *Gesell and Amatruda's developmental diagnosis: The evaluation and management of normal and abnormal neuropsychologic development in infancy and early childhood* (3rd ed.). New York: Harper & Row.

Knobloch, H., Stevens, F., & Malone, A. F. (1980). *Manual of developmental diagnosis: The administration and interpretation of the revised Gesell and Amatruda Developmental and Neurologic Examination*. Hagerstown, MA: Harper & Row.

Kopp, C. B., & McCall, R. B. (1982). Predicting later mental performance for normal at-risk, and handicapped infants. In P. B. Baltes & O. G. Brin (Eds.), *Life-span development and behavior* (Vol. 4). New York: Academic Press.

Langley, M. B. (1989). Assessing infant cognitive development. In D. Bailey & M. Wolery (Eds.), *Assessing infants and preschoolers with handicaps* (pp. 249–274). Upper Saddle River, NJ: Merrill/Prentice Hall.

Lefrancois, G. R. (1995). *Theories of human learning.* Pacific Grove, CA: Brookes/Cole.

Lerner, J. W., Lowenthal, B., & Egan, R. (1998). *Preschool children with special needs: Children at-risk, children with disabilities.* Needham Heights, MA: Allyn & Bacon.

Lerner, J., Mardell-Czudnowski, C., & Goldenberg, D. (1987). *Special education for the early childhood years* (2nd ed.). Upper Saddle River, NJ: Merrill/Prentice Hall.

Lewis, M., & Sullivan, M. W. (1985). Infant Intelligence and its assessment. In B. B. Wolman (Ed.), *Handbook of intelligence: Theories, measurements, and applications.* New York: Wiley.

Linder, T. (1993). *Transdisciplinary Play-Based Assessment: A functional approach to working with young children* (2nd ed.). Baltimore: Brookes.

Lipsitt, L. P. (1990). Learning and memory in infants. *Merrill-Palmer Quarterly, 36,* 53–66.

Lockman, J. J. (1983). Infant perception and cognition. In S. G. Garwood & R. R. Fewell (Eds.), *Educating handicapped infants: Issues in development and intervention* (pp. 117–164). Rockville, MD: Aspen.

Lowe, M., & Costello, A. J. (1976). *Manual for the Symbolic Play Test.* Windsor, England: NFR—Nelson.

McCall, R. B. (1994). What process mediates predictions of childhood IQ from infant habituation and recognition memory? Speculations on the role of inhibition and rate of information processing. *Intelligence, 18,* 107–126.

McCall, R. B., & Carriger, M. S. (1993). A meta-analysis of infant habituation and recognition memory performance as predictors of later IQ. *Child Development, 64,* 57–79.

McCallum, R. S. (1991). The assessment of preschool children with the Stanford-Binet Intelligence Scale: Fourth Edition. In B. Bracken (Ed.), *The psychoeducational assessment of preschool children* (2nd ed.) (pp. 107–132). Boston: Allyn & Bacon.

McCarthy, D. (1972). *McCarthy Scales of Children's Abilities.* New York: Psychological Corporation.

McCormick, K. (1996). Assessing cognitive development. In M. E. McLean, D. B. Bailey, & M. Wolery (Eds.), *Assessing infants and preschoolers with special needs* (pp. 269–304). Upper Saddle River, NJ: Merrill/Prentice Hall.

McCune, L. (1986). Symbolic development in normal and atypical infants. In G. Fein & M. Rivkin (Eds.), *The young child at play: Reviews of research* (pp. 45–61). Washington, DC: NAEYC.

McCune, L., Kalmanson, B., Fleck, M. B., Glazewski, B., & Sillari, J. (1990). An interdisciplinary model of infant assessment. In Samuel J. Meisels & Jack P. Shonkoff (Eds.), *Handbook of early childhood intervention* (pp. 219–245). New York: Cambridge University Press.

McCune-Nicolich, L. (1980). *A manual for analyzing free play: Experimental edition.* New Brunswick, NJ: Rutgers University.

McCune-Nicolich, L. (1983). *A manual for analyzing free play.* New Brunswick, NJ: Department of Educational Psychology, Rutgers University.

McLean, M., Bruder, M. B., Baird, S. M., & Dunst, C. J. (1991). Techniques for infants and toddlers with moderate or severe disabilities. In S. Raver (Ed.), *Strategies for teaching at-risk and handicapped infants and toddlers: A transdisciplinary approach* (pp. 234–259). Upper Saddle River, NJ: Merrill/Prentice Hall.

McLean, M., & McCormick, K. (1993). Assessment and evaluation in early intervention. In W. Brown, S. K. Thurman, & L. F. Pearl (Eds.), *Family-centered early intervention with infants and toddlers: Innovative cross-disciplinary approaches* (pp. 43–81). Baltimore: Brookes.

McLean, M., McCormick, K., & Baird, S. (1991). Concurrent validity of the Griffiths' Mental Development Scales with a population of children under 24 months. *Journal of Early Intervention, 15*(4), 338–344.

Mullen, E. M. (1991). *The Infant Mullen Scales of Early Learning: Instrument descriptions.* Cranston, RI: T.O.T.A.L. Child.

Murphy, M. D., & Brown, A. L. (1975). Incidental learning in preschool children as a function of level of cognitive analysis. *Journal of Experimental Psychology, 19,* 509–523.

Nehring, A. D., Nehring, E. F., Bruni, J. R., & Randolph, P. L. (1992). *Learning Accomplishment Profile Diagnostic Standardized Assessment.* Lewisville, NC: Kaplan School Supply Corp.

Neisser, U. (1967). *Cognitive psychology.* New York: Appleton-Century-Crofts.

Newborg, J., Stock, J., Wnek, L., Guidubaldi, J., & Svinicki, J. S. (1988). *The Battelle Developmental Inventory.* Chicago: Riverside.

Parks, S., Furuno, S., O'Reilly, K., Inatsuka, T., Hoska, C. M., & Zeisloft-Falbey, B. (1994). *Hawaii Early Learning Profile* (Birth to 3). Palo Alto, CA: VORT Corporation.

Piaget, J. (1952). *The origins of intelligence in children.* New York: International Universities Press.

Piaget, J. (1954). *The construction of reality in the child.* New York: Basic Books.

Piaget, J. (1962). *Play, dreams and imitation in childhood.* New York: Norton.

Raver, S. A. (1991). *Strategies for teaching at-risk and handicapped infants and toddlers: A transdisciplinary approach.* Upper Saddle River, NJ: Merrill/Prentice Hall.

Robinson, H. R., & Robinson, N. M. (1976). *The mentally retarded child* (2nd ed.). New York: McGraw-Hill.

Rosenblith, J. F. (1974a). Relations between neonatal behaviors and those at eight months. *Developmental Psychology, 10,* 779–792.

Rosenblith, J. F. (1974b). *Relations between newborn and four-year behaviors.* Paper presented at the meetings of the Eastern Psychological Association, New York.

Rosenblith, J. F. (1975). Prognostic value of neonatal behavioral tests. In B. Z. Friedlander, G. M. Sterritt, & G. E. Kirk

(Eds.), *Exceptional infant (vol. 3): Assessment and intervention*. New York: Brunner/Mazel.

Rossetti, L. M. (1990). *Infant-toddler assessment: An interdisciplinary approach*. Boston: College-Hill Press.

Rubenstein, J., & Howes, C. (1976). The effects of peers on toddler interaction with mothers and toys. *Child Development, 47,* 597–605.

Sattler, J. (1990). *Assessment of children* (3rd ed.). San Diego: Author.

Schneider, W., & Pressley, M. (1989). *Memory development between 2 and 20*. New York: Springer-Verlag.

Seifert, K. (1993). Cognitive development and early childhood education. In B. Spodek (Ed.), *Handbook of research on the education of young children* (pp. 9–23). New York: Macmillan.

Shantz, E. U. (1975). The development of social cognition. In E. M. Hetherington (Ed.), *The development of social cognition* (Vol. 5). Chicago: University of Chicago Press.

Shantz, E. U. (1975). The development of social cognition. In E. M. Hetherington (Ed.), *Review of child development research* vol. 5, pp. 257–353. Chicago: University of Chicago Press.

Shonkoff, J. (1983). The limitations of normative assessment of high-risk infants. *Topics in Early Childhood Special Education, 3,* 29–43.

Shonkoff, J. P., & Meisels, S. J. (1990). Early childhood intervention: The evolution of a concept. In S. J. Meisels & J. P. Shonkoff (Eds.), *Handbook of early childhood intervention* (pp. 3–31). New York: Cambridge University Press.

Siegler, R. (1983). Information processing approaches to child development. In P. Mussen (Ed.), *Handbook of child psychology* Vol. 1 (pp. 129–211). New York: Wiley.

Stodolsky, S. S. (1974). How children find something to do in preschools. *Genetic Psychology Monographs, 90,* 245–303.

Thorndike, R. L., Hagen, E. P., & Sattler, J. M. (1985). *Stanford-Binet Intelligence Scale: Fourth Edition*. Chicago: Riverside Publishing Co.

Umansky, W., & Hooper, S. R. (1998). *Young children with special needs* (3rd ed.). Upper Saddle River, NJ: Merrill/Prentice Hall.

Uzgiris, I., & Hunt, J. M. (1975). *Assessment in infancy: Ordinal scales of psychological development*. Urbana: University of Illinois Press.

VORT Corporation. (1995). *Hawaii Early Learning Profile* (HELP): HELP *for Preschoolers (3–6)*. Palo Alto, CA: VORT Corporation.

Vulpe, S. G. (1994). *Vulpe Assessment Battery, Revised Edition*. East Aurora, NY: Slosson Educational Publications.

Vygotsky, L. (1978a). *Mind in society*. Cambridge, MA: Harvard University Press.

Vygotsky, L. (1978b). *Thought and language*. Cambridge, MA: Harvard University Press.

Watson, M. W., & Fischer, K. W. (1977). A developmental sequence of agent use in late infancy. *Child Development, 48,* 828–836.

Wechsler, D. (1989). *Wechsler Preschool and Primary Scales of Intelligence-Revised*. San Antonio, TX: The Psychological Corp.

Woodcock, R. W., & Johnson, M. B. (1989). *Woodcock-Johnson Psychoeducational Battery-Revised*. Allen, TX: DLM.

Worobey, J., & Brazelton, T. B. (1990). Newborn assessment and support for parenting. In E. D. Gibbs & D. M. Teti (Eds.), *Interdisciplinary assessment of infants: A guide for early intervention professionals*. Baltimore: Brookes.

Wyly, M. V. (1997). *Infant assessment*. Boulder, CO: Westview Press.

Yarrow, L. J., Rubenstein, J. L., & Pedersen, F. A. (1975). *Infant and environment: Early cognitive and motivational development*. Washington, DC: Hemisphere.

Zelazo, P. R. (1979). Reactivity to perceptual-cognitive events: Application for infant assessment. In R. Kearsley & I. Sigel (Eds.), *Infants at risk: Assessment of cognitive functioning*. Hillsdale, NJ: Erlbaum.

Zelazo, P. R. (1982a). An information processing approach to infant cognitive assessment. In M. Lewis & L. T. Taft (Eds.), *Developmental disabilties: Theory, assessment, and intervention*. New York: Spectrum.

Zelazo, P. R. (1982b). Alternative assessment procedures for handicapped infants and toddlers: Theoretical and practical issues. In D. D. Bricker (Ed.), *Intervention with at-risk and handicapped infants: From research to application*. Baltimore: University Park Press.

15

Communication Assessment

Ellenmorris Tiegerman and Christine Radziewicz

During the past three decades, child language research has detailed the language acquisition process for children from birth to 5 years. Clinical research with young children with disabilities highlights the importance of language and communication intervention for children during the formative years as a critical foundation for later academic success.

In 1986, PL 99-457 extended the requirements, rights, and protections previously available only to school-aged children with disabilities downward to include infants and preschoolers from birth to age 5. Within the framework of this law, the professional skills of the speech-language pathologist became invaluable for youngsters with speech and language delays and their families. In 1990, the American Speech-Language-Hearing Association published a position statement on the role of the speech-language pathologist in service delivery to infants, toddlers, and their families. This position statement clarifies the roles and responsibilities of the speech-language pathologist as including:

- Screening and identification
- Assessment and evaluation
- Design, planning, direct delivery and monitoring of program
- Case management
- Consultation with and referral to agencies and other professionals providing services to this young population and their families

This position statement affirms the integral role of the speech-language pathologist in the identification, assessment, and remediation of the infant, toddler, or preschooler with a language or communication disorder. The speech-language pathologist is skilled in assessing the communication, speech, and language behavior of the child and the communicative interactions of the parents/caregivers, and can provide insights into enhancing and developing communication skills. For the young child, most early learning is mediated through language and, therefore, it is vital that children with speech impairments and their families participate in the assessment process to determine what assessment and intervention goals are most appropriate to enhance developmental patterns.

The passage of PL 99-457 and its subsequent amendments and reauthorizations has had a monumental impact on assessment. Previously, diagnostic teams focused on the child; however, now a more encompassing ecological perspective is needed in order to serve the child under age 5 years. A multidisciplinary assessment is required to meet the evaluation and treatment needs of children and families. As a result, a collaborative team of professionals performs an assessment with the child and family in order to determine whether or not the infant, toddler, or preschooler demonstrates age-appropriate skills in the areas of cognition, communication, motor development, physical development, and social emotional development. The outcome of this multidisciplinary assessment is the IEP, which is required for preschoolers, and the IFSP for infants and toddlers. These plans function as a contract and ensure that services will be provided to meet short-term and long-term developmental goals. The roles of the team members should be assumed in a comprehensive community-based program that is family-centered and is also coordinated with other services that families and their children may need or receive. The speech-language pathologist should be an integral member of any multidisciplinary team serving families and their young children (American Speech-Language-Hearing Association, 1990).

This chapter will focus on the assessment of communication development in infants, toddlers, and preschoolers. Questions to be addressed are: What assessment techniques, strategies, and instruments are suitable for this assessment process? Who is being evaluated and assessed? What is being evaluated and assessed? What is the role of the speech-language pathologist?

Parent-Child Interaction

An area of assessment that is of paramount importance to the speech-language pathologist is parent-child interaction. Previous research (Bell & Harper, 1977; Brazelton, 1982; Lewis & Rosenblum, 1974; Tronick & Ganino, 1986) has identified parent-child social interactions as bidirectional and homeostatic; that is, during a communicative interaction between parent and child, each is an active member of the interaction and each makes adaptations to the other's behavior. With an infant, the parent facilitates organization of the child's behavior and bears most of the responsibility for the interaction. As the child becomes older, he shares more responsibility for the interaction and learns to interact in a communicative style that matches the style of the parent. In optimal circumstances, there is a good fit or matching, and parent-child interchanges are pleasant and sustaining (Thomas & Chess, 1977). Because these early parent-child interactions lay the foundation for further language learning, it is imperative that the speech-language pathologist be skilled in assessing them. Assessment can be through observation and use of a parent-child interaction scale. Chapter 2 discusses many different types of parent-child interaction assessments that would be useful to the speech-language pathologist assessing the interaction of caregivers and child. Table 15–1 lists several specific instruments for assessing parent-child interaction with regard to communication between parents and children.

It should be noted that proper use of these scales requires a videotape recorder, a camera, and a playback monitor. These scales are effective in identifying strengths and weaknesses in the parent-child interactive dyad. This information enables the speech-language pathologist to work with the family in understanding their own interactive style as well as that of their child. Highlighting the behaviors that enhance communication empowers parents to become more effective teachers, models, and communication partners. The speech-language pathologist is particularly equipped to work with parents to enhance communicative styles and strategies. The speech-language pathologist's educational training background includes familiarity with areas such as prespeech, language, play, social routines, gestures, intentions, and parent-child interactions.

All of the information gained from observations, interviews, and parent infant assessment scales can readily be translated into intervention goals by the speech-language pathologist. Crais and Roberts (1991) developed a decision-making framework for early intervention that they refer to as decision trees. This framework is appropriate for children ages 3 months to 5 years and is an alternative to standardized testing. The decision trees include a sequenced set of questions followed by available response choices; they assess social interaction, comprehension, and production and have been recommended as guidelines for assessment and management by Yoder and Kent (1988). This highly organized framework is very convenient and suitable for the speech-language pathologist assessing and working with young children who are receiving early intervention services because many may be *chronologically* older than 3 years, but *developmentally* may be in the 3-month to 3-year age range. Figure 15-1 represents a decision tree that relates to the social interaction behaviors and comprehension behaviors of a child at the one-word utterance stage. Utilizing this decision tree will enable the speech-language pathologist to plan appropriate intervention strategies.

Child Assessment

When assessing the child, behavioral observations must be made and documented because behavioral observation is a critical diagnostic tool. It should be performed in a natural context. Observation is considered a critical aspect of

TABLE 15–1
Parent-Child Interaction Assessments

Assessment Instrument	Publisher/Source
Social Interaction Assessment/ Intervention	
Assesses communicative social interaction between the parent and the child (useful for children 2 to 34 mos)	McCollum (1984). *Child: Care, Health and Development, 10*, 301–315; McCollum & Stayton (1985). *Journal of the Division for Early Childhood, 9*(2), 125–135.
Interaction Rating Scale	
Assesses the parents' imitating, affect, gaze pattern, dyadic reciprocity, and interaction style.	Clark & Siefer (1985). *Infant Mental Health Journal, 6*, 214–225.
Teaching Skills Inventory	
Assesses the parents' verbal instructions and the child's interest level during interactions (useful for children 2 to 36 mos)	Rosenberg, Robinson, & Beckman (1984). *Journal of the Division for Early Childhood, 8*, 107–113.
Parent/Caregiver Involvement Scale	
Assesses 11 adult behaviors during play interactions with the child (useful for children 2 to 57 mos)	Farren, Kasari, Yoder, Harber, Huntington, & Comfort-Smith (1987). In T. Tamir (Ed.), *Stimulation and intervention in infant development.* London: Freund Publishing.

an assessment because it provides information about the way children actually use or do not use certain skills. Informal observation in a comfortable setting may be more important for speech and language assessment than the use of any specific standardized measure (McCune, Kalmanson, Fleck, Glazewski, & Sillari, 1990). The use of meaningful contexts is especially important in the assessment of young or low-functioning children. Contrived assessment situations reduce the probability that the language behaviors are typical of a child's everyday performance (Roth, 1990). Early language and communicative behavior is so dependent on the situation that children may be unwilling to display their skill to strangers in an unfamiliar environment. An advantage of language assessment through naturalistic observation is the ability to

FIGURE 15–1

Decision Tree for a Child at the One-Word Utterance Stage

Social Interaction

Assessment Questions		Intervention Activities
1 Does child verbally exhibit any earlier developing intentions (i.e., attention-seeking, requests, and protests) with familiar people?	-NO-	Go to Decision Tree for child at the pre-linguistic stage.
YES		
2 Does child nonverbally exhibit any intentions with unfamiliar people?	-NO-	Attempt to elicit attention by bringing out novel or action toys (e.g., windup toy). After demonstrating toy, allow it to stop and reinforce any signal from child indicating interest.
YES		
3 Does child verbally exhibit any intentions with unfamiliar person?	-NO-	Use "reported" verbally expressed intentions (e.g., "no") and play a game where at each turn child can respond "no" (e.g., offer wrong puzzle pieces). Begin by modeling and then wait for child's response.
YES		
4 Does child verbally express a variety of communicative intentions?	-NO-	During daily activities or play routines create a need for communication and model utterances to express a child's intentions (e.g., build a block tower and say "more block" when needs another and "block fall" when tower falls.
YES		
5 Does child initiate a familiar play routine related to the context and then take one turn in the interaction?	-NO-	Set up environment to encourage a familiar routine (e.g., position yourself for a tickle routine) and pause for child's turn. If no response, model approximate initiation (e.g., "tickle").
YES		
6 Does child maintain attention to a play activity or interaction for a continuous minute when playing with a "focused" adult?	-NO-	Select activity or game (e.g., pat-a-cake, horsie) the child enjoys and plays for an increasingly longer period of time, maintaining child's attention.
YES		

FIGURE 15–1
continued

7	Does child take turns in an interaction by exchanging social roles during game (e.g., adult tickles child, then child becomes the "tickler")?	-NO-	Play familiar game and model the initiator's role of the child (e.g., take child's hands and tickle yourself).

YES

8	Does child participate in play routines associated with daily activities (e.g., rubber duck jumps into bath and quacks at start of each bath time)?	-NO-	Begin repeating the same action or action/sound sequence at the same time during a daily activity.

YES

9	Does the child take three turns in an interaction or in a play activity initiated by an adult?	-NO-	Initiate a play activity or interaction (e.g., pat-a-cake, peek-a-boo), pause for child's response (e.g., with hands ready to clap), take another turn quickly (e.g., clap), and pause again.

Source: "Decision making in assessment and early intervention" by E. Crais and J. Roberts, 1991, *Language, Speech, Hearing Services in Schools, 22*, pp. 25–30, © American Speech and Hearing Association, Rockville, MD. Reprinted with permission.

assess many components of the language system simultaneously. As the child's language develops, all forms of assessment come to depend more and more on the use of language, both in understanding instructions and in producing responses.

To obtain a natural language sample in a setting outside the home or classroom, a play session between the baby and the caregiver may be set up with appropriate toys and picture books. This session could be recorded or videotaped and supplemented with observational notes. A home-based session allows more comfort and freedom on the part of the child and caregiver and, therefore, provides a richer language sample. The natural language sample becomes more important with age, and beyond 18 months becomes a critical feature of an assessment (McCune, et al., 1990). Roberts and Crais (1989) offered the following list of suggestions on how to manage the context and setting to engage children in interactions:

1. Choose developmentally appropriate toys and materials. Use play and motor scales to help in the selection.
2. Limit your own talking, especially questions. Pause often to encourage the child to initiate communication and take a turn.
3. Watch for and encourage any mode of communication demonstrated by child (eye gaze, point, shrug, word, etc.).
4. Parallel play with the child, mimicking her actions. Play animatedly with an object or toy and occasionally comment on an object or action.
5. Place a few items within eye gaze but out of reach; partially hide a few objects as well. If necessary, point to or comment on objects to encourage a comment or request by the child.
6. Let the child choose objects and/or activities, particularly in the beginning (and throughout the interaction if possible). Be

prepared to watch and interact/comment when the child shows interest.

7. Include parent of another child to help break the ice. Stay in the background and slowly get into the interaction.

8. Begin interaction with activities that require little or no talking, and gradually move to more verbal tasks.

9. Be genuine in your questions, and stay away from asking what is obvious to both you and the child.

10. Follow the child's lead in the interaction by maintaining the child's focus on particular topics and meanings.

11. Show warmth and positive regard for the child, and value his comments. (p. 351)

Observation of children interacting with care-givers in naturalistic contexts is one of the major means of sampling children's spontaneous communicative abilities. However, the result is often an incomplete picture of the young child's performance owing to the variable of the context, because not all behaviors of interest will occur, or may not occur with adequate frequency to provide sufficient data with which to make recommendations. The absence of a particular behavior is not necessarily an indication that the skill is not part of a child's repertoire. The skill also must be demonstrated frequently enough to assess it adequately. Therefore, the most complete sampling of language behaviors is obtained through a combination of naturalistic observations and structured elicitations (Roth, 1990).

Coggins, Olswang, and Guthrie (1987) and Wetherby and Rodriguez (1992) compared the use of elicitation procedures with sampling in natural contexts to obtain information. Elicitation tasks do not guarantee a response; they increase the probability that the young child will produce the desired behavior in a given situation. Both groups of researchers studied young children's expression of requests and comments in spontaneous play and from elicitation tasks. Coggins and colleagues found that the children

produced spontaneous comments in the play context but infrequently produced spontaneous requests. The results of both studies indicate that the elicitation tasks were more successful than the spontaneous-play context at sampling requests.

The inclusion of both low-structured observation and elicitation tasks supports the notion that multiple sources of information and multiple measures are the only adequate way to assess the communicative abilities of a young child. Therefore, the most complete sampling of language behaviors is obtained through a combination of naturalistic observations, elicitation tasks, and structured elicitations (Roth, 1990).

There are four areas that must be considered when assessing young children: cognitive development, communicative development, development of play, and motor development.

Cognitive Development

Piaget (1952) developed a model of the development of cognition that extends from birth to 14 years. This model is particularly interesting to educators in planning intervention techniques. Also of interest and use to the assessment team are scales that assess the earliest cognitive development. Several such scales have been developed that utilize this Piagetian framework; Uzgiris and Hunt (1975) developed six scales that pertain to the six branches of psychological development of infants (see Chapter 14 for assessing cognition).

An offshoot of Piagetian theory of cognitive development that is useful in assessing young children is information processing theory, which considers the mind as a complex cognitive system (Paget, 1989). This complex system is regarded in terms of mental processes that enable the child to problem solve and process cognition (see Chapter 14).

Play Development

Play is the child's domain. Assessment of play will give the assessment team valuable information about how the child interacts with his environment. Westby (1980) developed a scale that describes symbolic play and integrates expected language structures with play performance. A play scale developed by Garvey (1974) integrates Piaget's stages of cognitive development with play. Another play assessment instrument that looks at social play is Howes's Peer Play Scale (1980), which considers five developmental levels of play and allows the examiner to determine at what level the child is functioning based on observations of play.

Besides being an enjoyable activity, play serves as a vehicle to practice and solidify cognitive skills, promote emotional and social growth, refine gross and fine motor skills, and enhance communication development (Bailey & Wolery, 1989). As the child grows older it is expected that play schemas become more elaborate, complex, and interactive. When a child's level of play is assessed and understood, it is a valuable resource for facilitating development of other behaviors.

Motor Development

Normal motor development is well-documented (Chandler, 1979; Knoblock & Pasamanick, 1974); children pass through motor developmental milestones in an orderly fashion. Consequently, assessment of motor development is easily managed and is typically divided into assessment of fine motor skills and gross motor skills. The areas that should be considered when conducting a motor assessment include muscle tone, reflexes and reaction, movement and posture patterns, and functional abilities (Smith, 1989).

Recently much research has centered on the development of oral motor skills in the infant. Oral motor functioning includes reflexive oral motor abilities such as sucking and swallowing; assessment of feeding is especially important when working with the child who has suspected motor disabilities. In addition, study of the early vocal behaviors of the infant is

of particular interest to the speech-language pathologist. The chronology of oral motor feeding patterns is as follows.

Birth to 6 Months

Suckling: extension-retraction of tongue, up-and-down jaw movement, loose lip approximation.

Sucking: rhythmic up-and-down jaw movements with tongue tip elevation, tight approximation of the lips.

Rooting: head turns in response to tactile stimulation of lips or mouth.

Phasic bite reflex: rhythmic bite and release pattern when gums are stimulated.

6 to 24 Months

Munching: earliest level of chewing in which the tongue is flat and the jaw moves up and down.

Chewing: food is propelled between the teeth through spreading and rolling movements of tongue.

Tongue lateralization: the tongue moves to the sides of the mouth and propels food between teeth for chewing.

Rotary jaw movements: integration of vertical, lateral, diagonal, and circular movements of the jaw during chewing.

Controlled bite: easy closure of teeth on food with easy releasing of food for chewing (Jaffe, 1989).

Formal feeding assessment instruments include the *Feeding Assessment*, in English and Spanish versions (Morris & Klein, 1987); the *Pre-Speech Assessment Scale* (Morris, 1982); and the *Oral Motor Assessment* (Sleight & Niman, 1984). Each of these instruments will enable the speech-language pathologist to identify any strengths or needs associated with feeding.

The normally developing infant learns to shape vocalization into sound productions that approximate words and, eventually, multiword productions. For the infant with oral motor difficulties, the process does not necessarily occur with ease. Although there are no norms for articulatory and acoustic data on non-crying vocal behaviors in infancy, there are research studies that examine infant vocalizations (Delack & Fowlow, 1978; Oller, 1980, 1986). Proctor (1989) delineates five stages of vocal development and has developed a vocal assessment form.

Stage 1: More crying sounds than non-crying sounds; non-crying sounds are mostly vegetative.

Stage 2: Less crying; predominance of vocalic sounds, long-vowel (LV) productions.

Stage 3: Increased consonant productions; varied vowel productions; consistent consonant-vowel (CV) syllables; varied intonation contours.

Stage 4: Reduplicated babbling in the form of CV or consonant-vowel-consonant (CVC) structures; consistent variations in intonation contours.

Stage 5: Variety of CV and CVC combinations with sentence-like intonation; approximations of meaningful single words.

Utilization of a protocol such as Proctor's enables the speech-language pathologist to determine the level of vocal behavior development, compare it with oral motor feeding skill level development, and plan therapeutic intervention strategies.

Stoel-Gammon (1987) stated that by two years of age the normally developing child produces words using CV, CVC, CVCV, and CVCVC forms; produces a few consonant clusters; matches the consonant phonemes of adult words with 70 percent correctness; produces 9 or 10 different consonants in initial position; and produces five or six different consonants in the final position. This information is also useful to the speech-language

pathologist in determining whether intervention is needed.

Although there is considerable overlap of these three dimensions, each offers a somewhat different view of a child's communicative skills (Benner, 1992). Bailey (1989) indicated that there are seven characteristics to effective child assessment. McCormick and Schiefelbusch (1990) have adapted these seven characteristics so that they are focused on speech and language assessment. They state that the following characteristics indicate effective assessment:

1. The process incorporates multiple sources and multiple measures.
2. The process involves caregivers both as informants and significant partners.
3. The process is comprehensive, covering all important developmental and behavioral dimensions of language and considering performance across natural settings.
4. The process involves professionals from other disciplines.
5. The process is ecologically valid.
6. The process is nondiscriminatory.
7. The process is capable of providing continuous progress information.

Although all seven of these characteristics are useful for effective assessment, it is important to fully understand the impact the first three have on speech and language assessment. If an assumption is made that an effective assessment requires information from multiple sources, and measures, then it is assumed that information will be obtained by interviewing the family, observing the child in natural contexts, and administering formal and informal tests. Caregivers can give important information about the child's use of language at home, in situations professionals cannot observe, and with different communicative partners. Caregivers should also be asked to identify priorities for intervention.

Finally, to be effective, an assessment needs to be comprehensive, including information that concerns all aspects of language and communication performance across natural contexts. At the very least, language assessment must consider language comprehension, production, and use.

Child Assessment Instruments

A number of standardized norm-referenced instruments as well as standardized criterion-referenced instruments are available to the speech-language pathologist that are helpful in measuring speech, language, and communication development. These instruments are summarized in Table 15–1.

Dimensions of Speech and Language for a Comprehensive Assessment

A comprehensive assessment of infants at-risk for developmental problems must include a variety of speech and language techniques to assess a variety of components of speech, language, and communication. In addition, a speech-language pathologist should perform an oral-peripheral examination to determine the infant's neurological potential for efficient respiration and feeding and for appropriate, volitional sound production (McCune, et al., 1990).

TABLE 15–1
Standardized Norm-Referenced Child Assessment Instruments

Assessment Instrument	Description
Test of Auditory Comprehension of Language TACL:3 (Carrow-Woolfolk) Allen, TX: DLM Resources, 1999.	Measures the auditory comprehension of single words, teaching grammatical morphemes, and elaborated sentences, and can be administered to children 3 to 8.
Expressive One-Word Picture Vocabulary Test-R (Gardner) Novato, CA: AcademicTherapy Publications, 2000.	Measures expressive vocabulary. It is appropriate for children 2 to 11-11 years. It is available in English and Spanish.
Receptive One-Word Picture Vocabulary Test-R (Gardner) Novato, CA: Academic Therapy Publications, 2000.	Measures a child's single-word receptive vocabulary. It is appropriate for children 2 to 11-11 years. It is available in English and Spanish.
Test of Pragmatic Skills (Shulman) Tucson, AZ, Communication Skills Builders,1985.	Measures how children use their language in various communicative contexts. It is appropriate for children 3 to 8-11 years.
Test of Early Language Development (3rd Ed.) (Hresko, Reid, & Hammell) Austin, TX: PRO-ED, 1999.	Measures the understanding and expression of grammatical forms, language content, and semantic knowledge.
Behavioral Development Profile (Donahue. Montgomery, Keiser, Roecker, & Smith) Marshalltown, IA: Marshalltown Project, 1975.	Measures the development of children who are disabled and culturally deprived, ages birth through 3 years. The *Profile* consists of a communication scale, motor scale, and social scale.

Birth to Three Developmental Scales
(Bangs & Garrett)
Hingham, MA: Teaching Resources, 1979.

Provides baseline data for children ages birth to 3 years. It assesses social skills, motor skills, and receptive and expressive language.

Callier-Azusa Scales (Stillman, Ed.)
Dallas, TX: Callier Center for Communications Disorders, University of Texas at Dallas, 1975

Assesses motor development, perceptual development, daily living skills, language development, and socialization. This is a developmental scale designed specifically fordeaf, blind, and multidisabled children.

Carolina Developmental Profile (Lillie)
Winston-Salem, NC: Kaplan School Supply, 1975.

Assesses fine motor, gross motor, perceptual reasoning, receptive language, expressive language. This is a criterion referenced checklist of skills expected in children 2 to 5 years.

*Communicative Evaluation Chart
(Anderson, Miles, & Matheny)
Cambridge, MA: Educators Publishing Service, Inc., 1963.

Assesses comprehension and expression of language and motor skills. This checklist is a screening device for children birth to 5 years.

The Early Intervention Developmental Profile (D'Eugenio & Rogers)
Ann Arbor, MI: Early Intervention Project of Handicapped Infants and Young Children, 1975.

Assesses children birth to 36 months in the areas of language, motor development, cognitive development, and social-emotional development. It was designed for use by a multidisciplinary team consisting of psychologist or special educator, and occupational therapist, and a speech-language pathologist.

*Environment Prelanguage Battery
(Horstmeir & MacDonald)
Columbus, OH: Merrill,1978.

Assesses early prelinguistic communication skills such as play, gestures, imitation, following directions. It is appropriate for children 1 to 2-6 years.

Infant-Parent Training Program (Drezek)
Austin, TX: Infant-Parent Training Program, 1973.

Assesses the development level of children birth to 1 year in cognition, communication, social, and gross motor and self-help skills.

Informal Teacher Assessment Instrument
(Drezek)
Austin, TX: Infant-Parent Training Program, 1975.

Includes development checklist, skill checklists, observations guidelines, and checklist questions to determine developmental level of a child. It is appropriate for children birth to 6 years.

Koontz Child Developmental Program: Training Activities for the First 48 Months
(Koontz)
Los Angeles: Western Psychological Services, 1974.

Assesses a child's functioning level in gross motor, fine motor, social, and language skills areas for children birth to 48 months.

Learning Accomplishment Profile for Infants: Experimental Edition
(Griffen & Sanford)
Winston-Salem, NC: Kaplan School Supply Corp., 1975.

Assesses gross motor, fine motor, social, self-help, cognitive, and language areas. This assessment tool is designed to identify the developmental level of functioning in children birth to 3 years.

353

Portage Guide to Early Education, Revised Edition (Bluma, Shearer, Frohman, & Hilliard) Portage, WI: Portage Project, 1976.

To be used as an assessment instrument to identify a child's repertoire of behaviors. It can be used for children birth to 6 years.

*Receptive-Expressive Emergent Language Scale (2nd ed.) (Bzach & League) Baltimore: University Park Press, 1998.

Based on caregiver report and yields information on receptive and expressive language.

*Rossetti Infant Toddler Language Scale (Rossetti) East Moline, IL: Linguisystems, 1990.

Measures communication and interaction skills for children birth through 3 years. It looks at areas such as play, interaction attachment, pragmatics, gestures, language comprehension, and expression.

*Scales of Early Communication Skills for Hearing Impaired Children (Moog & Geers) St. Louis, MO: Central Institution for the Deaf, 1975.

Designed to assess speech and language development in hearing-impaired children ages 2 to 8 years.

Sequenced Inventory of Communicative Development-Revised (Hedrick, Prather, & Tobin) Seattle: University of Washington Press, 1984.

Assesses language skills such as sound awareness, comprehension, and verbal expression in children 3 months to 4 years.

*Goldman-Fristoe Test of Articulation (Goldman & Fristoe) Circle Pines, MN: American Guidence Service, 1986.

Measures a child's articulation of consonant sound. It is appropriate for ages 2 years to adult.

*Khan-Lewis Phonological Analysis (Khan & Lewis) Circle Pines, MN: American Guidance Service, 1986.

Measures phonological development. It is used in conjunction with the Goldman-Fristoe Test of Articulation and is appropriate for children $2\frac{1}{2}$ to 5 years.

*Peabody Picture Vocabulary Test-Revised (Dunn & Dunn) Circle Pines, MN: American Guidance Service, 1981.

Assesses receptive vocabulary in children ages $2\frac{1}{2}$ years to adult. It is available in English and Spanish.

*Clinical Evaluation of Language Fundamentals-P (Wiig, Secord, & Semel) San Antonio: Psychological Corporation, 1992.

Measures a range of expressive and receptive language skills in preschool children ages 3 through 6.

*Preschool Language Scale-3 (Zimmerman, Steiner, & Pond) San Antonio, TX: Psychological Corporation, 1992.

Assesses auditory comprehension and verbal language for children birth to 6-11 years. It is available in English and Spanish.

Early Language Milestone (ELM) Scale-2
(Caplan)
Ausin, TX: PRO-ED, 1993.

Considers several communicative behaviors
such as receptive, expressive, visual for children
birth to 36 months.

Utah Test of Language Development-3
(Mecham & Jones)
Austin, TX: PRO-ED, 1989.

Assesses the expressive and receptive
language of children ages 3 through 9.

---

*These assessment checklists/questionnaires assess only speech/language/communication development.

An audiological screening must also be done to obtain an estimate of hearing ability and to identify those children who should be referred for a complete audiological assessment (McCune, et al., 1990).

Assessing the Infant's Readiness to Communicate

In order to develop appropriate intervention goals for the parents and therapists who will eventually provide intervention services, it is important to consider the child's readiness to communicate. Socio-communicative skills involve maternal-infant interaction and attachment, as well as the child's overall ability to comprehend and process language (Rossetti, 1991). The social interaction that takes place between the infant and the caregiver provides the foundation for the child's intentional use of language (Bates, 1979; Bruner, 1981). A comprehensive language assessment needs to examine both the caregiver-infant interaction and the infant's readiness to communicate.

Many instruments have been developed to facilitate the assessment of infant-caregiver interaction. Note, however, that interactional styles vary across families and cultures and that it may be difficult to qualify and quantify the exact nature of infant-caregiver interactions. When interpreting results obtained using any of the measures, it is important for the assessor to focus on the positive behaviors of the caregiver and infant and the cultural variation in interaction patterns.

When assessing the infant's readiness to communicate, the following aspects need to be examined: the child's use of gaze, the attention to social stimuli and development of contingency, joint attention and joint action, and affective sharing.

Gaze is a powerful mode of communication. Infants respond to their caregiver's voice and face as early as 2 weeks of age, fixing their gaze on the caregiver's mouth or eyes (Owens, 1992; Tiegerman & Primavera, 1984). Reciprocal interactions that involve gaze are thus found early on in the infant's repertoire.

The development of reciprocal social and communicative interaction depends on the ability to understand contingency, that is, the fact that actions of others affect oneself and that one's own actions affect others (Klinger & Dawson, 1992). Through contingent, predictable, and repetitive interactions with caregivers, infants develop a sense of control over their environments (Lamb, 1981) and begin to perceive themselves as effective social agents (Schaffer, 1977). Thus, it is important to examine the contingency between the caregiver and the child. Likewise, the infant needs to be aware that social stimuli may signal the initiation of a communicative exchange.

Another aspect of early communication that needs to be documented is joint attention. Joint attention includes the triadic exchanges involving the caregiver, the infant, and objects. In these exchanges, caregivers and infants coordinate their attention around objects of mutual interest. Joint attention is observed through the use of referential looking between the object and caregiver

(Klinger & Dawson, 1992). Joint action or routinized interaction games such as peek-a-boo are another important aspect to early communication. These interactional games provide the infant the opportunity to learn and practice important aspects of communication (Ratner & Bruner, 1978). In these interactions, the infant learns about turn-taking, event initiation, and structure, and because there is a close relationship between what is said and what is done, the infant can begin to make sense out of the language he hears.

Affective sharing involves the interpersonal coordination of affective expression between an infant and his caregiver. Typically, they experience mutual interest and pleasure in each other's smiling and vocalizations (Klinger & Dawson, 1992).

Authentic Assessment

When assessing young children, assessors must choose their tools carefully and be certain that the appropriate children are identified as having communication delays or disorders. Specificity and sensitivity are two standards for assessment tools; specificity is the percentage of children correctly classified as having a positive outcome, and sensitivity is the percentage of children correctly classified as having a negative outcome (Barnes, 1982; Squires, Nickel, & Eisert, 1996). Authentic assessments are those which tease out any inherent biases in language and communication assessments. They are multidimensional and multiperspective, and do not rely on the results from one test type or have a single objective. Different types of assessment measures must be used when assessing the communication abilities of young children, including checklists, formal standardized measures, spontaneous speech samples, interviews, conversations, reviews of previous educational or diagnostic records and direct and indirect observations (Wiig, 2000). The communicative environment also must be examined to determine whether it is a source of stimulation for language development or is one that is not matched to the child's needs and thus does not enhance or facilitate the development of communication. This examination of the environment leads to an implementation of an ecobehavioral approach (McConnell, 2000), whereby the environment is shaped to create optimal conditions for stimulation, encouragement, opportunity, and reinforcement for attempts at communication.

Authentic assessments also help discriminate between communication difference versus disorder. The number of children of non-English-speaking backgrounds living in the United States today dictates that we must be prepared to identify exceptional children in their linguistic and cultural milieu (Bergin, 1980). The clinician must be sensitive to the cultural characteristics of a child's ethnic community; she must also be knowledgeable regarding acquisition and normative data on the child's first language.

As discussed in Chapter 3, speech-language clinicians need to have sufficient knowledge regarding cultural groups in order to provide competent clinical services to these children and their families. These groups have unique cultural characteristics; understanding of salient cultural and linguistic factors is necessary for assessment of communication disorders. Culture and language cannot be separated, and each culture defines what are deviant communication patterns within the perspective of the community. (Kayser, 1994). Therefore, it is essential that the assessment procedures used with children whose primary language is not English reduce or minimize the linguistic and cultural aspects that could negatively influence a diagnosis (Mattes & Omark, 1984; Omark & Erickson, 1983; Taylor & Payne, 1983; Terrell, 1983). The nonbiased assessment will distinguish the language-different child from the child who has a language disorder. There are two factors that impact upon the performance of culturally and linguistically diverse children during the assessment process: the language used in testing and the cultural relevance of the procedures selected. Conse-quently, it is imperative that assessments be conducted in the language in which a child is most proficient. Furthermore, assessment pro-cedures should be modified when necessary to accommodate the effects of the child's re-sponse patterns and experiences with the as-sessment materials used (Anderson, 1994). Only then will cultural and linguistic biases be reduced or eliminated.

Summary

Current thinking regarding early intervention and as-sessment must be revolutionized. It is no longer an issue of assessing the child; now the assessment ex-tends to the family. Because it is recognized that the parent is the front-line service provider and educator for the preschool child, the concerns and strengths of the family are now assessed. This enlarged view of the child as part of a family system (Bell & Harper, 1968) gives rise to an ecological view of development. Assessment of the family broadens the knowledge base related to the child. What are the cultural differ-ences of the family? What is the family structure and functioning? What areas of functioning need support or help?

When assessing the child, standardized crite-rion-referenced instruments are available. In addi-tion, informal or behavior observations are of para-mount importance in determining the child's functioning level. This type of assessment is au-thentic in that it captures the essence of the child performing in his environment. It gives invaluable clues as to how the child's disability impacts on his day-to-day living.

Services are no longer provided only to the child. Instead, assessors and interventionists work with the family and the child in order to determine and facili-tate development in multiple areas such as commu-nication, play and social interaction. Assessment is not static, but rather a work in progress. It must be in-sightful, nontraditional, creative, and flexible. It must provide a springboard for intervention. It must target goals that cross disciplines and meet children's needs. Assessment in the new millennium requires that we look into our therapy mirrors, our looking

glass, and go beyond what was—and enter into what can be.

References

American Speech-Language-Hearing Association. (1990). The roles of speech language pathologists in service de-livery to infants, toddlers, and their families. ASHA, 32 (Suppl. 2), 4.

Anderson, R. (1994). Cultural and linguistic diversity and language impairment in preschool children. Seminars in Speech and Language, 15(2), 115–124.

Bailey, D. B. (1989). Collaboration goal setting with families: Resolving differences in values and priorities for serv-ices. Topics in Early Childhood Special Education, 7(2), 59–71.

Bailey, D. B., & Wolery, M. (Eds.). (1989). Assessing infants and preschoolers with handicaps (pp. 1–21). Upper Saddle River, NJ: Merrill/Prentice Hall.

Barnes, K. E. (1982). Preschool screenings: The measurement and prediction of children at risk. Springfield, IL: Charles C. Thomas.

Bates, E. (1979). The emergence of symbols: Cognition and commu-nication in infancy. New York: Academic Press.

Bell, R. Q., & Harper, L. V. (1968). A reinterpretation of the direction of effects in studies of socialization. Psychologi-cal Review, 75, 81–95.

Bell, R. Q., & Harper, L. V. (1977). Child effects on adults. Hillsdale, NJ: Lawrence Erlbaum.

Benner, S. M. (1992). Assessing young children with special needs: An ecological perspective. New York: Longman.

Bergin, V. (1980). Special education needs in bilingual programs. Washington, DC: National Clearinghouse for Bilingual Education.

Brazelton, T. B. (1982). Joint regulation of neonatal-parent behavior. In E. Z. Tronick (Ed.), Social interchange in infancy: Affect, cognition, and communication (pp. 7–22). Baltimore: University Park Press.

Bruner, J. (1981). The social context of language acquisition. Language and Communication, 1, 155–178.

Chandler, L. (1979). Gross and fine motor development. In M. Cohen & P. Gross (Eds.), The developmental resource: Be-havioral sequences for assessment and program planning (Vol. 1, pp. 119–152). New York: Grune and Stratton.

Coggins, T. E., Olswang, L. B., & Guthrie, J. (1987). Assessing communicative intents in young children: Low struc-tured observation or elicitation tasks? Journal of Speech and Hearing Disorders, 52, 44–49.

Crais, E., & Roberts, J. (1991). Decision-making in assess-ment and early intervention. Language, Speech, and Hearing Services in Schools, 22(2), 19–30.

Delack, J. B., & Fowlow, P. J. (1978). The ontogenesis of differential vocalization: Development of prosodic contrastivity during the first year of life. In N. Waterson & C. Snow (Eds.), *The development of communication*. New York: Wiley.

Garvey, C. (1974). Some properties of social play. *Merrill Palmer Quarterly*, 20, 163–180.

Howes, C. (1980). Peer Play Scale as an index of complexity of peer interaction. *Developmental Psychology*, 16, 371–372.

Jaffe, M. (1989). Feeding at-risk infants and toddlers. *Topics in Language Disorders*, 10(1), 13–25.

Kayser, H. (1994). Preface for *Seminars in Speech and Language Communicative Impairments and Bilingualism*, 15(2), iv–v.

Klinger, L. G., & Dawson, G. (1992). Facilitating early social and communicative development in children with autism. In S. F. Warren & J. Reichle (Eds.), *Causes and effects in communication and language intervention* (pp. 157–186). Baltimore: Brookes.

Knoblock, H., & Pasamanick, B. (1974). *Gesell and Amatruda's developmental diagnoses: The evaluation and management of normal and neuropsychologic development in infancy and early childhood*. New York: Harper & Row.

Lamb, S. (1981). The development of social expression in the first year of life. In M. Lamb & L. Sherrod (Eds.), *Infant social cognition: Empirical and theoretical considerations* (pp. 155–176). Hillsdale, NJ: Lawrence Erlbaum Associates.

Lewis, M., & Rosenblum, L. (Eds.). (1974). *The effects of the infant on its caregiver*. New York: Wiley.

Mattes, L. J., and Omark, D. R. (1984). *Speech and language assessment of the bilingual handicapped*. San Diego: College Hill Press.

McConnell, S. R. (2000). Assessment in early intervention and early childhood special education: Building on the past to project into our future. *Topics in Early Childhood Special Education*, 20(1), 43–48.

McCormick, L., & Schiefelbusch, R. (1990). *Intervention processes and procedures in early language intervention*. New York: Merrill/Macmillan.

McCune, L., Kalmanson, B., Fleck, M. B., Glazewski, B., & Sillari, J. (1990). An interdisciplinary model of infant assessment. In S. J. Meisels & J. P. Shonkoff (Eds.), *Handbook of early childhood intervention* (pp. 219–245). New York: Cambridge University Press.

Morris, S. E. (1982). *Pre-Speech Assessment Scale*. Clifton, NJ: J. A. Preston.

Morris, S. E., & Klein, M. D. (1987). *Pre-feeding skills*, Tucson, AZ: Therapy Skill Builders.

Oller, D. K. (1980). The emergence of the sounds of speech in infancy. In G. A. Yer-Komshian, J. F. Kavanagh, & C. A. Ferguson (Eds.), *Child phonology* (Vol. 1: Production). New York: Academic Press.

Oller, D. K. (1986). Metaphonology and infant vocalization. In B. Lindblom & R. Zetterstrom (Eds.), *Precursors of early speech* (pp. 21–35). New York: Stockton Press.

Omark, D. R., & Erickson, J. G. (1983). *The bilingual exceptional child*. San Diego: College Hill Press.

Owens, R. E. (1992). *Language development: An introduction* (3rd ed.) New York: Merrill/Macmillan.

Paget, K. (1989). Assessment of cognitive skills in the preschool aged child. In D. B. Bailey & M. Wolery (Eds.), *Assessing infants and preschoolers with handicaps* (pp. 275–300). Upper Saddle River, NJ: Merrill/Prentice Hall.

Piaget, J. (1952). *The origins of intelligence in children*. New York: International Universities Press.

Proctor, A. (1989). Stages of normal noncry vocal development in infancy: A protocol for assessment. *Topics in Language Disorders*, 10(1), 26–42.

Ratner, N., & Bruner, J. (1978). Games, social exchange, and the acquisition of language. *Journal of Child Language*, 5, 391–402.

Roberts, J. E., & Crais, E. R. (1989). Assessing communication skills. In D. B. Bailey & M. Wolery (Eds.), *Assessing infants and preschoolers with handicaps* (pp. 339–389). Upper Saddle River, NJ: Merrill/Prentice Hall.

Rossetti, L. M. (1991). Infant toddler assessment: A clinical perspective. *Infant Toddler Intervention: The Transdisciplinary Journal*, 1, 11–28.

Roth, F. P. (1990). Early language assessment. In E. D. Gibbs & D. M. Teti (Eds.), *Interdisciplinary assessment of infants: A guide for early intervention*. Baltimore: Brookes.

Schaffer, R. (1977). *Mothering*. Cambridge: Harvard University Press.

Sleight, M., & Niman, C. (1984). *Gross motor and oral motor development in children with Down syndrome: Birth through three years*. St. Louis: St. Louis Association for Retarded Citizens.

Smith, P. (1989). Assessing motor skills. In D. B. Bailey & M. Wolery (Eds.), *Assessing infants and preschoolers with handicaps* (pp. 301–338). Upper Saddle River, NJ: Merrill/Prentice Hall.

Squires, J., Nickel, R., & Eisert, D. (1996). Early detection of developmental problems: Strategies for monitoring young children in the practice setting. *Developmental and Behavioral Pediatrics*, 17, 420–427.

Stoel-Gammon, C. (1987). Phonological skills of 2-year-olds. *Language, Speech, and Hearing Services in Schools*, 18, 323–329.

Taylor, O. L., & Payne, K. T. (1983). Culturally valid testing: A proactive approach. *Topics in Language Disorders*, 3, 8–20.

Terrell, S. L. (1983). Distinguishing differences from disorders: The past, present, and future of nonbiased assessment. *Topics in Language Disorders*, 3, 1–7.

Thomas, A., & Chess, S. (1977). *Temperament and development*. New York: Brunner/Mazel.

Tiegerman, E., & Primavera, L. H. (1984). Imitating the autistic child: Facilitating communicative gaze behavior. *Journal of Autism and Developmental Disorders*, 14(1), 27–38.

Tronick, E. Z., & Ganino, A. (1986). Interactive mismatch and repair: Challenges to the coping infant. *Zero to three*, 6(3), 1–6.

Uzgiris, I. C., & Hunt, J. (1975). *Assessment in infancy: Ordinal scales of psychological development.* Urbana: University of Illinois Press.

Westby, C. (1980). Assessment of cognition and language abilities through play. *Journal of Language, Speech, and Hearing Services in the Schools*, 11, 154–168.

Wetherby, A., & Rodriguez, B. (1992). *Communication and sym-bolic behavior scales.* Chicago: Riverside.

Wiig, E. (2000). Authentic and other assessments of language disabilities: When is fair fair? *Reading and Writing Quarterly*, 16, 179–210.

Yoder, D., & Kent, R. (1988). *Decision making in speech-language pathology.* Philadelphia: Decker.

$\sim$ 16 $\sim$

Assessing Social and Emotional Development

McEvoy and Odom (1996) described humans as social beings who come equipped with the "hardware" or neurological system to selectively attend to the social responses of their caregivers and, unconsciously at first, engage in behaviors that generate human responses. The caregivers' social responses begin to shape the "software" or cognitive processes in the ways that allow the infants to perceive and learn about the predictable nature of social behavior. Social and emotional development has been defined as the development of attachment, the growth of self, emergence of emotions, and the development of adaptive behaviors which include self care (Benner, 1992). The focus of assessment is on measures that reflect different aspects of a child's (1) characteristic traits, (2) emotional status, (3) sense of self, and (4) perceptions of others (Simeonsson, 1986). The assessment must consider the individual child's characteristics, the caregiver/parent-child interactions and relationships, and social and environmental factors.

Becoming an active member of the social world is a major developmental achievement for the infant or young child with disabilities (Odom & Munson, 1996). Difficulties in developing social skills often occur for children with disabilities. Roadblocks exist that prevent the development of these skills. Stress factors within and outside the family may at times influence the responsiveness of the caregivers. Factors such as adjustment to the diagnosis, additional caregiving demands, and financial pressures may affect initial parent-child interactions. In other cases, children are not allowed an optimal opportunity to establish a stable relationship with their primary caregiver. Infants who spend 4 to 10 weeks in an intensive care nursery use all of their physiological energy for survival. There is little energy left to develop a reciprocal relationship with any caregiver. Low birthweight infants spend considerable time during the first year in the hospital. Establishing optimal parent-infant interactional patterns in the early months of life with premature infants or infants who are medically fragile definitely will be difficult.

At times, it may be more difficult to establish a responsive relationship with young children with developmental disabilities. Infants with disabilities, motoric in particular, may not provide clear signals and enough information to the caregivers about when they are ready to interact (Yoder, 1987). Some infants may have delayed development of behavioral cues that are important for the caregiver. For example, infants who are blind, and thus have muted smiles and an absence of eye contact, may also have diminished, different, or delayed signals (Odom & Munson, 1996). Some infants with disabilities experience disrupted social relationships with their parents/ caregivers and are less socially accepted by peers than are normally developing children.

Research has shown that children with mild, moderate, or severe disabilities interacted less often with their peers than did normally developing children (Guralnick, 1980; Guralnick & Groom, 1985, 1987). These data suggest that most preschoolers with disabilities have social delays that exceed their developmental delays (Odom & McConnell, 1989). These peer relationships may not automatically develop even in integrated settings. Guralnick and Groom (1988) found that the success in social interaction experienced by children with mild disabilities decreased across the time that the children participated in the play group. This decrease suggested that as the group became more familiar with its members, deficits in social skills led to impaired interaction patterns for the children with disabilities. Children with more severe developmental delays appeared to engage in fewer mutual friendships (Buysee, 1993). Preschool teachers report that as many as 75 percent of their children with disabilities need to learn age-appropriate skills (Odom, McConnell, & Chandler, 1994). The development of social competence should be a primary goal for early intervention programs (Guralnick, 1990; Odom, McConnell, & McEvoy, 1992).

In this chapter, assessment strategies and instruments that provide useful information about the social and emotional performance of infants and young children with disabilities will be provided. The assessment must consider the individual child's temperament, readability, mastery motivation, the caregiver/parent-child interactions and relationships, and social and environmental factors. The chapter will begin by considering the child's emotional development and expand to consider aspects of social development.

General Considerations for Comprehensive Assessment

There are a variety of theoretical approaches to or philosophies of what should be assessed and measured by different tools or tests. Social-emotional behavior may be looked at quantitatively and qualitatively. For example, quantitatively, the examiner could derive a developmental level for social skills. Qualitatively, one might consider aspects of social-emotional development, e.g., behavioral style, temperament. The particular problems of children with disabilities require that assessment be flexible and comprehensive. Simply using a psychometric base for psychological testing is inadequate. No single measure is exhaustive or all-inclusive. A number of variables must be considered when assessing social-emotional development. These factors include the number and length of observations to be made, where the observations occur, and the characteristics of the child, such as temperament, readability, and motivational level. Figure 16–1 summarizes these variables.

Longitudinal

Observations made over time increase the likelihood of a more accurate assessment and enable the examiner and caregivers to have established sufficient trust to permit relatively ordinary family interactions to occur during the

FIGURE 16–1
Considerations for Comprehensive Assessment

Longitudinal
Natural settings
Child characteristics
 • Temperament
 • Readability
 • Mastery
  motivation

visits. Longitudinal social-emotional assessment can occur during the beginning weeks of intervention. The most appropriate approach to comprehensive assessment is a longitudinal procedure, including several unstructured observations in the home that can be used in conjunction with more formal assessment procedures (Fraiberg, 1980).

Natural Settings

The early interventionist who is collecting information on caregiver-infant interaction should observe the child and caregiver in a setting that is natural and comfortable for both; this is often the child's home. A play setting is an excellent time for observing. The time chosen should be when the child is active and alert. Using an unstructured approach has several advantages over formalized procedures as a means for assessing the social-emotional status of an infant and caregiver. The examiner is in a position to observe the infant's abilities and relationships with all members of the household. This procedure offers a much more valid and reliable picture of the baby's affective development.

Home visits also offer opportunities to observe the multiplicity of influences contributing to a developmental problem. Questions that might be considered are: Are there ample opportunities to explore the environment? Does the baby spend the day in the crib and lack adequate motor control and social experience? Are the effects of hospitalization or disability affecting the frequency or depth of interactions offered the infant? Home visits offer opportunities to inquire about parental perception of the baby's spontaneous behavior as it occurs. Recording the data collected during the home visit may be done through the use of a structured instrument such as the Home Observation for Measurement of the Environment Inventory (Bradley & Caldwell, 1980; Caldwell & Bradley, 1984) or the writing of clinical notes. The examiner should be sensitive so as not to detract from the spontaneity of the interaction. It is better to wait until after the visit for actual writing and note-taking. Additional considerations for conducting the diagnostic session are discussed in Chapter 5. Most assessment instruments provide instructions for collecting the needed information.

The caregivers' experiences with other professionals prior to and during referral influence the emotional tone that they present at the assessment. Their feelings about treatment by other professionals will influence their expectations about the assessment process and the team members. The initial interview should allow the caregivers the opportunity to ask questions in order to increase their security and sense of control. Assessment over a longer period of time allows the developmental history to be learned without immediately placing a questionnaire in front of the caregivers.

Observation in natural settings is a preferred strategy for assessing preschool social adjustment because it directly measures the behaviors of interest (Mudford, Beale, & Singh, 1990), does not impose artificial test room demands that young children are especially reactive to (Wittmer & Honig, 1994), and is not filtered through the biases and expectations of parents who may be heavily invested in assessment results (Iannotti, 1985; Kazdin, 1977).

Child Characteristics

Infants and young children show different patterns of behavior in temperament, readability, and behavior (Huntington, 1988). These characteristics can influence the relationships and thus affect caregiver behavior. Consideration must be given to these characteristics when assessing the social emotional development in young children.

Temperament. The term "temperament" is used to describe the behavioral style that contributes to infants' individual differences. An infant's temperament determines the way she reacts to her environment and the people around her. Individual differences can be seen very early in infants' prevailing moods, as well as in the intensity of their responses and their coping efforts (Wyly, 1999). Most formulations of temperament focus on individual expression of behaviors or the "how" rather than on the content of the behaviors, the "why" (Buss & Plomin, 1975). Researchers generally agree that temperament has a genetic basis, includes dimensions that can be identified in early infancy, is relatively stable, and can be modified by environmental influences (Wyly, 1999).

Thomas, Chess, and Birch (1968) identified 10 categories that can be used in assessing the temperament of infants and young children:

1. activity level (degree of activity displayed)
2. rhythmicity (regularity of behavioral patterns)
3. approach/withdrawal (tendency to approach or withdraw from new situation or person)
4. adaptability (ability to adjust to a new situation)
5. intensity of reaction (degree or level of reaction to different environmental situations)
6. threshold of responsiveness (degree of stimulation necessary to evoke a response)
7. quality of mood (general disposition)
8. distractibility (degree to which environmental stimuli can divert child's attention)
9. attention span (ability to keep attention focused)
10. persistence (tendency to stick with task despite obstacles)

Lerner and Dombro (2000) identified five specific traits that help describe a child's individual way of approaching the world:

1. How intensely the child responds to things
2. How active the child is
3. How the child interacts with others
4. How the child responds to change
5. How persistent or easily frustrated the child is (p. 25)

Readability. Readability is another pattern of behavior in infants and young children that may vary from child to child (Huntington, 1988). This characteristic involves the child's ability to provide caregivers with distinct signals and cues through overt behaviors (Benner, 1992). Infants with disabilities may provide unclear cues which may result in problems. Caregivers may not provide the appropriate response which may also result in problems in the infant-caregiver relationship. Readability is considered further in Chapter 15.

Mastery Motivation. The motivation the child shows as she attempts to learn new skills will directly influence her opportunity for development. There is a growing body of research on the techniques for the assessment of children's mastery motivation (Benner, 1992). These techniques can provide important information for the interventionist. Four forms of mastery motivation assessment are currently in use: (1) the structured mastery-task situation, (2) parental reports of observed mastery behavior, (3) global ratings of goal directedness, and (4) the free play situation (Brockman, Morgan, & Harmon, 1988). The purpose of assessing mastery motivation is to provide insight into the developmental domains on which the child is focusing energy. The examiner should assess the degree of persistence, approach to problem solving, and effectiveness of efforts in each developmental area.

Child Assessment Procedures

Assessing Child Characteristics

Formal checklists and rating scales are available which assess child characteristics. The *Temperament and Atypical Behavior Scale* (TABS) developed by Bagnato, Neisworth, Salvia, and Hunt (1999) is a rather new norm-referenced screening and assessment tool for infants and young children ages 11 to 71 months. The TABS is designed to identify temperament and self-regulation behavioral indicators by surveying key behavioral areas, including temperament, attention and activity, attachment and social behavior, neurobehavioral state, sleeping, play, vocal and oral behavior, senses and movement, and self-stimulatory behavior. The TABS Screener is a simple, 15-item form that parents complete in approximately 5 minutes. The TABS Assessment Tool is a 55-item checklist that is completed by parents or early childhood professionals; according to the authors, this checklist may be completed in 15 minutes. The results provide an assessment of atypical behaviors in four categories: detached, hypersensitive/active, underreactive, and dysregulated. An intervention guide included with the manual offers item-by-item strategies for minimizing problematic, atypical behaviors.

Child characteristics may also be observed during multidomain assessments. The *Transdisciplinary Play-Based Assessment* (TPBA) (Linder, 1993a) provides an excellent set of guidelines for observing social-emotional development. The TPBA furnishes worksheets for team members to use to make notes during the assessment. The following list gives examples from the TPBA for observation of child characteristics during the assessment.

Observation Guidelines for Social-Emotional Development[*]

I. Temperament
   A. Activity level

1. How motorically active is the child during the session?
2. Are there specific times during the session when the child is particularly active?
   a. Beginning, middle, or end
   b. During specific activities
B. Adaptability
   1. What is the child's *initial* response to new stimuli (persons, situations, and toys)?
      a. Shy, timid, fearful, cautious
      b. Sociable, eager, willing
      c. Aggressive, bold, fearless
   2. How does the child demonstrate his or her interest or withdrawal?
      a. Smiling, verbalizing, touching
      b. Crying, moving away, seeking security
   3. How long does it take the child to adjust to new situations, persons, objects, and so forth?
   4. How does the child adjust to new or altered situations after an initially shy or fearful response?
      a. Self-initiation (slowly warms up, talks to self)
      b. Uses adult or parent as a base of security (needs encouragement and reinforcement to get involved)
      c. Continues to resist and stay uninvolved
C. Reactivity
   1. How intense does the stimuli presented to the child need to be in order to evoke a discernible response?
   2. What type of stimulation is needed to interest the child?
      a. Visual, vocal, tactile, combination
      b. Object, social
   3. What level of affect and energy are displayed in response to persons, situations, or objects?
   4. What respone mode is commonly used?

5. What is the child's response to frustration?
II. Mastery Motivation
   A. Purposeful activity
      1. What behavior demonstrates purposeful activity?
      2. How does the child explore complex objects?
   B. Goal-directed behaviors
      1. What goal-directed behaviors are observed?
      2. How does the child respond to challenging objects or situations?
         a. Looking
         b. Exploring
         c. Appropriate use
         d. Persistent, task-directed
      3. How often does the child repeat successfully completed, challenging tasks?
      4. How persistent is the child in goal-directed behavior?
         a. With cause-effect toys
         b. With combinatorial tasks
         c. With means-end behavior
      5. Given a choice between an easy and more challenging task, which does the child select? (Examine if the child is over $3\frac{1}{2}$ years old.)
      6. How does the child demonstrate self-initiation in problem solving?
         a. How frequently is assistance requested?
         b. How does the child organize problem solving

---

[*]Linder, T. W. (1993). *The Transdisciplinary Play-Based Assessment: A Functional Approach to Working with Young Children* (Rev. ed., pp. 145–146). Baltimore: Paul H. Brookes Publishing Co.

General Procedural Considerations

Early interventionists should be reminded of general procedural considerations before assessment is begun. These basic considerations are:

- Social interaction skills are usually observed in natural contexts and recorded by an observer or reported by a caregiver. Administering test items from standardized assessments is not usually appropriate for social interaction skills.
- The setting will affect the social behavior of infants and children. A natural setting should be used, keeping in mind that even the presence of the examiner may cause children to respond differently.
- Social interaction is a reciprocal process. The interaction will be affected by the partners in the situation. The social context of the assessment should be reported when the information should be collected.
- Information should be collected from multiple sources. The more agreement there is across settings, the more confidence can be placed in the information provided.

Functional Developmental Approach

Greenspan (1996) recommended a functional developmental approach that assesses the whole child's core functional capacities in her most important everyday interactions with key caregivers. The *Functional Emotional Assessment Scale* (FEAS) (Greenspan, 1996) assesses the child's social, emotional, cognitive, and communicative capacities in the context of interactions with key caregivers. It is derived from an integrated understanding of the social, emotional, and cognitive development of infants and young children (Greenspan, 1979, 1989). This approach looks at the child's capacity for self-regulation, engagement, intentional communication, forming a complex sense of self, elaborating symbols and representations, and creating logical bridges or differentiations within her emerging symbolic world. The FEAS addresses six areas: primary emotional capacities; emotional range-sensorimotor (including speech); emotional range-affective; associated motor, sensory, language, and cognitive capacities; general infant tendencies; and overall caregiver tendencies (Greenspan, 1996).

The FEAS recognizes that the world of young children is a world of feelings and relationships. In this context of relationships with caregivers, infants and toddlers develop and demonstrate their cognitive, motor, and language skills (Greenspan, 1996). As in the other domains, the interaction between domains must be considered. The examiner must also keep in mind the influence of cognitive and language competence on social-emotional development as we tend to "see" or measure it. Examples of questions which should be asked are:

- Can the child comprehend thoughts/feelings?
- Can the child generalize from one experience to another?
- Can the child attend long enough to interact with the examiner?
- What is the influence of affective relationships at home (bonding, separation, identity issues)?

The assessment of a young child's emotional and social capacities provides families and professionals a rich profile of how a very young child experiences her physical and human environment, the ways in which the child uses her own resources and the support of the caregivers to engage with the world, and the challenges that confront the child (Greenspan, 1996). Information gained from this assessment approach suggests specific, individualized intervention approaches that will reinforce a child's and family's unique strengths and help them work effectively to overcome developmental challenges.

Social Development

A social interaction occurs when the social behavior of one partner is intentionally directed to the second partner. Social development is the acquisition of skills necessary for interacting competently with adults and peers. Social competence is the competent use of those skills in appropriate contexts (Odom & McConnell, 1989). Social competence involves social maturity, self-confidence, self-help skills, independence, and interaction with others. Young children's social and emotional development is apparent during the preschool years in their play, peer interaction, prosocial behavior, aggression, self-regulation, and expression of feelings (Bredekamp & Copple, 1997).

Two developmental skills or tasks must occur in social development. It is important that humans establish a positive working relationship or attachment with at least one primary caregiver. This relationship begins as early as 3 to 4 months and continues through adulthood. The second important task is to establish oneself as a member of a social network of peers. By age 3 years, children will show a preference for playing with peers rather than objects, and by age 5 will have developed fairly sophisticated social interactions (Odom & McConnell, 1989).

The child's self-concept is an important aspect of social emotional development during the early childhood years. Children's diminished egocentrism and improved reasoning ability help them to develop a more constant and stable perception of themselves despite the varied behavior and responses they receive from others. Children also have feelings and make judgments about themselves. These self-evaluations constitute their self-esteem. Helping children develop a sense of themselves as competent initiators of action is an important task for adults (Bredekamp & Copple, 1997).

Social development may break down for one of the following reasons: (1) the infant or child may lack the prerequisite skills for participating in successful social interactions (child may not have the motor skills or may not have learned how to share toys); (2) the partner may not have sufficient skills for participating in the successful interactions (e.g., child may be unable to engage her peers in mutually satisfying interactions because the peer group does not have the necessary skills); (3) both partners may have some social skills, but

there is a mismatch between the skills involved (e.g., the mother of a child who is blind may not understand that manual exploration is a social skill and may not respond to it). The assessment process should not only consider the level of development but also the reason the social development has broken down if the child is delayed in this area.

Adult-Infant Interactions

It is difficult to quantify the exact nature of the quality of adult-infant interactions. Although instruments have identified certain behaviors as representative of optimal interactional patterns, it is difficult to attach weighted values to these behaviors.

Interactional styles vary across families and cultures. Although caregiver-child interactional patterns show considerable variation, certain behaviors do seem to be important for the nurturing of the young child and may be worthwhile intervention goals. Generally, it is accepted that young children need experiences that support their emotional growth. According to Rossetti (1990), critical areas for socio-communicative intervention seem to be related to increasing and introducing experiences that foster the following in caregiver-child interactions:

- Attention and engagement;
- Intentional, reciprocal gestures and cues;
- Vocal/verbal turn-taking;
- Elaboration of emotional responsiveness; and
- Mutually pleasurable exchanges.

Eye contact, crying, quieting, attention to focus and voices, and body movements are interaction cues and responses of the normal newborn. In general, infant-caregiver interactions which are considered in synchrony with the infant's signals are thought to have beneficial long-term effects on cognitive, social, and linguistic skills (Sparks, Clar, Oas, & Erickson, 1988). (See also Chapter 15.)

Attachment. The relationship between the infant and parent or primary caregiver and its influence on shaping subsequent social relationships has been the focus of much research. Early parent-infant interactions are the foundation of infants' cognitive, social-emotional, and language development (Sparks, et al., 1988). There is agreement that the infant's positive relationship with the caregiver provides the basis for later social and emotional development (Barnard & Kelly, 1990; Beckwith & Cohen, 1984; Teti & Nakagawa, 1990). This first bond or attachment has been defined as "an enduring affective tie between infant and caregiver" (Sroufe, 1979, p. 495). Some of the terms used to refer to the attachment bonding are "mutuality," "falling in love," and "the dance" (Wyly, 1999). Research has shown that infants differentiate the primary caregiver very early (Lewis, 1987). Eventually attachment is established with secondary caregivers and family members. A stable affective bond is important for healthy emotional and cognitive development regardless of various child-rearing practices across cultures (Lewis, 1987). A lack of attachment during the early months can result in later caregiving deficiencies, such as child abuse, failure to thrive, etc. (Rossetti, 1990).

The attachment process involves reciprocal interactions between parents and infants. For example, a newborn baby opens her eyes and gazes at her mother, and her mother gazes back. Through these simple beginnings, a complex synchronous interaction system is built. The process requires both partners to pay attention, signal one another and continuously adjust their responses to each other's signals. These interactional systems become increasingly coordinated and involve verbal and gestural communication, facial expressions, turn taking, and mutual responsiveness (Sorce & Emde, 1982).

Assessment of Attachment. Researchers have identified elements essential to the interaction process. Identification of these elements now allows professionals to use parent-infant assessment scales to assess these interactions. Assessment of parent-infant interaction skills can provide information about the strengths of the interaction and target intervention activities to correct any interaction mismatches.

A number of empirically based scales have been developed to assess parent-infant functioning and to guide interventions with parents and infants with disabilities. Some of the scales were designed primarily for research or clinical purposes, and others were developed as part of specific infant intervention programs (Bromwich, 1981). The choice of an assessment procedure depends on the purpose of assessing the interaction and on the specific behaviors to be measured. The behaviors assessed by the various scales are typically behaviors that the research literature on parent-infant interactions has identified as essential to high-quality early relationships. Parent-infant interaction assessments vary in several dimensions. These variables include the setting of the observation, number of observations, types of behaviors observed, materials used, structure of the observation, and measurement format.

Methods for Assessing Parent-Infant Interactions. In general, an assessment of the parent-infant interaction pattern is part of a more comprehensive assessment that includes a structured assessment of the infant's developmental status. Information is also gathered from parents on the child's developmental history, medical conditions, and family history.

The setting used for observing interactions can be the infant's home environment, a clinic, or a laboratory observation room. Some assessment protocols specify exactly where observations must take place, whereas others are more flexible. Observing interactions in the home is an advantage in that the participants' behavior may be more realistic. Practical considerations may make this more difficult to arrange.

The structure of the observation is an important consideration in assessing parent-infant interaction. The structure of the assessment depends on the assessment goals. Parents and infants can be observed during bathing or feeding times (Barnard, 1979) or while playing. Some procedures require parents to teach their infants to do something (Mahoney, Powell, Finnegan, Fors, & Wood, 1986). On the other hand, parents might be observed for a specific time period doing what they would normally do in each other's presence.

The length of the observation is usually determined by the activities being observed. Some scales specify a minimum observation time while others have several 5- to 10-minute observations within one session. The total observation time in most assessments does not exceed 20 to 30 minutes.

Parent-infant behaviors are measured in several different ways. Some scales use a binary checklist in which the rater indicates the presence or absence of the specific behavior. Behavioral rating scales involving judgments about the quality of the observed behaviors are frequently used. Timed coding procedures may also be used to measure the frequency of specified behaviors as they occur within specific timed intervals.

Two levels of behavior can be measured by parent-infant assessments. Molar categories are global dimensions such as responsiveness, warmth, or directiveness. These behaviors establish the overall tone of the interactions. Ratings using molar scores provide a general summary of the observed interaction. Molecular categories are more specific parent or infant behaviors that constitute the overall interactions. Examples of molecular category behaviors are gestures, smiles, and eye contact. Molecular ratings can identify more narrowly defined behaviors that can be used in structuring interventions.

Parent-Infant Interaction Assessment Measures. The *Parent Behavior Progression* (PBP) (Forms I and II) (Bromwich, 1981) was constructed by the University of California, Los Angeles, Infant Studies Project to assess interactions between parents and their high-risk infants. The results are to be used as guides for intervention. The test has been used to sensitize interventionists to the unique properties of a parent-infant dyad and to promote increased parental enjoyment of their infants. Two forms are used. Form I is used with infants ages birth to 9 months, and Form II covers 9 to 36 months. The purpose of the scale is to serve as a diagnostic and intervention tool that focuses the examiner on positive behaviors in the interactions between parents and infant. Information from the assessment is then used to plan intervention strategies to assist parents in acquiring new behavior patterns. The focus is on the parents rather than the infant. The scales consist of a checklist of parent questions and structured observations of parents' interactions with their infants. Six hierarchical levels of parent involvement are identified according to increasing parental competencies.

The level sequence of the PBP follows the normal course of parent-infant involvement. For example, a level-one parent behavior would be that the parents enjoy the infant and the level-six behavior would be that the parents can independently generate new developmentally appropriate activities that are interesting to the infant. Bromwich (1983) pointed out that parent interventions do not have to strictly follow the PBP level sequence. Parents can be encouraged to engage in play activities with infants at Levels IV or V, which would result in mutually satisfying interactions and feelings of competence. Level IV indicates that the parents demonstrate an awareness of developmentally appropriate activities, and for Level V the parents initiate new play activities based on principles internalized from their own experience or modeled by an early interventionist.

The *Maternal Behavior Rating Scale* (MBRS) (Mahoney, Finger, & Powell, 1985) is a molar rating scale that assesses the quality of maternal interactive behaviors with 1- to 3-year-old children who are mentally retarded. A 10-minute mother-child play session is videotaped and then rated using the five-point Likert scale on

18 maternal behavior items and four child behaviors. The 18 maternal behavior items consist of behaviors such as expressiveness, enjoyment, warmth, sensitivity to child interest and state, and responsivity. Test observers should be trained to achieve 90 percent inter-rater reliability, and the free play situations should be as similar as possible. A seven-item shortened form of the MBRS (Mahoney, Powell, & Finger, 1986) has also been developed. The authors propose that the shortened form may be useful for evaluating the effects of intervention programs which are specifically designed for modifying mother-child play interactions.

The *Parent/Caregiver Involvement Scale* (PCIS) (Farren, Kasari, Yoder, Harber, Huntington, & Comfort-Smith, 1987) rates caregivers' involvement during a 20-minute live or videotaped observation. The focus is on the caregiver's interaction with the infant. Eleven behaviors, such as vocalization, physical responsiveness, control, and teaching behavior, are rated on a one-to-five Likert scale. The behaviors are assessed using three criteria: (1) the quality or effectiveness of the caregiver's behavior, acceptance, and warmth; (2) the amount of care, which refers to the level and quantity of the caregiver's behavior; and (3) the appropriateness or match between the infant and caregiver behaviors. The assessment includes an overall interaction rating. The PCIS has been used to develop individualized, family plans. One drawback of the PCIS is its focus on caregiver behavior without including information on the development of reciprocal exchanges between the parent and the child (Barnard & Kelly, 1990).

The *Nursing Child Assessment Teaching and Feeding Scales* (NCAST) (Barnard, 1979) are binary checklists designed to assess the reciprocity and contingency in parent-child interactions in two situations, feeding and teaching a task. The first or feeding situation is seen as a familiar activity that provides the most opportunities for interaction between parents and infant. In the second situation, caregivers are asked to teach two tasks to their infant, one task at age level and another that

is about 6 weeks above the infant's developmental level. The trained observer checks the behaviors observed after 3 to 5 minutes of observing the teaching or feeding. The feeding rating includes 76 yes/no items, and the teaching includes 73 yes/no items. The items are organized into six subcategories, which include four caregiver categories (sensitivity to cues, fostering social-emotional growth, fostering cognitive growth, and response to infant distress) and two child/infant categories (responsiveness and clarity of cues). The results are expressed as subscales for caregiver and infant and total scores.

The *Greenspan-Lieberman Observation System for Assessment of Caregiver-Infant Interaction During Semi-structured Play* (GLOS) (Greenspan, Lieberman, & Poisson, 1981; Greenspan & Lieberman, 1988) is another example of a test instrument that might be used in assessing a child's emotional functioning. This scale was developed to assess adaptive and maladaptive parent-infant interactions with multirisk families in a laboratory setting. The assessment is based on the Greenspan (1981) model of infant emotional development, which assumes that newborn infants begin to regulate and adapt to their environment. As their adaptation processes become more organized, they demonstrate the capacity to establish an attachment to caregivers. Although there are age-related adaptive behaviors, there are individual differences in the process, because infants use their unique coping skills to become invested in caregivers.

The GLOS scales measure specific behavioral criteria for assessing the quality of the infant-caregiver relationship from birth to 4 years of age. The caregiver behaviors include contingent responses to the infant, pleasurable or aversive tactile experiences with the infant, and level of stimulation with the infant. Infant behaviors focus on matters such as disengagement, seeking physical contact with the caregiver, and responses to caregiver behaviors. Trained observers code behaviors occurring in a 10-minute videotaped caregiver-infant play sequence filmed in a laboratory setting.

The complexity of the GLOS has prompted the development of a shorter version that employs a five-page rating system for 80 parent and infant behaviors.

The GLOS has been used principally as a research tool to describe the parenting interactions of adolescent and other groups of high-risk parents (Hofheimer, O'Grady, & Packer, 1988). The authors propose that the scale can provide useful clinical information for planning and implementing interventions for caregivers and infants with maladaptive interactions.

The *Mother-Infant Play Interaction Scale* (MIPIS) (Walker & Thompson, 1982) assesses the interactive strategies used by mothers and infants in an unstructured play situation. Play is considered to be a rich medium for interactive behaviors and subsequent attachment. The scale measures mutuality and responsiveness of mothers and infants between 4 and 6 weeks after birth. Qualities of play interactions are rated in a 5-minute live or videotaped session. The 16-item scale contains three subscales: maternal, infant, and dyadic. The maternal subscale includes maternal holding style, vocalization style, expression of affect, and visual interaction. The infant subscale consists of the predominant infant affect level, wakeful response, and visual interaction. Measures in the dyadic subscale include dyadic quality of interaction, interaction affect synchrony, and termination of interaction. Some examples from the MIPIS scale include maternal holding style, maternal caregiving style, predominant infant wakeful response level, and synchrony of affect. The MIPIS has been used as a research tool, and the authors provide instructions for clinical use of this instrument. The normative data on this scale are limited to normal mother-infant dyads and may not accurately reflect high-risk infant-mother behaviors.

The importance of parent-infant interaction has been acknowledged by researchers in early intervention by designing programs to enhance the dyadic interactions for infants with disabilities (Mahoney & Powell, 1988) and infants at risk for delay due to environmental or biological risks (Hans & Bernstein, 1990). Munson and Odom (1996) provided a thorough review of rating scales that measure parent-infant interaction. This review provides a description of instruments, evaluation data, and administration information (e.g., age range, location, method, cost, scoring format, etc.) as well as the readability level, norming population, purpose, reliability, and validity of 17 parent-infant interaction measures. Mahoney, Spiker, and Boyce (1996) warned that for parent-child assessment to become a routine practice, "it is critical that (a) there are reliable and valid instruments and/or clinical procedures for making judgments regarding parent-child relationships, (b) clinicians are adequately trained to conduct this activity in a manner that is sensitive and equitable to all parents, and (c) infant specialists have a compelling reason to engage in this practice" (p. 28).

Social Interaction Assessment

Dimensions of Social Interaction Assessment

Social interaction underlies all social and emotional development, including development of attachment, peer relations, social skills, and social competence. The basic capacity for social interaction is an essential prerequisite for all other aspects of social interaction such as social skills, social competence, and quality of social interaction. It is important to know about a child's basic capacity for social interaction to better understand normal development. Assessment of a child's basic capacity for social interaction is also helpful for evaluation and intervention purposes to identify deficits, develop specifically targeted interventions, and monitor the effectiveness of the intervention strategy (Ghuman, Peebles, & Ghuman, 1998).

Assessment can provide different views of a child's social development. A microscopic level looks at individual social behavior, and macroscopic looks at relationships or social status (Suen & Ary, 1989). The choice of assessment is determined by the purpose for which the information will be used. Microscopic assessment approaches might be used for planning or monitoring the effects of intervention programs, and more macroscopic approaches might be used for diagnosis or program evaluation (Odom & Munson, 1996).

Individual Social Behaviors. Individual social behaviors may be assessed in several ways: (1) frequency with which a social behavior occurs within a given time frame may be counted; (2) judgments of the affective quality of the social behavior may be made (i.e., positive or negative); and (3) indications by the examiner or data collector as to whether the child was initiating or responding to the social behavior of another child or adult.

Interactional Level. Interactions are the dynamic interchanges of behavior among partners in a social interaction. At the interactional level, social reciprocity is important. One form of social reciprocity is the immediate response of a social partner to a social behavior. In this type of social reciprocity, the sequence or order of behaviors in an interaction is important. Social behaviors that produce a response from a peer are reciprocal. Those behaviors that do not produce a response are not reciprocal. Examiners or data collectors identify the positive social behaviors that produce a response (Odom & McConnell, 1989).

Another type of reciprocity refers to the direction and frequency of social interactions with potential partners. To assess this type of reciprocity, the number of social behaviors a child directs to her peers and the number directed to her from peers are counted. This may also be done with caregivers and other children, such as strangers, older children, or siblings.

The duration of interactions also may be assessed. Duration may refer to the length of time

an intervention continues, as measured with a stopwatch, timing the beginning to the end of the interaction. The number of behaviors in a social interaction chain may also be measured by recording and counting the number of behaviors in each interaction. Usually when a child interacts frequently with a peer, and the peer in turn directs a large percentage of her interactions to the original child, it indicates the development of a friendship (Odom & Munson, 1996).

Social Relationships. Social relationships of infants and young children occur at the macroscopic level and may measure the success with which children achieve the benchmark social developmental tasks of attachment and social acceptance within a peer group. Infants are assessed based on achieving social developmental tasks, attachment, and social acceptance within a peer group. Attachment refers to the relationship that develops between infants and their caregivers. The purpose of the behaviors related to attachment, such as smiling, crying, locomotion to mother, and talking to mother, is to ensure that the child stays in close proximity to the attachment figure, especially when the child feels insecure (Bowlby, 1969; Ainsworth, Blehar, Waters, & Walls, 1978; Odom & Munson, 1996). Assessment of attachment was discussed earlier in this chapter. At the preschool level, social relationships with peers are most often measured by the use of a sociometric assessment. Such an assessment rates the popularity of the child as well as the level of acceptance that the child has achieved in the peer group (Asher & Taylor, 1981). Peer preferences or relationships can also be examined.

With sociometric assessment procedures, children are asked to provide general qualitative evaluations of the social acceptance, social preference, or likeability of other children. Teachers usually gather sociometric information from intact groups of children. Teachers should be cautious in interpreting information obtained from sociometric instruments, because such measures cannot necessarily be expected to offer stable estimates of social preference (McConnell & Odom, 1986).

Procedural Considerations in Assessing Social Interactions

The type of standardized assessment that is useful for measurement of development in the other domains, such as cognition and communication, is neither available nor appropriate for assessing social interaction skills (Odom & Munson, 1996). These skills are usually observed in natural contexts and recorded by an observer or reported by a parent. The characteristics of the natural setting may affect the information obtained, and the way in which the assessments are chosen or used will affect the ultimate usefulness of the information obtained (Odom & Munson, 1996). Odom and Munson (1996) discussed three important considerations in the procedures for assessing social interactions: (1) the setting, (2) the participants, and (3) the use of multiple measures.

Setting. It is important to assess children's social behavior in the most natural setting. The most natural setting for infants may be the home (Beal, 1991; Stern, 1974) or other location where parents and child feel most comfortable (Comfort, 1988). For infants who are in child care settings, observations in that setting with child care staff may provide additional information. Observers should not begin collecting data until they have established a positive rapport with the caregiver and child. Specific assessments for infants and caregivers were discussed earlier in this chapter.

The most typical setting for observing preschoolers' social interaction is during free play (Odom & Ogawa, 1992). The types of toys and activities available may well affect the play with peers (Odom & Munson, 1996). Children were found to be significantly more interactive during pretend play activities than during other activities during the day (Odom, Peterson, McConnell, &

Ostrosky, 1990). The structure of the activity also affects the level of interaction: that is, the number of children in the group and the definition of roles.

Participants. Children's social interaction will be affected by the partners with whom they interact and the history of that interaction. Both caregivers and infants contribute to the type of interactions occurring. The assessment used must capture the behavior of each participant. An infant will display very different behaviors with the mother, father, and other caregivers (Belsky, Gilstrap, & Rovine, 1984; Field, 1978; Power & Parke, 1986).

For preschool children, the skills of the peer group may affect the degree and nature of the interaction. Odom and colleagues (1990) found that the proportion of time spent in interaction was nearly twice as great in the early childhood education classes, which suggests that more interaction opportunities might occur when a nondisabled peer group is available. Assessments must report the participants in social interactions and measure the relative contribution of each for the interactions recorded (Odom & Munson, 1996).

Multiple Measures. Multiple sources of information should be collected on children's social performance, and this information should be provided by different informants. This approach will provide evidence of agreement or disagreement on socially competent behaviors from different perspectives and from different instruments. If agreement exists across assessments, then more confidence can be placed in the information obtained. For example, direct observation and teacher ratings of the child's social interactions might differ substantially owing to the difference in behaviors exhibited by the child in the home and school settings or to different standards used by the raters. Differences provide unique information about the child's social skills across settings, and a comprehensive assessment should capture such information (Odom & Munson, 1996).

Methods for Assessing Social Performance

Levels and Techniques for Assessment

Several levels and techniques exist for assessing the social interaction development of infants, toddlers, and preschoolers with disabilities. Each of the techniques provides slightly different information. Information may be obtained on individual social behaviors, relationships, or comparisons with established norms. The particular level or approach chosen is based upon the purpose of your assessment. Odom & Munson (1996) suggest that assessment information may be collected through: (1) observation of infants and young children in a social context, (2) rating scales, (3) sociometric nominations or ratings by peers, (4) curriculum-based assessments, and (5) norm-referenced tests. Table 16–1 provides a summary of assessment of social behavior and interaction of infants and young children with disabilities. The purpose of the assessment will determine the choice of assessment. A microscopic assessment approach might be used for planning or monitoring the immediate effects of intervention programs, and a macroscopic approach might be used for diagnostic or program evaluation (Odom & Munson, 1996). In Chapters 11 and 12, methods such as anecdotal data collection, direct observation, and rating scales are discussed.

Multimeasure Performance-Based Assessment

Odom and McConnell (1989) proposed a performance-based assessment of social competence that involved significant social agents in children's environments to make judgments about the competence of the children's social behavior. McConnell and Odom (1999) constructed and initially evaluated a performance-based approach for assessing social competence of young children with disabilities. A multimethod

assessment of children's social competence included direct observation, observer impressions, teacher rating, and peer ratings. The results of this study suggest that data drawn from multiple methods and agents can generate a performance-based assessment of peer-related social competence for preschool settings. This study supported the results of a previous study by Guralnick, Connor, Hammond, Gottman, and Kinnish (1995). The results of both studies point to the utility of social competence measures that systematically include variance from different specific sources and to the possibility that peer sociometrics represent a unique dimension of social competence.

Anecdotal Data Collection

Teachers sometimes keep notes on the social behavior of infants or children. The setting, activity, participants, and the behaviors observed should be recorded, and these notes should be written during the observation or immediately thereafter. Parents can also use anecdotal notes to describe interactive behaviors observed in the home. The *Systematic Anecdotal Assessment of Social Interaction* (SAASI) (Odom, McConnell, Kohler, & Strain, 1987) system can be used to provide structure to anecdotal reporting. In this system, the teacher identifies one child to observe in interactions with her peers. A simple form that has rows of boxes can be used to record each social interaction in which the targeted child participates. The form can then be analyzed in terms of behaviors of interest, such as frequency of initiations of social interactions and aggressive behaviors towards peers. Anecdotal note taking is discussed further in Chapter 11.

Questionnaires

Questionnaires may be used to gather information from individuals who are knowledgeable about the child's behavior. Questionnaires differ from rating scales in that they do not require

TABLE 16–1

Assessment of Social Behavior and Interactions of Infants and Young Children with Disabilities

Assessment Type	Title	Age Range	Information Generated	Description
Anecdotal	*Field Notes or Anecdotal Records*	Open	Behaviors determined by the teacher	Narrative recording or report of infants'/children's participation in social interaction with peers or caregivers
Questionnaires	*Early Childhood Friendship Survey* (Buysee, 1991)	Preschool	Mutual friendships Unilateral friendships Information about factors related to friendships	A questionnaire to be completed by caregivers (separate forms for parents and teachers)
	Assessment of Peer Relations (Guralnick, 1992)	Preschool	Range of information related to general overview of social behavior, emotional regulation, shared understanding, social strategies, tasks, and processes	A set of questionnaires to be completed by teacher or other individual knowledgeable about child's behavior. Both open-ended questions and rating forms included.
Direct Observation	*Social Interaction Assessment and Intervention* (McCollum & Stayton, 1985)	Infancy	Target behavior selected by assessor	Frequency count and overall rating
	Infant-Parent Social Interaction Code (Baird, Haas, McCormick, Carruth, & Turner, 1992)	Infancy	Parent (contingent responsivity, directiveness, intrusiveness, facilitation) Infant (initiation, participation, communication acts) Dyad (theme continuity)	Modified time sampling
	Parten/Smilansky Combined Scale (Rubin, et al., 1976)	Preschool	*Parten Scale* (unoccupied, onlooker, solitary, parallel, associative, cooperative) *Smilansky Scale* (functional, constructive, dramatic, games with rules)	An interval-sampling system designed to measure cognitive play within a social context
	Social Interaction Scan (Odom, et al., 1988)	Preschool	Isolate/unoccupied Proximity Interactive Negative Teacher interaction	A system for scanning classrooms of children. Designed to measure both interaction play and social integration.

	Instrument	Age Level	Behaviors	Comments
	Assessment of Peer Realations Guralnick & Groom (1988)	Preschool	Gains attention Uses peers as resource Leads peers Imitates Expresses hostility Competes for attention Shows pride Follows peers' activities	Event recording system for measuring peers' interactions
	Bronson Social and Task Profile (Bronson, 1994)	Preschool	Helps Shares Trades Takes turns Joint effort Suggests activity Assigns roles States rules	Event recording system
Rating Scales	*Parent-Child Observation Guide* (Bernstein, Hans, & Percansky, 1992)	Infancy	Parents (responsiveness to child's need and child's activity, positive feelings, helping child) Infant (expression, using parent involvement, positive feelings, language)	Binary scoring Three age levels (birth to 3 months, 4 to 15 months, and 16 to 36 months) Developed in project for infants and mothers at environmental risk
	Infant-Caregiver Interaction Scale (ICIS) (Munson & Odom, 1994)	Infancy	Environment (positioning, distractions, planning) Parent (participation, predictability, sensitivity/responsiveness/turn-taking, communicative intent, playful routines, imitation, affect) Infant (participation, predictability/consistency, sensitivity/responsiveness/turn-taking, communicative intent, playful routines, play behaviors, imitation, affect)	Five-point Likert scale Developed in a project for infants who were medically fragile
	Social Strategy Rating Scale (Beckman & Lieber, 1994)	Infancy and Preschool	21 social strategies, such as turn-taking, games, takes lead, invites, joins play	Rating scale completed after observing child in social interaction

TABLE 16–1
continued

Assessment Type	Title	Age Range	Information Generated	Description
Rating Scales	*Teacher Impressions Scale* (Vanderbilt/ Minnesota Social Interaction Project, 1993)	Preschool	16 social behaviors, such as converses appropriately, takes turns, plays cooperatively, smiles, shares materials	Rating scale completed after observing child in social interaction
	Social Skills Rating System (Gresham & Elliott, 1990)	Preschool	49-item scale that generates summary scores related to social skills and problem behavior	Alternate rating forms for teachers and parents
	Social Competence Scale (Kohn, 1988)	Preschool	Summary scores of cooperation vs. defiance and participation vs. disinterest	Scale completed by teacher or other individual familiar with the child
Sociometrics	McCandless & Marshall (1957)	Preschool	Summary score of peer nominations as friends	Peer nomination sociometric using photographs
	Asher, Singleton, Tinsley, & Hymel (1979)	Preschool	Summary score of peer rating by whole class	Peer rating scale using photographs
Curriculum-based Assessment	*The Carolina Curriculum for Infants and Toddlers with Special Needs* (2nd ed.) (Johnson-Martin, et al., 1991)	Infancy	Five developmental domains including social Social adaptation (self-direction, social skills, self-help skills)	Teaching activities correspond to each item in the assessment
	The Carolina Curriculum for Preschoolers with Special Needs (Johnson-Martin, et al., 1990)	Preschool	Five developmental domains including social Social adaptation (responsibility, self-concept, interpersonal skills)	Teaching activities correspond to each item in the assessment log
	Transdisciplinary Play-Based Assessment (rev. ed.) (Linder, 1993a)	Infancy and Preschool	Four developmental domains including social-emotional Social-emotional	Accompanying curriculum contains teaching activities (Linder, 1993b)

	Age range	Subdomains	Comments
AEPS (Bricker, 1993)	Infancy	(temperament, mastery, motivation, social interaction with parents, social interactions with facilitator, characteristics of dramatic play in relation to emotional development, humor and social conventions, social interactions with peers) Three subdomains related to interaction with adults, environment, and peers	Accompanying curriculum contains teaching activities (Cripe, Slentz, & Bricker, 1993)
Norm-referenced Assessment *Battelle Developmental Inventory* (Newborg, Stock, Wnek, Guidubaldi, & Svinicki, 1988)	Infancy and Preschool	Personal-social domains contain subdomains related to adult-interaction, expression of feelings—affect, self-concept, peer interaction, coping, social role	Provides standard scores and age-equivalence on social domain
Vineland Adaptive Behavior Scales (Sparrow, Ball, & Cicchetti, 1984)	Preschool	Age scores and percentile ranks for social age	General adaptive behavior scale with social competence subscale

Source: From Assessing social performance (pp. 408–411), by S. L. Odom and L. J. Munson, in *Assessing infants and preschoolers with special needs,* 2/e by M. E. McLean, D. B. Bailey, and M. Wolery (Eds.), © 1996. Reprinted by permission of Pearson Education, Inc. Upper Saddle River, NJ.

ratings on a numeric scale, usually do not have information related to reliability and validity, and sometimes are used as clinical instruments for designing interventions. For example, Buysee (1991) developed the *Early Childhood Friendship Survey,* which provides information about the friendships of young children as well as factors related to making friends. Another example is the *Assessment of Peer Relations* (APR) (Guralnick, 1992), an informal questionnaire which gathers information about children's involvement and purposes of interaction, emotional regulation, shared understanding, peer group entry behavior, conflict resolution, and maintenance of play. The APR was designed as a clinical tool for creating and monitoring intervention (Guralnick, 1992).

Direct Observation of Social Interaction

Direct observation systems require the assessor to directly observe and immediately record the social interaction behavior of the young children. The categories for observation are predetermined and the observations are made within a specific time frame. This differs from anecdotal records because the behavior to be observed is predetermined, and differs from rating scales in that no summary score is provided. Observation procedures that have been individually planned to meet a child's specific needs are more likely to be authentically related to the problem that led to the child's referral (Cone, 1986; Rushton, 1976).

Three types of direct observation systems exist for assessing children's social interactions: (1) momentary time sampling systems, (2) interval, and (3) event recording systems. Momentary time sampling systems require that the observer record at a specific point in time whether the infant, child, or parent is engaged in a specific social behavior or interaction. Interval sampling measures of social interaction require the observer to watch an infant or young child for a short period of time (6 to 15 seconds) and record whether the behavior occurred at all

during the interval. Event recording systems record each instance of a social behavior or interaction. These behaviors may be recorded within a specific time frame or interval. The assessor records all the behaviors that occur during the interval, rather than just the fact that the behavior occurred as in interval sampling. Each of these direct observation systems is discussed in Chapter 12 as well as the advantages and disadvantages of using these observation systems. The *Observational Assessment of Reciprocal Social Interaction* (McConnell, Sisson, & Sandler, 1984) is a direct observation instrument based on an interval sampling system, which can measure initiation behaviors, response behaviors, summative behaviors, and teacher behaviors.

The social behaviors of young children change rapidly in response to situational variables (Wittmer & Honig, 1994), requiring that observations be conducted across all relevant settings if a record of a child's social behavior is to be representative (Obrzut & Boliek, 1993). Behavioral samples collected must be large enough to represent accurately the entire time of interest. Doll and Elliott (1994) found that it would require at least five 10-minute observations across several weeks to adequately represent a preschooler's social behaviors. The predictability of different behaviors was quite variable. Incidence rates of certain behaviors were readily apparent, even after only two observations. For example, the degree to which a preschooler was physically aggressive or played or wandered alone was reliably predicted from two observation intervals. On the other hand, the degree to which a preschooler would share or engage in negative verbal behaviors was never adequately predicted from less than the completed observational record.

Behavior Rating Scales

Behavior rating scales typically contain a number of specific behaviors or correlates of behavior organized into empirically derived factors or scales which provide information about a child across numerous social-emotional behavior dimensions. These scales are usually developed from a review of the literature in the behavioral area of interest and by accessing behavioral descriptors of children who are representative of the target population.

Rating scales require observers to make a judgment about the quality or quantity of social behaviors or interactions that occur over a longer period of time, rather than simply recording behaviors as they occur. With rating scales, the developers define the construct assessed by the rating scale and the behaviors that compose those constructs. Numerical rating scales are used most often. Raters make judgments about the quantity or quality of behaviors represented by using a numerical scale, such as a Likert scale (Likert, 1932). Behavioral anchors provide the rater with a definition or description of what each number represents. These behavioral anchors may be very specific or general, but it is important that scale developers describe the behaviors, especially at the low and high ends of the scale (Finn, 1972). The rating scale may be completed immediately after observing the behavior, or judgments may be based on accumulated observation occurring over a longer period of time. Many rating scales include procedures for summarizing the ratings on individual items. The summary is computed by adding the ratings and computing a total score or by computing subscale scores. A rating scale will ideally provide information on the behaviors of both partners in the social interaction.

Odom and Munson (1996) summarized the advantages and disadvantages of using rating scales to measure social interaction. Advantages are that they usually (a) are easier to use than observational measures, (b) are relatively quick to administer and easy to score, and (c) require less training for raters than do observational measures. Therefore, rating scales may be useful for early interventionists in cases where time is an important consideration. For some

behaviors, rating scales may have higher predictive validity than do direct observation systems (Bakeman & Brown, 1980; Jay & Farran, 1981), or higher predictive validity over time (Schaefer, 1989; Clarke-Stewart & Hevey, 1981). Rating scales yield global information which may be useful for measuring general levels of social interaction when screening children, identifying current functioning level, or measuring change in behavior over time (Odom & Munson, 1996).

A disadvantage of using rating scales is the subjectivity of the rating, rather than using a direct observation system. Rating scales also provide less detailed information, which may make them less useful for designing and monitoring interventions. The rating scales currently available may not have complete validity and reliability data and training information (Odom & Munson, 1996).

Examples of Rating Scales. Achenbach and Edelbrock have developed two checklists that can be used with preschool-aged children. The *Child Behavior Checklist* (CBCL/2–3) (Achenbach, 1991; Achenbach & Edelbrock, 1981) is designed for children ages 2 to 3 years and consists of 99 items and one open-ended item describing various behaviors, emotional problems, or reactions to specific situations. It is completed by the child's parents. The Child Behavior Checklist (CBCL/4–18) for ages 4 to 18 years is actually somewhat different than the checklist for children from 2 to 3 years. The CBCL/4–18 has 118 problem statements and two open-ended items that are evaluated by parents along the same scale as the CBCL/2–3. The CBCL/4–18 also has a social competence section which assesses children's play and home activities, social interactions, school and academic status, and total social competence.

Conners' Behavior Rating Scales consist of Conners' Parent Rating Scales (CPRS) and Conners' Teacher Rating Scales (CTRS) (Conners, 1990). Although originally developed to help identify hyperactive children, Conners' Rating Scales are useful in characterizing and assessing other, related problem behaviors. There are two versions of each scale, a long and a short form. The short forms have normative data available at the preschool level. The CPRS consists of 48 items to be rated by parents on a scale of 0 to 3. Factor analyses have sorted the items into five scales: Conduct Problem, Learning Problem, Psychosomatic, Impulsive-Hyperactive, and Anxiety.

The *Social Skills Rating System* (SSRS) (Gresham & Elliott, 1990) is a multirater inventory designed to screen and assess children's social skills in different settings and to assist in the development of interventions when social skills deficits are identified. The SSRS assesses student social behaviors of preschoolers which may affect teacher-student relations, peer acceptance, and academic performance. The measure contains three behavior rating forms (teacher, parent, and student versions) and an integrative assessment and intervention planning record. The subdomains included in both the parent and teacher rating scales are cooperation, assertion, and self-control. The parent version also measures responsibility. Raters indicate how often a behavior occurs (never, sometimes, or very often). The SSRS demonstrates the potential to accurately assess the prosocial and problem behavior of preschoolers, across home and school environments and ratings, and to track these children's progress in these skills over time. The SSRS also may provide an important link between assessment and intervention, a critical need in preschool social emotional assessment (Knoff, Stollar, Johnson, & Chenneville, 1999).

The *Carolina Record of Individual Behavior* (CRIB) (Simeonsson, Huntington, Short, & Ware, 1982) is designed to assess the child's level of arousal or state as well as eight developmental behaviors, including social orientation, participation, motivation, endurance, receptive communication, expressive communication, object orientation, and consolability.

A brief checklist designed to determine a child's ability to function in an integrated setting based on social skills has been developed by Johnson and Mandell (1988). The *Social Observation for Mainstreamed Environments* (SOME) contains 15 items on which a child's performance and setting expectations are compared. Discrepancies are noted and resolutions developed. Samples of items included on the SOME are "plays well with others," "attends to tasks for short periods of time," and "practices turn taking." The instrument requires that the child be observed across multiple settings during different types of activities for a minimum of 10 minutes per observation, with a total observation time of approximately 50 minutes. The SOME can be useful in developing goals and objectives related to social development and in program planning for anticipated transitions (Benner, 1992).

The *Social Strategy Rating Scale* (Beckman & Lieber, 1994) was developed to provide a measure of key social strategies that are fundamental to the ability of young children to engage in socially competent exchanges with a variety of social partners. Twenty-one social strategies were identified that had been attributed to children from infancy through the preschool years. Children are rated across two dimensions: frequency with which the strategy is observed and appropriateness of the strategies used. Frequency is rated on a five-point scale ranging from "never" to "well-established." The appropriateness scale is used on those items receiving a frequency rating of 2 or above. It is a three-point scale that ranges from inappropriate to appropriate. Beckman and Lieber (1994) initially reported relatively high interobserver agreement, which was maintained over four data points and across three different social contexts. Good internal consistency was reported across contexts, and the scale detected differences in the children's social behavior with different partners.

The *Preschool and Kindergarten Behavior Scales* (PKBS) (Merrell, 1994–1996) were developed to address the lack of psychometrically sound behavioral assessment instruments available for use with the early childhood/preschool population and because of the desirability of assessing both social skills and problem behaviors with a single measure. Merrell (1996) reported that the PKBS appeared to be a psychometrically sound and clinically relevant instrument for screening and assessing social skills and social-emotional problems of young children. The author suggested the PKBS should facilitate practical and relevant descriptions of social skills deficits and problem-behavior excesses in individual assessment cases and should generate hypotheses regarding classification and intervention. The PKBS appears to compare favorably with other early childhood behavior rating scales (Bracken, Keith, & Walker, 1994; Merrell, 1995).

Sociometric Assessment

Sociometric assessment procedures provide general evaluations of the social acceptance, social preference, or likability of other children. Sociometric assessment requires information from intact groups of children, and thus, is useful only if the child is enrolled in a preschool or child care program.

Two general types of sociometric assessment instruments may be useful: peer nominations and peer ratings. For peer nominations, children are asked to identify those of their classmates who meet some general criterion ("best friend" or "the one liked the least"). Using positive and negative nominations allows the assessor to form two sociometric groups. The criteria may depend on the purpose of the assessment. Possible caregiver concerns should be considered when using negative nomination criteria.

When peer ratings are used, children provide general qualitative ratings for each child in the class or play group. The criteria depend on the purpose of the assessment but are used to gather general statements of preference (e.g., How much do you like to talk to or play with _____?) (Odom & McConnell, 1989). Ratings are usually on a three-point scale for preschoolers.

A child's peer rating is usually calculated as the sum or average rating received from all raters. Asher, Singleton, Tinsley, and Hymel (1979) developed and evaluated a picture rating procedure which has proved to be quite useful and is now widely accepted. Using this picture rating procedure, children sort photographs of their individual classmates into marked boxes to indicate their relative ratings.

Sociometrics are often used to measure social relationships with peers. These assessments may reveal the popularity and social acceptance of the child within the group (Odom & Munson, 1996). Because preschool children are the informants for sociometric procedures, concern has been expressed about the reliability or stability of these measures (McConnell & Odom, 1986; Odom & Munson, 1996). As stated previously in this chapter, young children with disabilities often have difficulty in developing social relationships. Therefore, any interpretation of the results should be based on all of the assessment data collected using a variety of tools and approaches in the assessment process.

Curriculum-Based Assessments

Curriculum-based assessments provide highly specific information regarding a child's current level of performance for multiple individual skills (Odom & McConnell, 1989). The purpose of a curriculum-based assessment is to provide a link among assessment, intervention, and evaluation. Skills are assessed across developmental domains and are usually ordered according to when they typically appear in a child's development. The social domain is usually one of the domains, with the CBA focusing on functional skills (Bricker, 1989). Some of the assessments include activities that early childhood special educators can use to support the child's acquisition of the skills identified as needing intervention.

Curriculum-based assessments provide information for planning individual interventions in the area of social development. Table 16–2 lists a number of curriculum-based assessments that have related curricula available. The early interventionist or early childhood special educator should carefully examine the social-emotional domain of the assessment to determine if the assessment is appropriate for the particular child. Assessment in this domain may address areas ranging from self-concept and locus of control to social competence and anxiety and temperament. McAllister (1991) noted several problems with using a curriculum-based assessment to assess the social-emotional domain. He proposes that the social skills domain is sometimes underrepresented, is merged with adaptive behavior items, may include too few items for a comprehensive assessment, and may not adequately reflect the social development of children with certain specific disabilities. Beckman and Lieber (1994) pointed out that curriculum-based assessments do not always focus on important social and cognitive strategies or on processes that may influence the emergence of the milestones. For example, typical items such as playing pat-a-cake may be included at the typical age for a child to acquire this skill. However, the social processes that make such an activity desirable (e.g., turn-taking, imitation) may not be described. The test chosen by the early interventionist must be selected based on the needs and strengths of the particular child. Subdomains and items within these subdomains should be reviewed before the assessment is chosen. A survey of the subdomains included in various multidomain curriculum-based assessments shows the wide range of behaviors included in the social-emotional domain. Table 16–2 summarizes subdomains included in some commonly used multidomain assessments.

Odom and McConnell (1989) provided the following guidelines for choosing criterion-referenced measures relative to assessing social-emotional development. The instrument must: (1) provide for direct and detailed assessment of a child's behavior across situations and settings; (2) focus on discrete social skills or components of social interaction (social initiation might include child's use of eye contact, proximity to peers during play, etc.); (3) arrange skills in a natural progression or heirarchy by task analysis or typical developmental progress; (4) be linked carefully to curricula or other intervention programs for children; and (5) be sensitive to small changes in behavior. A comprehensive assessment would use a curriculum-based assessment as only one part of the entire assessment process.

Norm-Based Assessments

When diagnosing or classifying a child, it is necessary to judge a child's social behavior against an established norm. In such cases, the examiner is concerned about the general performance of the child in relationship to the performances of other children, which requires the use of a norm-based instrument. Norm-based measures document a child's current level of functioning and thus may diagnose a social problem and possibly qualify a child for special services.

The majority of norm-based assessments of social behavior and competence usually describe the child's performance on broad dimensions of social development. These norms are used to compare the development of an individual child with the overall status of other children at a similar age. These are usually part of a broader assessment of development. Norm-based measures often rely on caregiver ratings, which are completed in interview formats, and teacher ratings completed in classroom situations.

The *Battelle Developmental Inventory* (BDI) (Newborg, Stock, Wnek, Guidubaldi, & Svinicki, 1988) includes measures of social development in the personal-social domain. The BDI assesses children from birth to 8 years and, therefore, few items are included for children

TABLE 16–2

Personal/Social Items on Assessment Instruments

Instrument	Domains/Subdomains
Assessment, Evaluation, and Programming System (Birth–3) Vol. 1 (Bricker, 1993); Vol. 2 (Cripe, Slentz, & Bricker, 1993)	Social (interaction with adults; interaction with environment; interaction with peers) Adaptive (feeding; personal hygiene; undressing)
Assessment, Evaluation, and Programming System (Three to Six) Vol. 3 (Bricker & Pretti-Frontczak, 1996); Vol. 4 (Bricker & Waddell, 1996)	Social Adaptive (dining; personal hygiene; dressing/undressing)
The Carolina Curriculum for Infants and Toddlers with Special Needs (2nd edition) (Johnson-Martin, Jens, Attermeier, & Hacker, 1991)	Social/Adaptation (self-direction; social skills; self-help—eating, dressing, & grooming)
The Carolina Curriculum for Preschoolers with Special Needs (Johnson-Martin, Attermeier, & Hacker, 1990)	Social/Adaptation (responsibility; self-concept; interpersonal skills; self-help skills—eating, dressing, grooming, & toileting)
Hawaii Early Learning Profile (Birth to 3) (Parks, Furono, O'Reilly, Inatsuka, Hoska, & Zeisloft-Falbey, 1994)	Social-Emotional Self-Help
Hawaii Early Learning Profile for Preschoolers (VORT, 1995)	Social-Emotional (attachment, separation, autonomy; development of self; expression of emotions & feelings; learning of rules & expectations; social interaction & play) Self-Help (oral-motor development; dressing; independent feeding; sleep patterns & behavior; grooming & hygiene; toileting; household independence & responsibility)
Early Learning Accomplishment Profile (Glover, Preminger, & Sanford, 1995)	Social-Emotional Self-Help
Learning Accomplishment Profile-Revised (Glover, Preminger, Sanford, & Zelman, 1995)	Personal-Social Self-Help
Transdisciplinary Play-Based Assessment (Linder, 1993a)	Social-Emotional (temperament; mastery motivation; social interactions with parent; social interaction with facilitator; characteristics of dramatic play in relation to emotional development; humor and social conventions; social interactions with peers)

younger than 12 months of age. The personal social domain targets peer interaction and also includes items related to self-concept, social roles, and expression of feelings. The number of items that specifically address children's interactions with others is relatively limited.

Norm-referenced assessments of adaptive behavior often include subsections related to social competence. For example, the *Vineland Adaptive Behavior Scale* (Vineland) (Sparrow, Balla, & Cicchetti, 1984) includes a survey form and an expanded edition that are completed during interviews with a parent or other informed adult. The socialization domain has three subdomains: (1) interpersonal relations, (2) play and leisure time, and (3) coping skills.

The *Developmental Teaching Objectives Rating Form-Revised* (DTORF-R) (Wood, 1992) is a norm-referenced rating scale, which is practical, easily administered, and classroom-oriented. The DTORF-R consists of 171 items measuring social-emotional development from birth through 16 years. There are four interactive subscales: Behavior, Communication, Socialization, and Academics/Cognition. The results provide a profile of sequential skills (items mastered) and deficits (items not yet mastered) for each subscale and also an aggregate score indicating the child's overall stage of social-emotional development. The items that are not yet mastered can be used for specific instructional objectives. The DTORF-R may be administered by teachers, psychologists, supervisors, and parents. The results can be used to:

1. Identify students in need of referral for special help
2. Make decisions about placement and grouping of children
3. Identify instructional objectives in the social emotional domain
4. Plan curriculum activities to foster social emotional competence
5. Document student progress in social emotional growth

6. Evaluate program effectiveness (Wood, 1992)

The Developmental Therapy curriculum described extensively in *Developmental Therapy in the Classroom* (Wood, Davis, Swindle, & Quirk, 1996) provides the goals and curriculum for each stage assessed by the DTORF-R. The DTORF-R is particularly useful with students whose behavior suggests serious emotional, social, or behavioral problems.

Additional examples of standardized, norm-referenced scales are the *Social Skills Rating System* (SSRS) by Gresham and Elliott (1990) (discussed earlier in this chapter) and the *Social Competence Scale* (Kohn, 1988). These standardized assessments yield standard scores and percentile ranks.

During the administration of a standardized instrument, the examiner may focus on the baby's relationship with her caregiver, which can give valuable information about social-emotional development. For example, McCune, Kalmanson, Fleck, Glazewski, and Sillari (1990) suggested the *Bayley Infant Behavior Record* (IBR) can be used as a psychosocial screening instrument to identify children at risk. Clinical observations made during a Bayley assessment can provide clues to social-emotional problems and to the impact of affective considerations on cognitive performance. McCune and colleagues (1990) gave the following examples of behavior which may indicate problems in social-emotional development:

- Does not take pleasure in interpersonal relationships
  - Mechanically builds tower
  - Does not look to parent or examiner as social reference point
  - Experiences private pleasure in tasks themselves, but does not share with others
  - Does not warm up to examiner
  - Unable to initiate a subsequent act without verbal encouragement

- Difficulty in self-organization
  - Unwillingness to relinquish toys as testing proceeds

- Unwillingness to engage sufficiently with a particular set of materials to complete a required task
- May seem unwilling to reach for or touch objects
- May appear highly distractible or unable to focus on one task
- May be easily frustrated and unable to persevere with tasks that are not easily mastered
- May operate only on their own agenda and cannot become interested in any items that are presented
- Difficulties in caregiver-infant relationship that may be observed may involve:
  - Caregiver's responsiveness to infant's bids for caregiver attention or involvement
  - Caregiver's capacity to provide appropriate social cues, such as reassurance or encouragement
  - Extremely anxious caregiver who is intrusive or tries to take over the assessment process
  - Overanxious parent may be unwilling to allow examiner to attend to baby by demanding constant attention from examiner
  - Caregiver who has withdrawn from relationship may turn baby over to examiner and act as if not present in room (McCune, et al., 1990, pp. 233–237)

The assessor should keep in mind that standardized measures are used to compare the behavior, performance, or development of an individual child with the overall status of other children at similar ages. Chapter 9 discusses the use of norm-based instruments with children with disabilities. The specific adaptations provided for children with disabilities should be reviewed. Care should be taken when using norm-based instruments with children with disabilities.

Using Social-Emotional Assessment Information

The assessment approaches discussed in this chapter are important for different purposes. The information gathered in social-emotional assessment may be used for screening and diagnosing, as well as in designing and monitoring instructional programs. The reader should refer to Table 16–1 for specific examples of each of these assessment approaches. Teacher rating scales seem to be the most efficient approach for screening preschool children (Odom & Munson, 1996). According to Odom and Munson (1996), social interaction assessment information may be used to document children's current skills and to diagnose a problem. This assessment information may be developed by using rating scales, norm-referenced instruments, or direct observation. Information from curriculum-based assessments, rating scales, and direct observation may be used to develop intervention plans and monitor a child's programming. Direct observation of young children in their natural setting may reveal valuable information about the nature of social exchanges and potential intervention targets. Direct observation, parent reporting, and rating scales may assist the teacher in monitoring an intervention program. Monitoring information must reflect the nature and quality of the interactive episodes. The teacher can observe preschool children with disabilities during play sessions with peers to note changes resulting from the intervention sessions and then write anecdotal notes, record systematic direct observation, or complete a rating scale (Odom & Munson, 1996).

It is important to remember that the parent should participate in identifying the difficulties in interaction and developing possible solutions. The early interventionist or early childhood special educator should communicate to the caregivers that the plans do not represent a negative judgment of their interactive skills. However, intervention plans probably will require caregivers to change their behavior because it is their behavior that is most amenable to change. Interventions should build on the positive behaviors already occurring in the interaction (Comfort, 1988; Odom & Munson, 1996). Any intervention plan must respect the cultural differences that influence the nature of infant-caregiver interactions.

Summary

A number of assessment methods may be used to collect information about the social-emotional development of infants, toddlers, and preschoolers with disabilities. The information gathered by these assessments may be used for different purposes. The assessor must match her choice of assessment instrument to the questions she is trying to answer about the child's social and emotional development. Investigation of an infant's attachment to a primary caregiver is accomplished through observations of infant-caregiver interactions. Assessment of a child's play and social interactions can involve observations, rating scales, sociometric procedures, curriculum-based assessments, and norm-referenced tests.

References

Achenbach, T. M. (1991). *Manual for the Child Behavior Checklist and Revised Child Behavior Profile.* Burlington, VT: University of Vermont Department of Psychiatry.

Achenbach, T. M., & Edelbrock, C. S. (1981). Behavioral problems and competencies reported by parents of normal and disturbed children aged four to sixteen. *Monographs of the Society for Research in Child Development*, 46 (Serial No. 188).

Ainsworth, M. D., Blehar, M. C., Waters, E., & Walls, S. (1978). *Patterns of attachment: A psychological study of the strange situation.* Hillsdale, NJ: Lawrence Erlbaum.

Asher, S. R., Singleton, L. C., Tinsley, B. R., & Hymel, S. (1979). A reliable sociometric measure for preschool children. *Developmental Psychology*, 15, 443–444.

Asher, S. R., & Taylor, A. R. (1981). Social outcomes of mainstreaming: Sociometric assessment and beyond. *Exceptional Education Quarterly*, 1, 13–30.

Bagnato, S. J., Neisworth, J. T., Salvia, J., & Hunt, F. M. (1999). *Temperament and Atypical Behavior Scale (TABS).* Baltimore: Brookes.

Baird, S., Haas, L., McCormick, K., Carruth, C., & Turner, K. (1992). Approaching an objective system for observation and measurement: Infant-parent social interaction code. *Topics in Special Education*, 12, 544–571.

Bakeman, R., & Brown, J. (1980). Early interaction: Consequences for social and mental development at three years. *Child Development*, 51, 437–447.

Barnard, K. E. (1979). *Instructor's learning resource manual.* Seattle: NCAST Publications, University of Washington.

Barnard, K. E., & Kelly, J. E. (1990). Assessment of parent-child interactions. In S. J. Meisels & J. P. Shonkoff (Eds.), *Handbook of early childhood intervention.* New York: Cambridge University Press.

Beal, J. (1991). Methodological issues in conducting research on parent-infant interaction. *Journal of Pediatric Nursing*, 6, 11–15.

Beckman, P. J., & Lieber, J. (1994). The Social Strategy Rating Scale: An approach to evaluating social competence. *Journal of Early Intervention*, 18(1), 1–11.

Beckwith, L., & Cohen, S. E. (1984). Home environment and cognitive competence in preterm children during the first 5 years. In A. W. Gottfried (Ed.), *Home environment and early cognitive development.* New York: Academic Press.

Belsky, J., Gilstrap, B., & Rovine, M. (1984). The Pennsylvania Infant and Family Development Project I: Stability and change in mother-infant and father-infant interaction in a family setting at one, three, and nine months. *Child Development*, 55, 692–705.

Benner, S. M. (1992). *Assessing young children with special needs.* White Plains, NY: Longman.

Bernstein, V., Hans, S., & Percansky, C. (1992). *Parent-Child Observation Guide.* (Available from Victor J. Bernstein, Department of Psychiatry, Box 411, The University of Chicago, Chicago, IL 60637).

Bowlby, J. (1969). *Attachment and loss: Attachment (Vol. 1).* New York: Basic Books.

Bracken, B. A., Keith, L. K., & Walker, K. C. (1994). Assessment of preschool behavior and social-emotional functioning: A review of thirteen third-party instruments. *Assessment in Rehabilitation and Exceptionality*, 1, 331–346.

Bradley, R., & Caldwell, B. (1980). The relation of home environment, cognitive competence and IQ among males and females. *Child Development*, 51, 1140–1148.

Bredekamp, S., & Copple, C. (Eds.). (1997). *Developmentally appropriate practice in early childhood programs* (Rev. ed.). Washington, DC: National Association for the Education of Young Children.

Bricker, D. (1989). *Early intervention for at-risk and handicapped infants, toddlers, and preschool children* (2nd ed.). Palo Alto, CA: VORT.

Bricker, D. (1993). *AEPS measurement for birth to three years.* Baltimore: Brookes.

Bricker, D., & Pretti-Frontczak, K. (Eds.). (1996). *Assessment, Evaluation, and Programming System (AEPS) for infants and children* (Vol. 3) AEPS *measurement for three to six years.* Baltimore: Brookes.

Bricker, D., & Waddell, M. (Eds.). (1996). *Assessment, Evaluation, and Programming System for infants and children* (Vol. 4) AEPS *curriculum for three to six years.* Baltimore: Brookes.

Brockman, L. M., Morgan, G. A., & Harmon, R. J. (1988). Mastery motivation and developmental delay. In T. D.

Wachs & R. Sheehan (Eds.), *Assessment of young developmentally disabled children*. New York: Plenum Press.

Bromwich, R. (1981). *Working with parents*. Austin, TX: PRO-ED.

Bromwich, R. (1983). *Parent Behavior Progression: Manual and 1983 supplement*. Northridge, CA: Center for Research Development and Services, Department of Educational Psychology, California State University.

Bronson, M. B. (1994). The usefulness of an observational measure of young children's social and mastery behaviors in early childhood classrooms. *Early Childhood Research Quarterly, 9*, 19–43.

Buss, A. H., & Plomin, R. (1975). *A temperament theory of personality development*. New York: Wiley Interscience.

Buysee, V. (1991). *Early Childhood Friendship Survey*. Chapel Hill, NC: Frank Porter Graham Center, University of North Carolina.

Buysee, V. (1993). Friendship of preschoolers with disabilities in community-based child care settings. *Journal of Early Intervention, 17*, 380–395.

Caldwell, B., & Bradley, R. (1984). *Home observation for measurement of the environment*. Little Rock: University of Arkansas.

Clarke-Stewart, K., & Hevey, C. (1981). Longitudinal relations in repeated observations of mother-child interactions from 1 to 2½ years. *Developmental Psychology, 17*, 127–145.

Comfort, M. (1988). Assessing parent-child interactions. In D. Bailey & R. Simeonsson (Eds.), *Family assessment in early intervention* (pp. 65–94). Upper Saddle River, NJ: Merrill/Prentice Hall.

Cone, J. D. (1986). Idiographic, nomothetic and related perspectives in behavioral assessment. In R. O. Nelson & S. C. Hayes (Eds.), *Conceptual foundations of behavioral assessment* (pp. 111–128). New York: Guilford Press.

Conners, C. K. (1990). *Conners' Behavior Rating Scales manual*. North Tonawanda, NY: Multi-Health Systems.

Cripe, J., Slentz, K., & Bricker, D. (1993). *Assessment, Evaluation, and Programming System (AEPS) for infants and children* (Vol. 2) AEPS *curriculum for birth to three years*. Baltimore: Brookes.

Doll, B., & Elliott, S. N. (1994). Representativeness of observed preschool social behaviors: How many data are enough? *Journal of Early Intervention, 18*(2), 227–238.

Farren, D. C., Kasari, C., Yoder, P., Harber, L., Huntington, G. S., & Comfort-Smith, M. (1987). Rating mother-child interactions in handicapped and at-risk infants. In T. Tamir (Ed.), *Stimulation and intervention in infant development*. London: Freund.

Field, T. (1978). Interaction behaviors of primary versus secondary caretaker fathers. *Developmental Psychology, 14*, 183–184.

Finn, R. (1972). Effects of some characteristics in rating scale characteristics on the means and reliabilities of ratings. *Educational and Psychological Measurement, 32*, 255–265.

Fraiberg, S. (Ed.). (1980). *Clinical studies in infant mental health: The first year of life*. New York: Basic Books.

Ghuman, J. K., Peebles, C. D., & Ghuman, H. S. (1998). Review of social interaction measures in infants and preschool children. *Infants and Young Children, 11*(2), 21–44.

Glover, E., Preminger, J., & Sanford, A. (1995). *Early Learning Accomplishment Profile (E-LAP)*. Chapel Hill, NC: Chapel Hill Training-Outreach Project.

Glover, E., Preminger, J., Sanford, A., & Zelman, J. (1995). *Learning Accomplishment Profile-Revised (LAP-R)*. Chapel Hill, NC: Chapel Hill Training-Outreach Project.

Goldsmith, H. H., Buss, A. H., Plomin, R., Rothbart, M. K., Thomas, H., Chess, S., Hinde, R. A., & McCall, R. B. (1987). Roundtable: What is temperament? Four approaches. *Child Development, 58*, 505–529.

Greenspan, S. I. (1979). Intelligence and adaptations: An integration of psychoanalytic and Piagetian developmental psychology. *Psychological Issues, 12* (3/4), Monograph 47/48. New York: International Universities Press.

Greenspan, S. I. (1981). *Psychopathology and adaptation in infancy and early childhood: Principles of clinical diagnosis and preventive intervention*. New York: Viking Press.

Greenspan, S. I. (1989). *The development of the ego: Implications for personality theory, psychopathology, and the psychotherapeutic process*. Madison, CT: International Universities Press.

Greenspan, S. I. (1996). Assessing the emotional and social functioning of infants and young children. In S. J. Meisels & E. Fenichel (Eds.), *New visions for the developmental assessment of infants and young children* (pp. 231–266). Washington, DC: Zero to Three/National Center for Infants, Toddlers, and Families.

Greenspan, S. I., & Lieberman, A. F. (1988). A clinical approach to attachment. In J. Belsky & T. Nezworski (Eds.), *Clinical implications of attachment* (pp. 387–424). Hillsdale, NJ: Lawrence Erlbaum.

Greenspan, S. I., Lieberman, A. F., & Poisson, S. S. (1981). *Greenspan-Lieberman Observation System for Assessment of Caregiver-Infant Interaction During Semi-structured Play (GLOS)*. Bethesda, MD: Mental Health Study Center, National Institute of Mental Health.

Gresham, F., & Elliott, S. (1990). *Social Skills Rating System*. Circle Pines, MN: American Guidance Service.

Guralnick, M. J. (1980). Social interaction among preschool handicapped children. *Exceptional Children, 46*, 248–253.

Guralnick, M. J. (1990). Social competence and early intervention. *Journal of Early Intervention, 14*, 3–14.

Guralnick, M. J. (1992). *Assessment of Peer Relations*. Seattle: Child Development and Mental Retardation Center, University of Washington.

Guralnick, M. J., Connor, R. T., Hammond, M. A., Gottman, J. M., & Kinnish, K. (1995). Immediate effects of mainstreamed settings on the social interactions and social integration of preschool children. *American Journal on Mental Retardation, 100*, 359–377.

Guralnick, M. J., & Groom, J. M. (1985). Correlates of peer-related social competence of developmentally delayed preschool children. *American Journal of Mental Deficiency*, 90, 140–150.

Guralnick, M. J., & Groom, J. M. (1987). The peer relations of mildly delayed and nonhandicapped preschool children in mainstreamed playgroups. *Child Development*, 58, 1556–1572.

Guralnick, M. J., & Groom, J. M. (1988). Friendships of preschool children in mainstream playgroups. *Developmental Psychology*, 24, 595–604.

Hans, S. L., & Bernstein, V. J. (1990). Planning programmes for high-risk infants: A facet analysis of parent-infant communication. *Applied Psychology: An International Review*, 39, 457–478.

Hofheimer, J. A., O'Grady, K. E., & Packer, A. B. (1988). Infants born to adolescents: Predicting development at four years from early interaction and social risk. Paper presented at the International Conference on Infant Studies, Los Angeles, March–April.

Huntington, G. S. (1988). Assessing child characteristics that influence family functioning. In D. B. Bailey & R. J. Simeonsson (Eds.), *Family assessment in early intervention* (pp. 45–64). Upper Saddle River, NJ: Merrill/Prentice Hall.

Iannotti, R. (1985). Naturalistic and structured assessments of prosocial behavior in preschool children: The influence of empathy and perspective taking. *Developmental Psychology*, 21, 46–55.

Jay, S., & Farran, D. (1981). The relative efficacy of predicting IQ from mother-child interactions using ratings versus behavioral count measures. *Journal of Applied Developmental Psychology*, 2, 165–177.

Johnson, R., & Mandell, C. (1988). A social observation checklist for preschoolers. *Teaching Exceptional Children*, Winter, 18–21.

Johnson-Martin, N. M., Attermeier, S. M., & Hacker, B. J. (1990). *The Carolina Curriculum for Preschoolers with Special Needs*. Baltimore: Brookes.

Johnson-Martin, N. M., Jens, K. G., Attermeier, S. M., & Hacker, B. J. (1991). *The Carolina Curriculum for Infants and Toddlers with Special Needs* (2nd ed.). Baltimore: Brookes.

Kazdin, A. E. (1977). Artifact, bias, and complexity of assessment: The ABC's of reliability. *Journal of Applied Behavioral Analysis*, 10, 141–150.

Knoff, H. M., Stollar, S. A., Johnson, J. J., & Chenneville, T. A. (1999). Assessment of social-emotional functioning and adaptive behavior. In E. Vazquez, I. Romero, & J. Kalesnik (Eds.), *Assessing and screening preschoolers: Psychological and educational dimensions* (2nd ed., pp. 126–160). Needham Heights, MA: Allyn & Bacon.

Kohn, M. (1988). *Kohn problem checklist/Kohn Social Competence Scale*. San Antonio: The Psychological Corporation.

Lerner, C., & Dombro, A. L. (2000). *Learning and growing together: Understanding and supporting your child's development*.

Washington, DC: Zero to Three/National Center for Infants, Toddlers, and Families.

Lewis, M. (1987). Social development in infancy and early childhood. In J. D. Osofsky (Ed.), *Handbook of infant development*. New York: Wiley.

Likert, R. (1932). A technique for the measurement of attitudes. *Archives of Psychology*, 22(140), 1–52.

Linder, T. W. (1993a). *The Transdisciplinary Play-Based Assessment* (Rev. ed.). Baltimore: Brookes.

Linder, T. W. (1993b). *The transdisciplinary play-based intervention*. Baltimore: Brookes.

Mahoney, G., Finger, I., & Powell, A. (1985). Relationship of maternal behavioral style to the development of organically impaired mentally retarded infants. *American Journal of Mental Deficiency*, 90, 296–302.

Mahoney, G., & Powell, A. (1988). Modifying parent-child interaction: Enhancing the development of handicapped children. *The Journal of Special Education*, 22, 82–96.

Mahoney, G., Powell, A., & Finger, I. (1986). The Maternal Behavior Rating Scale. *Topics in Early Childhood Special Education*, 6, 44–56.

Mahoney, G., Powell, A., Finnegan, C., Fors, S., & Wood, S. (1986). The transactional intervention program, theory, procedures and evaluation. In D. Gentry & J. Olson (Eds.), *The family support network series: Individualizing family services* (Monograph 4). Moscow, ID: Warren Center on Human Development, University of Idaho.

Mahoney, G., Spiker, D., & Boyce, G. (1996). Clinical assessments of parent-child interaction: Are professionals ready to implement this practice? *Topics in Early Childhood Special Education*, 16(1), 26–50.

McAllister, J. R. (1991). Curriculum-based behavioral intervention for preschool children with handicaps. *Topics in Early Childhood Special Education*, 11(2), 48–58.

McCandless, B. R., & Marshall, H. R. (1957) A sociometric picture for preschool children and its relation to teacher judgments of friendship. *Child Development*, 28, 139–147.

McCollum, J., & Stayton, V. (1985). Infant/parent interaction: Studies and intervention guidelines based on the SIAI model. *Journal of the Division for Early Childhood*, 9, 125–135.

McConnell, S. R., & Odom, S. L. (1986). Sociometrics: Peer-referenced measures and the assessment of social competence. In P. Strain, M. Guralnick, & H. Walker (Eds.), *Children's social behavior: Development, assessment, and modification* (pp. 215–286). New York: Academic Press.

McConnell, S. R., & Odom, S. L. (1999). A multimeasure performance-based assessment of social competence in young children with disabilities. *Topics in Early Childhood Special Education*, 19(2), 67–74.

McConnell, S. R., Sisson, L., & Sandler, S. (1984). *Category definitions for Observational Assessment of Reciprocal Social Interactions*. Unpublished observer training manual. University of Pittsburgh.

McCune, L., Kalmanson, B., Fleck, M. B., Glazewski, B., & Sillari, J. (1990). An interdisciplinary model of infant assessment. In S. J. Meisels & J. P. Shonkoff (Eds.), *Handbook of early childhood intervention* (pp. 219–245). New York: Cambridge University Press.

McEvoy, M. A., & Odom, S. L. (1996). Strategies for promoting social interaction and emotional development of infants and young children with disabilities and their families. In S. L. Odom & M. E. McLean (Eds.), *Early intervention/early childhood special education: Recommended practices* (pp. 223–244). Austin, TX: PRO-ED.

Merrell, K. W. (1994–1996). *Preschool and Kindergarten Behavior Scales.* Austin, TX: PRO-ED.

Merrell, K. W. (1995). Relationships among early childhood behavior rating scales: Convergent and discriminant construct validity of the Preschool and Kindergarten Behavior Scales. *Early Education and Development, 6,* 253–264.

Merrell, K. W. (1996). Social-emotional assessment in early childhood: The Preschool and Kindergarten Behavior Scales. *Journal of Early Intervention, 20*(2), 132–145.

Mudford, O. C., Beale, I. L., & Singh, N. N. (1990). The representativeness of observational samples of different durations. *Journal of Applied Behavior Analysis, 23,* 323–331.

Munson, L. J., & Odom, S. (1994). *Infant-Caregiver Interaction Scale (ICIS) manual.* Unpublished manuscript.

Munson, L. J., & Odom, S. L. (1996). Review of rating scales that measure parent-infant interaction. *Topics in Early Childhood Special Education, 16*(1), 11–25.

Newborg, J., Stock, J. R., Wnek, L., Guidubaldi, J., & Svinicki, J. S. (1988). *Battelle Developmental Inventory (BDI).* Chicago: Riverside.

Obrzut, J. E., & Boliek, C. A. (1993). Assessment of the child with social and emotional disorders. In J. J. Culbertson & D. J. Willis (Eds.), *Testing young children: A reference guide for developmental, psychoeducational, and psychosocial assessment* (pp. 345–382). Austin, TX: PRO-ED.

Odom, S. L. (1988). Research in early childhood special education: Methodologies and paradigms. In S. Odom & M. Karnes (Eds.), *Early intervention for infants and young children with handicaps: An empirical base* (pp. 1–21). Baltimore: Brookes.

Odum, S. L., Bender, M., Doran, L., Houden, P., McInnes, M., Deklyen, M., Speltz, M., & Jenkins, J. (1988). *Integrated preschool curriculum.* Seattle, WA: University of Washington Press.

Odom, S. L., & McConnell, S. R. (1989). Assessing social interaction skills. In D. B. Bailey & M. Wolery (Eds.), *Assessing infants and preschoolers with handicaps* (pp. 390–427). Upper Saddle River, NJ: Merrill/Prentice Hall.

Odom, S. L., McConnell, S. R., & Chandler, L. K. (1994). Acceptability and feasibility of classroom-based social interaction interventions for young children with disabilities. *Exceptional Children, 60,* 226–236.

Odom, S. L., McConnell, S. R., Kohler, F., & Strain, P. S. (1987). *Social interaction skill curriculum.* Unpublished curriculum manuscript. Pittsburgh: Early Childhood Research Institute, University of Pittsburgh.

Odom, S. L., McConnell, S. R., & McEvoy, M. A. (1992). Peer-related social competence and its implications for young children with disabilities. In S. Odom, S. McConnell, & M. McEvoy (Eds.), *Social competence of young children with disabilities* (pp. 3–36). Baltimore: Brookes.

Odom, S. L., & Munson, L. J. (1996). Assessing social performance. In M. E. McLean, D. B. Bailey, & M. Wolery (Eds.), *Assessing infants and preschoolers with special needs* (pp. 398–434). Upper Saddle River, NJ: Merrill/Prentice Hall.

Odom, S. L., & Ogawa, O. (1992). Direct observation of young children's social interaction with peers: A review of methodology. *Behavioral Assessment, 14,* 407–441.

Odom, S. L., Peterson, C., McConnell, S. R., & Ostrosky, M. M. (1990). Ecobehavioral analysis of early education/specialized classroom settings and peer social interaction. *Education and Training of Children, 13,* 316–330.

Parks, S., Furono, S., O'Reilly, K., Inatsuka, T., Hoska, C. M., & Zeisloft-Falbey, B. (1994). *Hawaii Early Learning Profile (Birth to 3).* Palo Alto, CA: VORT.

Power, T. G., & Parke, R. D. (1986). Patterns of early socialization: Mother-infant and father-infant interaction in the home. *International Journal of Behavioral Development, 9,* 331–341.

Rossetti, L. M. (1990). *Infant-Toddler Assessment.* Boston: Little Brown.

Rubin, K. H., Maioni, T. L., & Hornung, M. (1976). Free play behaviors in middle- and lower-class preschoolers: Parten and Piaget revisited. *Child Development, 47,* 414–419.

Rushton, J. P. (1976). Socialization and the altruistic behavior of children. *Psychological Bulletin, 83,* 898–913.

Schaefer, E. (1989). Dimensions of mother-infant interaction: Measurement, stability, and predictive validity. *Infant Behavior and Development, 12,* 379–393.

Simeonsson, R. J. (1986). *Psychological and developmental assessment of special children.* Boston: Allyn & Bacon.

Simeonsson, R. J., Huntington, G. S., Short, R. J., & Ware, W. B. (1982). The Carolina Record of Individual Behavior: Characteristics of handicapped infants and children. *Topics in Early Childhood Special Education, 2*(2), 43–55.

Sorce, J. F., & Emde, R. N. (1982). The meaning of infant emotional expression: Regularities in caregiving responses in normal and Down's syndrome infants. *Journal of Child Psychology and Psychiatry, 23,* 145–158.

Sparks, S., Clar, M., Oas, D., & Erickson, R. (1988). Clinical services to infants at risk for communication disorders. Paper presented at the annual convention of the American Speech-Language-Hearing Association, Boston, April.

Sparrow, S., Balla, D., & Cicchetti, D. (1984). *Vineland Adaptive Behavior Scales.* Circle Pines, MN: American Guidance Service.

Sroufe, L. A. (1979). Socioemotional development. In J. D. Osofsky (Ed.), *Handbook of infant development*. New York: Wiley.

Stern, D. (1974). Mother and infant at play: The dyadic interaction involving facila, vocal, and gaze behaviors. In M. Lewis & L. Rosenbaum (Eds.), *The effect of the infant on its caregiver* (pp. 187–213). New York: Wiley.

Suen, H. K., & Ary, D. (1989). *Analyzing quantitative behavioral observational data*. Hillsdale, NJ: Lawrence Erlbaum.

Teti, D. M., & Nakagawa, M. (1990). Assessing attachment in infancy: The strange situation and alternate systems. In E. D. Gibbs & D. M. Teti (Eds.), *Interdisciplinary assessment of infants: A guide for early intervention* (pp. 191–214). Baltimore: Brookes.

Thomas, A., Chess, S., & Birch, H. G. (1968). *Temperament and behavior disorders in children*. New York: New York University Press.

Vanderbilt/Minnesota Social Interaction Project (S. Odom and S. McConnell, Eds.). (1993). *Play time/social time: Organizing your classroom to build communication skills*. Tucson, AZ: Communication Skill Builders.

VORT Corporation. (1995). HELP *for Preschoolers*. Palo Alto, CA: VORT.

Walker, L. O., & Thompson, E. T. (1982). Mother-Infant Play Interaction Scale. In S. Smith-Humenick (Ed.), *Analysis of current assessment strategies on the health care of young children and childbearing families*. Norwalk, CT: Appleton-Century-Crofts.

Wittmer, D. S., & Honig, A. S. (1994). Play, story/song, and eating times in child care: Caregiver responses to toddlers and threes. In H. Goelman (Ed.), *Children's play in child care settings* (pp. 119–147). Albany, NY: State University of New York Press.

Wood, M. M. (1992). *Technical report for the Developmental Teaching Objectives Rating Form–Revised (DTORF-R)*. Athens, GA: Developmental Therapy Institute.

Wood, M. M., Davis, K. R., Swindle, F. L., & Quirk, C. (1996). *Developmental therapy-Developmental teaching: Fostering social-emotional competence in troubled children and youth* (3rd ed.). Austin, TX: PRO-ED.

Wyly, M. V. (1999). *Infant assessment*. Boulder, CO: Westview Press.

Yoder, P. (1987). Relationship between degree of infant handicap and clarity of infant cues. *American Journal of Mental Deficiency, 91*, 639–641.

Assessing Sensory-Motor Development

Shelly J. Lane

Sensory-Motor Versus Perceptual-Motor Assessment

In searching the literature for information pertinent to sensory-motor development and assessment, it will become quickly apparent that some confusion exists within this domain. Is sensory-motor the equivalent of perceptual-motor? If these terms are defined differently, does assessment of sensory-motor skill differ from assessment of perceptual-motor skill? Can sensory development and motor development be meaningfully studied as separate entities? Can we and should we, as practitioners, assess sensory processing and motor output individually? In reading the literature you will be able to find answers on both sides of each question. How best, then, can the child be served?

Strictly speaking, the terms "sensory" and "perceptual" do differ. An assessment of sensory systems alone implies testing the integrity of the sensory receptors and pathways to answer the question of whether or not the information is taken in at the receptor level and transmitted appropriately to the central nervous system (CNS). Perception extends beyond this aspect of sensory input to include the processing of sensory input within the CNS and the subsequent attachment of meaning to the input, in preparation for the development of a motor response (e.g., Movshon & Blakemore, 2000). However, when used together, as in "sensory-motor," there is an implication that the sensory input is processed and used to prepare the motor output or response. Thus, "sensory-motor assessment" often is used interchangeably with "perceptual-motor assessment"; functionally, for a child, these phrases are often equivalent.

Many of us continue to think in terms of "gross motor" and "fine motor" skills, with gross motor referring to big movements that use the whole body and fine motor to hand skills. This dichotomy is useful in categorizing motor skill, but does not extend well to the examination of sensory processing. This chapter will discuss both gross and fine motor skill development,

look at sensory processing and sensory skill, and discuss the interaction between sensory processing and the production of motor skills and motor planning.

Any assessment of motor skill requires some degree of sensory processing, or perception. Asking a child to perform a task requires that he process a verbal cue or direction; demonstrating a task with no verbal directions requires that the child process the task requirements visually and translate this into motor action; and even passively placing a child in a position or guiding his motor performance through a task requires that the child use his tactual/proprioceptive/kinesthetic senses to repeat the action. As a result, no assessment can be considered solely motor in nature, and the performance must be assessed based on both aspects of the task, the perceptual and the motor requirements.

What about "sensorimotor integration," and the assessment of this process? Sensory integration function is "the neurological process that organizes sensation from one's own body and from the environment and makes it possible to use the body effectively within the environment" (Ayres, 1979, p. 11). As conceptualized by Ayres, the founder of sensory integration theory, sensory integration function includes sensory modulation, sensory discrimination, and motor planning. Sensory modulation is the capacity to regulate and organize the degree, intensity, and nature of responses to sensory input in a graded and adaptive manner, so that individuals can maintain an optimal range of performance and adapt to challenges (Lane, Miller, & Hanft, 2000). Sensory discrimination is the capability to discern the qualities, similarities, and differences of sensory stimuli, including differentiation of the temporal or spatial qualities of sensory input (Lane, Miller, & Hanft, 2000). Finally, motor planning is the ability to conceptualize, organize, and execute nonhabitual motor tasks (Ayres, 1979, 1989; Lane, Miller, & Hanft, 2000). Thus, sensory integration function parallels the descriptions offered above, and indeed the processes must be considered similar. The differentiation comes in when one looks to assessment. Typically sensory-motor or perceptual-motor assessments focus on the *motor* aspect of the process; they look at the end product, the output: reflexes, pincer grasp, hopping and skipping, etc. Assessment of these skills is part of typical developmental evaluations. In contrast, assessments of sensory integration function look at the sensory input and processing aspect of the process: functions of the tactile system, the vestibular system (balance and equilibrium), etc. Generally, this form of assessment has not been a part of a typical developmental evaluation protocol, although tools are available that can be used (discussed later).

Thus, the domain of sensory-motor development and assessment in this chapter will include the processes involved in sensory intake, interpretation and integration of sensory input, the use of sensory input in the preparation of a motor response, and finally the motor response itself. Practitioners will rarely want, need, or be able to assess strictly sensory input. Instead, practitioners will be most helped, and therefore be best able to provide optimal guidance to the family and child, by assessing tools which consider combination of sensory input, processing, and motor output.

Development of Sensory-Motor Skills in Infancy

A part of the following section is devoted to the delineation of sensory and motor skills upon which sensory-motor assessments focus. Although not all chapters in this book take this approach, it has been done in this chapter as a means of linking motor to sensory skills. Numerous authors have documented motor development throughout infancy, and many excellent texts exist that provide the practitioner

with detailed information in this area (e.g., Alexander, Boehme, & Cupps, 1993; Short-DeGraff, 1988; Schuster & Ashburn, 1992). It is suggested that the practitioner commit to memory "key" aspects of development that will permit him to identify infants and children in need of detailed assessment of skills. Some of these key points in development will be covered below, although many clinicians prefer to develop their own list of developmental milestones that they consider to be critical. Sensory developmental milestones are more difficult to ferret out of the literature on infancy, and their relationship to motor skills is not always discussed. Responses to sensory input seem subtle and may be difficult for the untrained eye to identify. These will be covered in more detail below in order to give the practitioner some guidelines for knowing when to pursue assessment. Each area addressed is an area for potential assessment.

Newborns

Both sensory and motor activity can be seen prenatally, and these or similar responses and movements are seen at birth. The sensory systems of touch (tactile) and movement (vestibular-proprioceptive) predominate at birth, being the most mature. The vestibular system is the most mature and is fully functional at birth such that input in this system can be readily used to arouse or calm an infant. This system, along with proprioceptive and tactile inputs, is critical to reflexive movement. Although less mature in the newborn, smell contributes strongly to keeping the infant in close contact with the caregiver. Vision and audition are the least mature sensory systems in the newborn, although orienting reactions to both are present (Parham & Mailloux, 1996).

Flexion predominates at birth and as such the newborn posture is generally one of being curled up. Such a posture is more obvious when the newborn is on his stomach, because once placed on his back gravity pulls at least the trunk into greater extension. The flexion posture provides a base of support upon which some movement can take place.

Some cursory righting reactions are present owing to the maturity of the vestibular system, although muscle tone and strength are not sufficient to allow the newborn to resist the pull of gravity to any great degree. In addition, the newborn exhibits an automatic stepping reaction that occurs when pressure is placed on the feet and the center of gravity is placed slightly forward. In this position, alternating leg flexion and extension can be seen, resembling a walking pattern. This primitive walking pattern becomes adapted for more mature walking as the newborn matures. A strong grasp reflex is present at birth, but voluntary release develops over time (Cech & Martin, 1995).

From a motor perspective, newborn movements are reflexive and as such these movements are both stimulus dependent and involuntary. Primitive reflexes serve protective and survival functions, as can be seen in such things as the sucking and rooting reflexes. Postural reflexes, which would include the walking reflex described above, serve another function, the preparation for future movements (Payne & Isaacs, 1991). Other movements seen in the newborn are random, and not dependent on sensory input. These are considered a continuation of the movements documented in utero and include the head, trunk, and extremities. Sensory processing is most mature in the tactile and vestibular systems, and the infant uses these sensory systems extensively during the next several months.

Birth to 3 Months

Some key motor skills develop during this first quarter year that warrant mention. Many reflexes are present at birth that become integrated during the first year of life, including the rooting, grasp, and walking reflexes, as well as asymmetrical and symmetrical tonic neck reflexes. Head control develops throughout the first year, but infants should be able to lift their heads slightly and briefly when on their stomachs and turn their heads from side to side. The impetus for this is, in part, visual interest in the environment; thus, it may not be seen in infants with visual impairments.

When supported in a sitting position, infants should be able to both lift the head off the chest briefly and bring the head forward if it is dropped all the way back. Hand to mouth skills also begin at this early age. Despite the presence of the asymmetrical tonic neck reflex, infants can get at least one hand to the mouth and begin sucking on the fist early in development. By the end of 3 months, many infants can get both hands to their mouth and will likely enjoy the sucking activity that goes along with this.

During the first 3 months, babies do not seem to "do" much. They sleep a great deal and awaken primarily to eat. However, during this period of time when motor skills are at a minimum, sensory processing is not only highly active, it is highly important. At this age, babies enjoy being picked up and enjoy the comfort of close contact with a parent. Bath time should be a pleasant time as long as the infant is kept sufficiently warm. Even the newborn will respond to sounds and light in his environment. The response is often one of "stilling" of motor movement, along with some searching movements of the eyes. Infants can orient to changes in sound and light in their environment. This initial orientation may involve turning of the head or eyes in the direction of the new sound or change in light. Habituation to sounds and lights in the environment occurs with repeated or constant presence of the stimuli. This is an important skill because it allows the infant to block out sensory stimulation, which for the time being is meaningless, thereby permitting the rest and sleep that are critical for optimal development. Very young infants will also visually track an object up to 90 degrees, if the object is appealing (Schuster & Ashburn, 1992). As noted previously, infants are most attracted to visual objects with high contrast, hence the recent appearance of black-and-white infant toys and mobiles and infants' fascination with faces. Initially, visual acuity extends to only about 10 inches but gradually increases during the first few months of life. The ability to discriminate faces continues to develop through-out the first year of life. In addition to these visual skills, the infant is beginning to visually regard his hand and may begin to move the arm purposefully toward an object within the visual field. These skills are important because they lay the foundation for visually directed grasp and reach (Short-Degraff, 1988).

4 to 6 Months

Between 4 and 6 months of age, babies gain control of their heads and begin to get control of the trunk as well. As the vestibular system matures, they appear to be driven to conquer gravity and show high motivation in antigravity activities (Parham & Mailloux, 1996). Rolling—both prone to supine and supine to prone—develops during this period, as well as sitting, first with assistance and by 6 months independently. At this age, infants are still unable to get into and out of sitting independently. When placed on their stomach, 4-month-old babies will push up onto their hands and will be able to play with a toy for a brief period of time by shift-ing their weight to one arm, freeing the other arm for toy manipulation. This is also the period of time when babies find their knees, feet, and toes and develop the abdominal muscles needed to bring these body parts close to their hands and face. These activities are again driven by the visual system and may be delayed when visual deficits are present.

During this period, babies develop an inter-est in watching their hands and fingers move, indicating the integration of tactile and visual

inputs, and the fingers begin to move somewhat independently. The thumb is released during this stage to allow purposeful thumb-sucking and babies may be seen helping to hold the bottle with one or both hands, extending the ability developed in the first 3 months of getting hands to the midline of the body. This skill translates to bringing any number of graspable objects to the mouth, which is the primary tool of exploration at this age. Grasp is immature, and grasping small objects still presents a sig-nificant challenge to most babies. Accidental release of objects turns volitional at about 4 months of age, and leads to the transfer of ob-jects from one hand to the other. The begin-nings of motor planning are also observable as the infant works to produce novel actions and sounds with objects.

As the tactile system matures, tickling may now be responded to with a smile or even a gig-gle and some motor squirming. Bath time con-tinues to be fun for most babies. As they gain se-curity in the tub, babies of this age and older will often splash and play with vigor. Being held con-tinues to be an enjoyable activity. As the baby becomes more active, he may prefer to play in the parent's lap in addition to enjoying cuddling and close time. Most babies in this age range enjoy movement. They do not object to being picked up from sitting or lying down, and they often laugh with play that moves them quickly up and down. Visual and auditory skills are de-veloped such that they can see things across the room and will respond to auditory input by turn-ing the head and sometimes the body.

7 to 12 Months

During the last half of the first year, infants de-velop many new motor skills. Refinement of the infants' ability to interpret proprioceptive infor-mation from muscles and joints, as well as vestibular inputs, can be seen in the ongoing refinement of motor skills. Between 8 and 10 months, they begin to creep, thereby increasing their ability to explore the environment. An interesting skill that goes along with this new ability is the ability to get into and out of sitting and creeping postures. These transitional movements are critical both to overall motor development and to the babies' development of independence, and yet rarely are such transitional movements listed on a developmental scale. If a baby can sit very steadily, yet cannot get into and out of sitting, then it may be questioned whether or not sitting is truly a functional skill. Similarly, if a child can creep when placed on all fours but cannot get into the all-fours position independently, then minimal environmental exploration will take place with the baby's initiation.

By the end of the first year, creeping is expected to give way to walking. Pulling up to stand, cruising while holding onto furniture and walking with the hands held are skills that precede walking independently. The presence of these skills is a good sign that walking is soon to follow. It is critical to keep in mind that although the *average* baby will walk by 12 months, the *range* for walking is approximately 8 to 18 months. Variability in the time of skill attainment is present in most skills, but because walking is considered by many parents to be a pivotal skill, when a child does not walk by 12 months, some parents become unnecessarily worried. The clinical assessment at this point is critical in either identifying a delay or in putting the parents' minds to rest. A 12-month-old who is sitting independently, creeping and, more important, getting into and out of these positions but not yet walking may be merely a "late bloomer." Alternatively, if a 12-month-old seems stuck in a sitting or prone position or seems to have stiff or floppy muscles and is not walking, the practitioner may want to refer the child to an occupational or physical therapist for a more comprehensive assessment.

Hand skills blossom during the second half of the first year as the infant develops and refines both pincer and whole hand grasp. Along with skillful grasp comes the banging of objects on a table or tray and later the banging of two objects together at midline. In addition, peek-a-boo and pat-a-cake now become fun activities as the infant improves his midline hand skills. Toward the end of the first year, the pincer grasp and isolated finger movements are expressed and are accompanied by more refined tactile exploration of objects in the environment.

Within the sensory systems babies begin to demonstrate true intersensory integration. The visual guidance of reach and grasp has been discussed, and as the infant gains hand skills, the combination of visual and touch exploration of objects becomes more apparent. Although infants continue to obtain a great deal of touch information about objects with their mouths, the hands participate more and more, with the visual system taking a back seat to touch exploration. Twelve-month-old infants generally derive great pleasure from movement, both self-initiated and adult-initiated, and this is the time when "rough and tumble" play becomes popular. The explosion of movement skills and the incredible refinement of hand skills are both indications of improved motor planning abilities, and thus improved sensory integrative function.

12 to 24 Months

The drive to explore the environment continues to thrive and skills develop to support this drive. Thus, before they are 18 months old, children learn to manage stairs, first by crawling and later by walking both up and down. In addition, at this age babies learn to walk quickly, seeming to run from place to place. Supported by ongoing maturation of vestibular, proprioceptive, and visual processing, toddlers work on refining dynamic postural control (Parham & Mailloux, 1996). Fine motor skills also continue to improve, relying heavily on improvements in tactile discrimination, tactile-visual integration, and the ongoing development of motor planning skills.

As motor skills refine, the observer has greater opportunity to see the extent of perceptual development that has taken place. The ability to direct the foot in kicking a ball and the hand in throwing a ball indicates that visual motor skills are progressing. Fine motor skills such as putting pellets into a jar further indicate the precision of visual-tactile perception. Spatial perceptual skills become apparent as the child is able to correctly position a shape to place it into a simple form board, and develops the ability to imitate strokes with a crayon, first vertical and later horizontal. Activities demonstrated in this year point to the development of spatial and motor organization skills. Parham and Mailloux (1996) indicate that ideation, or "the ability to conceptualize what to do in a given situation" (p. 314), emerges in the second year of life. This can be observed in progress as a 20-month-old drags a ride-on toy to a couch and then uses it as a step-stool upon which to climb!

24 to 36 Months

Gross motor refinement occurs during this period, with the continued development of vestibular-proprioceptive and visual processing skills needed for balance, equilibrium, and muscle strength. Stair climbing using alternating feet going both up and down is an example of this integration and also points out the advances made in bilateral coordination. As trunk rotational movements become more readily accessible to the child, throwing begins to look more mature. The ability to weight shift while upright allows the child to stand very briefly on one foot, hop, and tiptoe walk. Although most children continue to be motivated to conquer gravity, some children may develop fears about movement during this year. They may dislike swinging high and feel insecure in other activities that take their feet off the ground. Although this may be worrisome to a parent, and in an older child may indicate a problem processing movement sensations, in many 2- to 3-year-old children it is a normal stage of gross motor development.

Fine motor skills are now closely linked with visual perception. Without formal assessment it may be difficult to determine at this age whether a fine motor deficit is due to poor motor performance or inadequate visual perception. As visual-tactile integration proceeds, writing implements can be held in the fingers rather than in the fist, and drawing takes on new precision. The maturation of visual perception, and its combination with motor planning, are seen in the child's ability to copy horizontal lines now rather than rely on imitation.

The motor control and visual-perceptual skills needed to construct a tower of 8 to 10 cubes should be present, and cubes may also be used to make other structures. Other fine motor refinements permit the acquisition of many fine motor self-help skills. However, performance of fine motor tasks is beginning to speed up, and thus accuracy may suffer to some degree. Visual-tactile integration is becoming more sophisticated at this point, and toward the close of the second year a child will be able to feel a familiar object and identify its picture without seeing the actual object. The continued cultivation of tactile perception is thought to be necessary as a foundation for more precise fine motor skill; unless the child has a good "feel" for objects used by the hand (pencils, scissors, etc.), manipulating them for skilled use may be less than adequate (Ayres, 1972).

All skills developed in the second year of life seem to require new and creative ideas of how to move, how to challenge oneself, and how to put together sequences of actions. These are all components of the process of motor planning. As much as motor planning is a reflection of the processes of sensory intake, processing, integration, and motor output, the production of such complex acts during the second year is a good indication of an intact nervous system.

36 to 48 Months

During the third year of life, children are working hard to refine their motor skills as they strive for independence. Ayres considered the period from 3 to 7 years of age as crucial for sensory integration. It is a period of receptiveness to input and one of maturation for the nervous system (Ayres, 1979). At times the observer will recognize frustration during this year because the desire to be independent is not matched by the motor and perceptual skills that would permit it. Gross motor skills are becoming more coordinated and more complex patterns of movement (e.g., reciprocal arm movements and longer strides during walking and running) are seen, so that the pattern more closely resembles that of an adult. The 2- to 3-year-old who seemed afraid of movement will likely begin to challenge himself again with swinging and climbing activities, as children are again driven to explore playgrounds and other play spaces. More trunk rotation is notable at this age in many activities, including kicking a ball and rising from the floor to standing using a half-kneel position. This is a good age to introduce the tricycle if it has not been done before. The 3-year-old can learn to pedal the tricycle and steer it to avoid running into things.

Within the fine motor domain, the 3-year-old is beginning to master reciprocal movements of the fingers, and usually to develop preference for handedness. Bilateral hand use is apparent both in scissor use and in activities such as stringing beads. The maturation of fine motor skills facilitates the development of daily living skills, which evolve along with the strong drive to "do it myself." Observers should bear in mind the effort taken in each of these tasks, irrespective of speed and accuracy, and the pride taken in "I did it myself" before they rush to aid or offer to fix the "error."

The visual system is becoming increasingly important as a tool for obtaining information from the environment and in the development of the above-mentioned fine motor skills. Visual-tactile perception refines and the child is able to identify three-dimensional shapes with his hand and find a match visually. Cuddling and close contact are still sought as a form of tactile comfort, even by the fiercely independent 3-year-old.

Ayres (1979) considered the third year to be the beginning of a period when sensory and motor skills were forming a foundation for higher intellectual functioning. The drive to challenge the vestibular and proprioceptive systems as well as the increasing complexity of movement activities and environmental exploration are further examples of the integration of sensory input with the creation and execution of complex motor activities.

48 to 60 Months

Improvements in all motor skills take place during this last preschool year. It is amazing to watch the 3-year-old struggle with climbing on a jungle gym, looking longingly at the older children who are able to maneuver themselves through and around the bars, transform into the 4-year-old with daring and skill. Development in balance, trunk rotational skills, and bilateral and reciprocal use of the arms and legs gives this child the ability to perform great motor feats. Later in the third and into the fourth years, children are often seen to be challenging their motor skills by attempting to discover new ways to accomplish the same old task. Thus, once a child has mastered a slide on his bottom he will then try to figure out how to go down the slide on his tummy, back, soles of the feet, or upside down. Children in this age range are seemingly unable to merely walk down the street. Instead they must walk sideways or backwards, balancing on the curb, or avoiding the sidewalk cracks. This drive to change the activity to challenge the developing motor skills is an excellent example of the development of motor planning skills in these preschoolers.

Fine motor skills become refined during this year. The 4-year-old's able fingers are also now readily engaged in more complicated songs with finger plays, and counting on the fingers becomes easier because the fingers are less awkward in independent movement.

Visual perceptual skills developed during this year will allow the child to connect vertical and horizontal lines to form squares and rectangles. These shapes were recognized before this time, but the ability to reproduce them is just now developing in most children. This advancement is needed to prepare the child for writing letters and numbers once he enters school. The drawing of diagonal lines may be learned at the age of 4, but is more likely to be seen in a 5-year-old child. Reproduction of block designs is now at the stage of the "gate" in which the child is asked to correctly perceive and position both blocks and spaces. The transfer of visual-tactile information has progressed to the point that children in this age range are beginning to be able to feel an object and point to the object's *picture*, rather than needing the three-dimensional object to be present.

Assessment

The most frequently used frame of reference in assessing sensory-motor skills is developmental, especially with children ages birth to 5 years. Sensory integration, motor control, and motor learning are other valid frames of reference to consider as this domain of development is approached. However, any assessment of these skills must be carried out within an overall systems approach to assist with the assessment of not just the child but also the environment. Assessing skills within an appropriate environment may be difficult to arrange, but the astute practitioner will quickly realize that it may not be relevant to the child or the family if the child cannot stack 8-inch cubes during the confines of an assessment. Failure to view the specific skills and deficits noted during a sensory-motor assessment from a systems perspective may make the results of such an assessment meaningless to the child and the family. A detailed discussion

of family-centered assessment and a systems approach to assessment is beyond the scope of this chapter and has been addressed in Chapter 11. In choosing and presenting the results of an assessment, the practitioner must integrate his findings into the real life of the child and family. By working to understand the system as well as the specifics of performance demonstrated by the child, the practitioner can ensure that the assessment results and recommendations meet the needs of the child and his family.

Several assessment tools will be briefly covered below. Not all of the assessments available for assessing sensory-motor function in the birth to 5-year-old population can be addressed, and so the reader should view those presented below as a sampling. Sensory-motor assessment is often a component of other assessment tools that examine general development, and the reader is referred to other chapters in this text for more information on general assessments.

The information to follow is not organized by age because many tools span several age ranges. Instead it is organized by assessment content. Tools that emphasize sensory processing are presented first; these may be the least familiar to the reader. The second section focuses on tools that primarily address motor skills. Finally, general developmental tools that include sensory-motor domains are addressed. A table follows each section which offers the reader a synopsis of each tool.

Assessment of Sensory Processing

In the period of time immediately following birth, several areas of development can be assessed, including sensory processing, muscle stiffness or tone, the presence of early reflexes, and state organization. Sensory processing in infancy is generally measured by looking at the infants' response to controlled sensory stimuli. Components of more general assessment tools often include such items. Beyond the newborn age, tools become somewhat more available, and the sophistication in assessing these areas continues to increase. However, especially for the very young child, this assessment domain is not rich with options.

One tool which attempts to assess sensory processing is the *Test of Sensory Function in Infants* (TSFI) (DeGangi & Greenspan, 1989). This assessment is currently used primarily by occupational therapists in an attempt to identify infants and young children experiencing over-sensitivity to touch or movement or difficulties with visual-tactile integration. According to DeGangi and Greenspan, while norms have been gathered on a small sample, it is best thought of as a criterion-referenced tool. It is useful with infants between 4 and 18 months of age. The variability in responses in the 4- to 6-month-old child makes the application to this population tenuous. The TSFI protocol can be learned by reading the manual, but it is recommended that further training and inter-rater reliability be established before it is used for clinical decision making (Benson & Lane, 1993). Administration time is approximately 15 to 20 minutes.

A more recent development is the *Infant/Toddler Symptom Checklist* (ITSC) (DeGangi, Poisson, Sickel, & Wiener, 1995), a screening tool designed to identify children potentially at-risk for the development of sensory integrative disorders, attentional deficits, emotional or behavioral problems. Items on this checklist tap into responses to sensory stimulation, as well as self-regulation, attention, modulation of arousal, attachment, and emotional functioning. There are five versions that apply to specific age ranges, encompassing the ages between 7 and 30 months. Like the TSFI, this tool is criterion-based rather than norm referenced, and it is recommended to be administered along with the TSFI. It is intended to be completed by a caregiver and should require only about 10 minutes. Interpretation should be done by a professional with knowledge of self-regulation, sensory integration, attention, and emotional regulation.

Visual perception is perhaps the most studied area of perception, yet few tools directly assess visual perceptual skills in young children. One tool which does attempt to measure these skills during early preschool is the *Test of Visual-Motor Integration* (VMI) (Beery & Buktenica, 1967; Beery, 1997). As shown in Table 17–1, this assessment is appropriate for children beginning at age 3 years. The VMI is designed as an early identification tool to assess difficulties with the integration of visual perception and motor skill. It can be administered in 10 to 15 minutes, either individually or in groups. The VMI is norm-referenced for children ages 3 to 17 years, 11 months, and has both a 27-item full assessment and an 18-item short version (for children ages 3 to 7). There are no specific training requirements for use of this tool; however, for interpretation of results, it is recommended that a professional with a background in education, psychology, learning disabilities, or a related profession be consulted.

Because the VMI is an assessment of visual-motor skills, the results of this assessment offer information about the processing of visual input to direct a motor response. Without further assessment, it is not possible to determine if identified problems are tied most closely to a visual processing deficit or to the motor aspect of test performance. Supplemental tests accompanying the fourth edition offer insight into visual perception and motor skill separately. Beery (1997) reports that when used in conjunction with other measures, the VMI can be valuable in predicting early academic achievement. For children 4 years of age, some assessment tools are available that address visual processing in the absence of motor skill, but these are not appropriate for the child in the birth to 3-year age range. Some evidence suggests that low VMI scores predict kindergarten-level reading difficulties (Klein, 1978); thus, it may be a useful tool in the early identification of some academic deficits.

Two additional standardized tools for assessment of visual perception are the *Test of Visual-*

Perceptual Skills-Revised (TVPS-R) (Gardner, 1996) and the *Motor-Free Visual-Perception Test-Revised* (MVPTR) (Colarusso & Hammill, 1996). Both tools are relatively simple to administer and interpret and provide more specific information about the processing of visual input. The TVPS-R divides visual processing into seven subcategories: figure-ground perception, spatial relations, visual sequential memory, visual memory, visual discrimination, form constancy, and visual closure. It is standardized for children ages 4 years, 1 month, to 13 years. It is designed to be language free, both in administration and in response, and thus can be used with children with language impairments. Although the time required for administration varies according to age, Gardner gives a range of 9 to 25 minutes. It should be noted that although the TVPS-R may assist in the identification of visual perceptual difficulties, it has not been shown to have good diagnostic or predictive validity.

The MVPT-R measures performance in five areas: spatial relations, visual closure, visual memory, figure-ground, and visual discrimination. These subdivisions may be helpful in identifying specific strengths and weaknesses in visual perceptual performance areas, although it is not entirely clear whether such division of the domain of visual perception is justified. The MVPT-R has been demonstrated to identify deficits in children with mental retardation and cerebral palsy; however, it may not correctly identify children with more subtle problems.

The most recently published tool that addresses sensory processing is the *Sensory Profile* (SP) (Dunn, 1999), which provides a standardized means of measuring the sensory processing abilities of children and offers practitioners a way to examine the impact of sensory processing dysfunction on the performance of daily activities. It is the outgrowth of, and a great improvement over, the older Sensory History forms. Although designed primarily for children ages 5 to 10 years, scoring adaptations have been included that make it useful for 3- and 4-year-old children.

The SP is a parent-oriented questionnaire which queries the parents as to their child's responses to sensory input in the auditory, visual, vestibular, and touch domains. It also includes a section addressing multisensory processing. Other sections ask the parents to rate their child's oral sensory processing, as well as sensory processing as it relates to endurance and muscle tone. The SP has three main sections: sensory processing, modulation, and behavioral and emotional responses. In addition to the full SP, a short version (the Short Sensory Profile) has been developed and is described in the manual.

The SP can be scored by system, and cut scores indicate if performance is typical or there is a "probable" or "definite" difference from typical children. In addition, the SP results can be interpreted based on factor scores. It is recommended that once the practitioner identifies the strengths and weaknesses in sensory processing experienced by the child, he should discuss these findings with the parents and be prepared to describe them in functional terms. For example, saying that a child is showing signs of tactile defensiveness is not very meaningful to most parents, but saying that the child appears to be very sensitive to touch is more helpful. This sensitivity may clarify for parents why the child resists activities such as hair combing, washing, and cutting. Telling parents that children who are very sensitive to touch prefer only certain types of soft clothing and get very angry when tickled puts the problem into useful terms and assists the parents in understanding both the problem and some of the behaviors the child exhibits.

Assessment of Motor Skills

Motor skill assessment is quite common, although many practitioners will incorporate it into a more global assessment of child strengths and needs. Many of the tools available will be familiar to the reader, but those that address

TABLE 17-1
Assessment Tools for Sensory Processing

Tool	Test of Sensory Function in Infants (DeGangi & Greenspan, 1989)	Infant/Toddler Symptom Checklist (DeGangi, Poisson, Sickel, & Wiener, 1995)	Developmental Test of Visual-Motor Integration (VMI) (Beery, 1997)	Test of Visual-Perceptual Skills—Revised (TVPS-R) (Gardner, 1996)	Motor-Free Visual Perception Test—Revised (MVPT-R) (Colarusso & Hammill, 1996)	Sensory Profile (SP) (Dunn, 1999)
Age range	4–18 mos	7–30 mos	3–17 yrs	4–13 yrs	4–11 yrs	5–10 yrs; special scoring available for ages 3–4 yrs
Testing time (minutes)	30	10	10–15	9–25	<10	30
Major sensory-motor areas tested						
Sensory processing—general	X	X				X
Tactile	X					X
Vestibular	X					X
Visual-motor integration	X		X			
Visual perception				X	X	
Reflexes						
Gross motor						
Fine motor						
Praxis	X					
Other areas tested		Self-regulation, arousal modulation, attachment, attention, emotional functioning				Modulation related to endurance, tone, body position and movement; modulation related to activity,

404

Category		Test 1	Test 2	Test 3	Test 4	Test 5	Test 6
Type of test							
	Norm-referenced	X	X	X	X		
	Criteria-referenced					X	X
	Informal/structured					X	X
	Observation	emotional responses; social-emotional responses, behavior, sensory threshold				Parent-completed questionnaire	
Scores obtained							
	Age level		Perceptual quotients; perceptual ages	Perceptual ages			
	Percentile			X	X		
	Standard			X	X		
	Other	Typical/probable difference/definite difference				Normal/deficient	Normal/at-risk/deficient
Psychometrics (as reported in the manual)							
	Reliability	Internal consistency	Test-retest Split-half	Internal consistency	Internal consistency Test-retest	None	
	Validity	Content, construct, convergent, discriminative	Content, construct	Content, construct, concurrent	Content, concurrent, construct, predictive	Construct, decision	

motor skills in the very young infant or newborn may be less so (see Table 17–1). It is only rarely that practitioners will likely be interested in solely a motor assessment, but there may be times when obtaining additional, more detailed information on motor skills is necessary. These tools may be useful at those times.

The Milani-Comparetti Motor Development Screening Scale (Milani-Comparetti & Gidoni, 1967; Kliewer, Bruce, & Trembath, 1977) looks primarily at reflex development, offering practitioners an insight into the integrity of the nervous system at an early age. This tool is designed to be used with children ages birth to 2 years. It examines both spontaneous and elicited reflex behaviors and can be administered within 10 minutes by an experienced examiner. It can be useful for examining this single domain of skill and for providing a vehicle for discussion with parents, because these reflexes are thought to be the foundation of what will develop in terms of motor skill later.

Another assessment tool focused on motor skills is the Movement Assessment of Infants (Chandler, Andrews, Swanson, & Larson, 1980). This assessment tool is most commonly used by occupational or physical therapists to assess muscle tone, reflex integration, and the development of automatic and volitional skills in the first year of life. It is a tool based on structured observation, with profiles of expected performance available for infants at both 4 and 8 months of age. The use of this tool may assist in the identification of motor abnormalities, rather than motor delays, within the first year.

The Toddler and Infant Motor Evaluation (TIME) is a comprehensive motor assessment tool that capitalizes on caregiver participation, examines motor skills in the context of functional activities, and reportedly is sensitive to incremental developmental gains (Miller & Roid, 1994). It is a standardized tool, designed for use with children ages 4 months to $3\frac{1}{2}$ years. Mobility, motor organization, and stability subtest sections are included, and social-emotional abilities are scored based on experiences during these three subtests. A function performance interview with the caregiver is included as an option. Additionally, three clinical subtests are included but are intended to be administered by advanced clinicians. Although specific administration directions are needed, flexibility is built into the TIME that will allow the examiner to obtain the best performance from the infant or young child. Although no specific examiner training is required, it is strongly recommended that examiners have a background in infant neuromotor development. A background in sensory integration is recommended as well.

The Peabody Developmental Motor Scales (2nd ed.) (PDMS-2) (Folio & Fewell, 2000) cover a broader age span than the tools previously discussed. Useful from birth through 72 months, the PDMS-2 is norm-referenced and includes activity cards which may be incorporated into an intervention program. Administration and interpretation of the PDMS-2 can be learned from the manual. It is divided into gross and fine motor sections, with subsections for each area that cover reflexes (for children up to age 11 months), stationary motor skills, locomotion, object manipulation, grasp, and visual-motor integration. The second edition of the PDMS includes expanded normative data, which are noted to be free of sexual and racial bias. A strength of this tool is that it has small age increments within the first 2 years of life and includes several skills at each age increment, thus providing the practitioner with a good overall picture of gross and fine motor development in the early years. Age-increment divisions enlarge after the first 2 years, which may dilute the ability to make specific statements about the child's strengths and weaknesses.

One final assessment tool in this area that examines both motor performance and aspects of visual perception is the Bruininks-Oseretsky Test of Motor Proficiency (BOTMP) (Bruininks, 1978), which is divided into gross and fine motor sections, each with its own subsections of function. It was intended to be used to assess children with mental retardation, learning disabilities, or developmental delays either as a diagnostic or screening tool. Standardized use of the test is for children ages $4\frac{1}{2}$ to $14\frac{1}{2}$ years. This broad range of ages may be viewed as both a strength and weakness of this assessment tool. The strength lies in the fact that it can readily be used to identify areas of growth and development, as well as areas that need intervention, over a long period of time. In fact, it is a commonly used assessment tool for school-aged children for this reason. However, any assessment tool that covers a 10-year age span is likely to be limited in the depth with which it can assess function, and the BOTMP falls prey to this weakness to some degree. The BOTMP total test score has been shown by Bruininks to have adequate reliability and decision validity. Administration and scoring can be learned from the manual, although it is recommended that examiner reliability be checked. Table 17–2 provides a summary of these tests of motor skills.

Assessments of General Development Including Sensory-Motor Domains

The *Neonatal Behavioral Assessment Scale* (NBAS) (Brazelton, 1984) was developed to distinguish individual differences between normal infants, especially with respect to social interactive behaviors. It has been adapted to be used with high-risk and premature infants and has been successfully applied to these populations. This tool contains 26 behavioral items, which cover the areas of interaction, motor skill, state control, and response to stress, and 20 reflex items. In examining performance on the items, one looks for "best" performance, not just the initial performance, and the response is graded as exceptional, average, or worrisome. No total score is obtained. Instead, examiners assess performance in the different areas and then identify strengths and weaknesses. A major focus of the NBAS is in teaching parents what to look for in the behaviors exhibited by the newborn. This tool was designed to be administered in the

presence of the parents to point out strengths, weaknesses, and general responses to the sensory input during the assessment process. In doing so, the NBAS has become a teaching tool to assist parents in understanding and working with their infants. A major shortcoming of this assessment tool is that it requires extensive examiner training, which is not available to all clinicians. Table 17–3 provides a listing of sensory-motor domains found in tests of overall development.

A second newborn assessment tool that covers similar areas is the *Neurological Assessment of Preterm and Full-Term Newborn Infants* (NAPFI) (Dubowitz & Dubowitz, 1981; Dubowitz, Dubowitz, & Mercuri, 1999). This criterion-referenced tool is suitable for use by many different professionals working with infants. It is appropriately applied to full-term or pre-term infants as they approach term age. The second edition of the NAPFI was designed to be quick (15 minutes) and easy to administer and to have a simple and objective scoring system. Unlike the NBAS, the NAPFI requires no specific training. It was designed to be reliable soon after birth, in order to assist in the identification of infants at-risk for later developmental delays. This tool is suitable for repeated examinations. Habituation to light and sound has been dropped from the second edition of this tool owing to the difficulty in administration. Additional changes made between first and second editions are delineated in the new manual.

Scores on the NAPFI are obtained for individual item responses in the areas of posture and tone, tone patterns, reflexes, movements, abnormal signs/patterns, and orientation and behavior. In addition, Dubowitz and colleagues designed a method of calculating an optimality score in each area, and a total optimality score for the assessment that may be used. The development of the latter methodology is new, and the use of the optimality score is under investigation. However, it offers the practitioner the advantage of obtaining a total performance score that can be compared with a typical population,

TABLE 17–2
Assessment Tools for Motor Skills

Tool	Milani-Comparetti Motor Development Screening Scale (Milani-Comparetti & Gidoni, 1967; Kliewer, Bruce, & Trembath, 1977)	Movement Assessment of Infants (Chandler, Andrews, Swanson, & Larson, 1980)	Toddler and Infant Motor Evaluation (TIME) (Miller & Roid, 1994)	Peabody Developmental Motor Scales (2nd ed.) (PDMS) (Folio & Fewell, 2000)	Bruininks-Oseretsky Test of Motor Proficiency (Bruininks, 1978)
Age range	0–24 mos	4 and 8 mos	4 mos–3$\frac{1}{2}$ yrs	0–72 mos	4$\frac{1}{2}$–14$\frac{1}{2}$ yrs
Testing time (minutes)	10	30	Varies	45–60	45–60
Major sensory-motor areas tested					
Sensory processing—General					
Tactile					
Vestibular					
Visual-motor integration				X	X
Visual perception					
Reflexes	X	X			
Gross motor		X	X	X	X
Fine motor				X	X
Praxis					X
Other areas tested		Muscle tone, automatic reactions, volitional movements, asymmetries are noted	Motor organization, stability, social-emotional abilities, functional performance (caregiver interview; additional subtests for advanced clinical assessment)		

Type of test				
Norm-referenced		X	X	X
Criteria-referenced	X			
Informal/structured	X			
Observation				
Scored as				
Age level			X	X
Percentile		X	X	X
Standard		X	X	X
Other	Reflexes	Risk score		
Psychometrics (as reported in manual)				
Reliability	None	Internal consistency Test-retest Decision consistency: Inter-rater	Test-retest Inter-rater	Test-retest Inter-rater (visual motor subtest)
Validity	None	Content, construct, factor analysis; criterion-related; discriminant; classification accuracy	Content, construct, original version	Content, construct, internal consistency, factor analysis

409

TABLE 17–3
Assessment Tools for Sensory and Motor Domains Within Tests of Overall Development

Tool	Neonatal Behavioral Assessment Scale (NBAS) (Brazelton, 1984)	Neurological Assessment of Preterm and Full-term Newborn Infants (NAPFI) (Dubowitz & Dubowitz, 1981)	Bayley Scales of Infant Development II (BSID-II) (Black, Matula, & Black, 1999)	Bayley Infant Neuro-developmental Screener (BINS) (Aylward, 1995)	Mullen Scales of Early Learning (Mullen, 1995)	Ages and Stages Questionnaires (Squires, Potter, & Bricker, 1999)	Developmental Indicators for the Assessment of Learning (DIAL-3) (Mardell-Czudnowski, & Goldenberg, 1998)	Miller Assessment for Preschoolers (MAP) (Miller, 1982)	FirsTEP (Miller, 1993)	Carolina Curriculum for Handicapped Infants and Infants At Risk (Johnson-Martin, Jens, Attermeier, & Hacker, 1991)
Age range	0–3 days from birth for full-term; up to 40 weeks gestational age for preterm	0–3 days from birth for full-term; up to 40 weeks gestational age for preterm		3–24 mos	Birth–68 mos	4–24 mos	3–6 yrs	2 yrs, 9 mos–6 yrs, 2 mos	2 yrs, 9 mos–6 yrs, 2 mos	12–36 mos
Testing time (minutes)	20–30	15	Varies	10	15–60, depending on age	Varies	30	45	15	Varies
Major sensory motor areas tested										
Sensory processing—general										
Tactile				X						
Vestibular										
Visual-motor integration								X	X	
Visual perception					X					
Reflexes	X	X								
Gross motor	X	X	X	X	X	X	X	X	X	X
Fine motor				X	X	X	X	X	X	X
Praxis								X	X	X

Other areas tested	Cognition communication/language, social skills adaptation, self-help	Cognition, communication; social-emotional scale; adaptive behavior checklist	Cognition (nonverbal), communication, complex tasks	Concepts, language, psychosocial skills	Personal-social, communication, problem solving	Receptive and expressive language	Muscle tone, quality of movement, basic neurologic functions, cognition	Posture and tone, abnormal signs/movements; orientation and behavior; state control	Interaction, state control and response to stress
Type of test									
Norm-referenced		X	X	X	X	X	X	X	
Criteria-referenced	X							X	
Informal/structured					Parent questionnaire			X	
Observation									X
Scored as									
Age level	X					X			
Percentile				X		X		X	
Standard				X		X		X	
Other	Results are used descriptively and tracked over time to note changes	Domain, composite; scaled scores: typical, possible need for further assessment, definite need for further assessment		Potential delay; OK	Typical; at-risk	Descriptive categories, developmental stages	High/moderate/low risk	Item performance report; optimality score	Identification of strengths and weaknesses in each area
Psychometrics (as reported in the manual)									
Reliability	None	Internal consistency Test-retest Inter-rater	Internal consistency Test-retest	Internal consistency Test-retest	Internal consistency Test-retest Inter-rater	Internal consistency Test-retest Inter-rater	Internal consistency Test-retest Inter-rater	None	Test-retest
Validity	None	content, construct, factor analysis, criterion, concurrent	Concurrent	Concurrent	Construct, concurrent	Construct, concurrent	Construct, convergent (with BSID II and Denver II), concurrent with clinical sample	None	None

an option that was not available in the first edition of this tool.

The examiner also has the option of rating behavioral state on each item as it is administered, and this rating can shed light on state modulation skills present in the infant. This tool can be administered, with practice, in about 15 minutes and thus may be an ideal tool for use in a busy clinic. No psychometric information is available on this tool, a sigificant shortcoming to an otherwise potentially useful tool.

It is important to understand that no assessment tool used in the newborn period is predictive of later outcomes. Instead such tools provide a glimpse of performance today, and some (the NBAS and the NAPFI, for instance) can be used to measure change over a short period of time. In addition, the findings of such assessments may provide guidance to parents in interaction with and handling of an infant in the early months of life.

The *Bayley Scales of Infant Development-II* (BSID-II) (Bayley, 1969, 1993; Black, Matula, & Black, 1999) also provide standardized assessment of motor development. A screening tool that draws from the BSID-II, the *Bayley Infant Neurodevelopmental Screener* (BINS) (Aylward, 1995) is designed to identify infants ages 3 to 24 months in need of additional assessment, and makes an excellent precursor to a recommendation for assessment using the BSID-II. An advantage of the BINS is its emphasis on the quality of skill performance and de-emphasis on whether the skill is actually present or absent. The BSID-II examines motor development as a whole, without separating fine and gross motor development when standard scoring is used. The BINS assesses basic neurological functions/intactness, focusing on muscle tone and quality of movement; receptive functions, which address visual, auditory, and tactile processing; expressive functions, which include fine and gross motor skills; and cognitive functions.

The *Mullen Scales of Early Learning* (Mullen, 1995) take a slightly different approach to general development, using an information processing model. According to Mullen, "The *Mullen Scales of Early Learning* represent the view that early cognitive development is best measured by a group of cognitive abilities that are distinct and well-defined in content, requiring different performances from infants and preschool children" (p. 9). Thus, this tool assesses gross motor skills as a basis on which other learning is developed; fine motor skills are linked to visual organization; and there is a visual "reception" scale that emphasizes visual decoding and downplays the need for a motor response. Receptive and expressive language is also assessed, which is applicable to children ages birth to 68 months. This tool can be used by any professional with training and practice in working with infants and young children. For the purposes of sensory-motor assessment, scores can be obtained for fine motor and visual reception. Because of the focus on process in this assessment, it adds a dimension to assessment in this age bracket that other similar tools do not offer.

One additional screening tool is worth mentioning here, the *Ages & Stages Questionnaires: A Parent-Completed Child Monitoring System* (2nd ed.) (Squires, Potter, & Bricker, 1999). This tool was developed as a monitoring system in which assessment could occur at regular intervals and accurately identify children at-risk or in need of further assessment. This tool includes parent-completed questionnaires that pertain to the major domains of development (communication, gross and fine motor, problem-solving, and personal-social skills) and can be completed at 2-month intervals between 4 and 24 months, at 3-month intervals from 27 to 36 months, and at 6-month intervals from 42 to 60 months. This instrument can be adapted for use in many different environments and thus can be used in the home or within programs. Scores are obtained for each domain, making it useful for the monitoring of sensory-motor development. As one would expect from a screening tool, there are minimal items for each domain at each age level and thus only a general sense of strengths and needs can be obtained.

The *Developmental Indicators for the Assessment of Learning* (3rd Ed.) (DIAL-3) (Mardell-Czudnowski & Goldenberg, 1998) offers a highly comprehensive standardized screening tool that includes a section on motor development. Embedded within the motor section are both fine and gross motor skills. The entire screening can be administered in 30 minutes, and it is appropriate for use with a 3- to 6-year-old population. In addition to examiner-administered items, the DIAL-3 includes a parent questionnaire and a rating scale for psychosocial behaviors that is completed by examiners during the screening. According to Mardell-Czudnowski and Goldenberg, this tool assesses skills that are directly related to classroom functioning.

The *Miller Assessment for Preschoolers* (MAP) (Miller, 1982) offers a unique perspective on preschool development by assessing sensory motor foundation skills, such as tactile and visual processing, as they relate to higher level domains of function such as motor planning and cognition. This standardized tool is applicable for children ages 2 years, 9 months through 5 years, 8 months, and was developed to identify children at-risk for the development of school-related problems. Although strictly speaking this tool was designed as a screening tool, it provides a great deal more information about skills than do most screening tests. The MAP assesses skills within five domains of functioning: neuromotor foundations, motor coordination, verbal, nonverbal, and complex tasks. Functionally, this screening test addresses areas of visual and tactual perception, balance and equilibrium, motor planning, and expressive and receptive language. Scoring of the MAP is based on percentile cut-off scores which place a child in a normal, questionable, or at-risk category. The MAP has been shown to have predictive validity for the identification of preschool children at-risk for academic difficulties, which makes it particularly useful. It is available to therapists, educators, and psychologists and can be learned by attendance at a training course.

Miller developed the FirstSTE*p* as a standardized screening tool that could be used as a companion to the MAP (Miller, 1993). This instrument is intended for individual administration to children ages 2 years, 9 months to 6 years, 2 months, and it provides a screening within cognition, communication, and motor domains. Individual domain scores can be obtained for each area. Within the motor domain, visual-motor integration, fine and gross motor planning, and balance items are included. In addition, caregiver questionnaires are included to address social-emotional and adaptive functioning, and an optional Parent/Teacher Scale can provide information on functioning in the home or school environment that may not be obtainable through the individual screening. The FirstSTEp was designed for use by individuals in a wide range of fields who are familiar with child development. Both the MAP and the FirstSTEp have been subjected to rigorous psychometric testing and show strong reliability and validity.

Criterion-based and curriculum-referenced assessment of sensory-motor development can also be found in general scales such the *Carolina Curriculum for Handicapped Infants and Infants At Risk* (Johnson-Martin, Jens, Attermeier, & Hacker, 1991), also discussed in Chapter 10. This tool offers assessment of fine and gross motor skill development, and is quick and easy to learn and administer. One shortcoming of such a tool is the small number of items for the younger age levels. This limits the practitioner's ability to identify areas of strength and weakness. However, a notable strength is that many of these tools are appropriate for repeated administration, making them very useful in updating knowledge of skills and setting goals. This can be very beneficial in planning and implementing programs for children with delays. As with most general developmental assessments, the tools listed above lend themselves well to multi- or interdisciplinary use which is so very important with children of this age.

Summary

During infancy and toddlerhood, sensory processing and motor output are the best windows available to view the integrity of the developing nervous system. Because sensory and motor development are inextricably linked, the assessment of sensory processing is often embedded in that of motor skill, but all too often the practitioner focuses only on the motor output and does not address the sensory input component of the process. As the child develops more cognitive skills that can be directly measured, assessment of sensory-motor skills is but one aspect of an overall assessment. Although sensory-motor skill may no longer correlate highly with cognitive performance, it is still an important aspect of development because environmental interaction is determined by these skills. Environmental interaction is very visible, and inadequate ability to interact with the environment may make a child look very much as though he has a disability. For instance, a 5-year-old child who cannot determine how to get on a swing, or who still has an overhand, fisted grasp of the crayon, is being impaired by his sensory-motor difficulties. This child may not have cognitive deficits, yet assessment and intervention would likely be very appropriate. Thus, assessment of strengths and weaknesses within the sensory-motor domain is an essential component of any evaluation. Clinically, it is often difficult to determine if the expression of a motor deficit is due to inadequate sensory processing or poor motor response accomplishment. The differentiation requires skill and experience as well as a thorough understanding of normal development in these areas. As knowledge in this area has grown, more tools that assist practitioners in distinguishing between sensory processing and motor output are available. The practitioner is encouraged to use these tools to best meet the needs of children and their families.

References

Alexander, R., Boehme, R., & Cupps, B. (1993). *Normal development of functional motor skills: The first year of life.* Tucson: Therapy Skill Builders.

Aylward, G. P. (1995). *Bayley Infant Neurodevelopmental Screener.* San Antonio: The Psychological Corporation.

Ayres, A. J. (1972). *Sensory integration and learning disorders.* Los Angeles: Western Psychological.

Ayres, A. J. (1979). *Sensory integration and the child.* Los Angeles: Western Psychological.

Bayley, N. (1969). *Bayley Scales of Infant Development.* San Antonio: The Psychological Corporation.

Bayley, N. (1993). *Bayley Scales of Infant Development-II* (2nd ed.). San Antonio: The Psychological Corporation.

Beery, K. E. (1997). *Beery-Buktenica Developmental Test of Visual-Motor Integration* (4th ed.). Parsippany, NJ: Modern Curriculum Press.

Beery, K. E., & Buktenica, N. A. (1967). *Beery-Buktenica Developmental Test of Visual-Motor Integration.* Cleveland: Modern Curriculum Press.

Benson, A., & Lane, S. J. (1993). The developmental effects of low level lead exposure. *Infants and Young Children,* 6(2), 41–51.

Black, M. M., Matula, K., & Black, M. M. (1999). *Essentials of Bayley Scales of Infant Development-II assessment.* New York: Wiley.

Brazelton, T. B. (1984). *The Neonatal Behavioral Assessment Scale.* Philadelphia: Lippincott.

Bruininks, R. H. (1978). *The Bruininks-Oseretsky Test of Motor Proficiency.* Circle Pines, MN: American Guidance Service.

Cech, D., & Martin, S. (1995). *Functional movement development across the life span.* Philadelphia: Saunders.

Chandler, L. S., Andrews, M. S., Swanson, M. W., & Larson, A. H. (1980). *Movement Assessment of Infants.* Rolling Bay, WA: Author.

Colarusso, R. P., & Hammill, D. D. (1972). *Motor-Free Visual-Perception Test (MVPT).* Novato, CA: Academic Therapy Publications.

Colarusso, R. P., & Hammill, D. D. (1996). *Motor-Free Visual Perception Test-Revised (MVPT-R).* Novato, CA: Academic Therapy Publications.

DeGangi, G. A., & Greenspan, S. I. (1989). *Test of Sensory Function in Infants.* Los Angeles: Western Psychological.

DeGangi, G. A., Poisson, S., Sickel, R. Z., & Wiener, A. S. (1995). *Infant/Toddler Symptom Checklist.* Tucson: Therapy Skill Builders.

Dubowitz, L., & Dubowitz, V. (1981). *The Neurological Assessment of Preterm and Full-Term Newborn Infants.* London: Cambridge University Press.

Dubowitz, L., Dubowitz, V., & Mercuri, E. (1999). *The Neurological Assessment of Preterm and Full-Term Newborn Infants* (2nd ed.). London: Cambridge University Press.

Dunn, W. (1999). *Sensory Profile.* San Antonio: The Psychological Corporation.

Folio, M. R., & Fewell, R. R. (2000). *Peabody Developmental Motor Scales* (2nd ed.). Allen, TX: Developmental Learning Materials Teaching Resources.

Gardner, M. F. (1996). *Test of Visual-Perceptual Skills (Non-Motor)-Revised.* Hydesville, CA: Psychological and Educational Publications.

Johnson-Martin, N., Jens, K. G., Attermeier, S. M., & Hacker, B. J. (1991). *The Carolina Curriculum for Handicapped Infants and Infants At Risk.* Baltimore: Brookes.

Klein, A. (1978). The validity of the Beery Test of Visual-Motor Integration in predicting achievement in kindergarten, first and second grades. *Educational and Psychological Measurement 38,* 457.

Kliewer, D., Bruce, W., & Trembath, J. (1977). *The Milani-Comparetti Motor Development Screening Test: Administration Manual.* Omaha: Meyer Children's Rehabilitation Institute.

Lane, S. J., Miller, L. J., & Hanft, B. E. (2000). Towards a consensus in terminology in sensory integration theory and practice (Pt 2): Sensory integration patterns of function and dysfunction. *Sensory Integration Special Interest Section Quarterly,* 23(2), 1–3.

Mardell-Czudnowski, C., & Goldenberg, D. S. (1998). *Developmental Indicators for the Assessment of Learning* (3rd ed.). Circle Pines, MN: American Guidance Services.

Milani-Comparetti, A., & Gidoni, E. (1967). A routine developmental examination in normal and retarded children. *Developmental Medicine and Child Neurology,* 9, 766.

Miller, L. J. (1982). *The Miller Assessment for Preschoolers.* Englewood, CO: KID Foundation.

Miller, L. J. (1993). *FirstSTEp Screening Test for Evaluating Preschoolers.* San Antonio: The Psychological Corporation.

Miller, L. J., & Roid, G. H. (1994). *The T.I.M.E.: Toddler and Infant Motor Evaluation.* Tucson: Therapy Skill Builders.

Movshon, J. A., & Blakemore, C. (2000). Sensory systems: Introduction. In M. S. Gazzaniga (Ed.), *The new cognitive neurosciences* (2nd ed., p. 251). Cambridge, MA: MIT Press.

Mullen, E. M. (1995). *Mullen Scales of Early Learning.* Circle Pines, MN: American Guidance Services.

Parham, D. L., & Mailloux, Z. (1996). Sensory integration. In J. Case-Smith, A. S. Allen, & P. N. Pratt (Eds.), *Occupational therapy for children* (3rd ed., pp. 307–355). St Louis: Mosby.

Payne, V. G., & Isaacs, L. D. (1991). *Human motor development: A lifespan approach.* London: Mayfield.

Schuster, C. S., & Ashburn, S. S. (1992). *The process of human development: A holistic life-span approach.* Philadelphia: Lippincott.

Short-DeGraff, M. A. (1988). *Human development for occupational and physical therapists.* Baltimore: Williams & Wilkins.

Squires, J., Potter, L., & Bricker, D. (1999). *The Ages & Stages Questionnaires: A parent-completed child monitoring system* (2nd ed.). Baltimore: Brookes.

18

Assessing Adaptive Behavior

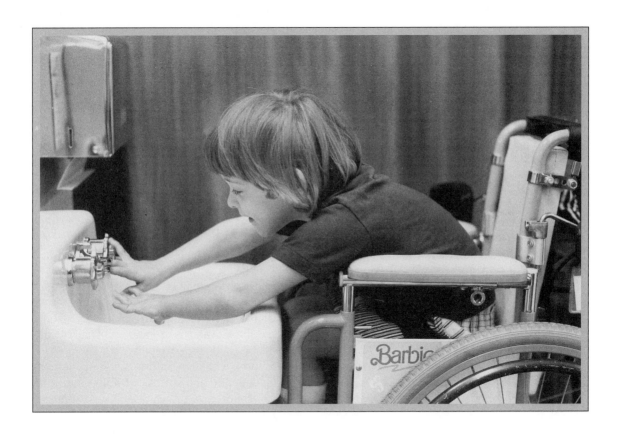

Adaptive behavior involves a child's ability to function independently to a developmentally appropriate degree, to effectively meet the social and natural demands of the environment wherein they interact, and to adjust and function within the cultural constraints of society (American Association on Mental Retardation, 1992; Sattler, 1992). Adaptive behavior may be defined physically, socially, and emotionally. Physical adaptive behaviors involve basic functions such as eating, keeping warm, and avoiding danger. Self-care skills are an important component of adaptive behavior. The major self-care skill areas are dressing/undressing, eating/feeding, toileting, and grooming. Social adaptive behaviors include communicating basic needs, cooperative play skills, and appropriate use of toys. Emotionally, adaptive behaviors include the formation of relationships that promote self-esteem and identity (Benner, 1992).

Cultural norms and age-related expectations influence this dynamic construct of adaptive behavior (Horn & Fuchs, 1987). The construct emphasizes the capacity to respond to demands in the immediate environment and the community. Adaptive behaviors at one developmental level are qualitatively different from those at another level. Adaptive behavior for a young child is acquiring skills such as walking, talking, and basic self-care. A school-age child must understand social rules in various settings. An adult must be able to hold a job, maintain a residence, and so on (Horn, 1996).

The concept of adaptive behavior has held a critical role in the assessment of persons with disabilities for many years (Harrison, 1987). The assessment of adaptive behavior is generally required before an individual may be classified as having mental retardation and, increasingly, before other disabilities are diagnosed (Frankenberger, 1984). In the IDEA Amendments of 1997 (PL 105-17), adaptive development is considered as a separate area from social and emotional development for determining eligibility for services. The inclusion of adaptive behavior as a criterion for defining developmental disability requires the assessment to include measures that give a clearer view of an individual's capabilities by assessing functioning under realistic situational demands. This approach is more practical and the focus for education becomes the acquisition of skills that will ensure functioning across appropriate environments and the provision of support or adaptations to ensure success (Luckasson, et al., 1992). A broad definition should be applied for adaptive behavior as a curriculum domain and should include skills for meeting the demands of the child's multiple unique environments (Horn, 1996; Horn & Childre, 1996).

Several rationales exist for assessing and teaching adaptive behavior in early childhood (Horn & Childre, 1996; Wolery & Smith, 1989). The reasons include:

- Independent participation in normal environments is an anticipated outcome of early intervention (Bailey & Wolery, 1992; Peterson, 1987; Wolery & Smith, 1989). A child with self-help skills has less caregiving demands, whereas a child with disabilities may have more intense needs. Caregiving demands are greater on parents of children with disabilities (Dyson & Fewell, 1986) and the duration is usually greater when a child has a disability.
- Children who can perform self-help skills independently appear less disabled and more like children without disabilities. Many of the behaviors defined as adaptive include personal/social behaviors, which are important for a child to be socially acceptable and thus more included in community settings.
- Some characteristics of adaptive behaviors provide logical support for their place in early childhood curricula. Many adaptive behaviors are acquired in early childhood. Mastery of these skills is part of daily routines, and the development of these skills takes a long time and reflects a hierarchical sequence of simple to complex.

- Many adaptive behaviors are visible skills (dressing, toileting, etc.), and their acquisition is obvious. Attainment of these adaptive behaviors may have an immediate concrete impact, safety issues, or economic benefits. For example, toileting eliminates the need for expensive infant diapers.
- Finally, self-care skills frequently are obvious examples of accomplishments. Becoming independent impacts the child's sense of competence and self-concept. Self-help skills such as learning to self-feed with a spoon, using the toilet, and putting on a coat will likely be noticed by others and be viewed as major accomplishments. Thus, a reason for assessing and teaching these skills is that children and caregivers will recognize the child's success; recognition of success may increase positive interactions.

The skills considered as adaptive behaviors are important for children to learn. The specific characteristics of these skills require consideration in the assessment of current functioning and future needs (Luckasson, et al., 1992). Skill levels should be determined in the context of natural environments which are typical of the child's age group. The assessment also must consider and make necessary adaptations for diversity in language or culture and for limitations or challenges. In addition, for the young child strengths and limitations may coexist, even within a single area. Finally, gains in the quality of life and independence in functioning generally occur for persons with disabilities when they are provided with appropriate supports over time (Horn & Childre, 1996).

Definition of Adaptive Behavior in Early Childhood

Adaptive behavior must be considered as a composite of a wide range of abilities that are dependent on one's age, environment, and cultural group at any moment (Luckasson, et al., 1992). The Task Force on Recommended Practices of the Division for Early Childhood (DEC) of the Council for Exceptional Children provided the following definition of adaptive behavior for early childhood (DEC Task Force on Recommended Practices, 1993):

> Adaptive behavior consists of changes in children's behavior as a consequence of maturation, development and learning to meet increasing demands of multiple environments. Independent functioning in these environments is the long-term goal. Instruction requires accommodating and adapting to support the specific strengths of individual children. Comprehensive intervention should address the following domains: self-care, community self-sufficiency, personal-social responsibility, and social adjustment. (p. 89)

The self-care subdomain addresses the sets of skills needed for independent functioning with regard to basic needs such as food and warmth. Specific skills include dressing/undressing, eating/feeding, toileting, and grooming (e.g., handwashing, facewashing, toothbrushing). The subdomain of community self-sufficiency refers to skills that promote age and culturally appropriate functioning with adult supervision in community environments, such as restaurants, grocery stores, and recreational areas. The personal-social subdomain includes basic environmental interactions play/self-occupation, peer cooperation and interaction, and the assumption of responsibility, such as demonstrating caution and avoiding danger. The final subdomain of social adjustment includes such behaviors as the ability to adjust to new situations, regularity of behavior patterns (e.g., eating, sleeping), general disposition, ability to stay on task, attention span and degree of distractibility, and amount of stimulation necessary to evoke a response (Horn & Childre, 1996). The wide range of abilities included in the adaptive domain requires a multidisciplinary approach to provide comprehensive assessment.

Interdisciplinary Involvement

Assessment of adaptive behavior includes many domains of a child's development. The child's functioning with adaptive and self-care skills greatly depends on the child's development in communication skills, gross and fine motor skills, and socialization skills. Critical skills of several of the subdomains are directly addressed in other developmental domains. Socialization skills in the adaptive scales refer to the broad domain of social functioning, which includes interpersonal relations, leisure time skills, and coping skills. For example, peer cooperation and interaction is a component of the social development domain. Therefore, a comprehensive assessment that looks at the whole child is essential.

Physical and occupational therapists need to participate in the assessment and intervention planning. Speech and language pathologists can assist in assessing the oral motor behaviors needed in eating as well as the necessary communication skills. Nutritionists can assess the child's diet. Of course, caregivers are essential in providing information related to choosing self-care objectives and teaching the appropriate self-care skills. In some cases, it may be appropriate to include medical personnel.

Considerations for Assessment

Generalization of Skills Across Settings

As with other developmental areas, it is necessary to assess adaptive behavior both formally and informally in a variety of settings. Using standardized procedures provides a direct assessment of a child's performance in a particular setting and at a particular time. Adaptive measures often rely on informants or third-party assessment by caregivers or teachers. Informal observation provides the opportunity for assessing behaviors in a variety of situations and allows the examiner to observe the child's

responses to the environment. It is important that a child is able to perform a particular skill appropriately in a variety of situations as the skill is needed. Assessors must use multiple methods and multiple informants to determine if the child has truly acquired the skill and is able to use the skill in a variety of settings.

Cultural Contexts

When assessing adaptive behavior, the assessment team must take into consideration whether the child can meet the demands of the current and future settings she encounters. The behaviors used to assess competence in adaptive behavior at a specific chronological age are identified from an analysis of the unique needs and lifestyle of the child and her family, peers, and community. This requires that the child must learn the cultural expectations for self-care and self-sufficiency necessary in group settings within and outside the home. Exactly what skills are learned is determined by the culture of the subsettings in which the family and the child participate on a regular basis. There is a significant variation in normal developmental sequences with heavy cultural influence. For example, the age at which transition from breast milk or formula to solid food occurs varies across generations, regions, and nationalities (Horn & Childre, 1996). The assessment team must develop a broad picture of the child's everyday contexts, including specific family, cultural, and community expectations for adaptive competence for her chronological age. The young child's acquisition of adaptive behaviors is embedded in the family's routines and their expectations. Therefore, families should know best their child's strengths and needs that impact his acceptability within and across settings. They can provide valuable information and validate information collected from other sources. Interviews and discussions with family members can be valuable for providing an opportunity for parents to indicate the adaptive behaviors they consider to be instructional priorities. Parents should be the primary source for identification of skills, priorities, and contexts for assessment and intervention (Horn & Childre, 1996).

Hierarchical Sequence

The adaptive behaviors acquired in the preschool years represent a hierarchical sequence from simple to complex. The sequence typically reflects changes in the amount of adult support needed and the efficiency of completing the task. Horn and Childre (1996) gave the example of feeding, with the child initially dependent on the adult in sucking liquid from the nipple; the child gradually becomes more efficient in latching onto the nipple and sucking. As the child's skills improve, she is able to drink from a sippie cup, gradually moves to drinking independently from a glass, and finally to pouring milk from a pitcher into a glass with minimal spillage.

There are four assessment implications in understanding this hierarchical sequence. First, team members must be competent in assessing skills across the full early childhood range. Second, team members must be knowledgeable of normal developmental sequences. They need to understand the significant variations in normal developmental sequences and the heavy cultural influence across generations, regions, and nationalities on these time frames. Finally, the team needs to be able to determine the probable cause of the absence of the skill. For example, is the failure to button a lack of fine motor coordination or limited exposure at home or in preschool?

Low-Frequency Behaviors

Some important adaptive behavior skills are used with relatively low frequency (e.g., dressing and undressing skills). However, these skills must become habitual to be truly functional. They must be performed fluently in response to natural cues, maintained by natural conse-

quences, and performed in a variety of settings and circumstances. This implies that the assessor may need to change the traditional assessment and instruction contexts to reflect the diversity of settings in which the skills naturally occur and adapt her schedule in order to increase the opportunities for observing these skills within the context of routines. The child must be given real-life opportunities to demonstrate habitual, generalized responses to natural cues provided across multiple current and future environments. The team members must assess not only the presence or absence of the skill but also fluency, generalization, and maintenance (Horn & Childre, 1996).

Behavior Chains

Many adaptive behaviors require physiological maturity and learned behavior (e.g., feeding and toileting skills). These skills are not discrete behaviors but rather a sequence of behaviors that result in a complex function. The assessment team must be skilled in analyzing the component parts of complex skills and appropriately assessing the child's current developmental and physiological status in relation to each of these component parts. It must first be determined if the required physiological components are present (e.g., ability to sit on the toilet seat). If they are not, then the team should determine if adaptations can be made that will bypass the component or if strategies can be developed to allow the child to learn to perform the component (e.g., teaching equilibrium responses for sitting). A sample task analysis that might be used in a preschool classroom is given in Figure 18–1.

Methods for Assessing Adaptive Behavior

The conceptual framework for assessing behaviors across subdomains of adaptive behavior is a functional ecological approach (DeStefano, Howe, Horn, & Smith, 1991; McDonnell & Hardman, 1988). The common themes are: (a) assessment

FIGURE 18–1
Sample Task Analysis

Toothbrushing

1. Child goes to sink area.
2. Child picks up toothbrush with her name.
3. Child uses toothbrush to scrape toothpaste onto toothbrush from bottom of cup.
4. Child brushes teeth for 10 to 20 seconds.
5. Child fills cup with water.
6. Child rinses out mouth with water.
7. Child throws paper cup into trash container.
8. Child rinses toothbrush with water from faucet.
9. Child returns toothbrush to holder.

---

items are referenced to the unique needs and lifestyle of the child, family, peers, and community; (b) assessment emphasizes skills that reflect increases in the child's ability to interact with the world; (c) assessment emphasizes skills that are useful immediately and in the future; and (d) assessment is conducted during multiple daily family and child routines and activities. There are many differences among cultures regarding the value placed on these skills and expectations for when they should be acquired (Peterson & Haring, 1989). The acquisition of these skills is dependent on the family's unique preferences and expectations. Therefore, the specific behaviors that determine competence in adaptive behavior should be identified based on the unique needs and lifestyles of the child, family, peers, and community.

Adaptive behavior is primarily assessed through adaptive behavior scales that integrate diagnostic interview, behavior checklist, behavior rating scale, and direct observation approaches. Observations in natural contexts and interviews with

significant adults are the primary sources of information. These indirect strategies include developmental scales, criterion-referenced lists, and ecological inventory methods.

Developmental Scales

Developmental scales are based on the normal sequence of development. Skills are sequenced according to the age at which they are acquired by normally developing children. There are many advantages to using developmental scales. Developmental test items are written in observable terms. These descriptive items assist in the reliable determination of the presence or absence of the skill. The scales can also be administered periodically as a measure of child change.

Because skills are listed in chronological order, they may provide information for determining the next skill to teach. The item following the last item passed in a subdomain becomes the target for instruction. The extensive listing of skills within the various subdomains reduces the risk of overlooking an important skill. The developmental age equivalents provided for clusters of skills assist teachers in determining whether the skills targeted for intervention are developmentally appropriate. For example, it would not be appropriate to expect a 2-year-old to be tying her shoes. Because developmental domains involve many disciplines, they may facilitate communication between disciplines.

The disadvantages involved in using developmental scales are related to the use of the information obtained. A major concern is the significant variation in the developmental sequences of some skills owing to the differences in childrearing from one culture to another, as well as geographic and generational differences. Some adaptive behaviors on developmental scales may be irrelevant in certain populations; for example, teaching a child to use a fork is not appropriate in China (Horn & Childre, 1996). The developmental items may need to be adapted so that the disability does not prevent assessment of the specific skill of interest. For example, a child who is blind may be able chew but cannot find the food on the plate. Another disadvantage relates to the use of the information obtained. Skills within and across subdomains may be seen in isolation. For example, the skill of scanning for objects, which may be assessed using one particular item on the scale, takes on more meaning in the context of looking for something in the child's environment. Some items are listed because of their high reliability at certain ages (White, 1985). The item which considers separating from caregiver and is often included in the social adjustment subdomain is not intended to address a lack of attachment by the child, but rather the child's ability to handle transitions and to self-regulate. It is often assumed that if an item is on an assessment, it must be meaningful for instruction. However, some items on many scales do not readily translate to intervention goals or the sequences of items may not be the best teaching sequence, especially for children with sensory and motor disabilities. There may also be large gaps between items (Horn & Childre, 1996).

Although developmental scales can serve an important role in the assessment process, the members of the assessment team must carefully evaluate the relevance of particular items for each child and each family. The child's age, interest, motor or sensory disabilities, and home and community environments must be considered in the assessment process and in the interpretation and use of results. Developmental scales are included in multidomain criterion-referenced assessments. Examples of these are discussed in the next section on criterion-referenced adaptive behavior scales and later in this chapter under multidomain assessments.

Criterion-Referenced Adaptive Behavior Scales

Criterion-referenced adaptive assessments measure a child's performance compared with a predetermined level of mastery. The items are chosen from an analysis of functional skills thought to be essential for young children to function independently and to cope with environmental demands.

It is preferred that the assessment be completed while observing the child in her typical setting or natural environment. This allows the assessment team to collect critical information about the responses the child uses in a functional manner, as well as when and how they are used. Most lists provide multiple-level scoring to reflect different levels of proficiency in using the skill. Because a standard presentation format does not have to be maintained, the assessment team is encouraged to find and use adaptations to assist the child in accomplishing the functional outcome. Criterion-referenced tests have fewer domains or age ranges but attempt to provide a comprehensive listing of skills with smaller increments to allow small changes to be reflected. Some criterion-referenced tests present items reflecting conceptual or response classes rather than singular, specific exemplar skills (Bricker, 1993). An example of this type of item is asking about adjustment to transitions, rather than the single item "separates easily from caregiver" (Horn & Childre, 1996). Narrower definitions and terminology, such as self-care or self-help skills, are frequently used in curriculum-based assessments.

The primary disadvantage of most criterion-referenced lists is that they do not provide norms for the test outcomes, which may be necessary for some aspects of eligibility determination, program evaluation, or progress monitoring. Another possible disadvantage is that the skills on the list still may not be relevant to the individual child and family contexts because they are generated to reflect the skills of large population groups and geographic areas.

Examples of Criterion-Referenced Adaptive Behavior Scales. The *Checklist of Adaptive Living Skills* (CALS) (Moreau & Bruininks, 1991) is an example of a criterion-referenced checklist of approximately 800 items in the areas of self-care, personal independence, and adaptive functioning. The CALS was developed to measure the adaptive behavior development of infants through adults. The CALS is divided into four domains: (1) personal living skills; (2) home living skills; (3) community living skills; and (4) employment skills. Each of these domains is organized into 24 specific skill strands. Each item covers a range of behaviors, and items are arranged in order of difficulty. The scale is administered as an interview and takes approximately 60 minutes to complete. Scoring requires simply checking items the child can perform independently according to the criterion. Because it is a criterion-referenced checklist, it may be readministered periodically.

The *Early Coping Inventory* (ECI) (Zeitlin, Williamson, & Szczepanski, 1988) measures the coping and adaptive behavior of children whose developmental level is between 4 to 36 months. *The Coping Inventory* (Zeitlin, 1985) can be used with children ages 3 to 16 years. The organization and administration of both are similar. The inventory is completed through direct observation of the child.

The ECI contains 48 items that are divided into the following three categories: sensorimotor organization (i.e., behaviors used to regulate psychophysiological functions and to integrate sensory and motor processes), reactive behavior (i.e., actions used to respond to the demands of physical and social environments), and self-initiated behavior (i.e., self-directed actions intended to meet personal needs and to interact with objects and people). The child is rated on a five-point scale according to the level of effectiveness that ranges from "the behavior is not effective" to "the behavior is consistently effective across situations." The manual provides many examples to clarify the rating scale that is based on the rater's subjective judgment. The ECI provides three types of information: sensorimotor organization, reactive behavior, and self-initiated behavior. The ECI yields three different types of clinically relevant information: (1) an adaptive behavior index, (2) a coping profile,

and (3) a listing of the most and least adaptive coping behaviors. The adaptive behavior index provides a global measure of the child's coping competence. The examiner may also determine the child's coping profile; it compares the child's level of effectiveness in the three behavioral categories (i.e., sensorimotor organization, reactive behavior, and self-initiated behavior). The profile helps to determine the primary focus for intervention by graphically depicting the child's unique behavioral patterns. It shows the relationships among the three categories of sensorimotor organization, reactive behavior, and self-initiated behavior. The range of scores indicates whether the child's behavior is consistent across these coping categories or if there are idiosyncratic patterns of strengths and vulnerability. The scorer also may list the most and least adaptive behaviors to identify the child's specific strengths and weaknesses. The list of least adaptive coping behaviors indicates the behavioral characteristics that need to be addressed in the IFSP. The list of most adaptive coping behaviors can be used to develop intervention strategies for enhancing the less adaptive behaviors and to expand the child's general coping effectiveness. Intervention then can build on the child's coping strengths (Zeitlin & Williamson, 1994).

The Coping Inventory (Zeitlin, 1985) is the same in its general format and scoring system as the ECI. The instrument has two categories: (1) Coping with Self, which includes the behaviors a child uses to meet personal needs; and (2) Coping with the Environment, which involves the behaviors used to adapt to external demands and pressures. In each of these categories, three bipolar dimensions are used to describe a child's coping style. The productive-nonproductive dimension assesses the child's capacity to be socially responsible, maintain self-esteem, and produce desired results. The flexible-rigid dimension assesses the child's ability to use a variety and range of strategies, to shift plans appropriately, or to reformulate ideas currently held. The active-passive dimension measures the child's ability to initiate and sustain mental or physical action when managing daily events. In summary, the ECI for infants and toddlers and the Coping Inventory for children and youth provide a structured, systematic approach to assessing a child's unique coping style (Zeitlin & Williamson, 1994). Figure 18–2 presents some examples of behaviors from the ECI and the Coping Inventory.

Examples of Multidomain Criterion-Referenced Assessments. Several criterion-referenced or curriculum-based, multidomain assessments address adaptive behavior development. Many global assessments offer subtests that are defined by the domains each attempts to measure. The *Assessment, Evaluation, and Programming System* (AEPS) (Bricker, 1993) includes fine motor, gross motor, adaptive, cognitive, social communication, and social skills, whereas the

FIGURE 18–2
Sample Items from the Early Coping Inventory: 4 to 36 Months and 3 to 16 Years

---

4 to 36 months

Sensorimotor organization
   Child demonstrates ability to self-comfort.

Reactive behavior
   Child demonstrates an awareness that own behavior has an effect on people and objects.

Self-initiated behavior
   Child applies a previously learned behavior to a new situation.

Source: From *Early Coping Inventory: A Measure of Adaptive Behavior* (p. 285), by S. Zeitlin, G. G. Williamson, & M. Szczepanski, 1988, Bensenville, IL: Scholastic Testing Service. Copyright 1988 by Scholastic Testing Service. Reprinted with permission.

3 to 16 years

Coping with self: Productive
   Child, when presented with a new or difficult situation, finds a way of handling it.

Coping with self: Active
   Child tells or shows others when he or she is angry or in disagreement.

Coping with self: Flexible
   Child can manage high-stress situations (finds ways to reduce feelings of stress or finds solution to the stress-causing situation).

Coping with environment: Productive
   Child functions with minimal amount of external structure (is self-directed, can create own routine or structure).

Coping with environment: Active
   Child is stimulating to others (gets others started, enthused, involved).

Coping with environment: Flexible
   Child accepts warmth and support (for example, responds to affection and encouragement from others, likes to be held, kissed, praised).

Source: From *Coping Inventory–Observation Form* (pp. 2–5) by S. Zeitlin, 1985, Bensenville, IL: Scholastic Testing Service. Copyright 1985 by Scholastic Testing Service. Reprinted with permission.

Learning Accomplishment Profile (LAP) (Nehring, Nehring, Bruni, & Randolph, 1992) includes fine and gross motor, language, self-help, and social-cognitive skills. These instruments do not necessarily include the same domains nor do they necessarily define the domains in the same way. A summary of some common curriculum-based assessments and the domains and subdomains included is shown in Figure 18–3.

Norm-Referenced Assessments

At the preschool level, the most frequently used and best adaptive behavior scales are standardized, normed, and psychometrically tested (Knoff, Stollar, Johnson, & Chenneville, 1999). They may use both parents and teachers as informants, and they may be interested exclusively in adaptive behavior or may be part of a comprehensive tool measuring multiple domains. (See Figure 18–3 for a listing of multiple domain norm-referenced assessments.)

Examples of Norm-Referenced Assessments. The *Adaptive Behavior Scales–School Edition* (ABS-S) (Lambert, Leland, & Nehira, 1993) was developed for children ages 3 to 16 years and is designed to measure a child's personal independence and social responsibility. It is divided into two parts. Part One focuses on personal independence, coping skills, and daily living skills. Nine domains are assessed: independent functioning, physical development, economic activity, language development, numbers and time, prevocational/vocational activity, responsibility, self-direction, and socialization. Part Two contains seven domains and assesses social maladaption. The domains are violent and antisocial behavior, rebellious behavior, untrustworthy behavior, stereotyped and hyperactive behavior, eccentric behavior, withdrawn behavior, and disturbed behavior. The second part of the ABS-S is administered as an interview.

The *Vineland Adaptive Behavior Scales* (Sparrow, Balla, & Cicchetti, 1984) are one of the most widely used instruments for assessing adaptive behavior

(Horn & Childre, 1996). There are three separate versions of the scales: a survey form, an expanded form, and a classroom edition. The survey form is designed to obtain an overview of adaptive behavior and is used with children ages birth to 18 years. The expanded form covers the same age range, but it is a comprehensive diagnostic instrument that provides in-depth information across a large sample of behaviors. The classroom edition addresses adaptive behaviors in classroom and school settings for children ages 3 to 12 years. All of the scales cover four adaptive behavior domains: (1) communication, (2) daily living skills, (3) socialization, and (4) motor skills. The primary caregiver who knows the child well is interviewed. The Vineland is probably the best-known measure of children's developmental skills based on parents' or other caretakers' reports (Mindes, Ireton, & Mardell-Czudnowski, 1996). The survey and classroom editions take approximately 20 to 60 minutes, while the expanded form takes 60 to 90 minutes. An optional maladaptive behavior scale is also included.

The *Scales of Independent Behavior-Revised* (SIB) (Bruininks, Woodcock, Weatherman, & Hill, 1984) use parents or teachers to assess the independent functioning of individuals, from infancy to late adulthood, in home, social, and community settings. The full form of the SIB contains 4 adaptive behavior clusters (Motor Behavior, Social Interaction and Communication Skills, Personal Living Skills, and Community Living Skills). These 4 clusters are broken down into 14 subscales. There are three problem behavior clusters with eight subscales: Internalized Maladaptive Behavior, Asocial Maladaptive Behavior, and Externalized Maladaptive Behavior. A Broad Independence cluster score is generated from the adaptive behavior areas and a Maladaptive Index is generated from the problem behavior areas. The full SIB takes about an hour to complete, but a 40-item short form can be completed for individuals at any developmental level. There is also an Early Developmental scale of adaptive behavior which was developed to assess children age 2½ or

FIGURE 18–3
Multiple Domain Assessments for Adaptive Behavior

Assessment Type	Specific Assessments	Age Range	Adaptive Domain Addressed
Norm-referenced	Battelle Developmental Inventory (BDI) (Newborg, Stock, Wnek, Guidubaldi & Svinicki, 1988)	Birth–8 yrs	Adaptive: attention, eating, dressing, personal responsibility, toileting
	Learning Accomplishment Profile–Diagnostic Ed. (Nehring, Nehring, Bruni, & Randolph, 1992)	Birth–6 yrs	Self-help
	Developmental Profile II (Alpern, Boll, & Shearer, 1980)	Birth–12 yrs	Adaptive skills (self-help)
	Kent Infant Development Scale (Reuter & Bickett, 1985)	Birth–12 mos	Self-help
Criterion-referenced	Assessment, Evaluation, and Programming System for Infants and Children: Vol. 1 (Bricker 1993); Vol. 2 (Cripe, Slentz, & Bricker, 1993)	Birth–3 yrs	Adaptive: feeding, personal hygiene, undressing
	Assessment, Evaluation, and Programming System for Infants and Children: Vol. 3 (Bricker, & Pretti-Frontczak 1996); Vol. 4 (Bricker & Waddell, 1996)	3–6 yrs	Adaptive: dining, personal hygiene, dressing and undressing
	BRIGANCE Diagnostic Inventory of Early Development-Revised (Brigance, 1991)	Birth–7 yrs	Adaptive (self-help)
	Carolina Curriculum for Infants and Toddlers with Special Needs (Johnson-Martin, Jens, Attermeier, & Hacker, 1991)	Birth–24 mos	Self-help: eating, grooming, dressing
	Carolina Curriculum for Preschoolers with Special Needs ((Johnson-Martin, Attermeier, & Hacker, 1990)	2–5 yrs	Self-help: eating, dressing, grooming, toileting; responsibility; self-control
	Hawaii Early Learning Profile (Parks, Furono, O'Reilly, Inatsuka, Hoska, & Zeisloft-Falbey, 1994)	Birth–36 mos	Self-help
	HELP for Preschoolers (VORT, 1995)	3–6 yrs	Self-help
	HICOMP (Willoughby-Herb & Neisworth, 1983)	Birth–5 yrs	Adaptive
	Early Learning Accomplishment Profile (Glover, Preminger, & Sanford, 1995)	Birth–36 mos	Self-help
	Learning Accomplishment Profile-Revised (Nehring, Nehring, Bruni, & Randolph, 1992)	3–6 yrs	Self-help; personal-social
	Vulpe Assessment Battery-Revised (Vulpe, 1994)	3–5 yrs to fifth grade	Adaptive behaviors; activities of daily living

younger or individuals who are developmentally functioning at the 2½-year-old level or younger.

Ecological Inventories

Ecological inventories examine the environment to determine needed skills rather than using commercially available lists of skills. The current and future environments relevant to the particular child are analyzed. The purpose of this examination is to identify functional routines and activities necessary for the child to participate in and then to estimate the child's ability to take part in these routines and activities. Assessment and curricular content are identified by assessing the skill requirements of relevant environments. Therefore, the environment or assessment site is the source for the skills listed.

The information used to identify and analyze routines and activities is collected by direct observation and interviews with significant individuals in the child's life, including the family, who can describe the child's present level of participation in daily routines and activities. The ecological inventory process is child-, family-, and culture-specific. The routines, activities, and skills identified reflect a child's capabilities, interests, and temperament, thus reflecting the uniqueness of each family and child. The routines and activities will vary from one child to another depending on such characteristics as the family members who are present in the home, work or school responsibilities, social/recreational interests and preferences, and interpersonal needs and strengths. Cultural diversity will be reflected in the family's lifestyle and similarly seen in the daily routines from which the assessment content is taken (Horn & Childre, 1996).

Horn & Childre (1996) listed five phases for the ecological inventory strategy: (1) associating the current level of functioning with major activities or settings (e.g., home living, leisure activities); (2) identifying current and future places where the child might participate (e.g., living and learning); (3) identifying subsettings in which the child currently participates or may in the future (e.g., bedroom or bathroom of home); (4) completing an inventory of each subsetting (e.g., bathroom with bathing, toothbrushing, etc.) and task-analyzing the activities into teachable units; and (5) assessing the child's performance of these sequences of behaviors, such as toothbrushing. An instructional program is designed and implemented based on this ecological inventory. This allows the assessment team to identify the skills that are most functional and relevant to the child and family.

A disadvantage of this process is that it does not offer structure or specific guidelines for the identification of skills. The skill sequences identified by a team led by a speech therapist may be very different from those identified by a team led by a physical therapist. It is important that teams identify not only the apparent skills but also more subtle social skills, such as smiling and making eye contact. Although these skills are not critical, they are important to socially acceptable performance.

As with other domains, it is important that information is generated from a variety of sources. The information generated from a developmental scale or a criterion-referenced assessment will provide the goals or next skills needed by the child. An ecological inventory will determine the relevance of the skills to the child's daily activities and settings and will be directed at maximizing participation in ongoing tasks. These approaches complement each other. The ecological inventory could be used to identify the activities and routines that the child needs to learn in order to participate in important natural environments such as home and preschool. A task analysis could be developed for any skills that the child may need additional assistance in acquiring. A developmental list or criterion-referenced list could be used to identify the specific skills across domains that are naturally embedded in these routines and that the child needs for successful participation. These skill lists could be validated by checking their appropriateness in the natural settings in which the child would use them. The list could then be used to assess the child's status and needs for intervention.

Assessment Within Subdomains

The DEC Recommended Practices (DEC Task Force on Recommended Practices, 1993) include five subdomains for the adaptive domain: self-care, community, self-sufficiency, personal-social responsibility, and social adjustment.

Self-Care

Self-care refers to dressing/undressing, eating/feeding, toileting, and grooming. The child acquires most of these basic skills by age 5 (Johnson-Martin, Attermeier, & Hacker, 1990). Self-care skills consist of sequences called chained responses, which means that simple skills may be linked together to perform more complex ones. The child needs to learn each step in the sequence; for example, dressing skills require sequencing behaviors such as putting on or taking off a jacket. Many assessments provide a list of skills and a system to record whether the child can or cannot perform the skills. These lists may not provide information as to the fluency with which the child can perform the tasks. The order or sequence of the tasks may vary, and the assessment may not allow for variation. Lists can serve as guides but should be individualized to accommodate the abilities and disabilities of each child. Direct observation and interviews with significant adults can determine if instruction is indicated in a given area at a specific time. Interventionists must carefully assess the skills and instructional procedures that need to be used for a particular child as well as the settings where the skills will be used. Decisions must be made about procedures, times for teaching, and teaching materials.

Self-care skills relate to the other developmental domains because they require discriminating the front of the shirt from the back, determining the appropriateness of the shirt for the weather or occasion, and control over a number of motor skills. Appropriate eating skills frequently are needed in social contexts where conversation is likely (Horn & Childre, 1996; Wolery & Smith, 1989).

Many criterion-referenced measures address self-care skills. The number of items for each of the self-care domains varies. The chained nature of self-care skills and the need to assess them at the times when they are needed limit the value of direct testing. Recording whether a child can or cannot do a skill does not provide much useful information for planning instruction. For example, two children could be scored as not putting on their shoes, but one child could do all of the required steps while the other child could do none of the required steps. This problem can be avoided by using a task-analytic data collection procedure and combining it with the levels of assistance needed by the child to complete each step. In addition, the fluency of the child's response also needs to be recorded. Self-care skills, such as taking off and putting on a garment, often can be accomplished by a separate sequences. For example, a jacket may be put on by using a crossed-arm method or one arm at a time. A different task analysis or sequence of steps is required for each of these methods. Neither of these sequences is incorrect, and each will produce the same effect. However, one of these may be easier for a given child than for another. The task in assessment is to identify which sequence will allow the child to learn most quickly.

Seven instructional decisions must be made in relation to self-care skills (Snell, 1987): (1) reinforcers, (2) procedures to control interfering behaviors, (3) self-care objectives, (4) instructional strategies, (5) monitoring procedures, (6) maintenance-facilitating procedures, and (7) generalization-facilitating procedures. Many of these decisions are made in response to assessment information from nearly all domains of the curriculum.

Community Self-Sufficiency

In early childhood the appropriate use of community resources includes skills that promote age- and culturally appropriate functioning with adult supervision. Specific skills included in this subdomain are provided in Figure 18–4. Related skills include communication of choices and needs, social interaction and behavior in the community, and the use of functional academics. The degree of independence, the range of settings, and the complexity are adjusted to reflect the developmental age and the cultural expectations. Community self-sufficiency for a

young child should include skills that promote age- and culturally appropriate functioning with adult supervision in community settings (e.g., stores, libraries, restaurants).

Community self-sufficiency skills overlap with other subdomains of adaptive behavior (e.g., eating, toileting) as well as other domains such as cognitive (e.g., problem solving), motor (e.g., mobility), social, and communication (Horn & Childre, 1996). The demands of the setting must be considered when measuring the competency of a given skill. Competence requires the ability to change behavior to suit the demands of the setting (Evans, 1991). The community environments of the young child and her access to them must be assessed to determine the appropriate level of participation. The future community environments that the infant or young child is likely to encounter must also be assessed to determine the specific skills that will be needed to participate in these settings. An example given by Horn and Childre (1996) is the feeding of an infant. The infant may be breast-fed at home but when out in the community a bottle is used. For this infant, bottle drinking is an adaptive community activity. The goals established must be made through consensus of the family and the interventionists, not simply by looking at a developmental checklist.

FIGURE 18–4
Adaptive Behavior Domain/Community
Self-Sufficiency Subdomain

Community Self-Sufficiency Skills

Traveling in the community

Grocery and general shopping at stores

Obtaining services from community businesses (doctors, dentists, clinics, restaurants, repair shops

Using public transportation

Using public facilities (e.g., school, libraries, post office, recreational areas)

Attending church or synagogue

Attending theaters and recreational events

Related skills:
    Communication of choices and needs
    Social interaction and behavior in the community
    Use of functional academics

Source: Adapted from Ford, A., Schnorr, R., Meyer, L., Davern, L., Black, J., & Dempsey, P. (1989). *The Syracuse community-referenced curriculum guide.* Baltimore, MD: Brookes.

Personal-Social Responsibility

The skills included in the personal-social responsibility subdomain include basic environmental interactions, self-directed behaviors, independent play–self-occupation, peer cooperation and interaction, and the assumption of responsibility (e.g., looking both ways before crossing the street). Figure 18–5 lists specific skills in this subdomain. Direct observation across multiple natural environments is the primary data collection stategy for the subdomain. The skills and level of independence should be documened across different settings, materials, and people. It is also important to collect information as to

FIGURE 18–5
Adaptive Behavior Domain/Personal-Social Responsibility Subdomain

---

Basic environmental interactions

Self-directed behaviors

- Making simple choices
- Learning and following a schedule
- Initiating and directing context-appropriate activities
- Completing necessary or required tasks
- Seeking assistance as needed
- Problem solving in familiar and novel situations
- Demonstrating appropriate assertive and self-advocacy skills

Independent play/self-occupation

- Developing a variety of leisure and recreational interests
- Choosing and self-initiating interests
- Using and enjoying home and community play activities
- Extending duration of play
- Expanding child's repertoire of interests, awareness, and skills

Peer cooperation and interaction

- Initiating a social interchange
- Learning to take turns
- Learning to end an interaction appropriately
- Increasing the duration of social interaction
- Appropriately refusing a social interchange
- Recognizing the rights, feelings, and needs of others

Assuming responsibility for one's behavior

- Controlling one's behavior
- Learning the rules of safety
- Demonstrating caution or avoiding danger
- Caring for property
- Functioning in the community

Sources: Adapted from Horn, E. M. (1996). Interventions to promote adaptive behavior skills. In S. L. Odom & M. E. McLean (Eds.), *Early intervention/early childhood special education: Recommended practices* (pp. 259–285). Austin, TX: PRO-ED; Horn, E. M., & Childre, A. (1996). Assessing adaptive behavior. In M. E. McLean, D. B. Bailey, & M. Wolery (Eds.), *Assessing infants and preschoolers with special needs* (pp. 462–490). Upper Saddle River, NJ: Merrill/Prentice Hall and McWilliam, R. A. (1991). Targeting teaching at children's use of time: Perspectives on preschoolers' engagement. *Teaching Exceptional Children, 23*(4), 42–43.

the degree to which the child's environments support the learning and demonstration of these skills. Does a child have the opportunity to interact with other children? Is the child allowed to make choices? A more complete discussion of social development is provided in Chapter 16.

Social Adjustment

The social adjustment subdomain includes abilities to adjust to new situations, regularity of behavior patterns (e.g., eating and sleeping), general disposition or temperament, ability to stay on task despite obstacles, attention span and degree of distractibility, and the amount of stimulation necessary for a child to make a response (see Figure 18–6). Positive adjustment reflects an integration and display of these skills in the context of the demands of the environment and personal needs (Zeitlin & Williamson, 1994). Effective adjustment fosters the acquisition of developmental skills, the development of a positive self-concept, and the ability to develop meaningful social relationships (Williamson, 1994). Effective social adjustment includes the ability to cope. Coping is the integration and application of developmental skills in the context of daily living (Williamson, 1996). Coping behaviors focus on nutrition, security, and a combination of activity and rest, combined with an opportunity to pursue interests and motivations to satisfy the drive to achieve mastery (Horn & Childre, 1996).

Assessing Coping Skills. Coping is the process of making adaptations in order to meet personal demands and respond to the demands of the environment. An infant must cope with family life, changes related to physical growth, and the many new experiences she faces every day. The goal is to increase feelings of well-being in situations which are seen as threatening or challenging. Children cope with situations in order to feel good about themselves. The more effectively a child copes, the more effectively she learns. A

child's adaptive competence is determined by the match between the needs or demands and the availability of resources to manage them (Williamson, 1996). The cluster of attributes, skills, and behaviors identified with coping in infants can be divided into three categories: sensori-motor organization, reactive behaviors, and self-initiated behaviors (Zeitlin, Williamson, & Szczepanski, 1988). Figure 18–6 lists specific behaviors in each of these three categories.

A thorough understanding of the child's coping style and strategies is necessary before initiating intervention. The ECI (Zeitlin, Williamson, & Szczepanski, 1988) may be used with infants and toddlers. The Coping Inventory (Zeitlin, 1985) may be used with preschoolers and older children. The child is observed in a variety of natural settings, such as during caregiving, free play, instructional, and small-group activities, to determine her coping behavior. The assessor should note the child's flexibility in the use of the behaviors, the circumstances under which they are applied, her success in managing specific stressors, and her feelings about the effectiveness of her efforts. Williamson (1996) suggested several issues that need to be considered when assessing a child's coping:

1. To what extent does the child engage in self-initiated behaviors, and are these coping behaviors productive?
2. Is the child able to use coping strategies flexibly across a variety of situations?
3. Is there a difference between the ability of the child to cope with inner demands and his ability to cope with the environment?
4. How does the child seem to evaluate the effectiveness of coping efforts? The answer to this question often indicates the status of the child's self-esteem. (p. 199)

Coping transactions have four components which contribute to the outcome of the coping process: (1) an internal demand (physical and emotional needs) or external demand (walking in a crowded store or obtaining a toy) that initiates the transaction; (2) the coping effort the child uses to

FIGURE 18–6
Adaptive Behavior
Domain/Social-Adjustment
Subdomain

Sources: Adapted from Horn, E.
M., & Childre, A. (1996). Assessing
adaptive behavior. In M. E.
McLean, D. B. Bailey, & M. Wolery
(Eds.), *Assessing infants and
preschoolers with special needs*
(pp. 462–490). Upper Saddle
River, NJ: Merrill/Prentice Hall and
Zeitlin, S., Williamson, G. G., &
Szczepanski, M. (1988). *Early
Coping Inventory.* Bensenville, IL:
Scholastic Testing Service.

Ability to Adjust or Cope with New Situations

Sensorimotor:

- Ability to attend
- Ability to self-comfort
- Ability to control activity level
- Ability to manage the intensity and variety of stimuli
- Ability to adapt to handling

Reactive behavior (responses to external demands):

- Ability to adjust to daily routines
- Ability to accept warmth and comfort from a familiar person
- Ability to respond to vocal and gestural directions
- Ability to adjust to changes in the environment

Self-initiated Behaviors:

- Ability to express likes and dislikes
- Ability to initiate actions for communicating a need
- Ability to persist during activities
- Ability to generalize skills to new situations

Regularity of behavior patterns

General disposition

Ability to stay on tasks despite obstacles

Attention span and degree of distractibility

Amount of stimulation necessary to evoke a response

---

manage the demand; (3) the environment's response to that effort; and (4) the child's reaction to the response (Williamson, 1996).

Interventions can then be planned based on this information. Three primary intervention options address the components of the coping process: (1) modify demands so that they are congruent with the child's capabilities; (2) enhance the child's coping resources; (3) provide appropriate, contingent feedback to the child's efforts. All three interventions are frequently used simultaneously (Williamson, 1996).

Assessing Survival Skills

As more and more young children are being served in regular preschools and as they move into kindergarten, greater emphasis is being placed on the skills children need to succeed in the regular kindergarten setting. As children move from preschool programs to school-age programs, the expectations of teachers change. Vincent, Salisbury, Walter, Brown, Gruenwald, and Powers (1980) defined preschool survival skills as behaviors that will facilitate referral to and maintenance in less restrictive environments when the child is ready for kindergarten or first grade. Behaviors that have been identified as survival skills were originally identified and researched by Walter (1979). Best practices literature for early childhood special education services advocates teaching skills that have future utility for young children (McDonnell & Hardman, 1988). Research conducted to explore the expectations of teachers in inclusive settings found that teachers in general education classrooms and child care centers focus more on social, behavioral, and functional skill areas (e.g., cooperative and nonaggressive behavior, caring for bathroom needs) than academic areas such as counting, and naming letters (Hains, Fowler, Schwartz, Kottwitz, & Rosenkoetter, 1989; Hemmeter & Rous, 1998; Johnson, Gallagher, Cook, & Wong, 1995; Murphy & Vincent, 1989). Early interventionists need to assess and then include survival skills in the preschoolers' instructional program.

It is essential that functional, social, and behavioral skills in young children with disabilities be assessed in light of developmentally appropriate expectations. The teacher must consider the age of the child, the child's individual needs, and the needs of the child's family when examining these expectations. This process must take into consideration the relationship of the cultural and social practices of the community. All of this information can be helpful in preparing the child for the next setting as well as adapting the next setting to meet the needs of the child.

McCormick and Kawate (1982) found that few of the behaviors considered important for participation in regular kindergarten and first grade classes are being assessed when using the most common preschool assessment instruments. They recommend that practitioners examine the instrument(s) currently in use in their settings to determine if these behaviors are being assessed. Figure 18–7 presents transition or survival skills that are related to successful transition from preschool to kindergarten.

The *Helpful Entry Level Skills Checklist* (HELS) (Byrd & Rous, 1990) was designed to assist teachers in selecting skills that would facilitate the transition of children from preschool into public school kindergarten and school-age programs. This instrument assesses the functional, social, and behavioral skills of children ages 3 to 6 years. The skills included on the checklist have been identified as important to the process of children transitioning into inclusive kindergarten and school-age settings (Hains, et al., 1989; Hemmeter & Rous, 1998; Johnson, et al., 1995). The skills selected for the HELS were seen as the most critical for facilitating children's successful transition from preschool to public school programs (Rous & Hallam, 1998). Five skill areas are included in the checklist: classroom rules, work skills, communication, social/behavioral, and self-management. The form includes a summary page for demographic information and skills targeted for intervention. The form also includes a general comment section and individual comment sections within each of the skill areas. The Classroom Matrix is used to help teachers organize daily and weekly lessons and activities around needed skills for the children. This matrix can also be used to assist in monitoring and documenting skill development. The checklist should be completed at the beginning of enrollment into a preschool program. The guidelines for administering the checklist allow for three possible responses: Yes (behavior well-established); No (behavior not observed); and I/E (inconsistent or emerging). Adaptations made (e.g., verbal

FIGURE 18–7

Transition Skills Related to
Successful Transition from
Preschool to Kindergarten

Source: Chandler, L. K. (1993). Steps
in preparing for transition: Preschool
to kindergarten. *Teaching
Exceptional Children, 25*(4) 52–55.

Social behaviors and classroom conduct

Understands role as part of group.
Respects others and their property.
Interacts and defends self without aggression.
Plays cooperatively; shares toys and materials.
Expresses emotions and affections appropriately.
Takes turn; participates appropriately in games.
Is willing to try something new.
Follows class rules and routines.
Lines up and waits appropriately.
Imitates peer actions.
Sits appropriately.
Plays independently.

Communication behaviors

Follows two- to three-part directions.
Initiates and maintains peer interactions.
Modifies behavior when given verbal feedback.
Asks peers or teachers for information or assistance.
Recalls and follows directions for tasks previously described.
Follows group instructions.
Relates ideas and experiences.
Answers questions.
Communicates own needs and wants.

Task-related behaviors

Finds materials needed for tasks.
Does not disrupt peers during activities.
Complies quickly with teacher instructions.
Generalizes skills across tasks and situations.
Follows task directions in small or large group.
Replaces materials and cleans up work space.
Monitors own behavior; knows when a task is done.
Begins and completes work at appropriate time without extra
    teacher attention.
Makes choices.
Stays in own space.
Follows routine in transition.
Uses a variety of materials.
Seeks attention appropriately.
Attends to teacher in a large group.

Self-help behaviors

Recognizes when a problem exists.
Locates and cares for personal belongings.
Avoids dangers and responds to warning words.
Takes outer clothing off and puts it on in a reasonable amount
    of time.
Tries strategies to solve problems.
Feeds self independently.
Cares for own toileting needs.

prompts, modeling, or physical support is needed) may be noted in the comment sections. Because many of the children who are experiencing developmental delays may need to spend more time acquiring the skills, teachers may begin planning for transition earlier (Rous & Hallam, 1998). Information from the HELS can provide valuable information for joint planning among families and professionals. Recommendations for families should respect family routines, schedules, and culture. The targeted skills should be shared with other child care providers and related service personnel to ensure consistency across environments.

Choosing Intervention Goals

The important aspect for developing intervention goals for adaptive behavior is not based on what the child knows or can do, but on how the child interacts with her environment (Horn & Childre, 1996). The assessment should provide information on (a) the specific skills mastered in the subdomains; (b) skills that are in the process of being acquired; (c) skills needed to meet the demands of current environments; (d) the environments that provide sufficient opportunity and support for learning the skill; and (e) related services, equipment, and aids that will facilitate the child's learning the skill. Adaptive behaviors should be selected that increase the child's participation and independence.

The adaptive domain requires team assessment and intervention. The team must first summarize the skills the child currently demonstrates in relation to the level of proficiency and the demands of her environments. The team should consider the child's chronological age, the manner in which peers perform the task, and the settings in which the skills will be used. The goals should reflect typical expectations for the child's chronological age level. It is important during intervention that opportunities are presented to learn and master skills that meet social

expectations. To increase a child's level of independence, intervention must target fluent responses, maintenance of acquired skills, and generalization of skills across situations and settings. Although adaptive behaviors are critical, they are often performed at a relatively low frequency. However, skills must be performed fluently and in response to natural cues, maintained by the natural consequences, and performed in a variety of settings. Therefore, the interventionist may need to change the traditional instructional settings to reflect the many settings in which the skills naturally occur and make adaptations in schedules to increase the opportunities for practicing these skills within the context of real-life routines.

Summary

The adaptive behavior domain should include skills that reflect chronologically age-appropriate behaviors for meeting the demands of the child's multiple environments. Acquisition of adaptive skills allows the child increased independence in her environment, decreased caregiving demands, more meaningful inclusion in community settings, and positive impacts on his sense of self-competence and self-concept (Horn & Childre, 1996). Adaptive behavior is a composite of a wide range of abilities and thus requires comprehensive assessment by a team of professionals and caregivers. The specific behaviors at any given developmental stage that determine competence in adaptive behavior should be identified from an analysis of the unique needs and lifestyles of the child, family, peers, and community. The goal of assessment is to lead to intervention that empowers the young child to cope with self and the environment in ways that foster personal well-being (Williamson, 1996).

References

Alpern, G., Boll, T., & Shearer, M. (1986). *Developmental Profile II.* Aspen, CO: Psychological Development Publications.

American Association on Mental Retardation (AAMR). (1992). *Definitions, classifications, and systems of supports* (9th ed.). Washington, DC: Author.

Bailey, D. B., & Wolery, M. (1992). *Teaching infants and preschoolers with disabilities* (2nd ed.). Upper Saddle River, NJ: Merrill/Prentice Hall.

Benner, S. M. (1992). *Assessing young children with special needs.* White Plains, NY: Longman.

Bricker, D. (1993). *Assessment, Evaluation, and Programming System (AEPS) for Infants and Children: vol 1. AEPS measurement for birth to three years.* Baltimore: Brookes.

Bricker, D., & Pretti-Frontczak, K. (Eds.). (1996). *Assessment, Evaluation, and Programming System (AEPS) for Infants and Children: vol. 3. AEPS measurement for three to six years.* Baltimore: Brookes.

Bricker, D., & Waddell, M. (Eds.). (1996). *Assessment, Evaluation, and Programming System (AEPS) for Infants and Children: vol. 4. AEPS curriculum for three to six years.* Baltimore: Brookes.

Brigance, A. H. (1991). BRIGANCE *Diagnostic Inventory of Early Development-Revised* (BDIED-R). N. Billerica: MA: Curriculum Associates.

Bruininks, R. H., Woodcock, R. W., Weatherman, R. F., & Hill, B. K. (1984). *Scales of Independent Behavior* (SIB). Allen, TX: DLM Teaching Resources.

Byrd, M. R., & Rous, B. S. (1990). *Helpful Entry Level Skills Checklist* (Rev. ed.). Lexington, KY: Child Development Centers of the Bluegrass.

Chandler, L. K. (1993). Steps in preparing for transition: Preschool to kindergarten. *Teaching Exceptional Children,* 25(4), 52–55.

Cripe, J., Slentz, K., & Bricker, D. (1993). *Assessment, Evaluation, and Programming System (AEPS) for Infants and Children: vol. 2. AEPS curriculum for birth to three years.* Baltimore: Brookes.

DEC Task Force on Recommended Practices. (1993). *DEC Recommended Practices: Indicators of quality in programs for infants and young children with special needs and their families.* Reston, VA: Council for Exceptional Children.

DeStefano, D. M., Howe, A. G., Horn, E. M., & Smith, B. A. (1991). *Best practices: Evaluating early childhood special education programs.* Tucson: Communication Skill Builders.

Dyson, L., & Fewell, R. R. (1986). Stress and adaptation in parents of young handicapped and nonhandicapped children: A comparative study. *Journal of the Division for Early Childhood,* 10(1), 25–34.

Evans, I. M. (1991). Testing and diagnosis: A review and evaluation. In L. H. Meyers, C. A. Peck, & L. Brown (Eds.), *Critical issues in the lives of people with severe disabilities* (pp. 25–44). Baltimore: Brookes.

Ford, A., Schnorr, R., Meyer, L., Davern, L., Black, J., & Dempsey, P. (1989). *The Syracuse community-referenced curriculum guide.* Baltimore: Brookes.

Frankenberger, W. (1984). A survey of state guidelines for identification of mental retardation. *Mental Retardation,* 22, 17–20.

Glover, E., Preminger, J., & Sanford, A. (1995): *Early Learning, Accomplishment Profile* (E-LAP). Chapel Hill, NC: Chapel Hill Training-Outreach Project.

Hains, A. H., Fowler, S. A., Schwartz, I. S., Kottwitz, E., & Rosenkoetter, S. (1989). A comparison of preschool and kindergarten teacher expectations for school readiness. *Early Childhood Research Quarterly,* 4, 75–88.

Harrison, P. L. (1987). Research with adaptive behavior scales. *Journal of Special Education,* 21(1), 37–68.

Hemmeter, M. L., & Rous, B. S. (1998). *Teachers' expectations of children transitioning into kindergarten or ungraded primary programs*: A national survey.

Horn, E. M. (1996). Interventions to promote adaptive behavior skills. In S. L. Odom & M. E. McLean (Eds.), *Early intervention/early childhood special education: Recommended practices* (pp. 259–285). Austin, TX: PRO-ED.

Horn, E. M., & Childre, A. (1996). Assessing adaptive behavior. In M. E. McLean, D. B. Bailey, & M. Wolery (Eds.), *Assessing infants and preschoolers with special needs* (pp. 462–490). Upper Saddle River, NJ: Merrill/Prentice Hall.

Horn, E., & Fuchs, D. (1987). Using adaptive behavior in assessment and intervention: An overview. *Journal of Special Education,* 21(1), 11–26.

Johnson, L. J., Gallagher, R. J., Cook, M. J., & Wong, P. (1995). Critical skills for kindergarten teachers. *Journal of Early Intervention,* 19(4), 315–327.

Johnson-Martin, N. M., Attermeier, S. M., & Hacker, B. (1990). *The Carolina Curriculum for Preschoolers with Special Needs.* Baltimore: Brookes.

Johnson-Martin, N. M., Jens, K. G., Attermeier, S. M., & Hacker, B. J. (1991). *The Carolina Curriculum for Infants and Toddlers with Special Needs* (2nd ed.). Baltimore: Brookes.

Knoff, H. M., Stollar, S. A., Johnson, J. J., & Chenneville, T. A. (1999). Assessment of social-emotional functioning and adaptive behavior. In E. Vazquez Nuttall, I. Romero, & J. Kalesnik (Eds.), *Assessing and screening preschoolers: Psychological and educational dimensions* (2nd ed., pp. 126–160). Needham Heights, MA: Allyn & Bacon.

Lambert, N. M., Leland, H., & Nehira, K. (1993). *Adaptive Behavior Scales-School: Second Edition* (ABS-S:2) Austin, TX: PRO-ED.

Luckasson, R., Schalock, R. L., Coulter, D. L., Snell, M. E., Polloway, E. A., Spitalnik, D. M., Reiss, S., & Stark, J. A. (1992). *Mental retardation: Definition, classification, and systems of support* (9th ed.). Washington, DC: American Association on Mental Retardation.

McCormick, L., & Kawate, J. (1982). Kindergarten survival skills: New directions for preschool special education. *Education and Training of the Mentally Retarded,* 17(3), 247–252.

McDonnell, A., & Hardman, M. (1988). A synthesis of "best practice" guidelines for early childhood services. *Journal of the Division for Early Childhood,* 12(4), 328–341.

McWilliam, R. A. (1991). Targeting teaching at children's use of time: Perspectives on preschoolers' engagement. *Teaching Exceptional Children,* 23(4), 42–43.

Mindes, G., Ireton, H., & Mardell-Czudnowski, C. (1996). *Assessing young children.* Albany, NY: Delmar.

Moreau, L. E., & Bruininks, R. H. (1991). *Checklist of Adaptive Living Skills.* Allen, TX: DLM Teaching Resources.

Murphy, M., & Vincent, L. J. (1989). Identification of critical skills for success in day care. *Journal of Early Intervention,* 13(3), 221–229.

Nehring, A. D., Nehring, E. F., Bruni, J. R., & Randolph, P. L. (1992). *Learning Accomplishment Profile-Diagnostic Standardized Assessment.* Lewisville, NC: Kaplan School Supply.

Newborg, J., Stock, J., Wnek, L., Guidubaldi, J., & Svinicki, J. (1998). *Battelle Developmental Inventory* (BDI). Allen, TX: DLM Teaching Resources.

Parks, S., Furono, S., O'Reilly, K., Inatsuka, T., Hoska, C. M., & Zeisloft-Falbey, B. (1994). *Hawaii Early Learning Profile* (HELP). Palo Alto, CA: VORT Corp.

Peterson, A. L., & Haring, K. (1989). Self-care skills. In C. Tingey (Ed.), *Implementing early intervention* (pp. 243–263). Baltimore: Brookes.

Peterson, N. (1987). *Early intervention for handicapped and at-risk children.* Denver: Love.

Reuter, J., & Bickett, L. (1985). *The Kent Infant Development Scale* (KIDS). Kent, OH: Developmental Metrics.

Rous, B., & Hallam, R. A. (1998). Easing the transition to kindergarten: Assessment of social, behavioral, and functional skills in young children with disabilities. *Young Exceptional Children,* 1(4), 17–26.

Sattler, J. M. (1992). *Assessment of children and families.* (3rd ed., rev.). San Diego: Author.

Snell, M. E. (1993). *Instruction of students with severe disabilities* (4th ed). Englewood Cliffs, NJ: Merrill/Prentice Hall.

Sparrow, S. L., Balla, D. A., & Cicchetti, D. V. (1984). *Vineland Adaptive Behavior Scales* (*Interview Edition*). Circle Pines, MN: American Guidance Service.

Vincent, L. J., Salisbury, C., Walter, G., Brown, P., Gruenwald, L. J., & Powers, M. (1980). Program evaluation and curriculum development in early childhood/special education: Criteria of the next environment. In W. Sailor, B. Wilcox, & L. Brown (Eds.), *Methods of instruction for severely handicapped students* (pp. 303–328). Baltimore: Brookes.

VORT Corporation. (1995). *HELP for Preschoolers.* Palo Alto, CA: Author.

Vulpe, S. (1994). *Vulpe Assessment Battery-Revised* (VAB-R). East Aurora, NY: Slosson Educational Publications.

Walter, G. (1979). *The "survival skills" displayed by kindergarteners and the structure of the regular kindergarten environment.* Unpublished master's thesis. University of Wisconsin, Madison.

White, O. R. (1985). The evaluation of severely mentally retarded individuals. In D. Bricker & J. Filler (Eds.), *Severe mental retardation: From theory to practice* (pp. 161–184). Reston, VA: Council for Exceptional Children.

Williamson, G. G. (1996). Assessment of adaptive competence. In S. J. Meisels & E. Fenichel (Eds.), *New visions for the developmental assessment of infants and young children* (pp. 193–206). Washington, DC: Zero to Three/National Center for Infants, Toddlers, and Families.

Willoughby-Herb, S. J., & Neisworth, J. T. (1983). *The HICOMP Curriculum.* San Antonio, TX: Psychological Corporation.

Wolery, M., & Smith, P. D. (1989). In D. B. Bailey & M. Wolery (Eds.), *Assessing infants and preschoolers with handicaps* (pp. 447–477). Upper Saddle River, NJ: Merrill/Prentice Hall.

Zeitlin, S. (1985). *Coping Inventory.* Bensenville, IL: Scholastic Testing Service.

Zeitlin, S., & Williamson, G. G. (1994). *Coping in young children: Early intervention practices to enhance adaptive behavior and resilience.* Baltimore: Brookes.

Zeitlin, S., Williamson, G. G., & Szczepanski, M. (1988). *Early Coping Inventory.* Bensenville, IL: Scholastic Testing Service.

⪜ Index ⪛